Artificial Intelligence and Integrated Intelligent Information Systems: Emerging Technologies and Applications

Xuan F. Zha
National Institute of Standards and Technology,
University of Maryland, USA & Shanghai JiaoTong University, China

IDEA GROUP PUBLISHING
Hershey • London • Melbourne • Singapore

Acquisition Editor: Kristin Klinger
Senior Managing Editor: Jennifer Neidig
Managing Editor: Sara Reed
Assistant Managing Editor: Sharon Berger
Development Editor: Kristin Roth
Copy Editor: Amanda O'Brien
Typesetter: Jessie Weik
Cover Design: Lisa Tosheff
Printed at: Yurchak Printing Inc.

Published in the United States of America by
Idea Group Publishing (an imprint of Idea Group Inc.)
701 E. Chocolate Avenue
Hershey PA 17033
Tel: 717-533-8845
Fax: 717-533-8661
E-mail: cust@idea-group.com
Web site: http://www.idea-group.com

and in the United Kingdom by
Idea Group Publishing (an imprint of Idea Group Inc.)
3 Henrietta Street
Covent Garden
London WC2E 8LU
Tel: 44 20 7240 0856
Fax: 44 20 7379 3313
Web site: http://www.eurospan.co.uk

Library of Congress Cataloging-in-Publication Data

Artificial intelligence and integrated intelligent information systems : emerging technologies and applications / Xuan F. Zha, editor.
p. cm.
Summary: "This book presents the recent advances in multi-mobile agent systems, the product development process, fuzzy logic systems, neural networks and ambient intelligent environments among many other innovations in this exciting field"--Provided by publisher.
Includes bibliographical references and index.
ISBN 1-59904-249-5 -- ISBN 1-59904-250-9 (pbk.) -- ISBN 1-59904-251-7 (eISBN)
1. Expert systems (Computer science) 2. Soft computing. 3. Artificial intelligence. I. Zha, Xuan F., 1965-
QA76.76.E95A75 2007
006.3'3--dc22

2006027707

British Cataloguing in Publication Data
A Cataloguing in Publication record for this book is available from the British Library.

Artificial Intelligence and Integrated Intelligent Information Systems: Emerging Technologies and Applications

Table of Contents

Foreword

At the start of the 20th century, national economies on the international scene were, to a large extent, agriculturally based. This was, perhaps, the dominant reason for the protraction on the international scene of the Great Depression, which began with the Wall Street stock market crash of October 1929. After World War II, the trend away from agriculturally based economies and toward industrially based economies continued and strengthened. Indeed, today, in the United States, approximately only 1% of the population is involved in the agriculture requirements of the U.S. and, in addition, provides significant agriculture exports. This, of course, is made possible by the greatly improved techniques and technologies utilized in the agriculture industry.

The trend toward industrially based economies after World War II was, in turn, followed by a trend toward service-based economies. In the United States today, roughly more than 70% of the employment is involved with service industries — and this percentage continues to increase. Separately, the electronic computer industry began to take hold in the early 1960s, and thereafter always seemed to exceed expectations. For example, the first large-scale sales of an electronic computer were of the IBM 650. At that time, projections were that the total sales for the United States would be 25 IBM 650 computers. Before the first one came off the production line, IBM had initial orders for more than 30,000. That was thought to be huge by the standards of that day, and today it is a very miniscule number, to say nothing of the fact that its computing power was also very miniscule by today's standards. Computer mainframes continued to grow in power and complexity. At the same time, Gordon Moore, of "Moore's Law" fame, and his colleagues founded INTEL. Then, around 1980, MICROSOFT was founded, but it was not until the early 1990s, not that long ago, that WINDOWS was created — incidentally, after the APPLE computer family started. The first browser was the NETSCAPE browser, which appeared in 1995, also not that long ago. Of course, computer networking equipment, most notably CISCO's, also appeared about that time. Toward the end of the last century the dot.com "bubble" occurred and "burst" around 2000.

Coming to the new millennium, for most of our history the wealth of a nation was limited by the size and stamina of the workforce. Today, national wealth is measured in intellectual capital. Nations possessing skillful people in such diverse areas as science, medicine, business, and engineering produce innovations that drive the nation to a higher quality of life. To better utilize these valuable resources, intelligent systems technology has evolved at a rapid and significantly expanding rate, and can be utilized by nations to improve their medical care, advance their engineering technology, and increase their manufacturing productivity, as well as play a significant role in a wide variety of other areas of activity of substantive significance.

The breadth of the major application areas of intelligent systems technology is very impressive. These include the following, among other areas: agriculture, electronics, business engineering, chemistry, environment, communications, geology, computer systems, image processing, education, information, management, military, law mining, manufacturing, power systems, mathematics, science, medicine, space technology, meteorology, and transportation.

It is difficult now to imagine an area that will not be touched by intelligent systems technology.

Artificial Intelligence and Integrated Intelligent Information Systems: Emerging Technologies and Applications edited by Xuan F. Zha, a leading contributor to intelligent systems technology, consists of five well-integrated broad subject area sections. There are four chapters in each section and, in all, there are 38 coauthors. These coauthors from academia and government institutions are among the leading contributors to intelligent systems technology on the international scene.

Intelligent systems technology has come a long way in a relatively short time. The early days were spent in a somewhat probing fashion, where researchers looked for ways to develop methods that captured human intelligence. After considerable struggle, they fortunately met with success. Armed with an understanding of how to design an intelligent system, they went on to solve real-world problems. At this point, intelligent systems took on a very meaningful role in the broad area of information technology. Along the way, there were a few individuals who saw the importance of publishing the accomplishments of intelligent systems technology, thus providing guidance to advance the field. Among this small group, I believe that Dr. Zha has made among the largest contributions to this effort. I believe his latest work in this volume he created and edited is one of his most valuable contributions to date and should be in the possession of all individuals involved in the field of intelligent systems technology.

Cornelius T. Leondes

Cornelius T. Leondes is an emeritus *professor at the School of Engineering and Applied Science, University of California, Los Angeles. He has served as a member or consultant on numerous national blue ribbon technical panels and scientific advisory boards, including the first five-man advisory board on the "Man on The Moon" project. He served as a consultant for numerous Fortune 500 companies and international corporations. He has published more than 200 technical journal articles and has edited and/or co-authored more than 120 books on high technology advances. He is a Guggenhein fellow, Fulbright research scholar, and IEEE fellow, as well as a recipient of the IEEE Baker Prize award and the Barry Carlton Award of the IEEE. He is regarded as a world-renowned expert in the theory and application of computer and control systems technology.*

Preface

For most of our history the wealth of a nation was limited by the size and stamina of the work force. Today, national wealth is measured in intellectual capital. Nations possessing skillful people in such diverse areas as science, medicine, business, and engineering produce innovations that drive the nation to a higher quality of life. Artificial intelligence (AI) has been studying the science and engineering of constructing intelligent systems. It is extensively used by combining with information science and technology. To better utilize these valuable resources, artificial intelligence (AI) technology has evolved at a rapid and significantly expanding rate. Nowadays, it is difficult to imagine the development of the modern world without extensive use of the AI and information technology and their integration that are rapidly transforming the global, knowledge-based economy as well as entire societies.

Overview on Recent Advances, Issues and Challenges in AI and IIIS

Most work in AI has focused on components of the overall system — such as learning, planning, knowledge representation, perception, and action. Information system/technology and intelligent knowledge management are playing an increasing role in business, science and technology. The breadth of the major application areas of intelligent, knowledge-based systems, and integrated intelligent information systems technologies is very impressive. These include, among other areas: agriculture, business, chemistry, communications, computer systems, education, electronics, engineering, environment, geology, image processing, information management, law, manufacturing, mathematics, medicine, metrology, military, mining, power systems, science, space technology, and transportation.

In recent years, with the advancement of artificial intelligence (AI) and information science and technology, there has been a resurgence of work in combining individual intelligent systems (knowledge-based systems, fuzzy logic, neural networks, genetic algorithms, case-based reasoning, machine learning and knowledge discovery, data mining algorithms, intelligent agents, soft computing, user intelligent interfaces, etc.) into integrated intelligent systems to solve complex problems. Hybridization of different intelligent systems is an innovative approach to construct computationally intelligent systems consisting of artificial neural network, fuzzy inference systems, approximate reasoning and derivative free optimization methods such as evolutionary computation and so on. The integration of different learning and adaptation techniques, to overcome individual limitations and achieve synergetic effects through hybridization or fusion of these techniques, has contributed to a large number of new intelligent system designs. Hybrid intelligent systems are becoming a very important problem solving methodology affecting researchers and practitioners in areas ranging from science, technology, business and commerce.

Specifically, there have been many attempts to solve decision making problems (assessment or evaluation and selection) by applying neural network and (fuzzy) rule-based expert systems techniques. The capabilities of rule-based (fuzzy) expert systems are inherently well suited for decision making problems. The major drawback, however, is that the programmer is required to define the functions underlying the multi-valued or ranked possibility optimization. Furthermore, expert-type rules use a comprehensive language system that may have built-in biases, embedded goals, and hidden information structures, which may result in errors. Neural networks using mathematical relationships and mappings to design and optimize systems are capable of statistical decision-making given incomplete and uncertain information, and can be used to adapt to the user/designer's requirements. Unlike rule-based (fuzzy) expert systems, they evaluate all the conflict constraints or fusion information simultaneously, and model/learn the knowledge base using black-box techniques. They do not use rules in the formal sense so the evaluation or decision making time can be greatly reduced from that of rule-based modeling. The strengths of neural networks accrue from the fact that they need not priori assumptions of models and from their capability to infer complex, nonlinear underlying relationships. From the statisticians' point of view, neural networks are essentially statistical devices to perform inductive inference and are analogous to non-parametric, nonlinear regression models. However, existing neural schemes use two or more separate neural networks to accomplish some tasks respectively, and need to train them separately. This is tedious and costly, and sometimes very difficult. In order to overcome the suffered shortcomings or difficulties above, more research endeavors are necessary to develop more general topologies of neural models, learning algorithms and approximation theories so that those models are applicable in the system modeling and control of complex systems. A new kind of hybrid neural networks is therefore required for decision support. It must also be conceded that rule-based (fuzzy) expert systems are much easier for humans to error-check than an ensemble of continuous equations in neural networks. In view of these practical requirements and current research status and future trend of intelligent decision support, an evolutionary neuro-fuzzy network or fuzzy neural network (FNN) model has been developed for supporting computational intelligent decision making and simulation. There is now a growing need in the intelligent community that complex decision making problems require hybrid solutions.

It is well known that intelligent systems, which can provide human-like expertise such as domain knowledge, uncertain reasoning, and adaptation to a noisy and time-varying environment, are important in tackling practical computing problems. Soft computing is an emerging collection of computing methodologies to exploit tolerance for uncertainty, imprecision and partial truth to achieve useable robustness, tractability, low total cost and approximate solutions. It is particularly efficient and effective for NP-hard problems. Recently, many different challenges posed by data mining have been solved by various soft computing methodologies. At this juncture, the principal constituents of soft computing are fuzzy logic, neuro-computing, evolutionary computing and probabilistic computing, simulating annealing, tabu search approach, swarm intelligence systems (such as particle swarm optimization, ant systems and ant colony systems) with the later subsuming belief networks, chaotic systems and parts of learning theory. Each of them contributes a revealable methodology which only in a cooperative rather than competitive manner for persuading problems in its field. Soft computing techniques facilitate the use of fuzzy logic, neuro-computing, evolutionary computing and probabilistic computing in combination, leading to the concept of hybrid intelligent systems. Such systems are rapidly growing in importance and visibility. In most cases, their purpose is not to replace the conventional techniques but to supplement and complement them so that a much wider range of situations can be adequately dealt with. Soft computing hybrid intelligent systems have a wide range of applications, such as synthetic battlefield agents for training, intelligent players and teams for computer entertainment, autonomous spacecraft, rovers, submersibles, and aerial vehicles, intelligent design and manufacturing. They can provide a unified, intelligent computational framework for human-machine system design and simulation. Systematic methodologies have also been proposed for the fusion of soft computing and hard computing. The principal research focus is on creating hybrid intelligent systems for real-world applications, and the core methodologies of soft computing are: evolutionary computation, fuzzy logic, and neural networks; with a representative collection of complementary hard computing techniques.

Petri net, coined by Professor C. A. Petri in 1962, is an important analytical and modeling tool for the discrete event dynamic systems. It has been modified, extended and analyzed in detail and possesses the potential to be integrated into an artificial intelligence (AI) framework. Petri nets not only can represent a variety of physical and synthetic process (e.g. design process, assembly process) well but also can be used for creation and development of integrated & hybrid intelligent information systems. To this connection, a new field, knowledge & intelligent Petri nets, is opened, in which the research is to investigate how to carry out knowledge /intelligent extension for Petri nets to build a unified, complete framework to represent multi-view knowledge and to perform reasoning and learning. For instance, a novel class of knowledge intensive Petri nets has been created by the editor and co-workers through combining artificial intelligence techniques with Petri nets, including knowledge Petri net, fuzzy knowledge Petri net, expert Petri net, fuzzy expert Petri net, neuro-fuzzy Petri net, and so forth. Such extended Petri net-based approach would be widely used in science, technology, business and commerce.

Reflecting the most fascinating AI-based research and its broad practical applications, integrated intelligent information system (IIIS) technologies, with the extensive use of the AI and information technology and their integration, are being utilized to advance engineering technology, increase manufacturing productivity, and improve medical care, as well as play a significant role in a very wide variety of other areas of activity with substantive significance. Integrated intelligent information systems (IIIS) are gaining better acceptance both in academia and in industry. The driving force behind this is that integrated and hybrid intelligence and distributed 3C (collaboration, cooperation, and coordination) allow the capture of human knowledge and the application of it to achieve high quality applications. Further motivation arises from steady advances in individual and hybrid intelligent-systems techniques, and the widespread availability of computing resources and communications capability through the world-wide web. However, the difficulties in distributed & integrated information systems development are increased due to the issues of intra- and inter- enterprise network communication, system heterogeneity, and information security, different engineering data formats and database formats. Many kinds of distributed information systems have been designed and implemented to address those difficulties in DIS development, which can provide an "information pipeline" that supports the sharing of information, specifically, in the context of collaborative/cooperative engineering. These systems are based heavily on industry standards (e.g., STEP, Standard for the exchange of product model data, officially ISO 10303) to provide an open and evolvable environment that can flow with, as well as contribute to, commercial best practices and trends.

The need for an infrastructure based upon distributed computing, information and communication technology (i.e., a cyber-infrastructure) becomes increasing paramount as we progress closer to a knowledge economy. A recent report of US National Science Foundation (NSF) indicates that such a cyber-infrastructure (CI) will play a pivotal role in supporting system design and realization. Factors in achieving seamless networks are: (1) connectivity, bandwidth for large scale data and information transfer; (2) reach, the ability to access and provide right information that is distributed across the networked enterprise; (3) interactivity, the ability to interact with people, computational tools and physical tools across time and space. Any cyber-infrastructure has to support along all these three aspects. Technical challenges in cyber-infrastructure for collaborative engineering applications (design and manufacturing) are (Ram Sriram at 2005 NSF EXCITED Workshop): (1) knowledge management, shared information and knowledge; (2) repositories, capture and reuse; (3) immersive environments; (4) standards; (5) constraint management; (6) negotiation tools and techniques; (7) database organization and access; (8) design and manufacturing supply chains; (9) remote monitoring and sharing; (10) security. An information repository/shared information system (IR/SIS), as an integrative information-sharing infrastructure, is crucial for information sharing, exchange and re-use in three dimensions: technology, functionality and information needs. This can be accomplished by addressing the following issues and challenges:

1. **Information needs.** Investigating the requirements for the shared information and classifying the information into two levels: full access and limited access. (1) Full access: Authorized partners have full access privilege to the specific information; (2) Limited access: Authorized partners can partially access to the specific information.
2. **Technological issues.** Investigating the information-sharing interface based on industry standards (STEP) and Extensible Markup Language (XML), web services for solutions to technological issues. (1) Multi-user interface: Partners perform diverse tasks, multiple information views need to be built from the same data storage and the same information storage may be updated from different partner views; (2) Heterogeneity: IR/SIS is constructed from a variety of different networks, operating systems, computer hardware, and programming languages; (3) Openness: IR/SIS is formed dynamically and allows arbitrary partner to communicate with another partner; (4) Security: IR/SIS is required to provide secure communication, against disclosure to unauthorized individuals and against un expected interference; (5) Concurrency control: The operation in IR/SIS is synchronized that its data remains consistent with multiple access from partners.

3. **Functionalities.** Investigating object-oriented database management system, universal description, discovery and integration (UDDI) for web services solutions to functionality requirements. (1) Distribution: application and data are spread out over more than one computer; (2) Storage: a repository is needed to keep and organize data in an organized way; (3) Sharing: A sharing mechanism (e.g., ontology) is required to facilitate interoperability between different partners; (4) Tracking: IR/SIS can document the up-to-date changes and provide disciplined backtracking capability.
4. **Modeling shared information space (SIS).** Developing SIS models and ontologies with Unified Model Language (UML/SysML), resource description framework (RDF), and Web Ontology Language (OWL).

The importance of integrating knowledge engineering (KE) practices into domains has been acknowledged by a number of researchers. Earlier studies focused on integrating reasoning mechanisms in domain specific support systems, mainly as diagnostic tools. Gradually, the research focus has shifted from the reasoning mechanism to the knowledge base. Recent studies focus on system and/or task structures, unified data and knowledge modeling and representation (e.g., UML/SysML), data management, standards, etc., concentrating on how these are integrated. Latest research indicates a trend towards semantic data and knowledge modeling for better interoperability. However, although these studies address the use of KE practices in the domains and some of them followed a uniform approach towards the development of knowledge bases, few of them can provide ontology-based knowledge management and reasoning services. As a result, a major limitation of the previous work is the lack of reusability and interoperability for common services. This challenge could be addressed if knowledge modeling were unified, formalized and enriched by employing ontological principles and semantics. Ontology and ontology-based computational services will be able to provide new kinds of knowledge management and reasoning services that facilitate the sharing and reuse of data and knowledge across various phases of system development. The current research focus is in developing formal ontologies with emerging semantic methods such as Process Specification Language (PSL), Web Ontology Language (OWL) and resource description framework (RDF), in support of these integration scenarios. This work will advance the research on ontology-based knowledge service, and is a step towards formalizing support system as a knowledge intensive system.

Topics and related issues of artificial intelligence, soft computing, and integrated intelligent information systems include but are not limited to the following:

1. Foundations and principles of data, information, and knowledge models
2. Methodologies for IIIS analysis, design, implementation, validation, maintenance and evolution
3. User models, intelligent and cooperative query languages and interfaces
4. Knowledge representation and ontologies, integration, fusion, interchange and evolution
5. Intelligent databases, object-oriented, extended-relational, logic-based, active databases, and constraint management
6. Intelligent information retrieval, digital libraries, and networked information retrieval

7. Distributed multimedia and hypermedia information space design, implementation and navigation
8. Visual interfaces, visual query languages, and visual expressiveness of IIIS
9. Machine learning, knowledge discovery, and data mining
10. Soft computing (including neural nets, fuzzy logic, evolutionary computing, probabilistic reasoning, and rough set theory) and hybrid intelligent systems
11. Uncertainty management and reasoning under uncertainty
12. Intelligent integration of information, information and knowledge repository
13. Distributed intelligent information systems, cooperative information systems, agent architectures and systems (including multi-agent scenarios)
14. Information and knowledge grid, grid computing, grid services for distributed systems integration
15. Ubiquitous computing, ambient intelligence, heterogeneous intelligent information systems interoperability
16. Industrial informatics, i.e., applications and case studies in novel applications, e.g., scientific databases, e-commerce, e-logistics, engineering design and manufacturing, product life cycle management and knowledge management, healthcare, education, etc.

The Overall Objective of the Book

There is a need for an edited collection of articles to reflect emerging intelligent technologies and their applications in areas: business, engineering, health care, management, and science, etc. The great breadth and expanding significance of AI and integrated intelligent information systems (IIIS) fields on the international scene require a major reference work for an adequately substantive treatment of the subject. This book aims to collect the relevant original works on the emerging technologies of artificial intelligence and integrated intelligent information systems and their applications in those areas above. The goal is to take a snapshot of the progress in the research and to disseminate recent developments and applications in different domains. The book provides relevant theoretical foundations, methodologies, frameworks and latest research findings in the areas for professionals who want to improve their understanding of the strategic role of artificial intelligence (AI) and integrated intelligent information systems (IIIS) at different levels of the information, knowledge and intelligence society, that is, trusts at the levels of the global economy, of networks and organizations, of teams and work groups, of information systems and, finally, of individuals as actors in the integrated (networked) environments. It brings together leading authoritative authors to address arguably most pressing challenge in the field-how to create and develop integrated intelligent information systems to serve our future needs.

The Organization of the Book

The focus of this book is on the integrated & hybrid intelligent methodologies, techniques, frameworks and systems. The chapters provide an integrated, holistic perspective on this complex set of challenges, combined with practice experiences of leading figures in industry. Some of the chapters provide rigorous research results, while others are in-depth reports from the field. All chapters are rigorously reviewed and carefully edited. There is a logical flow through this book, starting with emerging intelligent systems and soft computing then continuing hybrid intelligent systems and innovative computing, information and control followed by modeling and development of intelligent information systems and their applications for product design and development. The treatment of the subject in the book can be described as:

1. Examines emerging technologies and recent research results on AI and integrated intelligent information systems (IIIS), including integrated intelligent systems, hybrid intelligent systems, soft computing, distributed artificial intelligence (DAI), computer-integrated information systems (CIIS), intelligent computer-aided development systems, etc.
2. Presents theoretical fundamentals and implementation technology, as well as industrial applications.
3. Introduces new knowledge-intensive problem-solving strategies and their implementations based on AI and integrated and hybrid intelligent systems techniques.
4. Explores a few applications and case studies, including electro-mechanical systems, systems design, robot controller design, process control system, embedded and mechatronic systems design.

This book consists of the following distinctly titled and well integrated chapters. The contents of the book are organized into five parts consisting of 20 chapters. Each part has 4 chapters. A brief description of each of the chapters is provided.

Section I

Section I, *Emerging Intelligent Technologies and Applications*, addresses several emerging intelligent systems (such as agent-based ambient intelligence, parallelized ant colony algorithm, immunization systems, and knowledge grid-based approach) and their applications. The basic question is how accumulated data and expertise from business or medical operations can be abstracted into useful knowledge, and how such knowledge can be applied to on-going operations or services. The wide range of areas represented includes traveling salesman problem, human modeling, health care, data fusion and decision making.

Chapter I describes an agent-based ambient intelligence architecture able to deliver services on the basis of physical and emotional user status captured from a set of biometric features. Abstract representation and management is achieved thanks to two markup languages,

H2ML and FML, able to model behavioral as well as fuzzy control activities and to exploit distribution and concurrent computation in order to gain real-time performances.

Chapter II presents the work that parallelizes the ant colony systems and introduces the communication strategies so as to reduce the computation time and reach better solution for traveling salesman problem. The chapter also discusses a data clustering process using the constrained ant colony optimization (CACO). The CACO algorithm can resolve the problems of clusters with arbitrary shapes, clusters with outliers and bridges between clusters.

Chapter III reports the problem of spreading the normal state (rather than spreading of the abnormal state) that is formalized as cleaning a contaminated network by mutual copying. Repairing by copying is the "double edged sword" that could spread contamination when properly used. The chapter also introduces a framework for controlling copying involving a spatial prisoner's dilemma.

Chapter IV describes a grid-based method for data fusion with interactions among decision makers. This method takes advantages of observation of other decision makers' opinions and then modifies the result. The method simulates the process of human decision making. It involves decision making, decision fusion, discussion, and remaking, refuse. It can improve the reliability and flexibility of the fusion system.

Section II

Section II, *Hybrid Intelligent Systems and Applications*, explores hybrid intelligent systems of neural networks, fuzzy theory, and genetic algorithms and their applications in such areas as hierarchical fuzzy logic systems, text mining, classification system, and process control.

Chapter V presents an investigation into the design and development of a hierarchical fuzzy logic system. A new method using genetic algorithms for design of hierarchical fuzzy logic systems is proposed. This research study is unique in the way applied to design and development of hierarchical fuzzy logic systems. The proposed method is then applied to financial modeling and prediction. A hierarchical fuzzy logic system is developed to predict quarterly interest rates in Australia.

Chapter VI introduces a novel evolutionary model for intelligent text mining. The model deals with issues concerning shallow text representation and processing for mining purposes in an integrated way, and aims to look for interesting explanatory knowledge across text documents. The approach uses Natural-Language technology and genetic algorithms to produce explanatory novel hidden patterns. The proposed approach involves a mixture of different techniques from evolutionary computation and other kinds of text mining methods. Accordingly, new kinds of genetic operations suitable for text mining are proposed.

Chapter VII proposes a probabilistic learning technique, known as gated mixture of experts (MEs), made more adaptive by employing a customized genetic algorithm based on the concepts of hierarchical mixed encoding and hybrid training. The chapter outlines the main steps behind such novel hybrid intelligent system, focusing on its application to the nontrivial task of nonlinear time-series forecasting. Experiment results are reported with respect to three benchmarking time-series problems, and confirmed our expectation that the new integrated approach is capable to outperform, both in terms of accuracy and generalization, other conventional approaches, such as single neural networks and non-adaptive, handcrafted gated MEs.

Chapter VIII presents the applications of artificial intelligence (AI) in the process control of electro chemical discharge machining (ECDM). The aim of the study is to investigate the most suitable pulse classification architecture which provides the better classification accuracy with the minimum calculation time. A neural network pulse classification system (NNPCS), a fuzzy logic pulse classification system (FLPCS) and a neuro fuzzy pulse classification system (NFPCS) were developed for the pulse classification of the ECDM process. The NNPCS was selected as the most suitable pulse classification system for the ECDM process control system.

Section III

Section III, *Innovative Intelligent Computing, Information Processing and Control*, addresses the important question of how hybrid intelligent systems are applied in computing, information processing and control. Case studies examine a wide variety of application areas including vision-based intelligent systems, robot control, surveillance systems, sensor network design, and face detection and recognition.

Chapter IX describes a novel system that can track and recognize faces in real time using neural networks and genetic algorithms. The main feature of this system is a 3D facemask that combined with a neural network based face detector and adaptive template matching using genetic algorithms, is capable of detecting and recognizing faces in real time. Neural network learning and template matching enable size and pose invariant face detection and recognition while the genetic algorithm optimizes the searching algorithms enabling real time usage of the system.

Chapter X addresses the problem of combining color and geometric invariants for object description by proposing a novel colored invariant local feature descriptor. The proposed approach uses scale-space theory to detect the most geometrically robust features in a physical-based color invariant space. Building a geometrical invariant feature descriptor in a color invariant space grants the built descriptor the stability to both geometric and color variations. The proposed approach is applicable in any vision-based intelligent system that requires object recognition/retrieval.

Chapter XI discusses the need for automated detection and tracking for visual surveillance systems and proposes a solution using the capabilities of sensors network and the intelligence of multi-agent systems. This chapter introduces object detection and tracking system based on the multi-agent approach. Object detection is performed by means of the background subtraction techniques. After detection, a multi-agent tracking system tracks and follows the movement of each detected object. The proposed approach uses two types of agents: region agents and object agents. The region agents function as an arbiter between object agents. Object agents are responsible for keeping records of each detected object.

Chapter XII discusses probabilistic neural network (PNN) learning from information rich voice commands for controlling a robot. First, new concepts of fuzzy coach-player system and sub-coach for robot control with natural language commands are proposed. Then, the characteristics of subjective human decision making process and learning from such decisions are discussed. Finally, an experiment conducted with a PA-10 redundant manipulator in order to establish the proposed concept is described.

Section IV

Section IV, *Modeling and Development of Intelligent Information Systems*, considers application areas as modeling of mobile agent systems using a multi-level Petri net formalisms, formal approach for the modeling and verification of intelligent information systems using colored Petri nets, artificial intelligence approach to improve the efficiency of design pattern selection in developing object-oriented software, and the development of intelligent remote monitoring and maintenance systems.

Chapter XIII deals with the modeling of mobile agent systems evolving within structured environments using a multi-level Petri net based formalism, called n-LNS. In a n-LNS model the tokens of a net can be symbols or other nets allowing representing the behavior of mobile entities. The chapter introduces the formal definition of n-LNS and its application to the modeling of various kinds of discrete event systems, namely batch manufacturing systems, mobile robot communities, urban traffic micro-simulation, and software agents for e-commerce.

Chapter XIV presents an artificial intelligence approach to improve the efficiency of design pattern selection used in the development of object-oriented software. A prototype expert system was developed in order to automate this process of selecting suitable patterns to be applied to the design problem under consideration. The prototype system also provides the capabilities to browse patterns, view the relationship between patterns, and generate code based on the pattern selected. The routine application of such a system is viewed as a means to improve the productivity of software development by increasing the use of accepted design patterns.

Chapter XV presents a formal agent based approach for the modeling and verification of intelligent information systems using colored Petri nets. The use of a formal method allows analysis techniques such as automatic simulation and verification, increasing the confidence on the system behavior. The agent based modeling allows separating distribution, integration and intelligent features of the system, improving model reuse, flexibility and maintenance.

Chapter XVI presents methodologies and techniques for the development of an Internet server controller based intelligent remote monitoring and maintenance system. The discussion also involves on how to develop products and manufacturing systems using Internet-based intelligent technologies and how to ensure product quality, coordinate activities, reduce costs and change maintenance practice from the breakdown reaction to prevention. A hybrid intelligent approach using hardware and software agents (watchdog agent) is adopted. The server controller is web-enabled and its core is an embedded network model. The software agent is implemented through a package of smart prognostics algorithms.

Section V

Section V, *Integrated Intelligent Product Design and Development*, discusses applications of IIIS in product design and development, such areas intelligent design, feature-based semantic modeling, distributed CAD, new product innovation and development, intelligent knowledge management, and recommendation service in e-commerce.

Chapter XVII proposes a novel integrated intelligent framework for virtual engineering design and development based on the soft computing and hybrid intelligent techniques. An evolutionary neuro-fuzzy (EFNN) model is developed and used for supporting modeling, analysis and evaluation, and optimization tasks in the design process, which combines fuzzy logic with neural networks and genetic algorithms. The developed system HIDS-EFNN provides a unified integrated intelligent environment for virtual engineering design and simulation. The focus of this chapter is to present a hybrid intelligent approach with evolutionary neuro-fuzzy modeling and its applications in virtual product design, customization and simulation (product performance prediction).

Chapter XVIII presents a new feature-based modeling mechanism, document-driven design, to enable batch mode geometry construction for distributed CAD systems. A semantic feature model is developed to represent informative and communicative design intent. Feature semantics is explicitly captured as trinary relation, which provides good extensibility and prevents semantics loss. Data interoperability between domains is enhanced by schema mapping and multi-resolution semantics.

Chapter XIX proposes a design process for deploying intelligent recommendation services in existing e-markets, in order to reduce the complexity of such kind of software development. To demonstrate the applicability of this approach, the proposed process is applied for the integration of a wine recommendation service in a Greek e-market with agricultural products.

Chapter XX provides an analytical tool to assist organizations in their implementations of intelligent knowledge management systems (IKMS) along the new product development (NPD) process. The proposed framework outlines the technological and organizational path that organizations have to follow to integrate and manage knowledge effectively along their new product development processes. The framework is illustrated through an analysis of several case studies.

There are over 48 coauthors of this notable work and they come from 19 countries. The chapters are clearly written, self-contained, readable and comprehensive with helpful guides including introduction, summary, extensive figures and examples and future trends in the domain with comprehensive reference lists.

The discussions in these parts and chapters provide a wealth of practical ideas intended to foster innovation in thought and consequently, in the further development of technology. Together, they comprise a significant and uniquely comprehensive reference source for research workers, practitioners, computer scientists, academics, students, and others on the international scene for years to come.

The Target Audience

The contributors to this book clearly reveal the effectiveness and great significance of the AI and IIIS techniques and, with further development, the essential role that they will play in the future. Professionals and researchers working in the field of artificial intelligence, intelligent systems, information and knowledge management, in various disciplines, e.g., information and communication sciences, administrative sciences and management, education, computer science, information technology, engineering design, product development.

Moreover, the book provides insights and support executives concerned with the management of expertise, knowledge, information and organizational development in different types of work communities and environments. I hope that practitioners, research workers, students, computer scientists, and others on the international scene will find this volume to be unique and significant reference source for years to come.

Any opinions, findings, conclusions, or recommendations expressed in this material are those of the editor and authors. No approval or endorsement by the National Institute of Standards and Technology and University of Maryland is intended and implied.

Acknowledgments

The editor would like to acknowledge the help of all involved in the collation and review process of the book, without whose support the project would not have been satisfactorily completed.

Deep appreciation and gratitude is due to Ram D. Sriram, Group Leader at National Institute of Standards and Technology (NIST) for his support and help during my stay at NIST, and Cornelius T. Leondes, Professor Emeritus of University of California at Los Angeles for his kind encouragement and help over the years.

Most of the authors of chapters included in this also served as referees for articles written by other authors. Thanks go to all those who provided constructive and comprehensive reviews. However, some of the reviewers must be mentioned as their reviews set the benchmark. Reviewers who provided the most comprehensive, critical, and constructive comments include: Vincenzo Loia of Università degli Studi di Salerno, Italy; John Atkinson of Universidad de Concepción, Chile; Ernesto López Mellado of CINVESTAV Unidad Guadalajara, Mexico; Gary Moynihan of The University of Alabama, USA; Ashok Kumar of University of Louisiana, Lafayette, USA; Keigo Watanabe of Saga University, Japan; André Coelho of University of Fortaleza, Unifor, Brazi); and Constantina Costopoulou of Agricultural University of Athens, Greece. Support of the facility at NIST is acknowledged for archival server space in the completely virtual online review process.

Special thanks also go to all the staff at Idea Group Inc., whose contributions throughout the whole process from inception of the initial idea to final publication have been invaluable, in particular, to Kristin Roth, who continuously prodded via e-mail for keeping the project on schedule and to Mehdi Khosrow-Pour, whose enthusiasm motivated me to take on this project.

In closing, I wish to thank all of the authors for their insights and excellent contributions to this book. I also want to thank all of the people who assisted me in the reviewing process. Finally, I want to thank my family for their love and support throughout this project.

Section I:

Emerging Intelligent Technologies and Applications

Chapter I

Human-Based Models for Ambient Intelligence Environments

Giovanni Acampora, Università degli Studi di Salerno, Italy

Vincenzo Loia, Università degli Studi di Salerno, Italy

Michele Nappi, Università degli Studi di Salerno, Italy

Stefano Ricciardi, Università degli Studi di Salerno, Italy

Abstract

Ambient intelligence gathers best results from three key technologies, ubiquitous computing, ubiquitous communication, and intelligent user friendly interfaces. The functional and spatial distribution of tasks is a natural thrust to employ multi-agent paradigm to design and implement AmI environments. Two critical issues, common in most of applications, are (1) how to detect in a general and efficient way context from sensors and (2) how to process contextual information in order to improve the functionality of services. Here we describe an agent-based ambient intelligence architecture able to deliver services on the basis of physical and emotional user status captured from a set of biometric features. Abstract representation and management is achieved thanks to two markup languages, H2ML and FML, able to model behavioral as well as fuzzy control activities and to exploit distribution and concurrent computation in order to gain real-time performances.

Introduction

When designing ambient intelligence (AmI) environments (Aarts, 2004), different methodologies and techniques have to be used, ranging from materials science, business models, network architectures, up to human interaction design. However, as key technologies, AmI is characterized by:

- **Embedded.** Devices are (wired or unwired) plugged into the network (Ditze, 2004). The resulting system consists of several and multiple devices, compute equipments and software systems that must interact among them. Some of the devices are simple sensors; others are actuators owning a bunch of control activities in the environment (central heating, security systems, lighting system, washing machines, refrigerator, etc.). The strong heterogeneity makes it difficult a uniformed policy-based management.
- **Context awareness.** This term appeared for the first time in Schilit (1994), where the authors defined the context as locations, identities of nearby people and objects, and changes to those objects. Many research groups have been investigating on context-aware applications, but there is no common understanding on what context and context awareness exactly means.
- **Personalized.** AmI environments are designed for people, not generic users. This means that the system should be so flexible as to tailor itself to meet human needs.
- **Adaptive.** The system, being sensible to the user's feedback, is capable of modifying the corresponding actions that have been or will be performed (Astrom, 1987).

We have designed and implemented an intelligent home environment populated by intelligent appliance agents skilled to perform distributed and adaptive transparent fuzzy control. The agents interact and coordinate their activities using the Fuzzy Markup Language (FML) (Loia, 2005) as an abstract protocol over shared resources independently from hardware constraints. The agents compose an abstract layer that binds the instrumental scenario with the services, ensuring efficiency and adaptivity. This approach allows AmI designers to achieve useful goals:

- to customize the control strategy on a specific hardware through an automatic procedure;
- to distribute the fuzzy control flow in order to minimize the global deduction time and better exploit the natural distributed knowledge repositories; and
- to acquire at run time the user's behavior and the environment status in order to apply context-aware adaptivity.

This chapter proposes an ambient intelligence architecture being able to distribute personalized services on the basis of physical and emotional user status captured from a set of biometric features and modeled by means of a markup language based on XML. This language, namely *H2ML*, is a new tool to model human information usable at different abstraction levels inside the AmI architecture so as to reach transparency, uniformity, and abstractness in bridging multiple sensors properties to flexible and personalized actuators.

In this chapter we show that several layers composing the overall AmI architecture are used to achieve the aforesaid goal. Different layers serve to link the low-level details (the hardware layer) with the high-level view (software layer) by employing two classes of markup languages: FML and H2ML.

Fuzzy Markup Language

Initially, FML has been designed to act like a middleware between the legacy fuzzy environment and the real implementation platform. Legacy fuzzy environment module allows creating a fuzzy controller using a legacy representation (Acampora, 2005). An example of legacy fuzzy environment module is Matlab™ that produce a *.fis* file to represent the fuzzy control system. The obtained legacy fuzzy controller is passed to the FML converter module that translates it into a markup-based description (FML).

The next step concerns the real implementation of the fuzzy controller on a specific hardware. The Initial version of FML used XSLT languages translator to convert FML fuzzy controller in a general purpose computer language using an XSL file containing the translation description. At this level, the control is compilable and executable for the proposed hardware. Actually, FML can be considered as a standalone language used to model the fuzzy controllers from scratch. Now, the FML compiler is based on the integration of different techonologies to instantiate a run-time fuzzy controller without additional work. These technologies are: the *TCP/IP client/server application* and the *JAXB XML binding technology*. In particular, the JAXB XML binding technology allows generating a Java class hierarchy starting from the FML control description. The TCP/IP client/server application allows separating the real control from the controlled devices so as to obtain the total independence of the devices from the language used to code the fuzzy controller. In particular, a TCP server instantiates a Java objects collection representing the FML controller starting from the class hierarchy generated by a JAXB module. Using this object collection, the server will be able to apply the inference operators on the objects representing the fuzzy rule base, generating, in this way, a set of defuzzificated values representing the control results. The TCP Client, hosted on the controlled devices, is a simple standard TCP client able to send the sensor's values to server and to receive the control results; from this point of view, the Client does not know the details about the fuzzy control, it sees only a bidirectional data flow. The client/server communication is performed obviously by TCP sockets. Figure 1 shows the architecture of the proposed system. This choice allows obtaining a high level of abstraction showing one only gap: The client and the server have to agree on the exchange data format. In particular, the server has to know exactly the data format coming from the client and vice versa. The proposed system uses the classic string data type to solve the problem. In order to exchange

Figure 1. FML TCP/JAXB architecture

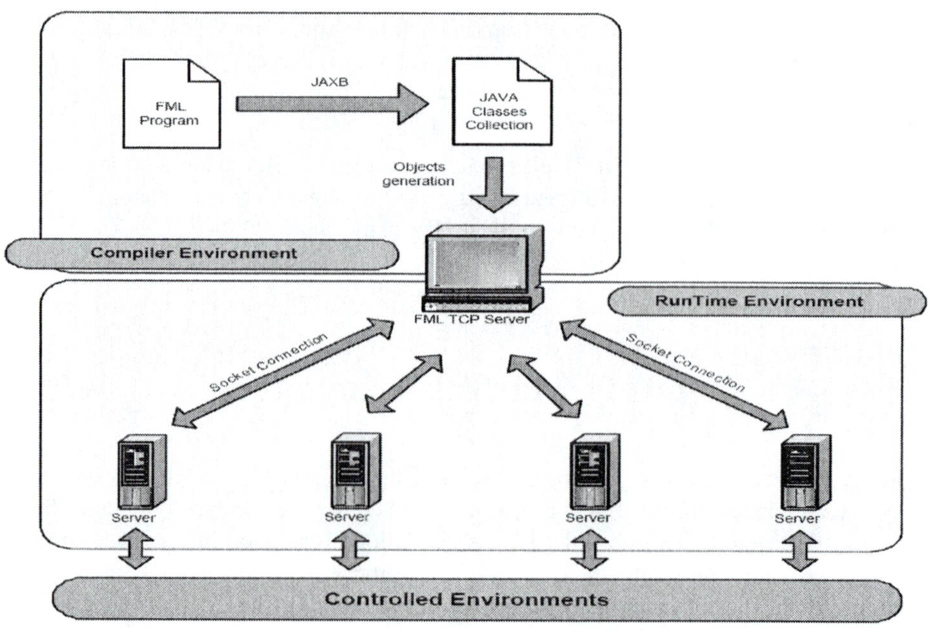

Figure 2. FML TCP/JAXB inference step

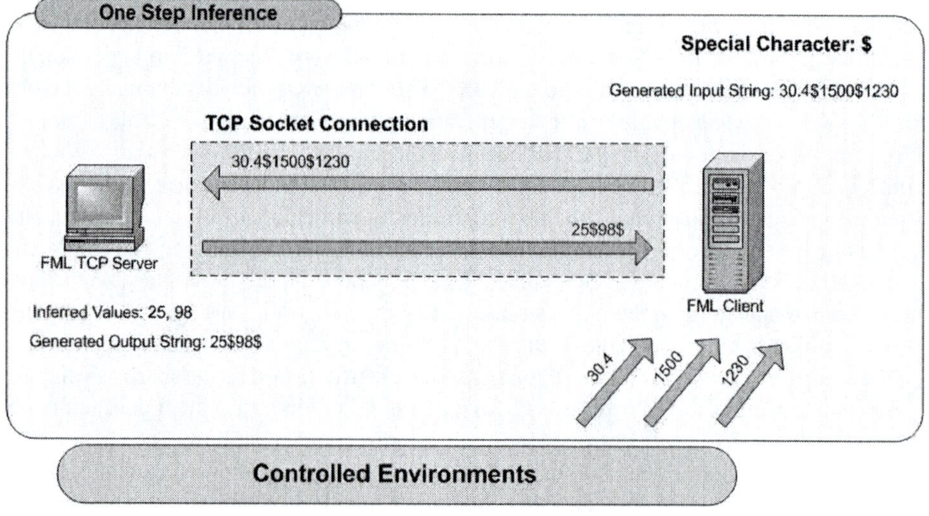

the sensors' values and the inferred results, the client and server have to choose a special character to create a communication data string. While the client uses this character to compose a string containing the sensors data, the server uses the same character to infer and to create a string containing the fuzzy control results. Client and server simply have to split the received string in order to use the data in a normal fashion. Figure 2 shows the communication step performed during a control iteration. In order to perform the JAXB/TCP/FML controller, it is necessary to create a TCP endpoint to identify in a direct and unambiguous way the FML server on the Internet. TCP defines an endpoint to be a pair of integers (host, port), where the host is the IP address for the FML server host and port is a TCP port where the server is executed on that host. The IP address depends on the network which hosts the FML server; the TCP port has to be defined in a univocal way to allow the FML clients to contact the server without problems. The FML server port is defined considering the concatenation of ASCII codes related to F, M and L characters modulo 65536 (available TCP ports) obtaining, in this way, the integer port number 12330. Some examples of FML/TCP endpoints are: (192.168.0.4, 12330), (193.205.186.85, 12330).

Fuzzy Markup Language and Fuzzy Logic Control

Since Zadeh's coining of the term fuzzy logic (Zadeh, 1965) and Mamdani's early demonstration of fuzzy logic control (FLC) (Mamdani, 1974), enormous progresses have been made by the scientific community in the theoretical as well as application fields of FLC. Trivially, a fuzzy control allows the designer to specify the control in terms of sentences rather than equations by replacing a conventional controller, say, a PID (proportional-integral-derivative) controller with linguistic IF-THEN rules. The main components of a fuzzy controller are:

- fuzzy knowledge base
- fuzzy rule base
- inference engine
- fuzzification sub-system
- defuzzification sub-system

The fuzzy knowledge base contains the knowledge used by human experts. The fuzzy rule base represents a set of relations among fuzzy variable defined in the controller system. The inference engine is the fuzzy controller component able to extract new knowledge from fuzzy knowledge base and fuzzy rule base. Extensible Markup Language (XML) (DuCharme, 1999) is a simple, very flexible text format derived from SGML (ISO 8879). Originally designed to meet the challenges of large-scale electronic publishing, nowadays, XML plays a fundamental role in the exchange of a wide variety of data on the Web, allowing designers to create their own customized tags, enabling the definition, transmission, validation, and interpretation of data between applications, devices, and organizations. If we use XML, we take control and responsibility for our information, instead of abdicating such control to product vendors. This is the motivation under FML proposal: to free control strategy from the device. FML uses:

- XML in order to create a new markup language for FLC
- XML schema in order to define the legal building blocks of an XML document
- XSLT in order to convert fuzzy controller description into a programming language code

Initially, FML used the XML document type definition (DTD) to realize the context free grammar for the new markup language. Actually, the FML grammar is defined by the XML schema in order to allow a direct integration with the JAXB techonology used in the FML compiling step. It is possible to use XML schema and JAXB to map a detailed logical structure of a fuzzy controller basic concepts of FLC into a tree structure, as shown in Figure 3, where each node can be modeled as a FML tag, and the link father-child represents a nested relation between related tags. This logical structure is called fuzzy object model (FOM).

Currently, we are using FML for modeling two well-known fuzzy controllers: Mamdani and Takagi-Sugeno-Kang (TSK) (Takagi, 1985).

In order to model the controller node of fuzzy tree, the FML tag <FUZZYCONTROL> is created (this tag opens any FML program). <FUZZYCONTROL> uses three tags: type, defuzzify method, and ip. The type attribute permits to specify the kind of fuzzy controller, in our case Mamdani or TSK; defuzzify method attribute defines the defuzzification method; ip can be used to define the location of controller in the computer network and, in the case of <FUZZYCONTROL> tag it defines the first member of TCP endpoint pair. Considering the left sub-tree, the knowledge base component is encountered. The fuzzy knowledge base is defined by means of the tag <KNOWLEDGEBASE> which maintains the set of fuzzy concepts used to model the fuzzy control system. <FUZZYVARIABLE> defines the fuzzy concept, for example, luminosity; <FUZZYTERM> defines a linguistic term describing the fuzzy concept, for example, low; a set of tags defining the shapes of fuzzy sets is related to fuzzy terms. The attributes of <FUZZYVARIABLE> tags are: name, scale, domainLeft, domainRight, type, ip. The name attribute defines the name of fuzzy concept (e.g., time of the day); scale defines how to measure the fuzzy concept (e.g., hour); domainLeft and

Figure 3. Fuzzy control tree

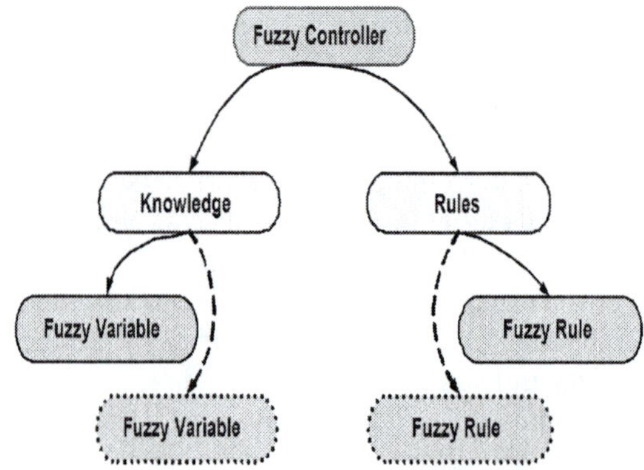

domainRight model the universe of discourse of fuzzy concept in terms of real values (e.g., [0000, 2400]); the role of variable (i.e., independent or dependent variable) is defined by type attribute; ip locates the position of fuzzy knowledge base in the computer network. <RULEBASE> permits to build the rule base associated with the fuzzy controller. The other tags related to this definiton are: <RULE>, <ANTECEDENT>, <CONSEQUENT>, <CLAUSEA>, <CLAUSEC>, <VARIABLE>, <TERM>, and <TSKPARAM>. The meaning of these tags appears evident and we do not further detail them here.

Distributed Fuzzy Control

Just to give a concrete example, considering automatic lighting system, we can model the knowledge base and rule base FML code portion, and in particular the lamp light level as shown in Listing 1 (Mamdani method).

Listing 1. FML sample program

```
<DOCTYPE FUZZYCONTROL SYSTEM "fml.dtd">
<FUZZYCONTROL d e f u z z i fyme t h o d = "CENTROID"
i p = "localhost" t y p e = "MAMDANI">
<KNOWLEDGEBASE IP = "localhost">
<FUZZYVARIABLE
    domainleft = "0" domainright = "1"
    i p = "localhost" name = "Luminosity"
    scale = "Lux"type = "INPUT">
    <FUZZYTERM name="low">
        <PISHAPE
            param1 = "0.0"
            param2 = "0 .45">
        </PISHAPE>
    </FUZZYTERM>
    <FUZZYTERM name="MEDIUM">
        <PISHAPE
            param1 = "0.49999999999999994"
            param2 = "0.44999999999999996">
        </PISHAPE>
    </FUZZYTERM>
    <FUZZYTERM name= "HIGH">
        <PISHAPE
            param1 = "0.5501" param2 = "1">
```

Listing 1. continued

```
            </PISHAPE>
        </FUZZYTERM>
</FUZZYVARIABLE>
</KNOWLEDGEBASE>
<RULEBASE
        inferenceengine = "MINMAXMINMAMDANI"
        i p = "localhost">
        <RULE connector = "AND" ip = "localhost"
            weight = "1">
            <ANTECEDENT>
                <CLAUSE not = "FALSE">
                    <VARIABLE> Luminosity </VARIABLE>
                        <TERM> low </TERM>
                </CLAUSE>
                <CLAUSE not = "FALSE">
                    <VARIABLE> hour </VARIABLE>
                        <TERM> morning </TERM>
                </CLAUSE>
            </ANTECEDENT>
            <CONSEQUENT>
                <CLAUSE not = "FALSE">
                    <VARIABLE>dimmer</VARIABLE>
                        <TERM>medium</TERM>
                </CLAUSE>
            </CONSEQUENT>
        </RULE>
▷▷▷
</RULEBASE>
</FUZZYCONTROL>
```

This bunch of FML code is useful to understand how it is possible to associate a fuzzy control activity (knowledge base and eventually the rule base) on a single host (in our example, localhost). In this naive example, a centralized Mamdani fuzzy controller is produced, but in real cases, a distributed approach is performed, as illustrated in Figure 4. This feature is useful to obtain several advantages:

- to parallelize the fuzzy inference engine reducing inference time and minimizing knowledge base and rule base occupancy;

Figure 4. Distributed fuzzy control tree

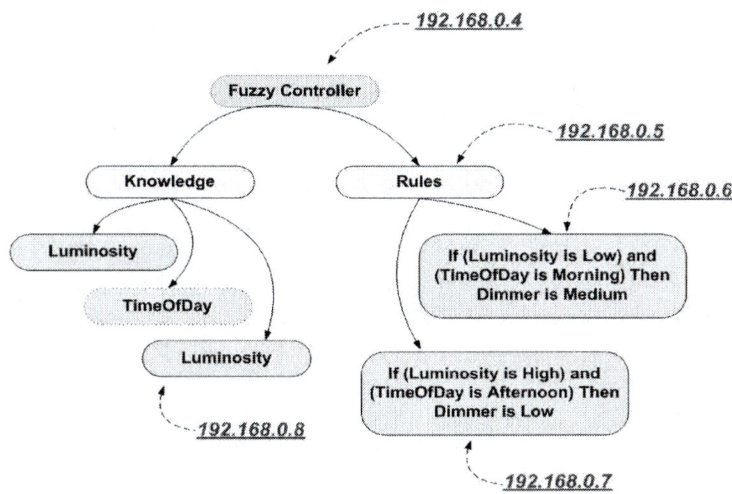

- to manage distributed knowledge environment, that is, environments in which the global knowledge is shared on many points of interested environment, as often happens in AmI;
- to exploit mobile agents as a natural and efficient technology to share data distribution and dispatch running code on a network.

In order to distribute fuzzy controller components on different hosts, we need to characterize the independent members of controller. In particular, working with Mamdani we identify the following components:

- fuzzy controller
- knowledge base
- fuzzy variable
- rule base
- fuzzy rule

The default value of ip attribute of <FUZZYCONTROL> tag is localhost. The Internet address value of the fuzzy controller is distributed toward the bottom in the parse tree related to fuzzy program. From this point of view, the Internet address of other independent components (knowledge base and rule base), if not defined, is overlapped by network address from <FUZZYCONTROL> tag. This distributive concept also is extended to the nodes of the parse tree related to the rule base and knowledge base: Each member of the controller is spread in a scalable and distributed way, as shown in Figure 4. Comparing Figures 3 and 4, we better note the strong differences between a centralized controller and a distributed one. In Figure 3, all components of the centralized controller are connected by straight lines indicating that all components (knowledge base, rule base, and related sub components) are maintained on the same host at the same time. Figure 4 shows a distributed fuzzy controller, whose members, connected by dotted lines, can be treated concurrently by different processes. In particular, Figure 4 shows a distributed fuzzy controller with luminosity and time of the day concepts hosted on 192.168.0.4, dimmer concept hosted on 192.168.0.8, and the rule base shared on 192.168.0.5, 192.168.0.6, and 192.168.0.7. In this way, we can distribute fuzzy rule base in the network and exploit distributed processing by minimizing inference. In order to address in a high-level way the issues of delocalization and concurrency, we map the distributed fuzzy model coded in FML on a multi-agents system. In particular, the agents that compose the system are: stationary fuzzy agent set, registry agent, and inference agent. The set of stationary fuzzy agent is used to manipulate in a distributed way the concept coded in FML program and modeled in the distributed fuzzy controller. These agents represent the run time containers able to execute the fuzzy logic operator on a modeled entity. Stationary fuzzy agents are hosted on the different hosts of the network; these hosts represent the fuzzy control network (FCN). The inference agent is a migrating agent able to apply the classic inference operator, like *Mamdani MinMaxMin* or *Larson Product* on hosts running the stationary agents. Due to the delocalization of rules, it is necessary to collect the partial inference results. This is done by the migration of inference agent that gathers the partial results available on each stationary. Just to give an idea of the gain from shifting a centralized to a decentralized evaluation, we give in Figure 5 the results from a testbed done by spreading the control over three computational nodes. On the axis x we report the number of fuzzy rules evaluated, the required inference time, expressed in milliseconds, is on axis y.

Figure 5. Mobile agent fuzzy improvements using three agents

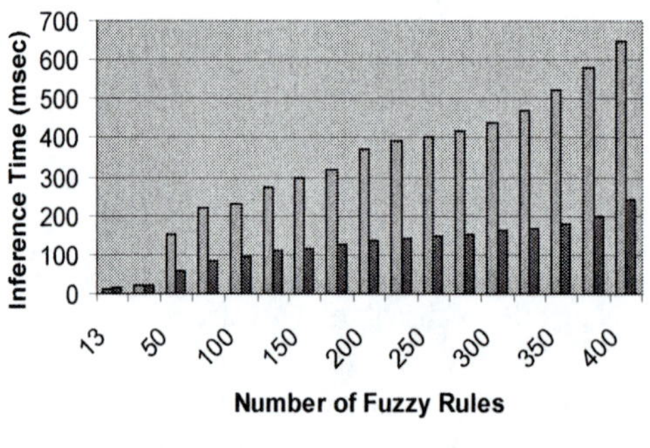

H2ML: Human to Markup Language

The proposed system architecture is organized in several layers, as depicted in Figure 6. In the first layer from top, ambient intelligence environment, a set of sensors and actuator wired via a domotic protocol is used to gather data about current user status (temperature, gait, position, facial expression, etc.). Part of information gathered at this stage is handled by morphological recognition subsystems (i.e., facial recognition eubsystem [8]) resulting in a semantic description. These kinds of information, together with the remaining information retrieved in the environment, are organized in a hierarchical structure based on XML technology in order to create a new markup language, called Human to Markup Language

Figure 6. Ambient intelligent architecture

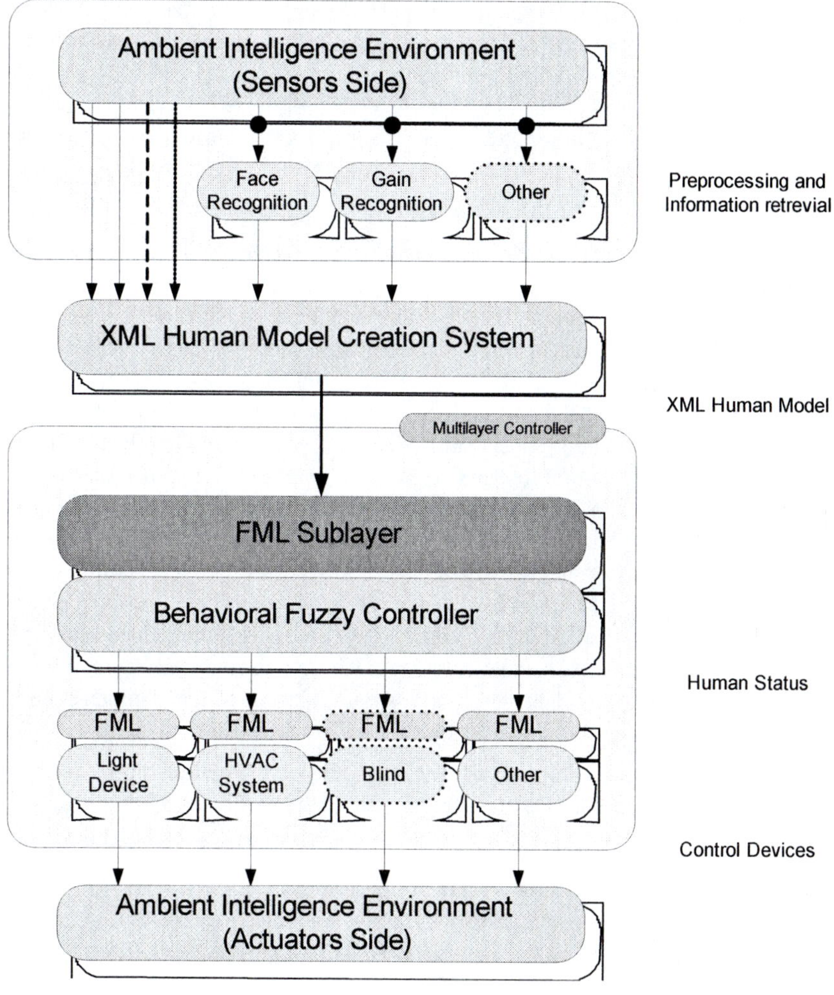

(H2ML). H2ML is a new tool to model human information allowing a transparent use in different intelligent frameworks.

The other layer, multilayer controller, based on the hierarchical fuzzy control, represents the core designed to distribute appropriate services related to the information contained in H2ML representation. Each fuzzy controller used in our architecture is coded in FML in order to achieve hardware transparency and to minimize the fuzzy inference time.

The ambient intelligence environment can be defined as the set of actuators and sensors composing the system together with the domotic interconnection protocol (Lontalk+IP in our case). The AmI environment is based on the following sensors and actuators: *internal* and *external temperature* sensors and *internal temperature* actuator, *internal* and *external luminosity* sensor and *internal luminosity* actuator, *indoor presence sensor*. Moreover, the system relies on a set of color cameras to capture information about gait and facial expression, and an infrared camera to capture thermal images of the users.

Recently, some approaches have been proposed to model the human aspect by using specific languages. Virtual Human Markup Language (VHML) (Marriot, 2002), and Multi-Modal Presentation Markup Language (Prendinger, 2004) are examples of languages proposed to simplify the human-computer interaction through a virtual Web assistant. While the mentioned languages are based on a high-level description of human status (i.e., happy and fear face concepts), H2ML is focused on detailed, low-level description of physical human features (i.e., closed and opened eyes or mouth). These features are important for AmI scenarios, in two wide applications:

- **Embodied conversational agents.** Conversational agents will be an integral part of ambient intelligent environments since they add a social dimension to man-machine communication and thus may help to make such environments more attractive to the human user. Earlier agent-based applications were characterized by a clear separation between the user's and the agent's world. Recently, there has been a trend, however, to merge the virtual and the physical space enabling completely new forms of interaction. Since agents embody inner features that underlie adaptive, robust and effective behavior, it is more natural for designer to mix together heterogeneous techniques to better represent and handle, at different levels of granularity and complexity, dynamic environments. Furthermore, the possibility to integrate useful pieces of intelligence into embedded artifact makes realizable scenarios of high-level ubiquitous computing. This vision has strongly stimulated the research community in envisaging agents stemmed with physical devices. These agents are named embedded agents, which were run in an embedded system or device. We believe that unifying conversational with embodied agents will represent a new paradigm for which a human is immersed in the proactive environment and vice versa (Churchill, 2000).
- **Context awareness.** Roughly, the system should own a certain ability to recognize people and the situational context, by processing human-oriented features.

In order to define language lexicon we have to describe a human in terms of morphological features. The H2ML implementation is based on tags referring to different nodes of the human representation tree. Each tag can use two different attributes: *value* and *status*. The value attribute is used to represent human features by a numeric continuous range, while status attribute is used to model information through a discrete set of labels.

Starting from the root, the <INDIVIDUAL> tag corresponding to the root tag of a H2ML program is created. Each child of this tag represents a specific structured biometric descriptor. In particular, the following set of tags is introduced: <PHYSICAL>, <FACE>, <THERMAL>, <SPEECH>, and <GAIT>.

The <PHYSICAL> tag refers to the height, weight, and build features of represented individual through corresponding tags <HEIGHT>, <WEIGHT>, <BUILD> and the related attributes *value* and *status*. The <FACE> tag is used to handle facial features. Such features are modeled by <EYES>, <EYEBROWS>, and <MOUTH> tags. The <EYES> tag has two child tags: <RIGHTEYE>, <LEFTEYE>. Eye features are modeled by <COLOR> tag. <EYEBROWS> tag is the root of a morphological subtree containing <LEFT> and <RIGHT> tags modeling the corresponding eyebrow. Finally, the <MOUTH> tag and its *status* attribute models the mouth-lips shape.

Body thermal features are represented through <TEMPERATURE> and <TMAP> tags nested in the <THERMAL> branch of the morphological tree. These tags use the *value* and *status* attribute to respectively model temperature and thermal distribution. The <SPEECH> tag represents voice features by <ACOUSTIC> and <SPECTRAL> nested tags. The last morphological subtree models motion features through the <GAIT> tag. Its child tags <POSITION>, <VELOTICY>, <ACCELERATION>, and <MOTION> are used to represent

Figure 7a. H2ML used to handle facial features

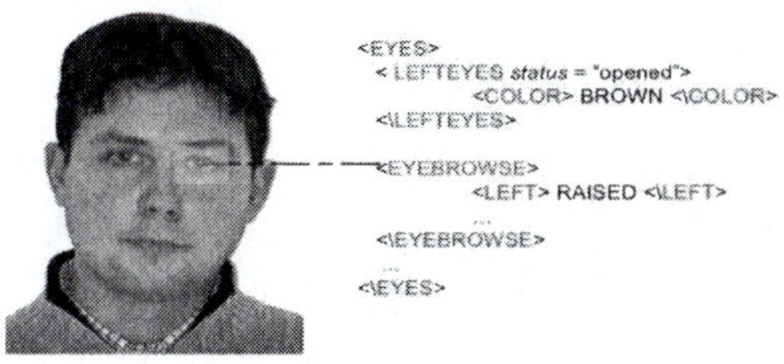

Figure 7b. H2ML used to handle body features

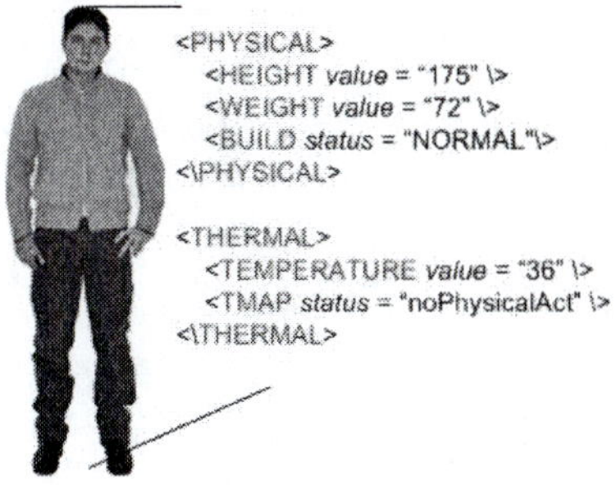

related physical properties. While the first three tags use the *value* attribute, the fourth one uses the *status* attribute to model the motion pattern property. Figures 7a and 7b show some examples of H2ML codes.

Vertical and Horizontal Fuzzy Distribution

The hierarchical structure of the proposed fuzzy controller is suited to apply a "divide et impera" strategy to the controlled system. Main goals are decomposed into sub-goals by partitioning the input space into a finite number of regions, each one featuring a specific sub-controller.

The divide et impera strategy leads to two different kinds of fuzzy rulebase distribution: *vertical* and *horizontal* distribution.

By "vertical fuzzy distribution" we mean a collection of dependent *control blocks* each ones represented by a single fuzzy controller or a set of horizontally distributed fuzzy controllers. The *dependency* relationship between control blocks is defined as follows: given a finite set of control block $\{CB_1, CB_2, \ldots, CB_i, \ldots, CB_n\}$ the output returned from the CB_i control block depends from the output computed from CB_{i-1} control block and so on. In particular, the defuzzified output of control block CB_{i-1} represents a fuzzy cutter for the aggregated, but not defuzzified, output of control block CB_i. The aim of the proposed vertical fuzzy distribution scheme is to separate fuzzy concepts not semantically related, emphasizing the fuzzy reasoning properties.

Through the "horizontal fuzzy distribution," we can parallelize inferences on different hosts, splitting a large semantically related rulebase by mobile agent technology, thus minimizing the fuzzy inference time (see the Fuzzy Markup Language section).

Experimental Results

Our scheme of fuzzy distribution allows separating the fuzzy variables related to human behavior from those related to domotic devices (vertical distribution). This distinction is thus used to parallelize the fuzzy inference applied to domotic controllers (horizontal distribution). More precisely, the first control block (vertical wise), named *behavioral fuzzy controller*, basically: (1) operates on H2ML program; (2) parses it; and (3) infers information about human status. The system adopts *singleton* fuzzy variables to model the behavioral concepts in fuzzy terms. *Sleeping*, *working*, and *relaxing* are only some examples of singleton behavioral fuzzy variables; the following rules are examples of behavioral rules:

IF velocity is LOW AND leftEye is CLOSED AND RightEye is CLOSED AND Speech is LOW AND Position is BED

THEN SLEEPING is ON

IF velocity is LOW AND leftEye is OPENED AND RightEye is OPENED AND Speech is LOW AND Position is Desk AND Acceleration is HIGH

THEN UserStatus is WORKING is ON

IF Velocity is LOW AND leftEye is OPENED AND rightEye is OPENED AND Speech is LOW AND Position is not BED

THEN RELAXING is ON

…

Figure 8. FML / H2ML application view

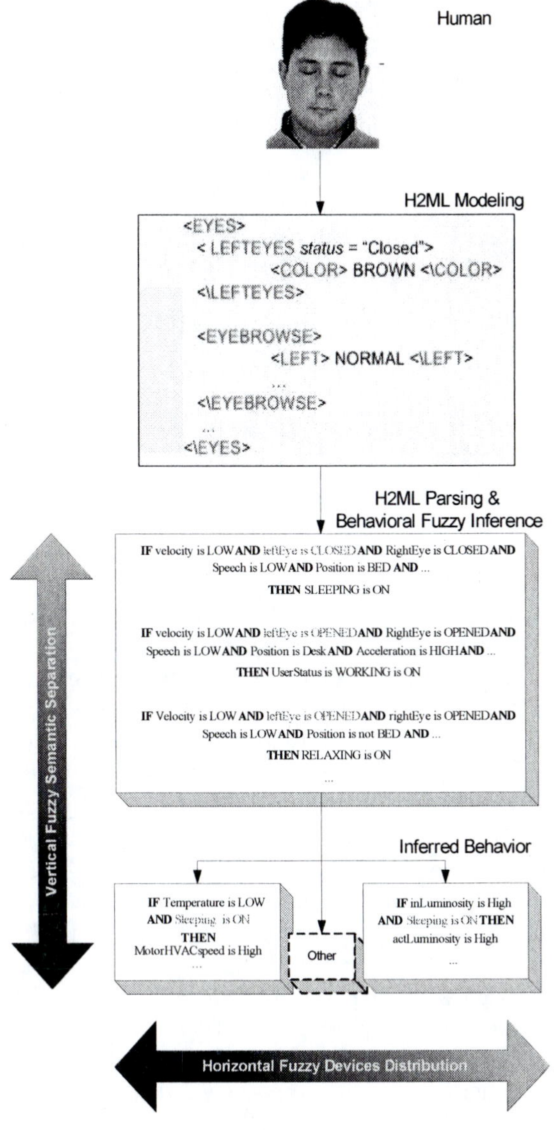

The information inferred at this stage will be used in the next level to control the actuator devices.

The second control block (vertical wise) is a set of semantically related controllers distributed using horizontal scheme. At this hierarchical level the system uses classic fuzzy controllers coded in FML. In particular, we code a whole fuzzy ambient intelligence controller distributing the related rules (e.g., HVAC rules or lighting system rules) on different hosts. Some examples of devices control distributed fuzzy rules are shown:

IF Temperature is LOW AND Sleeping is ON
THEN MotorHVACspeed is High

IF inLuminosity is LOW AND
Working is ON THEN actLuminosity is High
...

It is simple to note that information related to behavior inferred from root layer of hierarchic intelligence scheme is used merely to cut the fuzzy set composing the consequent part of rules so as to influence the device's operation. An application view of our framework is shown in Figure 8.

Conclusion

The importance of human body monitoring is fundamental for many sectors such as health, rehabilitation and gerontology, as well as domestic environments. In most cases, it is crucial to evaluate many indexes of activities, such as movement or acceleration of body segments, frequency of posture change, walking speed, and so forth. For this purpose, we find a growing set of instruments capable of capturing and tracking the human features. Even though many efforts are made for solving the several practical drawbacks arising from the use of these devices, minor experiences are reported to provide the abstract and problem-independent description model useful for the interoperability and adaptive control strategies. This issue is crucial for intelligent environment applications, but it is not fully supported by the currently available technologies. Sun JINI and Microsoft UPnP are two popular examples of network specifications for easy connection to home information appliances and computers, but they are rather primitive and demand a lot of complex works (in terms of several software layers) so as to bridge the framework with the sensor software level. Only recently, the scientific community is paying much attention to the problem of flexible and uniform utilization of sensors in advanced programmable controllers. The markup languages or in more general the formal conceptual description have played a key role in this direction. For the sake of simplicity we cite just two works (Noguchi, 2003; Fodor, 1998). In Noguchi (2003), the authors made a choice using XML to implement the sensor network middleware. This choice: allows achieving remarkable benefits for network transparency and flexible sensor management. A wider perspective has been deepened in Fodor (1998), where the concept and implication of an ontological controller are discussed. The ontological controller supervises a programmable controller in order to: (1) detect dynamically when the programmable controller is in a critical situation due to a violation of ontological assumptions and (2) move (when possible) the programmable controller into such a state from which it can regain its control (recovery operation). The combination of FML and H2ML in a multi-layered architecture represents a strong improvement for abstraction representation and efficient control management for real hardware AmI implementation (Echelon Lonworks, X10, Konnex, etc.). Moreover, the FML layer allows distributing fuzzy controller components on different hosts, thus providing a simple platform for real ubiquitous computing system.

References

Aarts, E. (2004, January-March). Ambient intelligence: A multimedia perspective. *IEEE Multimedia, 11*(1), 12-19.

Acampora, G., & Loia, V. (2005a, May 22-25). Using fuzzy technology in ambient intelligence environment. In *Proceedings of the IEEE International Conference on Fuzzy Systems*, Reno, NV.

Acampora, G., & Loia, V. (2005b). Fuzzy control interoperability and scalability for adaptive domotic framework. *IEEE Transactions on Industrial Informatics, 1*(2), 97-111.

Astrom, K. J. (1987). Adaptive feedback control. *Proceedings of the IEEE, 75*(2), 185-217.

Churchill E. (Ed.). (2000). *Embodied conversational agents*. Cambridge, MA: The MIT Press.

Ditze, M., Kamper, G., Jahnich, I., & Bernhardi-Grisson, R. (2004, June 24-26). Service-based access to distributed embedded devices through the open service gateway. In *Proceedings of the 2nd IEEE International Conference on Industrial Informatics*, Berlin, Germany (pp. 493-498).

DuCharme, B. (1999). *XML: The annotated specification.* Upper Saddle River, NJ: Prentice Hall.

Fodor, G. A. (1998). *Ontologically controlled autonomous systems: Principles, operations, and architecture*. Kluwer Academic.

Mamdani, E. H. (1974). Applications of fuzzy algorithms for simple dynamic plants. *Proceedings of IEEE, 121*, 1585-1588.

Marriott A., & Stallo, J. (2002, July 16). VHML: Uncertainties and problems, a discussion. In *Proceedings of the AAMAS-02 Workshop on Embodied Conversational Agents*, Bologna, Italy.

Noguchi, H., Mori, T., & Sato, T. (2003, October). Network middleware for utilization of sensors in room. In *Proceedings of IEEE/RSJ International Conference on Intelligent Robots and Systems,* Las Vegas, NV (Vol. 2, pp. 1832-1838).

Prendinger, H., Descamps, S., & Ishizuka, M. (2004). MPML: A markup language for controlling the behavior of life-like characters. *Journal of Visual Languages and Computing, 15*, 183-203.

Schilit, B., & Theimer, M. (1994). Disseminating active map information to mobile hosts. *IEEE Network, 8*(5), 22-32.

Takagi, T., & Sugeno, M. (1985) Fuzzy identification of systems and its applications to modeling and control. *IEEE Transactions on Systems, Man and Cybernetics, 15*(1), 116-132.

Zadeh, L. A. (1965). Fuzzy sets. *Information and Control, 8*, 338-353.

Chapter II

Intelligent Ant Colony System for Traveling Salesman Problem and Clustering

Shu-Chuan Chu, Cheng Shiu University, Taiwan

Jeng-Shyang Pan, Kaohsiung University of Applied Sciences, Taiwan, & Harbin Institute of Technology, China

Abstract

Processes that simulate natural phenomena have successfully been applied to a number of problems for which no simple mathematical solution is known or is practicable. Such meta-heuristic algorithms include genetic algorithms, particle swarm optimization, and ant colony systems and have received increasing attention in recent years. This work parallelizes the ant colony systems and introduces the communication strategies so as to reduce the computation time and reach the better solution for the traveling salesman problem. We also extend ant colony systems and discuss a novel data clustering process using constrained ant colony optimization (CACO). The CACO algorithm extends the ant colony optimization algorithm by accommodating a quadratic distance metric, the sum of K nearest neighbor distances (SKNND) metric, constrained addition of pheromone, and a shrinking range strategy to improve data clustering. We show that the CACO algorithm can resolve the problems of clusters with arbitrary shapes, clusters with outliers, and bridges between clusters.

History of Ant System and Ant Colony System

The Ant System algorithm (Colorni, Dorigo, & Maniezzo, 1991; Dorigo, Maniezzo, & Colorni, 1996) is a cooperative population-based search algorithm inspired by the behaviour of real ants. As each ant constructs a route from nest to food by stochastically following the quantities of pheromone level, the intensity of laying pheromone will bias the path-choosing decision-make of subsequent ants. It is a new member of the class of meta-heuristics joining algorithms such as simulated annealing (Kirkpatrick, Gelatt,, & Vecchi, 1983; Huang, Pan, Lu, Sun, & Hang, 2001), genetic algorithms (Goldberg, 1989; Pan, McInnes, & Jack, 1995), tabu search approaches (Golver, & Laguna, 1997; Pan, & Chu, 1996), particle swarm optimization (Eberhart, & Kennedy, 1995; Chang, Chu, Roddick,, & Pan, 2005] and neural networks (Kohonen, 1995; Kung, 1993). In common with many of these, the ant system algorithm is similarly derived from nature.

The operation of ant systems can be illustrated by the classical traveling salesman problem (see Figure 1). In the TSP problem, a traveling salesman problem is looking for a route which covers all cities with minimal total distance. Suppose there are n cities and m ants. The entire algorithm starts with initial pheromone intensity set to τ_0 on all edges. In every subsequent ant system cycle, or episode, each ant begins its trip from a randomly selected starting city and is required to visit every city exactly once (a Hamiltonian circuit). The experience gained in this phase is then used to update the pheromone intensity on all edges.

Given a finite set of cities and the distance between each pair of cities, the traveling salesman problem (TSP) aims to find a route through all cities by visiting each exactly once and returning to the initial city such that the total distance traveled is minimized. Assume m artificial ants travel through n cities. The operation of ant systems for the traveling salesman problem (*TSP*) is given next (Dorigo, Maniezzo, & Colorni, 1996; Dorigo & Gambardella, 1997):

Step 1: Randomly select the initial city for each ant. The initial pheromone level between any two cities is set to be a small positive constant. Set the cycle counter to be 0.

Step 2: Calculate the transition probability from city r to city s for the kth ant as:

$$P_k(r,s) = \begin{cases} \dfrac{[\tau(r,s)]\cdot[\eta(r,s)]^{\beta}}{\sum_{u\in J_k(r)} [\tau(r,u)]\cdot[\eta(r,u)]^{\beta}} & , \ if \ s \in J_k(r) \\ 0 & , \ otherwise \end{cases} \tag{1}$$

where r is the current city, s is the next city, $\tau(r, s)$ is the pheromone level between city r and city s, $\eta(r,s) = \dfrac{1}{\delta(r,s)}$ the inverse of the distance $\delta(r, s)$ between city r and city s, $J_k(r)$ is the set of cities that remain to be visited by the kth ant positioned on city r, and β is a parameter which determines the relative importance of pheromone level versus distance. Select the next visited city s for the kth ant with the probability $P_k(r, s)$. Repeat step 2 for each ant until the ants have toured all cities.

Figure 1. A traveling salesman problem with 12 cities

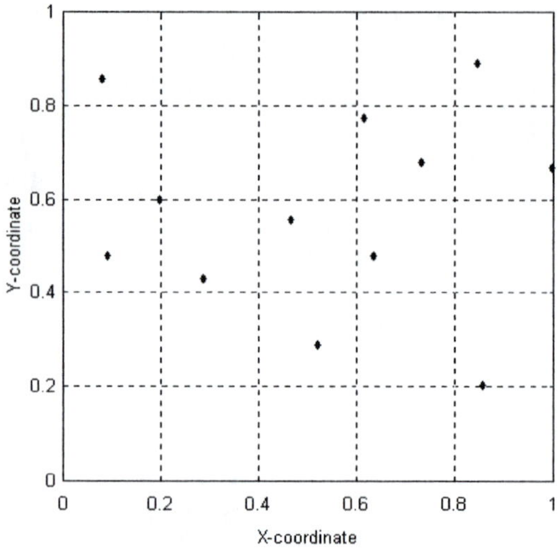

Step 3: Update the pheromone level between cities as:

$$\tau(r,s) \leftarrow (1-\alpha)\cdot \tau(r,s) + \sum_{k=1}^{m} \Delta \tau_k(r,s) \tag{2}$$

$$\Delta\tau_k(r,s) = \begin{cases} \dfrac{1}{L_k}, & if\,(r,s) \in route\ \ done\ \ by\ \ ant\ \ k \\ 0, & otherwise \end{cases} \tag{3}$$

$\Delta\tau_k(r, s)$ is the pheromone level laid down between cities r and s by the kth ant, L_k is the length of the route visited by the kth ant, m is the number of ants and $0 < \alpha < 1$ is a pheromone decay parameter.

Step 4: Increment cycle counter. Move the ants to the originally selected cities and continue Steps 2 to 4 until the behavior stagnates or the maximum number of cycles has reached, where a stagnation is indicated when all ants take the same route.

From Equation 1, it is clear ant system (AS) needs a high level of computation to find the next visited city for each ant.

Implementations of the ant system by applying program to the test problem in Figure 1 are given in Figures 2 and 3. Figure 2 reports a found shortest route of length 3.308, which is the truly shortest route validated by exhaustive search. Figure 3 gives a snapshot of the pheromone intensities after 20 episodes. A higher intensity is represented by a wider edge. Notice that intensity alone cannot be used as a criteria for judging whether a link is a constitute part of the shortest route or not, since the shortest route relies on the cooperation of other links.

Figure 2. The shortest route found by the ant system

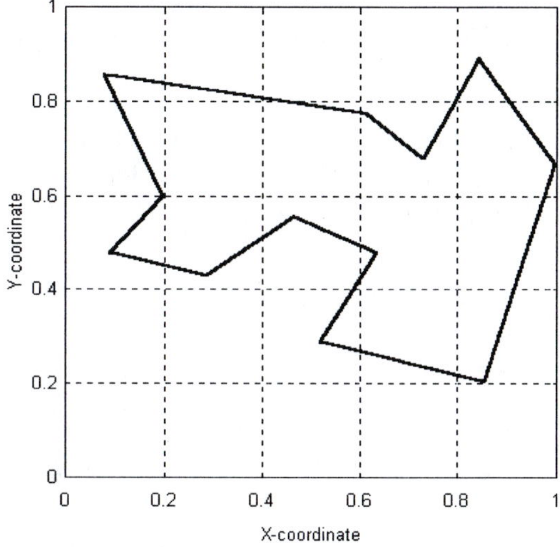

Figure 3. The snapshot of pheromone intensities after 20 episodes

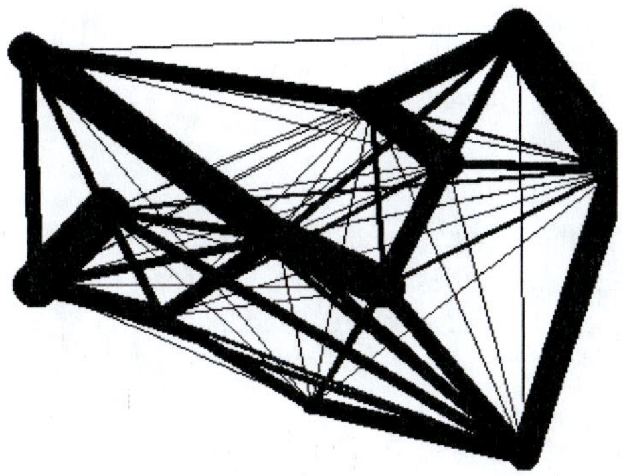

In order to improve the search efficiency, the ant colony system (ACS) was proposed (Dorigo, & Gambardella, 1997). ACS is based on AS but updates the pheromone level before moving to the next city (local updating rule) and updating the pheromone level for the shortest route only after completing the route for each ant (global updating rule). The algorithm of the ant colony system can be described as seen in the following steps.

Step 1: Randomly select the initial city for each ant. The initial pheromone level between any two cities is set to be a small positive constant τ_0. Set the cycle counter to be 0.

Step 2: Calculate the next city s to be visited for each ant according to:

$$s = \begin{cases} \arg\max_{u \in J_k(r)} [\tau(r,u)] \cdot [\eta(r,u)]^{\beta} & , \text{ if } q \le q_0 \quad (\text{exploitation}) \\ S & , \text{ otherwise} \ (\text{biased exploration}) \end{cases} \tag{4}$$

where q is a random number between 0 and 1, q_0 is a constant between 0 and 1, S is random variable selected using the probability distribution given in Equation 1 and β is a parameter which determines the relative importance of pheromone level versus distance.

Step 3: Update the pheromone level between cities as:

$$\tau(r, s) \leftarrow (1-\rho) \cdot \tau(r, s) + \rho \cdot \Delta\tau(r, s) \tag{5}$$

where $\Delta\tau(r, s) = \tau_0 = (n \times L_{nn})^{-1}$ and L_{nn} is an approximate distance of the route of all cities using nearest neighbour heuristic, n is the number of cities and $0 < \rho < 1$ is a pheromone decay parameter. Repeat Steps 2 and 3 for each ant until all cities are visited.

Step 4: Increment cycle counter. Update the pheromone level of the shortest route according to:

$$\tau(r, s) \leftarrow (1-\alpha) \cdot \tau(r, s) + \alpha \cdot \Delta\tau(r, s) \tag{6}$$

$$\Delta\tau(r,s) = \begin{cases} (L_{gb})^{-1} & , \text{ if } (r,s) \in \text{global best route} \\ 0 & , \text{ otherwise} \end{cases} \tag{7}$$

where L_{gb} is the length of the shortest route and α is a pheromone decay parameter. Move the ants to the originally selected cities and continue Steps 2 to 4 until the behavior stagnates or a maximum number of cycles has been reached, as before.

Ant Colony System with Communication Strategies

A parallel computer consists of a large number of processing elements which can be dedicated to solving a single problem at a time. Pipeline processing and data parallelism are two popular parallel processing methods. The function of the pipeline processing is to separate the problem into a cascade of tasks where each task is executed by an individual processor, while data parallelism involves distributing the data to be processed amongst all processors which then executes the same procedure on each subset of the data. Data parallelism has been applied to genetic algorithm by dividing the population into several groups and running the same algorithm over each group using different processor (Cohoon, Hegde, Martine, & Richards, 1987). The resulting parallel genetic algorithm has been successfully applied to noise reduction of vector quantization based communication (Pan, McInnes, & Jack, 1996a).

Parallelization strategies for AS (Bullnheimer, Kotsis, & Strauss, 1997) and ACS (Stützle, 1998) have been investigated, however, these studies are based on simply applying AS or ACS on the multi-processor, that is, the parallelization strategies simply share the computation load over several processors. No experiments demonstrate the sum of the computation time for all processors can be reduced compared with the single processor works on the AS or ACS.

In this work, we apply the concept of parallel processing to ant colony system (ACS) and a parallel ant colony system (PACS) is proposed. The purpose of the PAS and PACS is not just to reduce the computation time. Rather a parallel formulation is developed which gives not only reduces the elapsed and the computation time but also obtains a better solution. The artificial ants are firstly generated and separated into several groups. The ant colony system algorithm is then applied to each group and communication between groups is applied according to some fixed cycles. The basic idea of the communication is to update the pheromone level for each route according to the best routes found by neighbouring groups or, in some cases, all groups. Seven communication strategies are separately proposed for PACS. Experimental results based on the traveling salesman problem confirm the efficiency and effectiveness of the proposed PACS (Chu, Roddick, Pan, & Su, 2003; Chu, Roddick, & Pan, 2004).

Description

The ant colony system has been shown to be the improved version of the ant system by adding the local updating pheromone level immediately after moving each city for each ant and global updating pheromone level for the best route. We apply the idea of data parallelism to the ant colony system (ACS) and a parallel ant colony system (PACS) (Chu, Roddick, & Pan, 2004) is proposed. The parallel ant colony system (PACS) is described in the following steps.

Step 1: Initialization – Generate N_j artificial ants for the jth group, j=0, 1, ..., G-1. N_j and G are the number of artificial ants for the jth group and the number of groups, respectively. Randomly select an initial city for each ant. The initial pheromone level between any two cities is set to be a small positive constant τ_0. Set the cycle counter to be 0.

Step 2: Movement – Calculate the next visited city s for the ith ant in the jth group according to:

$$s = \begin{cases} \arg\max_{u \in J_{i,j}(r)} [\tau_j(r,u)] \cdot [\eta(r,u)]^{\beta}, & if \;\; q \le q_0 \;\; (exploitation) \\ visit\ city\ s\ with\ P_{i,j}(r,s) & , if \;\; q > q_0 \;\; (biased\ exploration) \end{cases}$$

$$P_{i,j}(r,s) = \begin{cases} \dfrac{[\tau_j(r,s)] \cdot [\eta(r,s)]^{\beta}}{\sum_{u \in J_k(r)} [\tau_j(r,s)] \cdot [\eta(r,s)]^{\beta}}, & if \;\; s \in J_{i,j}(r) \\ 0, & otherwise \end{cases}$$

where $P_{i,j}(r, s)$ is the transition probability from city r to city s for the ith ant in the jth group. $\tau_j(r, s)$ is the pheromone level between city r to city s in the jth group. $\eta(r,s) = \frac{1}{\delta(r,s)}$ the inverse of the distance $\delta(r, s)$ between city r and city s. $J_{i,j}(r)$ is the set of cities that remain to be visited by the ith ant in the jth group and β is a parameter which determines the relative importance of pheromone level versus distance. q is a random number between 0 and 1 and q_0 is a constant between 0 and 1.

Step 3: Local Pheromone Level Updating Rule – Update the pheromone level between cities for each group as:

$$\tau_j(r, s) \leftarrow (1-\rho) \cdot \tau_j(r, s) + \rho \cdot \Delta\tau(r, s)$$

$$\Delta\tau(r, s) = \tau_0 = (n \times L_{nn})^{-1}$$

where $\tau_j(r, s)$ the pheromone level between cities r and s for the ants in the jth group, L_{nn} is an approximate distance of the route between all cities using the *nearest neighbour heuristic*, n is the number of cities and $0 < \rho < 1$ is a pheromone decay parameter. Continue Step 2 and 3 until each ant in each group completes the route.

Step 4: Evaluation – Calculate the total length of the route for each ant in each group.

Step 5: Global Pheromone Level Updating Rule – Update the pheromone level between cities for each group as:

$$\tau_j(r, s) \leftarrow (1-\alpha) \cdot \tau_j(r, s) + \alpha \cdot \Delta\tau_j(r, s)$$

$$\Delta\tau_j(r,s) = \begin{cases} (L_j)^{-1} & , \ \textit{if} \ (r,s) \in \textit{best route of jth group} \\ 0 & , \ \textit{otherwise} \end{cases}$$

where L_j is the shortest length for the ants in the jth group and α is a pheromone decay parameter.

Figure 4. Update the pheromone level according to the best route of all groups

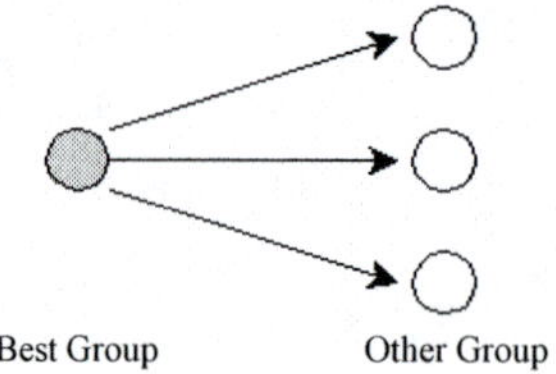

Step 6: Updating From Communication – Seven communication strategies are proposed next.

- **Strategy 1:** As shown in Figure 4, update the pheromone level between cities for each group for every R_1 cycles as:

  $$\tau_j(r, s) \leftarrow \tau_j(r, s) + \lambda \cdot \Delta\tau_{best}(r, s)$$

  $$\Delta\tau_{best}(r,s) = \begin{cases} (L_{gb})^{-1} & , \ if \ (r,s) \in best \ route \ of \ all \ groups \\ 0 & , \ otherwise \end{cases}$$

  where λ is a pheromone decay parameter and L_{gb} is the length of the best route of all groups, that is, $L_{gb} \leq L_j$, $j = 0, 1, ..., G - 1$.
- **Strategy 2:** As shown in Figure 5, update the pheromone level between cities for each group for every R_2 cycles as:

  $$\tau_j(r, s) \leftarrow \tau_j(r, s) + \lambda \cdot \Delta\tau_{ng}(r, s)$$

  $$\Delta\tau_{ng}(r,s) = \begin{cases} (L_{ng})^{-1} & , \ if \ (r,s) \in best \ route \ of \ neighbour \ group \\ 0 & , \ otherwise \end{cases}$$

  where *neighbour* is defined as being the group whose binary representation of the group number *j* differs by the least significant bit. λ is a pheromone decay parameter and L_{ng} is the length of the shortest route in the neighbour group.
- **Strategy 3:** As shown in Figure 6, update the pheromone between cities for each group for every R_3 cycles as:

  $$\tau_j(r, s) \leftarrow \tau_j(r, s) + \lambda \cdot \Delta\tau_{ng}(r, s)$$

  $$\Delta\tau_{ng}(r,s) = \begin{cases} (L_{ng})^{-1} & , \ if \ (r,s) \in best \ route \ of \ neighbour \ group \\ 0 & , \ otherwise \end{cases}$$

Figure 5. Update the pheromone level between each pair of groups

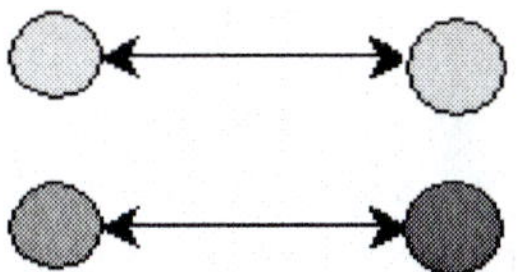

Figure 6. Update the pheromone level according to the ring structure

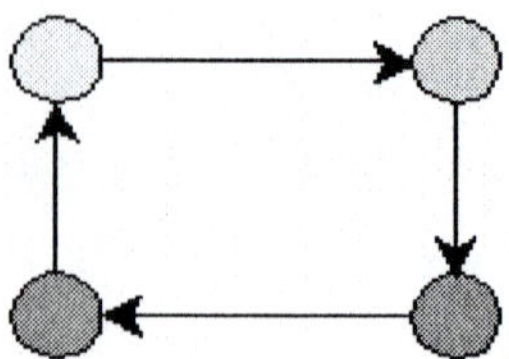

Figure 7. Update the pheromone level to the neighbours according to the group number j differs by one bit

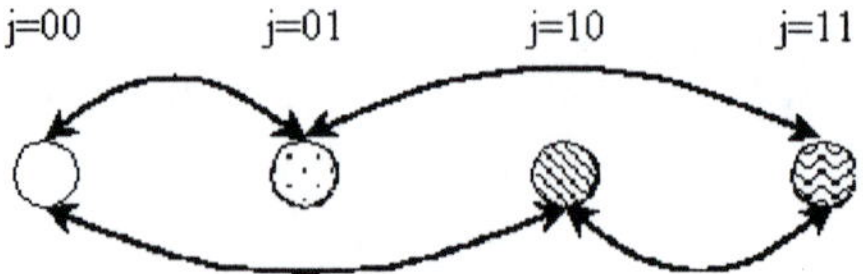

where *neighbour* is defined as being the group arranged as the ring structure. λ is a pheromone decay parameter and L_{ng} is the length of the shortest route in the neighbour group.

- **Strategy 4:** As shown in Figure 7, update the pheromone between cities for each group for every R_4 cycles as:

$$\tau_j(r, s) \leftarrow \tau_j(r, s) + \lambda \cdot \Delta\tau_{ng}(r, s)$$

$$\Delta\tau_{ng}(r,s) = \begin{cases} (L_{ng})^{-1} \ , \ \textit{if} \quad (r,s) \in \textit{best route of neighbour group} \\ 0 \ , \ \textit{otherwise} \end{cases}$$

where *neighbour* is defined as being those groups where the binary representation of the group number j differs by one bit. λ is a pheromone decay parameter and L_{ng} is the length of the shortest route in the neighbour group.

- **Strategy 5:** Update the pheromone between cities for each group using both Strategy 1 and Strategy 2.
- **Strategy 6:** Update the pheromone between cities for each group using both Strategy 1 and Strategy 3.
- **Strategy 7:** Update the pheromone between cities for each group using both Strategy 1 and Strategy 4.

Step 7: Termination – Increment the cycle counter. Move the ants to the originally selected cities and continue Steps 2 to 6 until the stagnation or a present maximum number of cycles has reached, where a stagnation indicated by all ants taking the same route.

Experimental Results for the Traveling Salesman Problem

To evaluate the effectiveness of PACS, we have performed an extensive performance study. In this section, we report our experimental results on comparing PACS with ant system (AS) and ant colony system (ACS). It is shown that PACS and various combinations outperform both ant system (AS) and ant colony system (ACS).

We used three generally available and typical data sets, EIL101, ST70 and TSP225 as the test material[1] to test the performance of the ant system (AS), ant colony system (ACS), and parallel ant colony system (PACS) for the traveling salesman problem.

To ensure a fair comparison among AS, ACS and PACS, the number of groups × the number of ants per group was kept constant — the number of ants for AS and ACS were set to be 80, one swarm with 80 ants, as reported by 1×80. For PACS, the number of ants was also set to be 80 that was divided into 4 groups with 20 ants in each group (i.e., 4×20) and 8 groups with 10 ants in each group (i.e., 8×10), respectively. The parameters were set to the following values: $\beta = 2$, $q_0 = 0.9$, $\alpha = \rho = \lambda = 0.1$ (Dorigo & Gambardella, 1997). The number of iterations for both EIL101 and ST70 were set to be 1000 and TSP225 was set to be 2000 as the cities of TSP225 are more than EIL101 and ST70 data sets. The number of cycles (i.e., R_1, R_2, R_3 and R_4) between updates of the pheromone level from communication for strategies 1 to 7 in PACS were set to be 30. In order to test the performance of the different approaches to the traveling salesman problem, variously proposed communication strategies for updating the pheromone level between groups in PACS were combined. Where appropriate, these seven communication strategies are applied to the PACS and compared to AS and ACS.

EIL101, ST70, and TSP225 are data sets with 101, 70, and 225 cities, respectively. Experimental results were carried out to the average shortest length for 10 seeds. The performance of PACS (i.e., ACS with communication strategy) is better by in comparison with AS and

Figure 8. Performance comparison among AS, ACS, and two arbitrarily chosen strategies for EIL101 data set

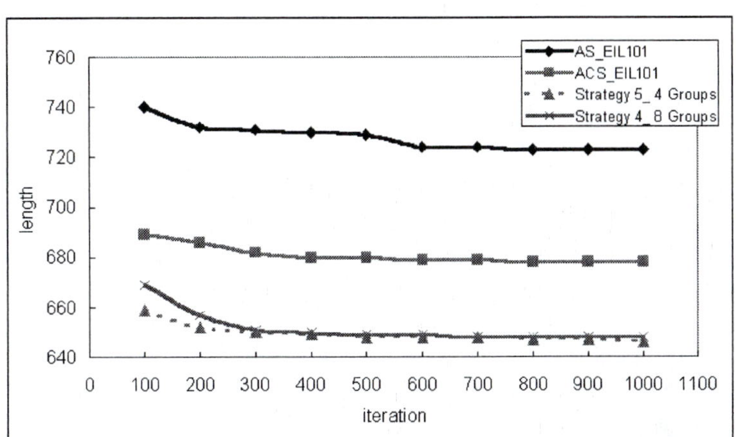

Figure 9. Performance comparison among AS, ACS, and two arbitrarily chosen strategies for ST70 data set

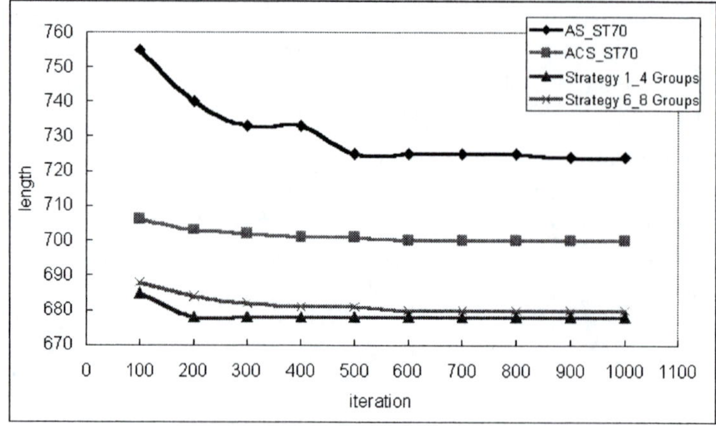

Figure 10. Performance comparison among AS, ACS, and two arbitrarily chosen strategies for TSP225 data set.

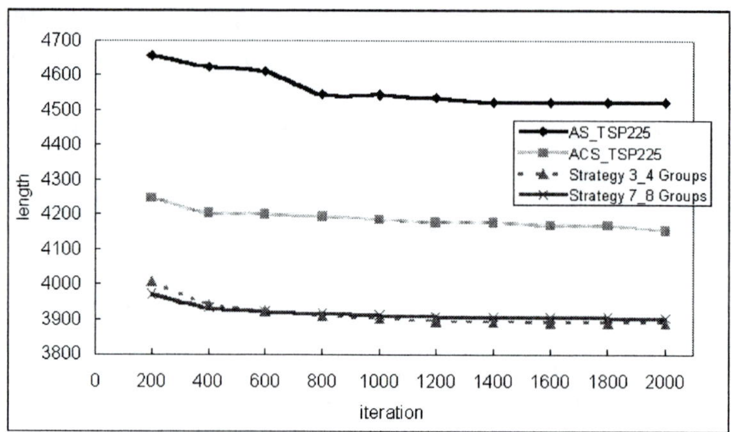

ACS can be illustrated by Figures 8, 9, and 10. As can be seen from Tables 1, 2, and 3, PACS outperforms both AS and ACS on effectiveness.

The EIL101 data set was used for the first experiment. As shown in Table 1, the average improvement on EIL101 for proposed Strategy 5 for four groups with 20 ants in each group by comparing with AS and ACS were much better up to be 10.57% and 4.70%, respectively. In comparison with AS and ACS, the average improvement on EIL101 for proposed Strategy 3 for eight groups with 10 ants in each group were 10.41% and 4.52%, respectively.

The ST70 data set was used for the second experiment. As we can see from Table 2, the average performance of proposed Strategy 3 for four groups with 20 ants in each group by compared with AS and ACS were 6.20% and 3.06%, respectively, and that of proposed Strategy 6 for eight groups with 10 ants in each group were 6.06% and 2.92%, respectively.

Finally, in the case of TSP225 data set, the experimental results shown in Table 3, compared with AS and ACS, shows that the average performance of proposed Strategy 3 for four groups with 20 ants in each group were 13.97% and 6.35%, respectively, and that of proposed Strategy 5 for eight groups with 10 ants in each group were 14.06% and 6.44%, respectively.

Table 1. The performance of ACS with communication strategies (Strategies 1 to 7) obtained in comparison with AS and ACS for EIL101 data set on TSP problem

Seed	AS	ACS	Strategy 1		Strategy 2		Strategy 3		Strategy 4		Strategy 5		Strategy 6		Strategy 7	
	1,80	1,80	4,20	8,10	4,20	8,10	4,20	8,10	4,20	8,10	4,20	8,10	4,20	8,10	4,20	8,10
1	730	683	657	655	648	653	649	645	654	644	646	651	646	653	647	646
2	730	680	657	655	650	647	643	648	647	649	641	650	660	643	648	643
3	731	681	644	646	655	655	641	646	653	646	641	648	646	645	648	642
4	720	678	645	648	651	654	651	647	647	647	643	646	642	647	650	652
5	727	676	641	643	648	663	648	656	651	651	644	650	647	651	647	647
6	727	673	656	655	648	644	645	655	648	649	647	653	651	653	644	655
7	698	675	642	644	649	658	646	648	651	650	650	646	647	648	645	645
8	726	679	646	651	653	662	658	645	647	645	653	650	647	653	652	655
9	721	672	645	646	651	656	652	642	649	650	652	647	649	651	646	650
10	718	685	643	651	654	647	645	645	652	651	646	647	646	652	650	648
Ave	723	678	648	649	651	654	648	648	650	648	646	649	648	650	648	648

Table 2. The performance of ACS with communication strategies (Strategies 1 to 7) obtained in comparison with AS and ACS for ST70 data set on TSP problem

Seed	AS	ACS	Strategy 1		Strategy 2		Strategy 3		Strategy 4		Strategy 5		Strategy 6		Strategy 7	
	1,80	1,80	4,20	8,10	4,20	8,10	4,20	8,10	4,20	8,10	4,20	8,10	4,20	8,10	4,20	8,10
1	734	701	679	680	683	684	678	683	681	683	684	679	680	677	682	681
2	721	700	681	681	677	686	688	681	677	681	679	681	677	681	677	681
3	722	700	681	682	678	683	678	681	678	681	677	681	681	682	678	677
4	717	701	677	688	682	687	678	682	679	694	685	683	656	681	681	689
5	721	703	678	684	678	686	678	681	678	678	678	679	682	683	677	682
6	713	702	691	690	694	683	678	682	678	678	692	681	689	684	689	686
7	714	700	682	683	678	683	677	683	681	677	681	682	678	677	677	677
8	730	701	677	682	677	679	677	682	681	683	681	677	678	678	678	683
9	730	696	677	681	679	685	678	678	677	682	683	679	683	677	678	681
10	736	699	678	693	682	688	678	681	681	682	680	691	682	678	677	690
Ave	724	700	680	684	681	684	679	681	679	682	682	681	682	680	680	683

Table 3. The performance of ACS with communication strategies (Strategies 1 to 7) obtained in comparison with AS and ACS for TSP225 data set on TSP problem

Seed	AS	ACS	Strategy 1		Strategy 2		Strategy 3		Strategy 4		Strategy 5		Strategy 6		Strategy 7	
	1,80	1,80	4,20	8,10	4,20	8,10	4,20	8,10	4,20	8,10	4,20	8,10	4,20	8,10	4,20	8,10
1	4587	4145	3907	3933	3913	3914	3879	3885	3903	3949	3882	3905	3866	3905	3884	3943
2	4492	4215	3903	3883	3879	3879	3883	3877	3955	3942	3916	3871	3902	3892	3891	3881
3	4454	4149	3888	3926	3900	3900	3889	3896	3953	3916	3906	3888	3878	3894	3919	3902
4	4609	4160	3892	3886	3908	3952	3889	3885	3895	3890	3871	3885	3866	3879	3919	3899
5	4538	4163	3881	3869	3888	3898	3879	3885	3879	3880	3882	3910	3878	3884	3886	3922
6	4483	4146	3942	3915	3916	3978	3892	3901	3961	3895	3883	3877	3901	3866	3882	3882
7	4555	4149	3904	3911	3876	3939	3881	3891	3881	3887	3881	3876	3892	3885	3882	3912
8	4491	4148	3950	3900	3912	3925	3950	3889	3890	3902	3957	3891	3936	3950	3952	3903
9	4500	4108	3903	3916	3903	3904	3889	3887	3896	3886	3882	3891	3904	3875	3881	3898
10	4521	4161	3877	3915	3875	3911	3877	3896	3876	3873	3884	3876	3919	3917	3895	3909
Ave	4523	4154	3905	3905	3897	3920	3891	3889	3909	3902	3894	3887	3894	3895	3899	3905

The main contribution of this section is to propose the parallel formulation for the ant colony system (ACS). Seven communication strategies between groups which can be used to update the pheromone levels are presented. For our preliminary experiments, the proposed parallel ant colony system (PACS) outperforms both ACS and AS based on three available traveling salesman data sets. In general, our presented systems based on data set with large data can get much better performance such that the average improvement of TSP225 is better than that of ST70. The proposed PACS may be applied to solve the quadratic assignment problem (Maniezzo & Colorni, 1999), data mining (Parpinelli, Lopes, & Freitas, 2002), space-planning (Bland, 1999), data clustering, and the combinatorial optimization problems.

Adaptive Ant Colony System for Data Clustering

Processes that simulate natural phenomena have successfully been applied to a number of problems for which no simple mathematical solution is known or is practicable. Such meta-heuristic algorithms include genetic algorithms, particle swarm optimization, and ant colony systems and have received increasing attention in recent years.

In this section, an advanced version of the ACO algorithm, termed the constrained ant colony optimization (CACO) algorithm, is proposed here for data clustering by adding constrains on the calculation of pheromone strength. The proposed CACO algorithm has the following properties:

- It applies the quadratic metric combined with the sum of K nearest neighbor distances (SKNND) metric to be instead of the Euclidean distance measure.
- It adopts a constrained form of pheromone updating. The pheromone is only updated based on some statistical distance threshold.
- It utilises a reducing search range.

Ant Colony Optimization with Different Favor (ACODF)

Ant colony optimization with different favor (ACODF) algorithm (Tsai, Wu, & Tsai, 2002) modified the ant colony optimization (ACO) (Dorigo & Gambardella, 1997) for data clustering by adding the concept of simulated annealing (Kirkpatrick, Gelatt, & Vecchi, 1983) and the strategy of tournament selection (Brindle, 1981). It is useful in partitioning the datasets for the clear boundaries among clusters, however, it is not suitable to partition the datasets for the clusters with arbitrary shapes, clusters with outliers and bridges between clusters.

Ant colony optimization with different favor (ACODF) applies ACO for use in data clustering. The difference between the ACODF and ACO is that each ant in ACODF only visits a fraction of the total clustering objects and the number of visited objects decreases with each cycle. ACODF also incorporates the strategies of simulated annealing and tournament selection and results in an algorithm which is effective for clusters with clearly defined boundaries. However, ACODF does not handle clusters with arbitrary shapes, clusters with outliers, and bridges between clusters well. In order to improve the effectiveness of the clustering based on the technique of ant colony optimization, our proposed CACO algorithm may solve these problems of clusters with arbitrary shapes, clusters with outliers, and bridges between clusters.

The Constrained Ant Colony Optimization (CACO)

An advanced version of ant colony optimization algorithm termed constrained ant colony pptimization (CACO) algorithm was proposed for data clustering by adding constrains for computing the pheromone strength. The CACO algorithm extends the ant colony optimization algorithm by accommodating a quadratic metric, sum of K nearest neighbor distances (SKNND), constrained addition of pheromone and a shrinking range strategy to improve the data clustering (Chu, Roddick, Su, & Pan, 2004). In order to improve the effectiveness of the clustering, the following four strategies are applied.

Strategy 1. While the Euclidean distance measure is used in conventional clustering techniques such as in the ACODF clustering algorithm, it is not suitable for clustering non-spherical clusters, (e.g.,, a cluster with a slender shape). In this work we therefore opt for a quadratic metric (Pan, McInnes, & Jack, 1996b) as the distance measure. Given an object at position O and objects X_i, $i = 1, 2, ..., T$, (T is the total number of objects), the quadratic metric between the current object O and the object X_m can be expressed as:

$$D_q(O, X_m) = (O - X_m)^t W^{-1} (O - X_m) \quad (8)$$

where $(O - X_m)$ is error column vector and W is the covariance matrix given as:

$$W = \frac{1}{T}\sum_{i=1}^{T}(X_i - \bar{X})(X_i - \bar{X})^t \quad (9)$$

here $\bar{X}$ is the mean of X_i, $i = 1, 2, ..., T$ defined as:

$$\bar{X} = \frac{1}{T}\sum_{i=1}^{T} X_i \quad (10)$$

W^{-1} is the inverse of covariance matrix W.

Strategy 2. We use the sum of K nearest neighbor distances (SKNND) metric in order to distinguish dense clusters more easily. The example shown in Figure 11 shows an ant located at A which will tend to move toward C within a dense cluster rather than object B located in the sparser region. By adopting SKNND, as the process iterates, the probability for an ant to move toward the denser clusters increases. This strategy can avoid clustering errors due to bridges between clusters.

Strategy 3. As shown in Figure 11, as a result of Strategy 2, ants will tend to move toward denser clusters. However, the pheromone update is inversely proportional to the distance between the visited objects as shown in Equations 5 and 6 and the practical distance between

Figure 11. Ant tends to move toward the object with dense cluster

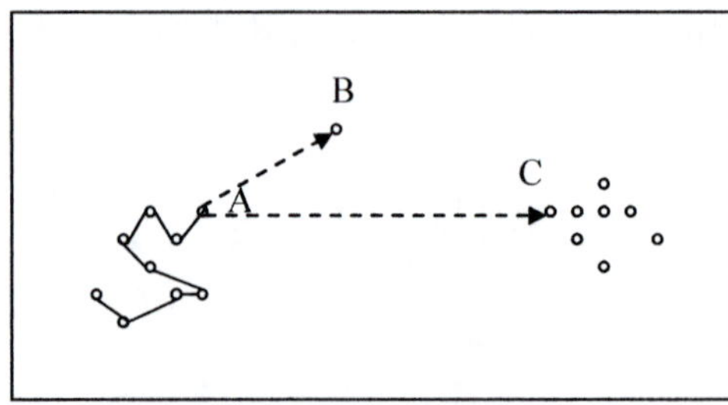

objects A and C could be farther than that between objects A and B reducing the pheromone level and causing a clustering error. In order to compensate for this, a statistical threshold for the kth ant is adopted.

$$L_{ts}^k = AvgL_{path}^k + StDevL_{path}^k \tag{11}$$

where $AvgL_{path}^k$ and $StDevL_{path}^k$ are the average of the distance and the standard deviation for the route of the visited objects by the kth ant expressed as:

$$AvgL_{path}^k = \frac{\sum L_{ij}^k}{E}, \text{ if } (X_i, X_j) \text{ path visited by the } k\text{th ant} \tag{12}$$

$$StDevL_{path}^k = \sqrt{\frac{\sum (L_{ij}^k - AvgL_{path}^k)^2}{E}}, \text{ if } (X_i, X_j) \text{ path visited by the } k\text{th ant} \tag{13}$$

where E is the number of paths visited by the kth ant. We may roughly consider object X_i and object X_j are located in different clusters if $L_{ij}^k > L_{ts}^k$. The distance between object X_i and object X_j cannot be added into the length of the path and the pheromone cannot be updated between the objects.

Strategy 4. Equation 1 is the conventional search formula between objects r and s for ant colony optimization. However this formula is not suitable for robust clustering as object s represents all un-visited objects resulting in excessive computation and a tendency for ants to jump between dense clusters as shown in Figure 12. In order to improve clustering speed and eliminate this jumping phenomenon, Equation 1 is modified to be:

$$P_k(r,s) = \begin{cases} \dfrac{[\tau(r,s)]\cdot[D_q(r,s)]^{-\beta}\cdot[SKNND(s)]^{-\gamma}}{\sum_{u\in J_k^{N_2}(r)}[\tau(r,u)]\cdot[D_q(r,u)]^{-\beta}\cdot[SKNND(u)]^{-\gamma}}, & if\ s \in J_k^{N_2}(r) \\ 0, & otherwise \end{cases} \tag{14}$$

Figure 12. Conventional search route using Equation 1

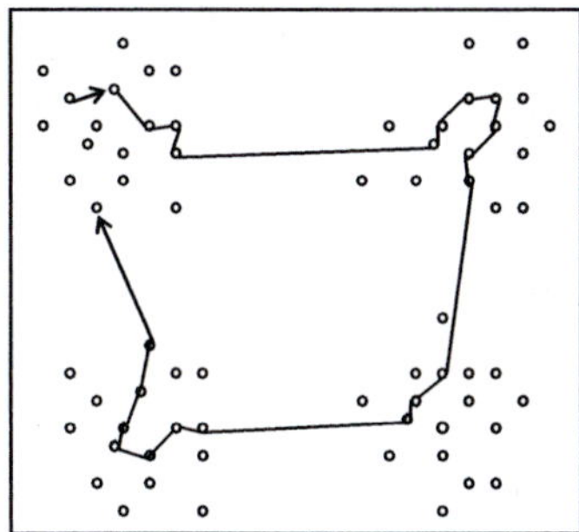

Figure 13. Shrinking search route using Equation 14

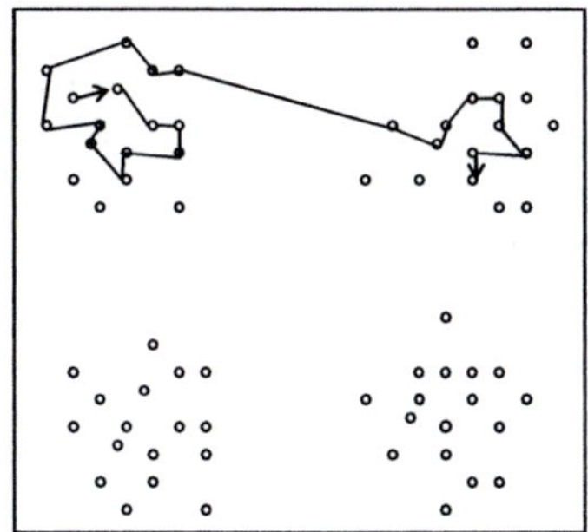

where $J_k^{N_2}(r)$ is to shrink the search range to N_2 nearest un-visited objects. N_2 is set to be $\frac{1}{10}$ objects. $D_q(r, s)$ is the quadratic distance between object *r* and object *s*. *SKNND*(*s*) is the sum of the distance between the object *s* and the N_2 nearest objects. β and γ are two parameters which determine the relative importance of pheromone level versus the quadratic distance and the sum of N_2 nearest neighbor distance, respectively. β is set to 2 and γ would be robust to set between 5 and 15. As shown in Figure 13, the jumping phenomenon is deleted after using the shrinking search formula.

The constrained ant colony optimization algorithm for data clustering can be expressed as seen in the following steps.

Step 1: Initialization – Randomly select the initial object for each ant. The initial pheromone τ_{ij} between any two objects X_i and X_j is set to be a small positive constant τ_0.

Step 2: Movement – Let each ant moves to N_1 objects only using Equation14. Here N_1 is set to be $\frac{1}{20}$ data objects.

Step 3: Pheromone Update – Update the pheromone level between objects as:

$$\tau_{ij}(t+1) = (1-\alpha)\tau_{ij}(t) + \Delta\tau_{ij}(t+1) \tag{15}$$

$$\Delta\tau_{ij}(t+1) = \sum_{k=1}^{T} \Delta\tau_{ij}^{k}(t+1) \tag{16}$$

$$\Delta\tau_{ij}^{k}(t+1) = \begin{cases} \dfrac{Q}{L_k}, & \textit{if } (i,j) \in \textit{route done by ant } k \textit{ and } L_{ij}^{k} < L_{ts}^{k} \\ 0, & \textit{otherwise} \end{cases} \tag{17}$$

where τ_{ij} is the pheromone level between object X_i and object X_j, T is the total number of clustering objects, α is a pheromone decay parameter and Q is a constant and is set to 1. L_k is the length of the route after deleting the distance between object X_i and object X_j in which $L_{ij}^{k} > L_{ts}^{k}$ of the kth ant.

Step 4: Consolidation – Calculate the average pheromone level on the route for all objects as:

$$Avg\tau = \frac{\sum_{i,j \in E} T_{ij}}{E} \tag{18}$$

where E is the number of paths visited by the kth ant. Disconnect the path between two objects if the pheromone level between these two objects is smaller than $Avg\tau$. All the objects connected together are in the same cluster.

Experimental Results for Data Clustering

The experiments were carried out to test the performance of the data clustering for ant colony optimization with different favor (ACODF), DBSCAN, CURE, and the proposed

Figure 14. Clustering result of CACO $(N_1 = \frac{1}{55})$

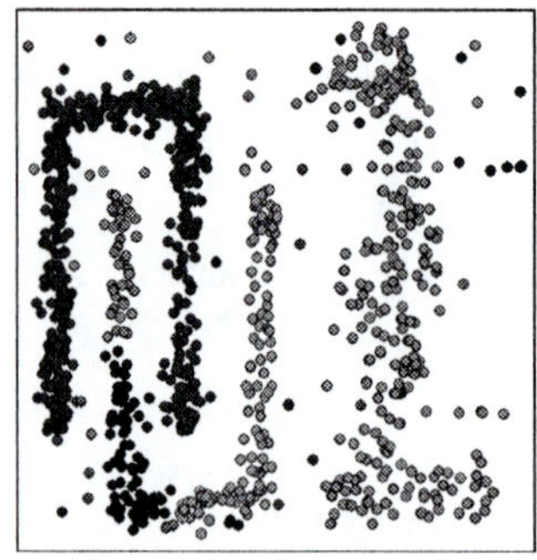

Figure 15. Clustering result of CACO $(N_l = \frac{1}{20})$

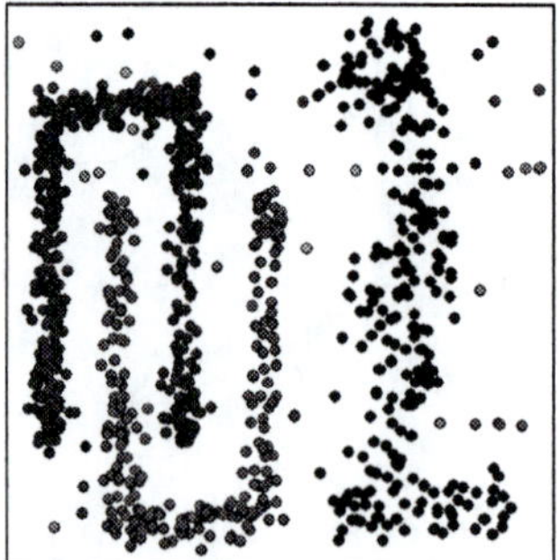

constrained ant colony optimization (CACO). Four data sets, four-cluster, four-bridge, smile-face, and shape-outliers were used as the test material consisting of 892, 981, 877, and 999 objects, respectively.

In order to cluster a data set using CACO, N_1 and γ are two important parameters which will influence the clustering results. N_1 is the number of objects to be visited in each cycle for each ant. If N_1 is set too small, the ants cannot finish visiting all the objects belonged to the same cluster resulting in a division of slender shaped cluster into several sub-clusters as shown in Figure 14. Our experiments indicated that good experimental results were obtained by setting N_1 to $\frac{1}{20}$ as shown in Figure 15.

γ also influences the clustering result for clusters with bridges or high numbers of outliers. As shown in Figure16, the four-bridge data set will be partitioned into just two clusters if γ is set to 1. By setting γ to 5, the four-clusters data set can be correctly partitioned as shown in Figure 17. We found that γ set between 5 and 15 provided robust results.

DBSCAN is a well-know algorithm that works well for clusters with arbitrary shapes. Following the recommendation of Ester, Kriegel, Sander, and XU (1996), *MinPts* was fixed to 4 and ε was changed during the experiments. *CURE* produces high-quality clusters in the existence of outliers, allowing complex shaped clusters and different size. We performed experiments with shrinking factor is 0.3 and the number of representative points as 10, which are the default values recommended in Guha, Rastogi, and Shim (1998).

Figure 16. Clustering result of CACO ($\gamma = 1$)

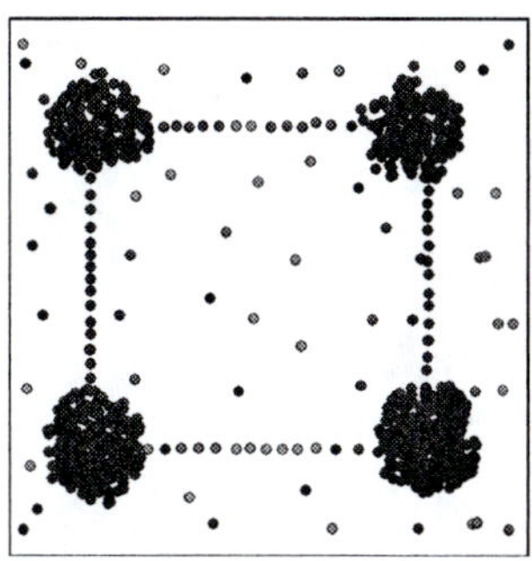

Figure 17. Clustering result of CACO ($\gamma = 5$)

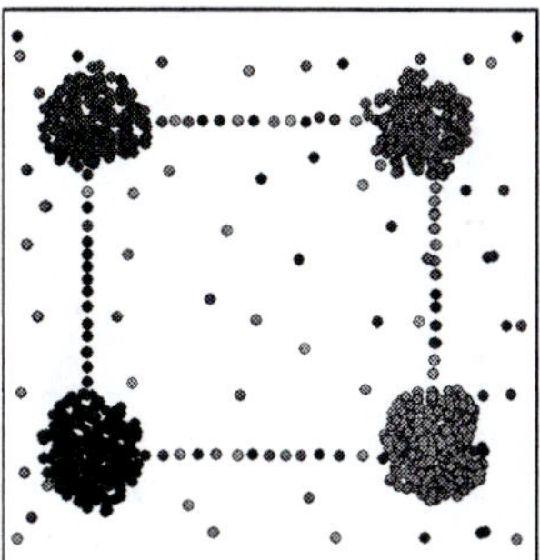

Figure 18. Clustering result of four-cluster by ACODF algorithm

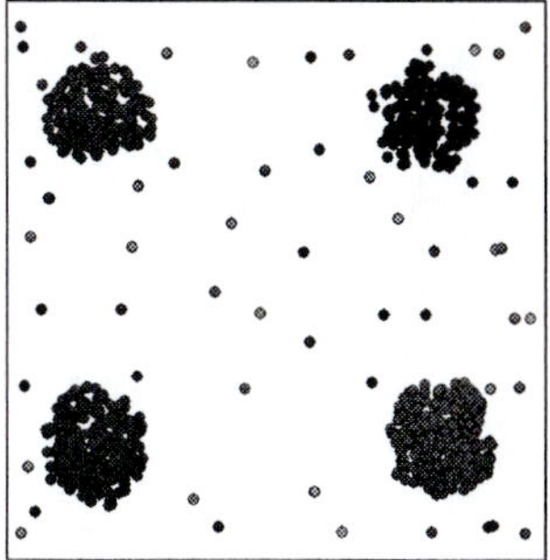

Figure 19. Clustering result of four-cluster by CACO algorithm

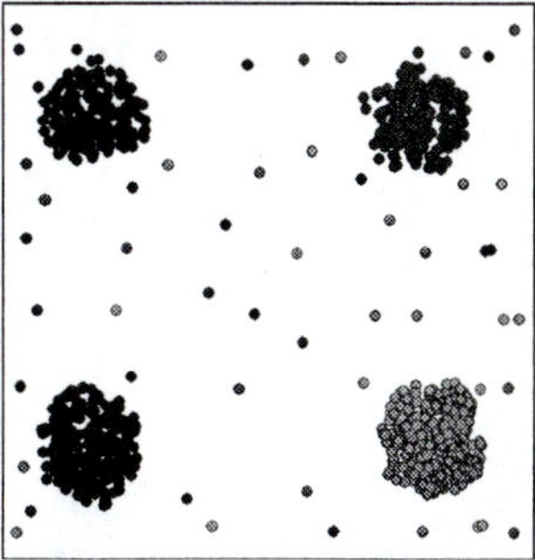

The first experiment tested the clustering performance of the four-cluster data set using the ACODF, DBSCAN, CURE, and CACO algorithms. As is illustrated in Figure 18, the ACODF algorithm was able to correctly cluster the four-cluster data set. Figure 19 shows the clusters found by CACO for four-cluster data set. For the results shown in Figure 20, DBSCAN worked well when the *MinPts* was fixed to 4 and $\varepsilon = 8.357$. CURE was able to find the right clusters, but some noises were present inside the clusters as shown in Figure 21.

Figure 20. Clustering result of four-cluster by DBSCAN algorithm

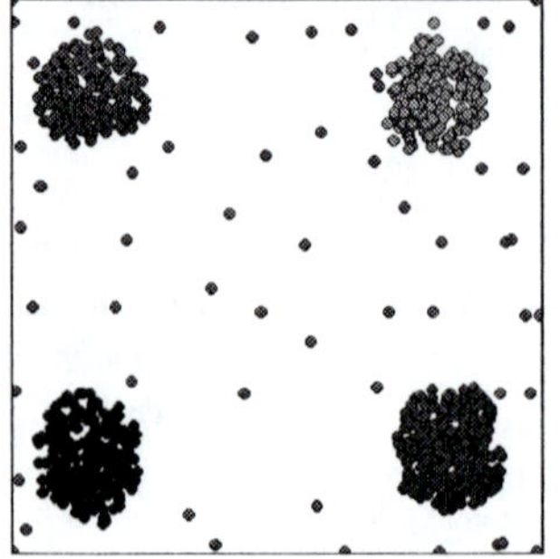

Figure 21. Clustering result of four-cluster by CURE algorithm

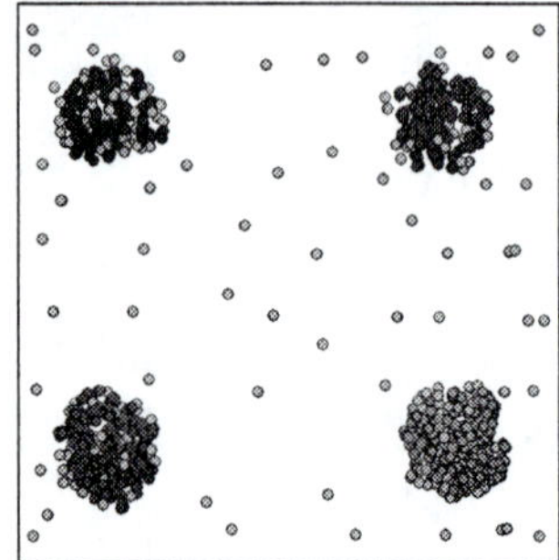

Figure 22. Clustering result of four-bridge by ACODF algorithm

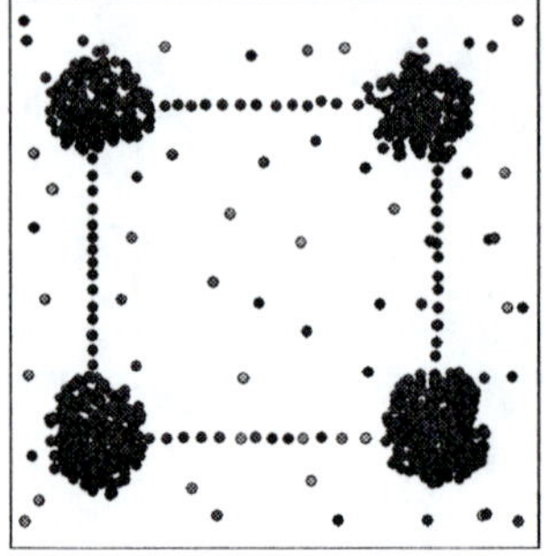

Figure 23. Clustering result of four-bridge by CACO algorithm

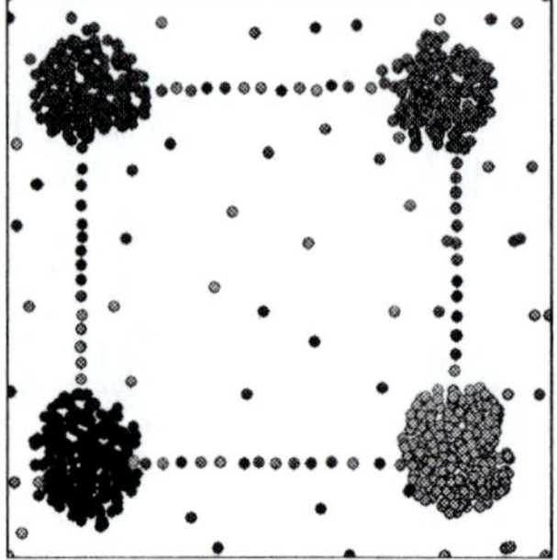

Figure 24. Clustering result of four-bridge by DBSCAN algorithm

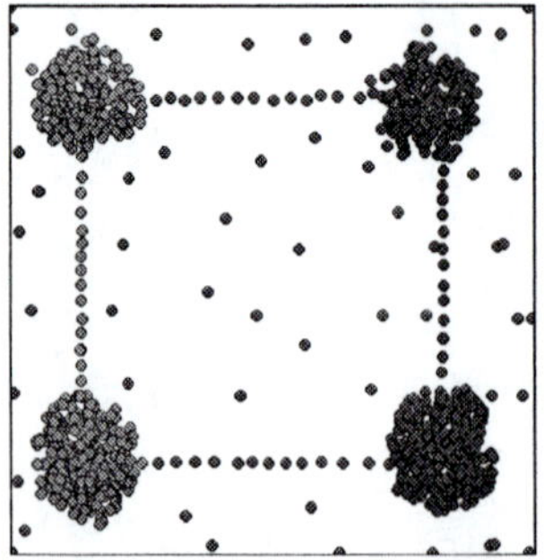

Figure 25. Clustering result of four-bridge by CURE algorithm

The second experiment was to partition the four-bridge data sets. As we can see from Figures 22 to 25, the ACODF algorithm puts the four spheres into the same clusters as the outlier points connecting these clusters while DBSCAN cannot correctly separate these clusters. In Figure 24, DBSCAN fails to perform well and puts the four spheres into two clusters because of the outlier points connecting these spheres. Although CURE clusters the data set into four clusters, there is noise inside and around these clusters shown in Figure 25. The CACO algorithm is able to separate this data set to four clusters as well as identify the rest as outlier points connecting the four spheres.

The third experiment was to test the smile-face data set. Figure 26 shows the results obtained by ACODF algorithm for smile-face data set, which partitions this data set as one cluster only. As shown in Figure 28, the results illustrate that DBSCAN is able to find eyes, nose and mouth clusters but it fails to find the outline cluster as the outline cluster has a few fragments. CURE cannot effectively find clusters shown in Figure 29 because the clusters in the data set are fragmented into a number of smaller clusters while the CACO algorithm can correctly partition the smile-face to five clusters shown in Figure 27.

The last experiment was to partition the shape-outliers data set. As in the previous experiment, the ACODF algorithm cannot correctly partition the shape-outliers data set shown in Figure 30. Figure 32 shows the clusters found by DBSCAN, but it also makes a mistake in that it has fragmented the clusters in the right-side "L"-shaped cluster. Figure 33 shows

Figure 26. Clustering result of smile-face by ACODF algorithm

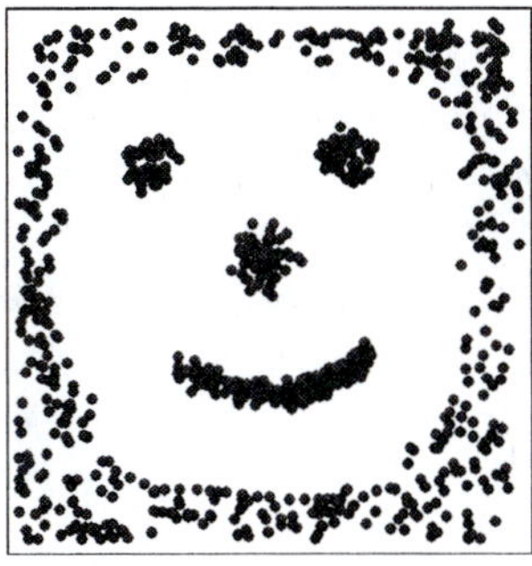

Figure 27. Clustering result of smile-face by CACO algorithm

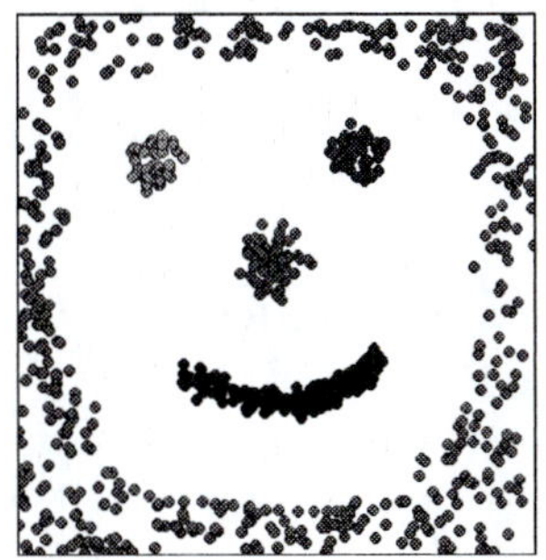

Figure 28. Clustering result of smile-face by DBSCAN algorithm

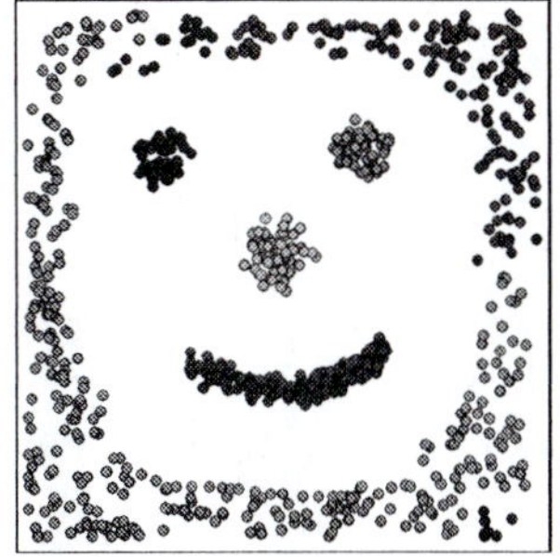

Figure 29. Clustering result of smile-face by CURE algorithm

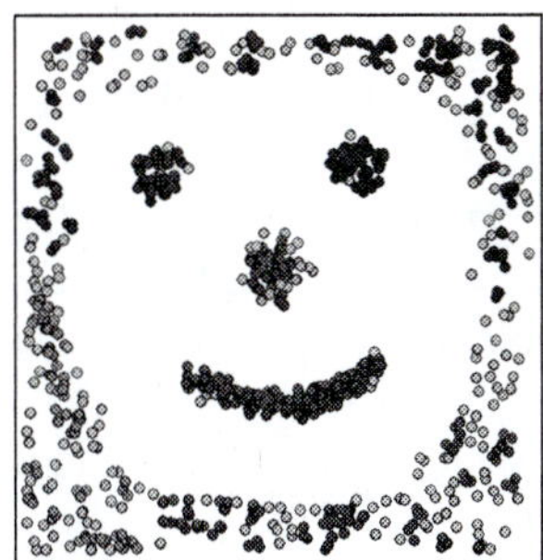

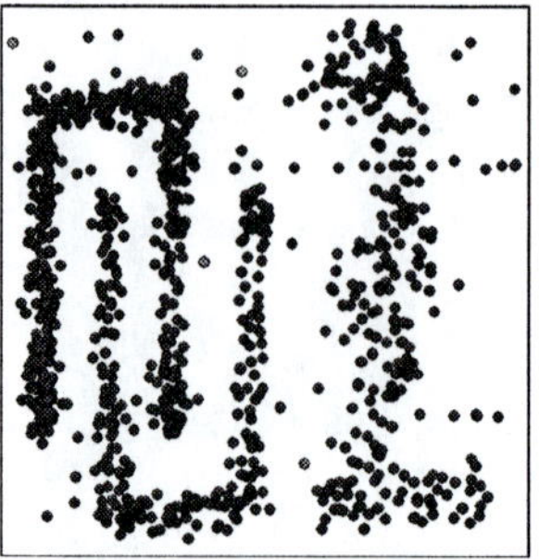

Figure 30. Clustering result of shape-outliers by ACODF algorithm

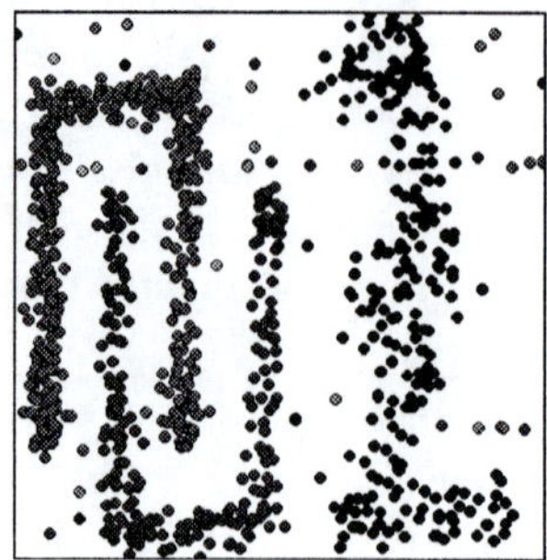

Figure 31. Clustering result of shape-outlier by CACO algorithm

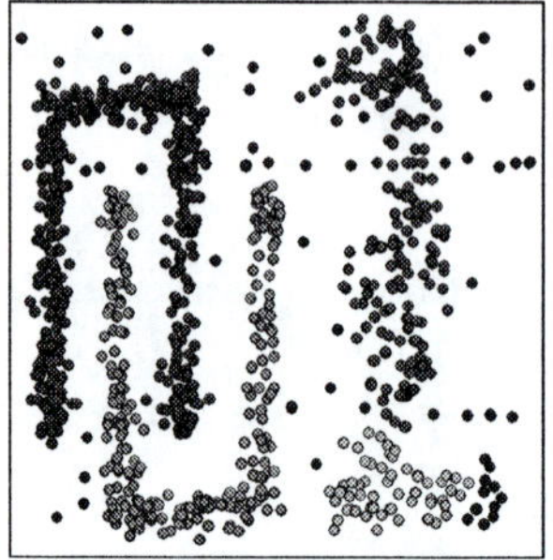

Figure 32. Clustering result of shape-outliers by DBSCAN algorithm

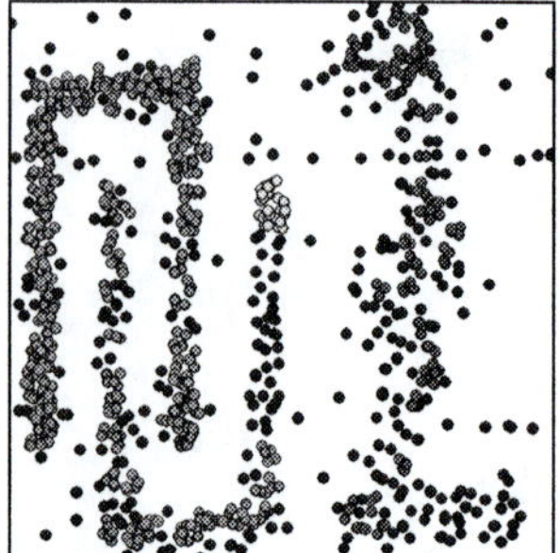

Figure 33. Clustering result of shape-outliers by CURE algorithm

that CURE fails to perform well on shape-outliers data set, with the clusters has fragmented into a number of smaller clusters. Looking at Figure 31, we can see that CACO algorithm correctly identifies the clusters.

Conclusion

The methodology of ant system and ant colony system are introduced. The parallel ant colony system (PACS) with communication strategies is presented for traveler salesman problem in this chapter for not only reducing the computation time but also obtain the better solution. The constrained ant colony optimization (CACO) is also presented for effective clustering by combining the ant colony system with quadratic distance metric, the sum of k nearest neighbour distances metric, constrained addition of pheromone and a shrinking range strategy. The proposed algorithms may also be applied to codebook design of vector quantization, job-shop scheduling, combinatorial optimization problems and intelligent information systems.

References

Bland, J. A. (1999). Space-planning by ant colony optimization. *International Journal of Computer Applications in Technology, 12*(6), 320-328.

Brindle, A. (1981). *Genetic algorithms for function optimization.* PhD thesis, University of Alberta, Edmonton, Canada.

Bullnheimer, B., Kotsis, G., & Strauss, C. (1997). *Parallelization strategies for the ant system.* Technical report POM 9/97, Institute of Applied Computer Science, University of Vienna, Austria.

Chang, J. F., Chu, S. C., Roddick, J. F., & Pan, J. S. (2005). A parallel particle swarm optimization algorithm with communication strategies. *Journal of Information Science and Engineering, 21*(4), 809-818.

Chu, S. C., Roddick, J. F., & Pan, J. S. (2004). Ant colony system with communication strategies. *Information Sciences, 167*(1-4), 63-76.

Chu, S. C., Roddick, J. F., Pan, J. S., & Su, C. J. (2003, October 28-31). Parallel ant colony systems. In *Proceedings of 14th International Symposium on Methodologies for Intelligent Systems*, Maebashi City, Japan (LNCS 2871, pp. 279-284).

Chu, S. C., Roddick, J. F., Su, C. J., & Pan, J. (2004, August 9-13). Serence on Artificial Intelligence. In *Proceedings of the 8th Pacific Rim Conference on Artificial Intelligence*, Auckland, New Zealand (LNAI 3157, pp. 534-543). Springer.

Cohoon, J. P., Hegde, S. U., Martine, W. N., & Richards, D. (1987). Punctuated equilibria: A parallel genetic algorithm. In J. J. Grefenstette (Ed.), *Proceedings of the 2nd International Conference on Genetic Algorithms and Their Applications* (pp.148-154). Hillsdale, NJ: Lawrence Erlbaum Associates.

Colorni, A., Dorigo, M., & Maniezzo, V. (1991). Distributed optimization by ant colonies. In F. Varlea & P. Bourgine (Eds.), *Proceedings of the First European Conference on Artificial Life,* Paris (pp.134-142). Elsevier Publishing.

Dorigo, J. M., & Gambardella, L. M. (1997, April). Ant colony system: A cooperative learning approach to the traveling salesman problem. *IEEE Transactions on Evolutionary Computation, 1*(1), 53-66.

Dorigo, M., Maniezzo, V., & Colorni, A. (1996, February). Ant system: Optimization by a colony of cooperating agents. *IEEE Transactions on Systems, Man, and Cybernetics-Part B: Cybernetics, 26*(1), 29-41.

Ester, M., Kriegel, H.-P., Sander, J., & Xu, X. (1996). A density-based algorithm for discovering clusters in large spatial databases with noise. In *Proceedings of the Second International Conference on Knowledge Discovery and Data Mining*, Portland, OR (pp. 226-231). AAAI Press.

Goldberg, D. E. (1989). *Genetic algorithm in search, optimization and machine learning.* New York: Addison-Wesley.

Golver, F., & Laguna, M. (1997). *Tabu search.* Boston: Kluwer Academic Publishers.

Guha, S., Rastogi, R., & Shim, K. (1998). CURE: An efficient clustering algorithm for large databases. In *Proceedings of the ACM SIGMOD International Conference on the Management of Data*, Seattle, WA (pp. 73-84).

Huang, H. C., Pan, J. S., Lu, Z. M., Sun, S. H., & Hang, H. M. (2001). Vector quantization based on genetic simulated annealing. *Signal Processing, 81*(7), 1513-1523.

Kennedy, J., & Eberhart, R. (1995). Particle swarm optimization. *IEEE International Conference on Neural Networks*, Piscataway, NJ (pp. 1942-1948).

Kirkpatrick, S., Gelatt, J. C. D., & Vecchi, M. P. (1983). Optimization by simulated annealing. *Science, 220*(4598), 671-680.

Kohonen, T. (1995). *Self-organizing maps*. Heidelberg: Springer.

Kung, S. Y. (1993). *Digital neural network*. Upper Saddle River, NJ: Prentice Hall.

Maniezzo, V., & Colorni, A. (1999, September/October). The ant system applied to the quadratic assignment problem. *IEEE Transactions on Knowledge and Data Engineering, 11*(5), 769-778.

Pan, J. S., & Chu, S. C. (1996). Non-redundant VQ channel coding using tabu search strategy. *Electronics Letters, 31*(17), 1545-1546.

Pan, J. S., McInnes, F. R., & Jack, M. A. (1995). VQ codebook design using genetic algorithms. *Electronics Letters, 31*(17), 1418-1419.

Pan, J. S., McInnes, F. R., & Jack, M. A. (1996a). Application of parallel genetic algorithm and property of multiple global optima to VQ codevector index assignment for noisy channels. *Electronics Letters, 32*(4), 296-297.

Pan, J. S., McInnes, F. R., & Jack, M. A. (1996b). Bound for minkowski metric or quadratic metric applied to VQ codeword search. *IEE Proceedings on Vision Image and Signal Processing, 143*(1), 67-71.

Parpinelli, R. S., Lopes, H. S., & Freitas, A. A. (2002). Data mining with an ant colony optimization algorithm. *IEEE Transactions on Evolutionary Computation, 6*(4), 321-332.

Stützle, T. (1998, September 27-30). Parallelization strategies for ant colony optimization. In *Proceedings of the Fifth International Conference on Parallel Problem Soving for Nature (PPSN-V)*, Amsterdam, The Netherlands (LNCS 1498, pp. 722-731). Springer-Verlag.

Tsai, C.-F., Wu, H.-C., & Tsai, C.-W. (2002, May 22-24). A new data clustering approach for data mining in large databases. In *Proceedings of the International Symposium on Parallel Architectures, Algorithms and Networks (ISPAN '02)*, Ateneo Professional Schools, Rockwell Center, Makati City, Metro Manila, The Philippines (pp. 315-320). IEEE Press.

Chapter III

Information Networks as Complex Systems: A Self-Repair and Regulation Model

Yoshiteru Ishida, Toyohashi University of Technology, Japan

Abstract

Complex networks such as scale-free networks and small-world networks, and their dynamics when information percolates through the networks, have been studied. This chapter reports the problem of spreading of the normal state (rather than spreading of the abnormal state) that is formalized as cleaning a contaminated network by mutual copying. Repairing by copying is a double-edged sword that could spread contamination when properly used. A framework for controlling copying involving a spatial prisoner's dilemma is introduced. A characteristic adaptation to the network environment has been observed.

Introduction

A new way of viewing networks from topological or structural viewpoints has been proposed. Many artificial and natural networks have been studied using this approach, and special attention has been paid to their structural properties, such as "scale-free" (Barabasi, 2002) or "small-world" (Watts, 2003). On the other hand, studies on the interaction in the network, or dynamics of the network (as opposed to structure), have also become an important topic. For example, information propagation in a scale-free network seems to be important.

In the context of fault-diagnosis, the scale-free network theory has shown that the Internet is robust against random faults, but vulnerable to selective attacks targeted at hubs (Dezso & Barabasi, 2002), and that viruses and worms may not be eradicated since the epidemic threshold is absent in the scale-free network (May & Lloyd, 2001; Pastor & Vespignani, 2001).

Malicious faults, such as viruses and worms, completely change the nature of faults. Machine faults are usually random faults, since their occurance is not "selective," and also they correspond to designed functions and hence are recovered when the parts covering the function are replaced. The point is that viruses and worms change the intended function rather than causing malfunction, hence they cannot be treated by usual redundancy and/or stand-by techniques. This drastic change of the aspect of faults calls for the design paradigm of the immune system, whose "self" is adaptive to the environment.

We have been studying the interaction of the network and proposed a dynamic relational network based on the immune network to increase robustness and adaptability to the dynamic environment (Ishida, 2004). In the framework, the network is double-sided and would raise the self-referential paradox in a flat logic without distribution, and hence subtle tuning is needed as in the immune system. Organizing responses to faults in large-scale systems has been proposed in a new approach of recovery-oriented computing (Brown & Patterson, 2001).

For physical systems such as mechanical systems, they are repaired by identifying the faulty components and replacing them with non-faulty ones. For information systems, however, they can be repaired by simply copying the clean system to the contaminated system. As the first step toward the adaptive defense of information systems, we consider self-repairing of the network by mutual copying (Ishida, 2005).

In self-repair systems with autonomous distributed units, abnormal units may adversely affect the system when they try to repair other normal units. Thus, the problem involves a double-edged sword similar to the immune system. We consider a critical phenomenon by modeling the problem by a probabilistic cellular automaton (pCA) which turns out to be a generalization of the well-known model (Domany & Kinzel, 1984). Self-repairing cellular automata have been attracting a widespread attention including in the field of statistical physics (Gacs, 2001).

Since the problem involves the double-edged sword leading to a critical phenomenon, repairs have to be decided giving consideration to the resources used and remaining in the system and the network environment. When the self-repair is done in an autonomous distributed manner, each unit does not voluntarily repair other units to save their own resources, thus leaving many abnormal units not repaired. This situation is similar to the dilemma that would occur in the prisoner's dilemma (Axelrod, 1984, 1987). Thus, we use a spatial version of the prisoner's dilemma (Nowak & May, 1992) for emergence of cooperative collectives and for controlling copying to save resources.

The next section explains the motivations and background of the models in this chapter. The approach of immunity-based systems involving the self-referential network is introduced. The approach inevitably leads to the double-edged sword. The problem of cleaning a network by mutual copying is formalized. However, the problem also has the aspect of a double-edged sword, and so there could be critical phenomena that occur at the boundary of eradication of abnormal nodes. The section "Probabilistic Cellular Automaton as a Model of a Self-Repairing Network" uses a probabilistic cellular automaton to analyze the critical phenomena. The double-edged sword requires careful regulation. The section "Regulating Mutual Copying by Spatial Strategies" introduces a game theory approach involving the spatial prisoner's dilemma for the regulation.

Background

An Introduction to Immunity-Based Systems

The self-nonself discrimination problem dealt with in the immune system would raise the self-referential problem as in statements such as: "I am a liar" and "This statement is false." To resolve this paradox, hierarchical logic or distribution of subjects could be done. We use the latter approach (Figure 1). Dividing subjects and placing them inside the system has been often discussed in autopietic systems (Maturana & Varela, 1980) and other complex systems. Placing the divided subjects in the system implies that the subjects have only local and unlabelled information in solving problems (Edelman, 1992). More importantly, the subject can be the object with which the subject operates and interacts.

It is still controversial whether the immune system actually needs to discriminate *self* and *nonself* in order to eliminate nonself (Langman & Cohn, 2000), however, elimination is actually done, hence, the double-sided property that the subject must be the object is unavoidable. Thus, the immune system is a double-edged sword.

It has been more than 30 years since the immune network was proposed by Jerne (1973). In the network theory, the immune system is not merely a "firewall" but a network of antigen-antibody reactions. That is, when antigen is administered, it stimulates the related cells and causes them to generate antibodies. However, the generated antibodies themselves are

Figure 1. Left figure corresponds to the statement: "I am a liar." Middle figure divides the subject into two. It is still not possible to identify the liar. By further distributing the subjects, it becomes possible to identify the liar. The arc indicates interaction.

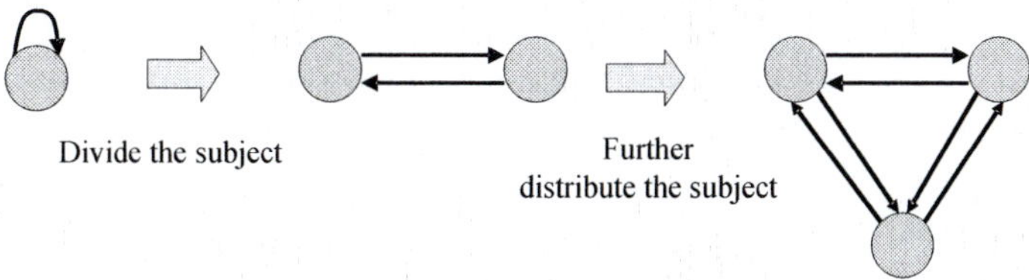

antigens to other cells and consequently result in another antibody generation. The antigen-antibody reaction percolates like a chain reaction and hence requires a regulation mechanism. An analogy of this problem in engineering design is the "alarm problem" of placing mutually activating and inactivating alarms whose sensitivity must be appropriately set to avoid mis-alarms (false negative) and false-alarms (false positive).

The challenge of immunity-based systems is to propose a design for placing these alarms which can autonomously tune themselves and adapt themselves to the environment. The immune system as an information system has been extensively studied (e.g., Edelman, 1992; Tauber, 1997; Farmer, Packard, & Perelson 1986). We are also studying the immune system as an information system, and proposed a design framework with the following three properties (Ishida, 2004):

- A **self-maintenance system** with monitoring not only of the nonself but also of the self
- A **distributed system** with autonomous components capable of mutual evaluation
- An **adaptive system** with diversity and selection

Probabilistic Cellular Automaton as a Model of a Self-Repairing Network

In information systems, the repairing units can repair others simply by copying their content, but could spread contamination if the repairing units themselves are contaminated. We consider the possibility of cleaning up the network by mutually copying. Repair by copying in information systems is also a double-edged sword, and it should be identified when the network can really eradicate abnormal elements from the system. We consider a probabilistic CA to model the situation where computers in a LAN mutually repair by copying their content.

The self-repairing network consists of units capable of repairing other connected units. We call the connected units "neighbor units" based on the terminology of CA. Although mutual repairing and other interactions involved may be done in an asynchronous manner, our model considers synchronous interactions for simplicity. Each unit tries to repair the units in the neighborhood, however, whether it can really repair or not depends on two factors: the state of the repairing unit and the success rate of the repair.

In a mathematical formulation, the model consists of three elements (U, T, R) where U is a set of units, T is a topology connecting the units, and R is a set of rules of the interaction among units. In simulations to come, a set of units is a finite set with N units, and the topology is restricted to the one-dimensional lattice as shown in Figure 2 for the model in this chapter's third section and the two-dimensional square lattice for the model in the fourth section. The network structure could be an n-dimensional array, complete graph, random graph, or even scale-free network. In our one- or two-dimensional lattice, each unit has S neighbors and the lattice with a boundary condition, that is, the structure of the lattice is a ring with unit 1 adjacent to the unit N in case of a one-dimensional lattice. Also, we restrict the case to each unit having a binary state: normal (0) and abnormal (1).

Figure 2. One-dimensional lattice with the neighborhood radius r. The next state of the cell will be determined by 2r+1 nodes in the neighborhood.

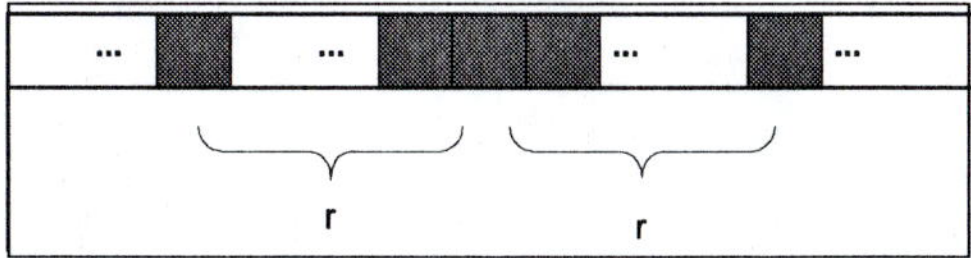

*Figure 3. Transition of the Domany-Kinzel model when both sides are 0 (left), one side is 1 (middle), and both sides are 1 (right). The symbol * is a wildcard that can match both 1 and 0.*

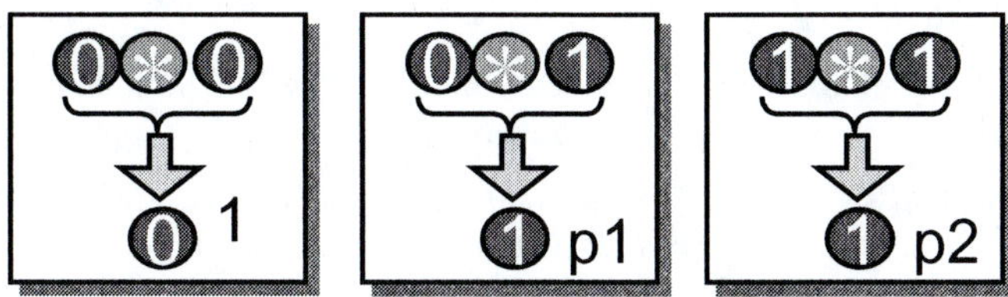

The Domany-Kinzel model (Domany & Kinzel, 1984) is a one-dimensional two state and totalistic probabilistic cellular automaton (pCA). The interaction is done in an alternated synchronous fashion: The origin cell with state 1 is numbered as 0. The numbering proceeds {1,2,.... } to the right, and {-1,-2,.... } to the left. At the N-th step the even numbered cells will act on the odd numbered cells and the odd numbered cells will act on the next step. The neighbor is two cells adjacent to oneself without self-interaction. As a probabilistic cellular automaton, the transition rules are as follows (Figure 3) where the self-state is the center in parentheses and the two neighbor states are on the left and on the right in parentheses. The self-state will change to the state indicated to the right of the arrow, with the probability indicated after the colon:

(0*0)→0:1, **(0*1)→1:**p1, **(1*1)→1:**p2

Spatial Prisoner's Dilemma as a Framework for Regulating Self-Repairing

In solving the problem of cleaning the contaminated network by mutual copying, another problem (other than the double-edged sword) is that each autonomous (and hence selfish) node may not repair others and may fall into a deadlock waiting for other nodes to be repaired. The situation is similar to that of the prisoner's dilemma that has been well studied in game theory and has been applied to many fields.

The prisoner's dilemma (PD) is a game played just once by two players with two actions (cooperation, C, or defect, D). Each player receives a payoff (R, T, S, P) as shown in Table 1 where $T > R > P > S$ and $2R > T+S$.

Table 1. The payoff matrix of the prisoner's dilemma. R, S, T, P are payoffs to player A.

		Player B	
		C	D
Player A	C	R (2)	S(0)
	D	T(4)	P(1)

In SPD, each player (and hence the strategy) is evaluated. In SPD, each site in a two-dimensional lattice corresponds to a player. Each player plays PD with the neighbors, and changes its action according to the total score it received.

The spatial prisoner's dilemma has been studied to investigate when, how, and why cooperation emerges among selfish agents (Nowak & May, 1992).

Our model generalizes SPD (gSPD) by introducing a spatial strategy (Ishida & Mori, 2005). Each player is placed at each lattice of the two-dimensional lattice. Each player has an action and a strategy, and receives a score. The spatial strategy determines the next action dependent upon the spatial pattern of actions in the neighbors. Each player plays PD with the neighbors, and changes its strategy to the strategy that earns the highest total score among the neighbors.

Our gSPD is done with spatial strategies: The next action will be determined based on the pattern of the neighbors' actions. The score is calculated by summing up all the scores received from PD with eight neighbor players. After r (strategy update cycle) steps of interactions with neighbors, the strategy will be chosen from the strategy with the highest score among the neighbors. Thus, the strategy will be updated at every r steps.

To specify a spatial strategy, the actions of the eight neighbors (the *Moore* neighbors) and the player itself must be specified (Figure 4), hence 2^9 rules are required. For simplicity, we restrict ourselves to a "totalistic spatial strategy" that depends on the number of D (defect) actions of the neighbor, not on their positions.

Figure 4. A strategy code for spatial strategies

The strategy code of the unit is expressed as a string consisting of nine characters of C's and D's (Matuo & Adachi, 1989) whose l-th element is C (D) if the action C (D) is taken when the number of D of the neighbor players is l (l=0,1,...,8). For example, *All-C* is [CCCCCCCCC], and *All-D* is [DDDDDDDDD]. As a typical strategy, we define *kD* that takes D if $l > k$ and C otherwise. For example, *2D* is [CCDDDDDDD]. This *kD* can be regarded as a spatial version of TFT where k seems to indicate the generosity (how many D actions in the neighbor are tolerated).

The strategy *kC* can be defined in the same manner: It takes C if $l > k$ and D otherwise. For example, a strategy code [CDDCCDCCC] is as shown in Figure 4. The number k in the strategy *kC* seems to indicate the contrariness that would cooperate even if k players in the neighbor defect. Further, *k1D-k2C* is a combination of *k1D* and *k2C*. For example, *2D-7C* is [CCDDDDDCC]. In our previous studies, the action error has an effect to favor more generous spatial strategies in the sense that more D actions should be forgiven in the neighbors' actions (Grim, 1995).

A Self-Repair Network and its Critical Phenomenon

A Model by Probabilistic Cellular Automata

The specific feature of the self-repair network is that repairing by an abnormal unit has an adverse impact. This adverse impact is implemented as a higher probability of contamination than that of successful cleaning in the model by probabilistic cellular automata.

Each unit tries to repair the units in the neighborhood in a synchronous fashion with a probability *Pr*. As shown in Figure 5, the repairing will be successful with the probability *Prn* when it is done by a normal unit, but with the probability *Pra* when done by an abnormal unit (*Pra* < *Prn*). In this chapter, we assume *Prn* = 1. The repaired units will be normal when all the repairing is successful. Thus, when repairing is done by two adjacent units, all repairing done by these two units must be successful in order for the repaired unit to be normal.

Figure 5. Probabilistic repair — P1'=P1+P0, P2'=P2+P0

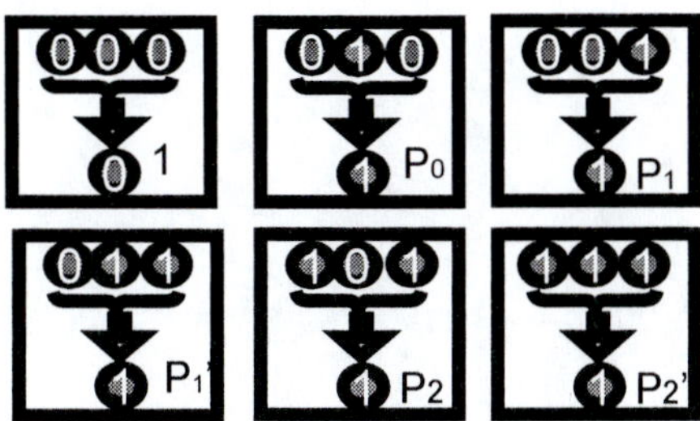

As a probabilistic cellular automaton, the transition rules are as follows:

(000)→0: 1, (010)→1: P0,

(001)→1: P1, (011)→1: P1+P0,

(101)→1: P2, (111)→1: P2+P0,

where **P0** = $(1 - \text{Pr})^2$, **P1** = Pr (1 - Pr *a*), and

P2 =2 (1 - Pr) **P1** + Pr^2 (1 - Pr a^2).

In such models, it is of interest to determine how the repairing probability *Pr* should be set when the probability of success by abnormal unit *Pra* is given. Also, when *Pr* is fixed to some value and *Pra* moves continuously to large values, does the number of abnormal units change abruptly at some critical point or does it just gradually increase? Further, when given some value of *Pra, Pr* should always be larger, which requires more cost.

Our model is a generalization of the Domany-Kinzel model. In fact, the model can be equated with the DK model when Pr = 1 (i.e. units always repair) with the parameters: *p1* = (1 - Pr *a*), *p2* = (1 - Pr a^2), that is, the case of the directed bond percolation.

Computer Simulations with a One-Dimensional Array

Computer simulations are conducted for one-dimensional CA with a boundary condition: that is, a ring-shaped network. Initially, only one unit is abnormal and is numbered as 0. The number of units is 500. One run stops at 800 steps. Figure 6 shows the number of normal units (averaged over 10 times).

Figure 6. Number of normal units after 800 steps plotted when the successful repair probability Pra varies. The three lines correspond to Pr = 0.3,0.6,1.0 from left to right.

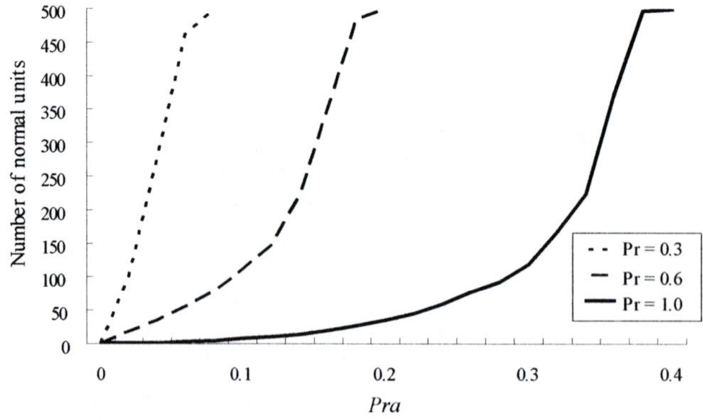

Figure 7. Frozen phase (left region where all the units are normal) and active phase (right region where some units remain abnormal) (Ishida, 2005)

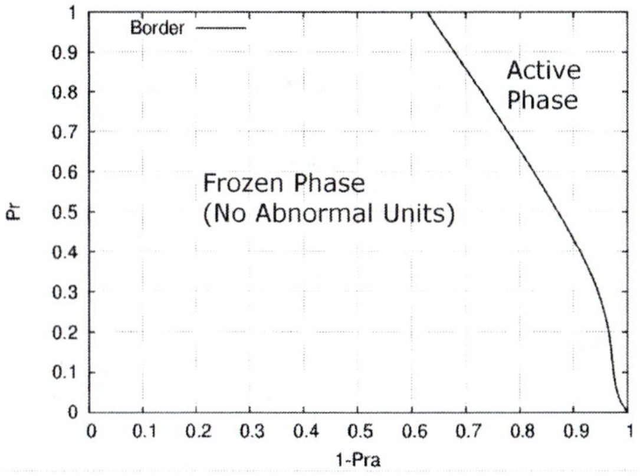

Under the approximation that the probability that the state of unit 0 is constant *p0* (mean field approximation and steady state), the following steady-state probability of *p0* is obtained:

$$p0 = \frac{\mathrm{Pr}\,a(2 - 2\,\mathrm{Pr} + \mathrm{Pr}\,a\,\mathrm{Pr})}{\mathrm{Pr}(1 - 2\,\mathrm{Pr}\,a + \mathrm{Pr}\,a^2)}$$

This steady-state probability also matches qualitatively the simulation results.

When *Pra* increases, the number of normal units rapidly increases. The steeper the curves, the smaller the probability *Pr*. That is, when *Pra* is less than 0.4, *Pr* should be small and hence repair should be done infrequently.

Further, there is a critical point of *Pra* that must be exceeded to clean up the network. The critical point becomes larger as the probability *Pr* becomes larger. In Figure 7, the critical points are plotted. The left region is the *frozen* region where all the units become normal, and the right region is the *active* region where some abnormal units remain in the network.

Regulating Mutual Copying by Spatial Strategies

A Model Incorporating SPD

In the model by pCA, units do not have a failure rate and do not become abnormal by themselves, however, the units in the model here do have a failure rate. The adverse impact of the abnormal units is implemented by raising the failure rate of the repaired units (when repaired by the abnormal units). Further, the units are assumed to use some resources while repairing. The units have to do the tasks assigned to them, but without doing repair, abnormal units increase and hence the performance of the system decreases, causing a dilemma.

A unit becomes abnormal depending on the failure rate λ. Each unit has a spatial strategy and repairs according to that code. Repairing is done depending on the repair rate γ and a repaired unit becomes normal. Also, the unit uses the quantity of resource Rγ for repairing. The unit is able to repair more than one unit, provided that the quantity of maximum resource Rmax is not exceeded. We call the resource that is not used for repairing the available resource Ra, and consider it as the *score* of a unit. If an abnormal unit repairs another unit, the failure rate λ of the repaired unit is increased by damage rate δ. Through the strategy update cycle r, the strategy of the unit is updated to that of the strategy that obtained the highest profit among the *Moore* neighborhood units. Each unit repairs (C) or does not repair (D). Parameters R, S, T, and P in the payoff matrix (Table 1) are respectively set to 1, 0, b ($1 < b < 2$) and 0 in the simulations below following Nowak-May's simulations (Nowak & May, 1992).

Figure 7 shows an example of a strategy code. The unit counts the number of D units in its *Moore* neighborhood in the previous step. In this case, five D units are present; then, in the next step, the unit does the action (C) represented in the fifth bit.

When the unit copies its content (software that can be copied and be contaminated), the strategy of the unit is also copied. Thus, the strategy will be changed at copying in addition to every strategy update cycle.

In the simulations, strategies are restricted to the *kC* strategy, which is composed of only nine among the 512 existing strategies. In the *kC* strategy, the unit does the action of D if the number of D units is less than *k*, and it does the action of C if the number of D units is greater or equal to *k*.

Computer Simulations with a Square Lattice

The simulation is done in a two-dimensional lattice space with a unit existing in each lattice. Throughout the simulations stated in this section, the parameters are: failure rate 0.001, repair rate 0.01, quantity of maximum resource 8, quantity of repair resource 2, damage rate 0.1 and strategy update cycle 200 (Table 2).

Table 2. List of parameters for simulations

	Description	Default value
$L \times L$	Size of the space	50×50
N	Number of nodes	2500
$N_f(0)$	Initial number of abnormal nodes	250
γ	Repairing rate	0.01
r	Strategy update cycle	200
Rmax	Quantity of maximum resource	8
Rγ	Quantity of resource used for repairing	2

Figure 8. A threshold in damage rate

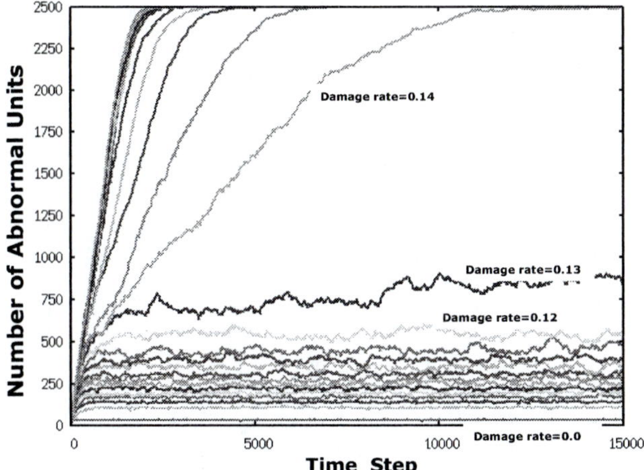

Efficacy of Repair

In this simulation, we only consider the strategy that always repairs (0C strategy), to observe the efficacy of repairing itself. It is expected that the repairing could contaminate the network when the damage rate is high.

Figure 8 plots the number of abnormal units (average number of 10 independent trials) with damage rate varying from 0.00 to 0.30. In this simulation, all the units are set to be normal initially. It can be observed that there is a threshold between 0.13 and 0.14 over which the number of abnormal units explodes. The threshold is also observed in the model presented in the previous section (Ishida, 2005). When the damage rate is less than 0.13, the number of abnormal units will be stabilized after some time steps, and hence the available resource is also stabilized. When the damage rate is more than 0.14, however, the number of abnormal units increases with further time steps.

This simulation indicates that the repairing by mutual copying is not effective to eradicate abnormal units when the damage rate is more than the threshold (0.14 in this simulation).

Efficacy of Strategic Repair

Since repairing itself cannot eradicate the abnormal units when the damage rate exceeds the threshold, it is obvious that even strategic repair will not clean the network. Figure 9 plots the evolution of the number of abnormal units when strategic repair and always repair are used when the damage rate is 0.2. Half of the units randomly selected are set to be abnormal initially. As observed in Figure 9, the strategic repair indeed could not clean the network. However, the strategic repair first succeeds in decreasing the number of abnormal units (around time step 200), and the contamination spreads more slowly than that by always repair. Figure 10 plots the available resources when the damage rate is 0.2.

Figure 9. Number of abnormal units when damage rate is 0.2

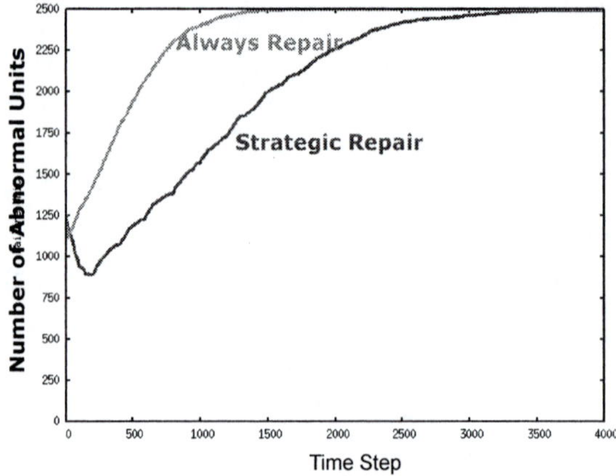

Figure 10. Available resources when damage rate is 0.2

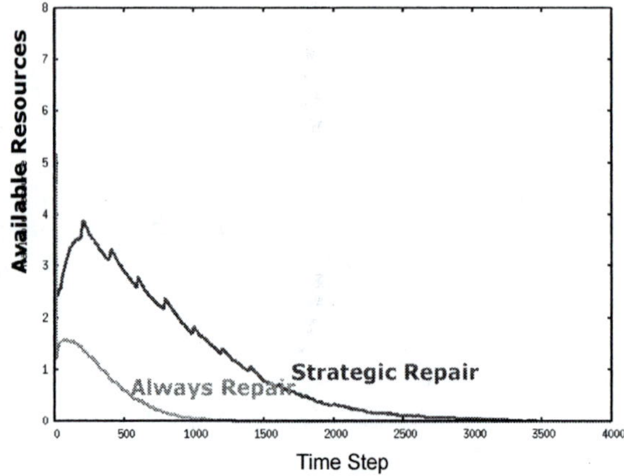

To further examine the superiority of the strategic repair, we compare it with two trivial strategies: one where the units always repair; and the other where the units never repair. We used the same parameters for these three strategies with the damage rate fixed at 0.1.

Figure 11 shows the evolution of the number of abnormal units, and Figure 12 shows the available resource (averaged over 40 independent trials) in each model. We can observe that both *the always repair* and *the strategic repair* become stable after some number of steps. (The oscillation observed in the strategic repair is due to the change of numbers in strategies at the strategy update cycle.) However, more resource remains available in *the strategic repair*. Moreover, *the strategic repair* becomes stable twice as fast.

Figure 11. Time evolution of a number of abnormal units when damage rate is 0.1

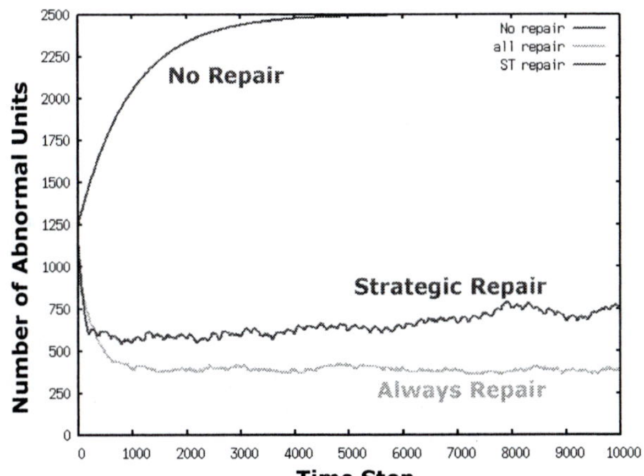

Figure 12. Time evolution of available resources when damage rate is 0.1

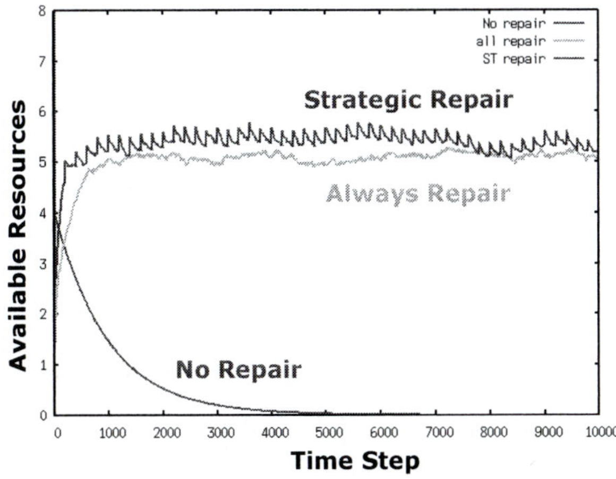

Adaptive Nature of the Strategic Repair

Figure 13 shows the number of units in each strategy of the *strategic repair*. It is observed that when the number of abnormal units increases, units with ease repairing strategies like *0C* also increase. Otherwise, units using hardly any repairing strategies like *8C* increase. This result suggests that the units choose an appropriate strategy depending on the environment. In fact, the efficacy (with respect to resource saving and abnormal unit eradication) of each strategy depends on the environment such as the failure rate and the number of abnormal units.

The adaptability of the strategic repair is more obvious when comparing Figure 13 and Figure 14, which show the cases with a high failure rate (0.004) and a low failure rate (0.001). More

Figure 13. Time evolution of the fraction of units with spatial strategies with failure rate 0.001

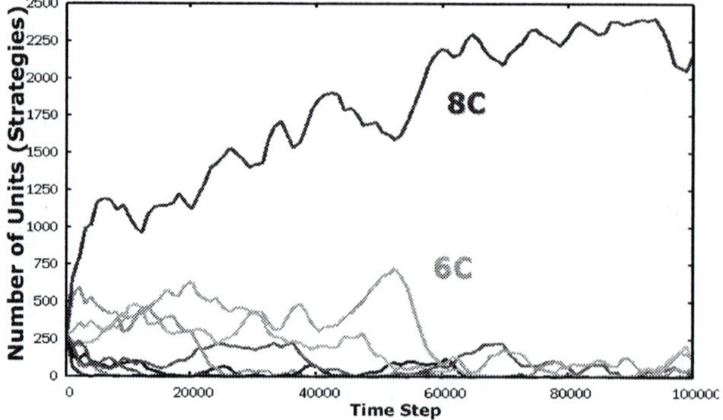

Figure 14. Time evolution of the fraction of units with spatial strategies with failure rate 0.004

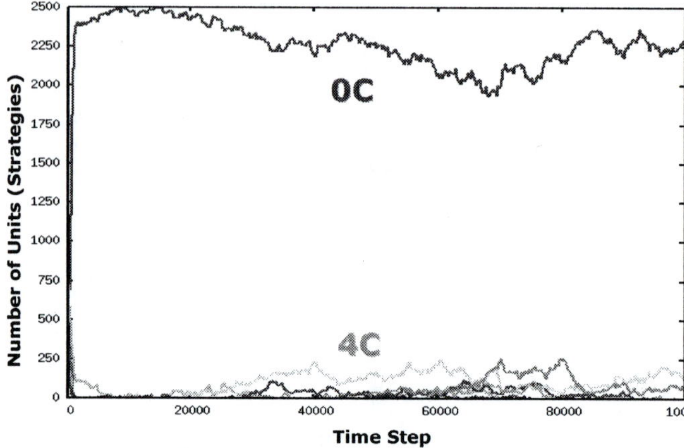

interestingly, Figure 14 indicates that the strategies 8C and 0C (or 1C) mutually support each other and are in a symbiotic relation. At a glance, the strategy 8C is dominant and may be sufficient as the optimal strategy in this environment; however, 8C alone cannot even survive and all the nodes end up with the abnormal state.

Future Trends

We presented a naive model for a naive problem of cleaning networks by mutual copying. When applied to existing information networks such as the Internet and sensor networks, self-repair networks should be able to deal with not only static regular networks but also dynamic growing networks such as Barabasi's scale-free networks, and should be able to deal with not only synchronous repair but also asynchronous repair.

Although threshold values of parameters for cleaning networks by mutual copying have been obtained by computer simulations, they should be determined with mathematical rigor. Also, theoretically, the model and results should be related to self-repairing cellular automaton by Gacs, but this problem was not considered in this chapter. Analogy to the immune system would suggest that node not only repair by copying (effector counterpart of the immune cells) but also recognize the abnormal nodes (receptor counterpart).

When the network is managed with autonomous distributed nodes using the game theory approach similar to the prisoner's dilemma, the adaptive character emerges. This adaptive nature is similar to the adaptive defense of the immune system that develops effective antibodies. Further, similar to ecological systems, symbiotic relations can be observed in the strategies that emerged. The similarities and differences from the biological systems will be carefully investigated in future work.

Conclusion

The problem of cleaning a contaminated network by mutual copying was studied by a model, which turned out to be a generalization of the probabilistic cellular automata proposed by Domany and Kinzel.

Cleaning by mutual copying is a double-edged sword, similar to the immune system, that could spread contamination rather than cleaning if not properly controlled.

When there are threshold values in parameters, they should be carefully regulated. Required is a framework of regulating mutual copying so that nodes (corresponding to computers) do not become selfish by only being repaired and also do not consume too many resources by often repairing. The framework involving a game theory approach of the spatial prisoner's dilemma turned out to be adaptive to the environment: strategies encouraging repairing emerges when the environment allows many abnormal nodes and opposite strategies emerge when the environment does not permit many abnormal nodes.

Acknowledgments

I am grateful to Toshikatsu Mori who helped to conduct the simulations. Some results in this chapter were presented in Ishida (2005), and Ishida and Mori (2005). This work was also partly supported by Grants-in-Aid for Scientific Research (B), 16300067; and by the 21st Century COE Program "Intelligent Human Sensing"' from the Ministry of Education, Culture, Sports, Science, and Technology of Japan.

References

Axelrod, R. (1984). *The evolution of cooperation.* New York: Basic Books.

Axelrod, R. (1987). The evolution of strategies in the iterated prisoner's dilemma. In L. Davis (Ed.), *Genetic algorithms and simulating annealing* (pp. 31-41). Pitman.

Barabasi, A.-L. (2002). *Linked: The new science of networks*. Perseus.

Brown, A., & Patterson, D. (2001). Embracing failure: A case for recovery-oriented computing (ROC). *High Performance Transaction Systems Workshop (TTPS '01).*

Dezso, Z., & Barabasi, A.-L. (2002). Halting viruses in scale-free networks. *Phys. Rev. E 65*, 055103.

Domany E., & Kinzel, W., (1984). Equivalence of cellular automata to Ising models and directed percolation. *Phys. Rev. Lett. 53,* 311.

Edelman, G. M. (1992). *Bright air brilliant fire: On the matter of the mind.* New York: Basic Books.

Farmer, J. D., Packard, N. H., & Perelson, A. S. (1986). The immune systems, adaptation and machine learning. *Physica D*, 22, 187-204.

Gacs, P. (2001). Reliable cellular automata with self-organization. *Journal Stat. Phys., 103*, 45-267.

Grim, P. (1995). The greater generosity of the spatialized prisoner's dilemma. *Journal theor. Biol., 173*, 353-359.

Ishida, Y. (2004). *Immunity-based systems: A design perspective.* Springer, GmbH.

Ishida, Y. (2005). A critical phenomenon in a self-repair network by mutual copying (LNAI 3682, pp. 86-92).

Ishida, Y., & Mori, T., (2005). Spatial strategies on a generalized spatial prisoner's dilemma. *Journal of Artificial Life and Robotics, 9*(3), 139-143.

Jerne, N. K. (1973). The immune system. *Scientific American, 229*(1), 52-60.

Langman, R. E., & Cohn, M. (Eds.). (2000). *Seminars in immunology.* Retrieved from http://www.idealibrary.com

Matuo, K., & Adachi, N. (1989). Metastable antagonistic equilibrium and stable cooperative equilibrium in distributed prisoner's dilemma game. In *Proceedings of the International Symposium Syst. Res., Infor. Cybern.*

Maturana, H., & Varela, F. (1980). *Autopoiesis and cognition: The realization of the living.* Dordrecht, D. Reidel.

May, R. M., & Lloyd, A. L. (2001). Infection dynamics on scale-free. *Phys. Rev. E, 64,* 066112.

Nowak, M. A., & May, R. M. (1992). Evolutionary games and spatial chaos. *Nature, 359*, 826-829.

Pastor R., & Vespignani, A. (2001). Epidemic spreading in scale-free networks. *Phys. Rev. Lett, 86,* 3200.

Tauber, A. I. (1997). *The immune self.* Cambridge, UK: Cambridge University Press.

Watts, D. J. (2003). *Six degrees: The science of a connected age.* W. W. Norton & Company.

Chapter IV

Soft Statistical Decision Fusion for Distributed Medical Data on Grids

Yu Tang, Georgia State University, USA

Yan-Qing Zhang, Georgia State University, USA

Abstract

This chapter introduces the decision fusion as a means of exploring information from distributed medical data. It proposes a new method of applying soft data fusion algorithm on the grid to analyze massive data and discover meaningful and valuable information. It could potentially help to better understand and process medical data and provide high-quality services in patient diagnosis and treatment. It allows incorporation of multiple physicians into one single case to recover and resolve problems, and integration of distributed data sources overcome some limitations of geographical locations to share knowledge and experience based on the soft data and decision fusion approach.

Introduction

Healthcare service is a complex industry nowadays. It is one of the most critical components of the modern human-oriented service. Informatics is an essential technology to health care (Dick & Steen, 1991) and has been applied to this field as long as computers have existed.

Information technology can be one of the major drivers of e-health activity, both directly and indirectly. E-health offers new opportunities to further improve the quality and safety of services because technology makes possible the high level of information management. However, it raises an important issue of how to utilize and integrate an impressive amount of medical data efficiently to provide high-quality and safe services.

Grid computing has emerged to address this issue. It was first developed in the scientific community and can be used as effective infrastructures for distributed high-performance computing and data processing (Foster, Kesselman, & Tuecke, 2001). The features of grid computing make the designation of an advance decision support system possible.

How to apply data fusion in a distributed medical decision system on the grid is still an open problem. In our previous research on this subject, the following observations were made that should guide our further work:

1. Massive data are collected in different organizations. With an explosion in size of database, discovering meaningful and valuable information from different datasets on grids is still a critical issue that affects decision-making in this area. There is an urgent need for a new computation technique to help service providers to process, analyze, and extract meaningful information from the rapid growing data.
2. The need for efficient, effective, and secure communication between multiple service providers for sharing clinical knowledge and experience is increasing. Traditional techniques are infeasible for analyzing large datasets that may maintain over geographically distributed sites.
3. The need for finding an efficient way to integrate data, knowledge, and decision from different parties is increasing.

These first two observations suggest an answer: build a grid-based system that enables the sharing of application and data in an open, heterogeneous environment. The last observation suggests an answer to build a soft fusion mechanism to do summarization, and it may result in higher accuracy of diagnosis and better treatment.

Related Work

There are several research groups whose work can contribute to grid-based data fusion on e-health. We first discuss decision support on the grid in the grid community, then we will introduce some related works about the medical decision support from the health community, and finally we will present some related works about soft data fusion and our proposal for solving this problem.

Decision Support on the Grid

A decision support system is defined as any computer program that assists decision-makers to utilize data and models to solve problems (Gorry & Morton, 1971; Keen & Morton, 1978; Sprague & Calson, 1980). Usually, it requires access to vast computation resources and processes a very large amount of data to make a decision. Grid computing is one approach to solving this problem. It has emerged as a paradigm with the ability to provide secure, reliable, and scaleable high-speed access to a distributed data resource. Compared to traditional distributed techniques, it has many advantages like resource sharing, high-performance services. The grid offers significant capability for designation and operation of complex decision support system by linking together a number of geographically distributed computers (Ong et al., 2004).

A grid-based decision support system can be used in a broad range of problems, from business to utilities, industry, earth science, health care, education and so on. Most researchers focus on simulation and visualization for specific processes such as air pollution (Mourino, Martin, Gonzalez, & Doallo, 2004), flooding crisis (Hluchy et al., 2004; Benkner, et al., 2003), and surgical procedures (Narayan, Corcoran-Perry, Drew, Hoyman, & Lewis, 2003; CrossGrid project) and then support decision-makers to make decisions on the basis of simulation results.

Medical Decision Support

The term medical decision support system describes a set of computer applications that are designed to assist health service providers in clinical decision-making. It can provide assessment or specifics that are selected from the knowledge base on the basis of individual patient characteristics (Hunt, Haynes, Hanna, & Smith, 1998; Delaney, Fitzmaurice, Riaz, & Hobbs, 1999). It is typically designed to integrate a medical knowledge base, patient data, and an application to produce case-specific advice.

The decision support system has been used in health care since the 1960s. There is evidence that using a medical decision support system may increase compliance with clinical pathways and guidelines and reduce rates of inappropriate diagnostic tests (Australia's Health Sector). It can support increased use of evidence by clinicians in direct patient care, resulting in better patient outcomes. However, the use of computerized medical decision systems is not commonplace. The results achieved have been rather low and the progress is slow (Reisman, 1996). Two identified barriers are lack of sources of knowledge and system development (Shortliffe, 1986), and lack of communication among profusion of different systems (Hobbs, Delaney, Carson, & Kenkre, 1996). As many researchers say, there is a rapidly growing need to improve medical decision-making in order to reduce practice variation, preventable medical errors (Poses, Cebul, & Wigton, 1995; Bornstein & Emier, 2001; Sintchenko & Coiera, 2003) and become feasible in the real world.

Soft Data Fusion

Data fusion is the amalgamation of information from multiple sources. It can be classified as either hard fusion and soft fusion.

All data fusion efforts are initiated to be used in particular research areas. It is still a "wide open field based on the difference in technology, the expectations by the users, and the kinds of problems that biologists and life scientists try to solve" (Freytag, Etzold, Goble, Schward, & Apweiler, 2003). Fusion system application can be found in the domain of hydrological forecasting (Abrahart & See, 2002), health care and medical diagnose (Laskey & Mahoney, 2003), and engineering (Chow, Zhu, Fischl, & Kam, 1993).

There are different approaches in the literature to fuse data. Some approaches use statistical analysis, while others use AI techniques like fuzzy logic (Chen & Luo, 1993), learning algorithms based on neural networks (Myers, Laskey, & DeJong, 1999), and Bayesian networks or uncertainty sets (Singhal & Brown, 1997) to handle the uncertainty.

Research Problem

In the healthcare industry, many organizations that could be located in different places collect data. In the traditional way, data is fragmented, and it is inconvenient for service providers to share experience and knowledge. Physicians would change medical decisions if they had enough "knowledge." Assume that they may collaborate under some agreements on some concerned problems. The following are some typical scenarios of example processes in e-health:

- Health service providers collaborate on the analysis of newly discovered disease or pathogenic bacteria.
- Health service providers collaborate on the estimate of the patient's state and providing appropriate treatments.
- Health service providers share the experience and knowledge with others.
- Health service providers get the support from others to make decisions for uncertain cases.

In these scenarios, collaboration across geographical location is needed to enable the sharing of data and knowledge and then make a decision. Greater benefits can be achieved if data integration is used rather than simply data collection (Sensmeier, 2003). Our research problems can be described as the following:

- **Quality of the medical decision.** Liability and reliability are two main issues of the medical decision system. Decision support tools must be carefully designed so that they are reliable and accurate (Sloane, Liberatore, & Nydick, 2002). How does one utilize grid computing to perform the data process? How does one use grid-based distributed data mining to discover knowledge? How does one make use of massive distributed data to improve the quality of service?

- **Collaboration.** How do the different parties collaborate with each other? How can we get data about patients and transmission through the Internet? Can data be integrated in different levels? How does one integrate the data, information, knowledge, and decisions from different organizations?

The following are our goals:

- **For service providers.** Share knowledge and experience to make high QoS decisions and choose the optimal treatment for the individual patient.
- **For patients.** Get better medical care that includes more accurate diagnosis results and better treatments.

Research Plan

In order to achieve all the requirements to make a system available, we need to integrate the network with multiple health service providers and patients. Grid computing allows flexible, secure, coordinated resource sharing among dynamic collections of individuals, institutions, and resources; it can be used as effective infrastructures for distributed high-performance computing and data processing (Foster, Kesselman, & Tuecke, 2001). The grid-based system of logical architecture is presented in Figure 1.

Figure 1 shows the logical architecture diagram of the system. The computers with service provider applications are the nodes of the grid. Health service providers communicate, exchange data, and share experience and knowledge through the grid service. Computers on the grid can be desktop, laptop, pocket PC, cell phone, and so on. Users of this system can be doctors, specialists, and assistants. They — users and computers — can communicate with each other through standard or wireless Internet. The typical data workflow is described in the following scenarios:

- Data of patient's current situation is sent to doctor.
- Decision support system starts to analyze data.
- Decision support system invites other doctor / system on the grid to participate in the diagnosis.
- Decision support system collects results from the grid and fuses results, then it generates decision.
- Doctor sends back results to patient.

Figure 1. Logical architecture

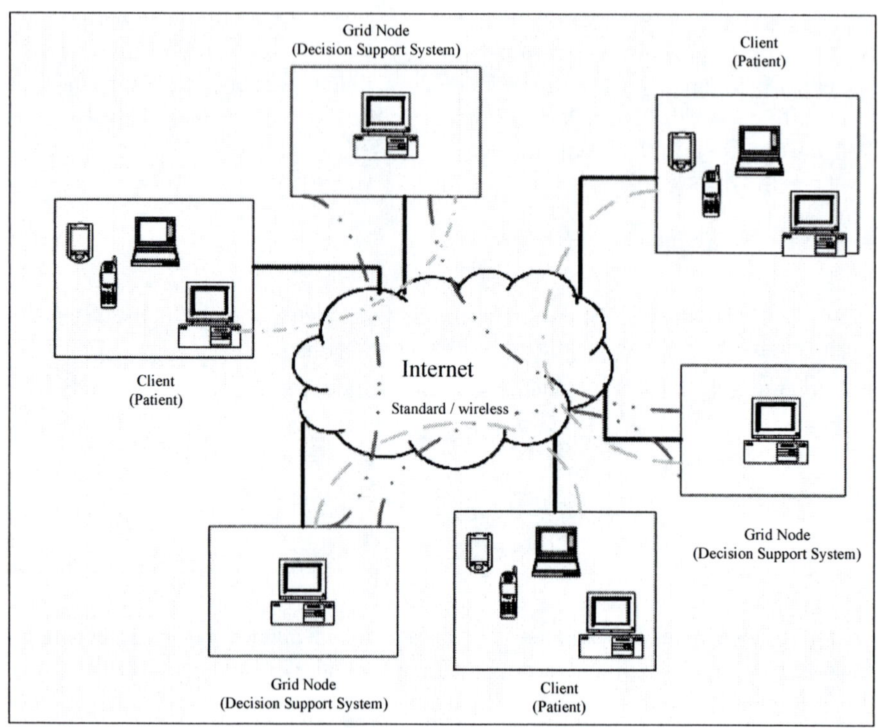

Figure 2. Software architecture

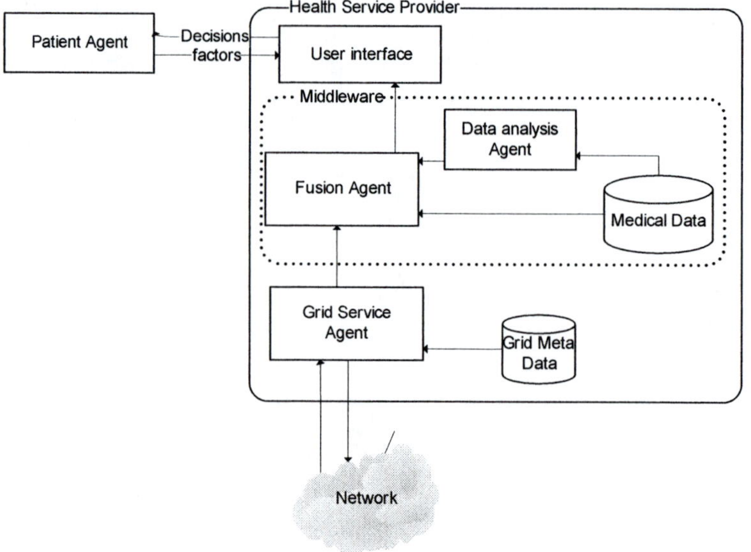

In order to perform such tasks, the decision support system has three integrated modules: grid service module, fusion service module, and user service module. The software architecture is shown in Figure 2.

Several modules work in the system to carry out tasks. The user friendly interface can accept tasks from and send back responses to users; the grid service agent module is used to provide basic services to manage the grid, coordinate actions, and resolve resources among nodes. The fusion agent module is used to implement different levels of data fusion. The data analysis agent module is used to analyze data and make diagnosis and decisions. Both fusion and data analysis modules work with the medical database. These three components are composed of middleware to provide services to the user.

To illustrate how this will work, we will first describe some key issues that are associated with grid-based distributed knowledge management technologies, as well as methodology for decision-making. We will then discuss plans to develop a feasible fusion mechanism for data, knowledge, and decision assembly.

Knowledge Management Technologies

Some factors that influence the quality of a medical decision system include: the quality of the underlying knowledge base used in the system; the incomplete dataset; and the conversion of knowledge into electronic form. Grid-based distributed data mining is used in this system to solve these problems and thus improve the quality of decisions. We will discuss these following issues:

- **Data privacy.** Medical data are sensitive and proprietary (Shamos, 2004); many hospitals and organizations treat health and medical data as their own property and are not willing to share with others. Proposed solutions to this issue include de-identification (Tracy, Dantas, & Upshur, 2004; Li & Chen, 2004; Kline, Johnson, Webb, & Runyon, 2004) and data-centered (Du & Zhan, 2002; Kantarcioglu & Clifton, 2002). We propose to follow both ways to protect data privacy.
- **Data preparation.** One barrier that influences the quality of a decision is the quality of medical data. They are often incomplete or out of time. The crucial information is missing when the decision is made. Data preparation is important to generate a high-quality decision. Conceptual reconstruction is one of options to be used to solve this problem (Aggarwal & Parthasarathy, 2001).
- **Data communication.** There is a security concern about this system. The use of grid security infrastructure (GSI) (Welch et al., 2003) allows secure authentication and data exchange over an opened network.
- **Data mining methods.** Using data mining in medical decisions can generate a decision of high accuracy (Kusiak, Kern, Kernstine, & Tseng, 2000). Several data mining algorithms are available for a decision-making system including: classification trees, case-based reasoning, neural network, genetic algorithm, fuzzy set approach, SVM, and so on. Our ongoing work is based on SVM and case-based reasoning. We will test and evaluate other algorithms in our future research.

Grid Toolkit

Grid computing is one of the innovative distributed computational models. It can offer high-performance computing and data processing abilities for the distributed mining and extraction of knowledge from data repositories. Grid applications are used in many fields including scientific computing, environmental monitoring, geohazard modeling, and business. It can be used as an effective infrastructure for distributed computing and data mining (Foster, 2001).

Grid technology is growing up very quickly and is going to be more and more complete and complex both in the number of tools and in the variety of supported applications (Cannataro, 2001). Compared to traditional distributed techniques, it has many advantages like resource sharing and high-performance services. Many existing tools are designed to provide functionalities of integration, resource management, access, process large datasets, and support the knowledge discovery process.

Globus Toolkit (Globus project group) is one candidate to implement grid management. It is a well-known grid middleware for providing grid resource management, security management, and other grid facilities. Globus Toolkit 3.0 is the first grid platform to fully support the OGSA/OGSI standard. It provides functionalities to discover, share, and monitor the resources. It also provides abilities for the mutual authentication of services and protection of data (Butler, 2000). The fusion module and application module are built on the base of Globus Toolkit.

Distributed Knowledge Discovery

The distributed knowledge discovery is a process that applies artificial intelligent theories and grid techniques to extract knowledge from distributed databases on the grid. Such processes can be implemented in the following steps:

1. **Data preparation.** The first step of this process is data preparation. Data retrieved from different databases on the grid needs to be pre-processed for two main reasons:
   - *Medical data is sensitive.* The data in this domain cannot be obtained without privileges. In order to protect data security, we follow two different ways: de-identification and data-centered. For de-identification, medical data in all organizations can be categorized into two parts: One part is pure medical data without any identified personal information of patients, it is accessible for all partners on the grid; the other part is full dataset with private patient information, it is only accessible for the owner. For data center, data processing is performed on a local data source. After processing, analysis results are based on data not data itself exchanged among the grid. Data and different levels of analysis results can be input of different level of fusion agent.
   - *Medical data may not be complete.* In order to minimize noise caused by incomplete data, pre-process data is necessary. The idea of conceptual reconstruction

Figure 3. Three-layer grid-based architecture

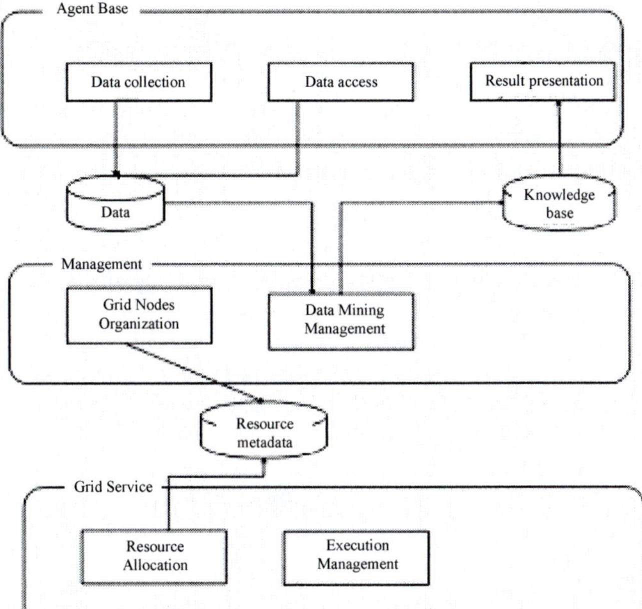

can be used to fill the missing data. One refill process is performed by calculating the mean and deviation of individual data values of each attribute; the other one is performed by finding the approximate patterns and calculating the mean of patterns. Different algorithms are used to calculate and fill missing values.

2. **Data exchange.** The second step of this process is data exchange. Grid tools provide secure, high-throughput data transfer. This model is set in terms of layer, just like many other grid-based knowledge discovery systems. Services provided by this model are set in a three-layer infrastructure as depicted in Figure 3.
3. **Data analysis.** The third step is data analysis. Several methods are used to analyze data. To take advantage of the grid, different data analysis applications can be used on different machines. Statistical algorithms and data mining algorithms are used to train medical data and generate results for a given case. In addition, they are used to discover useful knowledge on the distributed database. The knowledge explored includes membership functions and fuzzy rule sets. It aims to generate a number of fuzzy rules and membership functions by applying data mining algorithm to a collection of dataset on grids.
4. **Fusion analysis.** The system has the self-developing ability to analyze fusion results. Fusion logs are kept in a database, which enable system learning from outside resources.

Fusion Technologies

In real-world applications, a very large amount of data may be kept in the distributed database and can be accessed at an acceptable rate. Collaboration among many organizations is an important issue in making decisions with high accuracy. To combine data, information, and decisions from different parties, fusion is used in some research (Azuaje, Dubitzky, Black, & Adamson, 1999; Phegley, Perkins, Gupta, & Dorsey, 2002). The fusion technologies can be applied to different application domains.

We propose four possible levels of fusion with interactive discussion including different approaches to manage the fusion process. The integration of data and decision can occur in these four distinct levels — data, information, knowledge, and decision. Fusion service is based on basic grid mechanisms. It is built on top of grid services. Decisions made on the basis of local data are collected and fused. Such process aims to generate reliable decisions for health service providers by applying data mining algorithm and AI technologies to a collection of dataset on grids. It overcomes the disadvantages of human fusion and machine fusion: The former is limited by knowledge and subjective experience, while the latter is inflexible and relies on data excessively.

On account of the features of medical data, we propose soft fusion in our work, including fuzzy logic and simple weighting / voting. Neural network fusion and Bayesian fusion would be our future test.

Four-Level Fusion

A four-layer fusion framework is proposed for integration. It includes data fusion, information fusion, knowledge fusion, and decision fusion.

Figure 4. Four-layer fusion

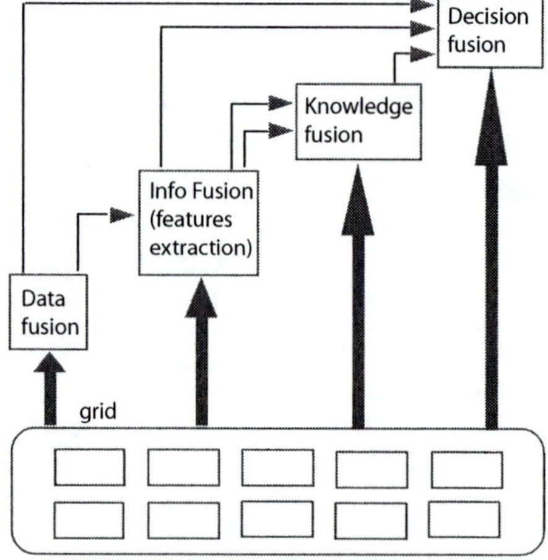

- **Data fusion.** This is the lowest level of fusion. The system collects data from multiple sources on the grid and provides categorized data that requires further processing and analysis to users. Users can make decisions or the system can generate decisions based on the process results of collected raw data.
- **Information fusion.** This is the second level of fusion. The system collects data that have common features from multiple sources on the grid and produces a more informative dataset for the users.
- **Knowledge fusion.** This is the third level of fusion. The system finds relevant features of data for each data source on the grid and summarizes knowledge from multiple nodes into a new knowledge base. Users can make decisions using knowledge base.
- **Decision fusion.** This is the highest level of fusion. The system gathers decisions and combines decisions coming from multiple nodes on the grid. The result is given as a system decision. In this chapter, we propose a dynamic decision fusion mechanism. The decision-making process is a negotiable process. It is not only a gather-and-combination procedure, but also allows decision-makers who have different opinions to discuss the issue of concern and make a final decision.

The four-layer frame work is presented in Figure 4.

Hybrid Interactive Fusion

To the best of the authors' knowledge, most of the current fusion systems have one feature in common: They fuse data or decisions on the basis of gathered items. They follow the simple flow — gather data, summarize, and give results. The limitation is clear; it is inflexible and relies excessively on computers.

We propose a dynamic fusion system with interactive discussion between different nodes on the grid. When the gathered decisions are not consistent, some further actions are performed. If service providers are available, they are invited to take a Web conference or telephone conference to discuss among each others. If they are not available, the system may be required to re-draw conclusions by exchanging training datasets or processing training datasets, including filter some unnecessary attributes using different algorithms to handle incomplete data. Compared to traditional fusion systems, it offers higher reliability and diagnosis accuracy by allowing users to confer with others in order to get consistency. This fusion process is described in Figure 5.

The dynamic fusion process simulates the human decision-making process. In the real world, such processes may involve decision-making, discussion, and re-decision-making. The dynamic fusion process is carried out as follows:

1. Systems analyze local datasets separately. Different data analysis applications, such as SVM, gene algorithm, and neuron network, can be used in different sites. The size of datasets varies from node to node.

Figure 5. Fusion process

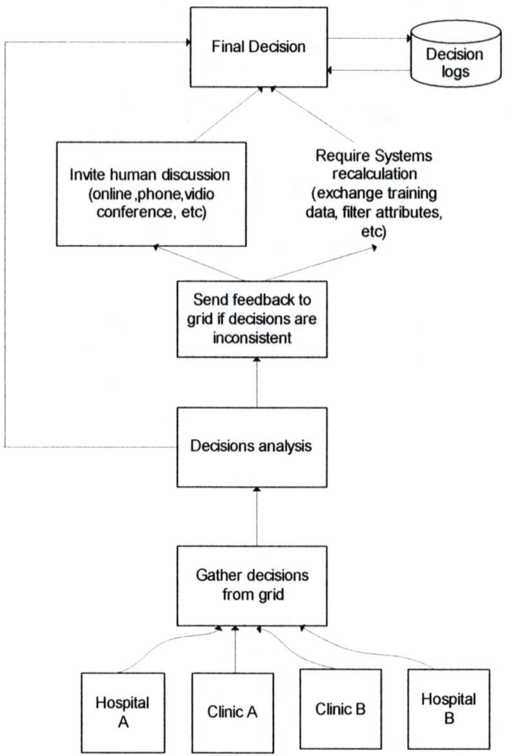

2. Consistent threshold is set by the user. It includes information about the number of users with consistent and confidence. It provides an indication of how certain we are about the decision fusion and what the acceptable fusion is. Consistent threshold is measured as <X, Y>. X and Y are values between zero to one. A value close to 1 for X means high consistency and for Y means high certainty. Similarly, a value close to 0 for X means low consistency and for Y means low certainty. <0.7, 0.7> is one example of consistent threshold, which means the acceptable result is that at least 70% of the decisions with average confidence 0.7 are identical. The higher the values of X, Y are, the more difficult to get satisfied answers but the more reliable results are.
3. Collect decisions from the grid and calculate consistent parameter <x, y>. Assume set S and set T are declared as decisions with the same results and total decisions, respectively.

   x = (size of S) / (size of T)

   y = mean of confidence values in S

   For example, there are eight systems in this medical group, and for some given case, six systems have the same diagnosis with confidence (0.8, 0.6, 0.5, 0.9,1, 0.75).

So, $x = 0.75$

and $y = 0.76$

4. If consistent confidence is less than consistent threshold, that is,

   $$<x, y> \; < \; <X, Y>, \quad x < X \text{ and } y < Y,$$

   the further fusion process is activated. Otherwise, results with confidence from different resources of the grid are input of fusion algorithm like voting/weight and neural network to generate the final system result.
5. Results come from the grid and the final system results are written into the database as fusion history. Every result counts in this system because it will be used as input by fusion algorithm and make contribution for future fusion. Systems accumulate knowledge in this way.

In the best case, all decision-makers on the grid have the same results in the first round of fusion. In this situation, no further fusion is needed. But in the worst case, decisions coming from different makers can be very different. Eight people may have eight different results for the same case. Exchange of opinions and discussion are necessary. Some decision-makers may change their decisions after discussion, and the fusion process is not implemented until it gets satisfied results.

Potential users of this system are doctors, physicians, specialists, and their assistants. The system can provide partial functionalities without human interactions in certain conditions. There are three types of the further fusion processes according to different types of users in the context of the grid:

- **Human-to-human.** The fusion process is implemented in a human-to-human environment. It occurs when users of systems are available and the system works as a decision assistant. The purpose of the system is to provide suggestions for users to make decisions by getting consistent results from group users. Once the system collects results from the grid, it determines the degree of consistency and compares it with the threshold. If it is lower than consistent, the system activates the further fusion including online discussion, e-mail, phone conference, and video conference. Doctors will discuss as to the given case just like the real-world situation. The system fusion decision starts again after some doctors change decisions.
- **Machine-to-machine.** The fusion process is implemented among machines. It occurs when systems work automatically without human interactions. Once the system determines to carry out the further fusion process, one of the two proposed methods can be implemented: re-analyze data using a different training dataset; or re-analyze data using the same training dataset, but only some important attributes are take into account. The first method involves data exchange and low-level data fusion, the latter one involves data preparation and middle-level information fusion. This process may repeat several times until it gets satisfied consistency.

- **Human-to-machine.** Not all doctors are available on the grid. The fusion process is implemented in a hybrid way. If the system needs to carry out the further fusion, it can have two parts: invite available doctors to discuss directly like in the human-to-human situation; or suggest system re-analyze data by providing part of the local set to remote systems or determining the attributes that are used for further analysis. Then, fuse the results again.

The proposed fusion mechanism follows the way humans make decisions. The AI technologies make it smarter and more reliable.

Conclusion

A novel method for data fusion with interactions among decision-makers is described. This method takes advantages of observation of other decision-makers' opinions and then modifies the result. This method simulates the process of human decision-making. It involves decision-making, decision fusion, discussion, and re-making, re-fuse. It can improve reliability and flexibility of the fusion system.

The goal of this project is to develop a generalized decision-making and fusion system on grid approach to improve accuracy of diagnose. A system using SVM for learning from medical data and fuzzy logic for making decisions is designed. Simulations based on Wisconsin Breast Cancer database and Heart Disease (UCI ML Repository) show that the new system is effective in terms of decision accuracy. Even more promising is that higher accuracies are possible if other AI techniques are used.

References

Abrahart, R. J., & See, L. (2002). Multi-model data fusion for river flow forecasting: An evaluation of six alternative methods based on two contrasting catchments. *Hydrology and Earth system science, 6*, 655-670.

Aggarwal, C. C., & Parthasarathy, S. (2001). Mining massively incomplete data sets by conceptual reconstruction. In *Proceedings of the 7th ACM SIGKDD International Conference on Knowledge Discovery and Data Mining* (pp. 227-232).

Australia's Health Sector. (2002). *Electronic decision support for Australia's health sector.* Report to Health Ministers by the national electronic decision support taskforce.

Azuaje, F., Dubitzky, W., Black, N., & Adamson, K. (1999). Improving clinical decision support through case-based data fusion. *IEEE Transaction on Biomedical Engineering, 46*(10).

Benkner, S., Engelbrecht, G., Backfrieder, W., et al. (2003). Numerical simulation for eHealth: Grid-enabled medical simulation services. In *Proceedings of the PARCO2003, Parallel Computing,* Dresden, Germany.

Bornstein B. H., & Emier, A. C. (2001). Rationality in medical decision-making: A review of the literature on doctors' decision-making biases. *Journal Eval. Clin. Pract., 7,* 97-107.

Butler, R., et al. (2000). Design and deployment of a national-scale authentication infrastructure. *IEEE Computer, 33*(12), 60-66.

Cannataro, M., Talia, D., & Trunfio, P. (2003). Design of distributed data mining on the knowledge grid. *CACM, 46*(1), 89-93.

Chen, T. M., & Luo, R. C. (1999). Multilevel multiagent based team decision fusion for autonomous tracking system. *Machine Intelligence & Robotic Control, 1*(2), 63-69.

Chow, J. C., Zhu, Q., Fischl, R., & Kam, M. (1993). Design of decision fusion rule for power system security assessment. *IEEE Transaction on Power System, 8,* 858-864.

CrossGrid Project. (n.d.) Retrieved from http://www.crossgrid.org

Delaney, B. C., Fitzmaurice, D. A., Riaz, A., & Hobbs, R. (1999). Can computerized decision support systems deliver improved quality in primary care. *BMJ, 319,* 1281.

Dick, R. S., & Steen, E. B. (Eds.). (1991). *The computer-based patient record: An essential technology for health care.* Washington, DC: National Academy Press.

Du, W., & Zhan, Z. (2002). Building decision tree classifier on private data. *IEEE International Conference on Data Mining workshop on Privacy, Security, and Data Mining, 14.*

Foster, I., Kesselman C., & Tuecke, S. (2001). The anatomy of the grid: Enabling scalable virtual organizations. *International Journal of Supercomputer Applications, 15*(3).

Freytag, J., Etzold, T., Goble, C., Schward, P., & Apweiler, R. (2003). Information and process integration: A life science perspective. *Schloss Dagstuhl International Conference and Research Center for Computer Science.* Retrieved from http://www.dagstuhl.de/03051/

Globus Toolkit. (n.d.). Retrieved from http://www.globus.org

Gorry, A., & Morton, M. S. (1971). A framework for information systems. *Sloan Management Review, 13,* 56-79.

Hluchy, L., Tran, V. D., Simo, B., Habala, O., Astalos, J., & Gatial, E. (2004). Flood forecasting in CrossGrid project. In *Proceedings of the 2nd European Across Grids Conference*, Nicosia, Cyprus.

Hobbs, F. D., Delaney, B. C., Carson, A., & Kenkre, J. K. (1996). A prospective controlled trial of computerized decision support for lipid management in primary care. *Family Practice, 13,* 133-137.

Hunt, D. L., Haynes, B. R., Hanna, S. E., & Smith, K. (1998). Effects of computer-based clinical decision support systems on physician performance and patient outcomes. *JAMA, 280,* 1339-1346.

Kantarcioglu, M., & Clifton, C. (2002). Privacy-preserving distributed mining of association rules on horizontally partitioned data. In *Proceedings of the ACM SIGMOD Workshop on Research Issue on Data Mining and Knowledge Discovery* (pp. 24-31).

Keen, P. G. W., & Morton, M. S. (1978). *Decision support systems: An organizational perspective.* Reading, MA: Addison-Wesley.

Kline, J. A., Johnson, C. L., Webb W. B., & Runyon, M. S. (2004). Prospective study of clinician-entered research data in the emergency department using an Internet-based system after the HIPAA privacy rule. *BMC Medical Informatics and Decision Making, 4,* 17.

Kusiak, A., Kern, J. A., Kernstine, K. H., & Tseng, B. L. (2000). Autonomous decision-making: A data mining approach. *IEEE Transaction on Information Technology in Biomedicine, 4*(4).

Laskey, K. B., & Mahoney, S. M. (2003). *Knowledge and data fusion in probabilistic networks.* Retrieved from http://ite.gmu.edu/~klaskey/papers/KDFML_Laskey_Mahoney.pdf

Li, Y. C., & Chen, S. (2004). Building Taiwan health grid for health decision making. *ISGC Workshop.*

Mourino, J. C., Martin, M. J., Gonzalez, P., & Doallo, R. (2004). Air pollution modeling in the CrossGrid Project. In *Proceedings of the Computational Science-ICCS 2004: 4th International Conference, Part 1*, Karkow, Poland (pp. 132-139).

Myers, J. W., Laskey, K. B., & DeJong, K. A. (1999). Learning Bayersian networks from incomplete data using evolutionary algorithms. In *Proceedings of the Genetic and Evolutionary Computation Conference.*

Narayan, S. M., Corcoran-Perry, S., Drew, D., Hoyman, K., & Lewis, M. (2003). Decision analysis as a tool to support an analytical pattern-of-reasoning. *Nursing and Health Sciences, 5*(3), 229-243.

Ong, M., Ren, X., Allan, G., Kadirkamanathan, V., Thompson, H. A., & Fleming, P. J. (2004). Decision support system on the grid. *International Conference on Knowledge-based Intelligent Information and Engineering System (KES2004),* New Zealand.

Phegley, J., Perkins, K., Gupta, L., & Dorsey, K. J. (2002). Risk-factor fusion for predicting multifactorial diseases. *IEEE Transaction on Biomedical Engineering, 49*(1).

Poses, R. M., Cebul, R. D., & Wigton, R. S. (1995). You can lead a horse to water — Improving physicians' knowledge of probabilities may not affect their decisions. *Med. Dec. Making,* 65-75.

Reisman, Y. (1996). Computer-based clinical decision aids. A review of methods and assessment of systems. *International Journal of Medical Informatics, 21*(3), 179-197.

Sensmeier, J. (2003, Fall). Advancing the state of data integration in healthcare. *Journal Healthc Inf. Manag, 17*(4), 58-61.

Shamos, M.I. (2004). *Medical and workplace privacy.* Retrieved from http://lorrie.cranor.org/courses/fa04/work2.ppt

Shortliffe, E. H. (1986). Medical expert systems-knowledge tools for physicians. *West J Med., 145*(6), 830-9.

Singhal, A., & Brown, C. (1997). Dynamic Bayes net approach to multimodal sensor fusion. In *Proceedings of the SPIE — the International Society for Optical Engineering* (Vol. 3209, pp. 2-10).

Sintchenko V., & Coiera, E. W. (2003). Which clinical decisions benefit from automation? A task complexity approach. *International Journal of Medical Informatics, 70*, 309-316.

Sloane, E. B., Liberatore, M. J., & Nydick, R. L. (2002). Medical decision support using the analytic hierarchy process. *Journal of Healthcare Information Management, 16*(4), 38-43.

Sprague, R. H., & Calson, E. D. (1980). Building effective decision support systems. *Management Information Systems Quarterly, 4*(4), 1-26

Tracy, C. S., Dantas G. C., & Upshur, R. E. (2004). Feasibility of a patient decision aid regarding disclosure of personal health information. *BMC Medical Informatics and Decision Making, 4*, 13.

UCI ML Repository. (n.d.). Retrieved from http://www.ics.uci.edu/~mlearn/MLSummary.html

Welch, V., Siebenlist, F., Foster, I., Bresnahan, J., et al. (2003). Security for grid services. *12th International Symposium on High Performance Distributed Computing (HPDC-12).* IEEE Press.

Section II:

Hybrid Intelligent Systems and Applications

Chapter V

Designing Layers in Hierarchical Fuzzy Logic Systems Using Genetic Algorithms

Masoud Mohammadian, University of Canberra, Australia

Russel Stonier, Central Queensland University, Australia

Abstract

In this chapter, the design and development of hierarchical fuzzy logic systems is investigated using genetic algorithms. This research study is unique in the way the proposed method is applied to the design and development of hierarchical fuzzy logic systems. The new method proposed determines the number of layers in the hierarchical fuzzy logic system. The proposed method is then applied to financial modeling and prediction. A hierarchical fuzzy logic system is developed to predict quarterly interest rates in Australia. The advantages and disadvantages of using hierarchical fuzzy logic systems for financial modeling is also considered. Good prediction of quarterly interest rate in Australia is obtained using this method. The number of fuzzy rules used is reduced dramatically, and the prediction of interest rate is improved.

Introduction

Traditionally the modeling of uncertain dynamic systems, such as that for prediction of interest rates, has relied on complex mathematical models to describe the dynamic system to be modeled. These models work well provided the system meets the requirement and assumption of synthesis techniques. However, due to uncertainty or sheer complexity of these systems, they are difficult to model and not easily adaptable to changes in the system which they were not designed for (Kosko, 1992; Mohammadian & Stonier, 1995; Zadeh, 1965). Computational intelligence techniques such as fuzzy logic, genetic algorithms (GAs), and neural networks have been successfully used in the place of complex mathematical systems (Cox, 1993; Kosko, 1992). Fuzzy logic is an active research area (Cordón, Herrera, Hoffmann, & Magdalena, 2001; Cox, 1993; Kosko, 1992; Lee, 1990; Mohammadian & Stonier, 1995; Zadeh, 1965). Fuzzy modeling or fuzzy identification has numerous practical applications in control, prediction, and inference. It has been found useful when the system is either difficult to predict and or difficult to model by conventional methods. Fuzzy set theory provides a means for representing uncertainties. The underlying power of fuzzy logic is its ability to represent imprecise values in an understandable form. The majority of fuzzy logic systems to date have been static and based upon knowledge derived from imprecise heuristic knowledge of experienced operators, and where applicable also upon physical laws that governs the dynamics of the process. Although its application to industrial problems has often produced results superior to classical control (Cox, 1993; Welstead, 1994), the design procedures are limited by the heuristic rules of the system. It is simply assumed that the rules for the system are readily available or can be obtained. This implicit assumption limits the application of fuzzy logic to the cases of the system with a few parameters. The number of parameters of a system could be large. The number of fuzzy rules of a system is directly dependent on these parameters. As the number of parameters increase, the number of fuzzy rules of the system grows exponentially (Mohammadian, 1996; Raju & Zhou, 1993). In fuzzy logic systems, there is a direct relationship between the number of fuzzy sets of input parameters of the system and the size of the fuzzy knowledge base (FKB). Kosko and Isaka (1993) call this the "Curse of Dimensionality". The "curse" in this instance is that there is exponential growth in the size of the FKB, $k = m^n$ where k is the number of rules in the FKB, m is the number of fuzzy sets for each input, and n is the number of inputs into the fuzzy system.

As the number of fuzzy sets associated with the input parameters increase, the number of rules increases exponentially. There are a number of ways that this exponential growth in the size of the FKB can be contained. The most obvious is to limit the number of inputs to the system. However, this may reduce the accuracy of the system, and in many cases, render the system being modeled unusable. Another approach is to reduce the number of fuzzy sets associate with each input variable. Again, this may reduce the accuracy of the system (Kosko, 1992). The number of rules in the FKB can also be trimmed if it is known that some rules are never used. This can be a time-consuming and tedious task, as every rule in the FKB may need to be examined. Raju and Zhou (1993) suggested using a hierarchical fuzzy logic structure for such fuzzy logic systems to overcome this problem. By using hierarchical fuzzy logic systems, the number of fuzzy rules in the system are reduced, thereby reducing the computational time while maintaining system robustness and efficiency.

This chapter considers the design and development of a hierarchical fuzzy logic system using genetic algorithms to model and predict interest rate in Australia. Genetic algorithms are employed as an adaptive method for design and development of such hierarchical fuzzy logic systems. They have been widely used for finding fuzzy rules and associated parameters (Anver & Stonier, 2004; Cordón et al., 2001; Thomas & Stonier, 2003). This chapter will show that they can be easily utilized to find the input and layer structure of a "best performing" hierarchical structure for interest rate prediction.

Hierarchical Fuzzy Logic Systems

The hierarchical fuzzy logic structure is formed by having the most influential inputs as the system input variables to the first level of the hierarchy, the next most important inputs to the second layer, and so on. If the hierarchical fuzzy logic structure contains n system input parameters and L number of hierarchical levels with n_i the number of variables contained in the ith level, the total number of rules k is then determined by: $k = \sum_{i=1}^{L} m^{n_i}$, where m is the number of fuzzy sets. This equation means that by using a hierarchical fuzzy logic structure, the number of fuzzy rules for the system is reduced to a linear function of the number of system variables n, instead of an exponential function of n as is the conventional case (Raju & Zhou, 1993). The first level of the hierarchy gives an approximate output, which is then modified by the second level rule set, and so on. This is repeated for all succeeding levels of the hierarchy. One problem occurs when it is not known which inputs to the system have more influence than the others. This is the case in many problems. In some cases, statistical analysis could be performed on the inputs to determine which ones have more bearing on the system.

Integrated Hierarchical Fuzzy Logic and Genetic Algorithms

Genetic algorithms (GAs) (Goldberg, 1989; Goonatilake, Campbell, & Ahmad, 1995) are powerful search algorithms based on the mechanism of natural selection and use operations of reproduction, crossover, and mutation on a population of strings. A set of possible solutions is the population. In this case, each solution is a coding of the fuzzy rules of a fuzzy logic system, represented as a string of numbers. New strings are produced every generation by the repetition of a two-step cycle. First, each individual string is decoded and its ability to solve the problem is assessed. Each string is assigned a fitness value, depending on how well it performed. In the second stage, the fittest strings are preferentially chosen for recombination to form the next generation. Recombination involves the selection of two strings, the choice of a crossover point in the string, and the switching of the segments to the right of this point, between the two strings (one-point cross-over). Figure 1 shows the combination of fuzzy logic and genetic algorithms for generating fuzzy rules.

Figure 1. Combination of fuzzy logic and genetic algorithms for fuzzy rule generation

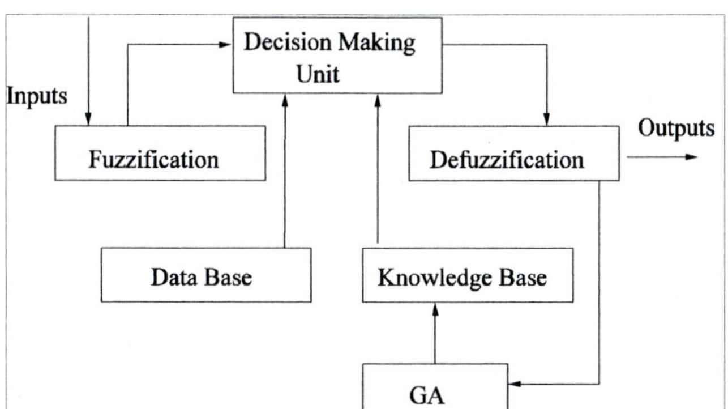

For encoding and decoding of the fuzzy rule for a fuzzy logic system, first, the ranges of the input parameters of the fuzzy logic system are divided into fuzzy sets. Assume that the fuzzy logic system has two inputs *a* and *b* and a single output *d*, and that the intervals of definition of the inputs and output of the system are divided into five fuzzy sets. The fuzzy logic system has a maximum of 25 fuzzy rules. The consequent for each fuzzy rule will be determined by genetic evolution.

In order to do so, the output fuzzy sets are encoded. (It is not necessary to encode the input fuzzy sets because the input fuzzy sets are assumed static and do not change.)

The consequent of each fuzzy rule can be any one of the five output fuzzy sets. Assume that the output fuzzy sets are: NB (negative big), NS (negative small), ZE (zero), PS (positive small), and PB (positive big). Then the output fuzzy sets are encoded by assigning 1 = NB, 2 = NS, 3 = ZE, 4 = PS, and 5 = PB. A string or individual in the population, representing all the fuzzy rules can then be defined as:

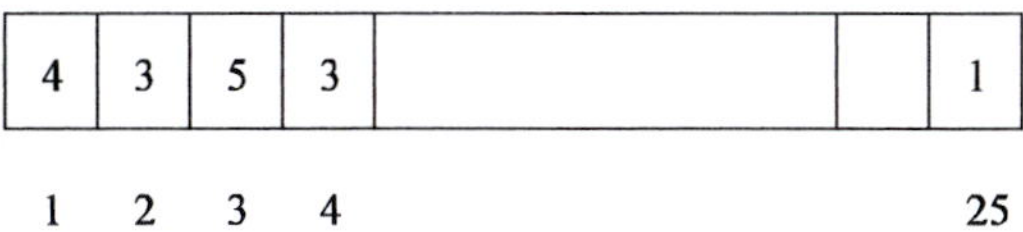

The initial population of the genetic algorithm is obtained by randomly encoding a set of strings. The fitness of each string is obtained by decoding each string into the fuzzy logic structure and determining a value defining its performance on the data given, see the later definition in relation to prediction of interest rate. In developing the population at the next generation, elitism is used with two or more copies of the best performing string from the parent generation included in the next generation to ensure that the best performing strings are not lost. The processes of selection, crossover, and mutation are then performed to add further individual strings to complete the population at this next generation. Selection and crossover are the same as in simple genetic algorithms (Goldberg, 1989), while the mutation operation is modified as shown. Crossover and mutation take place based on the probability of crossover and mutation, respectively. The mutation operator is changed to suit this problem, namely, an allele is selected at random and is replaced by a random number ranging from 1 to 5. The processes of selection, crossover, and mutation are repeated for a number of generations until a satisfactory fuzzy rule base is obtained. We define a satisfactory rule base as one whose fitness value differs from the desired output of the system by an acceptable small value. These general details are made more specific for the interest rate prediction in the next section.

Hierarchical Fuzzy Logic System for Interest Rate Prediction

There is much interest by investors and government departments in the ability to predict future interest rate fluctuations from current economic data. Economists and investors have been unable to find all the factors that influence interest rate fluctuations. It is agreed that there are some major economic indicators released by the Government (Goonatilake & Treleaven, 1995) that are commonly used to look at the current position of the economy. The indicators (see Mohammadian & Kingham, 1997; Mohammadian, Kingham, & Bignall, 1998) used in this chapter are:

- Interest rate is the indicator being predicted. The interest rate used here is the Australian Commonwealth government 10-year treasury bonds.
- Job vacancies is where a position is available for immediate filling or for which recruitment action has been taken.
- The unemployment rate is the percentage of the labour force actively looking for work in the country.
- Gross domestic product is an average aggregate measure of the value of economic production in a given period.
- The consumer price index is a general indicator of the rate of change in prices paid by consumers for goods and services.
- Household saving ratio is the ratio of household income saved to households' disposable income.
- Home loans measure the supply of finance for home loans, not the demand for housing.
- Average weekly earnings is the average amount of wages that a full-time worker takes home before any taxes.
- Current account is the sum of the balances on merchandise trade, services trade, income, and unrequited transfers.
- Trade weighted index measures changes in our currency relative to the currencies of our main trading partners.

- RBA commodity price index provides an early indication of trends in Australia's export prices.
- All industrial index provides an indication of price movements on the Australian Stock Market.
- Company profits are defined as net operating profits or losses before income tax.
- New motor vehicles is the number of new vehicles registered in Australia.

If we created a system that contains all these indicators, we should be in a much better position to predict the fluctuations in interest rates. A fuzzy logic system that used every indicator and had five fuzzy sets associated with every indicator would result in a large FKB consisting of more than six billion rules! As can be imagined, this would require large computing power to not only train the fuzzy logic system with a genetic algorithm, but also large storage and run-time costs when the system is operational. Even if a computer could adequately handle this large amount of data, there is still the problem in having enough data to properly train every possible rule. To overcome this problem, a hierarchical fuzzy logic structure for the fuzzy logic system can be constructed. By using a hierarchical fuzzy logic system, the number of fuzzy rules of the system is reduced, hence computational times are decreased resulting in a more efficient system. A novel way to tackle this problem would be to group the relevant indicators and to build a fuzzy knowledge base for each group. The first step is to divide the indicators into smaller-related groups. This problem was investigated in Mohammadian & Kingham (1997) and Mohammadian et al. (1998) and is described next:

1. Employment (job vacancies, unemployment rate)
2. Country (gross domestic product, consumer price index)
3. Savings (household saving ratio, home loans, average weekly earnings)
4. Foreign (current account, RBA index, trade weighted index)
5. Company (all industrial index, company profit, new motor vehicles)

The five fuzzy knowledge bases created from the top layer of the hierarchy are shown in Figure 2. The authors designed and connected together the fuzzy knowledge bases to form a final fuzzy knowledge base system. The final fuzzy knowledge base is shown in Figure 2; it uses the predicted interest rate from the five groups to produce a final interest rate prediction. The number of fuzzy rules for each group is shown in Figure 2.

The final hierarchical FKB contains 3,125 rules giving the total number of rules to be learnt as 5,250. This is a significant reduction from the six billion rules that would have been obtained using a single-layered fuzzy knowledge base. This allows quicker training time without the need for huge computer resources (Mohammadian & Kingham, 1997; Mohammadian et al., 1998).

The interest rate is included as input to each of the groups. To learn the fuzzy knowledge base for each group, a genetic algorithm was implemented as described. The genetic algorithm had a population size of 500 with a crossover rate of 0.6, a mutation rate of 0.01, and it was run for 10,000 generations over 10 years (a period of 40 quarters) of data. The fitness of

Figure 2. Hierarchical knowledge base flow

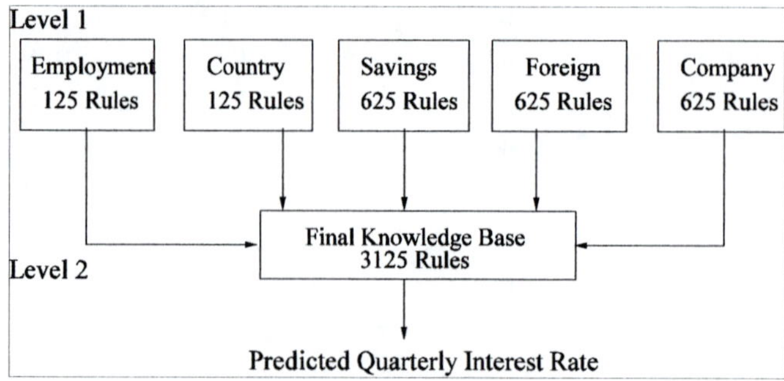

each string was calculated as the sum of the absolute differences from the predicted quarter and the actual quarter's interest rate. The fitness was subtracted from an "optimal" fitness amount, which was decided to be 30 as it was unlikely the error amount would be higher than this over 10 years (Mohammadian & Kingham, 1997; Mohammadian et al., 1998). The fitness is thus calculated by the following formula:

$$fitness = 30 - \sum_{i=0}^{30} abs(PI_i - I_{i+1}).$$

We refer the reader to the mentioned papers for a discussion on aspects of the fuzzy modeling that were used, including fuzzy membership sets for each of the key input variables, Mandami Max-Min inference engine, and center average defuzzification. Good prediction of Australian quarterly interest rate was obtained using the above system; see Mohammadian & Kingham (1997) and Mohammadian et al. (1998) for further details. The number of fuzzy rules used has been also reduced dramatically.

However, there is still a question: Does a two-layer hierarchical architecture provide the best solution?

To start to answer this question, one can start building and examining all three- or four-layer hierarchical fuzzy logic systems to find the correct number of layers required. This is a tedious exercise. Genetic algorithms can be used to solve this problem by determining the number of layers in the hierarchical fuzzy logic system and the correct combination of FKBs for each layer. We choose to develop hierarchical structures that have the form shown in Figure 3.

Using the economic indicators, five fuzzy logic systems were developed using the genetic algorithm approach described, one for each of the five groups described. Each system produces a predicted interest rate for the next quarter. For encoding and decoding of the hierarchical fuzzy logic system, first a number is allocated to each fuzzy logic system developed from the group of indicators. For this simulation, the number allocated to each group is shown in the following:

Figure 3. A three-layer hierarchical fuzzy logic system — 3,125 fuzzy rules

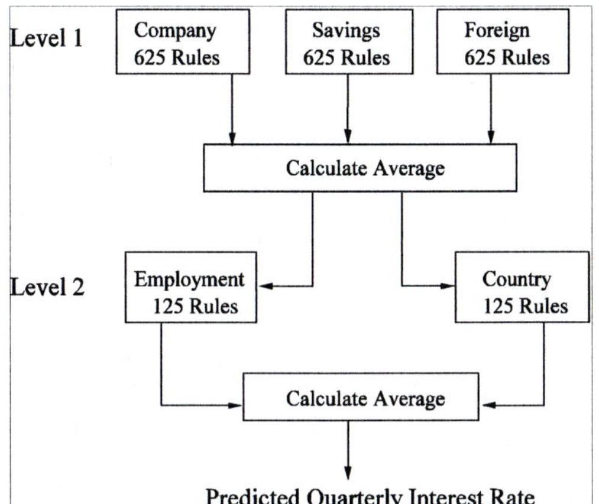

1 = Employment, 2 = Country, 3 = Savings, 4 = Foreign, 5 = Company

There are five layers possible so we can encode a string or individual in the population as follows:

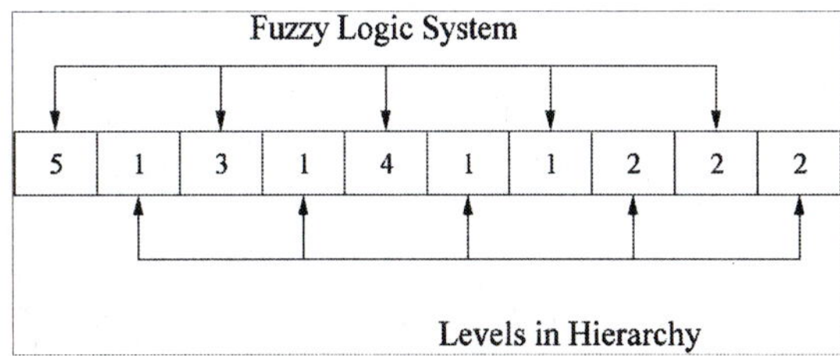

Here, Company (5) is in layer 1 of the hierarchy, Savings (3) is in layer 1 of the hierarchy and so on, finally, Country (2) is in layer 2. This string decodes to the hierarchical fuzzy logic system shown in Figure 3.

For this string, we evaluate its fitness based on the decoded hierarchical structure. It is the average error of the system for the training set and tests sets using the following formula (Mohammadian & Kingham, 1997; Mohammadian et al., 1998):

$$E = \frac{\sum_{i=1}^{n} abs(P_i - A_i)}{n},$$

where E is the average error, P_i is the predicted interest rate at time period i, A_i is the actual interest rate for the quarter and n is the number of quarters predicted.

Table 1. Comparison of average errors

	Training Error	Testing Error
HFL #1	0.356	0.659
HFL #2	0.343	0.663
HFL #3	0.289	0.494
HFL #4	0.274	0.441
HFL #5	0.291	0.398

Figure 4. Hierarchical fuzzy logic system — HFL #1

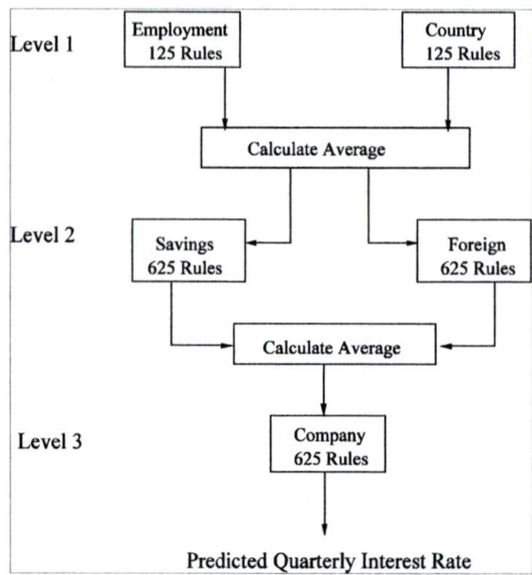

The initial population of the genetic algorithm is created with strings whose integer elements are randomly chosen between 1 and 5. The genetic algorithm is allowed to evolve as previously described until a satisfactory hierarchical fuzzy logic system defined by a small acceptable error E is obtained. The hierarchical fuzzy logic systems developed using the genetic algorithm predict the interest rate to different degrees of accuracy. It is now possible to choose the best hierarchical fuzzy logic system among those suggested by genetic algorithms.

The results of the five top performing hierarchical fuzzy logic systems designed by genetic algorithms are given in Table 1.

Comparison of average errors of these five best hierarchical fuzzy logic systems is also shown in Table 1.

The best performing structure is HFL #5, in terms of training and test errors. This is a much improved result when compared with the hierarchical model in Figure 2 which gave a training error of 0.402 and test error of 0.465. Figures 4, 5, and 6, show the structure of HFL #1, HFL #4, and HFL #5, respectively.

Figure 5. Hierarchical fuzzy logic system — HFL #4

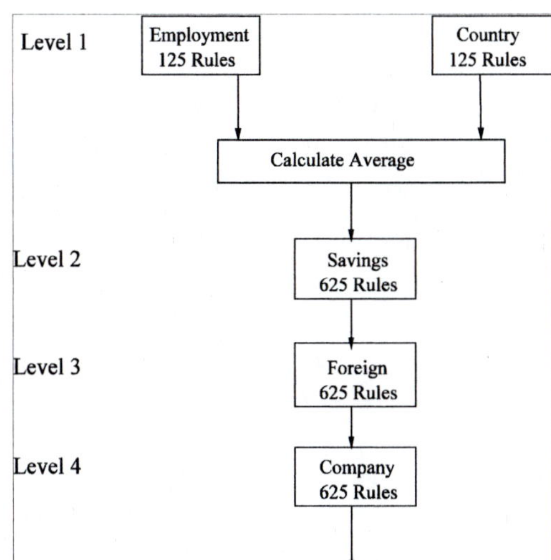

Figure 6. Hierarchical fuzzy logic system — HFL #5

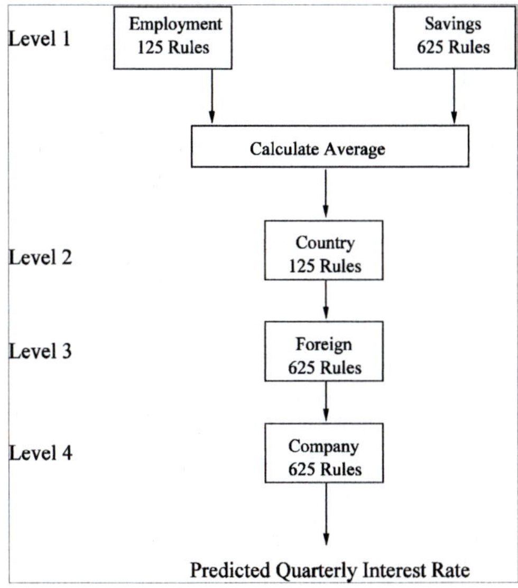

Conclusion and Further Investigations

In this chapter, an innovative method is used to design and develop hierarchical fuzzy logic systems. A genetic algorithm is used as an adaptive learning method to design a hierarchical fuzzy logic system to predict the fluctuations of the 10-year Australian Treasury bond using Australian economic data. Using hierarchical fuzzy logic systems, the number of fuzzy rules in the fuzzy knowledge base is reduced dramatically, hence computational times are decreased, resulting in a more efficient system.

From simulation results, it was found that the resulting hierarchical fuzzy logic systems determined by genetic evolution are capable of making accurate predictions of the following quarter's interest rate. The hierarchical fuzzy logic system used a fuzzy knowledge base which contains all the rules of the system, which allows an expert to inspect and make any modifications if necessary.

The research work performed in this chapter is unique in the way the hierarchical fuzzy logic systems are developed. However, it has assumed the original gathering together of the indicators in the five groups. It is not clear that even these groupings determined by an expert are the appropriate or best groupings. Further research needs to be undertaken on the full input structure with all 14 input variables, maximum number of layers possible in the hierarchy being 14. Research has recently been presented which has fully investigated the possible hierarchical structures for the control of the inverted pendulum, from the perspective of both the evolutionary learning and the convergence of state under the determined hierarchical controller (Zajaczkowski & Stonier, 2004).

The application of this method to several industrial problems, such as robotic control and collision avoidance of multi-robot systems, is currently under consideration.

References

Anver, M. M., & Stonier, R. J. (2004). Evolutionary learning of a fuzzy edge detection algorithm based on multiple masks. In *Proceedings of the 7th Asia-Pacific Complex Systems Conference (Complex 2004)*, Cairns, Australia (pp. 183-195).

Cordón, O., Herrera, F., Hoffmann, F., & Magdalena, L. (2001). Genetic fuzzy systems: Evolutionary tuning and learning of fuzzy knowledge bases. In *Advances in fuzzy systems: Applications and theory* (vol. 19). World Scientific Publishing.

Cox, E. (1993). Adaptive fuzzy systems. *IEEE Spectrum*, 27-31.

Goldberg, D. (1989). *Genetic algorithms in search, optimisation and machine learning*. Reading, MA: Addison Wesley.

Goonatilake, S., Campbell, J. A., & Ahmad, N. (1995). Genetic-fuzzy systems for financial decision making. In *Advances in Fuzzy Logic, Neural Networks and Genetic Algorithms, IEEE/Nagoya-University World Wisepersons Workshop* (LNAI). USA: Springer.

Goonatilake, S., & Treleaven, P. (1995). *Intelligent systems for finance and business*. USA: Wiley and Sons.

Kosko, B. (1992). *Neural networks and fuzzy systems, a dynamic system*. Englewood Cliffs, NJ: Prentice-Hall.

Kosko, B., & Isaka, S. (1993, July). Fuzzy logic. *Scientific American*, 76-81.

Lee, C. C. (1990). Fuzzy logic in control systems: Fuzzy controllers — Part I, part II. *IEEE Transactions on Systems, Man and Cybernetics, 2092*, 404-435.

Mohammadian, M., & Kingham, M. (1997). Hierarchical fuzzy logic for financial modelling and prediction. In *10th Australian Joint Conference on Artificial Intelligence* (pp. 147-156). Perth, Australia.

Mohammadian, M., Kingham, M., & Bignall, B. (1998). Hierarchical fuzzy logic for financial modelling and prediction. *Journal of Computational Intelligence in Finance*, UK.

Mohammadian, M., & Stonier, R. J. (1995). Adaptive two layer control of a mobile robot systems. In *IEEE International Conference on Evolutionary Computing* (Vol. 1, pp. 204-209). Perth, Australia.

Raju, G. V. S., & Zhou, J. (1993). Adaptive hierarchical fuzzy controller. *IEEE Transactions on Systems, Man & Cybernetics, 23*(4), 973-980.

Ruelle, D. (1989). *Chaotic evolution and strange attractors: The statistical analysis of time series for deterministic nonlinear systems*. Cambridge University Press.

Thomas, P. T., & Stonier, R. J. (2003, December). Hierarchical fuzzy control in robot soccer using evolving algorithms. In *Proceedings of the International Congress on Evolutionary Computation (CEC2003)* (Vol. 4, pp. 2434-2440). Canberra, Australia.

Welstead, T. (1994). *Neural networks and fuzzy logic applications in C/C++*. New York: Wiley.

Zadeh, L. (1965). Fuzzy sets. *Journal of Information and Control, 8*, 338-353.

Zajaczkowski, J., & Stonier, R. J. (2004, December). Analysis of hierarchical control for the inverted pendulum. In *Proceedings of the 7th Asia-Pacific Complex Systems Conference (Complex 2004)* (pp. 350-374). Cairns, Australia.

Chapter VI

Intelligent Text Mining: Putting Evolutionary Methods and Language Technologies Together

John Atkinson, Universidad de Concepción, Chile

Abstract

This chapter introduces a novel evolutionary model for intelligent text mining. The model deals with issues concerning shallow text representation and processing for mining purposes in an integrated way. Its aims are to look for interesting explanatory knowledge across text documents. The approach uses natural-language technology and genetic algorithms to produce explanatory novel hidden patterns. The proposed approach involves a mixture of different techniques from evolutionary computation and other kinds of text mining methods. Accordingly, new kinds of genetic operations suitable for text mining are proposed. Some experiments and results and their assessment by human experts are discussed which indicate the plausibility of the model for effective knowledge discovery from texts. With this chapter, authors hope the readers to understand the principles, theoretical foundations, implications, and challenges of a promising linguistically motivated approach to text mining.

Introduction

Like gold, information is both an object of desire and a medium of exchange. Also like gold, it is rarely found just lying about. It must be mined, and as it stands, a large portion of the world's electronic information exists as numerical data. Data mining technology can be used for the purpose of extracting "nuggets" from well-structured collections that exist in relational databases and data warehouses. However, 80% of this portion exists as text and is rarely looked at: letters from customers, e-mail correspondence, technical documentation, contracts, patents, and so forth.

An important problem is that information in this unstructured form is not readily accessible to be used by computers. This has been written for human readers and requires, when feasible, some natural language interpretation. Although full processing is still out of reach with current technology, there are tools using basic pattern recognition techniques and heuristics that are capable of extracting valuable information from free text based on the elements contained in it (e.g., keywords). This technology is usually referred to as text mining and aims at discovering unseen and interesting patterns in textual databases.

These discoveries are useless unless they contribute valuable knowledge for users who make strategic decisions (i.e., managers, scientists, businessmen). This leads then to a complicated activity referred to as knowledge discovery from texts (KDT) which, like knowledge discovery from databases (KDD), correspond to "the non-trivial process of identifying valid, novel, useful, and understandable patterns in data."

Despite the large amount of research over the last few years, only few research efforts worldwide have realised the need for high-level representations (i.e., not just keywords), for taking advantage of linguistic knowledge, and for specific purpose ways of producing and assessing the unseen knowledge. The rest of the effort has concentrated on doing text mining from an information retrieval (IR) perspective and so both representation (keyword based) and data analysis are restricted.

The most sophisticated approaches to text mining or KDT are characterised by an intensive use of external electronic resources including ontologies, thesauri, and so forth, which highly restricts the application of the unseen patterns to be discovered and their domain independence. In addition, the systems so produced have few metrics (or none at all) which allow them to establish whether the patterns are interesting and novel.

In terms of data mining techniques, genetic algorithms (GA) for mining purposes has several promising advantages over the usual learning / analysis methods employed in KDT: the ability to perform global search (traditional approaches deal with predefined patterns and restricted scope), the exploration of solutions in parallel, the robustness to cope with noisy and missing data (something critical in dealing with text information as partial text analysis techniques may lead to imprecise outcome data), and the ability to assess the goodness of the solutions as they are produced.

In order to deal with these issues, many current KDT approaches show a tendency to start using more structured or deeper representations than just keywords to perform further analysis so to discover informative and (hopefully) unseen patterns. Some of these approaches attempt to provide specific contexts for discovered patterns (e.g., "it is very likely that if X and Y occur then Z happens."), whereas others use external resources (lexicons, ontologies, thesaurus) to discover relevant unseen semantic relationships which may "explain" the discovered knowledge, in restricted contexts, and with specific fixed semantic relationships in mind. Sophisticated systems also use these resources as a commonsense knowledge base which along with reasoning methods can effectively be applied to answering questions on general concepts.

In this chapter, we describe a new model for intelligent text mining which brings together the benefits of evolutionary computation techniques and language technology to deal with current issues in mining patterns from text databases. In particular, the approach puts together information extraction (IE) technology and multi-objective evolutionary computation techniques. It aims at extracting key underlying linguistic knowledge from text documents (i.e., rhetorical and semantic information) and then hypothesising and assessing interesting and unseen explanatory knowledge. Unlike other approaches to KDT, the model does not use additional electronic resources or domain knowledge beyond the text database.

This chapter develops a new semantically-guided model for evolutionary text mining which is domain-independent but genre-based. Unlike previous research on KDT, the approach does not rely on external resources or descriptions, hence its domain-independence. Instead, it performs the discovery only using information from the original corpus of text documents and from the training data generated from them. In addition, a number of strategies have been developed for automatically evaluating the quality of the hypotheses ("novel" patterns). This is an important contribution on a topic which has been neglected in most of KDT research over the last years.

The model and the experimental applications provide some support that it is indeed plausible to conceive an effective KDT approach independent of domain resources and to make use of the underlying rhetorical information so as to represent text documents for text mining purposes. The first specific objective is to achieve a plausible search of novel / interesting knowledge based on an evolutionary knowledge discovery approach which makes effective use of the structure and genre of texts. A second objective consists of showing evaluation strategies which allows for the measuring of the effectiveness in terms of the quality of the outcome produced by the model and which can correlate with human judgments. Finally, the chapter highlights the way all these strategies are integrated to produce novel knowledge which contributes additional information to help one better understand the nature of the discovered knowledge, compared to bag-of-words text mining approaches.

Text mining or knowledge discovery from texts (KDT) can potentially benefit from successful techniques from data mining or knowledge discovery from databases (KDD) (Han & Kamber, 2001) which have been applied to relational databases. However, data mining techniques cannot be immediately applied to text data for the purposes of text mining (TM) as they assume a structure in the source data which is not present in free text. Hence, new representations for text data have to be used. Also, while the assessment of discovered knowledge in the context of KDD is a key aspect for producing an effective outcome, the evaluation / assessment of the patterns discovered from text has been a neglected topic in the majority of the KDT approaches. Consequently, it is not proved whether the discoveries are novel, interesting, and useful for decision-makers.

Despite the large amount of research over the last few years, only few research efforts worldwide have realised the need for high-level representations (i.e., not just keywords), for taking advantage of linguistic knowledge, and for specific purpose ways of producing and assessing the unseen knowledge. The rest of the effort has concentrated on doing text mining from an information retrieval (IR) perspective and so both representation (keyword based) and data analysis are restricted.

By using an evolutionary model for KDT, allows us to explore integrated approaches to deal with the most important issues in text mining and KDT. In addition, the model's implications for intelligence analysis are highlighted. In particular:

- Evolutionary computation techniques (Freitas, 2002) of search and optimization are used to search for high-level and structured unseen knowledge in the form of explanatory hypotheses.
- Different strategies are described so as to automatically evaluate the multiple quality goals to be met by these hypotheses (interestingness, novelty, etc.).
- Using a prototype system for looking for the best patterns, several experiments with human domain experts are carried out to assess the quality of the model and therefore the discovered patterns.

Overall, the approach put together information extraction (IE) technology and multi-objective evolutionary computation techniques. It aims at extracting key underlying linguistic knowledge from text documents (i.e., rhetorical and semantic information) and then hypothesising and assessing interesting and unseen explanatory knowledge. Unlike other approaches to KDT, we do not use additional electronic resources or domain knowledge beyond the text database.

Evolutionary Knowledge Discovery from Texts

Nahm and Mooney (2000) have attempted to bring together general ontologies, IE technology, and traditional machine learning methods to mine interesting patterns. Unlike previous approaches, Mooney deals with a different kind of knowledge (e.g., prediction rules). In addition, an explicit measure of novelty of the mined rules is proposed by establishing semantic distances between rules' antecedents and consequents using the underlying organisation of WordNet. Novelty is then defined as the average (semantic) distance between the words in a rule's antecedent and consequent. A key problem with this is that the method depends highly on WordNet's organisation and idiosyncratic features. As a consequence, since a lot of information extracted from the documents are not included in WordNet the predicted rules will lead to misleading decisions on their novelty.

Many approaches to TM / KDT use a variety of different "learning" techniques. Except for cases using machine learning techniques such as neural networks, decision trees, and so on, which have also been used in relational data mining (DM), the real role of "learning" in the systems is not clear. There is no learning which enables the discovery but instead a set of primitive search strategies which do not necessarily explore the whole search space due to their dependence on the kind of semantic information previously extracted.

Despite there being a significant and successful number of practical search and optimization techniques (Mitchell, 1996; Deb, 2001), there are some features that make some techniques more appealing to perform this kind of task than others, in terms of representation required, training sets required, supervision, hypothesis assessment, robustness in the search, and so forth.

In particular, the kind of evolutionary computation technique known as genetic algorithms (GA) has proved to be promising for search and optimization purposes. Compared with classical search and optimization algorithms, GAs are much less susceptible to getting stuck to local suboptimal regions of the search space as they perform global search by exploring solutions in parallel. GAs are robust and able to cope with noisy and missing data, they can search spaces of hypotheses containing complex interacting parts, where the impact of each part on overall hypothesis fitness may be difficult to model (De Jong, 2006).

In order to use GAs to find optimal values of decision variables, we first need to represent the hypotheses in binary strings (the typical pseudo-chromosomal representation of a hypothesis in traditional GAs). After creating an initial population of strings at random, genetic operations are applied with some probability in order to improve the population. Once a new string is created by the operators, the solution is evaluated in terms of its measure of individual goodness referred to as fitness.

Individuals for the next generation are selected according to their fitness values, which will determine those to be chosen for reproduction. If a termination condition is not satisfied, the population is modified by the operators and a new (and hopefully better) population is created. Each interaction in this process is called a generation and the entire set of generations is called a run. At the end of a run there is often one or more highly fit chromosomes in the population.

One of the major contributions of evolutionary algorithms (e.g., GAs) for an important number of DM tasks (e.g., rule discovery, etc.) is that they tend to cope well with attribute interactions. This is in contrast to the local, greedy search performed by often-used rule induction and decision-tree algorithms (Berthold & Hand, 2000; Han & Kamber, 2001). Most rule induction algorithms generate (prune) a rule by selecting (removing) one rule condition at a time, whereas evolutionary algorithms usually evaluate a rule as a whole via the fitness function rather than evaluating the impact of adding / removing one condition to / from a rule. In addition, operations such as crossover usually swap several rule conditions at a time between two individuals.

One general aspect worth noting in applying GAs for DM tasks is that both the representation used for the discovery and the evaluation carried out assume that the source data are properly represented in a structured form (i.e., database) in which the attributes and values are easily handled.

When dealing with text data, these working assumptions are not always plausible because of the complexity of text information. In particular, mining text data using evolutionary algorithms requires a certain level of representation which captures knowledge beyond discrete data (i.e., semantics). Thus, there arises the need for new operations to create knowledge from text databases. In addition, fitness evaluation also imposes important challenges in terms of measuring novel and interesting knowledge which might be implicit in the texts or be embedded in the underlying semantics of the extracted data.

We developed a semantically-guided model for evolutionary text mining which is domain-independent but genre-based. Unlike previous approaches to KDT, our approach does not

Figure 1. The evolutionary model for knowledge discovery from texts

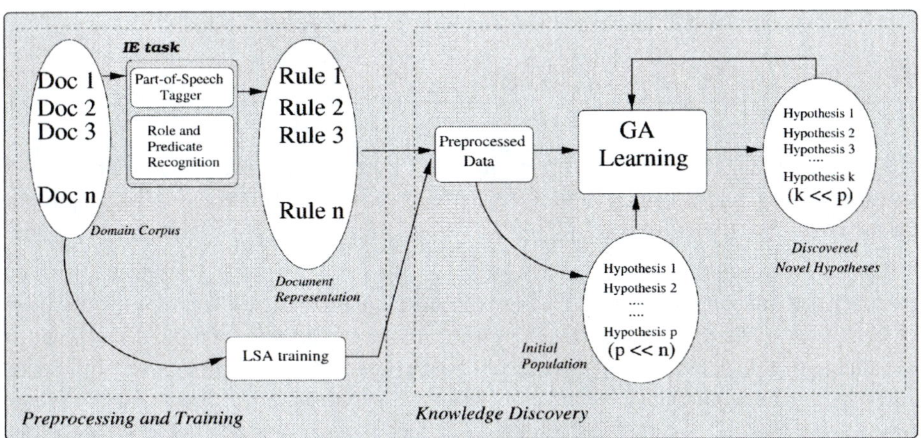

rely on external resources or descriptions hence its domain-independence. Instead, it performs the discovery only using information from the original corpus of text documents and from the training data generated from them. In addition, a number of strategies have been developed for automatically evaluating the quality of the hypotheses ("novel" patterns). This is an important contribution on a topic which has been neglected in most of KDT research over the last years.

In order to deal with issues regarding representation and new genetic operations so to produce an effective KDT process, our working model has been divided into two phases. The first phase is the preprocessing step aimed to produce both training information for further evaluation and the initial population of the GA. The second phase constitutes the knowledge discovery itself, in particular this aims at producing and evaluating explanatory unseen hypotheses.

The whole processing starts by performing the IE task (Figure 1) which applies extraction patterns and then generates a rule-like representation for each document of the specific domain corpus. After processing a set of *n* documents, the extraction stage will produce *n* rules, each one representing the document's content in terms of its conditions and conclusions. Once generated, these rules, along with other training data, become the "model" which will guide the GA-based discovery (see Figure 1).

In order to generate an initial set of hypotheses, an initial population is created by building random hypotheses from the initial rules, that is, hypotheses containing predicate and rhetorical information from the rules are constructed. The GA then runs for a number of generations until a fixed number of generations is achieved. At the end, a small set of the best hypotheses are obtained.

The description of the model is organised as follows: The next section presents the main features of the text preprocessing phase and how the representation for the hypotheses is generated. In addition, training tasks which generate the initial knowledge (semantic and rhetorical information) to feed the discovery are described. Then we describe constrained genetic operations to enable the hypotheses discovery, and proposes different evaluation metrics to assess the plausibility of the discovered hypotheses in a multi-objective context.

Text Preprocessing and Training

The preprocessing phase has two main goals: to extract important information from the texts and to use that information to generate both training data and the initial population for the GA.

In terms of text preprocessing (see first phase in Figure 1), an underlying principle in our approach is to be able to make good use of the structure of the documents for the discovery process. It is well-known that processing full documents has inherent complexities (Manning & Schutze, 1999), so we have restricted our scope somewhat to consider a scientific genre involving scientific / technical abstracts. These have a well-defined macro-structure (genre-dependent rhetorical structure) to "summarise" what the author states in the full document (i.e., background information, methods, achievements, conclusions, etc.).

Unlike patterns extracted for usual IE purposes such as in Hearst (1999, 2000) and Jacquemin & Tzoukermann (1999), this macro-structure and its roles are domain-independent but genre-based, so it is relatively easy to translate it into different contexts.

As an example, suppose that we are given the abstract of Figure 2 where bold sequences of words indicate the markers triggering the IE patterns.

Figure 2. An abstract and the extracted information

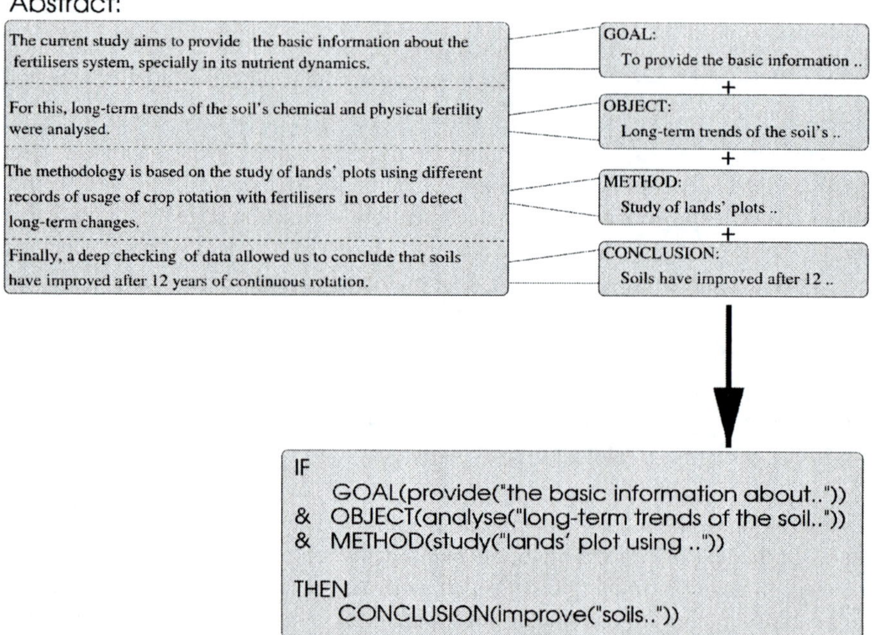

From such a structure, important constituents can be identified:

- **Rhetorical roles (discourse-level knowledge).** These indicate important places where the author makes some "assertions" about his or her work (i.e., the author is stating the goals, used methods, achieved conclusions, etc.). In the example, the roles are represented by goal, object, method, and conclusion.
- **Predicate relations.** These are represented by actions (predicate and arguments) which are directly connected to the role being identified and state a relation which holds between a set of terms (words which are part of a sentence), a predicate and the role which they are linked to. Thus, for the example, they are as follows:

  provide('the basic information ...'), analyse('long-term trends ...'), study('lands plot using ...'), improve('soil ...improved after ...').

- **Causal relation(s).** Although there are no explicit causal relations in the example, we can hypothesise a simple rule of the form:

  IF the current goals are G1, G2, ... and the means / methods used M1,M2, ... (and any other constraint / feature) THEN it is true that we can achieve the conclusions C1, C2, ...

  In order to extract this initial key information from the texts, an IE module was built. Essentially, it takes a set of text documents, has them tagged through a previously trained part-of-speech (POS) tagger, and produces an intermediate representation for every document (i.e., template, in an IE sense) which is then converted into a general rule. A set of hand-crafted domain-independent extraction patterns was written and coded.

  In addition, key training data are captured from the corpus of documents itself and from the semantic information contained in the rules. This can guide the discovery process in making further similarity judgments and assessing the plausibility of the produced hypotheses.
- **Training information from the corpus.** It has been suggested that huge amounts of texts represent a valuable source of semantic knowledge. In particular, in latent semantic analysis (LSA) (Kintsch, 2001), it is claimed that this knowledge is at the word level.

  LSA is a mathematical technique that generates a high-dimensional semantic space from the analysis of a huge text corpus. It was originally developed in the context of IR (Berry, 2004) and adapted by psycholinguistics for natural-language processing tasks (Landauer, Foltz, & Laham, 1998a).

  LSA differs from some statistical approaches for textual data analysis in two significant aspects. First, the input data "associations" from which LSA induces are extracted from unitary expressions of meaningful words and the complete meaningful utterances in which they occur, rather than between successive words (i.e., mutual information, co-occurrence). Second, it has been proposed that LSA constitutes a fundamental computational theory of the acquisition and representation of knowledge as its underlying mechanism can account for a longstanding and important mystery, the inductive property of learning by which people acquire much more knowledge than appears to be available in experience (Landauer, Laham, & Foltz, 1998b).

By keeping track of the patterns of occurrences of words in their corresponding contexts, one might be able to recover the latent structure of the meaning space, this is, the relationship between meanings of words: the larger and the more consistent their overlap, the closer the meanings.

In order to produce meaning vectors, LSA must be trained with a huge corpus of text documents. The initial data are meaningful passages from these texts and the set of words that each contains. Then, a matrix is constructed whose rows represent the terms (i.e., keywords) and the columns represent the documents where these terms occur. The cells of this matrix are the frequencies with which the word occurred in the documents. In order to reduce the effect of the words which occur across a wide variety of contexts, these cells are usually multiplied by a global frequency of the term in the collection of documents (i.e., logarithmic entropy term weight) (Berry, 2004).

These normalized frequencies are the input to LSA which transforms them into a high-dimensional semantic space by using a type of principal components analysis called singular vector decomposition (SVD) which compresses a large amount of co-occurrence information into a much smaller space. This compression step is somewhat similar to the common feature of neural networks where a large number of inputs are connected to a fairly small number of hidden layer nodes. If there are too many nodes, a network will "memorize" the training set, miss the generality of the data, and consequently perform poorly on a test set. Otherwise, this will tend to "capture" the underlying features of the input data representation.

LSA has also been successfully applied to an important number of natural-language tasks in which the correlations with human judgments have proved to be promising, including the treatment of synonymy (Landauer et al., 1998b), tutorial dialog management (Graesser, Wiemer-Hastings, & Kreuz, 1999; Wiemer-Hastings & Graesser, 2001), anaphora resolution (Klebanov, 2001), and text coherence measurement (Foltz, Kintsch, & Landauer, 1998).

In terms of measuring text coherence, the results have shown that the predictions of coherence performed by LSA are significantly correlated with other comprehension measures (Dijk & Kintsch, 1983) showing that LSA appears to provide an accurate measure of the comprehension of the texts. In this case, LSA made automatic coherence judgments by computing the similarity (*SemSim*) between the vector corresponding to consecutive passages of a text. LSA predicted comprehension scores of human subjects extremely well, so it provided a characterization of the degree of semantic relatedness between the segments.

Following work by Kintsch (2001) on LSA incorporating structure, we have designed a semi-structured LSA representation for text data in which we represent predicate information (i.e., verbs) and arguments (i.e., set of terms) separately once they have been properly extracted in the IE phase. For this, the similarity is calculated by computing the closeness between two predicates (and arguments) based on the LSA data (function *SemSim* ($P_1(A_1)$, $P_2(A_2)$)).

We propose a simple strategy for representing the meaning of the predicates with arguments. Next, a simple method is developed to measure the similarity between these units.

Given a predicate *P* and its argument *A*, the vectors representing the meaning for both of them can be directly extracted from the training information provided by the LSA analysis. Representing the argument involves summing up all the vectors representing the terms of the argument and then averaging them, as is usually performed in semi-structured LSA. Once this is done, the meaning vector of the predicate and the argument is obtained by computing the sum of the two vectors as used in (Wiemer-Hastings, 2000). If there is more than one argument, then the final vector of the argument is just the sum of the individual arguments' vectors.

Note that training information from the texts is not sufficient as it only conveys data at a word semantics level. We claim that both basic knowledge at a rhetorical, semantic level, and co-occurrence information can be effectively computed to feed the discovery and to guide the GA.

Accordingly, we perform two kinds of tasks: creating the initial population and computing training information from the rules.

1. **Creating the initial population of hypotheses.** Once the initial rules have been produced, their components (rhetorical roles, predicate relations, etc.) are isolated and become a separate "database." This information is used both to build the initial hypotheses and to feed the further genetic operations (i.e., mutation of roles will need to randomly pick a role from this database).

2. **Computing training information (in which two kinds of training data are obtained):**

    a. *Computing correlations between rhetorical roles and predicate relations.* The connection between rhetorical information and the predicate action constitutes key information for producing coherent hypotheses. For example, is, in some domain, the goal of some hypothesis likely to be associated with the construction of some component? In a health context, this connection would be less likely than having "finding a new medicine for ..." as a goal.

       In order to address this issue, we adopted a Bayesian approach where we obtain the conditional probability of some predicate *p* given some attached rhetorical role *r*, namely *Prob*($p|r$). This probability values are later used to automatically evaluate some of the hypotheses' criteria.

    b. *Computing co-occurrences of rhetorical information.* One could think of a hypothesis as an abstract having text paragraphs which are semantically related to each other. Consequently, the meaning of the scientific evidence stated in the abstract may subtly change if the order of the facts is altered.

       This suggests that in generating valid hypotheses there will be rule structures which are more or less desirable than others. For instance, if every rule contains a "goal" as the first rhetorical role, and the GA has generated a hypothesis starting with some "conclusion" or "method," it will be penalized, therefore, it is very unlikely for that to survive in the next generation. Since the order matters in terms of affecting the rule's meaning, we can think of the p roles of a rule, as a sequence of tags: $<r_1, r_2, ..., r_p>$ such that r_i precedes r_{i+1}, so we generate, from the rules, the conditional probabilities $Prob(r_p | r_q)$, for every role r_p, r_q. The probability that r_q precedes r_p will be used in evaluating new hypotheses, in terms that, for instance, its coherence.

Evaluation of Discovered Patterns

Our approach to KDT is strongly guided by semantic and rhetorical information, and consequently there are some soft constraints to be met before producing the offspring so as to keep them coherent.

The GA will start from a initial population, which in this case, is a set of semi-random hypotheses built up from the preprocessing phase. Next, constrained GA operations are applied and the hypotheses are evaluated. In order for every individual to have a fitness assigned, we use a evolutionary multi-objective optimisation strategy based on the SPEA algorithm (Zitzler & Thiele, 1998) in a way which allows incremental construction of a Pareto-optimal set and uses a steady-state strategy for the population update.

For semantic constraints, judgments of similarity between hypotheses or components of hypotheses (i.e., predicates, arguments, etc.) are carried out using the LSA training data and predicate-level information previously discussed in the training step.

Patterns Discovery

Using the semantic measure and additional constraints discussed later on, we propose new operations to allow guided discovery such that unrelated new knowledge is avoided, as follows:

- **Selection:** selects a small number of the best parent hypotheses of every generation (generation gap) according to their Pareto-based fitness (Deb, 2001).
- **Crossover:** a simple recombination of both hypotheses' conditions and conclusions takes place, where two individuals swap their conditions to produce new offspring (the conclusions remain).

  Under normal circumstances, crossover works on random parents and positions where their parts should be exchanged. However, in our case this operation must be restricted to preserve semantic coherence. We use soft semantic constraints to define two kind of recombinations:

  1. *Swanson's crossover.* Based on Swanson's hypothesis (Swanson, 1988, 2001) we propose a recombination operation as follows:

Figure 3. Semantically guided Swanson crossover

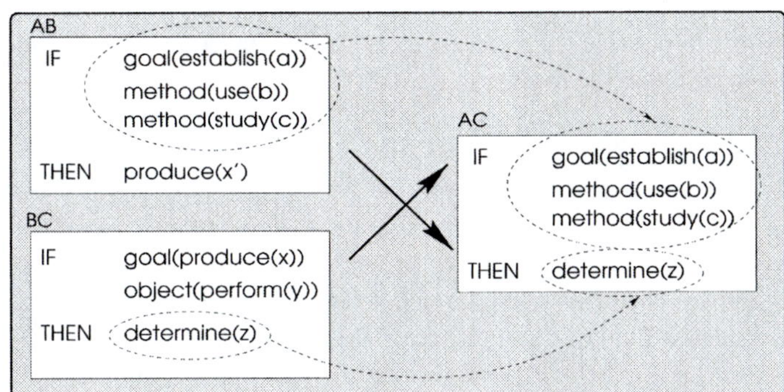

If there is a hypothesis (*AB*) such that "*IF A THEN B*" and another one (*BC*) such that "*IF B' THEN C*", (*B'* being something semantically similar to *B*) then a new interesting hypothesis "*IF A THEN C*" can be inferred, only if the conclusions of *AB* have high semantic similarity (i.e., via LSA) with the conditions of hypothesis *BC*.

The about principle can be seen in Swanson's crossover between two learned hypotheses as shown in Figure 3.

2. *Default semantic crossover.* If the previous transitivity does not apply then the recombination is performed as long as both hypotheses as a whole have high semantic similarity which is defined in advance by providing minimum thresholds.

- **Mutation:** aims to make small random changes on hypotheses to explore new possibilities in the search space. As in recombination, we have dealt with this operation in a constrained way, so we propose three kinds of mutations to deal with the hypotheses' different objects:
  1. *Role mutation.* One rhetorical role (including its contents: relations and arguments) is selected and randomly replaced by a random one from the initial role database.
  2. *Predicate mutation.* One inner predicate and argument is selected and randomly replaced by another from the initial predicate databases.
  3. *Argument mutation.* Since we have no information about arguments' semantic types, we choose a new argument by following a guided procedure in which we select predicate relations and then arguments at random according to a measure of semantic similarity via LSA (Wiemer-Hastings, 2000).
- **Population update:** We use a non-generational GA in which some individuals are replaced by the new offspring in order to preserve the hypotheses' good material from

one generation to other, and so to encourage the improvement of the population's quality. We use a steady-state strategy in which each individual from a small number of the worst hypotheses is replaced by an individual from the offspring only if the latter are better than the former.

Patterns Evaluation

Since each hypothesis in our model has to be assessed by different criteria, usual methods for evaluating fitness are not appropriate. Hence, evolutionary multi-objective optimisation (EMOO) techniques which use the multiple criteria defined for the hypotheses are needed. Accordingly, we propose EMOO-based evaluation metrics to assess the hypotheses' fitness in a domain-independent way and, unlike other approaches, without using any external source of domain knowledge. The different metrics are represented by multiple criteria by which the hypotheses are assessed.

In order to establish evaluation criteria, we have taken into account different issues concerning plausibility (Is the hypothesis semantically sound? Are the GA operations producing something coherent in the current hypothesis?), and quality itself (How is the hypothesis supported from the initial text documents? How interesting is it?). Accordingly, we have defined eight evaluation criteria to assess the hypotheses (i.e., in terms of Pareto dominance, it will produce an eight-dimensional vector of objective functions) given by: relevance, structure, cohesion, interestingness, coherence, coverage, simplicity, plausibility of origin.

The current hypothesis to be assessed will be denoted as H, and the training rules as R_i. Evaluation methods (criteria) by which the hypotheses are assessed and the questions they are trying to address are as follows:

- **Relevance.** Relevance addresses the issue of how important the hypothesis is to the target concepts. This involves two concepts (i.e., terms), as previously described, related to the question:

  What is the best set of hypotheses that explain the relation between <term1> and <term2>?

  Considering the current hypothesis, it turns into a specific question: How good is the hypothesis in explaining this relation?

  This can be estimated by determining the semantic closeness between the hypothesis' predicates (and arguments) and the target concepts[1] by using the meaning vectors obtained from the LSA analysis for both terms and predicates.

  Our method for assessing relevance takes these issues into account along with some ideas of Kintsch's Predication. Specifically, we use the concept of *strength* (Kintsch, 2001): $strength(A,I) = f(SemSim(A,I),SemSim(P,I))$ between a predicate with arguments and surrounding concepts (target terms in our case) as a part of the relevance measure, which basically decides whether the predicate (and argument) is relevant to the target concepts in terms of the similarity between both predicate and argument, and the concepts.

In order to account for both target terms, we just take the average of strength (*Str*) for both terms. So, the overall relevance becomes:

$$relevance(H) = (1/2)\sum_{i=1}^{|H|}\frac{Str[P_i, A_i, term1] = Str[P_i, A_i, term2]}{|H|}$$

in which $|H|$ denotes the length of the hypothesis H, that is, the number of predicates.

- **Structure (How good is the structure of the rhetorical roles?).** This measures how much of the rules' structure is exhibited in the current hypothesis.

  Since we have previous pre-processed information for bi-grams of roles, the structure can be computed by following a Markov chain (Manning & Schutze, 1999) as follows:

$$Structure(H) = Prob(r_1) * \prod_{i=2}^{|H|} Prob(r_1|r_{i-1})$$

  where r_i represents the *i-th* role of the hypothesis H, $Prob(r_i \mid r_{i-1})$ denotes the conditional probability that role r_{i-1} immediately precedes r_i. $Prob(r_i)$ denotes the probability that no role precedes r_i, that is, it is at the beginning of the structure (i.e., $Prob(r_i \mid <start>)$).

- **Cohesion (How likely is a predicate action to be associated with some specific rhetorical role?).** This measures the degree of "connection" between rhetorical information (i.e., roles) and predicate actions. The issue here is how likely (according to the rules) some predicate relation P in the current hypothesis is to be associated with role r. Formally, *cohesion for hypothesis H* is expressed as:

$$cohesion(H) = \sum_{r_i, P_i \in H}\frac{Prob[P_i|r_i]}{|H|}$$

  where $Prob(P_i \mid r_i)$ states the conditional probability of the predicate P_i given the rhetorical role r_i.

- **Interestingness (How interesting is the hypothesis in terms of its antecedent and consequent?).**

  Unlike other approaches to measure "interestingness" which use an external resource (e.g., WordNet) and rely on its organisation, we propose a different view where the criterion can be evaluated from the semi-structured information provided by the LSA analysis. Accordingly, the measure for hypothesis H is defined as a degree of unexpectedness as follows:

interestingness(H)= <Semantic Dissimilarity between Antecedent and Consequent>

That is, the lower the similarity, the more interesting the hypothesis is likely to be. Otherwise, it means the hypothesis involves a correlation between its antecedent and consequent which may be an uninteresting known common fact (Nahm & Mooney, 2002).

- **Coherence.** This metrics addresses the question whether the elements of the current hypothesis relate to each other in a semantically coherent way. Unlike rules produced by DM techniques in which the order of the conditions is not an issue, the hypotheses produced in our model rely on pairs of adjacent elements which should be semantically sound, a property which has long been dealt with in the linguistic domain, in the context of text coherence (Foltz et al., 1998).

  Semantic coherence is calculated by considering the average semantic similarity between consecutive elements of the hypothesis. However, note that this closeness is only computed on the semantic information that the predicates and their arguments convey (i.e., not the roles) as the role structure has been considered in a previous criterion. Accordingly, the criterion can be expressed as follows:

$$Coherence(H)=\sum_{i=1}^{|H|-1} \frac{SemSim[P_i[A_i], P_{i+1}[A_{i+1}]]}{(|H|-1)}$$

  where (|H|-1) denotes the number of adjacent pairs, and *SemSim* is the LSA-based semantic similarity between two predicates.

- **Coverage.** The coverage metric tries to address the question of how much the hypothesis is supported by the model (i.e., rules representing documents and semantic information).

  Coverage of a hypothesis has usually been measured in KDD approaches by considering some structuring in data (i.e., discrete attributes) which is not present in textual information. Besides, most of the KDD approaches have assumed the use of linguistic or conceptual resources to measure the degree of coverage of the hypotheses (i.e., match against databases, positive examples).

  In order to deal with the criterion in the context of KDT, we say that a hypothesis H covers an extracted rule R_i only if the predicates of H are roughly (or exactly, in the best case) contained in R_i.

  Formally, the rules covered are defined as:

$$RulesCovered(H)=\{Ri \in RuleSet | \forall Pj \in Ri \exists HPk \in HP:$$

$$(SemSim\{HP_k, P_j] \geq threshold \wedge predicate[HP_k]=predicate[P_j])\}$$

where $SemSim(HP_k, P_j)$ represents the LSA-based similarity between hypothesis predicate HP_k and rule predicate P_j, *threshold* denotes a minimum fixed user-defined value, *RuleSet* denotes the whole set of rules, *HP* represents the list of predicates with arguments of *H*, and P_j represents a predicate (with arguments) contained in R_i. Once the set of rules covered is computed, the criterion can finally be computed as:

$$Coverage(H) = \frac{RulesCovered[H]}{[RuleSet]}$$

where |*RulesCovered*| and |*RuleSet*| denote the size of the set of rules covered by *H*, and the size of the initial set of extracted rules, respectively.

- **Simplicity (How simple is the hypothesis?).** Shorter and / or easy-to-interpret hypotheses are preferred. Since the criterion has to be maximised, the evaluation will depend on the length (number of elements) of the hypothesis.
- **Plausibility of origin (How plausible is the hypothesis produced by Swanson's evidence?).** If the current hypothesis was an offspring from parents which were recombined by a Swanson's transitivity-like operator, then the higher the semantic similarity between one parent's consequent and the other parent's antecedent, the more precise is the evidence, and consequently worth exploring as a novel hypothesis. If no better hypothesis is found so far, the current similarity is inherited from one generation to the next.

  Accordingly, plausibility for a hypothesis *H* is simply given by:

$$\text{Plausibility (H)} = \begin{cases} S_p & \textit{If H was created from a Swanson's crossover} \\ O & \textit{If H is in the original population or is a result of another operation} \end{cases}$$

Note that since we are dealing with a multi-objective problem, there is no simple way to get independent fitness values as the fitness involves a set of objective functions to be assessed for every individual. Therefore the computation is performed by comparing objectives of one individual with others in terms of *Pareto dominance* (Deb, 2001) in which non-dominated solutions (Pareto individuals) are searched for in every generation.

Next, since our model is based on a multi-criteria approach, we have to face three important issues in order to assess every hypothesis' fitness: Pareto dominance, fitness assignment, and the diversity problem (Deb, 2001). Despite an important number of state-of-the-art methods to handle these issues (Deb, 2001), only a small number of them has focused on the problem in an integrated and representation-independent way. In particular, Zitzler and Thiele (1998) propose an interesting method, strength Pareto evolutionary algorithm (SPEA) which uses a mixture of established methods and new techniques in order to find multiple Pareto-optimal solutions in parallel, and at the same time to keep the population as diverse as possible. We have also adapted the original SPEA algorithm which uses an elitist strategy to allow for the incremental updating of the Pareto-optimal set along with our steady-state replacement method.

Analysis and Results

In order to assess the quality of the discovered knowledge (hypotheses) by the model a prolog-based prototype has been built. The IE task has been implemented as a set of modules whose main outcome is the set of rules extracted from the documents. In addition, an intermediate training module is responsible for generating information from the LSA analysis and from the rules just produced. The initial rules are represented by facts containing lists of relations both for antecedent and consequent.

For the purpose of the experiments, the corpus of documents has been obtained from a database for agricultural and food science. We selected this kind of corpus as it has been properly cleaned-up, and builds upon a scientific area which we do not have any knowledge about so to avoid any possible bias and to make the results more realistic. A set of 1,000 documents was extracted from which one-third were used for setting parameters and making general adjustments, and the rest were used for the GA itself in the evaluation stage.

Next, we tried to provide answers to two basic questions concerning our original aims: How well does the GA for KDT behave? How good are the hypotheses produced according to human experts in terms of text mining's ultimate goals: interestingness, novelty, usefulness, and so forth.

In order to address these issues, we used a methodology consisting of two phases: the system evaluation and the experts' assessment.

1. **System evaluation.** This aims at investigating the behavior and the results produced by the GA.

   We set the GA by generating an initial population of 100 semi-random hypotheses. In addition, we defined the main global parameters such as *mutation probability* (0.2), *cross-over probability* (0.8), *maximum size of Pareto set* (5%), and so forth. We ran five versions of the GA with the same configuration of parameters but different pairs of terms to address the quest for explanatory novel hypotheses.

   The different results obtained from running the GA as used for our experiment are shown in the form of a representative behavior in Figure 4, where the number of generations is placed against the average objective value for some of the eight criteria.

   Some interesting facts can be noted. Almost all the criteria seem to stabilise after (roughly) generation 700 for all the runs, that is, no further improvement beyond this point is achieved and so this may give us an approximate indication of the limits of the objective function values.

   Another aspect worth highlighting is that despite a steady-state strategy being used by the model to produce solutions, the individual evaluation criteria behave in unstable ways to accommodate solutions which had to be removed or added. As a consequence, it is not necessarily the case that all the criteria have to monotonically increase.

   In order to see this behavior, look at the results for the criteria for the same period of time, between generations 200 and 300 for Run 4. For an average hypothesis, the quality of coherence, cohesion, simplicity, and structure gets worse, whereas this improves for coverage, interestingness, and relevance, and has some variations for plausibility.

Figure 4. GA evaluation for some of the criteria

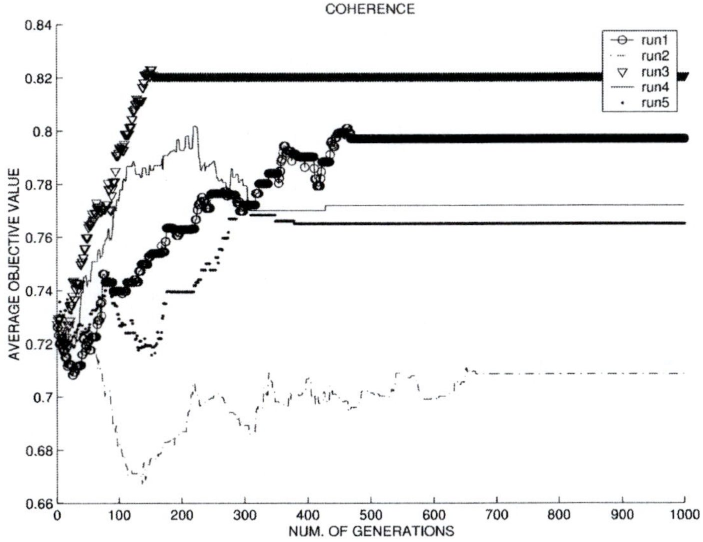

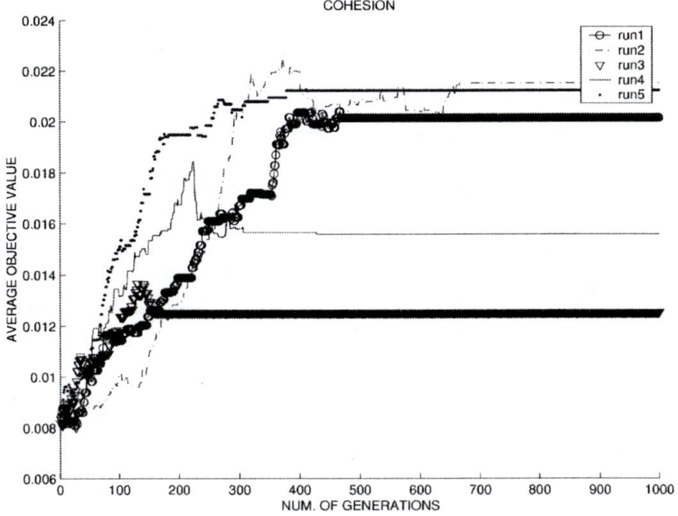

Figure 4. continued

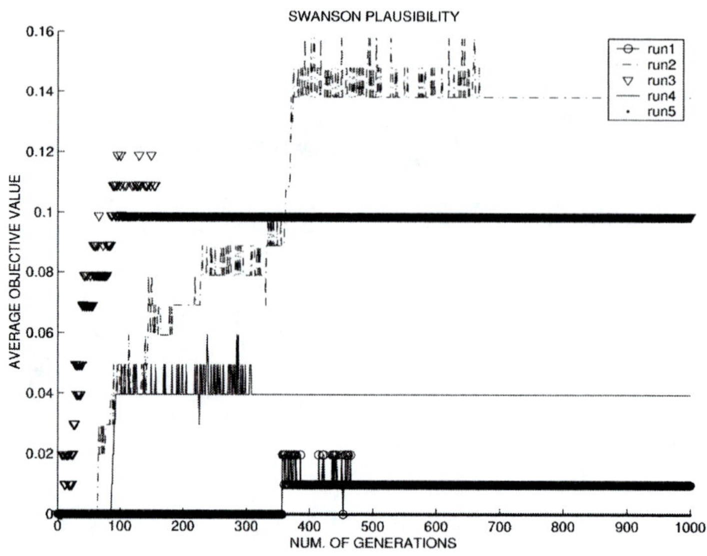

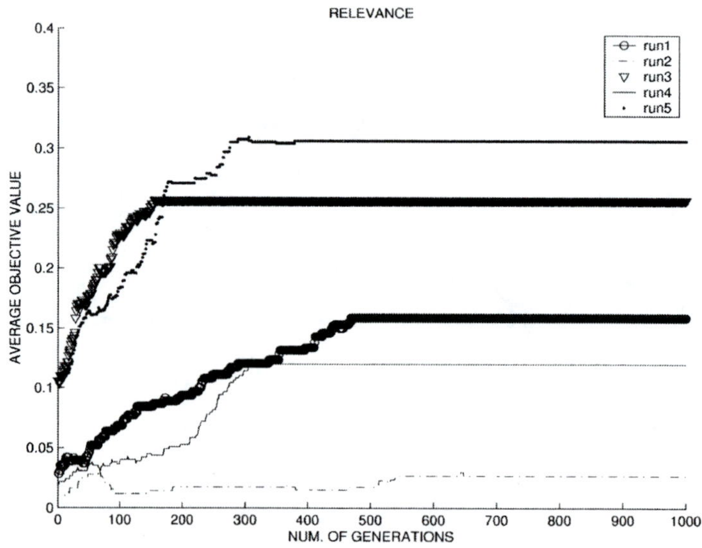

Table 1. Analysis of the behavior of the GA to different parameters

Run	P_m	P_c	AvgFitness	Std. Dev	Min.Fit.	Max.Fit.
1	0.025	0.50	0.0911	0.0790	0.0099	0.2495
2	0.075	0.50	0.0833	0.0746	0.0099	0.2495
3	0.125	0.50	0.0934	0.0746	0.0099	0.2495
4	0.175	0.50	0.0934	0.0740	0.0099	0.2297
5	0.2	0.50	0.0799	0.0701	0.0099	0.2297
6	0.025	0.60	0.0625	0.0601	0.0099	0.2188
7	0.075	0.60	0.0725	0.0600	0.0099	0.2188
8	0.125	0.60	0.0623	0.0602	0.0099	0.2188
9	0.175	0.60	0.0625	0.0600	0.0099	0.2188
10	0.2	0.60	0.0602	0.0583	0.0099	0.2188
11	0.025	0.70	0.0323	0.0617	0	0.2495
12	0.075	0.70	0.0358	0.0622	0	0.2495
13	0.125	0.70	0.0358	0.0619	0	0.2495
14	0.175	0.70	0.0316	0.0619	0	0.2495
15	0.2	0.70	0.0301	0.0958	0	0.4950
16	0.025	0.80	0.0230	0.0556	0	0.2495
17	0.075	0.80	0.0329	0.0553	0	0.2495
18	0.125	0.80	0.0240	0.0567	0	0.2495
19	0.175	0.80	0.0221	0.0543	0	0.2495
20	0.2	0.80	0.0209	0.0470	0	0.1881

The quality of the search process can also be analyzed by observing the typical behavior of the GA in terms of the performance of the genetic operators in generating fit solutions, its robustness (i.e., Does it always find good solutions?), and the quality of the hypotheses in terms of the objective functions.

In terms of genetic operators, the aim was to investigate how sensitive the GA is to different parameter values. Because of the large combination of parameter settings, we concentrated on the probabilities of crossover and mutation only, in terms of the fitness of the produced solutions. Note that because of the nature of the SPEA-based strategy, low fitness values are desired.

Test parameter values were established as shown in Table 1 for 20 runs of the GA, each up to 1,000 generations, with a initial population of 100 hypotheses. Here, different probabilities of mutation (*m*) and crossover (*c*) are tested, and the resulting average fitness of the population, its standard deviation, and the minimum and maximum values of fitness are shown (the rest of the parameters remain the same).

The parameters were systematically tested with steps of approximately 5% (starting from 0.025) for *m*, and 10% (starting from 0.50) for *c*. The final range for *m* is from 0.025 to 0.50, whereas for *m*, this is from 0.50 to 0.80. Thus, the table shows the different settings involved moving through the range for *m* and fixing a value for *c*. For example, the first 5 runs consider setting *c* fixed and testing with different values of *m*.

Some aspects of the resulting values are worth highlighting:

- Although finding good solutions is no guarantee that the search process is effective because human judgment is not considered, the GA seems to be able to find good hypotheses, that is, individuals with fitness zero or close to zero.
- Because of the constrained genetic operators, small changes in the parameter values do not have a significant effect on the best obtained fitness.
- Although higher values of *m* and *c* might improve the overall performance of the GA by decreasing the population fitness values, sometimes the maximum fitness values tend to increase despite the overall improvement of the population (see Runs 11 to 19, compared to Runs 6 to 10).
- As the parameter values increase, there is a tendency for the minimum fitness to decrease. However, note that because of the multi-objective nature of the model, having low (or zero) fitness values between Runs 11 and 20 does not necessarily imply that there are no changes in individual criteria of the best solutions. Indeed, considering individual objective values, the best solutions may be those with the lowest fitness values.
- Sudden peaks (e.g., average fitness of Run 3, 7, 12, etc.) can also be explained because of decisions on dominance (e.g., some less fit solutions leaving the Pareto set).

This analysis shows that increases in both mutation and crossover can have a positive effect on the quality of the solutions.

2. **Expert assessment.** This aims at assessing the quality (therefore, effectiveness) of the discovered knowledge on different criteria by human domain experts. For this, we designed an experiment in which 20 human experts were involved and each assessed five hypotheses selected from the Pareto set. We then asked the experts to assess the hypotheses from 1 (worst) to 5 (best) in terms of the following criteria: interestingness (INT), novelty (NOV), usefulness (USE), sensibleness (SEN), etc.

In order to select worthwhile terms for the experiment, we asked one domain expert to filter pairs of target terms previously related according to traditional clustering analysis (see Table 2 containing target terms used in the experiments). The pairs which finally deserved attention were used as input in the actual experiments (i.e., degradation and erosive).

Once the system hypotheses were produced, the experts were asked to score them according to the five subjective criteria. Next, we calculated the scores for every criterion as seen in the overall results in Figure 5 (for length's sake, only some criterion are shown).

Table 2. Pairs of target terms used for the actual experiments

Run	Term 1	Term 2
1	enzyme	zinc
2	glycocide	inhibitor
3	antinutritious	cyanogenics
4	degradation	erosive
5	cyanogenics	inhibitor

Figure 5. Distribution of experts' assessment of hypothesis per criteria

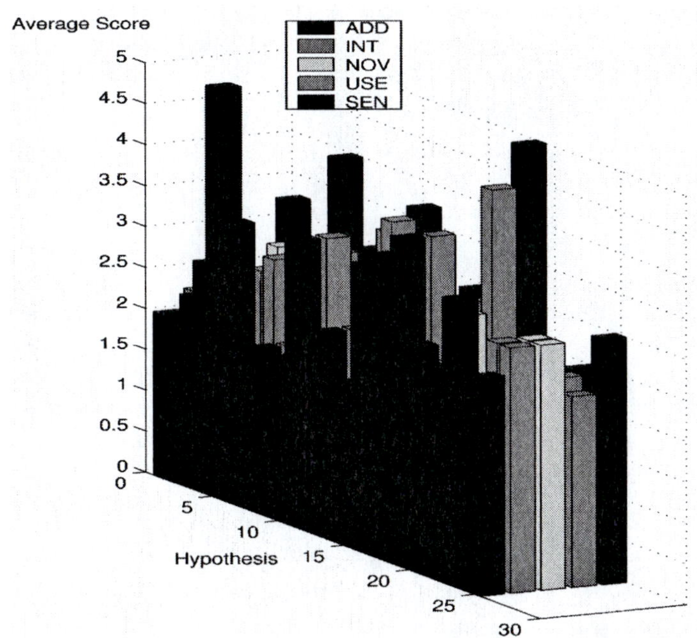

The assessment of individual criteria shows some hypotheses did well with scores above the average (50%) on a 1-5 scale. Overall, this supports the claim that the model indeed is able to find nuggets in textual information and to provide some basic explanation about the hidden relationships in these discoveries. This is the case for Hypotheses 11, 16, and 19 in terms of INT, Hypotheses 14 and 19 in terms of SEN, Hypotheses 1, 5, 11, 17, and 19 in terms of USE, and Hypotheses 24 in terms of NOV, and so forth.

These results and the evaluation produced by the model were used to measure the correlation between the scores of the human subjects and the system's model evaluation. Since both the expert and the system's model evaluated the results considering several criteria, we first performed a normalisation aimed at producing a single "quality" value for each hypothesis.

We then calculated the pair of values for every hypothesis and obtained a (Spearman) correlation $r = 0.43$ (*t-test* = 23.75, $df = 24$, $p<0.001$). From this result, we see that the correlation shows a good level of prediction compared to humans. This indicates that for such a complex task (knowledge discovery), the model's behavior is not too different from the experts'.

Note that in Mooney's experiments (Nahm & Mooney, 2000) using simple discovered rules, a lower human-system correlation of $r=0.386$ was obtained. Considering also that the human subjects were not domain experts as in our case, our results are encouraging as these involve a more demanding process which requires further comprehension of both the hypothesis itself and the working domain. In addition, our model was able to do it better without any external linguistic resources as in Mooney's experiments (Nahm and & Mooney, 2002).

In order to show what the final hypotheses look like and how the good characteristics and less desirable features as above are exhibited, we picked one of the best hypotheses as assessed by the experts (out of 25 best hypotheses) considering the average value of the 5 scores assigned by the user. For example, Hypothesis 65 of Run 4 looks like:

IF goal(*perform*(19311)) *and goal*(*analyze*(20811))
THEN establish(111)

where the numerical values represent internal identifiers for the arguments and their semantic vectors, and its resulting criteria vector is [0.92,0.09,0.50,0.005,0.7,0.00,0.30,0.25] (the vector's elements represent the values for the criteria relevance, structure, coherence, cohesion, interestingness, plausibility, coverage, and simplicity) and obtained an average expert's assessment of 3.74. In natural-language text, this can roughly be interpreted as (each item of the following NL description represents a predicate-level information of hypothesis):

- The **work** *aims* at *performing* the genetic grouping of seed populations and investigating a tendency to the separation of northern populations into different classes.
- The **goal** is to *analyse* the vertical integration for producing and selling Pinus Timber in the Andes-Patagonia region.
- As a **consequence**, the best agricultural use for land lots of organic agriculture must be *established* to promote a conservationist culture in priority or critical agricultural areas.

The hypothesis appears to be more relevant and coherent than others (relevance = 92%). However, this is not complete in terms of cause-effect. For instance, the methods are missing. It is also important to highlight that the high value for the coherence of the pattern (50%) is consistent with the contents of the predicates of the hypothesis. The three key paragraphs containing rhetorical knowledge indeed relate to the same topic: testing and producing specific Pinus trees. Even more important is the fact that despite having zero plausibility (novelty), the pattern is still regarded as interesting by the model (70%) and above the average by the experts. As for the target terms (degradant and erosive) and the way the discovered hypothesis attempts to explain the link between them, it can be seen that the contents of this patterns try to relate these terms with "agricultural areas," "seed populations," and so forth, so the discovery makes a lot of sense.

Other of the discovered patterns is given by Hypothesis 88 of Run 3, which is represented as follows:

IF goal(*present*(11511)) *and method*(*use*(25511))
THEN effect(1931,1932)

and has a criteria vector [0.29,0.18,0.41,0.030,0.28,0.99,0.30,0.50] and obtained an average expert's assessment of 3.20. In natural-language text, this can roughly be interpreted as:

- The **goal** is to *present* a two-dimensional scheme for forest restoration in which two regression models with Pinus and without Pinus are identified by inspiring in the natural restoring dynamics.
- The **method** is based on the *use* of micro-environments for capturing the kind of farm mice called *Apodemus Sylvaticusi,* and on the use of capture traps at a rate of 1,464 traps per night.
- Finally, in vitro digestion of three cutting ages in six ecotypes has an **effect** on "Big-alta" cuttings which got their higher performance in a 63-day period.

This hypothesis looks more complete (goal, methods, etc.) but is less relevant than the previous hypothesis despite its close coherence. Note also that the plausibility is much higher than for Hypothesis 65, but the other criteria seemed to be a key factor for the experts.

The hypothesis concerns with the production and cutting of specific kind of trees (Pinus) and forests where these lie. However, the second role ("the method is based...") discusses a different topic (mice capture) which apparently has nothing to do with the main issue and that is the reason for the pattern's coherence to be scored lower than the previous hypothesis (41% versus 50%). The model also discovered that there are organisms (and issues related to them) which are affecting the Pinus (and forest) restoration (i.e., mice). This fact has received a higher value for plausibility of origin or the novelty of the pattern (99%) and consequently, it is correlated with the experts opinion of the pattern (score=3.20).

Conclusion

Unlike traditional approaches to text mining, in this chapter, we show an innovative way of combining additional linguistic information and evolutionary learning techniques in order to produce novel hypotheses which involve explanatory and effective novel knowledge.

From the experiments and results, it can be noted that the approach supports the claim that the evolutionary model to KDT indeed is able to find nuggets in textual information and to provide basic explanations about the hidden relationships in these discoveries.

We also introduced a unique approach for evaluation which deals with semantic and data mining issues in a high-level way. In this context, the proposed representation for hypotheses suggests that performing shallow analysis of the documents and then capturing key rhetorical information may be a good level of processing which constitutes a trade off between completely deep and keyword-based analysis of text documents. In addition, the results suggest that the performance of the model in terms of the correlation with human judgments are slightly better than approaches using external resources as in (Nahm & Mooney, 2002). In particular criteria, the model shows a very good correlation between the system evaluation and the expert assessment of the hypotheses.

The model deals with the hypothesis production, and evaluation in a very promising way which is shown in the overall results obtained from the experts evaluation and the individual scores for each hypothesis. However, it is important to note that unlike the experts who have a lot of experience, preconceived concept models, and complex knowledge in their areas, the system has done relatively well only exploring the corpus of technical documents and the implicit connections contained in it.

From an evolutionary KDT viewpoint, the correlations and the quality of the final hypotheses show that the GA operations and the system's evaluation of the individuals may be effective predictions of really useful novel knowledge from a user perspective.

References

Berry, M. (2004). *Survey of text mining: Clustering, classification, and retrieval.* Springer-Verlag.

Berthold, M., & Hand, D. (2000). *Intelligent data analysis*. Springer.

Deb, K. (2001). *Multi-objective optimization using evolutionary algorithms*. Wiley.

De Jong, K. (2006). *Evolutionary computation: A unified approach.* MIT Press.

Dijk, T. V., & Kintsch, W. (1983). *Strategies of discourse comprehension*. Academic Press.

Foltz, P., Kintsch, W., & Landauer, T. (1998). The measurement of textual coherence with latent semantic analysis. *Discourse Processes, 25*(2), 259-284.

Freitas, A. (2002). *Data mining and knowledge discovery with evolutionary algorithms.* Springer.

Graesser, A., Wiemer-Hastings, P., & Kreuz, R. (1999). AutoTutor: A simulation of a human tutor. *Journal of Cognitive Systems Research*, (1), 35-51.

Han, J., & Kamber, M. (2001). *Data Mining: Concepts and techniques*. Morgan-Kaufmann.

Hearst, M. (1999). Untangling text data mining. *Proceedings of the 37th Annual Meeting of the ACL,* University of Maryland (invited paper).

Hearst, M. (2000). Text mining tools: Instruments for scientific discovery. *IMA Text Mining Workshop,* USA.

Jacquemin, C., & Tzoukermann, E. (1999). NLP for term variant extraction: A synergy of morphology, lexicon and syntax. In T. Strzalkowski (Ed.), *Natural language information retrieval* (pp. 25-74). Boston: Kluwer Academic.

Kintsch, W. (2001). Predication. *Cognitive Science, 25*(2), 173-202.

Klebanov, B. (2001). *Using lantent semantic analysis for pronominal anaphora resolution.* MSc thesis, School of Cognitive Science, Division of Informatics, University of Edinburgh.

Landauer, T., Foltz, P., & Laham, D. (1998a). An introduction to latent semantic analysis. *Discourse Processes, 10*(25), 259-284.

Landauer, T., Laham, D., & Foltz, P. (1998b). Learning human-like knowledge by singular value descomposition: A progress report. In M. Jordan, M. Kearns, & S. Solla (Eds.), *Advances in neural information processing systems* (Vol. 10, pp. 45-51). MIT Press.

Manning, C., & Schutze, H. (1999). *Foundations of statistical natural language processing.* MIT Press.

Mitchell, M. (1996). *An introduction to genetic algorithms*. MIT Press.

Nahm, U., & Mooney, R. (2000, August). Using information extraction to aid the discovery of prediction rules from text. *Proceedings of the 6th International Conference on Knowledge Discovery and Data Mining (KDD-2000) Workshop on Text Mining*, Boston (pp. 51-58).

Nahm, U., & Mooney, R. (2002, March). Text mining with information extraction. *AAAI 2002 Spring Symposium on Mining Answers from Texts and Knowledge Bases,* Stanford, CT.

Swanson, D. (1988). Migraine and magnesium: Eleven neglected connections. *Perspectives in Biology and Medicine*, (31), 526-557.

Swanson, D. (2001). On the fragmentation of knowledge. The connection explosion, and assembling other people's ideas. *Annual Meeting of the American Society for Information Science and Technology, 27*(3).

Wiemer-Hastings, P. (2000, August 13-15). Adding syntactic information to LSA. *Proceedings of the 22nd Annual Conference of the Cognitive Science Society*, Philadelphia (pp. 989-993)

Wiemer-Hastings, P., & Graesser, A. (2001). How latent is latent semantic analysis? In *Proceedings of the 16th International Joint Congress on Artificial Intelligence* (pp. 932-937). San Francisco: Morgan Kaufmann.

Zitzler, E., & Thiele, L. (1998). *An evolutionary algorithm for multiobjective optimisation: The strength Pareto approach.* Technical report 43, Swiss Federal Institute of Technology (ETH), Switzerland.

Endnote

[1] Target concepts are relevant nouns in our experiment. However, in a general case, these might be either nouns or verbs.

Chapter VII

An Evolutionary Framework for Nonlinear Time-Series Prediction with Adaptive Gated Mixtures of Experts

André L. V. Coelho, University of Fortaleza (Unifor), Brazil

Clodoaldo A. M. Lima, State University of Campinas (Unicamp), Brazil

Fernando J. Von Zuben, State University of Campinas (Unicamp), Brazil

Abstract

A probabilistic learning technique, known as gated mixture of experts (MEs), is made more adaptive by employing a customized genetic algorithm based on the concepts of hierarchical mixed encoding and hybrid training. The objective of such effort is to promote the automatic design (i.e., structural configuration and parameter calibration) of whole gated ME instances more capable to cope with the intricacies of some difficult machine learning problems whose statistical properties are time-variant. In this chapter, we outline the main steps behind such novel hybrid intelligent system, focusing on its application to the nontrivial task of nonlinear time-series forecasting. Experiment results are reported with respect to three benchmarking time-series problems and confirmed our expectation that the new integrated approach is capable to outperform — both in terms of accuracy and generalization — other conventional approaches, such as single neural networks and non-adaptive, handcrafted gated MEs.

Introduction

Time-series analysis and forecasting constitute an important research and application area. Much effort has been devoted over the past several decades to develop and improve generic models and methodologies capable to deal more properly with the complicated requirements commonly imposed by time-series analysis and forecasting (Weigend & Gershenfeld, 1994). Examples of well-established time-series models and methodologies include: (1) linear models such as moving average, exponential smoothing, and the auto-regressive integrated moving average (ARIMA) (Box, Jenkins, & Reinsel, 1994); (2) nonlinear models, such as neural networks, fuzzy systems, and, more recently, kernel-based models (Zhang, Patuwo, & Hu, 1998; Kim, Park, Hwang, & Kim, 1995; Cao, 2003); and (3) combined linear-nonlinear models (Zhang, 2003).

One of the neural-network-related techniques that has gained much attention recently, both in the areas of nonlinear regression and prediction, as well as on pattern classification, is referred to as mixtures of experts (MEs). Such conceptual learning framework, first introduced by Jacobs, Jordan, Nowlan, and Hinton (1991) and later extended by Jordan and Jacobs (1994), Xu, Jordan, and Hinton (1995), Weigend, Mangeas, and Srivastava (1995), and Meila and Jordan (1997), amount to a family of modular architectures devised to tackle complex problems in consonance with the divide-and-conquer principle: In a first stage, an original problem is divided into several smaller and simpler sub-problems that are subsequently solved independently; afterwards, solutions to those sub-problems are seamlessly integrated to form a complete solution to the original problem.

A single, non-hierarchical ME instance is composed of an array of supervised, competing modules, known as experts, whose activities are orchestrated by a mediator module, termed as gating. In the canonical ME model (Jacobs et al., 1991), the experts are assumed to be linear in nature whereas the soft-max function is adopted as the nonlinear activation function for producing the gating module's outputs. Conversely, in the gated ME variant, conceived by Weigend et al. (1995), a single nonlinear gating module is specified to coordinate competing nonlinear experts (implemented as multilayer perceptrons — MLPs) for dealing with different regimes of a given complex dynamic process. One advantage of using a nonlinear, instead of a linear, gating lies in the possibility of generating more elaborated time / space decompositions through nonlinear decision boundaries — something very attractive to cope with the nonstationarity and overfitting issues commonly present in nonlinear time-series prediction, for instance. Moreover, due to neural networks' universal approximation capabilities (Haykin, 1999), a well-configured nonlinear gating can, at least in theory, induce any sort of optimal problem decompositions. Therefore, gated MEs have achieved noticeable performance results in the identification of nonlinear systems (Lima, Coelho, & Von

Zuben, 2002) and in the modeling and segmentation of "real-world" time series showing different regimes with different levels of embedded noise (Mangeas, Weigend, & Muller, 1995; Srivastava, Su, & Weigend, 1998).

From a statistical sense, an ME model should be regarded as a mixture model (Titterington, Smith, & Makov, 1985) for estimating conditional probability distributions. Such interpretation is made possible by assuming that the expert outputs correspond to conditional component densities while the gating outputs correspond to input-biased mixture coefficients. Moreover, such interpretation leads to the possibility of employing a specific expectation-maximization (EM) formulation (Dempster, Laird, & Rubin, 1977) tailored for the estimation of the gating and expert parameters; this is accomplished through an iterative training process involving two complimentary steps defined over a log-based error function and encompassing the whole training dataset (Jordan & Jacobs, 1994).

In the work presented in this chapter, instead of following the prevalent strategy of designing ME models through a trial-and-error basis — which may be prone to unsuccessful results, as yet there are no general recipes indicating to the designer which architectural specification is more adequate to tackle the idiosyncrasies of a given problem in sight — we have conceived a novel genetic algorithm (GA) (Bäck, Fogel, & Michalewicz, 1997) based approach toward the automatic structural configuration and parameter tuning of gated MEs. This work, thus, is in line with the current trend of integrating intelligent methodologies into single frameworks (Goonatilake & Khebbal, 1995), particularly in the combining of evolutionary algorithms and neural networks (Yao, 1999).

In our customized GA, we have represented a whole gated ME instance (i.e., a composite of expert and gating modules) into a unique chromosome. By resorting to the concepts of regulatory genes and hierarchical codification (Dasgupta & McGregor, 1992; Kim et al., 1995), which allow the exclusion / inclusion of full blocks of genetic code relative to the expert modules, our evolutionary approach promotes the emergent pruning and growing of the number of neural experts. By this means, the complexity of the resulting gated ME model comes to be in direct rapport with the requirements imposed by the learning problem. Furthermore, in order to leverage the effectiveness of the novel hybrid intelligent scheme, as the space of feasible gated ME architectures may be too large to be dealt with, a local search refinement (a.k.a. hybrid training) is performed over each new generated ME individual via the gradient descent algorithm (backpropagation — BP) (Haykin, 1999), in such a manner as to further fine tune the experts' free configuration parameters. Both Lamarckian and Baldwinian types of hybrid learning (Whitley, Scott Gordon, & Mathias, 1994) are currently implemented within our evolutionary-adaptive gated ME framework.

With the aim to assess the performance of the adaptive gated ME models produced by our approach, some experiments considering three complicated time-series forecasting problems have been conducted, and the average results obtained are reported here. Our assessment is based on quantitative criteria, namely the accuracy and generalization of the final best models produced by the approach, providing comparisons with other alternative learning schemes, namely, simple neural networks and manually-shaped gated ME models.

The next section conveys background material supporting our work, whereas the third section conveys the pseudo-code and the main issues regarding our novel approach. Then, the fourth section in the sequel reports on the results achieved with the several experiments conducted on time-series prediction problems, whereas the last section is dedicated to some final remarks, situating the hybrid intelligent methodology presented here within the scope of this book and bringing some perspectives on future work.

Background

In the following, we first provide the reader with a brief outline of the main steps underlying a typical execution of genetic algorithms and discuss about two derived lines of research in this context, namely structured GAs and hybrid GAs. Afterwards, we introduce the main architectural and training issues related to ME models and comment upon some works focusing on their application to time-series forecasting.

Genetic Algorithms and their Structured and Hybrid Extensions

Genetic algorithms comprehend a very flexible, general-purpose metaheuristics premised on the evolutionary ideas of natural selection and population genetics (Bäck et al., 1997; Man, Tang, & Kwong, 1999). They are modeled loosely on the principles governing the evolution of species according to the "survival of the fittest" rule, employing a population of individuals (i.e., possible solution candidates for the optimization problem in hand) that undergo selection in the presence of variation-inducing operators, such as mutation, inversion, and recombination (also known as crossover). Such metaheuristics represents an intelligent exploitation of both random and direct search strategies within a well-defined search space to solve a certain computational problem.

The appeal of GAs comes from their simplicity and elegance as robust search algorithms as well as from their power to discover good solutions rapidly for difficult high-dimensional problems. GAs are particularly useful and efficient when (1) the search space is large, complex, or poorly understood; (2) domain knowledge is scarce or expert knowledge is difficult to encode to narrow the search space; (3) no mathematical analysis is available; and (4) traditional search methods fail (Bäck et al., 1997; Michalewicz, 1996).

A fitness function is used to evaluate the degree of adaptation of an individual to its environment (i.e., problem), and the reproductive successes of the group of such individuals vary with the values of fitness attributed to them. The coordinates of the individuals in the search space should be codified into chromosomes according to a given (generally tailored) solution representation, such as a set of string characters defined over a finite alphabet. A gene is a subsection of a chromosome which encodes the value of a single parameter (decision variable) being optimized. Typical encodings for such a gene are binary, integer, or real-valued numeric ones (Michalewicz, 1996).

In brief, the main steps behind the execution of canonical GAs are (Bäck et al., 1997; Michalewicz, 1996):

1. Randomly generate an initial population of solutions *Chrom*(0).
2. Compute and save the fitness *fit*(*m*) for each individual *m* in the current population *Chrom*(*t*).
3. Define selection probabilities $P_{sel}(m)$ for each individual *m* in *Chrom*(*t*) so that $P_{sel}(m)$ is proportional to *fit*(*m*).
4. From *Chrom*(*t*), produce new offspring via the application of genetic operators, according to additional probability rates: $P_{cross}(m)$, for crossover, and $P_{mut}(m)$, for mutation.
5. Generate a novel generation of individuals *Chrom*(*t* + 1) by probabilistically selecting individuals from the current population of parents and offspring in accord with a given generation gap (GGAP) parameter, that controls how many children will substitute for the current parents.
6. Repeat Step 2 until satisfying solution is obtained or a number of generations (*MAX_GEN*) is reached.

Despite their generally robust character, as the number of applications steadily increases, there have been found some domains of study where the performance of canonical GAs is below-average. Several modifications have been suggested to alleviate such difficulties (Bäck et al., 1997), amongst which two lines of research have deserved much attention recently, namely, how to better represent and manipulate the encoded information, and how to cooperatively integrate the evolutionary engine with other search / optimization techniques (either exact or approximate in nature) in order to boost the search process. While the second line of research is generally pursued through the conceptualization of novel schemes of hybrid GAs (Whitley et al., 1994; Whitley, 1996), one representative of the first line of research comes in the form of what has been called as structured (or hierarchical) GAs — sGAs (Dasgupta & McGregor, 1992; Kim et al., 1995).

The sGA model uses some complex mechanisms borrowed from the biological systems for developing a more efficient genetic search technique. Specifically, this model incorporates redundant genetic material and a gene activation mechanism which utilizes multi-layered genomic structures for the chromosome. The additional genetic material has many advantages in search and optimization, as it can maintain genetic diversity at all time during the search process, where the expected variability largely depends on the amount of redundancy incorporated in the encoding. Some aspects and advantages of structured GAs are summarized as follows (Dasgupta & McGregor, 1992):

- A chromosome is represented by a set of hierarchical levels in such a way that a block of genes pertaining to a certain level behaves as a kind of switch, controlling the expression (i.e., activation) of genes pertaining to downstream levels. During reproduction, the genes of all levels of the hierarchy are modified by the genetic operators — crossover and mutation — exactly as is done in canonical GAs.
- While decoding a chromosome into its phenotype, only those genes currently active in the chromosome contribute to the fitness calculation of the individual. The passive genes are apparently neutral and carried along as redundant genetic material during the evolutionary process.

- Genetic operations altering high-level genes result in changes to the active elements of the genomic structures. Particularly, the role of mutation is twofold: It changes the allele value of any gene, but when it occurs at a higher level it acts as a dominance operator and changes the expression of a set of gene values at the lower level.
- Even when a population converges to its phenotypic space, genotypic diversity still exists, which is a distinctive characteristic of the model. In most other GA models, phenotypic convergence implies also genotypic convergence, bringing the consequent impoverishment of diversity within the population.
- The sGA can maintain a good balance between exploration (i.e., the constant seeking for novel solutions) and exploitation (i.e., intensification of the search around the best points found so far), resulting in a more efficient search of potential areas of the phenotypic space. Being trapped at a local optimum, which causes premature convergence of the algorithm, can thus be avoided.
- The sGA hierarchical encoding provides a long-term mechanism for preserving and retrieving alternative solutions or previously-expressed building blocks within the chromosomal structures. Hence, in non-stationary optimizations, an sGA can provide a means for rapid long jump adaptation, avoiding the low rates of convergence shown by the canonical GA model.

Conversely, a hybrid GA model combines in some way a local search technique (either heuristic-based or not) with a more traditional genetic algorithm. The objective is generally one of threefold: (1) to generate initial solutions that already identify promising regions of the search space; (2) to restore the feasibility of the new solutions generated by the variation operators, mainly when the optimization problem has additional constraints on the values of the decision variables; and (3) to incorporate any extra knowledge gained about the problem in order to improve the quality of the new solutions generated by the variation operators.

In such context, it is worth it to distinguish between different classes of hybrid GAs. While the designation "memetic algorithms" alludes to extended GAs trying to model the social-cultural transmission of acquired information between successive generations of individuals (which indeed have some level of autonomy and are thus viewed as agents), both Lamarckian and Baldwinian types of hybrid GAs try to model the new sources of learning acquired by the individuals during their lifetimes and how such learned behavior can directly affect their fitness values (Ross, 1999; Whitley, 1996). Whereas the Lamarckian approach stipulates that the acquired behavior be coded back onto the genotype representation and passed along to offspring during reproduction, in the Baldwinian approach, only the fitness value of the individual is adjusted after the learning process takes place. According to Whitley et al. (1994), there are yet no general recipes for indicating whether a certain type of optimization problem is more appropriate to be dealt with through a Lamarckian or Baldwinian perspective; the better way to discover such appropriateness is still through the conduction of systematic empirical simulations for the problem domain under investigation. Such kind of comparison was performed for our adaptive gated ME approach when tackling the nonlinear time-series forecasting problems and the results are presented in a section that follows.

Mixtures of Experts and their Application on Time-Series Prediction

ME models are particularly useful for coping with mapping problems in which the form of the mapping is different for distinct regions of the input space (Jacobs et al., 1991; Weigend et al., 1995; Haykin, 1999). Even though applying a single neural network or other non-linear predictor could provide a reasonable global solution for these problems, the strategy of assigning different expert subnetworks to distinct regions seems to be more effective in such undertaking. This is accomplished in MEs (Figure 1) by employing a separate gating module in charge of deciding, based on the input data and its degrees of confidence on the experts' capabilities, which of the competing experts should be recruited to determine the overall system's output.

Formally stating, given an input sample **x**, each expert k ($k = 1, \ldots, K$) produces an output $\mathbf{y}_k$ in accordance with its local conditional probability function $\phi_k(\mathbf{t} \mid \mathbf{x})$, where **t** is the target output vector, and then the final system output **y** is given as the weighted sum of the estimated probabilities from all experts, namely,

$$\mathbf{y}(\mathbf{x}) = \sum_{k=1}^{K} g_k(\mathbf{x})\mathbf{y}_k(\mathbf{x}), \tag{1}$$

where $g_k(x)\left(g_k \geq 0, \sum_k g_k = 1\right)$ is the gating's confidence level on assigning the given input sample to the k-th expert.

Essentially, each expert is adaptively trained to extract relevant features of its associated space whereas the gating module is trained to produce fair global weights for combining the experts' outputs and to softly partition the input space. The decoupled training between gating and expert modules becomes possible by resorting to the EM algorithm (Dempster et al., 1977; Jordan & Jacobs, 1994), whose formulation to estimate the gating and experts' parameters comprehends two well-delimited steps defined over a log-based error function, given by:

Figure 1. The typical mixture of experts framework

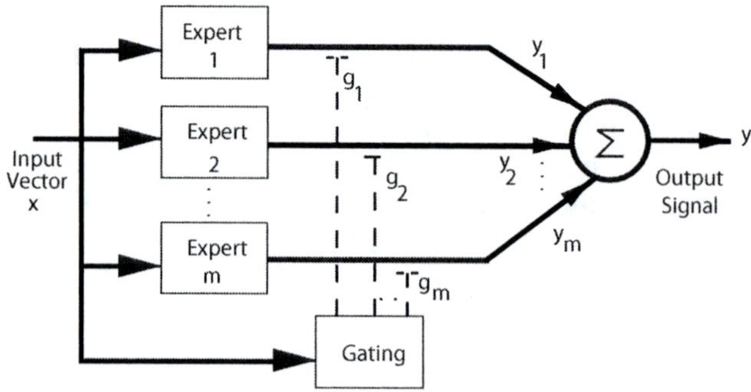

$$E = -\sum_{n=1}^{N} \log \sum_{k=1}^{K} g_k \phi_k , \tag{2}$$

where n is the index of the training samples. The tricky idea to be employed here is that the minimization of this error function can be simplified if each pattern could be allocated to exactly one expert module; this is made possible by utilizing some latent variables that equal to one for one component and zero for the others. The EM steps are:

E-Step. Here, we should calculate the expected values for the latent variables $h_k^{(n)}$, assuming that all the other free parameters (from the gating and experts) are fixed and known:

$$h_k^{(n)}\left(\mathbf{t}^{(n)} | \mathbf{x}^{(n)}\right) = \frac{g_k\left(\mathbf{x}^{(n)}\right)\phi_k\left(\mathbf{t}^{(n)} | \mathbf{x}^{(n)}\right)}{\sum_{j=1}^{K} g_j\left(\mathbf{x}^{(n)}\right)\phi_j\left(\mathbf{t}^{(n)} | \mathbf{x}^{(n)}\right)}. \tag{3}$$

M-Step. The cost function to be minimized for the gating module is:

$$E_{gate} = -\sum_{n=1}^{N}\sum_{k=1}^{K} h_k^{(n)}(\mathbf{t}^{(n)} | \mathbf{x}^{(n)}) \log(g_k(\mathbf{x}^{(n)}) \tag{4}$$

and for the expert j is:

$$E_{expert} = -\sum_{n=1}^{N}\sum_{k=1}^{K} h_k^{(n)}(\mathbf{t}^{(n)} | \mathbf{x}^{(n)}) \log(\phi_k(\mathbf{t}^{(n)} | \mathbf{x}^{(n)})), \tag{5}$$

where, for regression problems, the conditional probability density of the k-th expert ϕ_k is usually given by:

$$\phi_k(\mathbf{t}^{(n)} | \mathbf{x}^{(n)}) = \frac{1}{(2\pi)^{d/2}(\sigma_k^2)^{1/2}} \exp\left\{ -\frac{(\mathbf{t}^{(n)} - \mathbf{y}_j^{(n)})^T(\mathbf{t}^{(n)} - \mathbf{y}_j^{(n)})}{2\sigma_j^2} \right\} ,$$

where d is the dimension of $\mathbf{t}$, σ_k^2 denotes the variance of the k-th expert's outputs, and $\mathbf{y}_k$ is a function of some of its parameters (usually, its connection weights).

The formalization may be applied to either conventional or gated ME (also known as society of experts) models. In the latter variant, each of the expert modules becomes associated with local adaptive variances σ_k^2 that do not depend upon the input signal $\mathbf{x}$; the role of such variances is to provide a better calibration in the modeling of the data regions allocated to each expert. Likewise, such second-order statistics can be interpreted as the level of confidence that each expert has on the accuracy of its own outputs.

For time-series forecasting, the employment of these local variances is readily justifiable since it enhances the whole temporal segmentation process (areas of dissimilar predictability are grouped together) and also prevents overfitting, as the experts learn to match their variances to their local noise levels. Moreover, in this application scenario, the role of the gating is to discover the different temporal regimes, as well as the switching between them, commonly present in multi-stationary time series (Weigend & Gershenfeld, 1994), whereas the role of the experts is to properly model the data distribution associated with each regime.

Weigend et al. (1995), Mangeas et al. (1995), and more recently Srivastava et al. (1999) have applied gated ME variants for dealing with intricate time-series problems, such as chaotic series (as the Laser, studied in this work) and electricity load series. Typically, the gating and expert parameters are obtained in the M-step of the EM algorithm by employing a nonlinear optimization algorithm, such as gradient descent (Haykin, 1999). In the next section, we present an alternative, genetic-based mechanism for the automatic structural and parametric configuration of Gated MEs also for time-series prediction.

In this regard, it is interesting to mention that Hong, Oh, Kim, and Lee (2002) have already investigated the performance of an evolutionary algorithm, namely, the evolutionary structured optimization (ESO) method, developed by the authors, on the training of ME models for nonlinear time-series prediction. However, instead of considering the gated ME variant, the authors focused on the localized ME variant, as proposed by Xu et al. (1995) which is composed of linear experts and gating modules. Furthermore, amongst the various ME parameters that could be susceptible to automatic adaptation, only those related to the gating module (centers and widths of probability density functions) were actually calibrated through artificial evolution, and no automatic structural configuration (i.e., number, types, and dimensions) of the expert modules was taken into consideration in Hong et al.'s approach. Conversely, such issues were taken into account when of the formulation of the evolutionary methodology presented in the next section.

Adaptive Gated Mixture of Experts

Figure 2 brings the pseudo-algorithm with the main steps behind the proposed evolutionary approach for automatically designing gated ME models. As an extended GA-based adaptive framework (Bäck et al., 1997), the key conceptual issues underlying it involve:

- the (quasi-) hierarchical encoding of a whole Gated ME instance into a given chromosome with the possibility to automatically undertake the pruning / growing of the number of expert modules
- the definition of the fitness function to discern between adequate and non-adequate individuals within a population of candidate solutions
- the definition of the genetic operators (and their associated rates)
- the possibility to perform local training refinement over the gating and expert modules, in such a way as to leverage the genetic search efficiency (exploitative / explorative behavior)

Figure 2. The main steps comprising our evolutionary approach for designing gated ME models

1. Randomly generate the initial population (*Chrom*);
2. Decode *Chrom*, apply the EM algorithm, and then train each ME with gradient descent (BP)
   (a) *New_Chrom*←BPtrain(*Chrom*, τ_1);
3. *If (Lamarckian Search OR Baldwinian Search)*
   (a) *Chrom*←*New_Chrom*;
4. Evaluate *Chrom*
   (a) *fit*(*Chrom*) ← *-Likelihood function*;
5. While (*gen* ≤ MAX_GEN)
   (a) *fit*(*Chrom*) ← *Ranking*(*fit* (*Chrom*));
   (b) *Offspring* selection (GGAP);
   (c) *Offspring* recombination (P_{cross});
   (d) *Offspring* mutation (P_{mut});
   (e) Train parents (*Chrom*) τ_1 times;

   $$\tau_1(gen) \leftarrow \tau_1(gen-1) - \left\lfloor \tau_1(0) \times \frac{(gen)}{MAX\_Gen} \right\rfloor$$

   (f) Train children (*Offspring*) τ_2 times;
   (g) Evaluate *Chrom* and *Offspring*;
   (h) *If (Lamarckian Search)*
      i. *Chrom*←*New_Chrom*;
      ii. *Offspring*←*New_Offspring*;
   (i) *If (Baldwinian Search)*
      i. *Chrom*←*New_Chrom*;
   (j) Join *Chrom* and *Offspring* in a common pool and cutoff the worst individuals;
   (k) *gen*←*gen* + 1;

In the following subsections, we touch upon such issues.

Codification and Fitness Function

The codification scheme we have adopted for our approach is highly influenced by the ideas brought forth by Dasgupta and McGregor (1992) in the conceptualization of structured GAs. Such nonlinear interpretation of linear strings has two distinctive characteristics that seem particularly useful for the evolution of gated ME architectures: (i) as a single change at a higher level of the hierarchy enables multiple changes at lower levels, bringing about the possibility of large variations in the phenotypes from one generation to the other, the gated ME adaptation process can exhibit patterns of evolutionary "jumps" across the fitness land-

Figure 3. The mixed-encoding representation of a chromosome

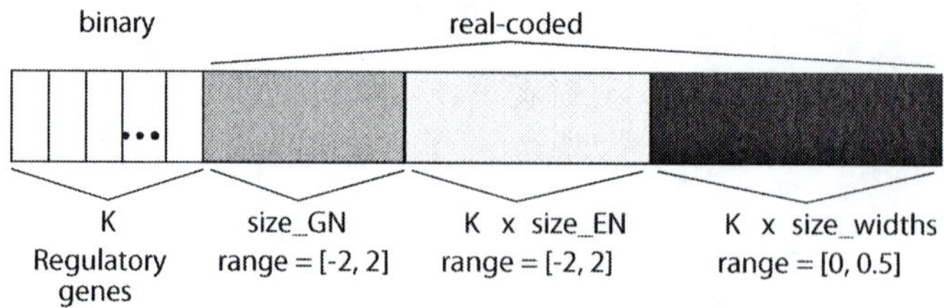

scape, in such a manner as to try to match the complexity of the model with that required by the problem; and (ii) although not active in one generation, important building blocks (a.k.a. "junk genes") may still persist in the chromosome structure and be carried in a neutral and apparently redundant form to subsequent generations, something very interesting to ensure the continuous coadaptation of the ME chromosome's parts and to maintain higher levels of genetic variability (thus, preventing from premature convergence problems).

Figure 3 shows how a gated ME instance is represented as a mixed-encoding chromosome. As it is noticeable, there are only two levels in our hierarchy. At the higher level, there are K regulatory bits, where the k-th bit indicates whether the k-th expert (and its associated parameters, represented via real-coded genes at the lower level) will be considered as active ('1') or not ('0'), while phenotypically interpreting a certain ME individual. (As there is only one gating for each gated ME, its parameters — connection weights — will always be considered as active.) Also shown in Figure 3 are the ranges associated with real-coded decision variables (free parameters of the gating and expert modules).

As indicated in the pseudo-code of Figure 2, in the minimization process pursued by our evolutionary approach, we have made use of the negative of the log-likelihood error function defined in (2) as the metric to assign fitness values among competing chromosomes. This agrees with the ME philosophy, since (2) serves as an adequate (entropy-related) measure to evaluate the quality of the interactions between gating and expert modules in the problem decomposition and solution.

Genetic Operators and Rates

In our extended GA model, the stochastic universal sampling (SUS) algorithm proposed by Baker (1987) is applied to select individuals to mate and to produce new offspring. The idea behind SUS is to make a single draw from a uniform distribution and use this to determine how many offspring to assign to each parent, a strategy that minimizes chance fluctuations. Moreover, we have also made use of a linear ranking operator to better discriminate between the chromosomes' fitness values (Bäck et al., 1997). Ranking selection has the desirable property that it is invariant under any monotonic mapping of the fitness function. Contrasted to steady-state GAs, where only one parent can be replaced by one child in each generation, in our modified GA, the number of individuals in the current population that should replaced by their offspring is controlled by the generation gap constant discussed earlier; in this way, the best among parents and children are then holded for next iteration.

Novel ME chromosomes are produced via recombination and mutation, with rates given by $P_{cross}(\cdot)$ and $P_{mut}(\cdot)$, as discussed. As our extended GA employs a mixed "binary-real" codification scheme, different genetic operators were recruited to deal with the different levels of the ME chromosome's hierarchy. For the binary (regulatory genes) level, one-point crossover and simple bit mutation operators were used. For the real-coded (gating and experts' parameters) level, arithmetic crossover and an EP-based mutation operator were employed (Michalewicz, 1996). The latter stipulates a new value for a given variable by adding to its current amount a small random perturbation (with normal distribution) that fits within the variable's range. In contrast to recombination operators that exchange information between mates, arithmetic crossover attempts to blend, via a convex sum, the component variables of two given parents, say x_{1i} and x_{2i}, resulting in a new individual $\mathbf{x}'$ given by: $x_i^{'} = \alpha \times x_{1i} + (1-\alpha) \times x_{2i}$, where $\alpha \in [0, 1]$.

Hybrid Training

In our evolutionary framework, we have exploited the potentialities bring forth by Lamarckian and Baldwinian types of hybrid learning in the evolution of gated ME instances by applying, in each generation of the main GA cycle, the gradient descent algorithm (Haykin, 1999) at each module (gating or expert) of each chromosome separately. This is done in an iterative basis, where the several configuration parameters (weights and variances) of both parents and offspring are locally optimized through the backpropagation algorithm for τ_1 and τ_2 iterations, respectively. In order to promote fairness when comparing parents with their offspring and also to avoid overtraining and loss of computational resources, the former parameter is made adaptive and shows a linear decaying behavior with rate proportional to the number of generations already executed (refer to Figure 2).

Simulation Experiments and Results

In order to compare the performance exhibited by gated ME models designed via our evolutionary approach to that exhibited by single MLPs and by manually-shaped gated ME models trained only with BP, we conducted three series of experiments, each one considering a different nonlinear time-series problem. In the first group of experiments, we assessed our approach in the prediction of a chaotic time series generated via the Mackey-Glass differential delay equation (Mackey & Glass, 1977), which is defined as $x_{MG}(t) = \frac{0.2x(t-\tau)}{1+x^{10}(t-\tau)} - 0.1x(t)$. The aim is to anticipate the value of a future point in $k = t + P$ having as background the points generated up to $k = t$. The conventional method for this type of prediction is to create a direct mapping from D points of the time-series spaced Δ units of time apart from each other, that is, $\{x(t - (D-1)\Delta), \ldots, x(t - \Delta), x(t)\}$, to a predicted future value $x(t + P)$. From $x_{MG}(t)$, we extracted 1,000 input-output data samples of the form $[x(t-18), x(t-12), x(t-6), x(t); x(t + 6)]$, where t varies from 118 to 1,117. The first 500 contiguous samples were used for training and the rest for test.

In the second group of experiments, we considered the laser dataset, representing a series of 2,000 measurements of chaotic intensity fluctuations (Weigend & Gershenfeld, 1994). Following Zhang and Joung (1999), we have partitioned the laser series into two mutually-exclusive datasets, one for training, containing the first 1,000 contiguous samples, and the other for test, with the remaining samples. Three contiguous values (lags) [$x(t$-3), $x(t$-2), $x(t$-1)] were used as input for predicting the target value $x(t)$.

The last group of experiments involved the one-step-ahead prediction of the daily exchange rate between the U.S, dollar and British pound (USD / GBP) currencies, in a total of 784 samples covering a period of three years (January 1991 to December 1993), from which the first 600 observations were used as training data and the others make up the test set. Such time series is referred to here as Forex, and as it is prone to trending problems, we have followed the guidelines of Anastasakis and Mort (2000) and worked upon a modified time series (with a smoother envelope), whose form is given by $x_{FX}(t) = p_t - \frac{1}{5}\sum_{i=1}^{5} p_{t-i}$, where p_t is the actual price at time t of the USD / GBP exchange rate.

In ME applications, when using a large number of expert modules, there is a great chance to have experts focusing on arbitrarily small subsets of the data, which may lead to overfitting problems. Likewise, when the distribution of missing data becomes sharp, focusing on few data points at a time, it is also possible to have the whole architecture overfitting the training data through the gates of the gating module. These problems can be counteracted by properly setting some configuration and training parameters, such as the number of hidden neurons of the gating (h_g) and experts (h_e), the number of EM iterations (t_{EM}), the number of training epochs used in the M-step (t_M) of the EM algorithm, and the maximum number of experts allowed per gated ME instance (K_M) (Lima et al., 2002).

In the simulations, aiming at uniformity in the comparison, we have applied the control parameters summarized in Table 1 when experimenting with gated ME models (produced either through BP or through our evolutionary approach) for all the time series under consideration. In our evolutionary approach, referred to here as GATED-EVOL, t_{EM} refers to each generation, while t_M is given by τ_1 (for parents) and τ_2 (for offspring) (see Figure 2). Conversely, simple MLPs were designed with five hidden neurons and were trained until reaching 2,000 epochs in BP with fixed learning rate (Haykin, 1999). Moreover, we normalized all training / test datasets in the range [-1; +1] and the forecasting performance metrics, as defined below for univariate time series, were calculated in the resulting normalized series (Zhang et al., 1998):

Table 1. Parameter settings in gated ME experiments

Parameter	Gated-BP	GATED-EVOL
h_g, h_c	5 neurons	5 neurons
t_{EM}	200 steps	3 (parents), 10 (offspring) steps
t_M (τ_2, $\tau_1(0)$)	500 iterations	500 iterations
K_M	{3,5} experts	5 experts
Chrom	(fixed)	25 individuals
P_{mut}	....	30%
P_{cross}	....	75%
GGAP	....	90%
MAX_GEN	....	100

- sum of squared errors (SSE): $E_{SSE} = \sum (e_t)^2$;
- mean square error (MSE): $E_{MSE} = \frac{1}{N}\sum (e_t)^2$;
- mean absolute error (MAE): $E_{MAE} = \frac{1}{N}\sum |e_t|$;
- mean absolute percentage error (MAPE): $E_{MAPE} = \frac{1}{N}\sum \left|\frac{e_t}{y_t}\right| \cdot 100$;
- root mean square error (RMSE): $E_{RMSE} = \frac{1}{N}\sqrt{\sum (e_t)^2}$
- normalized root mean square error (NRMSE): $E_{NRMSE} = \sqrt{\sum \frac{(e_t)^2}{\sum (\mu_y - y_t)^2}}$;
- Theil's coefficient: $T_r = \sqrt{\frac{\sum (e_t)^2}{\sum (d_t - d_{t-1})^2}}$; and
- mean reversion: $T_\mu = \sqrt{\frac{\sum (e_t)^2}{\sum (\mu_d - d_{t+1})^2}}$.

In such definitions, d_t and y_t refer to the desired and achieved mapping outputs at time t, $e_t = d_t - y_t$, N is the number of observations considered, and $\mu_s = \sum s_t / N$ is the mean value of time series $s = \{d, y\}$. Armstrong and Collopy (1992) and Refenes (1995) provide a good qualitative discussion on the statistical properties analyzed by such metrics. For instance, with the Theil's coefficient, one can compare the performance exhibited by any novel predictor with that shown by a naive predictor based on the random-walk hypothesis; this is particularly interesting to gauge for economic time series such as the Forex. Any predictor whose T_r value is less than one is doing better than repeating the last actual observation of the series as a prediction of the next value. By other means, the mean reversion metric compares the generated predictor with another trivial one, which is the historic mean value of the whole time series.

Figures 4 through 12 present several results related to the application of our evolutionary approach toward the automatic design of gated ME models. As quite the same qualitative behavior was observed for the Lamarckian and Baldwinian versions, most of the times we show graphs related to only one of the configurations (except given to Figure 12).

Figures 4, 6, and 9 are similar in nature and show the same steadily-decreasing behavior of the log-likelihood function (i.e., the increasing of the fitness value) of the best gated ME model across the GA generations, for all studied time series. Conversely, Figures 5 and 11 contrast the target and predicted time series (in the test dataset) for the Mackey-Glass and Laser scenarios, while Figures 7 and 12 display the absolute error of prediction for each timepoint (also in the test set) of the Forex and Laser cases. Finally, Figures 8 and 10 depict

Figure 4. Fitness of the best model across GA generations for the best run — Lamarckian and Mackey-Glass

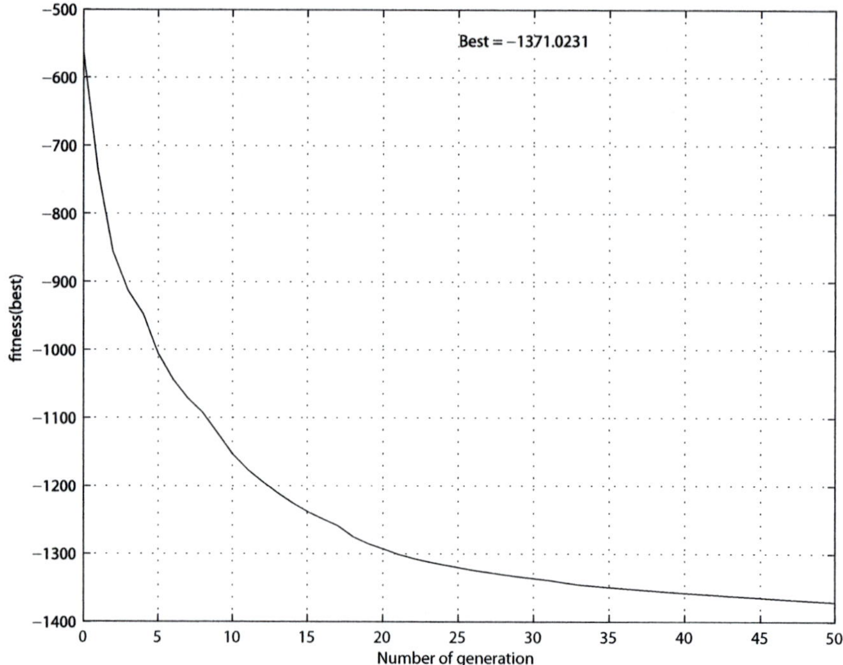

Figure 5. Window of prediction of the best Gated-Evol model (Baldwinian) in test set — Mackey-Glass

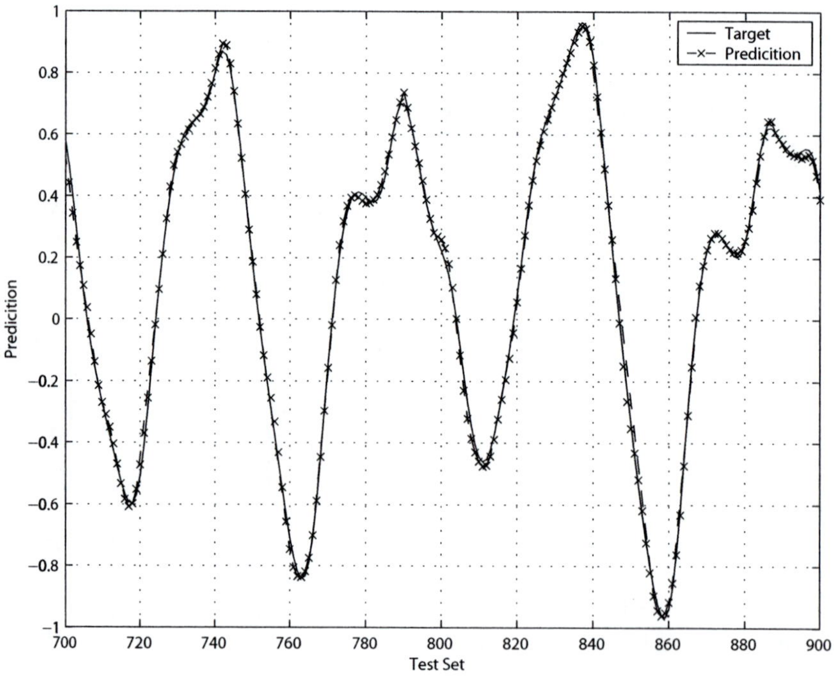

Figure 6. Fitness of the best model across GA generations for the best run — Baldwinian and Forex

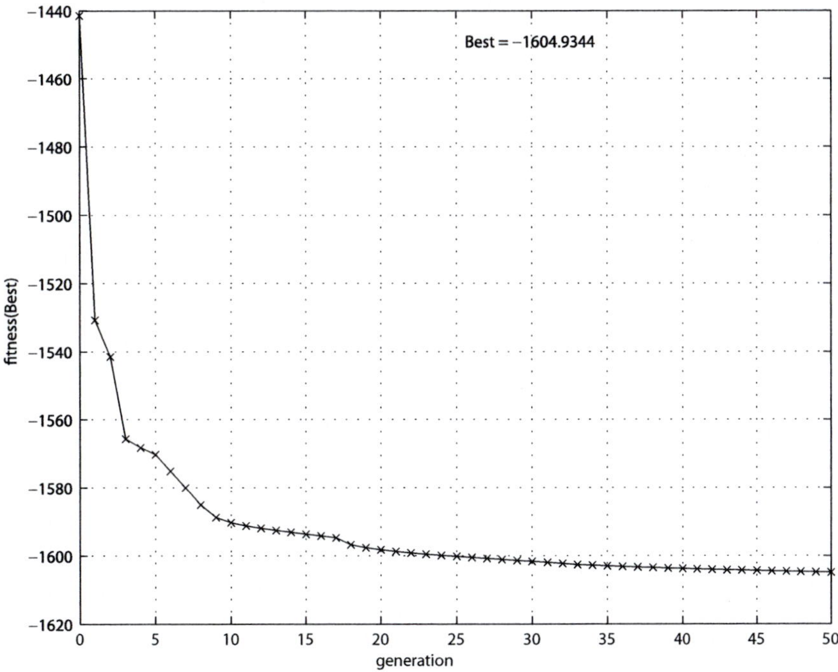

Figure 7. Absolute prediction error in the test for the best GATED-EVOL *model — Lamarckian and Forex*

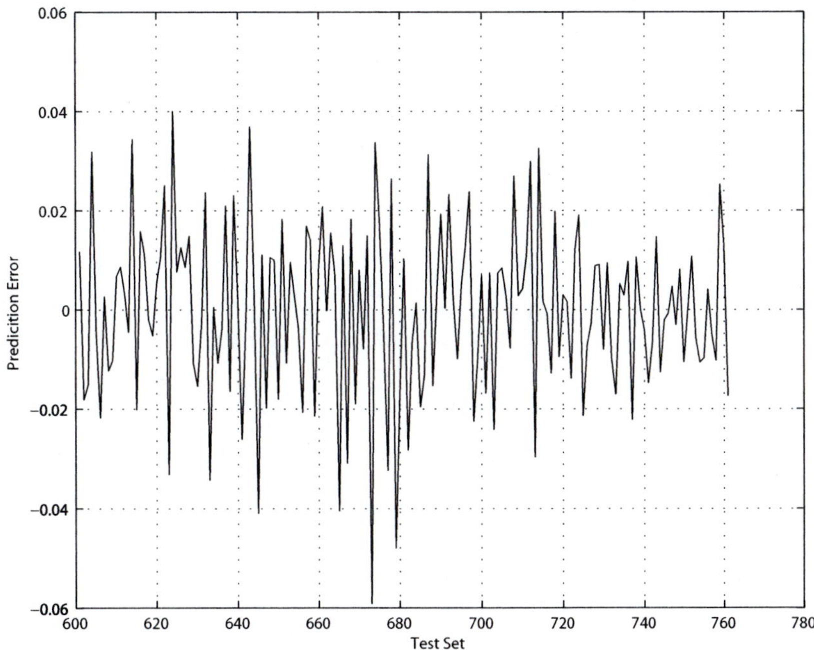

Figure 8. Dynamic growing and pruning behavior of our evolutionary approach: Average number of expert modules present in the 10% best gated ME models in each generation — Lamarckian and Forex

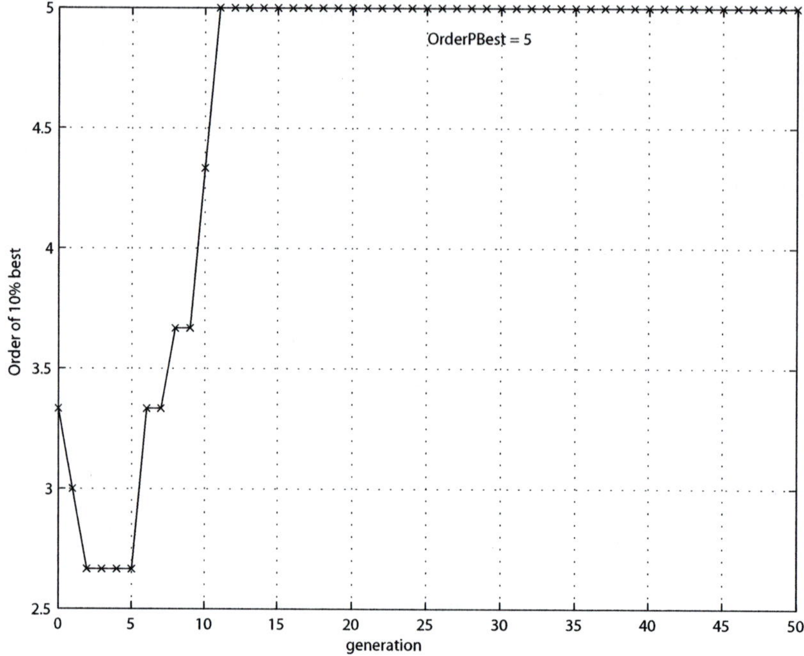

Figure 9. Fitness of the best model across GA generations for the best run — Lamarckian and Laser

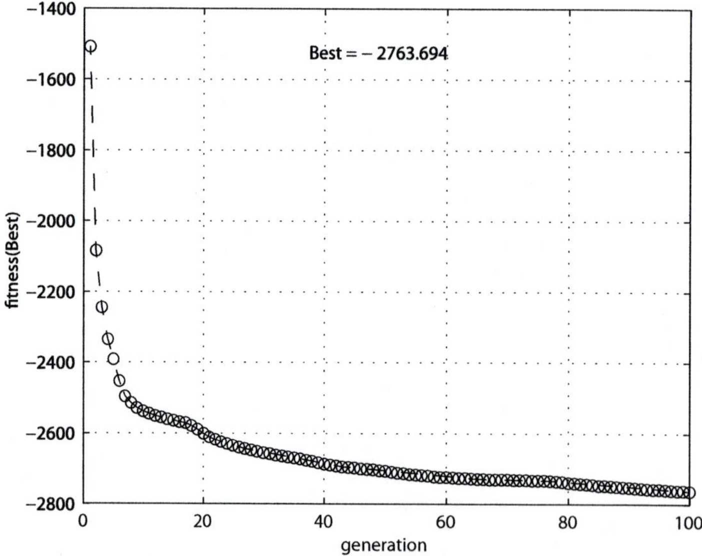

Figure 10. Dynamic growing and pruning behavior of our evolutionary approach: Average number of expert modules present in the 10% best gated ME models in each generation — Lamarckian and Laser

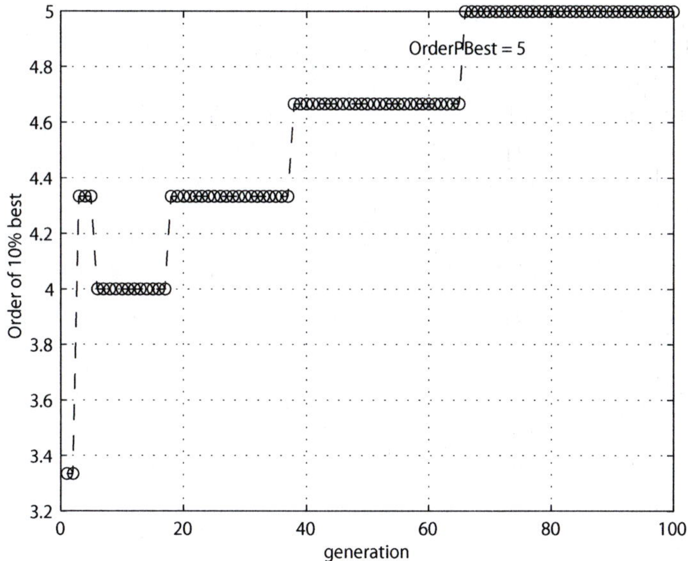

Figure 11. Target and predicted time series — Lamarckian and Laser

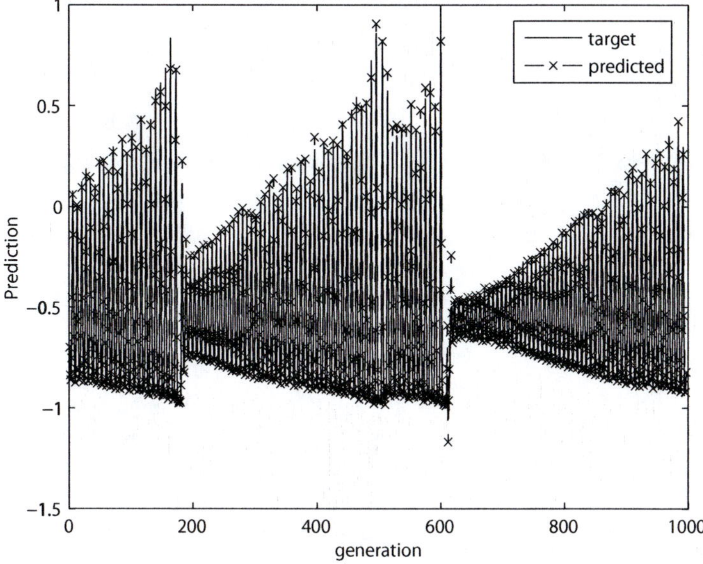

Figure 12. Comparison of prediction errors in the Laser test set produced by the best GATED-EVOL *models trained according to Lamarckian (a) or Baldwinian (b) perspectives*

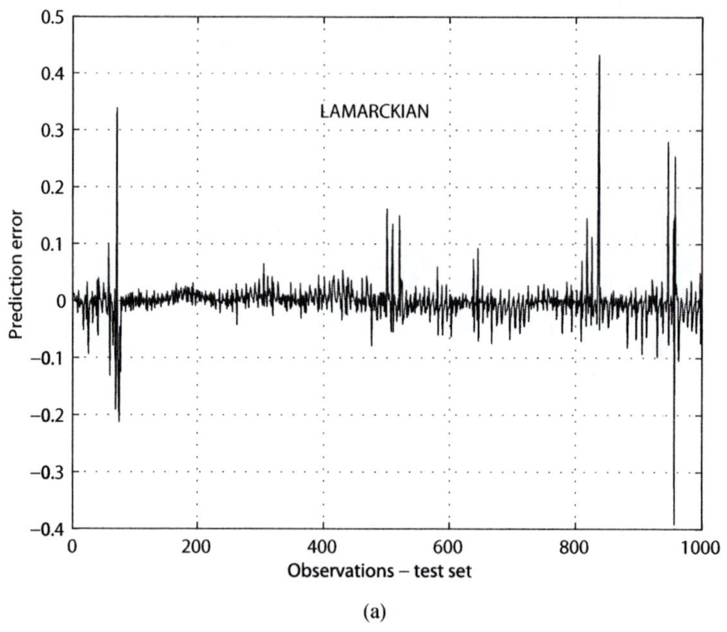

(a)

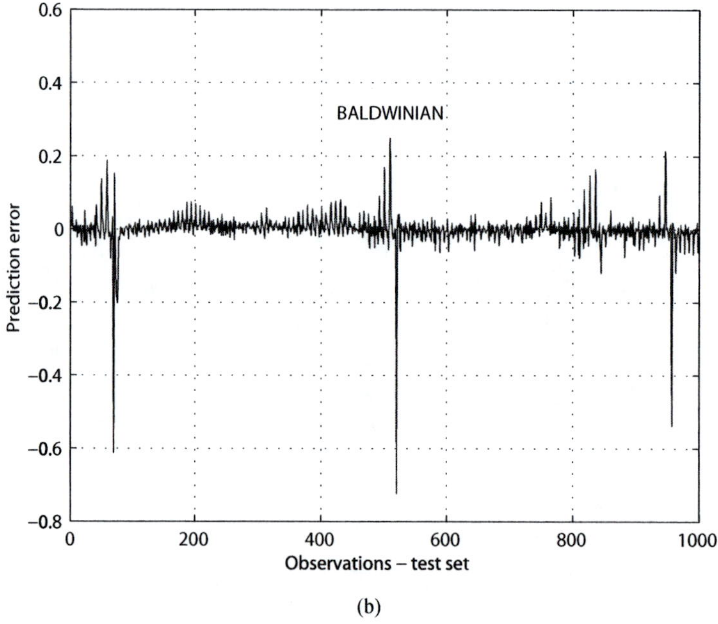

(b)

the growing and pruning process promoted by our evolutionary approach toward the emergent definition of the right size (complexity) of the best gated ME model. In such regard, it is pertinent to mention that both hybrid-training versions of our approach, Lamarckian and Baldwinian, have achieved, in most of the times, the same levels of complexity (i.e., numbers of expert modules) of the best final gated ME model for all three time-series problems under consideration. For Mackey-Glass time series, the number of experts in the best final model was four, while, for the Forex and Laser time series, such number was five, that is, the maximum number of experts allowed was indeed necessary (see Table 1).

By other means, Tables 2 and 3 contrast the performance of the best final models produced by our evolutionary approach with that exhibited by the models produced by two contestant approaches, viz. single neural networks (MLPs) and manually-crafted gated MEs trained only with BP, in both training (accuracy) and test (generalization) phases. For all approaches, the average performance in five (5) trials is reported considering all the metrics discussed earlier.

As can be noticed, our evolutionary approach was very effective in automatically assembling gated ME structures for tackling the aforementioned forecasting problems. The models produced via Lamarckian hybrid-training mode was, in average, a bit better than those produced via Baldwinian hybrid-training mode for all scenarios. The comparative results have confirmed our previous expectations that the novel evolutionary hybrid framework could, in average, outperform the other non-adaptive contestant approaches. It is interesting to mention that the average results achieved with both hybrid-training versions of our approach, Lamarckian or Baldwinian, were, in the great majority of the cases, superior to those exhibited by non-adaptive gated ME models produced exclusively with BP, despite the fact that the latter were trained exhaustively for more than 100,000 BP epochs ($t_M \times t_{EM}$) and the maximum number of BP iterations allowed for each novel chromosome of our GA was only 5,000 ($\tau_2 \times t_{EM}$). Moreover, most of the times, the performance achieved by our evolutionary models in the test datasets were equivalent to that acquired in the training phase, reflecting the good generalization capability promoted by the evolutionary hybrid approach. Overall, we can ascertain that the results produced via the gated ME models (adaptive or not) are quite comparable (and sometimes much better) to those produced by other related approaches discussed in the literature (Anastasakis & Mort, 2000; Hong et al., 2002; Weigend et al., 1995; Zhang & Joung, 1999).

Future Trends

The methodology of coping with hard problems through the proper integration (i.e., combination, fusion, and/or transformation) of the theoretical resources provided by different and complimentary intelligent techniques, also known as intelligent systems hybridization (Goonatilake & Khebbal, 1995), has proved to be very promising in several domains of application in the recent years and, thus, it deserves to be constantly discussed, evaluated, and disseminated as a prominent artificial intelligence (AI) principle in the literature. The whole work presented in this chapter gives a further step in such direction, as it congregates different lines of AI research within the same conceptual framework, namely, genetic algorithms,

Table 2. Average results concerning all experiments — training phase. "SD" means standard deviation, calculated in relation to MSE, "L" means Lamarckian, and "B" means Baldwinian.

	Training								
	SSE	MSE	MAE	MAPE	RMSE	NRMSE	T_r	T_u	SD
					Mackey-Glass				
Gated-EVOL (*L*)	0.02537	0.00005	0.00503	4.55874	0.00032	0.01399	0.0961	0.01396	7.72%
Gated-EVOL (*B*)	0.02976	0.00006	0.00576	4.88533	0.000345	0.01434	0.10415	0.01512	10.22%
Gated-BP (3)	0.03074	0.00006	0.00607	8.31403	0.00035	0.01537	0.1059	0.0154	5.21%
Gated-BP (5)	0.03141	0.00006	0.00568	4.76386	0.00035	0.01555	0.1070	0.0155	3.59%
MLP	0.42851	0.00086	0.02384	14.10222	0.00131	0.05751	0.3952	0.0574	1.12%
					Forex				
Gated-EVOL (*L*)	0.18830	0.00031	0.01307	1.41884	0.00072	0.79367	0.79494	0.69610	4.13%
Gated-EVOL (*B*)	0.27085	0.00045	0.01387	1.52755	0.00087	0.67046	0.83105	0.72772	7.93%
Gated-BP (3)	0.18522	0.00031	0.01300	1.41109	0.00072	0.75574	0.9132	0.6001	4.80%
Gated-BP (5)	0.18589	0.00031	0.01301	1.41209	0.00072	0.76076	0.9148	0.6011	3.94%
MLP	0.32304	0.00054	0.01717	1.86215	0.00095	2.50417	1.2060	0.7925	1.07%
					Laser				
Gated-EVOL (*L*)	0.97096	0.00097	0.01602	13.82342	0.00099	0.08443	0.08708	0.08430	7.44%
Gated-EVOL (*B*)	2.53601	0.00254	0.01916	20.50788	0.00160	0.13661	0.14074	0.13624	12.88%
Gated-BP (3)	2.71745	0.00273	0.02180	19.97744	0.00165	0.14284	0.1457	0.1410	3.21%
Gated-BP (5)	1.99276	0.00200	0.01868	18.43002	0.00142	0.12104	0.1248	0.1208	5.03%
MLP	11.01982	0.01105	0.06979	69.43926	0.00333	0.30169	0.2934	0.2840	2.81%

neural networks, and probabilistic learning, for dealing with a class of non-trivial scientific problems, namely, nonlinear time-series forecasting (Weigend & Gershenfeld, 1994).

As the complexity and diversification of the problems being tackled by AI techniques steadily increases, we envisage that novel forms of hybridization will emerge in the following years, aiming to exploit the peculiarities of each problem and the potentialities of each technique. Modular archetypes of such hybrid intelligent systems will become even

Table 3. Average results concerning all experiments — test phase. "SD" means standard deviation, calculated in relation to MSE, "L" means Lamarckian, and "B" means Baldwinian.

	Training								
	SSE	MSE	MAE	MAPE	RMSE	NRMSE	T_r	T_μ	SD
	Mackey-Glass								
Gated-EVOL (*L*)	0.02359	0.00005	0.00477	4.01224	0.00031	0.01356	0.0927	0.01352	10.12%
Gated-EVOL (*B*)	0.02881	0.00006	0.00551	4.26988	0.00034	0.01479	0.1024	0.01494	13.77%
Gated-BP (3)	0.02921	0.00006	0.00593	6.94126	0.00034	0.01504	0.1032	0.0150	5.92%
Gated-BP (5)	0.03093	0.00006	0.00546	4.25430	0.00035	0.01549	0.1062	0.0155	7.11%
MLP	0.42131	0.00084	0.02347	18.45716	0.00130	0.05721	0.3918	0.0571	2.3%
	Forex								
Gated-EVOL (*L*)	0.04111	0.00026	0.01250	1.35078	0.00126	0.95020	0.95020	0.70283	6.56%
Gated-EVOL (*B*)	0.04330	0.00026	0.01274	1.37768	0.00125	0.90729	0.90729	0.71167	10.77%
Gated-BP (3)	0.04194	0.00026	0.01260	1.36130	0.00127	0.89032	0.89032	0.7118	4.88%
Gated-BP (5)	0.04171	0.00026	0.01261	1.36239	0.00127	0.90925	0.90925	0.7098	4.14%
MLP	0.05670	0.00035	0.01514	1.63759	0.00148	2.64111	1.0579	0.8276	1.97%
	Laser								
Gated-EVOL (*L*)	1.43045	0.00143	0.01809	14.44745	0.00120	0.09872	0.10146	0.09871	6.89%
Gated-EVOL (*B*)	2.41858	0.00242	0.02112	12.78808	0.00156	0.12911	0.13153	0.12835	13.55%
Gated-BP (3)	2.66299	0.00266	0.02312	26.44303	0.00163	0.13769	0.1384	0.1347	5.78%
Gated-BP (5)	1.82348	0.00182	0.02033	14.57271	0.00135	0.11247	0.1146	0.1114	9.12%
MLP	13.93351	0.1393	0.07549	54.71098	0.00373	0.33622	0.3167	0.3081	3.26%

more apparent, allying the benefits of the hybridization principle with that shown by the "divide-and-conquer" precept.

As future work, we shall extend our evolutionary framework to also deal with localized MEs (Xu et al., 1995) as well as with hierarchical ME models (Jordan & Jacobs, 1994). Other application areas, like pattern classification, are also under investigation. Furthermore, we are currently working toward the integration of swarm intelligence techniques (Kennedy & Eberhart, 2001) with our evolutionary framework.

Conclusion

In this work, we have presented a novel evolutionary methodology, based on the concepts of structured (Dasgupta & McGregor, 1992; Kim et al., 1995) and hybrid (Whitley et al., 1994; Whitley, 1996) GAs, for the automatic and constructive design (i.e., architectural specification and parameter calibration) of gated mixture of experts models (Weigend et al., 1995; Mangeas et al., 1995; Srivastava et al., 1999). Moreover, several experiments over three non-trivial forecasting problems were conducted in order to evaluate the potentials of the novel approach, and the main results were discussed in detail here. The results are indeed promising and empirically testify that the devised hybrid evolutionary approach could keep up well with the hard task of automatically designing gated ME models for dealing with predictive issues.

Acknowledgment

CNPq / Funcap and Fapesp have sponsored the first two authors via post-doctorate scholarships # 23661-04 and # 04/09597-0, respectively.

References

Anastasakis, L., & Mort, N. (2000, October). Applying a feedforward neural network for the prediction of the USD/BGP exchange rate. In *Proceedings of 3rd Conference in Technology and Automation*, Piraeus, Greece (pp. 169-174). T.E.I. of Piraeus.

Armstrong, J., & Collopy, F. (1992). Error measures for generalizing about forecasting methods — Empirical comparisons. *International Journal of Forecasting, 8*(1), 69-80.

Bäck, T., Fogel, D., & Michalewicz, Z. (Eds.). (1997). *Handbook of evolutionary computation.* New York: Oxford University Press.

Baker, J. (1987). Reducing bias and inefficiency in the selection algorithm. In J. Grefenstette (Ed.), *Proceedings of the Second International Conference on Genetic Algorithms and Their Applications* (pp. 14-21). Hillsdale, NJ: Lawrence Erlbaum Associates.

Box, G., Jenkins, G. M., & Reinsel, G. (1994). *Time series analysis: Forecasting & control* (3rd. ed.). Upper Saddle River, NJ: Prentice Hall.

Cao, L. (2003). Support vector machines experts for time series forecasting. *Neurocomputing, 51*, 321-339.

Dasgupta, D., & McGregor, D. (1992, June). Designing application-specific neural networks using the structured genetic algorithm. In *Proceedings of the International Conference on Combinations of Genetic Algorithms and Neural Networks,* Baltimore (pp. 87-96). Los Alamitos, CA: IEEE Computer Society Press.

Dempster, A. P., Laird, N. M., & Rubin, D. B. (1977). Maximum likelihood from incomplete data via the EM algorithm. *Journal of the Royal Statistical Society B, 39*(1), 1-38.

Goonatilake, S., & Khebbal, S. (1994). *Intelligent hybrid systems*. New York: John Wiley & Sons.

Haykin, S. (1999). *Neural networks — A comprehensive foundation* (2nd ed.). Upper Saddle River, NJ: Prentice Hall.

Hong, S.-G., Oh, S.-K., Kim, M.-S., & Lee, J.-J. (2002). Evolving mixture of experts for nonlinear time series modelling and prediction. *Electronics Letters, 38*(1), 34-35.

Jacobs, R., Jordan, M., Nowlan, S., & Hinton, G. (1991). Adaptive mixtures of local experts. *Neural Computation, 3*(1), 79-87.

Jordan, M., & Jacobs, R. (1994). Hierarchical mixtures of experts and the EM algorithm. *Neural Computation, 6*(2), 181-214.

Kennedy, J., & Eberhart, R. (2001). *Swarm intelligence*. San Mateo, CA: Morgan Kaufmann.

Kim, K.-H., Park, J.-K., Hwang, K.-J., & Kim, S.-H. (1995). Implementation of hybrid short-term load forecasting system using artificial neural networks and fuzzy expert systems. *IEEE Transactions on Power Systems, 10*(3), 1534-1539.

Lima, C. A. M., Coelho, A. L. V., & Von Zuben, F. J. (2002). Mixture of experts applied to nonlinear dynamic systems identification: A comparative study. In *Proceedings of the VII Brazilian Symposium on Neural Networks* (pp. 162-167). Recife, Brazil: IEEE Computer Society Press.

Mackey, M., & Glass, L. (1977). Oscillations and chaos in physiological control systems. *Science, 197*(4300), 287-289.

Man, K. F., Tang, K. S. & Kwong, S. (1999). *Genetic algorithms: Concepts and design*. New York: Springer-Verlag.

Mangeas, M., Weigend, A. S., & Muller, C. (1995). Forecasting electricity demand using nonlinear mixture of experts. In *Proceedings of the World Congress on Neural Networks* (pp. 48-53). Washington, DC.

Meila, M., & Jordan, M. I. (1997). Markov mixtures of experts. In R. Murray-Smith & T. A. Johansen (Eds.), *Multiple model approaches to modelling and control* (pp. 145-166). Taylor and Francis.

Michalewicz, Z. (1996). *Genetic algorithms + data structures = Evolution programs* (3rd ed.). Berlin, Germany: Springer-Verlag.

Peter Zhang, G. (2003). Time series forecasting using a hybrid ARIMA and neural network model, *Neurocomputing, 50*, 159-175.

Peter Zhang, G., Patuwo, B. E., & Hu, M. Y. (1998). Forecasting with artificial neural networks: The state of the art. *International Journal of Forecasting, 14*(1), 35-62.

Refenes, A. N. (1995). *Neural networks in the capital markets*. New York: John Wiley & Sons.

Ross, B. J. (1999). A Lamarckian evolution strategy for genetic algorithms. In L. D. Chambers (Ed.), *Practical handbook of genetic algorithms-complex coding systems* (pp. 1-16), Boca Raton, FL: CRC Press.

Srivastava, A. N., Su, R., & Weigend, A. S. (1999). Data mining for features using scale-sensitive gated experts. *IEEE Transactions on Pattern Analysis and Machine Intelligence, 21*(12), 1268-1279.

Titterington, D., Smith, A., & Makov, U. (1985). *Statistical analysis of finite mixture distributions*. New York: John Wiley & Sons.

Weigend A. S. & Gershenfeld, N. A. (Eds.) (1994). *Time series prediction: Forecasting the future and understanding the past.* Reading, MA: Addison-Wesley.

Weigend, A. S., Mangeas, M., & Srivastava, A. N. (1995). Nonlinear gated experts for time series: Discovering regimes and avoiding overfitting. *International Journal of Neural Systems, 6*(4), 373-399.

Whitley, D. L. (1996). Modeling hybrid genetic algorithms. In G. Winter, J. Periaux, M. Galan, & P. Cuesta (Eds.), *Genetic algorithms in engineering and computer science* (pp. 191-201). Chichester, UK: John Wiley & Sons.

Whitley, D. L., Scott Gordon, V., & Mathias, K. E. (1994). Lamarckian evolution, the Baldwin effect and function optimization. In Y. Davidor, H.-P. Schwefel, & R. Männer (Eds.), *Parallel problem solving from nature — PPSN III* (LNCS 866, pp. 6-15). Berlin: Springer.

Xu, L., Jordan, M. I., & Hinton, G. E. (1995). An alternative model for mixtures of experts. In G. Tesauro, D. S. Touretzky, & T. K. Leen (Eds.), *Advances in neural information processing systems 7* (pp. 633-640). Cambridge, MA.

Yao, X. (1999). Evolving artificial neural networks. *Proceedings of the IEEE, 87*(9), 1423-1447.

Zhang B.-T., & Joung J.-G. (1999, September). Time series prediction using committee machines of evolutionary neural trees. In *Proceedings of IEEE International Conference on Evolutionary Computation,* Washington, DC (pp. 281-286). Piscataway, NJ: IEEE Press.

Chapter VIII

Applications of Artificial Intelligence in the Process Control of Electro Chemical Discharge Machining (ECDM)

T. K. K. R. Mediliyegedara, Glasgow Caledonian University, UK

A. K. M. De Silva, Glasgow Caledonian University, UK

D. K. Harrison, Glasgow Caledonian University, UK

J. A. McGeough, The University of Edinburgh, UK

Abstract

This chapter presents the applications of artificial intelligence (AI) in the process control of electro chemical discharge machining (ECDM). The performance of the ECDM process depends on the pulse shape of the voltage and current waveforms. However, the type of the pulse and shape of the voltage and current waveforms are highly nonlinear and complex in nature. Therefore, the intelligent pulse classification systems are required for the achieve-

ment of better performance of the ECDM process. The aim of the study is to investigate the most suitable pulse classification architecture which provides the better classification accuracy with the minimum calculation time. A neural network pulse classification system (NNPCS), a fuzzy logic pulse classification system (FLPCS), and a neuro fuzzy pulse classification system (NFPCS) were developed for the pulse classification of the ECDM process. However, the NNPCS was selected as the most suitable pulse classification system for the ECDM process control system as it provides the smallest calculation time and reasonable classification accuracy.

Introduction

Fierce competition and higher customer expectations are forcing manufacturing businesses to improve quality, lower selling price, and shorten time to market. To achieve such objectives, novel techniques and tools are used in the manufacturing industry. Artificial intelligence (AI) is a novel technique that is becoming popular in various industrial applications to increase efficiency and quality and reduce the cost of production. Since the early 1960s, AI has found its way into industrial applications, mostly in the area of expert knowledge-based decision-making for the monitoring and controlling of manufacturing processes. That fact has been enhanced with advances in computer technology and the advent of fast micro-processes. The concept of intelligent control was first introduced in late 1970s. In recent years, intelligent control has emerged as one of the most active and fruitful areas of research and development within the spectrum of engineering disciplines with a variety of industrial applications.

Various manufacturing processes, such as machining, casting, forming, forging, spinning, and fabrication, are employed in the manufacturing industry. The conventional machining processes are often based on removing materials using tools harder than the workpiece. However, there are many limitations of such conventional machining processes when advanced and hard materials (e.g., hastalloy, nimonic, etc.) are to be machined economically. Unconventional manufacturing processes, such as electro discharge machining (EDM), electro chemical machining (ECM), and so forth, are used to machine very hard materials that are difficult to machine with conventional machining processes. Electro chemical discharge machining (ECDM) combines the features of EDM and ECM. Due to the inherent complex nature of the ECDM process, the applicability of conventional control approaches, which are used in ECM and EDM, are limited. Therefore, there is a need for more advanced intelligent process control approaches to improve the performance of the ECDM process. The prime objective of this chapter is to present the applications of AI in the process control of ECDM.

Background

Electro Chemical Discharge Machining

Non-conventional machining processes were developed after World War II that apply machining principles based on physical or chemical phenomena which differ substantially from those applied in traditional machining (Kruth, 1995). ECM and EDM are two of the well-established, nonconventional manufacturing processes of today. EDM is also known as electric-erosion machining or electric-spark machining, in which the material removal is achieved by the thermal action of electric discharges occurring between a tool electrode and the workpiece. ECM is a nonconventional metal removal process in which current is made to pass between a cathode tool and an anode workpiece through an electrolyte solution. In recent years, however, attention has turned toward the application of hybrid non-conventional machining processes. A hybrid nonconventional machining process is a machining process which combines two or more nonconventional machining processes. ECDM is such a hybrid nonconventional manufacturing process, combining the features of ECM and EDM. One of the major advantages of ECDM, over ECM or EDM, is that the combined metal removal mechanisms in ECDM yields a much higher machining rate (De Silva, 1988).

The ECDM process consists of a cathodic tool and an anodic workpiece (WP), which are separated by a gap filled with electrolyte, and pulsed direct current (DC) power applied between them (Figure 1). This leads to electrical discharges between the electrodes, thus achieving both electrochemical dissolution and electro discharge erosion of the workpiece (De Silva, 1988). Figure 32 of Appendix A shows the ECDM process showing the tool positioning system, pulsed power supply, and graphical user interface.

Figure 1. Schematic diagram of the electro chemical discharge machining (ECDM) process

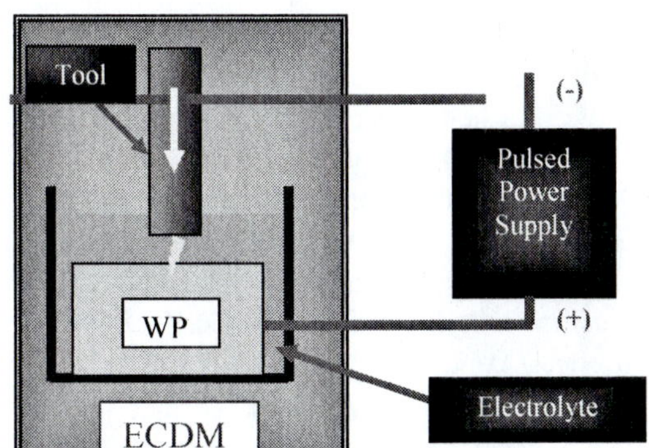

Control Problem

The performance of ECDM, in terms of surface finish and rate of machining, is affected by many factors (Mediliyegedara, De Silva, Harrison, & McGeough, 2004a). As far as the metal removal mechanism of an EDCM process is concerned, it is necessary to control the inter electrode gap (IEG) (the gap between the tool and the workpiece), electrolyte flow rate, temperature of the electrolyte, electrolyte concentration, and pulse parameters of the pulsed power supply at an optimum level to obtain higher performance in terms of the machining accuracy, the surface finish, and the metal removal rate (MRR) (Mediliyegedara, De Silva, Harrison, & McGeough, 2004b). On the other hand, it is necessary to have a secure control system to ensure the safe operation of the machine. The IEG control mechanism plays a crucial role in the ECDM process.

Knowledge of the actual gap width is necessary when generating a reference signal for the tool position control system, but there is no direct approach to measure the IEG. Therefore, it is necessary to devise a method to estimate the IEG. In the past, researchers have proposed various techniques to estimate the gap width for the EDM process and the ECM process. Average gap voltage, average working current, ignition delay time, and so forth have been used to estimate the IEG and hence act as feedback signals for the EDM process. However, it is necessary to investigate a mechanism to estimate the IEG condition of the ECDM process, which is a combination of both EDM and ECM.

One can identify five distinct types of pulses in the ECDM process: electro chemical pulse (ECP), electro chemical discharge pulse (ECDP), spark pulse (SP), arc pulse (AP), and short circuit pulse (SCP) (see Figure 2). De Silva (1988) has presented a detailed analysis of various pulses in ECDM. Mediliyegedara et al. (2004a) argued that the information about the pulse type could be used for process optimisation of the ECDM process. For this purpose, an effective and efficient pulse classification system is required. There are many approaches in the pulse classification of the EDM process such as neural networks, fuzzy logic, and so forth.

Various neural network architectures have been utilized in the past for pulse classification and modeling the EDM process. Tasi and Wang (2001) have utilised ANNs to model the metal removal rate in electro-discharge machining. Both Liu and Tarng (1997) and Kao and Tarng (1997) employed feed-forward neural networks for the online recognition of pulse types in the EDM process. Based on their results, discharge pulses were identified and then employed for controlling the EDM process.

On the other hand, researchers have employed fuzzy logic for the pulse classification and modeling the EDM process. Zheng et al. (2002) has employed a fuzzy controller to control the EDM process. They have shown that extracting fuzzy rules from dynamic data on the off-line basis makes fuzzy rules more practical than creating fuzzy rules based on the experts experience. Tarng, Tseng and Chung (1997) employed a fuzzy pulse discriminating system for EDM. Lin, Chung, and Huang (2001) showed that the accuracy of wire EDM can be improved by using fuzzy logic. Behrens and Witzak (1995) have integrated fuzzy technology in EDM process control.

However, there is still a need for an intelligent pulse classification system for the purpose of ECDM process control. This study is focused on development of an intelligent pulse classification system for pulse classification of the ECDM process. First of all, a neural

Figure 2. Ideal voltage waveforms and current waveforms for (a) ECP, (b) ECDP, (c) SP, (d) AP, and (e) SCP

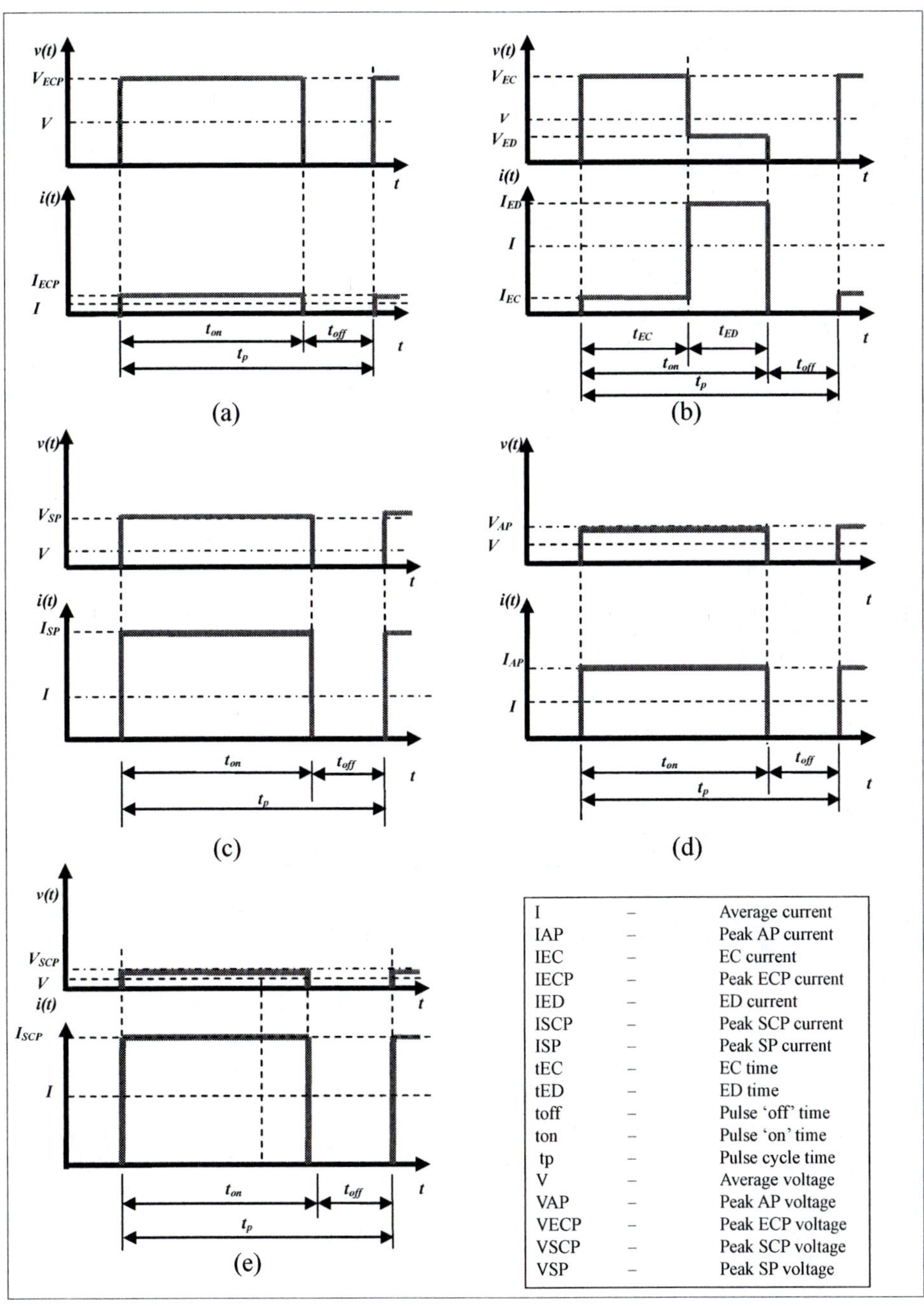

network pulse classification system (NNPCS) is developed. Then, a fuzzy logic pulse classification system (FLPCS) is developed. Finally, a neuro fuzzy pulse classification system (NFPCS) is developed.

To evaluate the performance of the pulse classification system (PCS), it is necessary to have a method to measure the classification accuracy of the PCS. The term classification accuracy (CA) is introduced to compare the performance of the PCS. One can define CA of the PCS as the average CA of each type of pulses. In general, the CA of a 'X' type pulse can be defined as follows:

$$\mathrm{CA} = \left\{ \frac{\sum_{i=1}^{n_x} x_i}{n_x} - \frac{\sum_{i=1}^{n_y} y_i}{n_y} \right\} \times 100\% \tag{1}$$

where:

x_i simulated output value from 'X' output for i^th pulse when the input values corresponds to 'X ' type pulses,

y_i simulated output value from all other outputs for the ith pulse when the input corresponds to 'X' type pulses,

n_x number of 'X' type of pulses, and

n_y number of all other type of pulses.

Neural Network Pulse Classification System (NNPCS)

When an ANN is used for the pulse classification, it is necessary to identify the most appropriate neural network architecture. As far as real-time implementation is concerned, there are many important parameters that must be investigated. First, a suitable neural network architecture must be identified. Second, one has to identify the pulse features that can be effectively used to classify pulses. Third, it is necessary to prepare a suitable training data set and a test data set. Fourth, the optimum number of layers and the number of neurons in each layer has to be decided. Fifth, it is necessary to investigate an activation function that is easy to implement, while providing acceptable classification accuracy. Finally, a training algorithm, which provides efficient training, has to be identified. In this particular application, training can be performed off-line at the designing phase. Therefore, this application does not demand an investigation of efficient training algorithms.

Neural Network Architecture

In the past, researchers have found that the feed-forward neural network architecture will provide the better performance in the pulse classification of EDM process (Liu & Tarng, 1997; Kao & Tarng, 1997). Therefore, it was decided to use a feed-forward ANN to classify pulses in the ECDM process. One of the most widely used artificial neural networks is the feed-forward neural network architecture also known as multi-layered perception (MLP) (Bermak & Bouzerdoum, 2002). The popularity of the MLP architecture stems from the existence of efficient training techniques based on the back-propagation algorithm. In a feed-forward architecture, the information propagates from the input to the output in a feed-forward manner, passing through intermediate processing layers called hidden layers. A feed-forward architecture may contain one or more hidden layers. Each hidden layer comprises processing elements, or neurons, that receive inputs only from the neurons in the preceding layer; there is no information flow between neurons residing in the same layer.

Feature Extraction

Four different features were considered when classifying pulses: peak voltage (PV), average voltage (AV), peak current (PC), and average current (AC). Since the four features were used as inputs, four neurons were used in the input layer such as I_1, I_2, I_3 and I_4. Similarly, since there are five distinct types of pulses, five output neurons are used in the output layer such as O_1, O_2, O_3, O_4 and O_5. The architecture of the NNPCS is shown in Figure 3 (Mediliyegedara, De Silva, Harrison, & McGeough, 2004c).

Figure 3. The architecture of the neural network pulse classification system (NNPCS)

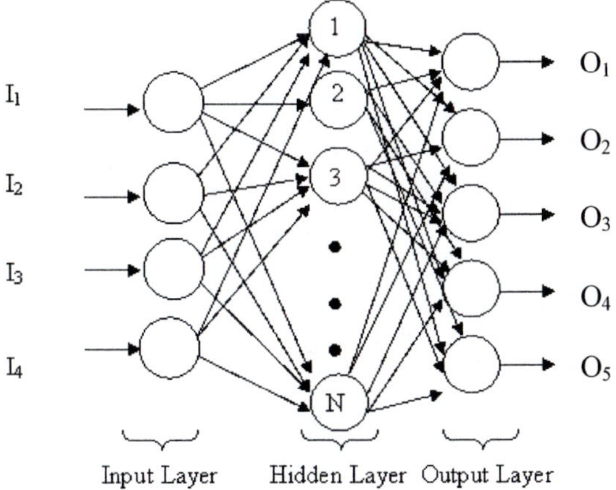

The Preparation of a Training Data Set and a Test Data Set

One hundred pulses were selected from each pulse type, and the values were calculated. PV, AV, PC, and AC were used as the features (inputs) in the ANN. Then, the numerical values of the features and the corresponding pulse types were tabulated as shown in Table 1. The second column (PV), the third column (AV), the fourth column (PC), and the fifth column (AC) in Table 1 were used as the input matrix of the ANN. Outputs of the ANN were prepared as follows. If a pulse belongs to ECP, '1' is assigned to the ECP and '0' is assigned to the other pulses. Similarly, 'ones' and 'zeros' are assigned to all the pulse types to prepare an output matrix.

The third column, the fourth column, the fifth column, the sixth column, and the seventh column of Table 2 were used to form the output matrix of the ANN. The data set was divided into two sets, the training data set and the test data set. The training data set and the test data set consist of 70 and 30 data points, respectively, for one type of pulse. Therefore, altogether, the training data set and the test data set consist of 350 and 150 data points.

Table 1. Input matrix and corresponding pulse type

Sample	PV (I_1)	AV (I_2)	PC (I_3)	AC (I_4)	Pulse Type
1	54.0178	30.6049	23.0178	14.0178	ECP
2	11.1502	24.7862	22.609	5.8516	ECDP
3	67.1547	19.4378	25.3923	7.1961	SP
4	20.607	15.7936	31.9426	14.7936	AP
5	4.3707	3.4037	36.0184	20.6126	SCP
-	-	-	-	-	-
-	-	-	-	-	-
500	2.5351	2.2427	30.2135	16.1162	SCP

Table 2. Output matrix and corresponding pulse types

Sample	Pulse Type	ECP (O_1)	ECDP (O_2)	SP (O_3)	AP (O_4)	SCP (O_5)
1	ECP	1	0	0	0	0
2	ECDP	0	1	0	0	0
3	SP	0	0	1	0	0
4	AP	0	0	0	1	0
5	SCP	0	0	0	0	1
-	-	-	-	-	-	-
-	-	-	-	-	-	-
500	SCP	0	0	0	0	1

Number of Layers and Number of Neurons in Each Layer

In the real-time implementation point of view, the fewer the number of layers, the fewer the calculation cycle time. Therefore, a FFNN with one hidden layer was considered in this study. There are four inputs in the input layer. PV, AV, PC, and AC were used as the inputs. There are five outputs: ECP, ECDP, SP, AP, and SCP. Now, one has to investigate the optimum number of neurons in the hidden layer and the best activation function having less complexity.

Investigation of the Optimum Number of Neurons in the Hidden Layer

In this section, our objective is to find out the optimum number of neurons in the hidden layer. Now, one has to select an activation function to train and simulate an ANN. In the past, researchers have found that the logistic sigmoid function (LOGSIG) gives better performance in classification applications (Bermak & Bouzerdoum, 2002). Therefore, LOGSIG were used as the activation functions throughout the neural network. The number of neurons in the hidden layer (N) was varied from one to ten. Therefore, altogether, 10 different FFNNs were created.

Training and Simulation of the Neural Networks

First, a FFNN with one hidden layer was created and trained using the training data set. In the training phase, 10000 epochs were used, and the final root mean square error goal was set to be 0.00001. Then, the trained neural network was simulated using a test data set. The structure of the test data set is shown in Table 3.

After that, CA was calculated using Equation 1. Similarly, 10 FFNNs were created, trained, and simulated by increasing the number of neurons in the hidden layer by one at a time. Figure 4 shows the root mean square error curve (RMSE) when training the ANN (with N=6).

Table 3. Structure of the test data set

Data Points	1-30	31-60	61-90	91-120	121-150
Pulse Type	ECP	ECDP	SP	AP	SCP

Figure 4. Root mean square error vs. number of epochs

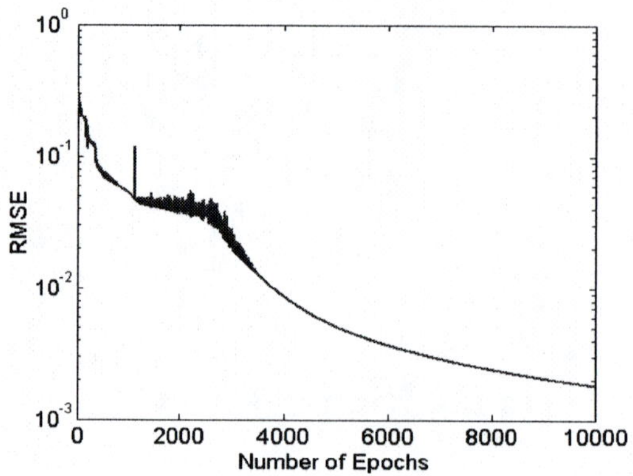

Figure 5. Classification accuracy vs. number of neurons in the hidden layer

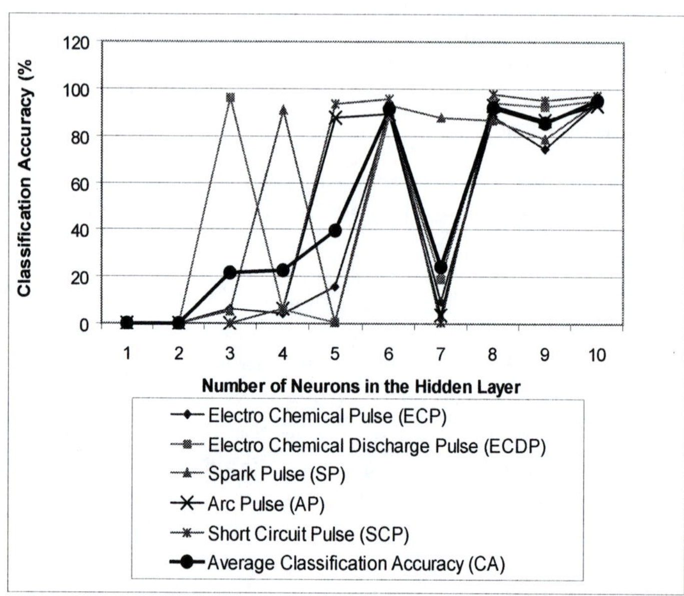

Classification Accuracy vs. Number of Neurons in the Hidden Layer

Figure 5 shows classification accuracy (CA) versus number of neurons in the hidden layer (N). It is possible to identify from Figure 5 that the average classification accuracy (ACA) is a maximum when N=6 and N=10.

As far as the implementation is concerned, N=6 is a more suitable network architecture. Therefore, an ANN with six neurons was used to simulate the test data set.

Simulated Results

The simulated results, which are shown in the following Figures 6 through 10, are corresponding to a trained ANN having six neurons in the hidden layer (i.e., N=6). Vertical axes (Y) of following graphs indicate the output values of the neural network. In the ideal situation, if a pulse is an ECP, then the output value from node O_1 should be equal to '1'. Other output values (O_2, O_3, O_4 and O_5) should be equal to '0'. Figure 6 shows the output O_1 is nearly equal to '1', for the first 30 pulses. This means the first 30 pulses have been classified as ECP by the ANN. Similarly Figures 7 through 10 show the output values from node O_2, O_3, O_4 and O_5, respectively.

Table 4 summarises the classification accuracies for the five different pulse types mentioned. The overall classification accuracy of the proposed neural network is 91%.

Figure 6. Simulated output from node O_1

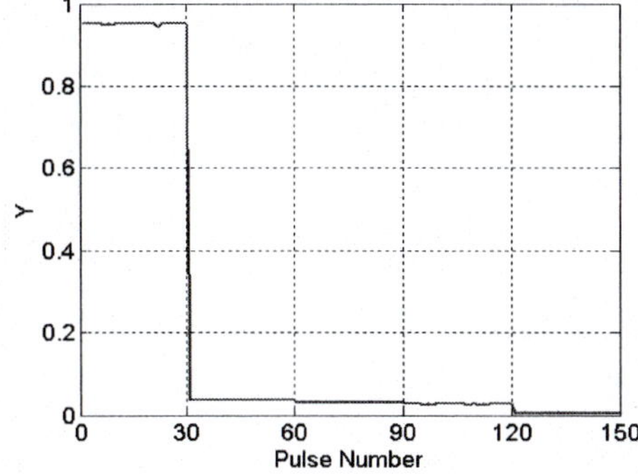

Figure 7. Simulated output from node O_2

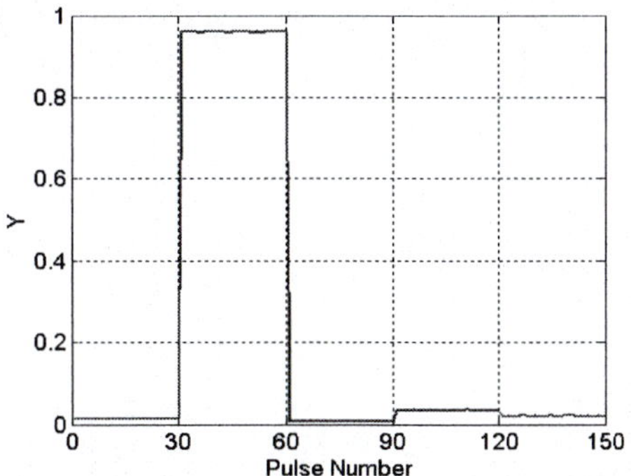

Figure 8. Simulated output from node O_3

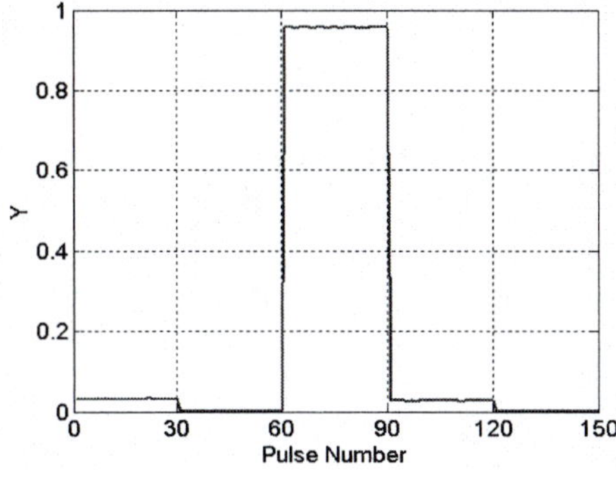

Figure 9. Simulated output from node O_4

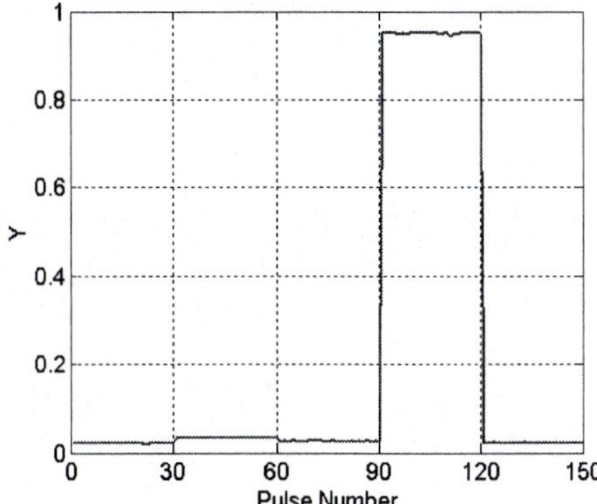

Figure 10. Simulated output from node O_5

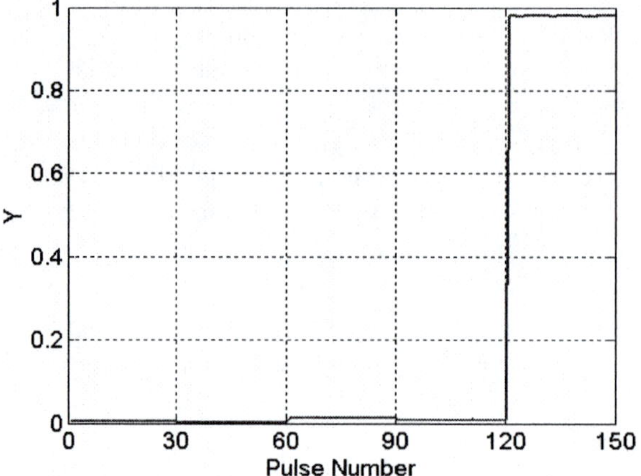

Table 4. Classification accuracies

Pulse Type	Classification Accuracy (%)
EC P	90.24
ECDP	88.05
SP	92.93
AP	89.31
SCP	95.43
Average	91.19

Fuzzy Logic Pulse Classification System

As far as real-time implementation of FLPCS is concerned, many important parameters must be investigated. First, it is necessary to investigate suitable features, which describe the pulse shapes effectively. Those features can be used as inputs of the FPCS. FPCS is composed of three calculation steps: fuzzification, fuzzy inference, and defuzzification. The linguistic rule base of the classifier implements the classification strategy.

The block, in which the fuzzification is performed, is known as a fuzzifier. The second step where the linguistic rule base is derived is known as fuzzy inference. The block, in which the fuzzy inference is performed, is known as an inference engine. The last step is the defuzzification step in which the linguistic variables are translated back into real numerical values. The block, in which the defuzzification is performed, is known as a defuzzifier.

Figure 11. A block diagram of the fuzzy logic pulse classification system (FLPCS)

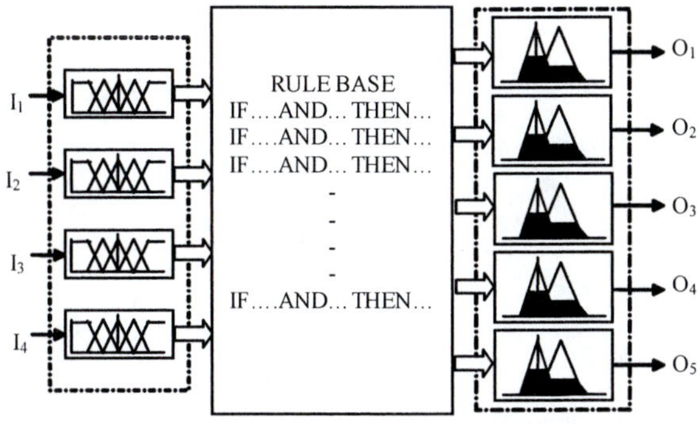

Selection of Input and Output Variables

A block diagram of a fuzzy logic pulse classification system (FLPCS) is shown in Figure 11 (Mediliygedara et al., 2004d). There are four input variables: I_1, I_2, I_3, and I_4. Normalised values of peak voltage (PV), average voltage (AV), peak current (PC), and average current (AC) of a pulse were used as I_1, I_2, I_3 and I_4 respectively. There are five outputs: O_1, O_2, O_3, O_4, and O_5, corresponding to ECP, ECDP, SP, AP, and SCP.

Fuzzification

Five linguistic terms were used to create the input linguistic variables so that the fuzzy rule base can be developed easily: very small (VS), small (S), medium (M), large (L), and very large (VL). Membership functions of input variables, such as normalised values of I_1, I_2, I_3, and I_4, are shown in Figures 12 through 15.

Figure 12. Membership functions of the normalized peak voltage (I_1)

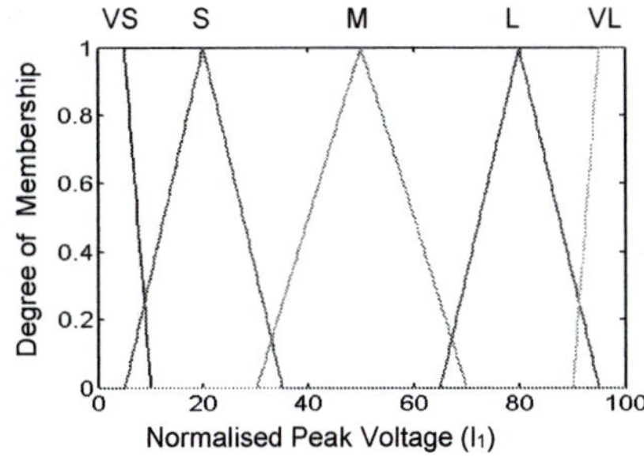

Figure 13. Membership functions of the normalized average voltage (I_2)

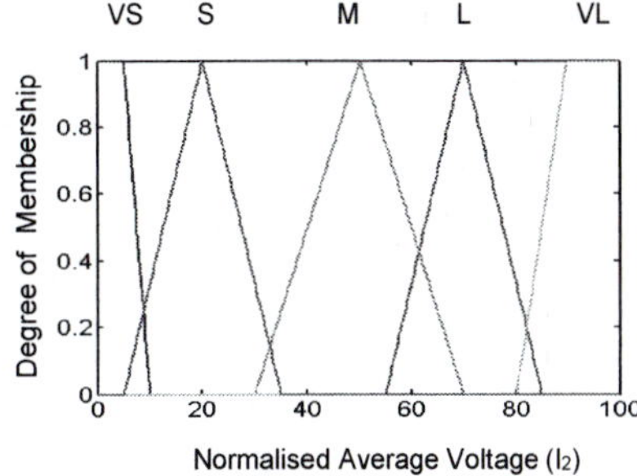

Figure 14. Membership functions of the normalized peak current (I_3)

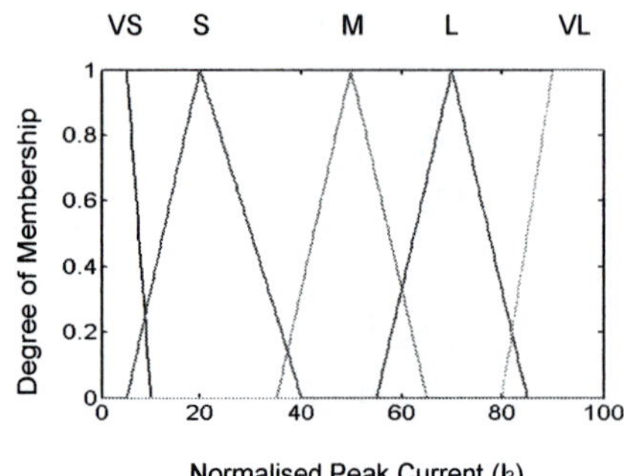

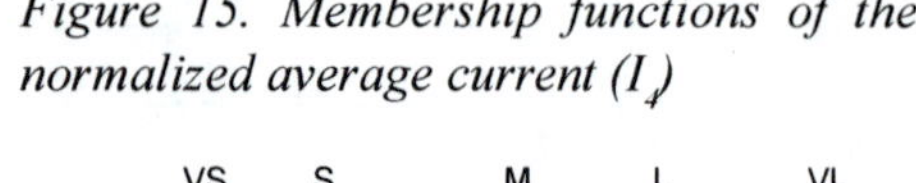

Figure 15. Membership functions of the normalized average current (I_4)

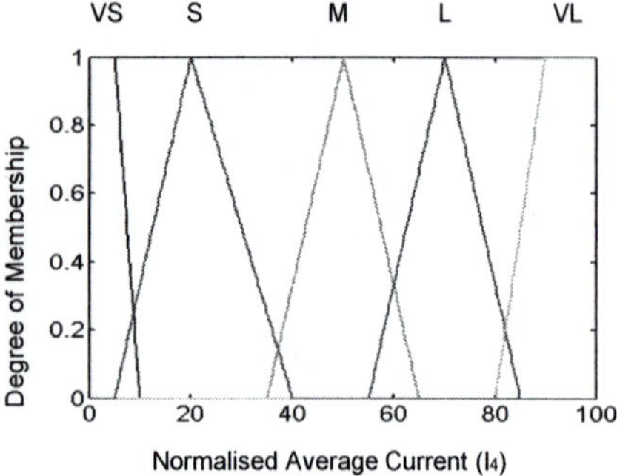

Table 5. Fuzzy rule base for the pulse classification of the ECDM process

	ECP	ECDP	SP	AP	SCP
PV	L	S	L+VL	S	VS
AV	L+VL	L	M	M	S
PC	M	M	L+VL	L+VL	L+VL
AC	M+L	S	S	M+L	L+VL

Fuzzy Rule Base

The fuzzy rule base contains the expert knowledge, which is necessary to classify pulses. In the pulse classification of the ECDM, there are four input variables each having five linguistic terms. Therefore, the number of possible rules is $5^4 = 625$, but some rules do not exist in the normal operation. So, it is possible to identify fuzzy rules which are relevant to the normal operation conditions. If PV, AV, PC, and PV are S, L, M, and S, respectively, then the corresponding pulse is ECDP and so on. The complete rule base is shown in Table 5.

Defuzzification

The mean of the maximum defuzzification method was employed. Two linguistic terms were used to create the output linguistic variables such as 'Yes' (Y) and 'No' (N). Membership functions of all output variables (O_1, O_2, O_3, O_4 and O_5) are in the same shape. Figure 16 shows the membership functions of the output corresponding to ECP (O_1) of the fuzzy pulse classification system.

Figure 16. Membership functions of the outputs O_1, O_2, O_3, O_4, O_5

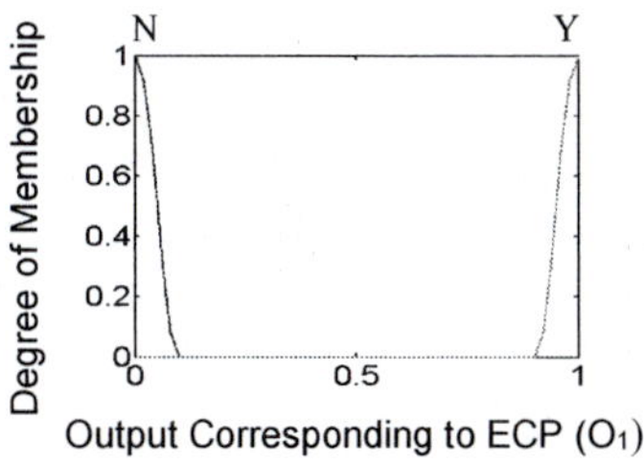

Table 6. Structure of the test data set

Data Points	1-30	31-60	61-90	91-120	121-150
Pulse Type	ECP	ECDP	SP	AP	SCP

Preparation of Test Data Set

Thirty pulses were selected from each pulse type. The normalised values of PV, AV, PC, and AC were calculated and were used as the inputs for FPCS. The test data set, the structure of which is shown in Table 6, consists of 150 data points.

Simulated Results

The simulated results are shown Figures 17 through 21. The vertical axes (Y) of the graphs indicate the output values of the FLPCS. In the ideal situation, if a pulse is an ECP, then the value of the output O_1 should be equal to '1'. Other output values (O_2, O_3, O_4, and O_5) should be equal to '0'. Figure 17 shows the output O_1 is nearly equal to '1', for the first 30 pulses.

Figure 17. Simulated values for output corresponding to electro chemical pulses (O_1)

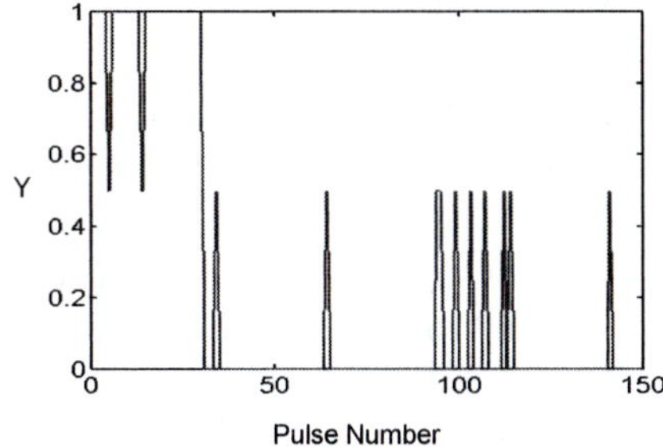

Figure 18. Simulated values for output corresponding to electro chemical discharge pulses (O_2)

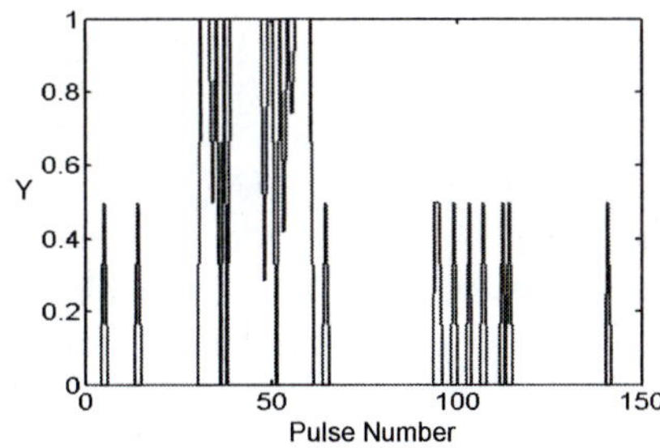

Figure 19. Simulated values for output corresponding to spark pulses (O_3)

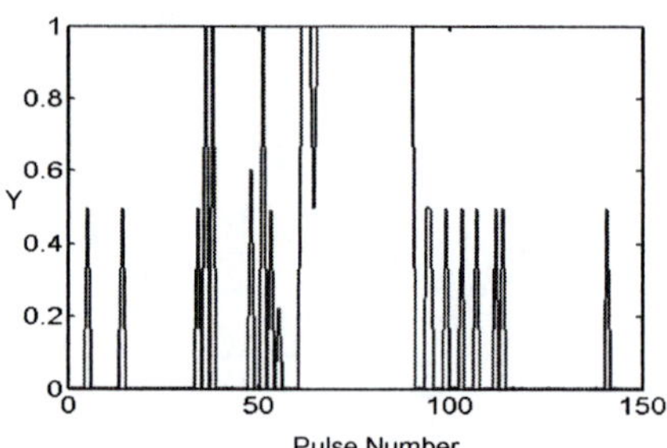

Figure 20. Simulated values for output corresponding to arc pulses (O_4)

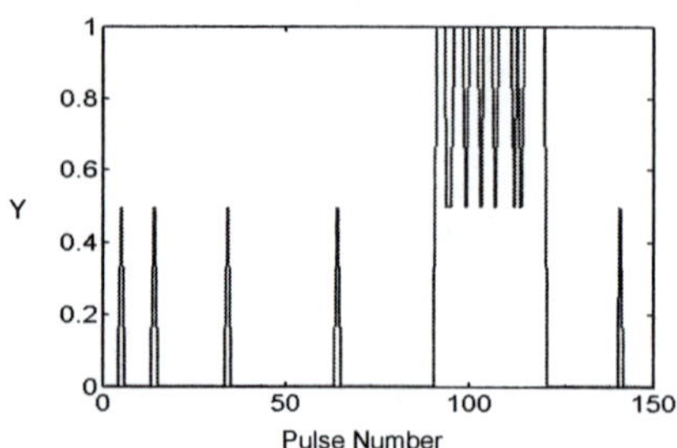

Figure 21. Simulated values for output corresponding to short circuit pulses (O_3)

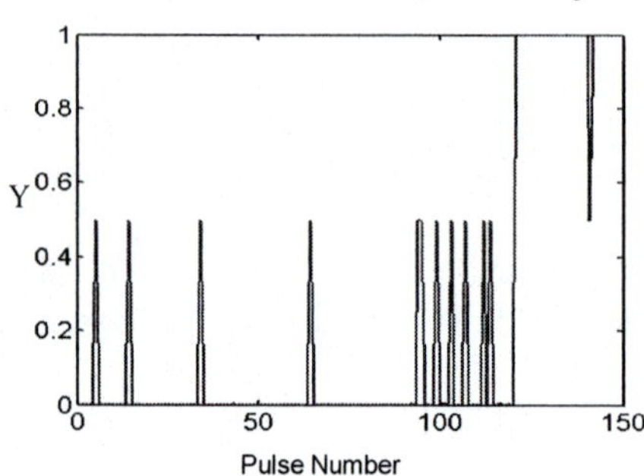

Table 7. Classification accuracies

Pulse Type	Classification Accuracy (%)
EC P	92.50
ECDP	78.56
SP	89.99
AP	86.11
SCP	93.60
Average	88.15

This means the first 30 pulses have been classified as ECP by the FPCS. Similarly, Figure 18, Figure 19, Figure 20, and Figure 21 show the values of the output O_2, O_3, O_4, and O_5.

Table 7 summarises the classification accuracies for the five different pulse types mentioned. The average classification accuracy of the FLPCS is 88 %.

Neuro Fuzzy Pulse Classification System (NFPCS)

Adaptive Neuro Fuzzy Inference Systems

An adaptive neuro fuzzy inference system (ANFIS) provides a method for the fuzzy modeling procedure to learn information about a data set, in order to compute the membership function parameters that best allow the associated fuzzy inference system to track the given input / output data. The parameters associated with the membership functions will change through the learning process. The computation of these parameters is facilitated by a gradient vector, which provides a measure of how well the fuzzy inference system is modeling the input / output data for a given set of parameters. As far as real-time implementation is concerned, many important parameters must be investigated. First, it is necessary to investigate suitable features which describe the pulse shapes effectively. Those features can be used as inputs of the ANFIS. Second, the architecture of the fuzzy inference system must be investigated.

A Neuro Fuzzy Pulse Classification System (NFPCS) for the ECDM Process

The neuro fuzzy pulse classification system (NFPCS) is composed of five ANFISs, namely, ANFIS1, ANFIS2, ANFIS3, ANFIS4, and ANFIS5 (Figure 22) (Mediliyegedara, De Silva, Harrison, & McGeough, 2004e).

There are four input variables: peak voltage (PV), average voltage (AV), peak current (PC), and average current (AC). There is one output per each ANFIS, namely, O_1, O_2, O_3, O_4, and O_5. Outputs O_1, O_2, O_3, O_4, and O_5 are corresponding to ECP, ECDP, SP, AP, and SP, respectively.

Preparation of Data Set

The second column (PV), the third column (AV), the fourth column (PC), and the fifth column (AC) in Table 8 are used as the input matrix for the NFPCS. The outputs of the NFPCS are prepared as follows. If a pulse belongs to ECP, '1' is assigned to the ECP and '0' is assigned to the other pulses. Similarly, 'ones' and 'zeros' are assigned to all the pulse types to prepare an output matrix.

Figure 22. Achitecture of the neuro fuzzy inference system

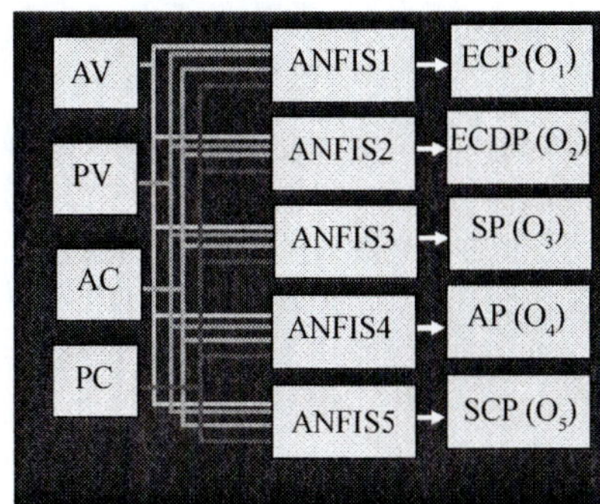

Table 8. The training data set

Sample	PV	AV	PC	AC	Pulse Type	Outputs				
						O_1	O_2	O_3	O_4	O_5
1	54.0	30.6	23.0	14.0	ECP	1	0	0	0	0
2	11.1	24.7	22.6	5.8	ECDP	0	1	0	0	0
3	67.1	19.4	25.3	7.1	SP	0	0	1	0	0
4	20.6	15.7	31.9	14.7	AP	0	0	0	1	0
5	4.3	3.4	36.0	20.6	SCP	0	0	0	0	1
-	-	-	-	-	-	-	-	-	-	-
-	-	-	-	-	-	-	-	-	-	-
500	2.5	2.2	30.2	16.1	SCP	0	0	0	0	1

Results

The ANFIS has generated four bell curve shape membership functions per each input. Figures 23 through 26 show the membership functions for PV, AV, PC, and AC, respectively.

The test data set was prepared as follows. Data points from 1 to 30 correspond to the ECPs. Data points from 31 to 60 correspond to the ECDPs, and so on. In all, there are 150 data points. The structure of the data set is shown in Table 9.

The simulated results are shown in Figures 27 through 31. The vertical axes (Y) of the graphs indicate the output values of the NFPCS. In the ideal situation, if a pulse is an ECP, then the value of the output O_1 should be equal to '1'. Other output values (O_2, O_3, O_4 and O_5) should be equal to '0'. Figure 27 shows the output O_1 is nearly equal to '1', for the first 30 pulses. That means the first 30 pulses have been classified as ECP by the NFPCS. Similarly, Figures 28 through 31 show values of the output O_2, O_3, O_4, and O_5.

Table 10 summarises the classification accuracies for the five different pulse types mentioned. The average classification accuracy of the NFPCS is 97 %.

Cycle times of the classification systems were obtained. Table 11 summarises average classification accuracy and cycle time of the pulse classification systems.

From Table 11, it is possible to observe that the average classification accuracy of NFPCS outperformed that of NNPCS and FLPCS. However, NNPCS provides the smallest cycle time, hence the minimum calculation overhead. Therefore, NNPCS was selected as the most suitable pulse classification system for the ECDM process.

Figure 23. Membership functions of the normalised peck voltage (PV)

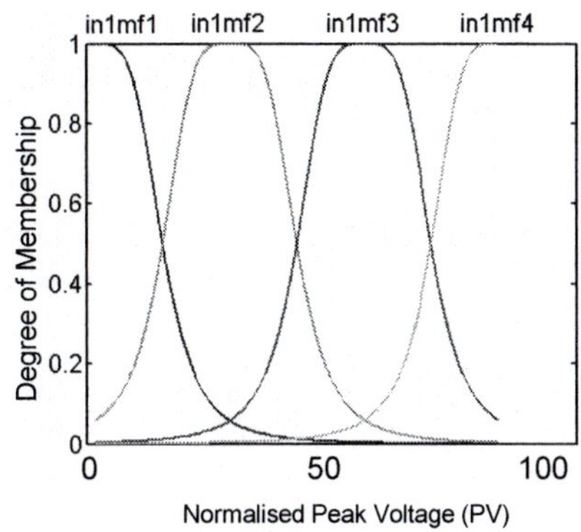

Figure 24. Membership functions of the normalised average voltage (AV)

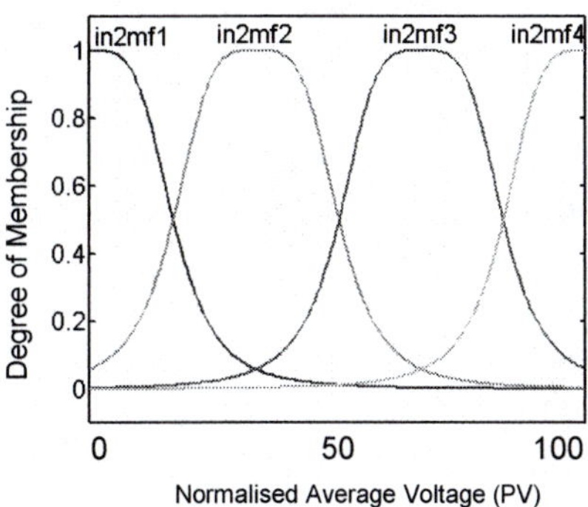

Figure 25. Membership functions of the normalised peck current (PC)

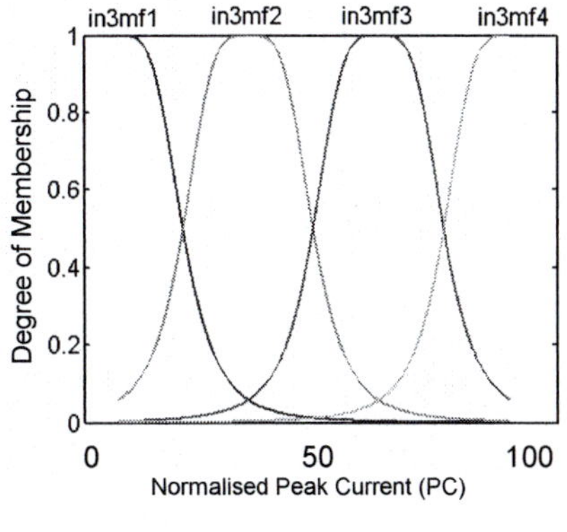

Figure 26. Membership functions of the normalised average current (AC)

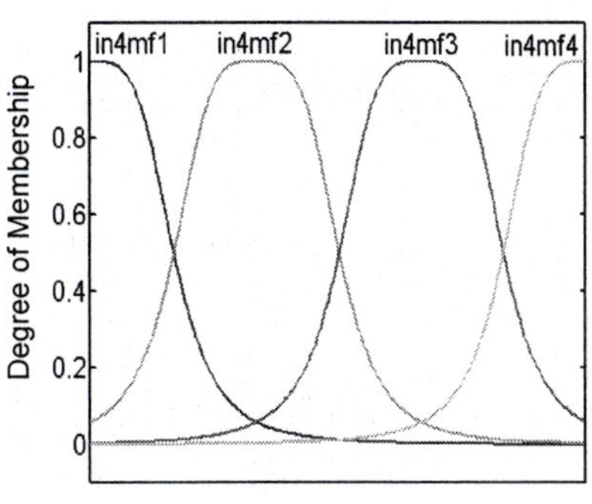

Normalised Peak Current (PC)

Figure 27. Simulated values from the output O_1

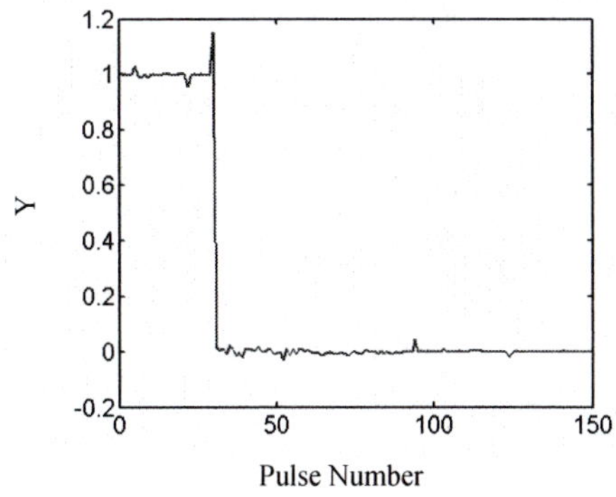

Figure 28. Simulated values from the output O_2

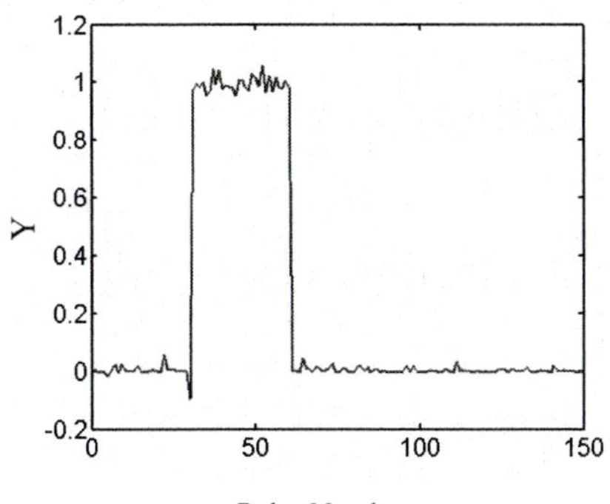

Table 9. Structure of the test data set

Data Points	1-30	31-60	61-90	91-120	121-150
Pulse Type	ECP	ECDP	SP	AP	SCP

Figure 29. Simulated values from the output O_3

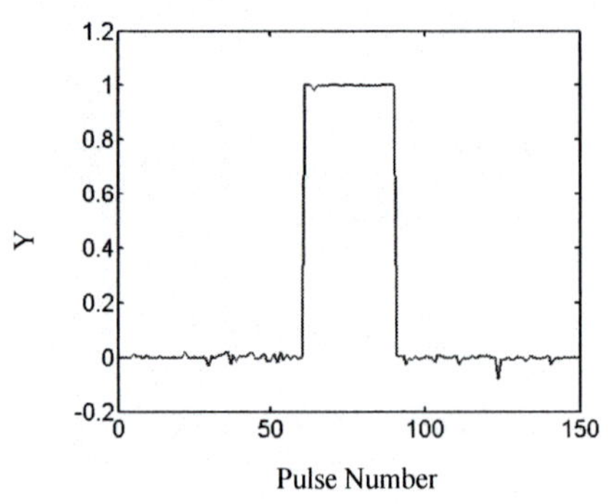

Figure 30. Simulated values from the output O_4

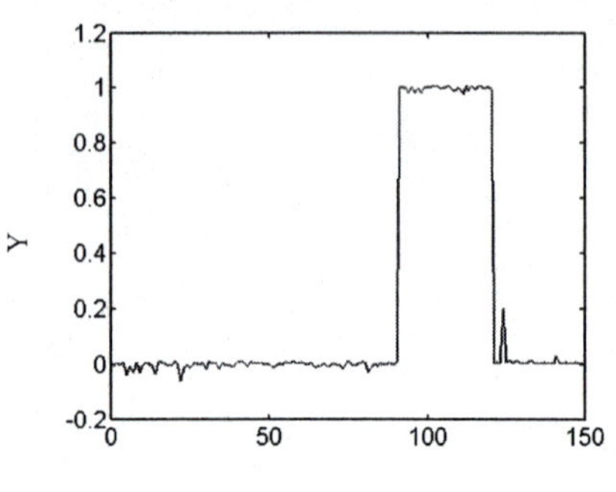

Figure 31. Simulated values from the output O_5

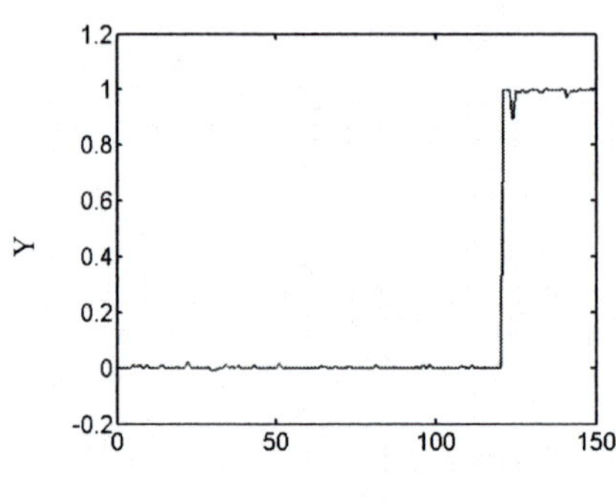

Table 10. Classification accuracies

Pulse Type	Classification Accuracy (%)
ECP	96.2
ECDP	97.1
SP	96.6
AP	98.1
SCP	97.6
Average	97.1

Table 11. Average classification accuracy and cycle time of the pulse classification systems

Pulse Classification System	Average Classification Accuracy (%)	Cycle Time (ms)
NNPCS	91	0.26
FLPCS	88	1.71
NFPCS	97	2.52

Implementation

The ECDM process (Figure 32) consists of three main systems: pulsed power supply system (PPSS), working fluid circulation system (WFCS), and pulse classification and control system (PCCS). The pulsed power supply is responsible for providing electrical energy to the inter electrode gap (IEG) in a controlled manner.

It is possible to set the maximum current and the maximum voltage of the pulsed power supply. The fluid circulation system is responsible for maintaining electrolyte parameters such as conductivity, pH, and so forth at a constant level and maintaining the electrolyte flow rate through the IEG. The WFCS consists of a high pressure pump, a main working fluid tank, and a filtering system. The process control system is responsible for monitoring the IEG conditions and maintaining the IEG at an optimum level. The overall architecture of the pulse classification and process control system is shown in Figure 33.

A NI-PCI-7342 motion controller was used to implement the control algorithm of the TPCS. A NI-PCI-5112 8-Bit digitiser was used to obtain the voltage and current waveform parameters in the inter-electrode gap. A CV3-200 / SP8 voltage transducer (VT) and a CSNP-661 current transducer (CT) were employed to obtain the inter-electrode gap voltage and the working current waveforms. A PC having Intel Pentium IV 2 GHz processor and a 512 Mb random access memory (RAM) was used to implement the process control algorithm. A PIC 18F512 micro controller based pre-processing unit was employed to isolate, filter, and process the voltage and current signals. In the pre-processing stage, the peak values

Figure 32. The ECDM process showing tool positioning system, pulsed power supply, and graphical user interface (GUI)

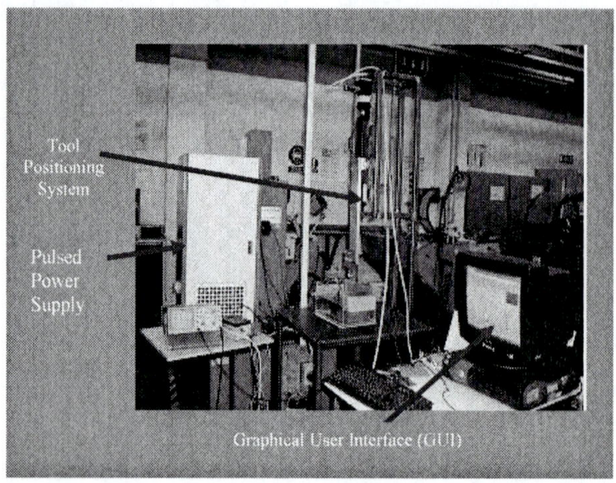

Figure 33. A block diagram of the intelligent process control system of the ECDM process

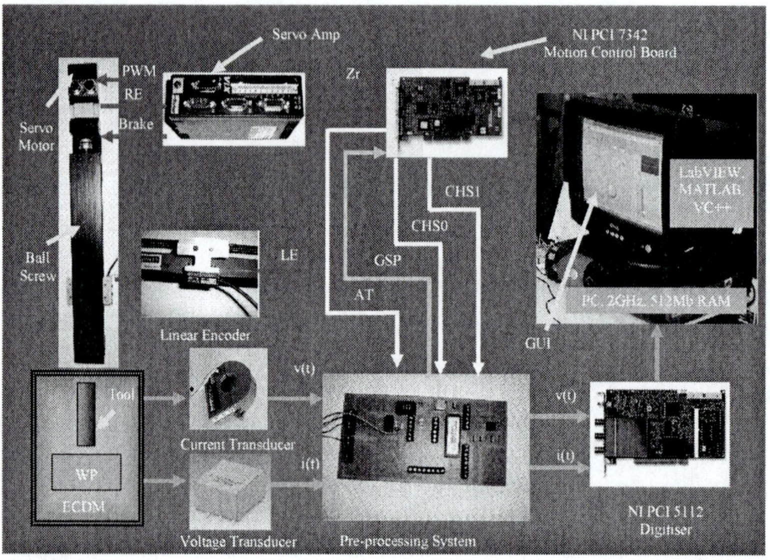

and the root mean square (RMS) values of current and voltage waveforms were calculated. The motion controller and the digitiser were fitted to the PC via the peripheral component interconnect (PCI) bus. The LabVIEW 7 package was used to develop the graphical user interface (GUI) and pulse classification system, and the process control algorithm was implemented in LabVIEW by embedding a MATLAB script.

Future Trends

There are many potential applications of AI in non-conventional manufacturing processes such as EDM, ECM, ECDM, and so forth. Since the system dynamics of EDM, ECM, and ECDM are highly nonlinear, stochastic, and complex in nature, AI can be applied for the process optimisation. On the other hand, the process performance, such as material removal rate (MRR) and surface finish (SF), can be predicted using integrated intelligent information systems (IIIS). Future research work by the authors will be focused on the applications of IIIS systems in process optimisation and prediction of performance of the EDM, ECM, and ECDM processes.

Conclusion

A neural network pulse classification system (NNPCS), a fuzzy logic pulse classification system (FLPCS), and a neuro fuzzy pulse classification system (NFPCS) for the pulse classification of the ECDM process have been established and analysed based on the process variables. Four features — PV, AV, PC, and AC — were used successfully for the classification of pulses in the ECDM process. The term classification accuracy (CA) was defined to measure the performance of a pulse classification system. The simulation results showed that the feed-forward network with six neurons in the hidden layer could be successfully used in the pulse classification of the ECDM process with average classification accuracy of 91%. Further, it was observed that the CA of the FLPCS is 88%. FLPCS consists of four inputs, five outputs, and 28 fuzzy rules. The CA of NFPCS, which consists of five ANFISs, is 97%. However, NNPCS provides the smallest cycle time, hence the minimum calculation overhead. Therefore, NNPCS was selected as the most suitable pulse classification system for the ECDM process, conclusively showing an effective pulse classification tool has been established for the real-time process control of the ECDM process.

References

Behrens, A., & Witzak M. P. (1995). Integrating fuzzy technology in EDM process control. *11th International Symposium for Electromachining (ISEM-XI),* Lausanne, Switzerland (pp. 287-293).

Bermak, A., & Bouzerdoum, A. (2002). VLSI implementation of a neural network classifier based on the saturating linear activation function. In *Proceedings of the 9th International Conference on Neural Information Processing*, Orchid Country Club, Singapore.

De Silva, A. K. (1988). *Process developments in electrochemical arc machining.* Unpublished doctoral dissertation, University of Edinburgh, UK.

Kao, J. Y., & Tarng, Y. S. (1997). A neural network approach for the on-line monitoring of the electrical discharge machining process. *Journal of Material Processing Technology, 69*, 112-119.

Kruth, J. P. (1995). Rapid prototyping — A new application of physical and chemical processors for material accretion manufacturing. In *Proceedings of the 11th International Symposium for Electro Machining (ISEM XI)*, Lausanne, Switzerland (pp. 3-27).

Lin, C. T., Chung, I. F., & Huang, S. Y. (2001). Improvement of machining accuracy by fuzzy logic at corner parts for wire-EDM. *Fuzzy Sets and Systems, 122*, 499-511.

Liu, H. S., & Tarng, Y. S. (1997). Monitoring of the electrical discharge machining process by adaptive networks. *International Journal of Advance Manufacturing Technology, 13*, 264-270.

Mediliyegedara, T. K. K. R., De Silva, A. K. M., Harrison, D. K., & McGeough, J. A. (2004a). An intelligent pulse classification system for electro chemical discharge machining (ECDM) — A preliminary study. *Journal of Material Processing Technology, 149*, 499-503.

Mediliyegedara, T. K. K. R., De Silva, A. K. M., Harrison, D. K., & McGeough, J. A. (2004b). An intelligent gap with controller for electro chemical discharge machining (ECDM) machine. In *Proceedings of the 4th CIRP Seminar on Intelligent Computation in Manufacturing Engineering (ICME 2004)*, Sorrento, Italy (pp. 473-478).

Mediliyegedara, T. K. K. R., De Silva, A. K. M., Harrison, D. K., & McGeough, J. A. (2004c). Feature extraction and pulse classification electro chemical discharge machining (ECDM) — Artificial neural network Approach. In *Proceedings of the 9th Online World Conference on Soft Computing in Industrial Applications.*

Mediliyegedara, T. K. K. R., De Silva, A. K. M., Harrison, D. K., & McGeough, J. A. (2004d). Fuzzy logic approach for the pulse classification of electro chemical discharge machining (ECDM) machine. In *Proc. of the 34th Int. MATADOR Conference*, Manchester, UK (pp. 161-166).

Mediliyegedara, T. K. K. R., De Silva, A. K. M., Harrison, D. K., & McGeough, J. A. (2004e). An adaptive fuzzy inference system for the process control of electro chemical discharge machining (ECDM) process. In *Proceedings of the 4th International Conference on Monitoring and Automatic Supervision in Manufacturing (AC'04)*, Zakopane, Poland.

Mediliyegedara, T. K. K. R., De Silva, A. K. M., Harrison, D. K., McGeough, J. A., Hepburn D., & McKenna P. (2004f). Design and development of an intelligent process controller in LabVIEW environment for electro chemical discharge machining (ECDM). *Control 2004. Symposium*, Bath, UK.

Tarng, Y. S., Tseng C. M., & Chung, L. K. (1997). A fuzzy pulse discriminating system for electrical discharge machining. *International Journal of Machine Tool Manufacture, 37*(4), 511-522.

Tasi, K. M., & Wang, P. J. (2001). Comparisons of neural network models on material removal rate in electrical discharge machining. *Journal of Materials Processing Technology, 117*, 111-124.

Zheng, H., Liu, Q. B., Gou, Y. F., Zhao, W. S., Kong, Z. Y., & Liu, J. C. (1998). A fuzzy controller for EDM process. In *Proceedings of the 12th International Symposium for Electromachining (ISEM-XII)*, Aachen, Germany (pp. 185-191).

Section III:

Innovative Intelligent Computing, Information, and Control

Chapter IX

Neural Networks and 3D Edge Genetic Template Matching for Real-Time Face Detection and Recognition

Stephen Karungaru, University of Tokushima, Japan

Minoru Fukumi, University of Tokushima, Japan

Norio Akamatsu, University of Tokushima, Japan

Abstract

This chapter describes a novel system that can track and recognize faces in real-time using neural networks and genetic algorithms. The main feature of this system is a 3D facemask that, combined with a neural network-based face detector and adaptive template matching using genetic algorithms, is capable of detecting and recognizing faces in real-time. Neural network learning and template matching enable size and pose invariant face detection and recognition, while the genetic algorithm optimizes the searching algorithms, enabling real-time usage of the system. It is hoped that this chapter will show how and why neural networks and genetic algorithms are well suited to solve complex pattern recognition problems like the one presented in this chapter.

Introduction and Background

Given a real-time visual scene, the process of automatically detecting and recognizing faces can be very complex. This is because of the many factors that must be taken into account when attempting such a task. These factors range from scene characteristics (e.g., lighting, background, etc.) to facial factors (e.g., expression, size, orientation, and location). Other factors include system accuracy, speed, reliability, and the ability to easily change or upgrade the system to adapt to the ever-changing situations. However, if accomplished, real-time face tracking and recognition can find numerous application areas at home, in the office, in cars, security, surveillance, entertainment, computer interface, robotics, and so forth.

This chapter describes how genetic algorithms and neural networks can be used for real-time face detection and recognition. The basic face detector is a three-layered back propagation-trained neural network using frontal face images of a fixed size (40x40 pixels). Faces that are larger than this size and of other orientations can be searched for using a genetic algorithm-guided 3D face template matching. For the system to perform well on real-time images, genetic information inheritance is used to estimate the position, size, and pose of the face in the next frame. Genetic information inheritance aids the genetic algorithm in converging rapidly, allowing more time for face recognition. Face recognition is carried out using a hybrid system made up of a neural network and template matching methods.

The use of genetic information inheritance from frame to frame and robust searching using genetic algorithms are the main points in this chapter. The methods provide this system with high speed and detection rates. In addition, color information is only used mainly at the beginning of the search to initialize the genetic algorithm. Another strong point of this system is the use of similar methods and features for both face detection and recognition. At a rate of 60 milliseconds per frame, it is not easy to tune different methods to perform both functions effectively. Moreover, a random sampling method is used to increase the data used to train the neural networks, reducing the number of face samples that must be collected beforehand.

This work was carried out using a Sony IEEE1394 SDK FWLink-4001 digital camera at 15 frames per second. The selected image size was 320x240 pixels. The camera data is in YCrCb format, accessed using a MFC application. A Dell Precision 370 Pentium IV computer was used to perform computer simulations.

The rest of this chapter is organized as follows. The third section looks at other works related to this one. Face detection including all the processes required for size and pose invariance (e.g., genetic algorithms) are described in the fourth section. The next section is dedicated to face recognition where the neural network and template matching methods are explained. Results and discussions are in the sixth section and the seventh section concludes this chapter. The last section offers an insight on the future direction this research area is likely to go.

Related Work

A robust real-time object detector using an integral image is proposed by Viola and Jones (2004) that achieved good results. However, their system is rather complex because it involves a combination of a wide range of methods. Bartlett, Littlewort, Fasel, and Movellan (2003) propose a real-time face detection system based on Viola's work. The system was trained using 8,000 face examples and millions of non-face examples. However, the system is for frontal faces only and has to sweep the image several times to detect faces larger than the training size. Fasel, Fortenberry, and Movellan (2004) propose a probabilistic model of image generation and apply it to real-time face and eye blink detection. In this method, again, the faces need to be almost frontal and the subjects need to be near the camera. Rowley, Baluja, and Kanade (1998) propose a face classifier using neural networks for still images. Yang, Kriegman, and Ahuja (2002) offers a comprehensive survey of face detection methods. Off-line face recognition has been the center of research in many a researchers work for a long time. Li and Lu (1999) present a novel classification method called the nearest feature line that achieved a 3.125% error rate for the ORL database. A method using wavelet sub band representation and kernel associative memory is proposed by Zhang, Zhang, Li, and Cheng (2004). Yan, He, Hu, Zhang, Li, and Cheng (2004) use Bayesian shape localization for local and global textures to recognize faces. A 96% accuracy on the Yale database is reported. Face recognition using independent component analysis of Gabor features is proposed by Liu and Wechsler (2003). Sukthakar (2000) reports on biologically inspired approaches for face recognition and discusses five methods. These are neuro-physiological (Desmore, 1998), principal component analysis (Turk & Pentland, 1991), elastic bunch graph matching (Wislott, Fellous, Kruger, & Malsbnurg, 1997), human perception (Hancock, Bruce, & Burton, 1998), and nearest neighbor (Sim, Sukthakar, Miller, & Baluja, 1999).

The requirement of the face to be frontal and its proximity to the camera is what really separates the work described in this chapter from these works. The system here attempts to detect and recognize faces in spite of these conditions. In fact, apart from limiting the number of subjects in the camera view at any time to a maximum of three, this work has no other special requirements.

Face Detection

For most processes dealing with the face, the position, size, and orientation of the face in a visual scene must be initially extracted. In this section, a neural network-based face detector (NND) that can detect faces of frontal orientations and fixed size will be discussed. Then, a method to extend the NND to detect faces of all orientations and sizes using a 3D facemask and genetic algorithms will be presented.

Neural Network-Based Face Detector

Neural networks have been shown to be excellent classifiers in complex pattern classification problems. One such challenge is face detection because of the many factors that must be resolved. A face detection system should detect all faces regardless of their rotation, size expression, or the illumination present. Moreover, since face detection is a step before face recognition, it must work at high speeds and accuracy, otherwise the results of face recognition will not be satisfactory.

Structure and Input Image Size

The speed of training and testing the neural network depends on its structure and number of nodes in its layers (especially the input layer). After trying out many neural network structures with speed and accuracy in mind, the face detector was selected to be a three-layered back propagation trained neural network. The size of the training samples was set at 40x40 pixels because experimentation showed that this is the smallest size offering the best trade-off between speed and accuracy of the system and also because facial edges could be extracted accurately.

The edges of the image are used to represent the inputs. The edges are extracted using Laplacian of Gaussian and median filters and then matched to the best fitting edge model. The Laplacian of Gaussian (LoG) filter is applied first to smooth and detect the edges of the facial features. In this filter, a large kernel (e.g., 15x15) produces good edge detection (Figure 1a), but its computation time is high due to the large kernel size. After several experiments, a trade-off kernel of 7x7 was employed, but a lot of noise was produced (Figure 1b). Therefore, a 3x3 medium filter was then applied to reduce this noise. The cost of calculation for a 7x7 LoG filter followed by a 3x3 medium filter is 30% less than for a 15x15 LoG that produced similar results (Figure 1c). Edges found are highlighted using white and non-edges using black. The edges around the eyes and the mouths are further enhanced using the best fitting oval (Figure 1d).

The image reduces to binary form with 800 pixels. Therefore, the input layer of the neural network has 800 nodes. The neural network design calls for each hidden layer unit to learn the characteristics of a region of the face. The input sample is therefore subdivided into 16 regions each 10x10 pixel in size. The 10x10 pixel regions allow each node in the hidden layer to learn the characteristics of that region. The teacher signal is set to 0.95 for a face input and 0.05 for a non-face input. Therefore, the hidden layer has 16 nodes and the output layer has one node. The size (number of weights) of the neural network is then 1,633 weights. That is, each of the 16 10x10 pixel regions has 100 pixels, therefore, 101 weights (one for biasing). Note that as opposed to the conventional fully connected neural network, this system connects each of the areas to their own independent hidden layer node. The overall size of the network is reduced by 11,200 weights from 12,833, for fully connected, to 1,633.

Figure 1. Edge detection, (a) 15x15 LOG, (b) 7x7 LOG, (c) 7x7 LOG and median filter, (d) best fitting ovals around the eyes and mouth

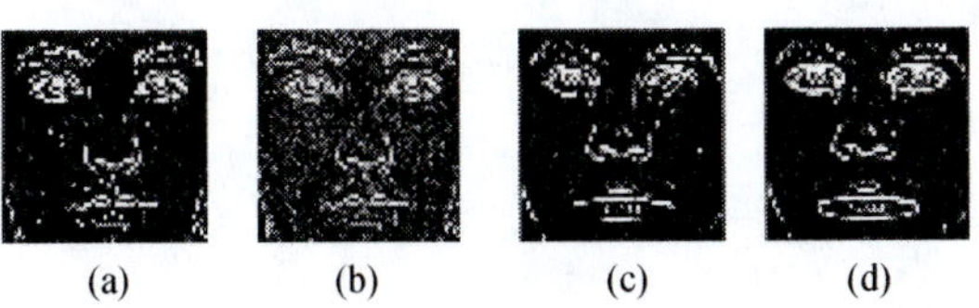

Training Data

Although neural networks are excellent classifiers, one of the major problems during training is insufficient training data. Many samples are required during training to achieve good classification. However, it was not practical to collect all the data required to successfully train the face detector. The original face and non-face images used for training were gathered from the University of Oulu database (Soriano, Marszalec, & Pietikainen, 2000), scanning printed photographs in newspapers and books and pictures taken using a digital camera. These images contained faces of various orientations, positions, and lighting intensities. Initially, 400 face and 600 non-face examples were prepared to train the neural network

Increasing the Face Data Samples

The 400 input face samples prepared are not sufficient to successfully train this neural network. To increase the number of face samples, new samples are created using a random sampling method. A new sample is constructed from three samples selected at random from the 400 input images available. In this method, each of the face samples is subdivided into three regions. The upper and lower regions each occupy 40% of the face regions respectively. The center region occupies the remaining 20%. The selection of the boundaries was chosen such that the upper region contained the eyes, the center region to include the nose, with the mouth in the lower region. The first sample selected contributes the upper region of the new face, the second sample the center and the third sample the lower part, Figure 2. Using this method, we created another 1,000 input images for the training.

Since it is very difficult to represent all the non-faces, another 1,100 examples of non-faces are introduced to the system using the bootstrapping method proposed by Sung (1996).

Before the samples collected can be used for training the neural network, they undergo several preprocesses. The preprocesses include normalization of the face feature positions in the 40x40 pixels face region, image mirroring, equalization, and lighting normalization to take care of lighting variation using histogram matching and rotation of the samples 0 to 5 degrees in the clockwise and counter-clockwise directions (for some frontal rotational invariance).

The back propagation (Rumelhart, Hinton, & Williams, 1986) and structural learning (Ishikawa, 1993) algorithms were used for training the face detection neural network. Structural

Figure 2. Images (a), (b) and (c) are lighting fitted example samples from the original database. Image (d) shows the new sample created by our method.

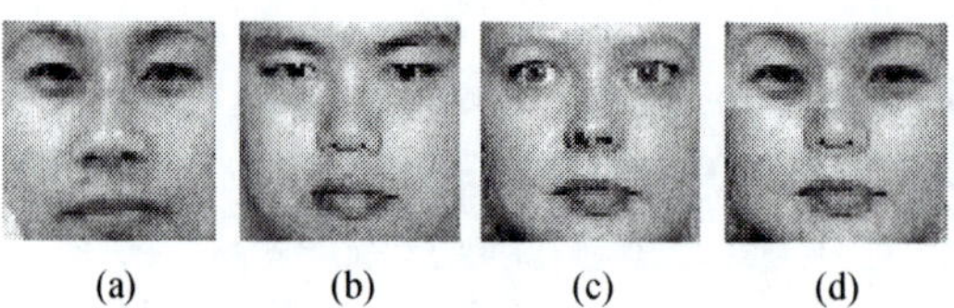

(a) (b) (c) (d)

learning is used to further reduce the size of the neural network by eliminating unused (near zero in value) weights.

Search Space Control: Face Candidates

The speed of this system is proportional to the number of times the neural network detector must be run per frame. For each possible face position in the scene, the neural network detector must be run. Conventionally, these positions equal the total number of pixels in the frame. To improve the speed, the search positions should be reduced. It is assumed that the faces to be searched for contain some skin color. Therefore, face searching becomes a two-step process. First, search for skin color regions called face candidates, and, second, search for faces inside the face candidates. Another advantage of using face candidates is that it allows the genetic algorithm to search for more than one face per scene.

A missed skin color region introduces the likelihood that a face will be missed during the search. Therefore, it becomes very important that the all skin color regions be accurately extracted. In fact, the number of face candidates is equal to or more than the actual number of faces that can be detected in an image.

Skin color detection is accomplished using a threshold filter that uses the YCrCb color system (Poynton, 2003; Plataniotis & Venetsanopoulo, 2000) and a neural network-based skin color detector. The camera used in this work uses the YCrCb color system. In this color system, skin color occupies a well-defined region that can be described using thresholds. These thresholds are:

$$110 \leq Cr \leq 140 \quad (1)$$

$$125 \leq Cb \leq 150 \quad (2)$$

This is a general filter that, although fast, detected all the skin color regions but also generated a lot of noise (near skin color regions).

The skin color detector filter is a more specialized filter that can also be used to detect skin color regions. The skin color detector filter is designed to be a three-layer neural network with two inputs (Y, Cr+Cb), four hidden units, and one output. The performance of the skin color detector filter is far better than that of the threshold filter. Its shortcoming is that it takes more time to search.

The face candidates are therefore extracted using a hybrid skin color detection filter. The hybrid filter works by first applying the threshold filter to the whole image and then running the skin color detector filter on the areas segmented by the threshold filter. The effect of applying the skin color detector filter last is that it removes the near skin color regions from the segmented areas, thereby further reducing the size of the face candidates. Although the skin color detector filter alone can achieve the same result as the hybrid filter, the hybrid filter runs faster. By noting that it is unlikely for faces to be contained in small area face candidates, the face candidates can be further trimmed by eliminating those areas that are less than 10x10 pixels in size.

Pose and Size Invariance: 3D Face Model

In real-time face tracking, the camera is usually mounted on a spot above the subjects. In such a scenario, it is virtually impossible to capture the frontal view of the subject's face unless the subject looks up directly at the camera. Moreover, the subjects may turn their head randomly while their image is being captured. Therefore, although it is possible to extend the neural network face detector to capture rotated frontal faces using a genetic algorithm (Karungaru, Fukumi, & Akamatsu, 2005), such a system cannot suffice in this case. A new system to capture the pose is required. By using 3D edge genetic algorithm-guided edge template matching this problem can be solved.

A 3D facemask is constructed from the average of 100 subjects' frontal and side profile edges. The objective is not to create an accurate 3D face model but a mask that can help estimate the pose of the face. Using edge information, it becomes possible to estimate the orientation of a face by matching the edges to the 3D facemask using a genetic algorithm.

However, not all edges can be extracted from the face in all orientations. Using the 100 face images of different orientations, edge extraction was carried out to determine which of the edges could be extracted most often (over 90%). These edges, called the core edges, are the full or parts of eclipses around the eyes and mouth, the area around the nose, and the line extending from the tip of the nose to the center of the eyes (nose line). The core edges are used during matching.

The 3D facemask is then constructed using the two averaged face profiles (side profile is used for depth), the core points, the general relationships between them, and Bezier curves (Demidov, 2003) (Figure 3).

Figure 3. Different views of the general mask that was constructed; xyz:angle represent the rotation vector and the rotation angle along the vector.

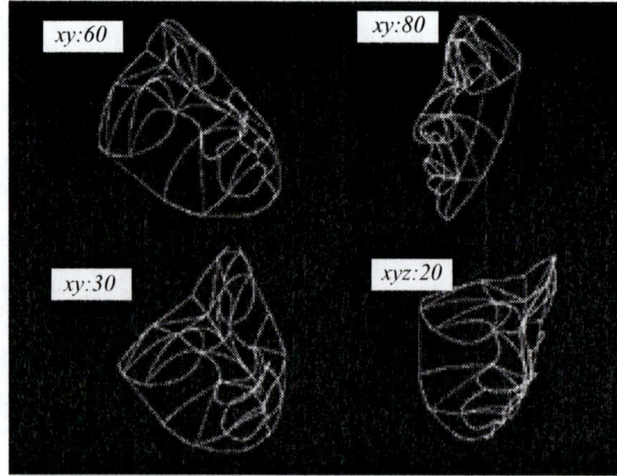

Note that not all the edges shown in Figure 3 are used during matching. The orientation angle and the core edges determine the edges that are "visible" and thus can be used during matching.

GA-Guided Template Matching

The main point of using the genetic algorithm is to optimize the search by automatically selecting the position, orientation, and the size of the 3D facemask edge template for matching, since initially, it is not possible to estimate the pose or size of the face in the visual scene. Once a match is found, the template is rotated to the frontal position and rescaled to 40x40 pixels, and then it is tested using the neural network to confirm the result.

The frame size is 320x240 pixels. Since the face is assumed to be enclosed in a square, the largest size of a face to be encountered in this system is then 240x240 pixels. This information is used to determine the length of the GA chromosome. The GA (binary coded) determines the position, orientation, and size of each sample. The chromosome bits representing the position are coded using 9 (320) and 8 (240) bits for the x- and y-axis, respectively. These are decided from the size of the target image. The orientation angle range is from -128 to 128 degrees. This requires 8 bits (first bit represents the sign) to code for each of the three possible dimensions. Since the maximum size of the face is 240x240 pixels, the maximum possible scale is 6 times. This requires 4 bits to code.

Therefore, the chromosome length is 45. For every face candidate region, the size of the initial population is 20. The GA is set to terminate after 200 generations. Since genetic algorithms are global optimizers, with the search starting at multiple positions instead of one, the chances of being trapped in a minimum are small. This parallel search means the search can be terminated before the 200 generations if an elite solution is found. However, because fast convergence sometimes leads to false solutions, the minimum number of generations before termination was set to 75.

In this GA, the probability of crossover is 0.73 (bit number 34) and the rate of mutation is set at 0.01.

During reproduction, the elite solution is saved and the rest of the population reproduced. The first parent is selected from the top 8 fittest individuals and the other parent from the whole population. By controlling the selection of parents, the GA is forced to also include the weaker genes, improving the search. The selection method used is the roulette wheel.

The fitness of the genetic algorithm is calculated using the sum of pixel color difference between the "visible" core edges and the edges in the target image. As the sum approaches zero, the fitness approaches one.

Face Recognition

Unlike face detection that involves searching in unknown space, face recognition is a matching problem. In this work, face recognition uses many preprocessing methods already performed during face detection saving some processing time. Face recognition is accomplished using a hybrid face recognizer consisting of a neural network and edge template matching.

Feature Extraction

The results of face detection can be used to aid the facial features extraction. The features of interest are both eyes, the tip of the nose, and the lips. The feature extraction process proceeds as follows:

1. Using the results of skin color detection from the face candidate extraction section, extract the position of the eyes. That is, search for holes (non-skin color regions) in the skin color regions above the center of the face (Figure 4a).
2. Search for the position of the lips from the bottom third area of the face. To do this, use the YCrCb thresholds equation 1 and 2 and the following RGB color space threshold to detect the lips region, Figure 4b.

   RGB: $B \leq 40$ (3)

3. Match the eye and the mouth regions to the best fitting ovals.
4. Extract the edges from the face. This has already been done during face detection.

Test Database

The test database consists of five subjects. The five subjects include four men and one woman. The woman and two of the men are of Japanese descent, while the remaining two men are of African and central Asian descent, respectively. Each of the images is processed for its edges and the eyes and mouth fitted using ovals. Therefore, each subject has two images in the database, the original frontal image and the edges image.

Moreover, based on the sizes of the edge ovals and the distance between them, the database is further subdivided into two parts. Part 1 consists of a man and woman both of Japanese

Figure 4. Feature extraction (a) eyes, (b) lips

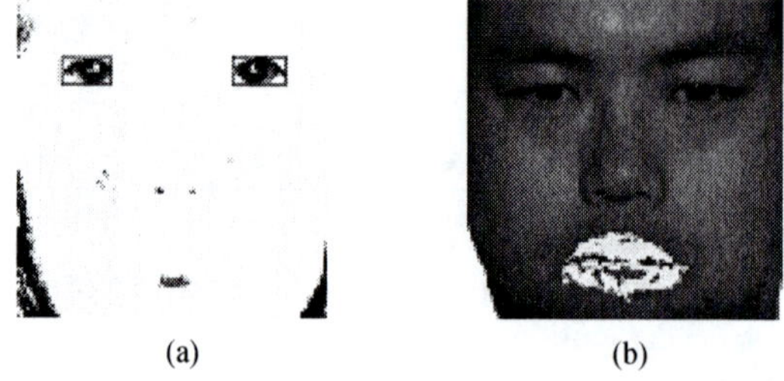

(a) (b)

descent, and Part 2 groups the remaining three persons together. The reason for this separation is to increase the speed of searching through the database using the hybrid method where the template matching decides the group and the neural network recognizes a subject.

Neural Network

In most practical situations, a face recognition database usually has only one image per subject. This presents a problem for neural network-based recognition systems because of insufficient training data. A data increasing method is therefore necessary. In this work, the original image is preprocessed using several methods to increase the data available for neural network training. These methods are image mirroring, images created using the left part and right part of the face.

Note that there are now a total of four images to train the neural network for each original image. That is, the best oval fitted eyes and mouth edge information images of the original, its mirror, left side, and the right half images. Also, note that the neural network is trained using the edges information only.

The neural network consists of three layers. The size of the face image used is 40x40 pixels. Since the training images are grayscale, the neural network's input layer has 800 nodes and the hidden layer 30 nodes. This system is tested using five subjects. Hence, the output layer has six nodes, one each for the five subjects and the remaining one to represent the group to which the subject belongs.

The neural network was then trained using the information constructed from a data set of five images.

Template Matching

The template used is the one constructed using the best oval fitting the eyes and mouth edges, the same as the one used to train the neural network. Template matching is performed with the help of a genetic algorithm to automatically test several positions around the target and also adjust the size and orientation of the template as the matching process progresses.

The purpose of the template matching used here is to reduce the search area of the face database. In the database, the faces are classified into two groups depending on the size and distance between the eyes, nose, and mouth.

Recognition Procedure

The two processes of face detection and recognition described are combined as follows to perform real-time face recognition. Step A describes the face detection process, and Step B the face recognition process. Note that, Steps A and B are repeated every second.

Step A

1. From the first frame, determine face candidate regions.
2. Extract the edges of the region.
3. Run the GA to select the position size and orientation of the sample.
4. If the 3D facemask produces a good fit, normalize the sample by rotating and scaling it to the frontal position.
5. Confirm face region using the neural network detector.

This initial search takes about 0.6 seconds, that is, about 10 frames depending on the number of face candidates.

Step B

1. For the extracted face position, use the edges information extracted to perform template matching. This helps reduce the search area in the database. Then, perform the neural network preprocesses and run the recognition neural network. Note that a genetic algorithm that sets the size and orientation of the sample before it is processed guides the template matching and the neural network processes.
2. Process the next frame using information inherited from the earlier frame. This includes the face detection information, that is, the position, size, and orientation of the faces (GA parameters) and the results of face recognition.
3. Repeat Step A, except the search for face candidates. It is assumed that the face candidates will not vary greatly between frames. Continue until the last frame (15th frame).

Beginning in the next second, repeat the whole process including face candidate area extraction. The process can then continue in real-time (15 frames per second), assuming no further significant increase in the number of face candidates.

Results and Discussion

Computer simulations in this work are performed in a normal office environment without controlling the background or the room lighting. However, since the camera is stationary, the movement of the subjects is limited to within the camera's field of view. By pointing the camera in a different direction, the background can be altered. The following experimental conditions were used.

1. Two camera positions, Pos A and Pos B, different backgrounds
2. Test time of 5 minutes per session at 15 frames per second
3. Four sessions per camera position

There is no determined order or number of times that a subject should be in the field of view of the camera. The only requirements are that a subject must appear at least once every 15 seconds and no more than three subjects should appear simultaneously.

To calculate the accuracies, the video streams for a five-minute span was saved, and the results manually verified. Since the camera was run at 15 frames per second, the total number of frame saved per session was 4,500. This system was tested using a database consisting of five members of our research group. Table 1 shows the results.

From Table 1, the real-time face detection accuracies of Pos A and Pos B are 92.3% and 92.5%, respectively. Also, their respective face recognition accuracies are shown as 89.3% and 90.5%. The average face detection accuracy is 92.4%, and recognition accuracy is 89.9%. Please note that the face recognition results shown here are based on the results of face detection.

From these results, it can be seen that face detection is unaffected by the background because the average accuracies at Pos A and Pos B are almost the same. Individual results show the worst results for the African descent subject. The reason was that face candidate extraction mostly failed for this subject because of the skin color thresholds (equations 1 and 2) that were selected. Better results could be obtained by adjusting the thresholds. However, the lowered thresholds increased the number of face candidates rapidly making real-time detection impossible. The best result was from the only woman in the database because her edge extraction results were the best.

Table 1. Simulation results

Session	Camera Position			
	Pos A		Pos B	
	Accuracy %		Accuracy %	
	Detection	Recognition	Detection	Recognition
1	95	92	89	87
2	92	89	94	92
3	93	89	94	91
4	89	87	93	92
Average	92.3	89.3	92.5	90.5

Conclusion

In this chapter, a real-time face detection and recognition system using neural networks and genetic algorithms guided 3D template matching was presented. Size and orientation invariance capabilities of the system were achieved using genetic algorithms guided search. To show the effectiveness of the proposed method, computer simulations were carried out using five subjects. The average face detection accuracy achieved was 92.4% and the recognition accuracy was 89.9%. Although this chapter concentrated on the human face, the approach presented here can be used to search and recognized other objects like vehicle registration plates and so forth. Edge and face candidate region extractions results contributed heavily to the faces missed.

In the future, it is hoped that a better skin color segmentation invariant of illumination and better edge detection methods using neural filters will be used to improve the results of this work. Other future works include the extension of this system to include more test subjects and application of these results for autonomous humanoid robot control.

Future Trends

Automatic pose and size invariant face detection and recognition have very many areas of application. For this reason, this technology will continue to develop especially with integration with other technologies. In security control, especially at night, the imaging device could be changed from the normal camera to an infrared one that would be more effective. This technology will also be made portable. One way is by utilizing it in robots or making it available simultaneously to security personnel on the ground and those manning the terminals. This will lead to improved response time in case of threats. Also, in entertainment, especially in games and movies, this technology is likely to make an impact. One example is using online face detection to become a character in games or in movies.

References

Bartlett, M. S., Littlewort, G., Fasel, I., & Movellan, J. R. (2003). Real time face detection and facial expression recognition: Development and applications to human computer interaction. *Conference on Computer Vision and Pattern Recognition Workshop, 5*(5), 53-58.

Desmore, R. (1998). Face-selective cells in the temporal cortex of monkeys. *Journal of Cognitive Neural Science, 3*, 1-8.

Demidov, E. (2003). *An interactive introduction to splines.* Retrieved April 10, 2005, from http://www.ibiblio.org/e-notes/Splines/Intro.htm

Fasel, I., Fortenberry, B., & Movellan J. (2004). A generative framework for real time object recognition and classification. *Computer Vision and Understanding, 98*, 182-210.

Hancock, P., Bruce, V., & Burton, M. (1998). A comparison of two computer based face identification systems with human perception of faces. *Vision Research,* (38), 2277-2288.

Ishikawa, M. (1993). Structural learning with forgetting. *Neural networks, 9*(3), 509-521.

Karungaru, S., Fukumi, M., & Akamatsu, N. (2005). Face detection: Size and rotation invariance using genetic algorithms. In *Proceedings of the RISP International Workshop on Nonlinear Circuits and Signal Processing* (pp. 211-214).

Li, S. Z., & Lu, J. (1999). Face recognition using the nearest feature line method. *IEEE Transactions on Neural Networks*, (10), 439-443.

Liu, C., & Wechsler, H. (2003). Independent component analysis of Gabor features for face recognition. *IEEE Transactions on Neural Networks, 14*(4), 919-928.

Plataniotis, K., & Venetsanopoulos, A. (2000). *Color image processing and applications*. Springer.

Poynton, C. (2003). *Frequently asked questions about color.* Retrieved September 15, 2004, from http://www.inforamp.net

Rowley, H., Baluja, S., & Kanade, T. (1998). Rotation invariant neural network based face detection. In *Proceedings of the IEEE Computer Society Conference on Computer Vision and Pattern Recognition* (pp. 38-44).

Rumelhart, D. E, Hinton, G. E, & Williams, R. J. (1986). Learning internal representations by back propagation. *Parallel distributed processing: Exploration into microstructure of cognition, 1*, 318-362.

Sim, T., Sukthakar, G., Miller, M., & Baluja, S. (1999). *High performance memory based face recognition for visitor identification.* Technical report JPRC-TR-1999-001-1, *Just Research.*

Soriano, M., Marszalec, E., & Pietikainen, M. (2000). Physics-based face database for color research. *Journal of Electronic Imaging, 9*(1), 32-38.

Sukthakar, G. (2000). *Face recognition: A critical look at biologically-inspires approaches*. Technical report CMU-RI-TR-00-04, Robotic Institute, Carnegie Mellon University.

Sung, K. (1996). *Learning and example selection for object and pattern recognition.* PhD Thesis, MIT AI Lab.

Turk, M., & Pentland, A. (1991). Eigenfaces for recognition. *Journal of Cognitive Neuroscience, 3*, 71-86.

Viola, P., & Jones, M. J. (2004). Robust real-time face detection. *International Journal of Computer Vision, 57*(2), 137-154.

Wislott L., Fellous, J., Kruger, N., & Malsbnurg, C. (1997). Face recognition by elastic bunch graph matching, *The IEEE Transactions on Pattern Analysis and Machine Intelligence, 19*(7), 775-779.

Yan, S., He, X., Hu, Y., Zhang, H., Li, M., & Cheng, Q. (2004). Bayesian shape localization for face recognition using global and local textures. *IEEE Transactions on Circuits and Systems for Video Technology*, (14), 102-113.

Yang, M., Kriegman, D. J., & Ahuja, N. (2002). Detecting faces in images: A survey. *The IEEE Transactions on Pattern Analysis and Machine Intelligence, 24*(1), 34-58.

Zhang, B., Zhang, H., & Ge, S. (2004). Face recognition by applying wavelet sub band representation and kernel associative memory. *IEEE Transactions on Neural Networks*, (15), 166-177.

Chapter X

Colored Local Invariant Features for Distinct Object Description in Vision-Based Intelligent Systems

Alaa E. Abdel-Hakim, University of Louisville, USA

Aly A. Farag, University of Louisville, USA

Abstract

This chapter addresses the problem of combining color and geometric invariants for object description by proposing a novel colored invariant local feature descriptor. The proposed approach uses scale-space theory to detect the most geometrically robust features in a physical-based color invariant space. Building a geometrical invariant feature descriptor in a color invariant space grants the built descriptor the stability to both geometric and color variations. The comparison between the proposed colored local invariant features and gray-based local invariant features with respect to stability and distinction supports the potential of the proposed approach. The proposed approach is applicable in any vision-based intelligent system that requires object recognition / retrieval. At the end of this chapter, we present a case study of a local features-based camera planning platform for smart vision systems.

Introduction

Distinct object description is a common goal for most vision-based intelligent systems. Robotic vision, driver support systems, visual tracking, panoramic vision, camera self-calibration, and camera planning are few out of many examples of the applications and intelligent systems that need robust object description and recognition methodologies. However, object description and matching is not an easy task in the presence of variations in real imaging conditions. Several kinds of variations can affect the image of an object. These variations are categorized into two main types: geometric and photometric. The geometric variations include changes in translation, rotation, scaling, and affine and / or projective transformations, whereas the photometric variations include changes in illumination direction, illumination intensity, illumination color, and highlights. Therefore, the challenge for any approach to object description is to build a feature descriptor that is invariant to both the geometric and photometric changes simultaneously.

Color is valuable information in object description and matching tasks. Many objects can be misclassified if their color contents are ignored. Nevertheless, most of the existing approaches use gray geometric-based feature extractors. Contrastingly, color-based image retrieval approaches neglect the geometrical characteristics of objects. Combining both geometrical and color information in object description has been growing rapidly. In most cases, the approaches that combine color and geometric contents are stronger either at one of the geometry side or the color side.

In this chapter, we address the problem of distinct description of objects using local invariant features. Particularly, we focus on embedding the color information in traditional geometrical feature descriptors and its impact on the performance of different types of vision-based intelligent systems.

Problem Statement and Chapter Overview

The problem of object description can be looked at as a transformation between two spaces. The first space is the object image, either gray or color, where the object is represented as a 2D signal. The other space is the feature space in which the object is represented by a reduced vector representation whose length varies depending on the feature extraction approach used.

In contrast to the image space, the object representation in the feature space should not be affected by the variations of the imaging conditions. In other words, for perfect object description, the multiple representations of the object in the image space, under different imaging conditions, should be mapped to a unique representation in the feature space. This condition is called "feature invariance." Feature invariance represents the biggest challenge for any object description approach.

In the background section of this chapter, we review some of the existing approaches in feature extraction. In sections "Geometrical Invariant Features" and "Photometric Invariance", we explain well-known approaches for geometrical and photometrical / color invariant techniques, respectively. In these two sections, we highlight the advantages and disadvantages of the existing geometric and photometric invariant approaches. In the section "Combining Photometrical and Geometrical Invariants", we focus on embedding colors in geometrical-invariant feature descriptors and highlight our contribution to the field of combining geometric and photometric local invariant features. We explain in detail our method for building colored local invariant feature descriptors that combines both color and geometrical invariants in a way that is more robust to both geometric and photometric changes in imaging conditions (Abdel-Hakim & Farag, 2006). Also, we show that this method is more distinctive in feature matching and object recognition applications. We end this section with an evaluation study which illustrates the robustness and distinction of our approach when compared with other approaches. Next, we present a case study for applying local invariant features in a particular intelligent system. Specifically, we present a general local invariant features-based camera planning platform for vision-based intelligent systems. Last, we give a glimpse of the future trends in using colored local invariant features in intelligent systems.

Background

Most of the feature extraction approaches for object recognition and matching problems have been focusing on geometrical or luminance features. The geometric features of an object are extracted in high informative regions like edges or corners (Canny, 1986; Besl & Jain, 1985; Harris & Stephens, 1988). Other kinds of approaches use the luminance signature in order to describe an object (Schmid & Mohr, 1997). Color histograms (Swain & Ballard, 1991) and gray histograms (Schiele & Crowley, 1996) are well-known examples of luminance-based approaches. The color histograms concept has been extended to include some sort of illumination invariance by using color ratios of neighboring pixels (Nayar & Bolle, 1996) or by using illumination-invariant moments for color histogram distributions (Finlayson, Chatterjee,& Funt, 1996). Color and gray histograms belong to the "global features" family. Global features have limitations with occlusion and partial appearance. Moreover, they are not distinct features in many cases, as shown in Figure 1.

Figure 1. Global features may fail in distinguishing different objects (a) two different objects, (b) gray histograms of the objects of (a).

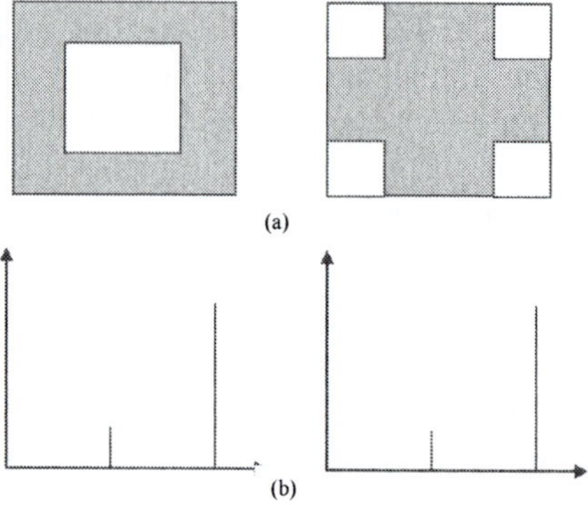

For all of those approaches, the invariance with respect to imaging conditions represents the biggest challenge. Specifically, the extracted features should be invariant with respect to geometrical variations, such as translation, rotation, scaling, and affine and/or projective transformations. At the same time, these features should be invariant to photometric variations such as illumination direction, intensity, colors, and highlights. Therefore, several research studies in the literature have been presented to develop feature descriptors that are as robust as possible to these variations.

In geometrical invariant approaches, local features are preferred because of their robustness to partial appearance and their lower sensitivity to global displacements in the image (Harris & Stephens, 1988; Lowe, 1999; Schmid & Mohr, 1997). Nearly all geometrical invariant approaches avoid dealing with colored images since colors add another layer of difficulty represented in the color constancy problem. However, many research studies have been presented to solve this problem. For example, the normalized RGB representation (Funt, Barnard, & Martin, 1998) has been used to partially achieve the illumination invariance in a geometrical invariant feature descriptor. Some other invariant color representations have been developed depending on statistical-based transformations (Ohta, Kanade, & Sakai, 1980; Vandenbroucke, Macaire, & Postaire, 1998). As a more sophisticated approach, various physical-based color invariants have been developed in Geusebroek, Boomgaard, Smeulders, and Geerts (2001) for invariant color representations under different imaging conditions.

It is obvious that considering gray values for geometrical invariant approaches discards valuable color information of objects, as shown in the example in Figure 2. Hence, pure geometrical-based approaches may fail in differentiating between many objects. Moreover, they have difficulties in describing "non-geometric objects" (Schmid & Mohr, 1997).

Figure 2. Neglecting the color content may affect the object distinction; note the similarity between the two magnified corners occurs when discarding the color information (Source: Geusebroek, Burghouts, & Smeulders, 2005)

On the other hand, due to the global nature of luminance-based approaches, they suffer from partial visibility and "extraneous features" (Schmid & Mohr, 1997). In spite of their relatively few numbers, some approaches in the literature have been presented to combine geometrical and color features. For example, in Gevers and Smeulders (2000), color and shape invariants are combined for image retrieval. However, the color invariants in that approach are very sensitive to the noise around their singularities. Also, the geometrical invariants are primitive when compared to the pure gray-based approaches. In Brown and Lowe (2002), the normalized RGB model has been used in combination with scale invariant feature transform (SIFT) to achieve partial illumination invariance beside its geometrical invariance. As one of our contributions to this field, a multi-stage recognition approach has been developed for the purpose of achieving both color and geometrical invariance (Farag & Abdel-Hakim, 2004).

Geometrical Invariant Features

Geometrical invariance means the robustness of the extracted features to geometric changes represented in translation, rotation, scaling, and affine transformations as well as occlusion and partial appearance. In other words, for a specific object, a feature $F(\vec{x})$ at a location $\vec{x} = (x, y)$ should satisfy the following condition:

$$F(\vec{x}) = F(T\vec{x}) \tag{1}$$

where *T* is a transformation that includes translation, rotation, scaling, and affine transformation.

Building a good geometrical invariant feature descriptor starts from the selection of the object points which are less affected by geometrical variations. Then, distinct characteristics, which also should be invariant to geometrical changes, are collected somehow to build the feature descriptor. Matching these feature descriptors is the final stage of the object retrieval process.

Interest Point Detectors

The ideal way to describe an object using local features is to have a feature descriptor for every point in the objects. Obviously, this is completely inadequate for object recognition applications because the extremely huge number of features will lead to very slow and inefficient matching procedures. Moreover, the image of any object has a large portion of it with uninteresting points for local description (e.g., the homogeneous edgeless and textureless regions). Therefore, some "interest points" should be carefully selected to construct a usefully distinct set of features for the object which they describe. Interest points are usually selected in highly informative locations such as edges and corners.

Figure 3. Harris corner detector using shifting windows

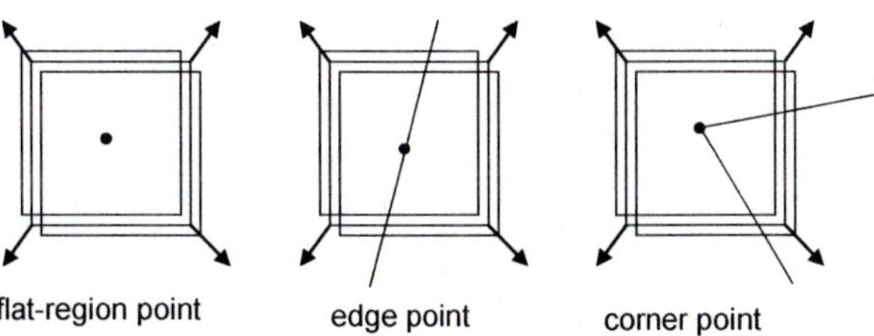

In the context of feature invariance, interest points should be selected so that they achieve the maximum possible repeatability under different imaging conditions. Several kinds of interest point detectors have been developed in literature (Canny, 1986; Harris & Stephens, 1988; Lowe, 1999; Schmid & Mohr, 1997).

The Canny edge detector (Canny, 1986) is one of the well-known early techniques to extract edges with relatively good robustness to noise. The Canny edge detector depends on double thresholding the image gradient maxima. The larger threshold is used to detect the strong edges, whereas the smaller one is used to detect the weak edges. Then, the weak edges are filtered to exclude the edges which are not connected to strong ones.

To detect both of edges and corners, the well-known Harris corner detector (Harris & Stephens, 1988) has been developed. The Harris corner detector depends on shifting a window in different directions and tracking the changes in the intensities. Corners should give strong response, that is, significant change, in all directions, whereas edges give strong response in a specific direction and flat regions do not give a strong response at all (Figure 3). Harris corner detector provides a good stability against rotation. However, it is weak with respect to scale changes.

Scale-space theory offers the main tools for selecting the most robust feature locations, or the interest points, against scale variations.

Scale-Space Theory and Scale Invariant Interest Points

Given a signal $f: R^N \rightarrow R$ then scale-space representation $L: R^N \times R_+ \rightarrow R$ is defined as:

$$L(\vec{x},t) = g(\vec{x},t) * f(\vec{x}) \tag{2}$$

where $L(\vec{x},0) = f(\vec{x}) \forall \vec{x} \in R^N$ and $g(\vec{x},t)$ is the scale-space kernel which is usually Gaussian.

The scale-space representation, $L(\vec{x},t)$, of a signal $f(\vec{x})$ is analogous to letting an initial heat distribution f evolve over time t in a homogenous medium. Hence, fine-scale details disappear and signals become more diffuse when the scale parameter increases. This analogy implies that the scale-space representation can equivalently be defined as the solution of the *diffusion equation*, shown in Equation 3, with initial condition $L(\vec{x},0) = f(\vec{x})$ (Lindeberg, 1994b).

$$\partial_t L = \frac{1}{2}\nabla^2 L \qquad (3)$$

For scale invariance, Lindeberg (1994a) showed that the normalization of the Laplacian of Gaussian, $\nabla^2 g$, with factor $\sigma^2 = t$ is necessary for scale invariance. Later, Mikolajczyk and Schmid (2002) proved experimentally that the maxima and minima of $\sigma^2\nabla^2 g$ produce the most stable image features (Lowe, 2004).

$$\sigma^2\nabla^2 g = \sigma\frac{\partial g}{\partial\sigma} \approx \sigma\frac{g(x,y,k\sigma) - g(x,y,\sigma)}{k\sigma - \sigma} \qquad (4)$$

$$g(x,y,k\sigma) - g(x,y,\sigma) \approx (k-1)\,\sigma^2\nabla^2 g \qquad (5)$$

As shown in Equation 5, the σ^2 normalization of the Laplacian of Gaussian can be approximated by difference-of-Gaussian (Lowe, 2004). In other words, the locations of the maxima and minima in the difference-of-Gaussian pyramid correspond to the most stable features with respect to scale changes.

Feature Descriptors

Many approaches have been developed in the literature for geometrical invariant features, for example, steerable filters (Freeman & Adelson, 1991), differential invariants (Koenderink & Doom, 1987), complex filters (Schaffalitzky & Zisserman, 2002), moment invariants (Gool, Moons, & Ungureanu, 1996), affine invariant features (Mindru, Moons, & Gool, 1999; Obdrz´alek & Matas, 2002; Tuytelaars & Gool, 1999), rotation invariant features (Harris & Stephens, 1988), and scale invariant features (Lowe, 1999, 2004).

Scale invariant feature transform (SIFT) (Lowe, 1999, 2004) includes almost all the geometric invariants and it has been proven to have the best performance over the other local invariant feature descriptors (Mikolajczyk & Schmid, 2003).

In SIFT, a canonical orientation is assigned to each detected interest point. The assigned canonical orientation is used as a reference orientation for a histogram of gradient orientations of the interest point neighborhood. Computing the histogram of gradient orientations using orientations calculated relative to the assigned canonical orientation guarantees the robustness of the SIFT against rotation changes.

After building the feature descriptors for the object, they are appended to a feature database of different objects for the purposes of later recognition. During the online recognition process or the object retrieval, a query image for an unknown object is processed in the same manner to extract and build a set of feature descriptors. Then, matching to the feature database is done. Euclidian distance matching (Lowe, 2004), Mahalanobis distance matching (Schmid & Mohr, 1997), or best-bin-first search (Beis & Lowe, 1997) can be used for feature matching. The matched features are used to estimate the pose of the retrieved object. Generalized

Table 1. Percentage detection rate for different descriptors using different interest point detector for false positives $\leq 1\%$

Geometrical Change	Interest point detector	Differential Invariants	Complex Filters	Moment Invariants	Cross Correlation	Steerable Filters	SIFT
Rotation 45°	Harris	85.6	86.7	93.9	97.8	99.1	99.1
	Harris-Laplace	77.8	88.3	93.3	97.8	96.0	99.1
Scale 2.5 + Rotation 45°	Harris-Laplace	65.6	76.1	91.2	73.3	96.7	99.6
	DoG	66.7	76.7	94.4	73.8	96.8	100
V.point 60°	Harris-Affine	53.9	58.0	77.8	47.3	82.2	86.7

Hough transform (Ballard, 1981) and RANSAC (Fischler & Bolles, 1981) are famous tools for rejecting outliers and estimating the most accurate pose of the retrieved object.

Performance Evaluation

Mikolajczyk and Schmid (2003) have performed a detailed performance evaluation for a number of local invariant feature descriptors using different interest point detectors. They concluded that the SIFT descriptor performs best under different geometric changes. Table 1 shows some of the results which have been obtained during this study.

Photometric Invariance

Photometric invariance is the stability of the detected features against photometric changes. Photometric changes include variations in illumination intensity, illumination direction, illumination color, and highlights.

In this section, we explore two approaches of photometric invariance. The first one is developed by Schmid and Mohr (1997) for gray-value invariants. The other one is developed by Geusebroek et al. (2001) for color invariance.

The approach developed by Schmid and Mohr (1997) uses Harris corner detector to detect the interest points in the image. Each feature descriptor is built by using image derivatives which describe the neighborhood of an interest point. The image derivatives are computed by convolution with Gaussian derivatives. The descriptor entries are as shown in Equation 6.

$$V = \begin{bmatrix} L \\ L_i L_i \\ L_i L_{ij} L_i \\ L_{ii} \\ L_{ij} L_{ji} \\ \varepsilon_{ij}(L_{jkl} L_i L_k L_l - L_{jkk} L_i L_l L_l) \\ L_{iij} L_j L_k L_k - L_{ijk} L_i L_j L_k \\ -\varepsilon_{ij} L_{jkl} L_i L_k L_l \\ L_{ijk} L_i L_j L_k \end{bmatrix} \tag{6}$$

where $L_{i_1 \ldots i_n}(\mathbf{x},\sigma)$ is the image convolution with the Gaussian derivatives and $i_k \in \{x, y\}$, $\varepsilon_{12} = -\varepsilon_{21} = 1$ and $\varepsilon_{11} = \varepsilon_{22} = 0$.

Yet, this descriptor is still a gray value-based feature descriptor. Obviously, color is an important source of distinction between objects. On the opposite side, dealing with colors is more difficult than gray-level representation. This is because the instability of color representations with respect to variations in imaging conditions. Therefore, color invariance is a crucial problem which has to be solved for distinct object description and recognition. Many research studies have been presented for color constancy (e.g., D'Zmura & Lennie, 1986; Brainard & Freeman, 1997). In this section, we give a brief description for the invariants in the model developed by Geusebroek et al. (2001).

In this model, the color invariants depend on the old Kubelka-Munk theory which models the reflected spectrum of colored bodies (Kubelka, 1948). Kubelka-Munk theory models the photometric reflectance as given by:

$$E(\lambda,\vec{x}) = e(\lambda,\vec{x})(1-\rho_f(\vec{x}))^2 R_\infty(\lambda,\vec{x}) + e(\lambda,\vec{x})\rho_f(\vec{x}) \tag{7}$$

where λ is the wavelength and $\vec{x}$ is a 2D vector that denotes the image position. $e(\lambda,\vec{x})$ denotes the illumination spectrum and $\rho_f(\vec{x})$ is the Fresnel reflectance at $\vec{x}$. $R_\infty(\lambda,\vec{x})$ denotes the material reflectivity. $E(\lambda,\vec{x})$ represents the reflected spectrum in the viewing direction. Some special cases can be derived from Equation 7. For example, the Fresnel coefficient can be neglected for matte and dull surfaces. By assuming equal energy illumination, the spectral components of the source are constant over the wavelengths and variable over the position, which is applicable for most of the practical cases. Then, Equation 7 will be:

$$E(\lambda,\vec{x}) = i(\vec{x})[\rho_f(\vec{x}) + (1-\rho_f(\vec{x}))^2 R_\infty(\lambda,\vec{x})] \tag{8}$$

By differentiating Equation 8 with respect to λ, we get:

$$E_\lambda = i(\vec{x})(1-\rho_f(\vec{x}))^2 \frac{\partial R_\infty(\lambda,\vec{x})}{\partial\lambda} \tag{9}$$

and

$$E_{\lambda\lambda} = i(\vec{x})(1-\rho_f(\vec{x}))^2 \frac{\partial^2 R_\infty(\lambda,\vec{x})}{\partial\lambda^2} \tag{10}$$

By dividing Equation 9 by Equation 10, we get:

$$H = \left(\frac{E_\lambda}{E_{\lambda\lambda}}\right) = \frac{\partial R_\infty(\lambda,\vec{x})}{\partial\lambda} / \frac{\partial^2 R_\infty(\lambda,\vec{x})}{\partial\lambda^2} = f(R_\infty(\lambda,\vec{x})) \tag{11}$$

Thus, $H = \left(\frac{E_\lambda}{E_{\lambda\lambda}}\right)$ is the reflectance property which is independent of viewpoint, surface orientation, illumination direction, intensity, and Fresnel reflectance coefficient.

By considering only matte and dull surfaces for the model in Equation 7, that is, $\rho_f \approx 0$ and $E = i(\vec{x})R_\infty(\lambda, x)$ (which is the Lambertian model under the constraint of equal energy illumination), another object reflectance property $C_\lambda = \left(\frac{E_\lambda}{E}\right)$ is provided as an invariant to the viewpoint, surface illumination, illumination direction, and illumination intensity. By adding an assumption of planar objects to the previous assumptions, $W_x = \left(\frac{E_x}{E}\right)$ is given as an invariant to the changes in the illumination intensity. For matte and dull surfaces with single illumination spectrum, $N_{\lambda x} = \left(\frac{E_{\lambda x}E - E_\lambda E_x}{E^2}\right)$ is given as an object reflectance property that is independent of the view point, surface orientation, illumination direction, illumination intensity, and illumination color. Hence, $N_{\lambda x}$ determines material transition regardless of illumination color and intensity distribution. Higher order derivatives for these invariants are used for more robust representations. For detailed derivation of these invariants, the reader is referred to Geusebroek et al. (2001).

To calculate these invariants from the known RGB color space, the Gaussian color model is used as a general model for representation of spectral information and local image structure. In this model, a linear transformation from the RGB space is used to obtain *spectral differential quotients* $(\hat{E}, \hat{E}_\lambda, \hat{E}_{\lambda\lambda})$. Then, *spatial differential quotients* $(\hat{E}_x, \hat{E}_{\lambda x}, \hat{E}_{\lambda\lambda x})$ are obtained by convolution with Gaussian derivative filters. Using the product of two linear transformations, one from RGB to XYZ and the other from XYZ to the Gaussian color model (Geusebroek et al., 2001), the desired implementation of the Gaussian color model in terms of RGB can be obtained as shown in Equation 12. Measurement of the color invariants is obtained by substitution of E, E_λ and $E_{\lambda\lambda}$ by $\hat{E}, \hat{E}_\lambda$ and $\hat{E}_{\lambda\lambda}$ at a given σ_x.

$$\begin{pmatrix} \hat{E} \\ \hat{E}_\lambda \\ \hat{E}_{\lambda\lambda} \end{pmatrix} = \begin{pmatrix} .06 & .63 & .27 \\ .30 & .04 & -.35 \\ .34 & -.60 & .17 \end{pmatrix} \begin{pmatrix} R \\ G \\ B \end{pmatrix} \tag{12}$$

Combining Photometrical and Geometrical Invariants

As shown in the previous section, "Geometrical Invariant Features", object recognition using local invariant features involves three main stages: interest points detection, descriptor building, and descriptor matching.

Interest Points Detection

As proved earlier, the extrema in the Laplacian pyramid, which is approximated by difference-of-Gaussian for the input image in different scales, have been proven to be the most robust interest points detector with respect to geometric changes (Burt & Adelson, 1983; Mikolajczyk & Schmid, 2003). Because of the existence of a Gaussian filter at the beginning of the process of calculating the color invariants, we do not need a pre-smoothing filter for the input image as gray-based approaches do (Lowe, 1999). However, we expand the input image by factor of two before building the pyramid to preserve the highest spatial frequencies. For the Gaussian color model, we use $\sigma_x = 1.5$, whereas $\sigma = 1.1$ for the Gaussian filter of the pyramid levels.

For the input image, we use the H color invariant, which is presented in the previous section, to achieve the stability of the detected features to photometric changes (Abdel-Hakim & Farag, 2006). The geometric stability is achieved by using a difference-of-Gaussian pyramid to detect the interest points and the way in which the feature descriptors are built, as shown in the next subsection.

Descriptor Building

After localizing the interest points, feature descriptors are built to characterize these points. We build our descriptor in a way similar to SIFT. Instead of using gray gradients in building the keys, we use the gradients of the color invariants which are discussed in the previous subsection. We show the results obtained using the H invariant only since it is stable to most of the photometric changes that an object image may have. Currently, we are working in investigating more color invariants. Building our descriptors in this way makes them obtain inherently the robustness of SIFT to different geometrical transformations, which has been proved as the best among other known feature extractors (Mikolajczyk & Schmid, 2003), as shown in the third section. At the same time, the use of color invariants in the feature descriptors, instead of using gray values, guarantees the robustness to photometric changes.

Feature Matching

The matching process is performed for the built local descriptors by finding the nearest neighbor of each feature descriptor in a given feature descriptors-database. The collection of location, scale, and canonical orientation of the matches provides estimation for a rigid 2D transformation of the object. After rejecting outliers, the generalized Hough transform (Ballard, 1981) is used to find a peak cluster among the estimated 2D transformations. Hence, the pose of the object is detected.

Figure 4. Sample images of a colored from ALOI object under different illumination directions and intensities: (a-e) one light source from different directions; (f) two light sources from the right direction; (g) two light sources from the left direction; (h) all light sources are on

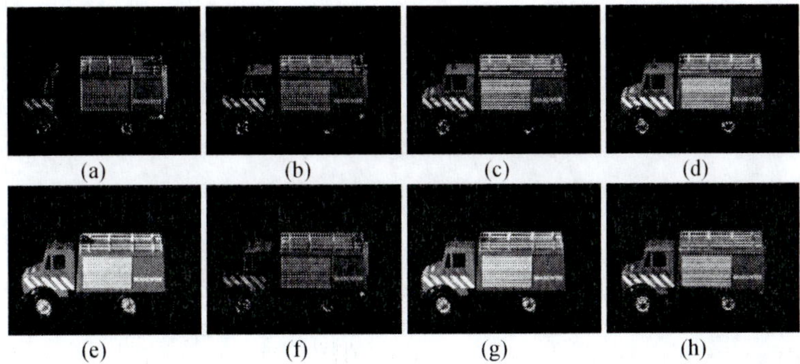

Figure 5. Detected features for a specific object under different illumination directions and intensities: (left two columns) — original images; (middle two columns) — detected features in color invariant space; (right two columns) — detected features in using gray values

Experimental Results

To evaluate our approach, we use the "Amsterdam Library of Object Images" (ALOI) (Geusebroek, Burghouts, & Smeulders, 2005), which is an image database of colored objects. Figure 4 shows a sample object under different illumination directions and intensities. It is noted that there is a large variation in the image content with respect to the illumination changes. Therefore, we found that this database is a good data set in order to prove the potential of our proposed approach.

For evaluation purposes, we compare the performance of our approach with the performance of the SIFT approach as the analogous gray-based approach to ours and as the most stable gray-based descriptor. For fair comparison, we assign the optimum values to the SIFT parameters, as described in Lowe (2004). Since the geometrical-feature structure of SIFT and the proposed descriptor are very close to each other, we focus on the comparison results between them with respect to photometric variations. Figure 5 shows the detected features of a sample object under different illumination directions and intensities using the H color invariant space versus those obtained using gray level.

Figure 6. Evaluation results of features repeatabilities and matching under varying illumination conditions. Results are obtained for 384x288 object images.

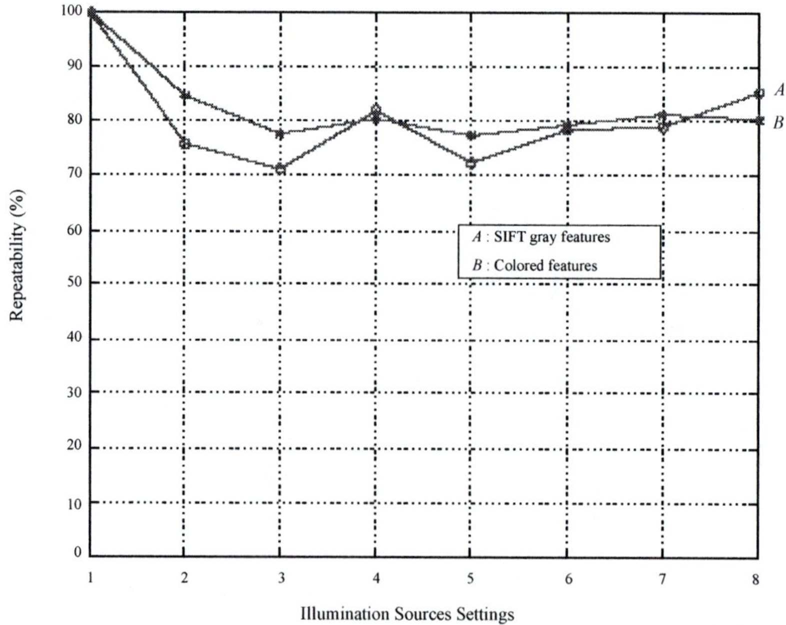

(a) Percentage repeatability of the detected features under different illumination directions and intensities

Figure 6. continued

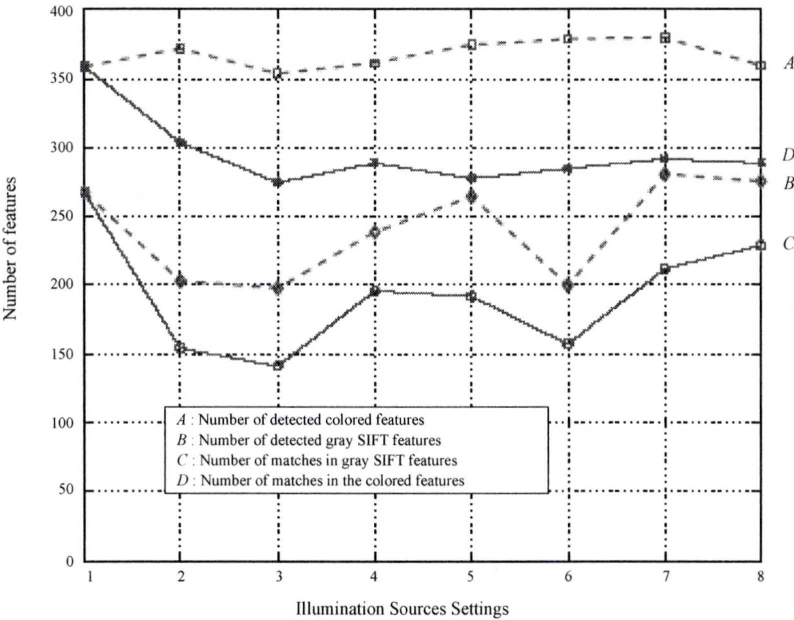

(b) Number of the detected and matched features under different illumination directions and intensities

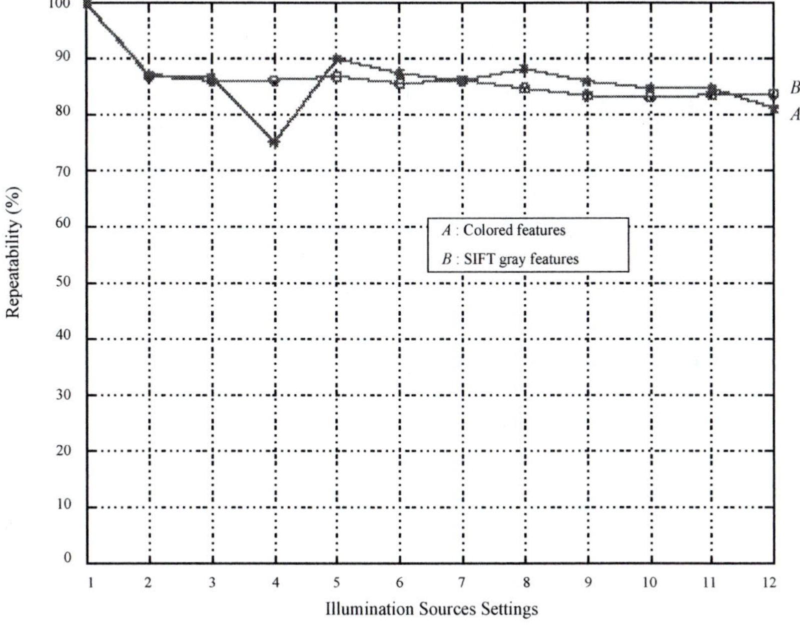

(c) Percentage repeatability of the detected features under different illumination colors

Figure 6. continued

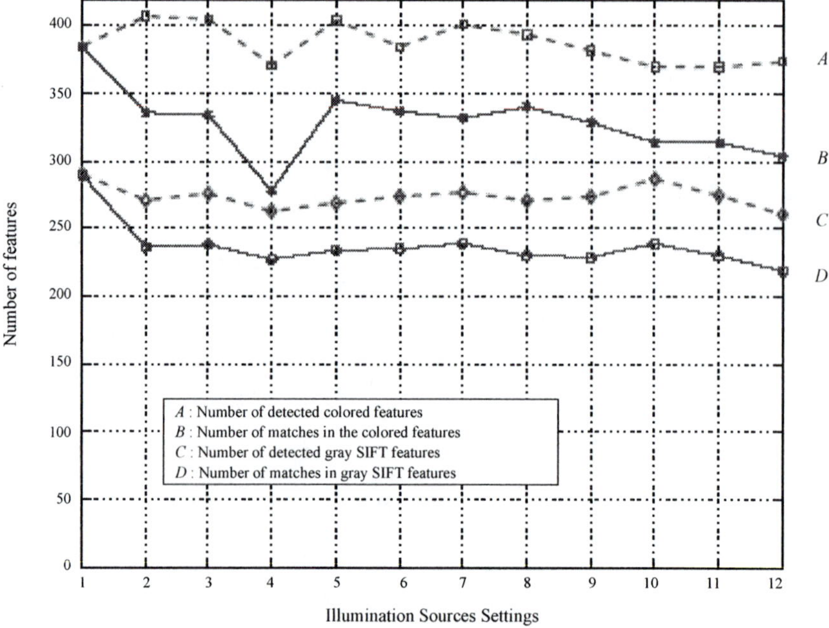

(d) Number of the detected and matched features under different illumination colors

It is known that as the number of detected features increases, the performance of the recognition process is enhanced. Therefore, it is noted from the first glance at Figure 5 that the proposed approach performs better with respect to the number of the detected features. The most important result appears in the complete missed areas (lower left corner in some gray images) which are caused as a result of depending on gray values, whereas the features are repeated in the whole object in the colored case.

Figure 6 shows quantitative evaluation results for the proposed approach versus the SIFT approach. In this figure, we show the repeatability and the matching results for objects imaged under different illumination conditions. Although the percentage repeatability of SIFT may be higher than the proposed approach in a few cases, the number of matched features of our approach is much larger than those of SIFT, as shown in Figure 6b. This is because the number of the detected features in our approach is much higher than SIFT. This high number of detected features supports the potential of the proposed approach in object recognition.

When matching an object under combinations of general geometric and illumination changes to a database of features, the number of the correct matched features increases by a factor of about 2.5 times the number of the correct matches achieved by using SIFT. Therefore, we can conclude that the proposed approach performs better than the gray-based approach.

Case Study: Virtual Force Model for Camera Planning in Smart Vision Systems

In this section, we show a case study for application of local invariant feature descriptors in vision-based intelligent systems. We present a robust model for camera planning in smart vision systems (Farag & Abdel-Hakim, 2005; Abdel-Hakim & Farag, 2005). Camera planning can be viewed as the problem of assigning proper values for camera parameters to achieve some visual requirements.

The presented framework is based on applying virtual forces to control the pan-tilt units carrying the camera such that one or more desired objects appear within a specific area of interest in the acquired image(s).

Camera Planning Problem

Definition: Given a vision system with K cameras (C_k; k =1... K) and n parameters or degrees-of-freedom, (d_i; i =1... n) and given an application A with r constraints, ($R_j(A)$; j = 1... r). Then, a set of specific settings for the n camera parameters, $P(C, A)$, is said to be the solution of the camera planning problem if all the r constraints are satisfied with those settings. This definition can be rewritten as shown in Equation 13.

$$P(C, A) = \{p_{ki}, k = 1...K, i = 1...n \\ : R_j(A) = true \forall j = 1..r\} \tag{13}$$

As an example, consider a 3D reconstruction system using a stereo vision module with two independent pan-tilt units, that is, $k = 2$. Each camera has two degrees-of-freedom, that is, n=2x2=4. For 3D reconstruction using stereo vision application, we have two constraints, that is, r=2. The first constraint $R_1(A)$ = *true*, when the overlap is the maximum. The second one $R_2(A)$ = *true*, when a disparity between the two images exists. According to Equation 13, the solution for camera planning problem is a set of the pan and tilt displacement values for the first camera and the pan and tilt displacement values for the second camera, $p11$, $p12$, $p21$ and $p22$, respectively, such that $R_1(A)$ and $R_2(A)$ are satisfied.

Virtual Forces

In the real world, physical forces are generated by some effectors to change the mechanical status of an object. The case of springs is a good illustration of the force operation. As shown in Figure 7, when the spring is at rest, the external applied force (F) to the spring is zero. Hence, its energy, (E), and its internal force are zeros. When an external force is applied to the spring, some displacement, Δd, will occur in the free end of the spring causing

Figure 7. The spring model

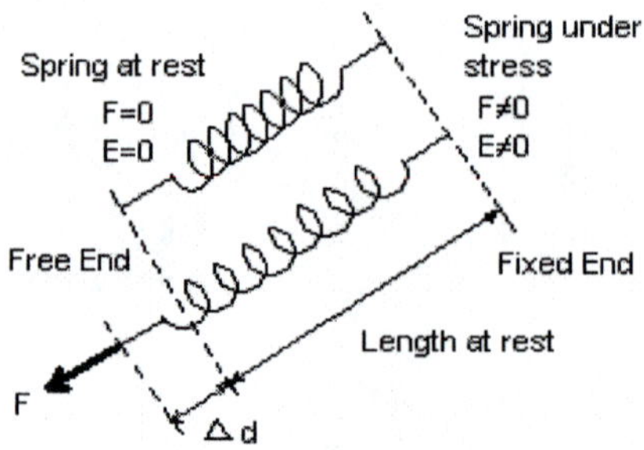

a change in its length. The relation between the applied force and the displacement is given by Hook's law, as shown in Equation 14.

$$F = k_s \Delta d \qquad (14)$$

where F is the applied force, k_s is the spring stiffness , and Δd is the displacement of the free end.

Virtual forces are developed to simulate the physical forces. In virtual forces-based applications, some effectors apply a virtual force to the subject. Hence, a displacement of that subject occurs according to the value of that virtual force and the characteristics of the subject. Therefore, the spring model is attractive to be adopted in virtual forces applications. Then, Equation 14 precisely describes the relation between the applied virtual force and the resulted displacement. The key issue here is how to select the spring stiffness k_s. In the real world, this stiffness depends on the physical characteristics of the spring material. In the virtual models, it is estimated according to the application's nature and the parameters to be changed.

Virtual Forces Model

Assume that we have a target object which appears, completely or partially, in the captured image of the camera to be planned. The main goal is to find the pan and the tilt angular displacements of the camera to get the image of that target object into some area of interest in the captured image. To simplify the mathematical derivation and the operation of the model, assume that the planning process is aimed at getting a certain point (m) into some desired coordinate in the image, which we call "attractor." Therefore, the problem became how to find the pan and the tilt angular displacements (ϕ) and (θ), respectively, for the camera to achieve that goal.

According to the spring model, assume that the virtual force F, which is necessary to displace m by (Δd) in pixels, is composed of two components: a horizontal component F_p and a vertical one F_t.

$$F = F_p\vec{x} + F_t\vec{y} \tag{15a}$$

$$F_p = k_{sp}\Delta u \tag{15b}$$

$$F_t = k_{st}\Delta v \tag{15c}$$

The needed pan displacement is a function of the horizontal component of the virtual force. Similarly, the needed tilt displacement is a function of the vertical component, as shown in the following lemma.

Lemma (1): The pan and the tilt angular displacements equal to the inverse tangent of the horizontal and vertical components of the applied virtual force, respectively, given that the stiffness value associated with each component equals the reciprocal of the correspondent focal length in pixels.

In other words,

$$\phi = \tan^{-1} F_p \tag{16a}$$
$$\theta = \tan^{-1} F_t \tag{16b}$$

given that:

$$k_{sp} = \frac{1}{\alpha_u} \tag{17a}$$

$$k_{st} = \frac{1}{\alpha_v} \tag{17b}$$

where α_u and α_v are the correspondent focal lengths in pixels. For the detailed proof, the reader is referred to Abdel-Hakim and Farag (2005).

To validate this lemma, we have measured pixel displacements in images of a calibrated camera, caused by known pan and tilt angles, as shown in Figure 8. Figures 9a 9b show the plot of Δu and Δv versus the pan and tilt displacements, respectively. The circles, in Figure 9, represent the displacement results for near points, the crosses represent the results for far points and the solid line represents the ground truth. The closeness of the circles to the crosses confirms the assumption of the ineffective depth change on the pixel displace-

Figure 8. (a) The horizontal pixel displacement due to a pan shift=±15°; (b) the vertical pixel displacement due to a tilt shift=±15° (①: a near point, ②: a far point)

(a)

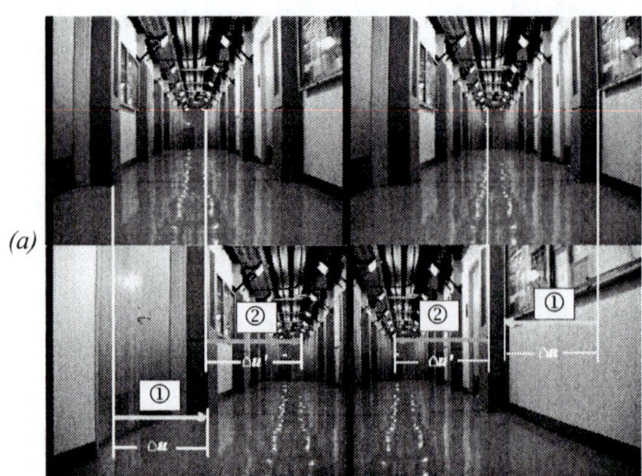

(b)

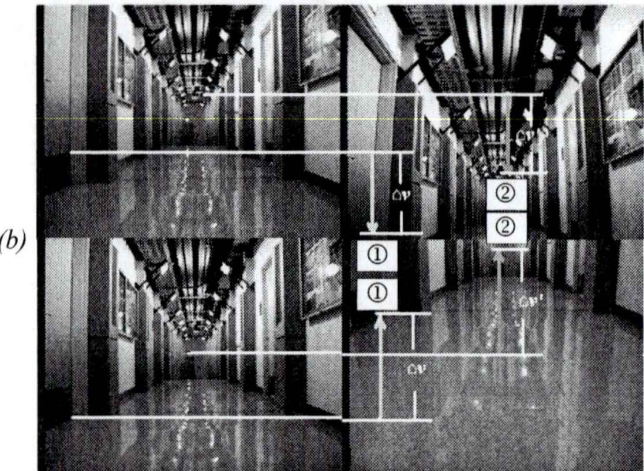

ment. From these figures, we can see that the experimental results conform with the lemma within acceptable accuracy.

In the model's practical operation, if the camera parameters, namely α_u and α_v, are unknown, the previous experiment is done as a simple "stiffness calibration" process to get the stiffness values. Overestimation of the stiffness causes the camera to oscillate around the attractor, while its underestimation causes the camera to get to the attractor slowly. The actual value of the focal length affects the error in this case. Specifically, as the focal length increases, zooming in, the pixel displacements become more sensitive to the camera rotation.

Camera Planning Using Virtual Forces

The approach presented in this case study employs the contents of the captured image and previous knowledge about a target object to direct the camera to a proper position relative

Figure 9. Validation results for lemma (1); (a) pure pan; (b) pure tilt

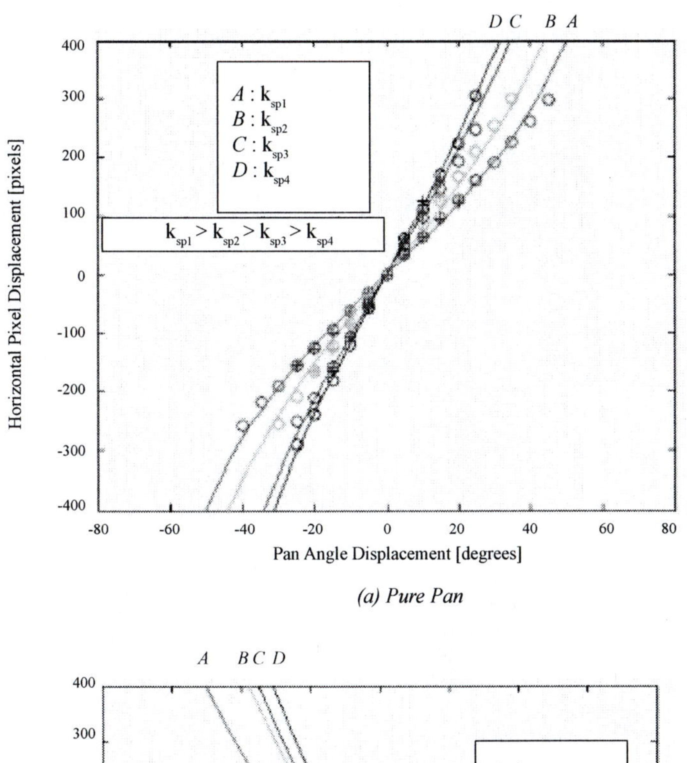

(a) Pure Pan

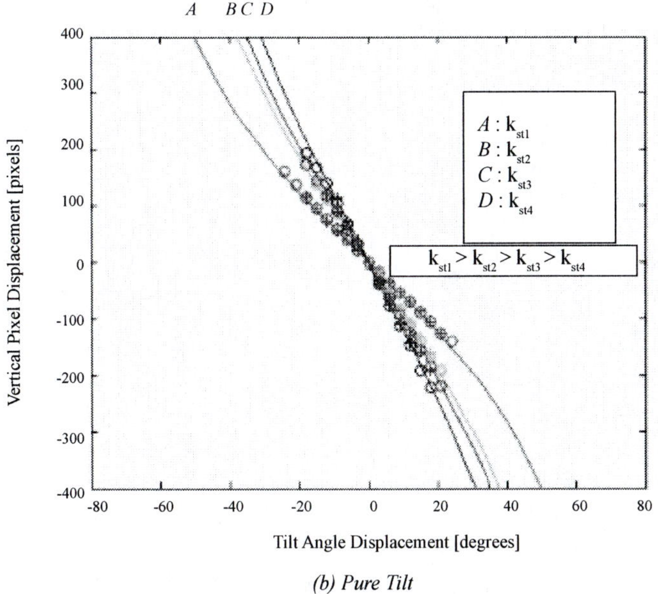

(b) Pure Tilt

Figure 10. The virtual force and its components between the attractor and the centroid

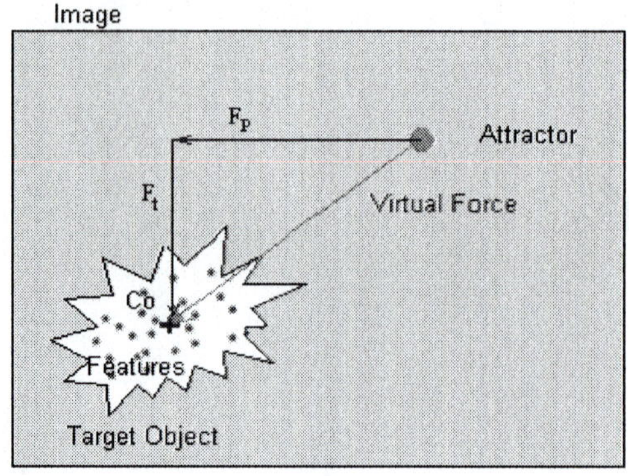

Algorithm 1. General description of the proposed approach

1: Calculate the stiffness values
2: Acquire an image G for the target object(s)
3: Extract the points of interest (*Pe*) in G
4: ∀*Pe*, build a feature descriptor *fe*
5: Capture an image G*c* using the camera to be planned
6: Extract the points of interest (P*c*) in G*c*
7: ∀P*c*, build a feature descriptor (*fc*)
8: Match *fc*'s to *fe*'s to get a total of *Mp* matched points P*m*'s
9: **if** *Mp* <ε **then**
10: stop,(The target object does not exist in the captured image)
11: **end if**
12: Calculate the centroid *Co* of P*m*'s
13: Calculate the displacement Δu and Δv between *Co* and the attractor
14: Calculate *Fp;Ft* from Equation 15
15: Using *Fp;Ft* , calculate the planning parameters of the system (ϕ and θ)
16: In case of partial target appearance in the unplanned image, the centroid position will be changed. Then repeat from Step 5, till ϕ and θ<*Certain Threshold*

to that target object. Two pre-operation steps should be performed off-line. The first step is the stiffness calibration as described earlier. The stiffness calibration can be skipped if the used camera is already calibrated for its intrinsic parameters. In this case, α_u and α_v are known. So, the stiffness values can be calculated as shown in Equation 17. The second step is capturing an image (G) of the target object. Then, some points of interest in this target object (P_e) are extracted and feature descriptors (f_e) are built.

In the online operation of the system, a matching between the acquired image (G_e) and the target object is performed. By the matching process, the coordinates of the matched points in the captured image (P_m) are determined and the centroid (C_o) of those matched points is calculated, as shown in Equation 18.

$$C_o = \frac{1}{M_p}\sum_{i=1}^{M_p} P_m(i) \tag{18}$$

where M_p is the total number of the matched points.

Then, the spring model of Equation 15 is applied to calculate the necessary virtual force to bring the centroid of the matched features to the "attractor," as shown in Figure 10. Then, by using lemma (1), the needed pan and tilt displacements are obtained. A general description of the above approach is given in Algorithm 1.

The use of the centroid of the matched features, as the subject of the virtual force action, achieves several benefits. The first one is to avoid the estimation of the object pose and hence the consequent slowness in performance. The second one is supporting the robustness of the proposed approach against possible weaknesses in the matching algorithm.

The proposed camera planning approach has the following advantages over the previous approaches:

- **Portability.** The proposed approach is setup-independent and can be applied to any vision system for any application with any number of cameras.
- **Expandability.** It can be used with any current or even future feature extraction and matching algorithm. Also, it can be used with any camera planning application.
- **Robustness.** It is robust to any weakness in the matching algorithm used. Also, it can work with very poor initial settings (e.g., partial appearance of the target object, occlusion, etc.). The results section will illustrate this.
- **Flexibility.** It is flexible to accommodate any hardware constraints (e.g., correlating some parameters with each other like panning both of the cameras, in some stereo systems, by setting the same angle with opposite sign). Also, the stiffness estimation process is much simpler than conventional calibration methods in the previous approaches.
- **Simplicity.** The concept of the approach is simple enough to be developed for any vision system.

Experiments

We have applied this model on two different vision systems. The first one is a monocular vision system with two degrees of freedom. The other system is a stereo vision system with four degrees of freedom, two for each camera.

Experiments Design

The first setup is a monocular vision system consisting of a Sony EVI D30 pan / tilt color video camera mounted on ATRV-Mini robot. The purpose of this experiment is to get the

Figure 11. The target objects

(a)

(b)

Table 2. Specifications of the PTU-46-17.5

	Pan	Tilt
Resolution	0.051433°	0.051433°
Maximum	170.0°	30.0°
Minimum	-170.0°	-30.0°

Figure 12. The ATRV2 robot with its pan-tilt units

target object of Figure 11a into the center of the captured image. This experiment is a simple illustration of the operation of the proposed model.

The second setup is a stereo system of ATRV2 robot, shown in Figure 12. The pan-tilt units used are two motion-independent Directed Perception PTU-46-17.5 units. Thus, we have two degrees-of-freedom for each unit, as shown in the top part of Figure 12. Table 2 shows the specifications of those pan-tilt units.

The purpose of this experiment is to get the target object of Figure 11b into the field of view of the two cameras to achieve the maximum overlap between the left and the right images with respect to that target object. At the same time, a certain disparity between the stereo image pair should exist. Those two constraints facilitate the consecutive 3D reconstruction of the target object. The attractors are set on coordinates of 40 pixels to the right and the left of the centers of the right and the left images, respectively. This experiment illustrates the applicability of the proposed model on a well-known vision system (i.e., stereo vision). The points of interest-, in the two experiments, are extracted using the feature descriptors shown in the first part of this chapter.

To show the robustness of our approach with respect to weak matching algorithms, the matching threshold has been set such that a number of false matches could be obtained.

Results

Here, we show the planning results obtained using both of the setups described before. These results have been obtained while keeping the robots stationary during the planning process.

Figure 13 shows the results obtained using the first setup, while Figure 14 shows the results obtained using the second setup. The resolutions of the acquired images are 320x240 and 640x480 for the first and the second setup, respectively. Figure 13a and Figure 14a show the acquired images before applying our planning algorithm. It is clear that with this initial position, the detection of the target object is too hard even for the human eye. We intentionally

Figure 13. Results for monocular setup, (a-c) before planning and (d-f) after planning

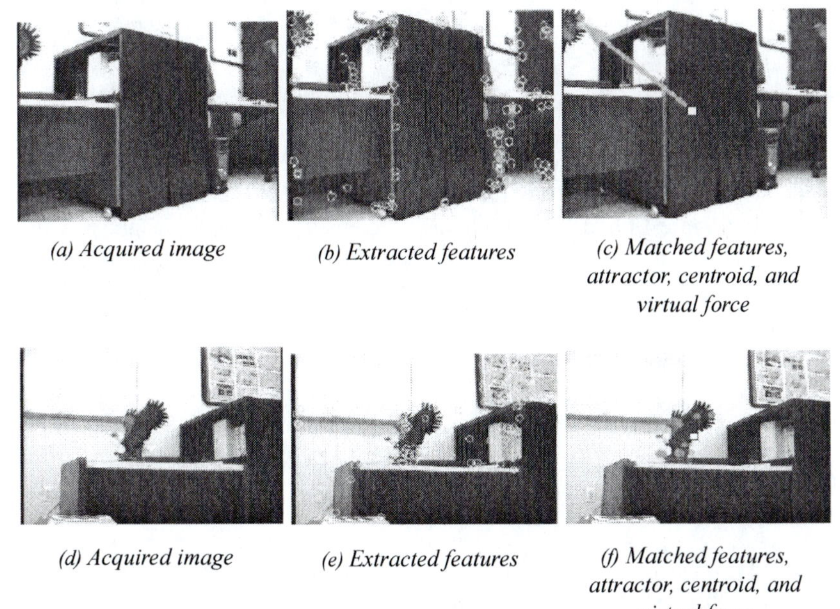

(a) Acquired image *(b) Extracted features* *(c) Matched features, attractor, centroid, and virtual force*

(d) Acquired image *(e) Extracted features* *(f) Matched features, attractor, centroid, and virtual force*

Figure 14. Results for stereo setup, (a,c,e) before planning, note the partial appearance of the target object and (b,d,f) after planning. Legend: Yellow circles: points-of-interest; Blue cross: centroid; Red circles: mismatched points; White square: attractor; Green circles: correct matched points; and Cyan arrow: virtual force

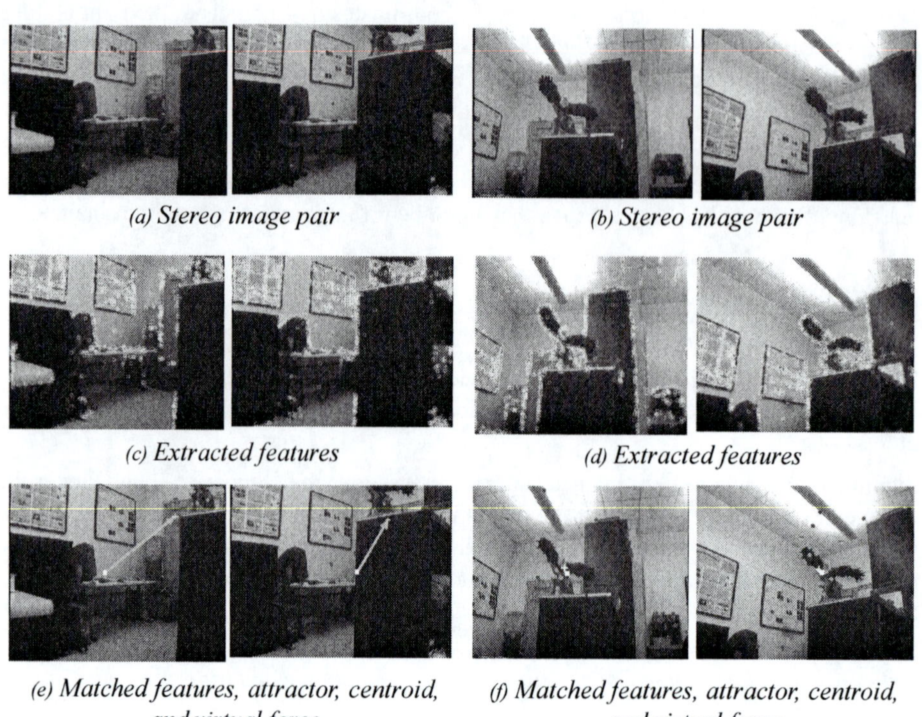

(a) Stereo image pair *(b) Stereo image pair*

(c) Extracted features *(d) Extracted features*

(e) Matched features, attractor, centroid, and virtual force *(f) Matched features, attractor, centroid, and virtual force*

use a poor initialization to show the efficiency of the proposed model. Actually, the matching algorithm plays a great role in such cases of poor initial camera positions. Figure 13b and Figure 14c show the detected points-of-interest in the initial images. Figure 13c and Figure 14e show the points matched for the target object with the calculated virtual forces. It is clear from Figure 13 and 14 that although there is a number of mismatches, the planning algorithm could find the correct desired direction of the virtual force and hence of the camera motion. As discussed in the previous section, this is due to the use of the centroid of the matched features. Figures 13d, 13e, 13f, 14b, 14d, and 14f show the same set of results obtained after planning.

Future Trends

Object description and recognition is a common part in most vision-based intelligent systems. Once a more robust and efficient object description technique is developed, it is adopted in most of the vision-based intelligent systems. Dozens of applications have been using local invariant features, such as robotic vision-based navigation, tracking, camera-self calibration, panoramic vision, face recognition, surveillance systems, and driver support systems.

Colored local invariant features are essential for the systems whose color is a major component of their input data, such as face recognition, driver support systems, and several surveillance systems. For example, color cannot be ignored in road sign recognition systems. To overcome the problems of using gray-based local invariant features in road sign recognition, we have developed a multi-stage system to detect and recognize road signs (Farag & Abdel-Hakim, 2004). In the first stage of that system, the category of the road sign is detected by labeling the colors of the input image using Baye's classifier. Then, the SIFT gray-based local invariant feature descriptor is used for recognition. We plan to use the developed colored local invariant feature descriptor in a single-stage road sign recognition system.

Conclusion

In this chapter, we explored the problem of object description and recognition using local invariant feature descriptors and its applications in intelligent vision-based systems. We illustrated the significance of embedding color information in object description for better recognition performance. We presented our most recent contribution to the field of combining color and geometrical invariant features, and we showed the improvements in the performance of object description that are achieved by using color information. A case study of a robotic camera planning intelligent system that uses local invariant feature descriptors in its operation was also presented.

References

Abdel-Hakim, A. E., & Farag, A. A. (2005). Robust virtual forces-based camera positioning using a fusion of image content and intrinsic parameters. In *Proceedings of the 8th International Conference on Information Fusion*, Philadelphia (pp. 540-547).

Abdel-Hakim, A. E., & Farag, A. A. (2006, June 17-22). CSIFT: A SIFT descriptor with color invariant characteristics. In *Proceedings of the IEEE International Conference on Computer and Pattern Recognition (CVPR'06),* New York (pp. 1978-1983).

Ballard, D. (1981). Generalized Hough transform to detect arbitrary patterns. *IEEE Transactions on Pattern Analysis and Machine Intelligence*, *13*(2), 111-122.

Beis, J., & Lowe, D. (1997). Shape indexing using approximate nearest-neighbour search in high-dimensional spaces. In *Proceedings of the Conference On Computer Vision and Pattern Recognition,* Washington, DC (pp. 1000-1006).

Besl, P., & Jain, R. (1985). Three-dimensional object recognition. *ACM Comput. Surv.*, *17*(1), 75-145.

Brainard, D., & Freeman, W. (1997). Bayesian color constancy. *Journal of Optical Society of America*, *14*(7), 1393-1411.

Brown, M., & Lowe, D. (2002). Invariant features from interest point groups. In *Proceedings of the British Machine Vision Conference* (pp. 656-665).

Burt, P., & Adelson, E. (1983). The Laplacian pyramid as a compact image code. *IEEE Transactions on Communications, 31*(4), 532-540.

Canny, J. (1986). A computational approach to edge detection. *IEEE Transactions on Pattern Analysis and Machine Intelligence, 8*(6), 679-698.

D'Zmura, M., & Lennie, P. (1986). Mechanisms of color constancy. *Journal of Optical Society of America, 3*(10), 1662-1672.

Farag, A. A., & Abdel-Hakim, A. E. (2004). Detection, categorization and recognition of road signs for autonomous navigation. *Advanced Concepts in Intelligent Vision Systems*, Brussel, Belgium (pp. 125-130).

Farag, A. A., & Abdel-Hakim, A. E. (2005). Virtual forces for camera planning in smart vision systems. *IEEE Workshop on Applications of Computer Vision*, Breckenridge, CO (pp. 269-274).

Finlayson, G., Chatterjee, S., & Funt, B. (1996). Color angular indexing. In *Proceedings of the 2nd European Conference on Computer Vision* (p. 16-27).

Fischler, M., & Bolles, R. (1981). Random sample consensus: A paradigm for model fitting with applications to image analysis and automated cartography. *Communications of the ACM, 24*(6), 381-395.

Freeman, W., & Adelson, E. (1991). The design and use of steerable filters. *IEEE Trans. Pattern Analysis and Machine Intelligence, 13*(9), 891-906.

Funt, B., Barnard, K., & Martin, L. (1998). Is machine colour constancy good enough? In *Proceedings of the 5th European Conference on Computer Vision,* London (Vol. 1, pp. 445-459).

Geusebroek, J., Boomgaard, R. van den, Smeulders, A., & Geerts, H. (2001). Color invariance. *IEEE Transactions on Pattern Analysis and Machine Intelligence, 23*(12),1338-1350.

Geusebroek, J. M., Burghouts, G., & Smeulders, A. (2005). The Amsterdam library of object images. *International Journal on Computer Vision, 61*(1), 103-112.

Gevers, T., & Smeulders, A. W. M. (2000). Pictoseek: Combining color and shape invariant features for image retrieval. *IEEE Transactions on Image Processing, 9*(1), 102-119.

Gool, L. J. V., Moons, T., & Ungureanu, D. (1996). Affine/photometric invariants for planar intensity patterns. In *Proceedings of the 4th European Conference on Computer Vision,* London (Vol.1, pp.642-651).

Harris, C., & Stephens, M. (1988). A combined corner and edge detector. In *Proceedings of the 4th Alvey Vision Conference* (pp. 147-152). Manchester University.

Koenderink, J. J., & Doom, A. J. van. (1987). Representation of local geometry in the visual system. *Biological Cybernetics, 55*(6), 367-375.

Kubelka, P. (1948). New contribution to the optics of intensely light-scattering materials, part I. *Journal of Optical Society of America, 38*(5), 448-457.

Lindeberg, T. (1994a). Scale-space theory: A basic tool for analysing structures at different scales. *Journal of Applied Statistics, 21*(2), 224-270.

Lindeberg, T. (1994b). *Scale-space theory in computer vision.* Norwell, MA: Kluwer Academic Publishers.

Lowe, D.(1999). Object recognition from local scale-invariant features. In *Proceedings of the International Conference on Computer Vision,* Corfu, Greece (Vol. 2, pp. 1150-1157).

Lowe, D. (2004). Distinctive image features from scale-invariant keypoints. *International Journal Computer Vision, 60*(2), 91-110.

Mikolajczyk, K., & Schmid, C. (2002). An affine invariant interest point detector. In *Proceedings of the 7th European Conference on Computer Vision-Part I,* London (pp. 128-142).

Mikolajczyk, K., & Schmid, C. (2003). A performance evaluation of local descriptors. In *Proceedings of the International Conference on Computer Vision & Pattern Recognition* (Vol. 2, pp. 257-263).

Mindru, F., Moons, T., & Gool, L. J. V. (1999). Recognizing color patterns irrespective of viewpoint and illumination. In *Proceedings of the International Conference on Computer Vision & Pattern Recognition* (pp. 1368-1373).

Nayar, S., & Bolle, R. (1996). Reflectance based object recognition. *International Journal Computer Vision, 17*(3), 219-240.

Obdrz′alek, S., & Matas, J. (2002). Object recognition using local affine frames on distinguished regions. In *Proceedings of the British Machine Vision Conference* (pp.113-122).

Ohta, Y. I., Kanade, T., & Sakai, T. (1980). Color information for region segmentation. *Computer Graphics and Image Processing, 13*, 222-241.

Schaffalitzky, F., & Zisserman, A. (2002). Multi-view matching for unordered image sets, or how do I organize my holiday snaps?. In *Proceedings of the 7th European Conference on Computer Vision-Part I,* London (pp. 414-431).

Schiele, B., & Crowley, J. L. (1996). Object recognition using multidimensional receptive field histograms. In *Proceedings of the 4th European Conference on Computer Vision* (pp. 610-619).

Schmid, C., & Mohr, R. (1997). Local grayvalue invariants for image retrieval. *IEEE Transactions on Pattern Analysis and Machine Intelligence, 19*(5), 530-535.

Swain, M. J., & Ballard, D. H. (1991). Color indexing. *International Journal of Computer Vision, 7*(1), 11-32.

Tuytelaars, T., & Gool, L. J. V. (1999). Content-based image retrieval based on local affinely invariant regions. *Visual Information and Information Systems* (pp. 493-500).

Vandenbroucke, N., Macaire, L., & Postaire, J. (1998). Color pixels classification in an hybrid color space. In *Proceedings of the International Conference on Image Processing,* Chicago (Vol. 1, pp. 176-180).

Chapter XI

Automated Object Detection and Tracking for Intelligent Visual Surveillance Based on Sensor Network

Ruth Aguilar-Ponce, University of Louisiana - Lafayette, USA

Ashok Kumar, University of Louisiana - Lafayette, USA

J. Luis Tecpanecatl-Xihuitl, University of Louisiana - Lafayette, USA

Magdy Bayoumi, University of Louisiana - Lafayette, USA

Mark Radle, University of Louisiana - Lafayette, USA

Abstract

The aim of this research was to apply an agent approach to a wireless sensor network in order to construct a distributed, automated scene surveillance. A wireless sensor network using visual nodes is used as a framework for developing a scene understanding system to perform smart surveillance. Current methods of visual surveillance depend on highly trained personnel to detect suspicious activity. However, the attention of most individuals degrades after 20 minutes of evaluating monitor-screens. Therefore, current surveillance systems are prompt to failure. An automated object detection and tracking was developed in order to build a reliable visual surveillance system. Object detection is performed by means of a background subtraction technique known as Wronskian change detection. After discovery, a multi-agent tracking system tracks and follows the movement of each detected object. The proposed system provides a tool to improve the reliability and decrease the cost related to the personnel dedicated to inspect the monitor-screens.

The Need for Automated Surveillance Systems

Automated visual surveillance is becoming an increasingly interesting topic for the scientific community because of the changing security needs. The need for developing computer systems that can provide enough information to take rapid action against security threats is greatly felt. Typically, visual surveillance systems consist of several cameras distributed through an area connected to monitors in a central operator room, where highly qualified personnel are in charge of reviewing and analyzing the video stream of each camera to observe suspicious activities. A high-level sketch of such a system is illustrated in Figure 1a. However, with the increasing number of cameras to monitor a huge number of installations of interest, there is simply not enough pairs of eyes to keep track of all information. Moreover, a recent study concludes that after 20 minutes of evaluating monitor-screens, the attention of most individuals degrades to below acceptable levels (Green, 1999). Another factor to be considered is the cost because cameras are cheap and ubiquitous but the personnel required to analyze them are highly expensive. Therefore, the video captured by the cameras serves more as an archive to refer to after an event has occurred. A current trend in the research is to design *smart surveillance systems* capable of preventing untoward incidents rather than investigating after the incidents have occurred. However, there are many challenges to be overcome before a reliable automated surveillance system is realized (Dick, 2003). These technical challenges include system design and configuration, architecture design, object identification, tracking and analysis, restrictions on network bandwidth, physical placement of cameras, installation cost, privacy concerns, reliable object detection, and trustworthy identification of individual.

There are several events that a smart surveillance system has to detect in real-time such as motion, abandoned object alert, object removal, and observation of any other abnormal activity or behavior. Motion detection alerts when objects are moving in the specified zone. Also, the system must identify the characteristics of the motion such as velocity, acceleration, and direction of movement. Another event of interest is an abandoned object that constitutes a potential threat such as bombs. It is also of interest to investigate when an object has been removed from the area under surveillance such as expensive equipment being stolen. The system must be capable of alerting against behavior that deviates from the norm such as a vehicle going over or under the speed limits in a parking lot.

Two core issues for *automated surveillance* are *object detection* and *tracking*. Surveillance cameras provide video stream that suffer from low resolution and low frame rate. Moreover, the quality of the video depends on the lighting conditions. Also, suspicious activity must be detected at the time of occurrence, therefore, object detection must be performed in real-time.

Figure 1. (a) Typical surveillance system; (b) proposed approach to surveillance systems

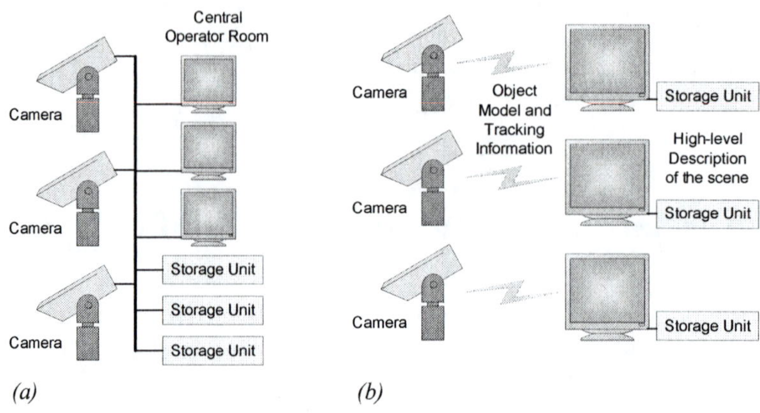

These characteristics make object detection a challenge. Object detection may be performed by *background subtraction* and *optical flow* techniques. The optical flow is capable of detecting object movement even when the background is also moving. However, this technique is computationally complex and resource demanding, hence, it is difficult to be implemented in real-time. On the other hand, background subtraction is more suited to detecting movements or changes on the scene, yielding to a low complexity implementation. A fixed background is required for this type of detection. The background subtraction is done in several steps. First, the raw image is changed into a format that can be processed. Then, a background model is built based on the previous frames. Next, the comparison between input frame and the background model is performed. As a result, a foreground mask is built up.

In a surveillance system, several cameras could capture the same object. Therefore, cooperation among them has to be achieved in order to track such objects over an extended distance and time. Since tracking has to be performed over an extended period of time, lighting conditions and background variations arise as problems to be solved. A smart surveillance system must be capable of continuously tracking the identity, location, and activity of people and vehicles within the supervised area (Hampapur, 2003).

This chapter is organized as follows. The next section describes the previous research efforts on automated visual surveillance. Then, we explain the basis of our approach and discuss our proposed solution to object detection and tracking. We talk about the proposed multi-agent system for tracking detected objects and then depict future trends on this area. Finally, conclusions are presented.

Previous Efforts on Automated Surveillance Systems

There have been several efforts made to create an automated surveillance system. Some of these efforts are summarized in this section.

Video Surveillance and Monitoring (VSAM)

An early research effort made to address this problem was a system proposed by Collins, Lipton, Fujiyoshi, and Kanade (2001) at Carnegie Mellon University entitled "Video Surveillance and Monitoring" (VSAM). The architecture of VSAM consists of an operator central unit, several sensor processing units, a graphical user interface (GUI), and several visualization nodes.

The sensor processing units perform object detection by means of adaptive background subtraction and three-frame differencing. This information is sent to the operator central unit. That is, the operator control unit receives the processed data from the entire sensor processing units distributed over the area of interest. Once the operator control unit acquires results from the sensor-processing units, this information is integrated with a site model and a database of known objects to infer information of interest to the user. The resulting data is sent to the GUI and the visualization nodes. The user must indicate surveillance tasks to be performed. The operator control unit serves / acts as an arbiter, indicating which unit must perform a given task. The tasks include tracking a given object, displaying views fields, and / or creating a region of interest.

This system has advantageous characteristics such as providing several points of visualization through the network, saving bandwidth by sending symbolic information about the detected object. However, the system still needs human supervision. The tracking of moving objects is only performed when the user assigns the task. The operator control unit acts as an arbiter. Therefore, tasks cannot be completed if it fails. The architecture detects and classifies objects present on the scene and shows all this information in a report to the user. Then, the system waits for the user to assign new tasks.

Distributed Intelligence for Visual Surveillance

Framework based on cooperative agents for visual surveillance was proposed by Remagino, Shihab, and Jones (2004) at Kingston University. The system consists of several cameras distributed over the area of interest where the view field of the cameras can be overlapped. The framework defines three agents: ground plane agent, camera agent, and object agent. The ground plane agent is responsible for calibrating the camera to a common ground plane coordinate system to allow integration across multiple cameras. The camera agent is responsible for detecting and tracking all moving object crossing its field of view. The detection of object is done by classifying each pixel as moving or static compared with the previous frame. Once an object has been detected, the system computes the three-dimensional (3D) trajectory of the object and extracts the set of sub-images containing the event in each frame. If multiple agents are tracking the same event, then they must merge and inherit the data channels from multiple camera agents

The detection algorithm employs classification of each pixel as a moving or static one. However, it is not clear whether this detection algorithm will discard shadows cast by a moving object or if the algorithm is robust against changes of illumination. Several cameras may instantiate a number of agents tracking the same event, which may result in waste of resources until the agents merge. Also, the camera agent is responsible for detecting the moving objects, extracting parameter models, and assigning objects to the object agents, while the object agent just stores the values of parameters. Therefore, the burden of processing resides only on the camera agent.

Computer Vision System for Modeling Human Interaction

A real-time computer vision and machine learning system for modeling human behavior and interaction in a visual surveillance system is proposed by Oliver, Rosario, and Pentland. (2000) at MIT. Visual surveillance requires understanding how humans behave and interact among them to achieve a secure area. This approach models the person-to-person interaction using statistic learning techniques known as hidden Markov (Rabiner, 1986, 1989) and coupled hidden Markov models (Brand, 1997) to teach the system to recognize the normal single-person behaviors and person-to-person interactions. The system employs a camera with wide field of view watching a dynamic outdoor scene. Once an image has been acquired, motion detection is performed by subtracting a background model from the current scene. The background model is built up by averaging N previous frames. This technique is known as eigenbackground subtraction. The tracking of each event is performed by a Kalman filter that predicts the event positions and velocity in the next frame. The computer vision module extracts a feature vector for each detected object describing its motion and heading as well as spatial relationship to all nearby moving objects. The hidden Markov models take the feature vector to classify the perceived behavior. The eigenbackground subtraction method used to detect objects requires N previous frames, covariance matrix, and mean background image. Therefore, the system will require massive amount of resources to achieve real-time operation.

All those previous approaches fail to establish a trade-off between complexity, accuracy, and automation. Surveillance systems require automated detection and tracking that can be implemented in real-time while consuming a moderate amount of resources. The information that can be shared through the network must be limited to relevant data. Moreover, the communication must be restricted to nodes that share the same monitoring area giving the opportunity of discarding redundant information and saving energy.

Basis for the Proposed Development Approach: Distributed Sensor Network

Automated surveillance systems must perform three basic tasks: *object detection, tracking,* and *threat analysis*. The proposed surveillance system consists of a network of cameras spatially distributed, therefore, object detection and tracking requires distributed computing and cooperation among the nodes to perform their tasks. In order to perform threat analysis, a high-level description of the area under surveillance is also provided. The proposed framework can provide distributed computing, cooperation among nodes, and a high-level description of the monitored area. In essence, the backbone of the proposed system is a *distributed sensor network.*

A *distributed sensor network* is a large collection of sensors distributed through an area of interest where each sensor possesses a processing capability. The sensors cooperate in an ad-hoc manner to communicate information with each other. A sensor collects data and performs basic processing on the collected data. The information of interest is a general view of the monitoring area rather than a single view of one sensor. Therefore, the information collected from all parts of the network is merged by means of a *data fusion system*. The resulting data is then used to infer the state of the monitoring area. Since there are several hundreds of sensors distributed over an area, multiple instantiations of the same event is possible. In order to avoid transmission of redundant information of the same event, sensors must cooperate to detect such instantiations and merge those different datasets into one single set. There are several applications that can benefit from the proposed framework such as surveillance of battlefields, intrusion detection, improvement of intelligibility under noisy conditions, automatic control of air-conditioners and humidifiers in buildings, environmental monitoring, and remote health monitoring. Several applications are discussed by Iyengar (2005).

Figure 2. A sensor node in the proposed system

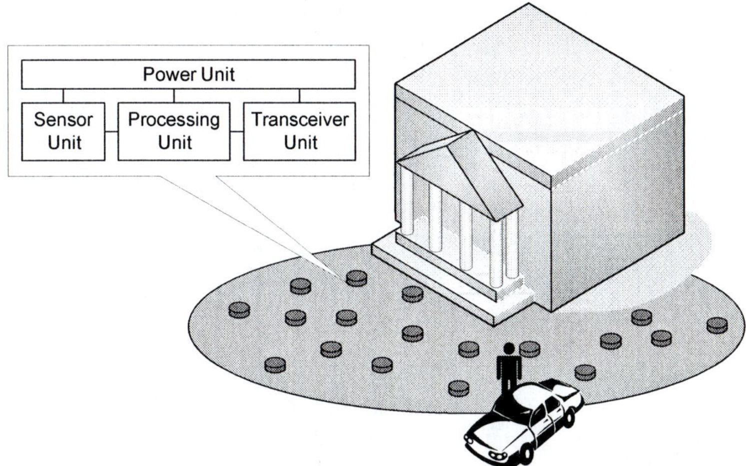

The *wireless sensor network* must comply with several characteristics such as intelligence in each node implemented by a processing unit, the performance must not degrade because of the spatial distribution, the network must be able to accommodate diverse sensors, and the network must operate even if some nodes have failed. Data processing must be done in real-time, because sensor data are time-sensitive. In summary, distributed sensor networks must be intelligent, reliable, and robust. In sensor networks, the data is stored and retrieved from several nodes spatially distributed by means of the query processing system as explained by Woo (2004).

Each sensor node is a tiny embedded device composed of four basic units: sensor, processing, communication and power unit, illustrated in Figure 2. The sensor unit may include any of the following sensors: seismic, acoustic, radar, infrared, humidity, light, temperature, pressure, vibration, and radioactivity sensors. The processing unit is composed of a digital signal processor (DSP) or ARM processor capable of performing pre-processing on the collect data. The communication unit is formed for a transceiver and gives the nodes the capability to communicate among them to achieve their goal. Finally, the power unit is in charge of supplying voltage for the entire node operation. Changing batteries for sensors in short intervals of time is infeasible due to the large amount of nodes. Therefore, durable sources of energy have been studied over the years (Meninger, 2001; Lal, 2004). Also, several techniques for efficient use of the energy inside the node have also been studied (Wentzloff, 2004; Sinha, 2001).

Proposed Approach for Automated Object Detection and Tracking

A hierarchical distributed sensor network approach is proposed to enable automated object detection and tracking. In the proposed approach, there are two units: object processing unit (OPU) and scene processing unit (SPU).

OPU is an embedded system capable of detecting moving object in the area under surveillance. It contains an image sensor to provide raw video data to be processed by a background subtraction system to obtain a foreground mask. The *foreground mask* contains moving objects, appearing and disappearing objects while discarding changes due to illumination variations. Once an object has been detected, the information is passed to a multi-agent tracking system. The multi-agent tracking system extracts object model parameter values and stores them until the time to send them to SPU.

SPU is a high-level analysis and storage node. It receives information from several OPUs distributed throughout the area of interest. The information that SPU receives consist of object model values, object segments, and the tracking history. Then, SPU classifies each object into predetermined sets. The sets are broadly organized into human-individuals, animals, and vehicles. Once this information is obtained, it is used to analyze if a threat pattern exists.

OPUs are organized into clusters to ensure high correlation between data collected for nodes within a group. A cluster-head is elected for each cluster. The cluster-head is in charge of

Figure 3. Overall proposed architecture

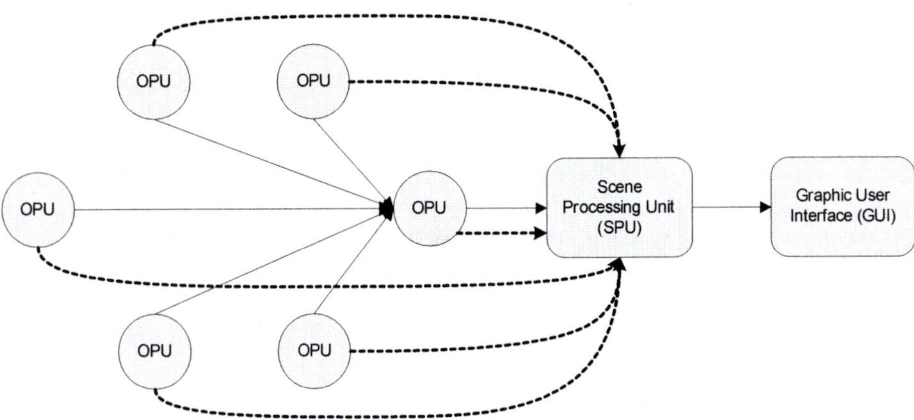

Figure 4. Connectivity of the whole system (all connections are wireless)

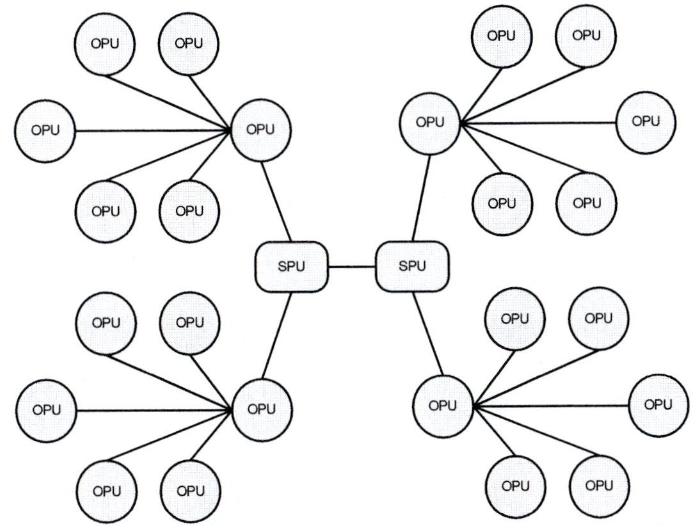

merging cluster data before sending them to SPUs. Therefore, cluster-heads function as a gateway between the cluster and the SPU. The overall organization of the proposed approach is illustrated in Figure 3. Each SPU includes a graphic user interface (GUI), to provide several visualization points through the network. It is noted that an SPU can be connected to more than one cluster as illustrated in Figure 4. The SPUs and OPUs have independent functionalities. However, a meaningful cooperation can be achieved through coordination between them. In order to track moving objects, cooperation is needed between OPUs. When an object moves out of the area monitored by an OPU, then the information is sent to the next corresponding OPU the previous OPU does not suspend detection and tracking. SPU analyzes further the information sent by the OPUs. Also, it is in charge of requests information to the OPUs such as video footage.

The information that flows through the network is only the object parameter values, that is, no video is transmitted from the OPUs to SPU. This way, the use of bandwidth is optimal. However, the architecture allows the possibility of viewing the actual video footage on the cameras. At a given time the user can indicate by means of the GUI his or her desire of watching the video footage of a given camera. The OPU will then suspend processing and compress the video in order to send it to the SPU. Therefore, each OPU has two action modes. The *default processing mode* will detect and track objects and send only the object model information. The second mode is *video mode* in which the OPU sends compressed video to the SPU.

Object Processing Unit

OPU is a low level sensor node consisting of an embedded system containing an image sensor. OPU obtains raw video stream processed by a background subtraction technique known as *Wronskian change detector*. Then, a foreground mask of the scene under surveillance is sent to the *multi-agent tracking system*. Agents are in charge of obtaining the *object model* parameters. Object model consists of the velocity, acceleration, and direction of movements as well as segments of the image containing the detected objects. Once an object has been detected, the agent system initiates a tracking file for each object and records the object model information. This information must be stored until the transmission to the SPU takes place. OPU functions are decomposed into video and processing mode. *Video mode* takes raw video stream and compresses it using *discrete cosine transform* (DCT). *Processing mode* performs the functions already described here. Processing mode is the default operation mode. Figure 5 illustrates the functional diagram of the OPU.

SPU requires a high-level interpretation of the data acquired by the OPUs rather than individual data of each cell; therefore, the data aggregation is performed before sending the information. OPUs are connected into static clusters. Clusters are created beforehand to ensure the maximum correlation. The data aggregation technique is used to combine the

Figure 5. General functions performed at OPU

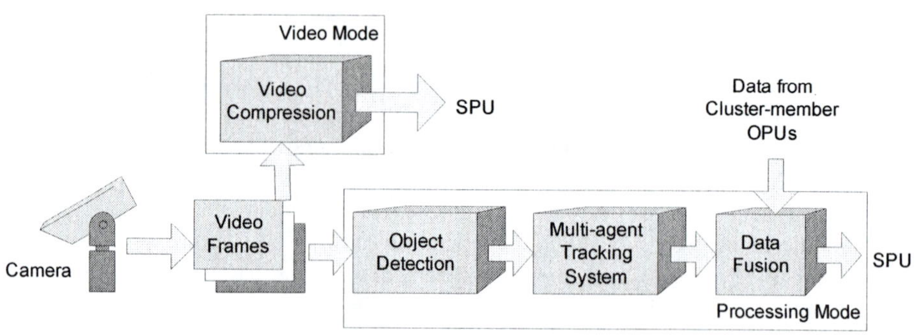

object model information into a smaller set that retains all effective data. In each cluster, one unit acts as a cluster-head. A cluster-head is responsible for data aggregation and information transmission to SPU. Also, a cluster-head acts as a gateway between a cluster and a SPU. Since the cluster-head has more activities than the cluster-members, being a cluster-head is more energy-intensive than being a cluster-member only. A rotation of the cluster-head position is done in order to maximize lifetime of each node. The information is sent to the SPU in rounds; each round begins with a cluster-head selection. The duration of each round is kT, where T is a fixed interval of time and k is a positive integer. After the cluster-head selection, the aggregation and transmission of information is done. The selection of cluster-head is realized by using a modified LEACH cluster head selection algorithm provided in (Heinzelman, 2002).

Cluster members retain the information sent to the cluster-head until they receive a successful transmission message. Then, the information will be discarded in order to have enough space for new information. The cluster members wait for the successful transmission message from the cluster-head for a limited interval of time. While waiting, the cluster members still perform their actions. If they do not receive the message within this interval, a new cluster-head will be elected and information will be re-sent.

Scene Processing Unit

SPU is a high-level analysis and storage node dedicated to perform threat identification based on the information sent by multiple OPUs. SPU has a broader look at the scene under observation because it receives the information from several OPUs. Thus, the SPU can perform accurate detection of suspicious activities. Along with object model and tracking information, a segment of the image containing the detected object is received by the SPU. This segment could be used by the classification and decomposition procedure. The object could be classified into person, animal, or vehicle sets. A person set contains a single person or a group of persons, while the vehicle set contains sedan, truck, delivery truck, or 18

Figure 6. Functional diagram of SPU tasks

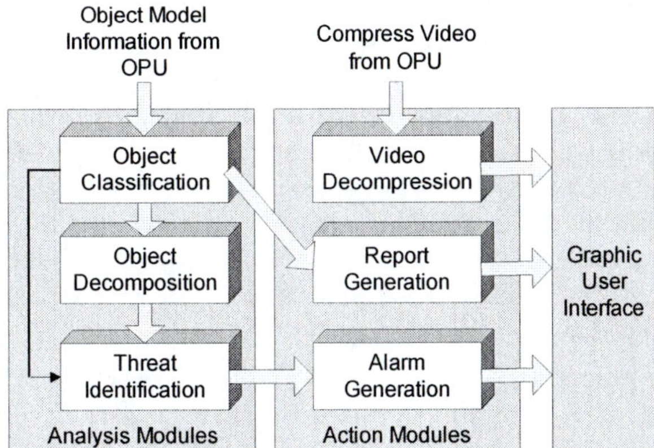

wheelers. If the detected object has been classified into person set, then the decomposition procedure will take place and a person will be decomposed into legs, arms, and trunk. This decomposition is performed in order to determine if the person has a hazardous material in his arms, or strapped on his trunk, like a weapon. The information will be sent to the threat detection procedure. Based on that information the SPU will decide what action will be taken, such as taking a closer look on the scene or an alarm detonation.

Figure 6 shows a functional diagram of the activities performed at the SPU. The tasks performed by the SPU are computationally complex, thus they require high computation capabilities and memory as well as a database of threat patterns. SPU functions are classified into analysis and action modules. Analysis modules contain object classification, object decomposition, and threat identification, while video decompression, report generation, and alarm generation are action modules.

Graphic User Interface

The graphic user interface (GUI) provides a daily report of actions in the area of interest. The report includes all information collected from OPUs on the particular object observed. It also provides a tool to observe video from the cameras. The video information is sent compressed to the SPU, which is in charge of decompressing the video and showing it by means of GUI.

The Proposed Multi-Agent Object Detection and Tracking System

A smart tracking system requires intelligence to perform its activities, which a *multi-agent system* can provide. Since the early 1990s, agent paradigms have been the subject of intense study. *Agents* are an extension of the object-oriented paradigm and have been suggested as a breakthrough of computer science (Jennings, 1998). An agent is a computer system capable of autonomous action in its environment in order to achieve its goal. An agent must be capable of controlling its state and behavior as well as interacting with the other agents. Agent-based systems are designed by first recognizing which part of the program can be a candidate for an agent. The entities that are the best candidates must be autonomous, social, responsive, and proactive. Autonomous entities do not require human interventions to perform their tasks, while they are socially capable of interacting intelligently with other entities. They must be responsive to their environment and capable of taking initiative (i.e., proactive). The problems that are suitable for multi-agent solutions include problems requiring interoperability and interconnection, such as decision support systems, and problems whose solutions are drawn from distributed autonomous experts, for example, healthcare providers as suggested by Nwana (1999) and Dietl (2001).

Agents can effectively address several applications, such as mobile computing environment on database systems (Pissinou, 1997). This architecture employs agents as a representative of mobile system. Agents can provide an analysis tool for team behavior (Nair, 2004). Agents have also been employed in marketplace modeling. One of the major research topics in these applications is the negotiation protocol. The agent-based system improves user's ability to manage information, especially if the information is distributed through a network and is changing daily. A framework for mining information based on agents is presented in Palaniappan (1992). Another popular application of agents is in automation of different tasks. Automated system for multiple sensor placement based on coordination of intelligent agents is presented in Hodge (2003).

The agent framework is well suited for application to our scene understanding because it has multiple desirable characteristics, such as:

- It provides a mechanism for binding together a set of tasks related to a particular input.
- It allows a clear specification of the interface between these sets.
- It facilitates an event-driven process control.

Tracking people passing through an area of interest cannot be done by a single agent since the information is temporally and spatially distributed. Cooperating agents that collect spatial and temporal information through the entire area are used to solve the problem.

Our approach to scene understanding incorporates agents under the following scheme. The area of interest is divided into several sub-areas in agreement with camera range view as illustrated in Figure 6. Each region corresponds to a sub-area where the camera has the best view. Each sub-area has assigned a camera and a *region agent.* A fixed video camera with a wide range of view delivers the raw video stream to be analyzed. The object detection block delivers a foreground mask containing only the event of interest. This foreground mask is sent to the region agent.

The region agent segments the image using the foreground mask. Each segment is sent to the *object agents* that have been already spawned by the region agent. If any object agent does not recognize a segment, then a new agent is spawned to track that object. The object agent is responsible for updating the object model based on information subtracted from

Figure 7. Segmentation of the area of interest for two different camera dispositions

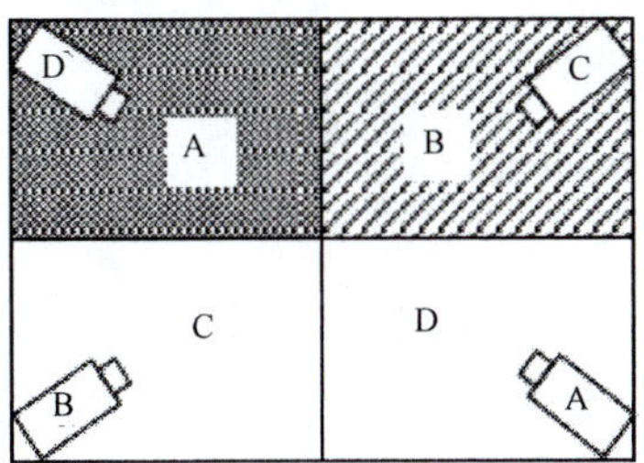

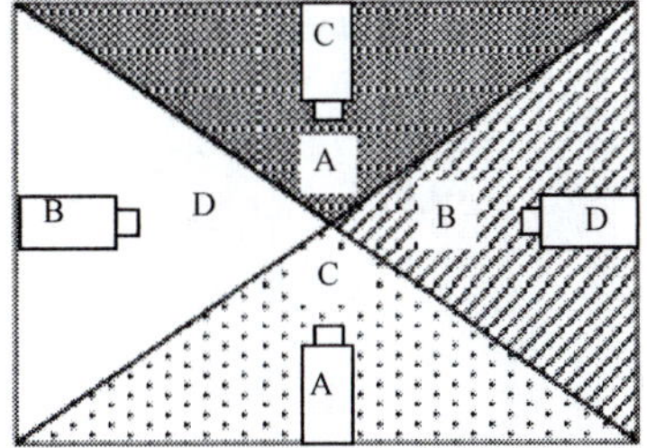

Figure 8. Region agents model

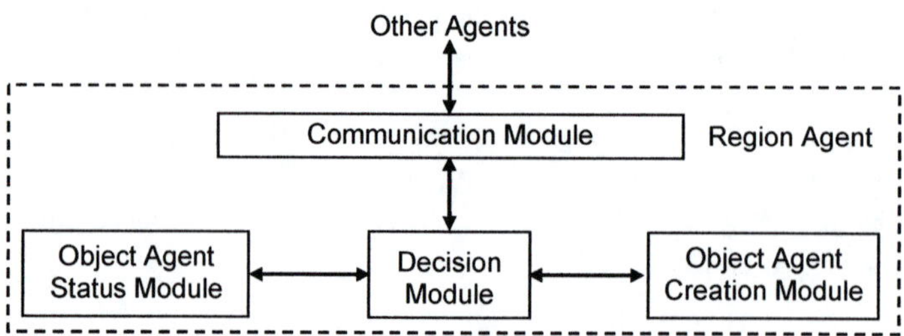

several frames. When an object approaches the border of the area monitored by the region agent, this agent must communicate with the proper agent to send all the information on the object to it. The region agent negotiates proper handoff of moving objects leaving its area with its neighbor.

Each object agent has its *tracking database* to store all the values of the model parameters. The task of the object agent is to identify its assigned object and update image segment as well as trajectory in its tracking database, while the region agent is responsible for creation of object agents and assignment of detected object.

Region Agent Model

The region agent is responsible for monitoring its area as well as coordinating object agents already assigned to the detected objects. In order to perform its activities, a region agent consists of four modules: communication module, object agent status module, object agent creation module, and decision module. Figure 7 describes the agent model. When a new event has been sensed, the region agent must create a new object agent responsible for tracking and updating the object model of the recently detected event.

Object Agent Status Module

The region agent (RA) functions as a coordinator for all the object agents (OAs) that have been created by it. In order to perform its activities, the RA must know the status of the OA. When a new frame has arrived, the RA is responsible for segmenting the frame. Each segment of the frame contains a detected object. The RA marks all the OAs as *not-identified* to indicate that none of the OAs has identified the object present at the scene. When an OA recognizes its object, it will send an acknowledgment message to the RA, then update its status as *positive-identification*.

Decision Module

The decision module is in charge of generating all messages for the other agents. When a new frame arrives, the OA status must be updated and messages are sent to OAs announcing the arrival of a new frame. Then, this module decides the order of transmission to the OAs. When a segment has not been identified for the OAs already created, a new OA must be spawned. When an object is approaching the border of the area, communication with the proper RA is engaged. The decision is based on the heading of the object.

Communication Module

The communication module allows the RA to exchange information with the other agents via a predefined set of messages. The decision module chooses the types of messages and their contents. The agents in the proposed system utilize a protocol based on the Knowledge Query Manipulation Language (KQML) proposed by Finin (1992). KQML is based on *speech act theory* (Searle, 1970) and is a popular protocol that is being used widely for communication among agents (Huhns, 1998; Weiss, 1999). All the necessary information for the correct interpretation of the message is included in the transmission.

Object Agent Model

An OA is responsible for determining if its assigned objects appear on the scene. Also, it is responsible for updating the model and informing the RA that a positive match was established. To execute its task, the OA uses communication, object matching, and decision modules. This agent also contains a tracking database to store all the previous values of the velocity, acceleration, and heading of the detected object. The OA model is depicted in Figure 8. The update module is responsible for updating the new object parameter values in the tracking database. The decision module generates the message to communicate with the RA. The OA must inform when a positive match has been established. Also, the decision module chooses when the update process must be performed.

Figure 9. Region agents model

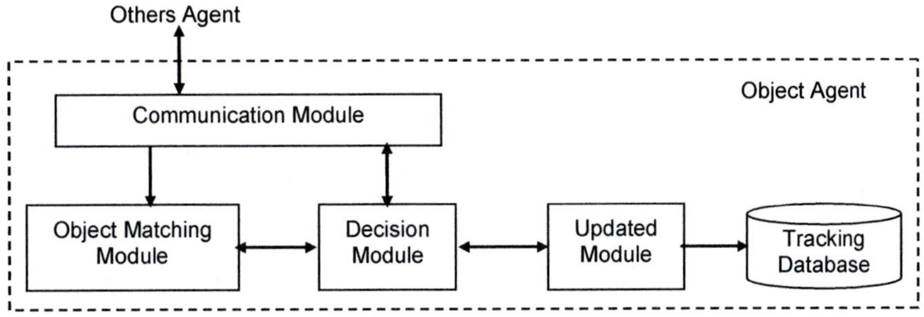

The object matching module recognizes if the segment contains the assigned object. The decision is made based on the Mahalanobis distance. The Mahalanobis distance is a technique to determine similarity between a set of values and an unknown sample (Kamei, 2002). The Mahalanobis distance takes the information of the variance and covariance between variables. This means that the interaction between variables and the range of acceptability is used to determine the similarity between the two sets of values. The distance is calculated by using Equation 1, where I represents the matrix containing the values of the image of the segment, m_t is the vector of the means of the variable of the detected object, and S_t is the with-in group covariance of the detected object.

$$D_M(I) = (I - m_t) S_t^{-1} (I - m_t) \qquad (1)$$

Ontology for the Multi-Agent System

The simulation of the cooperative agents is done by ZEUS toolkit (Collins, 1998). ZEUS toolkit provides tools for simulation and development of cooperative agents in form of Java classes' package. ZEUS provides different default role modeling to implement the function-

Table 1. Fact definition

Fact	Attributes	Default	Meaning
Image_Segment	Segment: Matrix containing a image segment	Null	Segment containing the object to be match
Position_on_Frame	Coordinates x, y: integer	(0,0)	Position coordinates of the upper left corner of the segment
Distance_to_Border	Distance: real	Max	Distance of the object to the border
Approaching_Border	Approach: Boolean	False	Flag for object approaching border area
Velocity	Velocity: real	0	Velocity of the detected object
Acceleration	Acceleration: real	0	Acceleration of the detected object
Heading	Heading: integer	0	Heading of the detected object
Positive_id	ID: Boolean	False	Positive match of the segment with the assigned object
Number_NegID	NO_ID: integer	0	After all the segments have been analyzed by the agent, increments this value to indicated that its object was not present on the current scene
NoSegment	NoSeg: Boolean	False	Indicated to Object Agent that there are no more segments to analyze
ObjectAgentID	Name: string	Null	Name of the Object Agent
RegionAgentID	Name: string	Null	Name of the Region Agent

ality inherent to a multi-agent application. The role model for this particular application is *shared information space*. This model allows each agent to be a publisher and subscriber simultaneously. The responsibilities for every publisher include sending information to subscribers, responding to information sent for subscribers and performing its specific activities. Subscribers must respond to the publisher and perform their activities. RA publishes image segments and each OA takes an image segment and identifies if it corresponds to its assigned object. If a part of the object cannot be identified by any OA, then the RA creates a new OA for that particular object.

The ontology is the shared understanding of the interest domain. Agents communicate among each other to cooperatively solve a designated problem. The communication is performed via messages. Each message contains parameters that possess a meaning in the problem domain. In order for the agents to understand these messages, they must share a common knowledge. The definition of the ontology is defined to be a set of facts. Table 1 presents the set of facts defined for this application.

Object Detection through Background Subtraction Technique

Change detection plays a key role in real-time image analysis. Detection on the scene under observation includes moving, adding, or removing objects. The detection procedure must be able to differentiate between noise or illumination variations and actual movement. One key issue is robustness against illumination changes. A review of several approaches has been studied by Cheung (2004). The most instinctive technique is *frame differencing,* followed by thresholding. Change is detected if the difference of the corresponding pixels exceeds a preset threshold. The advantage of this technique is its low computational complexity. However, it is very susceptible to noise and illumination changes.

Median filter is one of the most popular background subtraction techniques (Cucchiara, 2003). The median of each pixel of all the frames in the buffer constitutes the background estimation. Background pixels are considered to be those that stay on more than half of the frames on the buffer. However, this technique requires a buffer large enough to store L frames. *Recursive background subtraction techniques* do not require a buffer of previous frames. They recursively update the background model based on each input frame. Any error in the background estimation can remain for a long period of time due to its recursive nature. The most popular recursive technique is *Mixture of Gaussian (MoG)* (Friedman, 1997). This method models each background pixel by a mixture of K Gaussian distributions (K is a number between 3 and 5). Different Gaussians are assumed to represent different colors. The weight parameter of the mixture represents the time proportions that those colors stay in the scene. The probable background colors are the ones that stay longer and more static. However, the technique is computationally intensive; its parameters require careful tuning, and it is very sensitive to sudden changes in global illumination.

Wronskian change detector (WCD) employs the Wronskian of intensity ratios as a measure of change (Durucan, 2001). A large mean or large variance of the intensity ratios increases the Wronskian value. This method can detect object interiors and structural changes. Also, WCD is robust against illumination changes. WCD is a suitable algorithm to be implemented

Table 2. Background subtraction techniques

Method	Adaptability	Precision	Complexity	Tuning	Global Illumination Changes	Storage Requirement
Frame Differencing	High	Low	Low	Simple	Sensitive	1 frame
Median Filter	High	Medium	Medium	Simple	Less sensitive	L frames
Mixture of Gaussian	Low	High	High	Complex	Sensitive	None
Wronskian Change Detector	High	Medium	Medium	Simple	Robust	1 frame

Figure 10. Simulation results for background subtraction of an outdoor image, (a) background image, (b) image containing a moving object (truck), (c) results with a 3×3 window, and (d) results with a 5×5 window

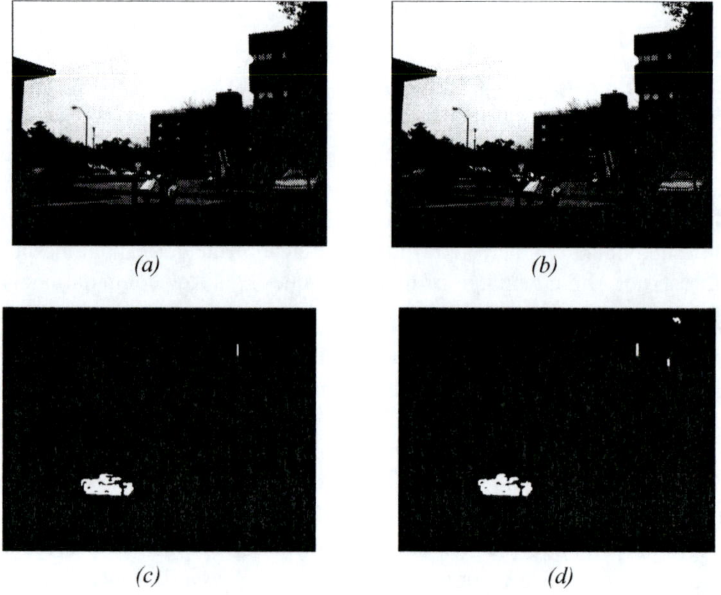

in real-time due to its low complexity. Also, this technique requires only one previous frame; therefore, we adopt it for application in which resources are limited. A comparison of the discussed methods is presented in Table 2. WCD offers a tradeoff between complexity and storage requirements while achieving medium precision and robustness against global illumination changes.

WCD is a non-recursive background subtraction technique that distinguishes changes based on intensity values. Consequently, WCD requires conversion of images into luminance values. Changes are detected based on intensity ratios variance. In order to determine if a change has occurred, a region of support is assigned to each pixel. The size of the region of support can vary from 3×3, 5×5, and 9×9 pixels. The center pixel of the region of support is replaced by the vector formed with the pixel and its neighbors.

If two vectors are linearly independent, then a change can be assumed. A simple and rigorous test for determining the linear dependency of vectors is the Wronskian determinant. WCD exploits the fact that the ratio of luminance values from two light sources helps to quantify the difference between the light sources. The WCD is computed by the Equation 2, where x_i and y_i are the components of the vector for the current frame and the previous frame respectively and n is the dimension of the vector. TH represents the value of the threshold.

$$W\left(\frac{x_i}{y_i}\right) = \frac{1}{n}\left(\sum_{i=1}^{n}\frac{x_i^2}{y_i^2} - \sum_{i=1}^{n}\frac{x_i}{y_i}\right) \leq T \tag{2}$$

$W(x/y)$ detects changes corresponding to dark zones, while its inverse ratio $W^*(x/y)$ finds if a change has occurred in bright zones. Therefore, computing both values allows robust detection against global illumination changes.

Figure 11. Simulation results for background subtraction of an indoor image, (a) background image; (b) image containing a moving object (person); (c) results with a 3×3 window; and (d) results wtih a 5×5 window

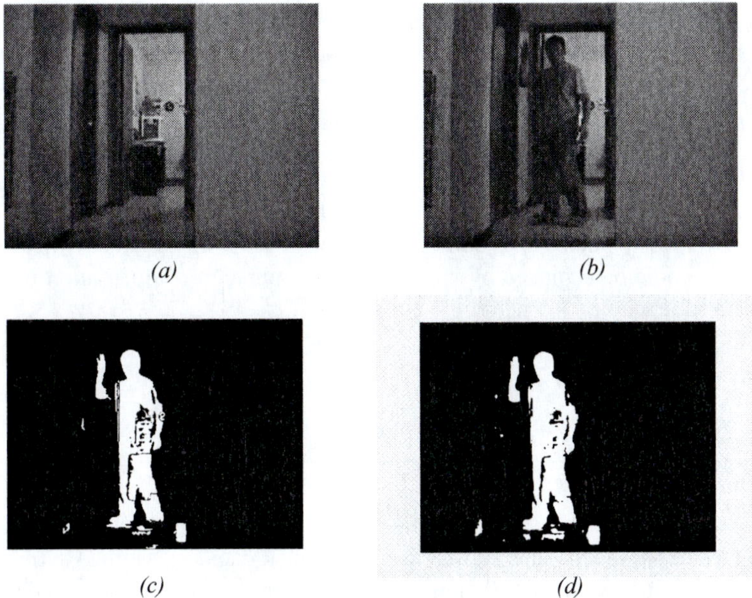

(a) (b) (c) (d)

Figure 12. Detection performance for different luminance values, (a) results for indoor scenes; (b) results for outdoor scenes

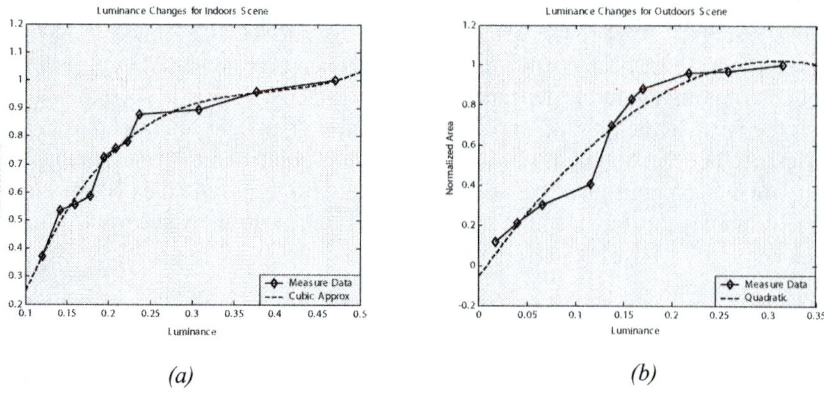

(a) *(b)*

Simulation results show that regions of support larger than 3×3 do not provide better results but require more resources. Therefore, in our approach a fixed 9-dimension vector has been selected. Our simulation accepts frames in JPEG format from the camera where each frame size is 640 × 480 pixels images. Each pixel is an 8-bit value ranging from 255 to 0. The original image is in RGB format that is converted to a luminance value. The resulting foreground mask has zero values for elements on the background and 255 values for detecting moving objects. Figure 9 shows result for an outdoors image using window size of 3 × 3 and 5 × 5. Figure 10 illustrates simulation results for background subtraction of an indoor image. The results for two different size windows are almost the same in these cases.

The background subtraction algorithm must be robust against the change of global illumination. In order to measure the performance of the Wronskian detector, images with different luminance average values were tested. The results are shown in Figure 11 for indoor and outdoor scenes. Luminance average values give a measure of the global illumination of the scene. A factor of 0.47 was obtained at noon when the brightest light can be observed for outdoor. The brightest indoor scene has a factor of 0.31. Since the system will be deployed on building and parking lots, a medium change of illumination can be assumed. Based on the results, Wronskian detector is sufficiently robust for our application. However, further improvement could be achieved by including an illumination compensation block before background subtraction.

Future Trends

Threat recognitions must be done by analyzing behaviors of detected objects. There are two main sources of attack: humans and vehicles. A human displays criminal activity such as hitting or gun pointing, while a car poses a threat when its velocity exceeds the limits set for the area. Therefore, a spatio-temporal pattern detection approach must be employed. Statistical learning techniques such as the hidden Markov model can be employed to detect the criminal pattern activity. However, the nature of these events imposes several challenges such as small and imbalanced training sets. In view of the fact that criminal activity is a rare event, the amount of training data is small. Furthermore, it is desirable that new criminal patterns can be detected without explicit retraining. Since the amount of data containing a threat is smaller than the data containing normal activity, the training set may be uneven.

Statistical learning models can be classified into generative or discriminative ones. The generative models such as the hidden Markov model learn a class density for each class. When a new event is present, these techniques select the most likely class by using a maximum a posterior class. On the other hand, the discriminative models estimate the posterior for each class without modeling the class density. Solutions to these problems have been proposed in Maciel (2000) and Heisele (2003). The coupled hidden Markov and hidden Markov models have been applied toward behavioral analysis and agent have been employed to provide training set for these models (Meninger, 2001).

Another issue to consider is security in the sensor network. Since nodes are limited in energy, computation, and communication capabilities and interact with their physical environment and people, they are prompt to a variety of attacks. These attacks include node capture, physical tampering, and denial of service. Data encryption and access control is one approach to guarantee security and privacy.

Current public-key cryptographic primitives are expensive in terms of computational complexity; therefore, it is not suitable to employ such technique in computational-limited nodes. A new random-key predistribution scheme that is resilient against node compromise is needed as well as the hardware support for such approach (Dimitrijevic, 2003). Denial of service attack disrupts the network's operation by broadcasting a high-energy signal. If the transmission is strong enough, the entire network communication could be jammed. A defense against jamming is to employ spread-spectrum or frequency hopping communication scheme. Therefore, a cryptographically secure spread-spectrum of frequency hopping radio is greatly needed.

An essential service for sensor network is routing and data forwarding. However, routing protocols are susceptible to node-capture attacks. A big step toward a secure network will be achieved by creating secure routing protocols. Sensor network require solutions that are fully distributed and incurred in low cost in terms of communication, power, and memory resources. Several issues related to security and privacy on sensor network are presented by Perrig (2004) and Chang (2003).

Conclusion

A distributed scene understanding architecture has been presented. The architecture consists of a hierarchical sensor network comprising two units: object processing unit and scene processing unit.

OPU is a low-level embedded system containing an image sensor that provides a video stream used to automatically detect and track object present on the scene. Object detection is performed by means of Wronskian change detector. WCD delivers a foreground mask containing detected objects. This foreground mask is employed by the multi-agent system to track each object. Multi-agent system extracts object model values and stores it until they are transmitted to SPU.

SPU is a high-level analysis and storage node dedicated to identifying threat patterns. In order to perform its task, detected objects are classified into predefined sets. Then, the objects are decomposed and the information is supplied to a threat identification block along with the tracking information. If a threat is identified then an appropriate action will be taken. SPU continuously generates a report of activities containing the detected object and tracking information.

The proposed architecture represents an effort toward an intelligent surveillance system capable of automatically detecting suspicious activity using wireless sensor networks. Continued research in this direction will allow preventing catastrophic events. The more intelligence is incorporated into a surveillance system, the closer we will achieve a secure environment. Ethical issues related to this technology have to be addressed by a mixture of technological and social efforts.

Acknowledgments

The authors acknowledge the support of the U.S. Department of Energy (DoE), EETAPP program DE97ER12220, the Governor's Information Technology Initiative, the DoE award DE-FGO2-04ER46136, and the Louisiana Board of Regents contract DOE/LEQSF (2004-07)-ULL, as well as the support of the National Science Foundation NSF, INF 6-001-006 and NSF OISE-0512403.

References

Brand, M., Oliver, N., & Pentland, A. (1997). Coupled hidden Markov models for complex action recognition. In *Proceedings of IEEE Computer Society Conference on Computer Vision and Pattern Recognition*, San Juan, Puerto Rico (pp. 994-999).

Chan, H., & Perrig, A. (2003). Security and privacy in sensor network. *IEEE Computer, 36*(10), 103-105.

Cheung, S-C. S., & Kamath, C. (2004, January). Robust techniques for background subtraction in urban traffic video. In *Proceedings on Video Communication and Image Processing SPIE Electronic Imaging*, San Jose, CA, UCRL-JC-153846-ABS, UCRL-CONF-200706.

Collins, R. T., Lipton, A. J., Fujiyoshi, H., & Kanade, T. (2001, October) Algorithm for cooperative multisensor surveillance. In *Proceedings of IEEE, 89*(10), 1456-1477.

Collis, J. C., Ndumu, D. T., Nwana, H. S., & Lee, L. C. (1998). The ZEUS agent building toolkit. *BT Technology Journal, 16*(3), 60-68.

Cucchiara, R., Piccardi, M., & Prati, A. (2003). Detecting moving objects, ghost and shadows in video stream. *IEEE Transaction on Pattern Analysis and Machine Intelligent, 25*(10), 1337-1342.

Culler, D. E., & Hong, W. (2004). Wireless sensor networks. *Communication of the ACM, 47*(6), 30-33.

Dick, A. R., & Brooks, M. J. (2003, December). Issues in automated visual surveillance. In *Proceeding of 7th Digital Image Computing: Technique and Applications*, Sydney, Australia (pp. 195-204).

Dietl, M., Gutmann, J. S., & Nebel, B. (2001, November). Cooperative sensing in dynamic environments. In *Proceeding of International Conference on Intelligent Robots and Systems*, Hawaii (Vol. 3, pp. 1706-1713).

Dimitrijevic, Z., Wu, G., & Chang, E. Y. (2003, December). SFINX: A multi-sensor fusion and mining system. In *Proceedings of the IEEE Pacific-rim Conference on Multimedia. Singapore* (pp. 15-18).

Durucan, E., & Ebrahimi, T. (2001). Change detection and background extraction by linear algebra. *Proceedings of the IEEE, 89*(10), 1368-1381.

Finin, T., McKay, D., & Fritzon, R. (1992). *An overview on KQML: A knowledge query and manipulation language* (Technical Report No. CS-94-12). MD: University of Maryland, Computer Science Department.

Friedman, N., & Russell, S. (1997). Image segmentation in video sequences: A probabilistic approach. In *Proceedings of the 13th Annual Conference on Uncertainty in Artificial Intelligence* (pp. 175-181). Morgan Kaufmann Publisher Incorporated.

Green, M. W. (1999). *The appropriate and effective use of security technologies in U.S. schools. A guide for schools and law enforcement agencies* (Tech. Rep. No. NCJ178265). Sandia National Laboratories.

Hampapur, A., Brown, L., Connel, J., Pankanti, S., Senior, A., & Tian, Y. (2003, December). Smart surveillance: Application, technologies and implications. In *Proceeding of ICICS-PCM* (pp. 1133-1138).

Heinzelman, W. B., Chandrakasan, A. P., & Balakrishnan, H. (2002). An application-specific protocol for wireless microsensor networks. *IEEE Transaction on Wireless Communication, 1*(4), 660-670.

Heisele, B. (2003). Visual object recognition with supervised learning. *IEEE Intelligent Systems, 18*(3), 38-42.

Hill, J., Horton, M., Kling, R., & Krishnamurthy, L. (2004). The platforms enabling wireless sensor networks. *Communication of the ACM, 47*(6), 41-45.

Hodge, L., & Kamel, M. (2003). An agent-based approach to multisensor coordination. *IEEE Transactions on Systems, Man, And Cybernetics — Part A: Systems and Humans, 33*(5), 648-662.

Huhns, M. N., & Singh, M. P. (1998). *Readings in agents*. San Francisco: Morgan Kaufmann.

Iyengar, S. S., & Brooks, R. R. (2005). *Distributed sensor networks.* Boca Raton, FL: Chapman & Hall/CRC Press Company.

Jennings, N., & Wooldridge, M. (1998). Applications of intelligent agents. *Agent technology: foundations, applications, and markets* (pp. 3-28). Berlin, Germany: Springer-Verlag.

Kamei, T. (2002). Face retrieval by an adaptive Mahalanobis distance using a confidence factor. In *Proceedings of International Conference on Image Processing* (Vol. 1, I-153 - I-156).

Lal, A., & Blanchard, J. (2004). The daintiest dynamos. *IEEE Spectrum, 41*(9), 36-41.

Maciel, B. D., & Peters, R. A. (2000) A comparison of neural and statistical techniques in object recognition. *Proceeding of IEEE International Conference on Systems, Man and Cybernetics* (Vol. 4, pp. 2833-2838).

Meninger, S., Mur-Miranda, J. O., Amirtharajah, R., Chandrakasan, A. P., & Lang, J. (2001). Vibration-to-electric energy conversion. *IEEE Transactions on VLSI Systems, 9*(1), 64-76.

Nair, R., Tambe, M., Marsella, S., & Raines T. (2004). Automated assistant for analyzing team behaviors. *Autonomous Agents and Multi-Agents Systems Journal, 8*(1), 69-111.

Nwana, H. S., & Ndumu, D. T. (1999). A perspective on software agents research. *The Knowledge Engineering Review, 14*(2), 1-18.

Oliver, N. M., Rosario, B., & Pentland, A. P. (2000). Bayesian computer vision system for modeling human interactions. *IEEE Transaction on Pattern Analysis and Machine Intelligence, 22*(8), 831-843.

Palaniappan, M., Yankelovich, N., Fitzmaurice, G., Loomis, A., Haan B., Coombs, J. et al. (1992). The envoy framework: An open architecture for agents. *ACM Transaction on Information Systems, 10*(3), 233-264.

Perrig, A., Stankovic, J., & Wagner, D. (2004). Security in wireless sensor networks. *Communication of the ACM, 47*(6), 53-57.

Pissinou, N., Makki, K., Hong, M., Ji, L., & Kumar, A. (1997, November). An agent based mobile system. In *Proceeding of the 16th International Conference on Conceptual Modeling*, Los Angeles, CA (pp. 361-374).

Rabiner, L., & Juang, B. (1986). An introduction to hidden Markov models. *IEEE Acoustic Speech and Signal Processing Magazine, 3*(1), 4-16.

Rabiner, L. R. (1989). A tutorial on hidden Markov models and selected applications in speech recognition. *Proceedings of the IEEE, 77*(2), 257-286.

Remagnino, P., Shihab, A. I., & Jones, G. A. (2004). Distributed intelligence for a multi-agent visual surveillance. *The Journal of the Pattern Recognition Society, 37*(4), 675-689.

Searle, J. R. (1970). *Speech acts: An essay in the philosophy of language*. Cambridge University Press.

Sinha, A., & Chandrakasan, A. (2001). Dynamic power management in wireless sensor networks. *IEEE Design and Test of Computer, 18*(2), 62-74.

Vieira, M. A. M., Coelho, C. N., da Silva, D. C., & da Mata J. M. (2003, September). Survey on wireless sensor network devices. In *Proceedings of IEEE Conference on Emerging Technologies and Factory Automation*, Lisbon, Portugal (pp. 537-544).

Weiss, G. (1999) *Multiagent system: A modern approach to distributed artificial intelligence*. Cambridge, MA: Massachusetts Institute of Technology Press.

Wentzloff, D. D., Calhoun, B. H., Min, R., Wang, A., Ickes, N., & Chandrakasan A. P. (2004, January). Design considerations for next generation wireless power-aware microsensor nodes. In *Proceedings of 17th International Conference on VLSI Design*, Mumbai, India (pp. 361-367).

Woo, A., Madden, S., & Govindan, R. (2004). Networking support for query processing in sensor networks. *Communication of the ACM, 47*(6), 47-52.

Chapter XII

Fuzzy Coach-Player System for Controlling a Robot Manipulator

Chandimal Jayawardena, Saga University, Japan

Keigo Watanabe, Saga University, Japan

Kiyotaka Izumi, Saga University, Japan

Abstract

Natural language commands are information-rich and conscious because they are generated by intelligent human beings. Therefore, if it is possible to learn from such commands and reuse that knowledge, it will be very effective and useful. In this chapter, learning from information-rich voice commands for controlling a robot is discussed. First, new concepts of fuzzy coach-player system and sub-coach for robot control with natural language commands are proposed. Then, the characteristics of subjective human decision-making process and learning from such decisions are discussed. Finally, an experiment conducted with a PA-10 redundant manipulator in order to establish the proposed concept is described. In the experiment, a probabilistic neural network (PNN) is used for learning.

Introduction

In recent years, there has been increased interest on research related to human-robot interaction. Even socially interactive robots who can demonstrate human-like behavior through natural language communication, understanding gestures, and so forth have received attention (Fong, Nourbakhsh, & Dautenhahn, 2003).

Among recent related works, two lines of research, both of which are equally important in achieving true human-like behavior, can be identified. This is a result of having two viewpoints for the same problem (i.e., human-robot cooperation).

The first line of research concentrates on embedding robots with more human-like cognitive capabilities. For example, Oates, Schmill, and Cohen (2000) presented an unsupervised learning method that allowed a robotic agent to identify and represent qualitatively different outcomes of actions. They used human experience to evaluate the method. Roy (2003) presented a computational model which was able to learn words from multisensory data. In a more recent interesting work presented in Roy, Hsio, and Mavridis (2004), they proposed a set of representations and procedures that enable a robotic manipulator to maintain a "mental model" of its physical environment by coupling active vision to physical simulation with the view of creating an interactive robot which could engage in a cooperative task with a human. Ballard and Yu (2003) and Yu and Ballard (2004) presented a multimodal interface that was able to learn words from human users in an unsupervised manner in which users perform everyday tasks while providing natural language descriptions of their tasks. This line of research is very important, however, due to extremely demanding technical requirements and theoretical developments, such systems still have a long way to go in order to be applied in practical domains.

The other line of research concentrates on controlling ordinary robots by human-friendly means. Here, ordinary robots are the robots which are controlled by conventional methods and are already being utilized for useful work. For example, Lin and Kan (1998) proposed an adaptive fuzzy command acquisition method for controlling machines using natural language commands such as "move forward at a very high speed." In Pulasinghe, Watanabe, Izumi, and Kiguchi (2004), similar commands were used to control a mobile robot handling out-of-vocabulary words. Pulasinghe, Watanabe, Izumi, and Kiguchi (2003) demonstrated a complex human-robot cooperative assembly task using a robot manipulator controlled by natural language commands. The advantage of this line of research is that it enables us to develop human interfaces for existing robotic systems. Some of the potential areas for such applications are nursing and aiding, helping humans in complex tasks such as surgery, and implementing space-restricted systems where other input-output devices are not feasible.

The work presented in this chapter is different from both of these views. It is related to the second one in the sense that it concentrates on controlling ordinary robotic systems by human-friendly means rather than developing a robot with human-like cognitive capabilities.

In natural language communication, encountering words and phrases with fuzzy implications is inevitable. Therefore, any system which accepts true natural language commands should be able to understand their fuzzy meanings. On the other hand, being generated by experienced humans, natural language commands are inherently information rich. Therefore, they can be very usefully and efficiently employed in machine control fine-tuning the performance of the machine. For example, a command like "move slowly" may concisely convey information regarding the nature of terrain, distances to obstacles, and so forth. Therefore, if it is possible to learn from such commands and reuse that knowledge effectively, it will be very efficient and useful. This chapter proposes a method of learning from information-rich fuzzy voice commands for controlling a robot.

First of all, two new concepts, fuzzy coach-player system and sub-coach (Jayawardena, Watanabe, & Izumi, 2003), are introduced. The analogy between the fuzzy coach-player system concept and the real-world relationship between a coach and a player is discussed. The sub-coach concept is proposed to eliminate the limitations of the fuzzy coach-player system. The possibility of learning from natural language commands is then discussed. Inherent subjective nature of natural language commands is discussed and a mathematical model which enables learning from such commands is proposed.

Coach-Player Systems

If controlling a robot with voice commands to perform a non-trivial task is considered, a duplex communication should exist between the robot and the human. Flow of information from human to robot is via verbal commands and the same from robot to human is via visual observation.

The user may make the robot complete a certain task in several steps by issuing a series of commands while observing the robot's behavior at each step. This is analogous to the real-world relationship between a coach and a player in training of a sport. Therefore, this type of a system can be called a coach-player system; in particular, it can be called a fuzzy coach-player system if fuzzy voice commands are used. This concept is illustrated in Figure 1.

There are three important features in a coach-player system:

1. **Command interpretation and execution by the player.** Player contextually interprets the user commands and performs an action. Consequently, the state of the robot and the environment may change.

Figure 1. Concept of fuzzy coach-player system

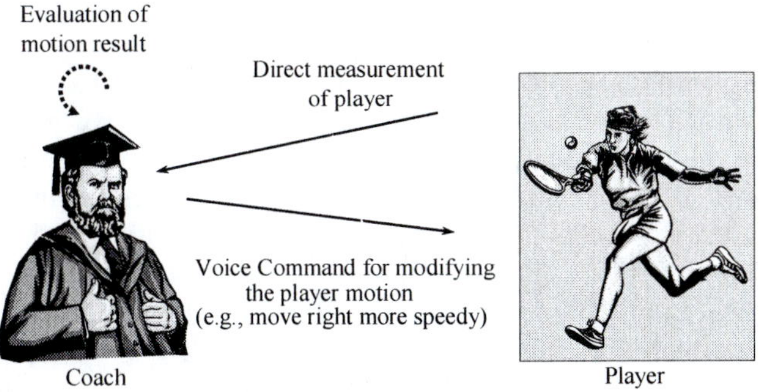

Figure 2. Coach-player system model

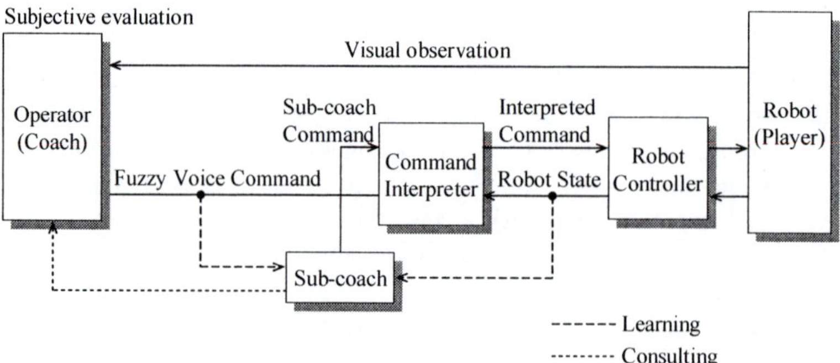

2. **Evaluation of the player by the coach.** Coach observes and subjectively evaluates the state change of the robot and the environment. This subjective evaluation depends on the coach's knowledge, experience, attitude, and so forth. The next command will be influenced by this evaluation.

3. **Improvement of the player's performance.** As a result of accepting the coach's commands, the player will improve its performance toward the coach's intended direction. This may continue until the coach is satisfied with the player's performance.

Figure 2 shows the implementation model of a coach-player system when it is applied to robot-control. Command interpreter module will interprets fuzzy voice commands of the user. For example, a user command may be "move little right." After the interpretation of this, a crisp command will be sent to the robot controller in the required format. Consequently, the robot controller will issue the respective low-level command.

Sub-coach is a software agent that stands in between the user (coach) and the robot (player). Initially, the sub-coach acts just as an observer. It learns from user commands and the corresponding robot states as indicated in Figure 2. Once it gained a sufficient knowledge, it can directly issue commands to the command interpreter, as the user does, consulting the user only when required. This is indicated with dotted arrows in the figure.

Learning from Fuzzy Voice Commands

Voice commands controlling a robot depend on the robot world state. Here, the robot world includes the robot itself, the working environment, and the final objective to be achieved. The user evaluates the world state, subjectively based on his or her knowledge and experience, and issues the most suitable command according to his or her understanding. For example, when controlling a mobile robot to navigate through obstacles, if the user thinks that the robot might clash with an obstacle ahead when it continues to travel at the current velocity, he or she might say "robot, slow down." In response, the robot will reduce the speed. Consequently, the world state will change, thus, avoiding the collision. Therefore, the process of controlling a robot using a series of voice commands can be seen as changing the robot world state repetitively until the required target is achieved.

Robot World State

Robot world state can be defined using two kinds of parameters. One is the kind of parameters which defines the state of the robot itself (e.g., velocity, position, etc.). The other is the kind of parameters which indicate the closeness to the final objective (e.g., distance to the target point to be reached, the depth of a hole drilled, etc.).

Let S be the complete set of all possible world states and S_i be a general element of the set. Then, it follows that:

$$S_i = \{x_1, x_2, \ldots, x_p, y_1, y_2, \ldots, y_r\} \qquad (1)$$

Here, $x_1, x_2, \ldots, x_p$ are the parameters that define the state of the robot itself, where p is the number of such parameters. $y_1, y_2, \ldots, y_r$ are the parameters which indicate the closeness to the final objective and r is the number of such parameters. $(p + r)$ is the total number of parameters required to define a world state. Thus, a world state is a $(p + r)$ dimensional entity and it is a member of a $(p + r)$ dimensional state-space. All these parameters are scalar quantities. Whenever a vector is involved, its components are used as different parameters. More concrete definitions will be found in the section under which implementation details are discussed.

Learning

Let C be the complete set of all valid user commands and C_j be a general element of the set. Assume that the command issued in response to the world state S_i is C_j. Then, we have:

$$f : S \rightarrow C \qquad (2)$$

Here, f is a subjective function which depends on the knowledge, experience, attitude, and so forth of the user. For example, C_j can be something like "go very little."

Since the robot world state may depend on the values of various continuous parameters, S would be continuous. Thus, S may contain an infinite number of points. On the contrary, due to the limitations of any feasible system, the number of valid commands is limited. Therefore, it can be assumed that C is discrete and finite. Thus, f is a serjective function as shown in Figure 3.

The objective of learning by the sub-coach is to learn the subjective function f so that in a later case it can find the correct command corresponding to a world state not encountered during learning. However, since C contains only a finite number of elements, this problem

Figure 3. Relationship between robot world state and commands

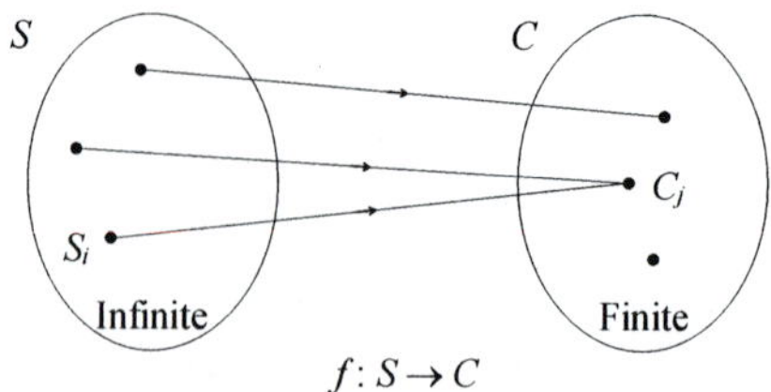

is reduced to a pattern classification problem where the number of classes is equal to the number of valid commands. Thus, if the sub-coach can classify an incoming pattern correctly, it can make correct decisions.

Theoretically, any element in *S* can be mapped to any element in *C*. Since *S* contains an infinite number of elements, if the abrupt decision changes between very close states tend to be frequent, the classification will fail. However, this argument for decision-making based on classification is further supported by the inherent subjective nature of human decisions.

Subjective Human Decision-Making

Human voice commands are fuzzy in their very nature. Although a state of a robot can be defined with various measurable parameters, a human observing that state may not understand it numerically. Instead, his or her evaluation would be subjective and context dependent. As a result, his or her decisions also would not be objective; rather they would be subjective decisions.

As an example, let us consider the illustration shown in Figure 4. Assume that the user wants to guide a robot manipulator to move its tip from source to target. Also, assume that the user can move the manipulator tip either up / down (y axis) or left / right (x axis) using verbal commands. As the first step, user might say "move left" or "move up." In this case, the exact coordinate positions are *Source* = (597.94, -291.93) and *Target* = (450.80, -132.55). But for his or her decision, the user does not use these accurate details. Instead, he might think "what is the best way to move from the source area to the target area." Thus, the user may take the same decision to move from any point in the source area to any point in the target area.

This concept is not valid only for moving between points. In this example, the subjective decision of the user depends only on the source position and the target position. Therefore, a state can be defined using *x*, *y* coordinates of *Source* and *Target*, that is, they are s_x, s_y, t_x and t_y. Then, according to Equation 1, a state can be defined as $\{s_x, s_y, t_x, t_y\}$, whose dimension is four. Thus, in this case, a state is a member of a four-dimensional state-space. According to the explanation, for two sufficiently closer members in the state-space, the user may make similar decisions. Thus, it should be valid for any state-space as far as the user decisions are subjective.

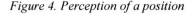

Figure 4. Perception of a position

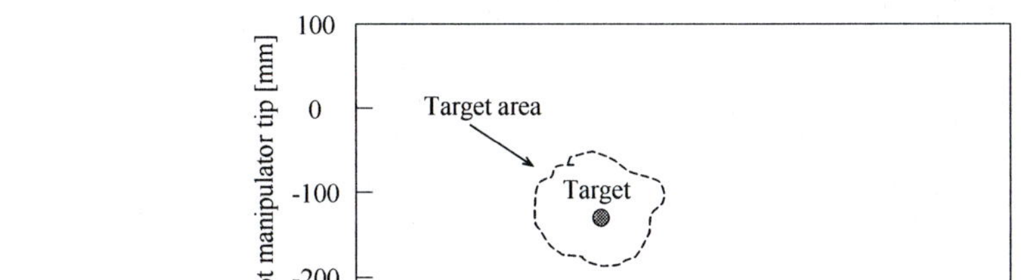

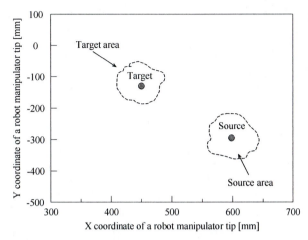

Therefore, according to the previous discussion, although S may contain an infinite number of continuous values, the frequency of abrupt decision changes among sufficiently closer states is much smaller than the theoretical maximum. Thus, the classification problem becomes less complex.

Overview of the Experiment

An overview of the sample experiment conducted to demonstrate the concept is given here. In this experiment, a human user was able to command a robot manipulator with voice commands to pick objects placed on a table and to place them in a bin, avoiding obstacles. To do this, the tip of the manipulator had to be moved from one point to another in 3D space.

When controlling through voice commands is considered, the task of moving from one point to another has to be performed in a step-by-step fashion. At each step, there are two decisions to be made. They are:

1. moving direction
2. moving distance

After making these decisions, the user has to issue a voice command which includes both direction and distance information. Out of these two components of the command, the direction command component is a non-fuzzy decision. The direction decision commands used in the experiment were left, right, forward, backward, up, and down. By looking at the present tip position of the robot, the bin and the placement of the obstacles, the user could subjectively decide the best direction to move.

Table 1. Fuzzy commands used by the human user

Direction command component (D_i)	Distance command component (d_i)
go up go down go right go left go forward go backward	very little little medium Far

Figure 5. The experimental setup

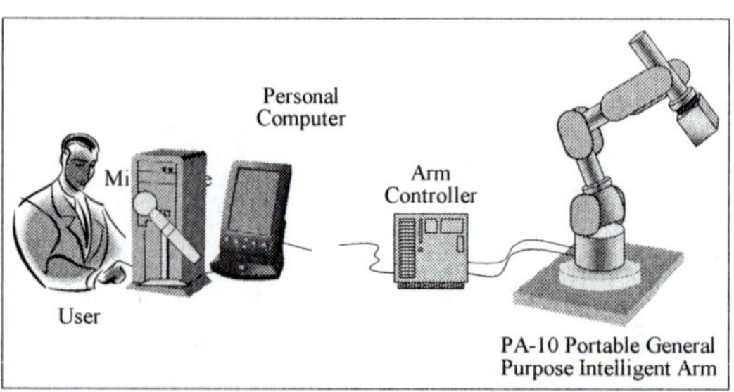

On the other hand, the distance command component is a fuzzy command. That is because, when natural language commands are used to instruct distances, commands such as "move little" are more convenient than the ones containing numerical values. A set of distance commands used in the experiment is shown in Table 1. Any combination of a direction command component and a distance command component was valid. For example, "go very little right" was a valid command. After learning, the sub-coach was capable of generating similar commands.

The commands used to catch and release objects (i.e., "close gripper" and "open gripper") are not shown in the table because they are not relevant to the learning process described later. Interpreting fuzzy voice commands is one of the additional, but important tasks need to be performed. The method used to interpret these fuzzy commands and the details of the inference procedure are explained in the Appendix.

The experimental setup is shown in Figure 5. It consists of a microphone, a personal computer, a PA-10 portable general purpose intelligent arm, and the arm controller. The speech recognition software, the sub-coach program, and the operational control program of PA-10 are hosted in the personal computer whose operating system is Windows XP. The speech recognition is performed using IBM Via Voice SDK. A view of the experimental setup is shown in Figure 6.

The flowchart presented in Figure 7 shows the operation of the sub-coach. There, S_i is the current state for which a decision is required. C_i is the suitable command corresponding to the state S_i.

Figure 6. View of the experimental setup

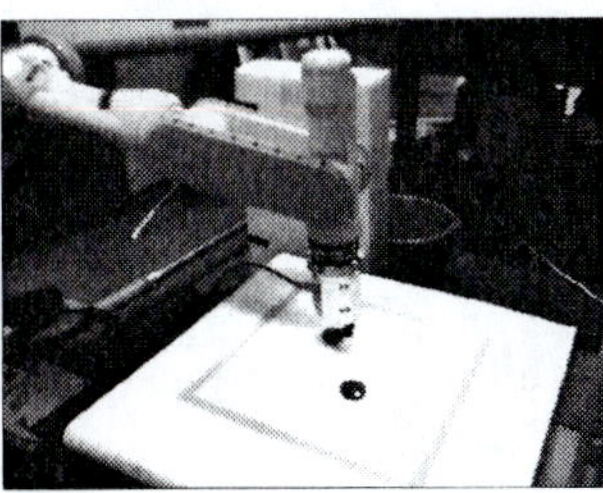

Figure 7. Command generation of the sub-coach using the knowledge base

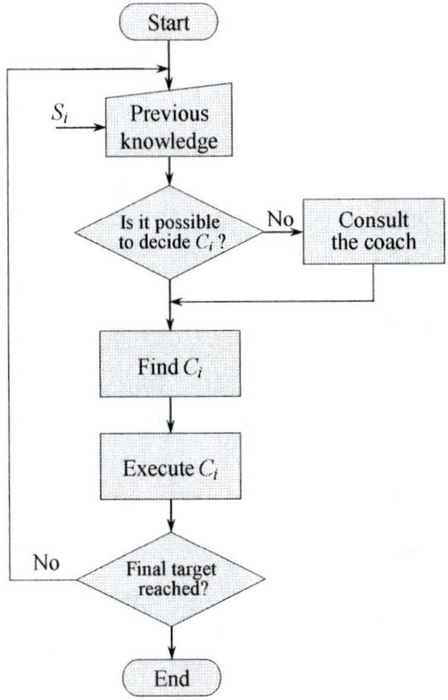

Implementation of Sub-Coach

Knowledge Acquisition

The robot-world state for the motions in 3*D* space is defined as:

$$S_i = \{\mathbf{s}_i^T, \mathbf{t}_i^T\} \tag{3}$$

where $\boldsymbol{s}_i$ is the current position vector of the robot, $\boldsymbol{t}_i$ is the final target position vector, and:

$$\boldsymbol{s}_i^T = [s_{x_i}, s_{y_i}, s_{z_i}] \tag{4}$$

$$\boldsymbol{t}_i^T = [t_{x_i}, t_{y_i}, t_{z_i}] \tag{5}$$

where $(s_{x_i}, s_{y_i}, s_{z_i})$ and $(t_{x_i}, t_{y_i}, t_{z_i})$ are x, y, z coordinates of the current position and the final target, respectively. Command C_i is defined as:

$$C_i = \{D_i, d_i\} \tag{6}$$

where D_i is the direction command component and d_i is the distance command component.

Possible values of D_i and d_i are shown in Table 1. As explained in the Appendix, to interpret fuzzy distance commands, the actual distance traveled in response to the previous command is used. Let the actual previous distance traveled when C_i is issued be l_i. Possible values of l_i are *low*, *medium*, and *high*.

Knowledge acquisition by the sub-coach is the same as learning the function *f*. For this purpose, a probabilistic neural network (PNN) is used. However, to learn the function *f*, any suitable method may be used. In more complex domains, more sophisticated classification methods should be employed. The main factors which motivated the use of PNN are its simplicity, fast response, and the suitability for online training.

Three object moving motions are shown in Figure 8. Here, the coordinates of the object with reference to the object table are assumed to be known in advance by some other means.

Figure 8. Sample training movements

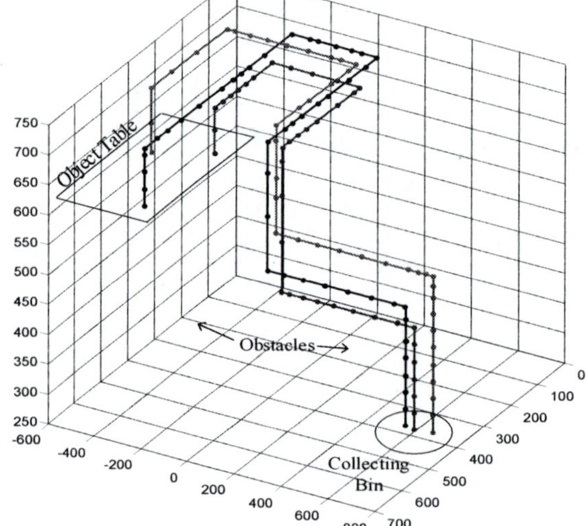

Figure 9. Convergence of learning

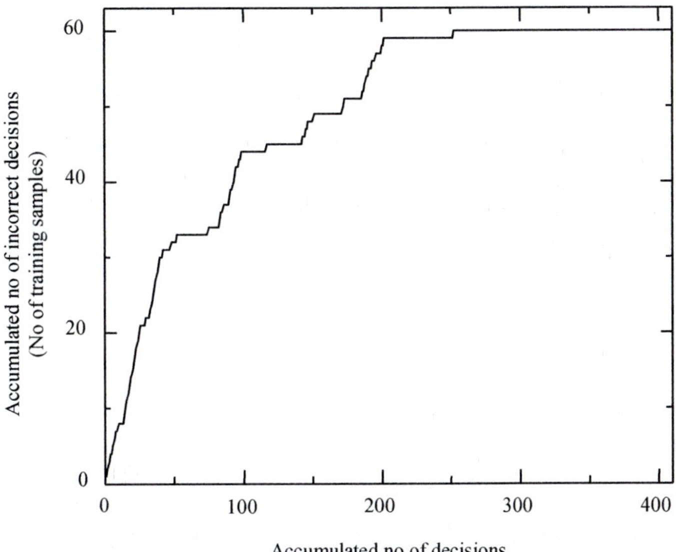

For example, object coordinates on the table can be calculated using an image taken from a camera placed above the table. So, in this experiment what is learned is the path from the table to the bin avoiding surrounding obstacles.

During online training, objects placed in different places of the table were moved to the bin. At the points marked with circles in the Figure 8, decisions were made. First, sub-coach made the decision, and if it is correct according to human evaluation, it was executed. If it is incorrect, a human user issued the correct command.

Figure 9 shows the total number of incorrect decisions made by the sub-coach versus the total number of decisions made during nine pick and place operations. Once the sub-coach made an incorrect decision, the knowledge base of the sub-coach is updated using the correct human user command. Thus, the number of incorrect decisions is equivalent to the number of training samples for the PNN.

It can be observed that initially the number of errors is high due to lack of knowledge. As the knowledge base grows, the rate of increase of the accumulated error is reduced and finally the accumulated error is saturated.

A portion of the training data collected during online training is shown in Table 2.

Decision-Making

The PNN architecture used in this chapter is a modified version of the original PNN architecture. The PNN was first proposed in Specht (1990). Because of ease of training and a sound statistical foundation in Bayesian estimation theory, PNN has become an effective

Table 2. Training data for PNN

i	State (S_i)						C_i		l_i
	s_{x_i}	s_{y_i}	s_{z_i}	t_{x_i}	t_{y_i}	t_{z_i}	D_i	d_i	
...	...	...	...	...	...	...	...	...	...
2	+366.35	-270.14	+619.44	+455.00	+703.00	+277.00	B	l	H
3	+366.33	-270.14	+657.99	+455.00	+703.00	+277.00	B	l	M
...	...	...	...	...	...	...	...	...	...
57	+401.17	+735.61	+309.57	+455.00	+703.00	+277.00	D	m	M
58	+496.44	-400.16	+715.42	+455.00	+703.00	+277.00	B	m	M
59	+408.17	-399.96	+723.50	+455.00	+703.00	+277.00	B	f	M
60	+408.17	+59.82	+723.31	+455.00	+703.00	+277.00	F	m	H
...	...	...	...	...	...	...	...	...	...

B: backward; D: down; F: forward; l: little; m: medium; f: far; H: high; M: medium

tool for solving many classification problems (Raghu & Yegnanarayana, 1998; Ganchev, Fakotakis, & Kokkinakis, 2003; Romero, Touretzky, & Thibadeau, 1997; Musavi, Chan, Hummels, & Kalantri, 1994).

One of the principal advantages of the PNN approach is that it is much faster than the well-known back propagation approach, for problems in which the incremental adaptation time of back propagation is a significant fraction of the total computation time (Specht, 1990; Duda, Hart, & Stork, 2004; Mao, Tan, & Ser, 2000).

The decision-making process of the sub-coach is essentially a pattern classification problem. The input for the decision-making algorithm is the robot world state. For example, if the direction decision is considered, each state is associated with a direction decision. Since the number of direction decisions is finite, selecting the most suitable decision is the same as categorizing the input state into the correct category. Deciding the most suitable distance and the most possible previous distance is performed in the same manner.

The PNN architecture used is shown in Figure 10. The summation layer and the decision layer are composed of three parallel segments because this network is used to find three different values in parallel. That is, finding the most appropriate direction command, D_i, the most appropriate distance command, d_i, and the most appropriate actual distance associated with d_i, l_i is equivalent to three pattern classifications. These three segments can be called as segment D, segment d, and segment l.

Figure 10. Probabilistic neural network architecture

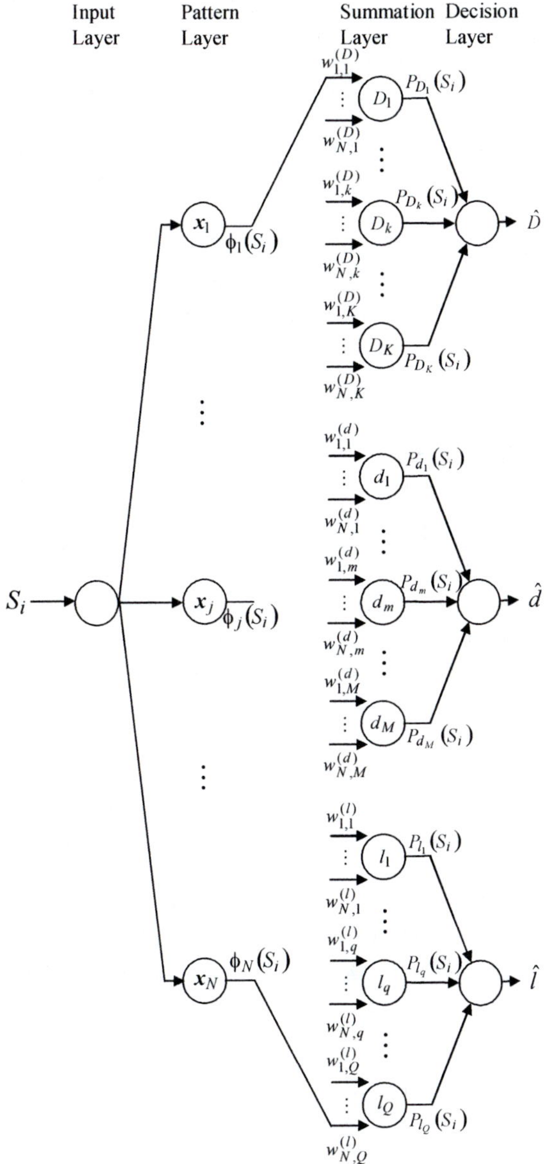

In the figure:

N number of neurons in the pattern layer, or number of learned states (number of entries in the knowledge base)

K number of neurons in the segment *D* of the summation layer, or number of possible direction decisions

M number of neurons in the segment d of the summation layer, or number of possible distance commands

Q number of neurons in the segment l of the summation layer, or number of possible distances traveled in response to the previous command.

Assume that S_i is the input received by the PNN. The input neurons are merely distribution units that supply the same input value to all the pattern neurons.

Each neuron in the pattern layer corresponds to a previously learned state. For example, the weight vector x_i associated with the jth neuron of the pattern layer is composed of the jth state of the training data set. Each neuron in the pattern layer forms the dot product of the input pattern vector S_i with its weight vector x_j and then performs a nonlinear operation on the dot product. Thus, the output of the jth neuron is given by:

$$\phi_j(S_i) = \exp\left\{\frac{-(S_i - x_j)^T (S_i - x_j)}{2\sigma^2}\right\} \tag{7}$$

where σ is a smoothing parameter. Although other methods can be employed to determine σ, in this case, the method proposed by Cain (1990) is used due to its simplicity. According to Cain, σ of any class is proportional to the mean value of the minimum distances among the training vectors in the class. The proportionality constant is usually in the range of 1.1 and 1.4.

Here, it should be observed that the number of neurons in the pattern layer is equal to the number of training samples. As the training data set becomes larger, the network size may grow proportionally. Thus, one of the outstanding issues associated with PNN is determining the network size. Various research have been carried out on reducing the number of neurons in the pattern layer (Raghu & Yegnanarayana, 1998; Romero et al., 1997). However, in this chapter, this issue has not been addressed because the number of training samples is of a manageable size (i.e., 60). On the other hand, it is a topic for a separate research which is out of the scope of the present work.

Weights that connect the pattern layer and the summation layer are defined as follows:

$$w_{j,k}^{(D)} = \begin{cases} 1 & \text{if } D_j = D_k \\ 0 & \text{otherwise} \end{cases} \tag{8}$$

where $k = 1, 2, \ldots, K$,

$$w_{j,m}^{(d)} = \begin{cases} 1 & \text{if } d_j = d_m \\ 0 & \text{otherwise} \end{cases} \tag{9}$$

where $m = 1, 2, \ldots, M$, and

$$w_{j,q}^{(l)} = \begin{cases} 1 & \text{if } l_j = l_q \\ 0 & \text{otherwise} \end{cases} \tag{10}$$

Each neuron in the pattern layer connects to the each neuron in each segment of the summation layer. For example, $w_{j,k}^{(D)}$ is the weight that connects the jth neuron of the pattern layer to the kth neuron in the segment D of the summation layer. If the direction decision D_j associated with the state j is equal to D_k, then $w_{j,k}^{(D)}$ is 1. Otherwise, it is 0.

Neurons in the summation layer compute the maximum likelihood of D_i, d_i, and l_i associated with the state S_i being equal to D_k, d_m, and l_q. It is given by:

$$P_u(S_i) = \frac{\sum_{j=1}^{N} \phi_j(S_i) w_{j,u}}{\sum_{j=1}^{N} w_{j,u}} \tag{11}$$

where $u = D_k, d_m, l_q$.

The decision layer classifies the state S_i based on the output of all neurons in the summation layer by using:

$$\hat{D} = D_k \text{ if } P_{D_k}(S_i) = \max\{P_{D_1}(S_i), \ldots, P_{D_K}(S_i)\} \tag{12}$$

$$\hat{d} = d_m \text{ if } P_{d_m}(S_i) = \max\{P_{d_1}(S_i), \ldots, P_{d_M}(S_i)\} \tag{13}$$

$$\hat{l} = l_q \text{ if } P_{l_q}(S_i) = \max\{P_{l_1}(S_i), \ldots, P_{l_Q}(S_i)\} \tag{14}$$

where $\hat{D}$, $\hat{d}$, and $\hat{l}$ denote the most probable direction command, the most probable distance command, and the most probable distance traveled in response to the previous command respectively.

Here, $\hat{l}$ needs further explanation. The most probable distance command $\hat{d}$ is decided using the distance commands associated with previous states in a small neighborhood of the current state. However, the meanings of these fuzzy commands are context dependent; that is, according to our fuzzy command interpretation method described in the Appendix, they depend on the corresponding previous distances traveled. Consequently, the command estimated based on past data is valid only for a certain context. $\hat{l}$ is the context, that is, the immediate previous distance for which the command $\hat{d}$ is valid.

To deduce the correct distance command d_i from these values, the algorithm shown in Figure 11 is used. In the algorithm L is *Low*, M is *Medium* and H is *High*.

Assume that $\hat{d}$ and $\hat{l}$ are *medium* and L, respectively. As explained, these are the distance command and the actual distance traveled in response to the previous command corresponding to a small neighborhood. In other words, for the neighborhood, the distance command had been "medium" in the context in which the distance traveled in response to the previous

Figure 11. Algorithm to deduce d_i from $\hat{d}$

```
IF d̂= very little THEN d_i= very little
ELSE IF d̂= little THEN
    IF l̂= L THEN
        IF l_i= L THEN d_i= little
        ELSE d_i= very little
    ELSE IF l̂= M THEN
        IF l_i= L or M THEN d_i= little
        ELSE d_i= very little
    ELSE d_i= very little
ELSE IF d̂= medium THEN
    IF l̂= L THEN
        IF l_i= L THEN d_i= medium
        ELSE d_i= little
    ELSE IF l̂= M THEN
        IF l_i= L or M THEN d_i= medium
        ELSE d_i= little
    ELSE d_i= medium
ELSE
    IF l̂= L THEN
        IF l_i= L THEN d_i= far
        ELSE d_i= medium
    ELSE IF l̂= M THEN
        IF l_i= L or M THEN d_i= far
        ELSE d_i= medium
    ELSE d_i= far
```

command was *L*. The user had issued that command after observing that the actual distance traveled in response to the previous command was *low*. Assume that, after interpreting this command, the robot had traveled 25 mm.

For the current state also, the sub-coach needs to issue a similar command. For that, the only knowledge it has is the this fact. Whatever the distance command, its interpreted crisp value should be less than 25 mm because beyond that point, the sub-coach does not know whether there are any obstacles or not. On the other hand, it should command the robot to travel the maximum possible distance to ensure the highest efficiency. Thus, if l_i is *low*, then sub-coach can issue "medium" as the next command. However, if l_i is *medium* or *high*, then it has to issue "little," because otherwise, the interpreted crisp distance will be more than 25 mm.

As explained, the direction decisions made by the sub-coach are non-fuzzy. They are, *up*, *down*, *right*, *left*, *forward*, and *backward*. Assuming that the conditions which influence the direction decision (e.g., distance to obstacles) are the same for all the members in a small neighborhood, the sub-coach can use $\hat{D}$ as the actual direction command (D_i) suitable for the current state.

Conclusion

The learning of sub-coach has been discussed in the framework of fuzzy coach-player system by applying a probabilistic neural network. First, the importance of learning from information-rich natural language commands was discussed and the new concepts of fuzzy coach-player system and sub-coach were introduced. Then, the characteristics of subjective human decision-making process were discussed and a mathematical model which was suitable for subjective decision-making was developed.

The sub-coach was trained online with movements covering different areas of the working space of the robot where the working space of the robot consisted of an object table, a bin, and obstacles. The objective was to pick the objects from the object table and place them in the bin located away from the object table. In doing so, the user commanded the robot to move its tip from a position in the table to the bin avoiding obstacles. At each step, the sub-coach took two decisions, that is, direction to move and distance to move, and these decisions were evaluated by the human user. If the decision was correct, it was executed, whereas if it was incorrect, the correct decision was issued by the human; thus, improving the knowledge of the sub-coach.

It was observed that after about 60 training samples, the learning was converged for this particular task. Thus, it can be observed that it is possible to hand over certain tasks to the sub-coach while assisting him or her only when needed. This can largely reduce the burden of a user who controls a robot with voice commands. On the other hand, a user can control more than one robots at the same time, just monitoring and helping them as needed.

Using this system, it is possible to improve the usability of redundant manipulators by controlling them using fuzzy voice commands. Additionally, the same method may be suitably applied for other robotic systems, too, though it was illustrated for a PA-10 redundant manipulator in this chapter. The most important feature of the proposed method is that it utilizes the inherent fuzzy nature of spoken language commands to generate possible commands for unknown cases.

Future Trends

In this section, some of the most important current research directions related to the natural language usage in human-robotic interaction are summarized.

Generally, there are three key components which would contribute to the success of human-friendly robotic systems. They are visual interfaces, natural language communication, and safety.

In human communications, vision, and language are not totally independent. The shared context among the parties involved in conversation plays an important role in conveying the meaning of the speech. Although some important research has been performed on the relationship between vision and language considering speaker point of view in Roy et al. (2004), achievement of joint attention in Imai, Ono, and Ishiguro (2003), use of spatial relationship to establish a natural communication in Skubic et al. (2004), and so forth; there is a long way to go.

However, there are situations where natural language usage may not be desirable and ask for additional requirements. A good example was the World Trade Center (WTC) rescue operation which provided an opportunity to use and evaluate some of the robots working in cooperation with humans in a real-world situation (Casper & Murphy, 2003). It was observed that although natural language usage was useful for human-robot interactions in general, due to the environmental conditions during such rescue operations, natural language usage was impractical. Instead, more research on perceptual user interfaces, representing robot and world states, using same robot platform for multiple tasks, and many other research directions have been emphasized.

References

Ballard, D. H., & Yu, C. (2003). A multimodal learning interface for word acquisition. In *Proceedings of IEEE International Conference on Acoustics, Speech, and Signal Processing* (Vol. 5, pp. 784-787).

Burrascano, P. (1991). Learning vector quantization for the probabilistic neural network. *IEEE Transactions on Neural Networks, 2*(4), 458-461.

Cain, J. B. (1990). Improved probabilistic neural network and its performance relative to the other models. *Proceedings of SPIE, Applications of Artificial Neural Networks*, 1294 (pp. 354-365).

Casper, J., & Murphy, R. R. (2003). Human-robot interactions during the robot-assisted urban search and rescue response at the World Trade Center. *IEEE Transactions on Systems, Man, and Cybernetics-Part B: Cybernetics, 33*(3), 367-385.

Duda, R. O., Hart, P. E., & Stork, D. G. (2004). *Pattern classification* (2nd ed.). New York: Wiley.

Fong, T., Nourbakhsh, I., & Dautenhahn, K. (2003). A survey of socially interactive robots. *Robotics and Autonomous Systems, 42*(3-4), 143-166.

Ganchev, T., Fakotakis, N., & Kokkinakis, G. (2003). Impostor modeling techniques for speaker verification based on probabilistic neural networks. In *Proceedings of IASTED International Conference on Signal Processing, Pattern Recognition, and Applications*, Rhodes, Greece (pp. 185-190).

Imai, M., Ono, T., & Ishiguro, H. (2003). Physical relation and expression: Joint attention for human-robot interaction. *IEEE Transactions on Industrial Electronics, 50*(4), 636-643.

Jayawardena, C., Watanabe, K., & Izumi, K. (2003). Probabilistic neural network based learning from fuzzy voice commands for controlling a robot. In *Proceedings of the International Conference on Control, Automation, and Systems*, Bangkok, Thailand (pp. 2011-2016).

Lin, C. T. & Kan, M. C. (1998). Adaptive fuzzy command acquisition with reinforcement learning. *IEEE Transactions on Fuzzy Systems, 6*(1), 102-121.

Mao, K. Z., Tan, K. C., & Ser, W. (2000). Probabilistic neural-network structure determination for pattern classification. *IEEE Transactions on Neural Networks, 11*(4), 1009-1016.

Mitsubishi Heavy Industries Ltd., PA-10 portable general purpose intelligent arm programming manual - rev.1.

Musavi, M. T., Chan, K. H., Hummels, D. M., & Kalantri, K. (1994). On the generalization ability of neural-network classifier. *IEEE Transactions on Pattern Analysis and Machine Intelligence, 16*(6), 650-663.

Oates, T., Schmill, M. D., & Cohen, P. R. (2000). A method for clustering the experiences of a mobile robot that accords with human judgment. In *Proceedings of the 17th National Conference on Artificial Intelligence*, Austin, TX (pp. 846-851).

PA-10 Portable General Purpose Intelligent Arm. *Programming manual*. Mitsubishi Heavy Industries Ltd. Retrieved from http://www.mhi.co.jp

Pulasinghe, K., Watanabe, K., Izumi, K., & Kiguchi, K. (2003). Control of redundant manipulators by fuzzy linguistic commands. In *Proceedings of the SICE Annual Conference*, Fukui, Japan (pp. 2819-2824).

Pulasinghe, K., Watanabe, K., Izumi, K., & Kiguchi, K. (2004). A modular fuzzy-neuro controller driven by spoken language commands. *IEEE Transactions on Systems, Man, and Cybernetics-Part B: Cybernetics, 34*(1), 293-302.

Raghu, P. P., & Yegnanarayana, B. (1998). Supervised texture classification using a probabilistic neural network and constraint satisfaction model. *IEEE Transactions on Neural Networks, 9*(3), 516-522.

Romero, R. D., Touretzky, D. S., & Thibadeau, R. H. (1997). Optical Chinese character recognition using probabilistic neural networks. *Pattern Recognition, 30*(8), 1279-1292.

Roy, D. (2003). Grounded spoken language acquisition: Experiments in word learning. *IEEE Transactions on Multimedia, 5*(2), 197-209.

Roy, D., Hsio, K., & Mavridis, N. (2004). Mental imagery for a conversational robot. *IEEE Transactions on Systems, Man, and Cybernetics-Part B: Cybernetics, 34*(3), 1374-1383.

Skubic, M., Perzanowski, D., Blisard, S., Schultz, A., Adams, W., Bugajska, M., & Brock, D. (2004). *IEEE Transactions on Systems, Man, and Cybernetics — Part C: Applications and Reviews, 34*(2), 154-167.

Specht, D. F. (1990). Probabilistic neural networks. *Neural Networks, 3*(1), 109-118.

Yu, C., & Ballard, D. H. (2004). A multimodal learning interface for grounding spoken language in sensory perceptions. *ACM Transactions on Applied Perceptions, 1*(1), 57-80.

Appendix: Interpreting Fuzzy Motion Commands

All natural language commands are fuzzy in their very nature. Their meanings are subjective and context dependent. For example, what is meant by "move little" by a human is not a fixed value.

In this implementation, it is assumed that the actual amount to be traversed in response to a distance command is dependent on the distance traversed immediately before that. This assumption is based on the observation of natural human tendency.

For example, a human who just traveled 10 km may consider another 1 km as a short distance while another one who just traveled 100 m may consider the same 1 km as a long distance. This kind of an approach has been adopted in Pulasinghe et al. (2003). The similarity between that and the approach in this chaptert comes from the fact that, in both systems the actual response to the previous command is used as an input when interpreting the present command. However, in the system discussed in this chapter, simple fuzzy reasoning is used, while in Pulasinghe et al. (2003), a fuzzy neural network has been used.

In the process of interpreting the meanings of fuzzy distance commands, the following 12 rules are used for fuzzy reasoning:

R^1 If a is '*very little*' and l is L then h is VVS

R^2 If a is '*very little*' and l is M then h is VS

R^3 If a is '*very little*' and l is H then h is S

R^4 If a is '*little*' and l is L then h is S

R^5 If a is '*little*' and l is M then h is B

R^6 If a is '*little*' and l is H then h is VB

R^7 If a is '*medium*' and l is L then h is VB

R^8 If a is '*medium*' and l is M then h is VVB

R^9 If a is '*medium*' and l is H then h is F

R^{10} If a is '*far*' and l is L then h is F

R^{11} If a is '*far*' and l is M then h is VF

R^{12} If a is '*far*' and l is H then h is VVF

where a is distance command character variable, l is previous distance, and d is new distance. Fuzzy labels for the previous distance and the new distance are defined by:

- ***VVS*:** very very small
- ***VS*:** very small
- ***S*:** small
- ***B*:** big
- ***VB*:** very big

- ***VVB*:** very very big
- ***F*:** far
- ***VF*:** very far
- ***VVF*:** very very far
- ***L*:** low
- ***M*:** medium
- ***H*:** high

Distance command character variable a represents the support set of distance command component and its membership value is either 1 or 0, that is, a has singleton membership functions. The membership functions for a and l are shown in Figures 12 and 13, respectively. Consequent part gives the new distance, d and the membership functions are shown in Figure 14.

The firing strength of the ith rule, α_i is computed as:

$$\alpha_i = \mu_{AM_i}(a) \cdot \mu_{PD_i}(l) \tag{15}$$

Here, "." is the algebraic product. Using Larsen's product operation rule as the fuzzy implication function, the ith rule leads to the decision:

Figure 12. Membership functions for action modification

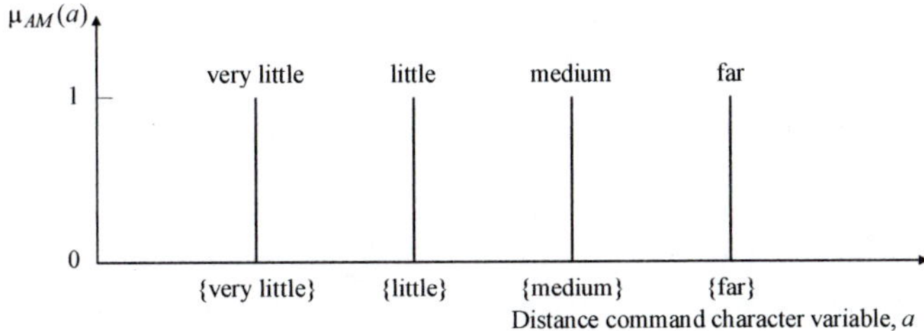

Figure 13. Membership functions for previous distance

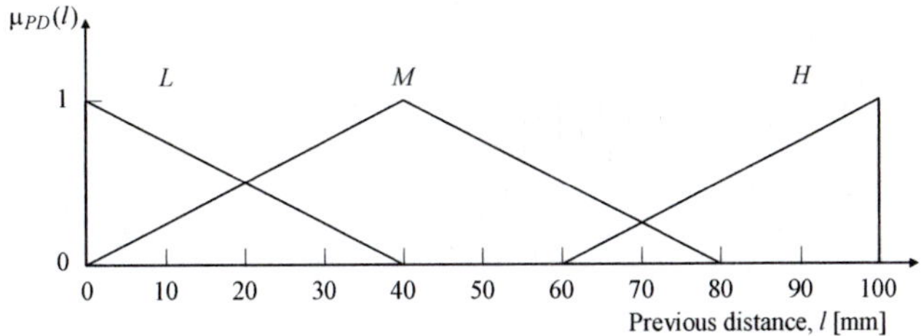

Figure 14. Membership functions for new distance

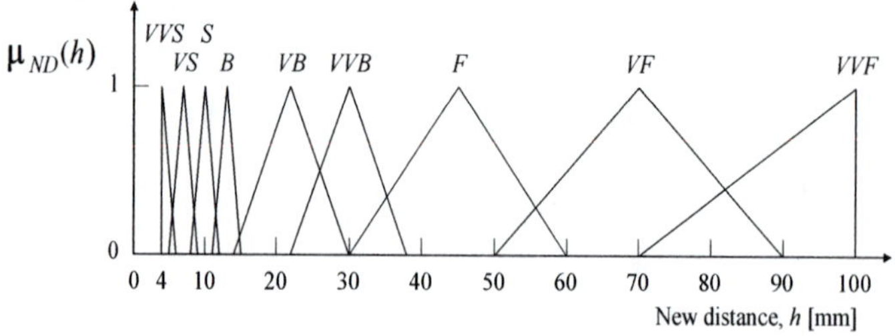

$$\mu_{ND'_i}(h)=\alpha_i \cdot \mu_{ND_i}(h) \tag{16}$$

Consequently, the membership function $\mu_{ND'}$ of the inferred consequence is given by:

$$\mu_{ND'}(h)=\mu_{ND'_1}(h)\vee \ldots \vee \mu_{ND'_{12}}(h) \tag{17}$$

$$\mu_{ND'}(h)=\alpha_1 \cdot \mu_{ND_1}(h)\vee \ldots \vee \alpha_{12} \cdot \mu_{ND_{12}}(h) \tag{18}$$

To obtain the crisp output value, a defuzzification strategy is required. Using the well-known Center-of-Area method, the crisp output value of the new distance, h_0 is obtained as follows:

$$h_0 = \frac{\int_{-\infty}^{+\infty}\sum_{i=1}^{12}\alpha_i h \mu_{ND_i}(h)\,dh}{\int_{-\infty}^{+\infty}\sum_{i=1}^{12}\alpha_i \mu_{ND_i}(h)\,dh} \tag{19}$$

After the crisp value of the distance to be traversed, h_0 is decided, it can be directly used to control the tip position of the PA-10 manipulator using its tip position deviation control mode (PA-10). Initially, there is no distance traveled in response to the previous command. Therefore, the initial input value was decided according to the workspace of the manipulator.

Section IV:

Modeling and Development of Intelligent Information Systems

Chapter XIII

Multi-Level Modeling of Multi-Mobile Agent Systems

Ernesto López-Mellado, CINVESTAV Unidad Guadalajara, Mexico

Abstract

This chapter deals with the modeling of mobile agent systems evolving within structured environments using a multi-level Petri net-based formalism, called n-LNS. In a n-LNS model the tokens of a net can be symbols or other nets allowing representing the behaviour of mobile entities. The chapter introduces the formal definition of n-LNS and its application to the modeling of various kinds of discrete event systems, namely batch manufacturing systems, mobile robot communities, urban traffic micro-simulation, and software agents for e-commerce. A case study is included regarding the coordination of an e-market place.

Introduction

Nowadays, organisations and processes operate supported by computer systems which are quite complex because of their largeness and versatility of the provided services. Furthermore, functioning requirements may change often.

The proposed solutions for addressing the design of these distributed systems take advantage of object-oriented methodologies allowing modularity and software reutilisation. This requires concurrent processing which is distributed among several networked computers.

In the last few years, the multi-agent systems (MAS) paradigm has been adopted for developing distributed systems (Ferber, 1999). Agent-based technology has been welcome with a great interest of many research groups because it is a promising approach for conceiving software systems applied in e-commerce, information retrieval, and manufacturing systems automation. MAS appears in these kinds of problems in which some agents have the ability to displace within the computer network; they are called mobile agents (DiMarzo, 1998; Milojicic, 1999).

For these kinds of systems, formal methods are useful for specifying and verifying the functioning of MAS during the earliest stages of the development life cycle. For this purpose Petri nets (PN) and their extensions have been widely used in software systems development because these formalisms allow representation in a clear and compact manner complex behaviour including concurrence, synchronization, resource allocation, and information exchange; particularly, in MAS, high-level PNs have been adopted for modeling partially the behaviour of agents.

In Moldt (1997), coloured PN (CPN) were used for modeling MAS; however, it is difficult to describe important elements such as the environment where the agents evolve or the agents mobility. In order to cope with these problems, a CPN extension was proposed for specifying MAS (Xu, 2000); in this work, the agent mobility is modeled through the updating of references. This approach brings the specification near to software implementation despite the loss of clearness of the description.

Recently, the approach of "nets within nets" has been held in several works for modeling systems with mobile entities. In Valk (1998), a two-level elemental object system (EOS) is proposed; the first level model is a PN state machine while tokens may be ordinary PN or integers.

Holding the same notion of nets within nets, in Hiraishi (2000) PN^2, a two-level formalism similar to the Valk's definition, is proposed; also, in Lomazova (2000), nested PN is proposed; at the same time, in Kummer (2001) and Kölher (2001), reference nets as a support of a simulation tool in which the tokens are references to other nets are proposed.

Following this approach, EOS has been extended; a less restrictive definition of a three-level net formalism for the modeling of mobile physical agents has been proposed (Almeyda, 2002). Later, this definition has been extended; a multi-level PN system, nLNS, was proposed (Villanueva, 2003; Sánchez, 2004), where an arbitrary number of levels can be defined. Also, we added a more complete interaction mechanism allowing the description of conversations among agents.

In this chapter, we present the definition of nLNS and a methodology for modeling mobile agent-based systems. The methodology is outlined and illustrated through a case study from the field of e-commerce.

The remainder of this chapter is organized as follows: the next section presents the definition of the multi-level system. Then, there is an overview of the application of n-LNS to the modeling of various systems including mobile entities. The next section illustrates the application of the proposed formalism to a case study regarding an electronic marketplace. Finally, implementation issues using the JADE framework are briefly discussed.

A Multi-Level Net Formalism

An n-LNS model consists mainly of an arbitrary number of nets organized in n levels according to a hierarchy; n depends on the degree of abstraction that is desired in the model. A net may handle as tokens, nets of deeper levels and symbols; the nets of level n permits only symbols as tokens, similarly to CPN. Interactions among nets are declared through symbolic labelling of transitions.

n-Level Net System Definition

The definition of n-LNS includes the description of the components (structure and marking), declaring of interaction (transition labelling), and the enabling and firing rules (including the synchronization mechanism).

Petri Net Structure

Definition. A PN structure is a bipartite digraph denoted by a triple G = (P, T, F) where P and T are finite nonempty set of vertices called places and transitions, respectively, $P \cap T = \varnothing$, and $F \subseteq P \times T \cup T \times P$ is a flow relation of the net. Pictorially, places are represented as circles and transitions as bars or rectangles.

Type Nets

Definition. A type-net of level i is a tuple $typenet_i = (G, TOKEN_i, LABEL_i, VAR_i, \tau, \lambda, \pi)$ for $1 \leq i \leq n$, where:

- G is a PN structure
- $TOKEN_i$ is a finite non empty set of type-nets and symbols permitted into the places of a net level i: $TOKEN_i \subseteq \{typenet_{j,k} \mid i<j\leq n,\ 1\leq k\leq r\} \cup SYMBOL_i$
  - n is the number of levels of a multi-level net system
  - r is the number of different type-nets allowed into places of a net of level i
- $SYMBOL_i$ is a finite set of symbols allowed into the places of a net of level i
- $LABEL_i$ is a finite set of labels defined for a net level i; $LABEL_i \subseteq LABELS$
- $VAR_i = \{x, y, ...\} \subseteq VARS$ is a finite set of variables defined to a net of level i, where:
  - $Type$: $VAR_i \rightarrow (TOKEN_i - SYMBOL_i)$ assigns types to variables.
- τ: $P_i \rightarrow 2^{TOKEN\,i} - \varnothing$ is an assignment function of types to places.
- λ: $T_i \rightarrow 2^{(LABEL\,i \times \mathrm{ATTRIB})} - \varnothing$ is an assignment function of labels to transitions, where:
  - If i = 1 then $ATTRIB = 2^{\{\downarrow\}}$

- If $2 \leq i \leq n\text{-}1$ then $ATTRIB = 2^{\{\equiv, \downarrow, \uparrow\}}$
- If $i = n$ then $ATTRIB = 2^{\{\equiv, \uparrow\}}$

- π: $F_i \times LABEL_i \rightarrow M_{VARi \cup SYMBOLi}$ is a weighting function that assigns to every arc, a multi-set of variables and symbols, with respect to transition labels. If $label \notin \lambda(t)$, $\pi((p, t), label) = \pi((t, p), label) = \varnothing$. Moreover if i=n then $VAR_i = \varnothing$, so that π: $F_n \times LABEL_n \rightarrow M_{SYMBOLn}$.

A type-net $typenet_i$ is a PN structure with additional information that declares and handles data defined in $TOKEN_i$, according to the pre and post conditions established by π and λ.

Nets of Level *i*

Definition. A net of level i is a type-net $typenet_i$ with a marking μ_i : $NET_i = (typenet_i, \mu_i)$; $1 \leq i \leq n$, where:

- $typenet_i$ is a type-net of level i.
- $\mu_i : P_i \rightarrow M_{NETSTOKENi \cup SYMBOLi}$ is a marking function for the type-net of level i.
  - $NETS_{TOKENi} \subseteq \{NET_{i+1}, NET_{i+2}, \ldots, NET_n\}$.

Figure 1. Piece of a 4-LNS model

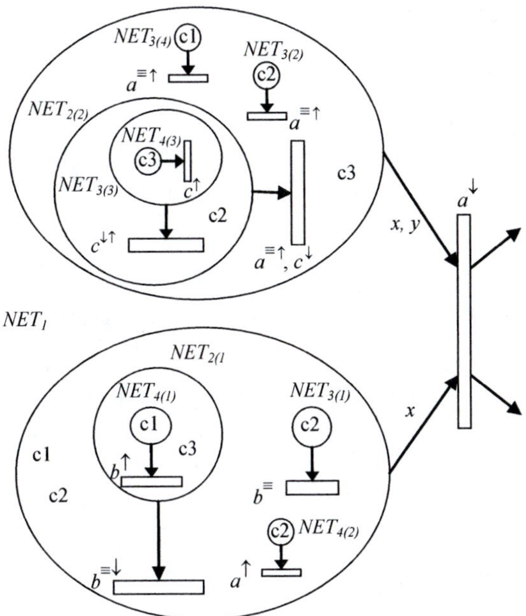

Net System

A n-LNS model, called net system, is the set of all the defined nets at all the levels.

Definition. A n-level net system is a n-tuple NS= (NET_1, NET_2, ... NET_n) where NET_1 is the highest level net, and $NET_i = \{NET_{i,1}, NET_{i,2}, ..., NET_{i,r}\}$ is a set of r nets of level i.

Figure 1 sketches pieces of the components of a 4-LNS. The level 1 is represented by the net NET_1, the level 2 by the nets $NET_{2,1}$ and $NET_{2,2}$, the nets $NET_{3,1}$, $NET_{3,2}$, $NET_{3,3}$, and $NET_{3,4}$ compose the level 3, and the nets $NET_{4,1}$, $NET_{4,2}$, $NET_{4,3}$ form the level 4.

Net System Evolution

The components of a model may interact among them through synchronization of transitions. The synchronization mechanism is included in the enabling and firing rules of the transitions; it establishes that two or more transitions labeled with the same symbol must be synchronized. In order to define the enabling conditions and firing of transitions, we introduce first the notion of variable binding.

Definition. A binding *b* on a variable set *VARS* = {x, y, ...} is a function *b*: *VARS*→ NET-S_{TOKENi}; for a $v \in VARS$, b(*v*) is a lower level net whose the type is *Type*(v). b_t maps every variable defined on the weight of the input arc to the transition t, with respect to a label. $m_{<b>}$ denotes a multiset of nets resulting of instancing a multiset of variables m with b.

Enabling Rule

Definition. A transition *t* of a net of level i NET_i is enabled with respect to a label $lab \in \lambda(t)$ if:

- There exists a binding b_t: $VAR_t \rightarrow NETS_{TOKENi}$, where VAR_t is the set of variables appearing in all $\pi((p, t), lab)$.
- It must fulfil that $\forall p \in \bullet t$, $\pi((p, t), lab)_{<bt>} \subseteq \mu_i(p)$.
    - (<b_t> is not necessary when the level net is *n*).
- The conditions of one of the following cases are fulfilled:
    - **Case 1.** If $lab = (l, \varnothing)$. The firing of *t* is autonomously performed.
    - **Case 2.** If $lab \neq (l, \varnothing)$ one must consider one of the following situations:
        - $lab = (l, \{\equiv\})$. It is required the simultaneous enabling of the transitions labelled with $l^{\equiv}$ belonging to other nets into the same place *p'* of the next upper level net. The firing of these transitions is simultaneous and all the (locally) synchronized nets remain into *p'*.
        - $lab = (l, \{\downarrow\})$. It is required the enabling of the transitions labelled with $l^{\uparrow}$ belonging to other lower level nets into $\bullet t$. These transitions fire simultane-

ously and the lower level nets and symbols declared by $\pi((p, t), lab)_{<bt>}$ are removed.

- $lab = (l, \{\uparrow\})$. It is required the enabling of at least one of the $t' \in p'\bullet$, labelled with $l^{\downarrow}$, of the upper level net where the *NETi* is contained. The firing of *t* provokes the transfer of *NETi* and symbols declared into $\pi((p', t'), lab)_{<bt>}$.

The rest of the subsets of ATTRIB represent combinations of these clauses. So, $(l, \{\equiv,\downarrow,\uparrow\})$ indicates that a transition must be synchronized locally, internally, externally respect to the symbol $l^{\equiv\downarrow\uparrow}$.

Firing Rule

The firing of transitions in all level nets modifies the marking by removing $\pi((p, t), lab)_{<bt>}$ in all the input places and adding $\pi((t, p), lab)_{<bt>}$ to the output places.

In Figure 1, NET_1 is synchronized through the transition labelled with $a^{\downarrow}$ with $NET_{2,2}$, $NET_{3,2}$, $NET_{3,4}$ and $NET_{4,2}$ by mean the transitions (locally synchronized) labelled with $a^{\uparrow}$; all these transitions must be enabled to fire. The simultaneous firing of the transitions removes these nets from the input places.

$NET_{2,1}$, $NET_{3,1}$, and $NET_{4,1}$ are synchronized through the transitions labelled with $b^{\downarrow}$, $b^{\equiv}$, $b^{\uparrow}$ respectively; the firing of the transitions changes the marking of $NET_{2,1}$ and $NET_{3,1}$; $NET_{4,1}$ is removed from the place of $NET_{2,1}$.

$NET_{3,3}$ is removed from the input place of $NET_{2,2}$ and $NET_{4,3}$ is removed from $NET_{3,3}$; this interaction is established by $c^{\downarrow}$, $c^{\downarrow\uparrow}$, $c^{\uparrow}$, respectively.

Modeling Mobile-Agent Systems

Modular and Hierarchical Modeling

The use of nLNS induces a modular and hierarchical modeling methodology, describing separately the behaviour of all the involved components and then integrating such models into a global one by means the synchronization of transitions.

We consider that the minimum number of levels in a nLNS model of a large MAS is three: The first level structures the environment where the agents move through; the second level represents the behaviour of the agents (mobile or stationary); and the third level describes the functioning of specific items of an agent, such as interaction protocols, plans, intentions, and so forth; the lower level may specify other entities not included in the agent model such as resources. According to the size of the MAS or depending on the adopted hierarchy, more levels can be defined.

It is important to point out that the models of the agents describe only the general reactive behaviour of these entities; many agent activities such as perceiving, learning, decision-making, or planning are performed by specialised processes based on appropriated techniques and methods. Nevertheless, the reactive behaviour involves several tasks inherent to interactive agents namely navigation, cooperation, and negotiation which can be described by PN modules.

Case Study: Multi-Agent Marketplace

System Description

Consider the system depicted in Figure 2; it represents a computer network where a host acts as a marketplace. Within this environment, there exist stationary agents and mobile agents. The mobile agents arrive to the marketplace from other hosts and interact among them in order to buy or sell goods or services on behalf of users. When the trade process finishes, the agents return to the origin host to deliver the result of its transaction to the user. In the scheme, arrows represent the connection between two computers which allows communication and transfer of agents (Chavez, 1996).

For the sake of illustration, it is assumed that the negotiation is performed among one buyer and two sellers, and one kind of product is traded. (Sánchez, 2004).

Figure 2. Agents in an electronic market place

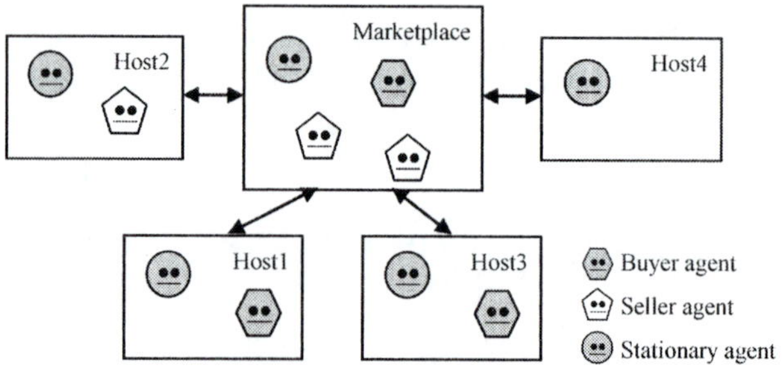

Figure 3. Model architecture

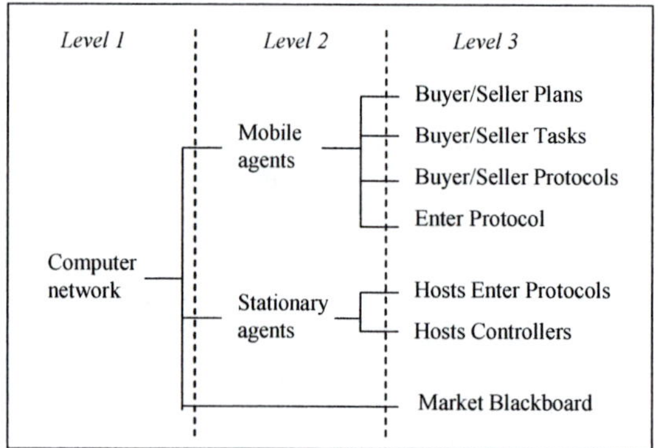

System Modeling/Model Structure

The model is organised at three levels: the level 1 net describes the topology of the computer network where the agents evolve; three nets of level 2 represent the behaviour of agents; and several nets of level 3 model the entities that guide the agents' behaviour, namely, the plan, tasks, and interaction protocols. Figure 3 shows the model structure in which the nesting relationship among the model components is stated.

The Environment Model

The network model *EnvNet* = (*TypeEnvNet*, μ_{EnvNet}) is shown in Figure 4; it is obtained straightforward from the scheme of Figure 2. Every place represents a host of the network, and the transitions represent either the transfer of token-nets or the communication between two hosts (that joined by bidirectional arcs). The labels attached to the transitions t1, t4, t7 have the form MvM, representing the movement of the agent to the market, and the labels attached to the transitions t2, t5, t8 have the from MvHk (k=0,1,2) representing the movement of the agent to a host k. All the labels have the attribute of internal synchronisation.

The initial marking shown in the figure represents the distribution of the stationary and mobile agents and the blackboard. One stationary agent exists in every host; also, a mobile

Figure 4. Network model

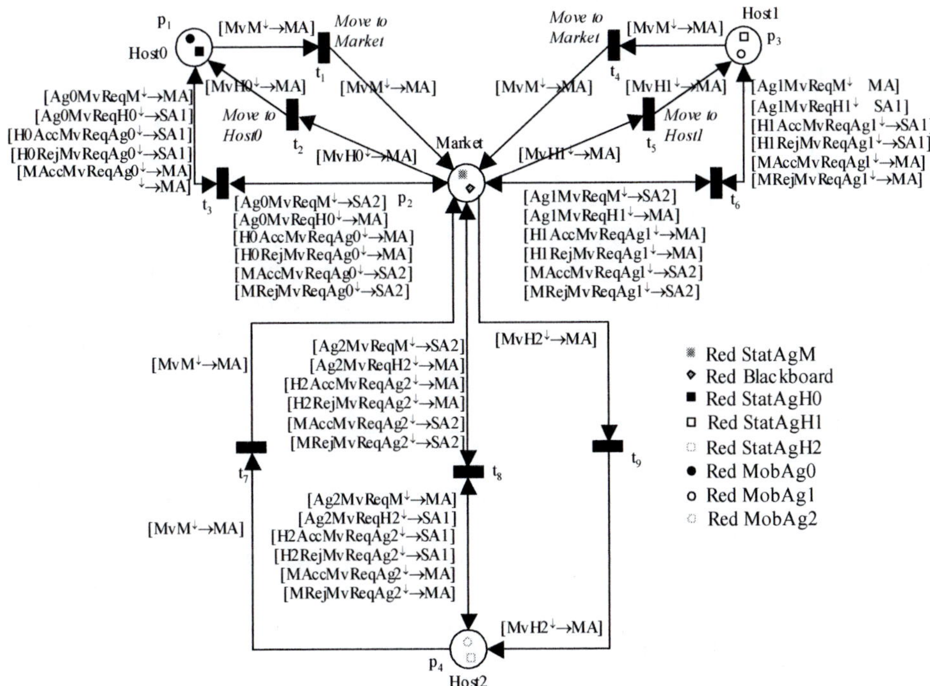

Figure 5. Stationary agent model

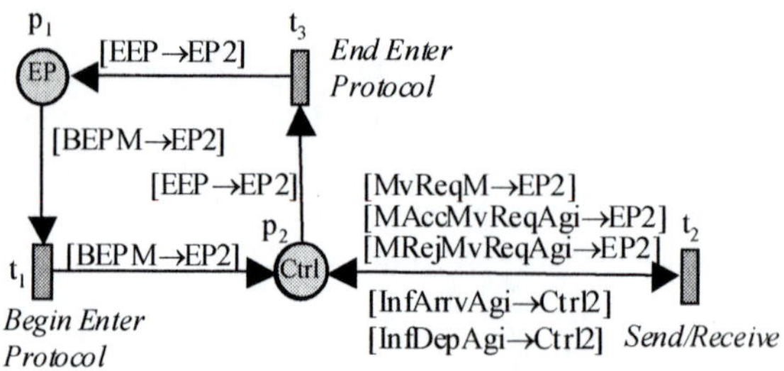

Table 1. Functions λ y τ fo the net TypeEnvNet

TypeEnvNet	
λ	
$\lambda(t_1)=\lambda(t_4)=\lambda(t_7)=\{MvM^{\downarrow}\}$	$\lambda(t_2)=\{MvH0^{\downarrow}\}$
$\lambda(t_3)=\{Ag0MvReqM^{\downarrow}, Ag0MvReqH0^{\downarrow}, H0AccMvReqAg0^{\downarrow}, H0RejMvReqAg0^{\downarrow}, MAccMvReqAg0^{\downarrow}, MRejMvReqAg0^{\downarrow}\}$	$\lambda(t_5)=\{MvH1^{\downarrow}\}$
$\lambda(t_6)=\{Ag1MvReqM^{\downarrow}, Ag1MvReqH1^{\downarrow}, H1AccMvReqAg1^{\downarrow}, H1RejMvReqAg1^{\downarrow}, MAccMvReqAg1^{\downarrow}, MRejMvReqAg1^{\downarrow}\}$	$\lambda(t_8)=\{Ag2MvReqM^{\downarrow}, Ag2MvReqH2^{\downarrow}, H2AccMvReqAg2^{\downarrow}, H1RejMvReqAg2^{\downarrow}, MAccMvReqAg2^{\downarrow}, MRejMvReqAg2^{\downarrow}\}$
$\lambda(t_9)=\{MvH2^{\downarrow}\}$	
τ	
$\tau(p_1)=\tau(p_3)=\tau(p_4)=\{TypeMobAg\mathit{i}, TypeStatAgH\mathit{i}\}$ $i \leq 3$	$\tau(p_2)=\{TypeMobAg\mathit{i}, TypeStatAgM\}$ $i \leq 3$
VAR	
Type(MA) = {TypeMobAg*i*} $i \leq 3$ *Type*(SA1) = {TypeStatAgH*i*} $i \leq 3$ *Type*(SA2) = {TypeStatAgHM}	

agent exists in every host except to the market (p_2). Furthermore, there is a net of level 3 within p2, which models a simple blackboard. In this example, MobAg0 acts as the buyer, and MobAg1 and MobAg2 are the sellers. Additional data that completes the model are included in Table 1.

Stationary Agent Model

The behaviour of stationary agents is simple: They receive access request from mobile agents, decide to grant or deny the permission, and send the answer. A protocol similar to Request Interaction Protocol (FIPA, 2002b) is used for this purpose. Furthermore, stationary agents take the record of the agents in the host. Refer to Figure 5 to see a presentation of the structure of the stationary agent of the market. Agent models of other hosts are similar, but they have different labels in some of their transitions.

Figure 6. Enter task

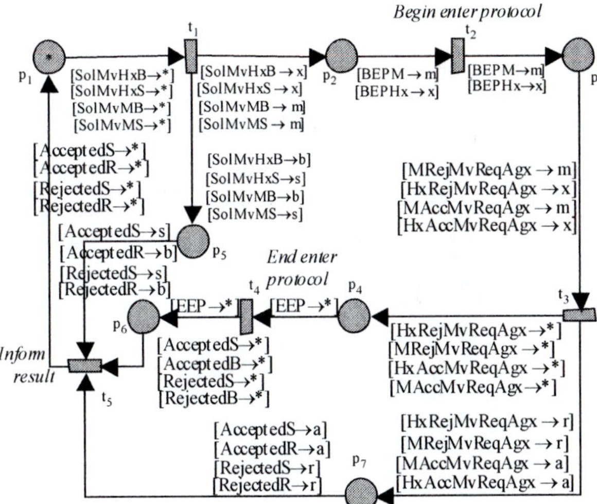

Figure 7. Net CtrlHx

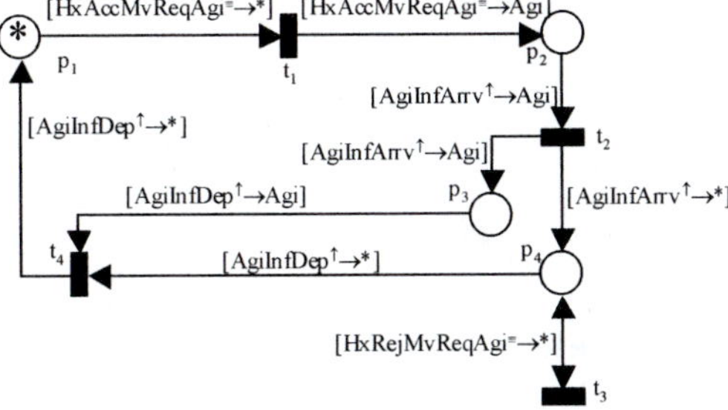

The tokens marking the places of the stationary agent are nets of level 3: one net representing the *participant role* in the Request Interaction Protocol (see Figure 6), and the other net of type *TypeControl*, (Figure 7) where the record of the agents in the host is taken.

Mobile Agents

The behaviour of the mobile agents is more complex; it is described by a net of level 2 that moves through the environment model. This behaviour is guided by the plans of the agents. A plan describes the sequences of tasks to be executed by the agent for the achievement of its goal (in this case, to sell or buy a product).

The structure of the mobile agents is shown in Figure 8. Its plans are contained into p1, the tasks are included into p2, and the protocols used by the agent to interact with other agents are contained into p4. When an agent wants to enter into the market, transition t2 is fired, removing the plan and the pertinent task from p1 and p2, respectively. The task

Figure 8. Mobile agent model

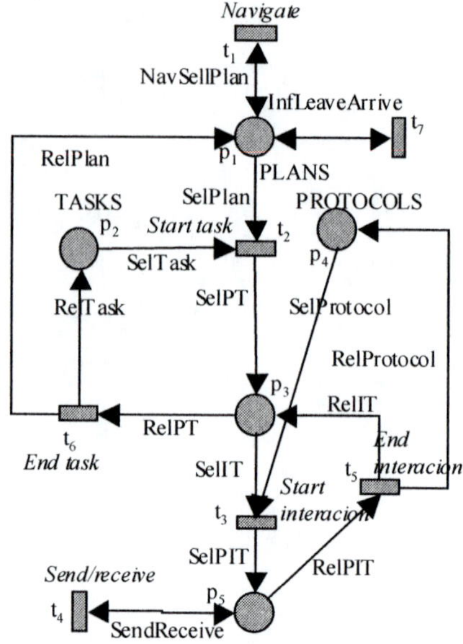

Figure 9. Plan for buying

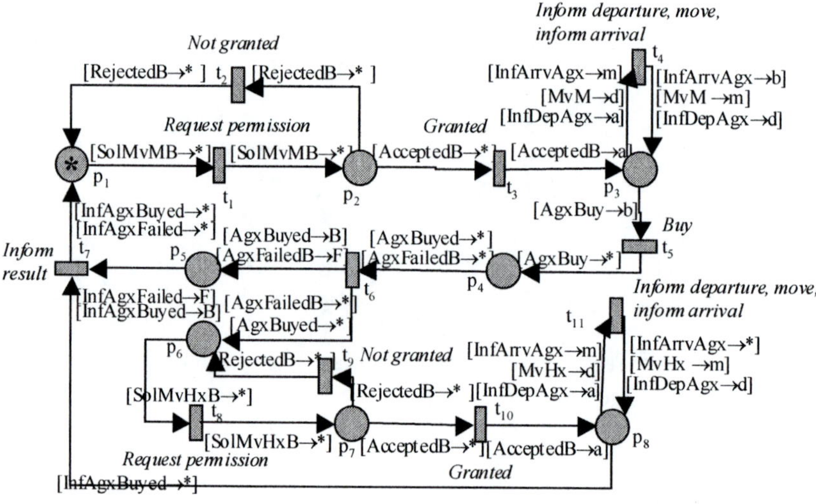

starts the necessary protocol to request access to the host, sending and receiving messages using t4. Once the protocol finished t3 fires, and when the task finishes, t6 fires, returning the plan and task to their corresponding places. If the access is granted, the agent informs its departure to the stationary agent of its host (t7), it moves to the market (t1), and informs its arrival (t7). Then the agent begins the negotiation process, firing t2 again, selecting the

Figure 10. Request Protocol (participant role)

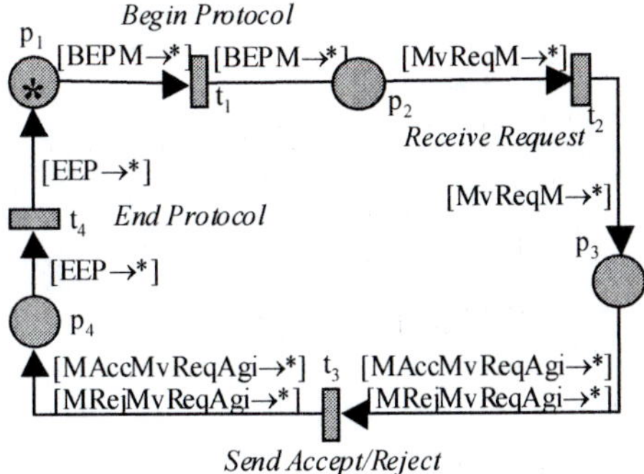

Figure 11. Buy task

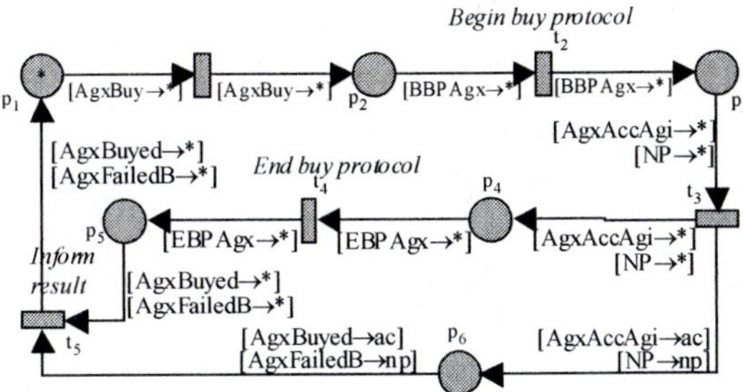

appropriate task, according to its plan (selling or buying); the task in execution selects the appropriate protocol.

The MAs have different plans, depending if they have to buy or sell a product. These plans are modeled with nets of level 3. Figure 9 depicts the plan of a buyer agent. The plan of the seller is similar, but in the case if it does not find a buyer, the agent tries to sell its product again. Roughly speaking, the buyer plan consist of the following actions: request permission to enter to the market, move to the market, try to buy, request permission to return to its original host, move to the host, and inform the result.

The tasks an agent can carry out are: buy, sell, and enter to a host. Figures 10 and 11 show the nets of level 3 that model the buying and the entering tasks, respectively. The selling task is similar to the buy task.

Interaction Protocols and Blackboard

The interaction protocols used in this example are Request Interaction Protocol (FIPA, 2000a) and Contract Net Interaction Protocol (FIPA, 2000b). The former is used for requesting access to a host, and the latter for the trading of a product. Figure 12 depicts the

Figure 12. Enter Protocol (initiator role)

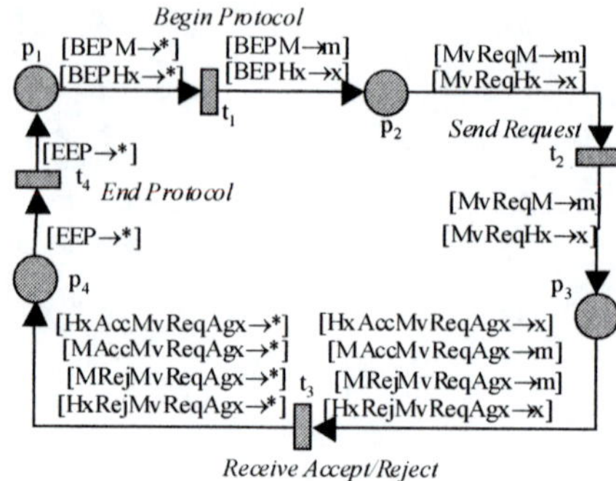

Figure 13. BuyProt$_x$: Contract net protocol (initiator role)

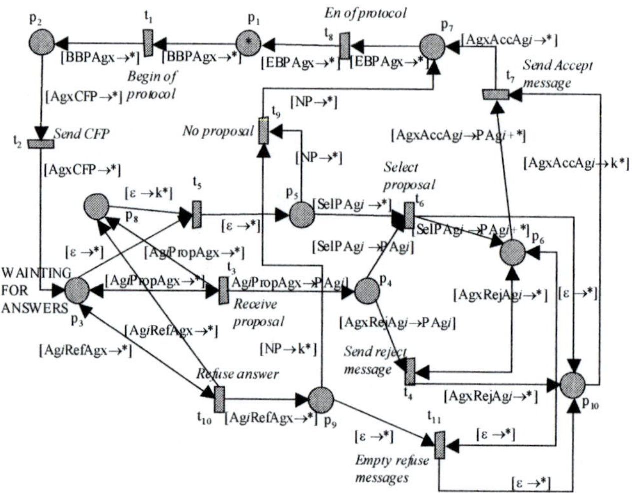

net for the participant role in the Request Interaction Protocol. The initiator role is played by the MA, and it is described in Figure 13. The initiator role in contract net is played by the buyer agent, and the participant role by the seller. The buyer sends the call for proposal (CFP), including the specification of the product it wants to buy. The seller can refuse the CFP, or accept it, and then send a proposal. The buyer receives the proposals and the refuse messages, and then it evaluates the proposals, selecting the best one. Then, the buyer notifies its decision to the accepted and rejected sellers, and the protocol ends. If no agent sends a proposal, the protocol ends, the buyer returns to its original host, and informs that it failed in buying the good.

An agent model may interact with other agent models and with nets of level 3 representing resources or other abstract entities such as blackboards. In this case study, we consider the

Figure 14. Blackboard model

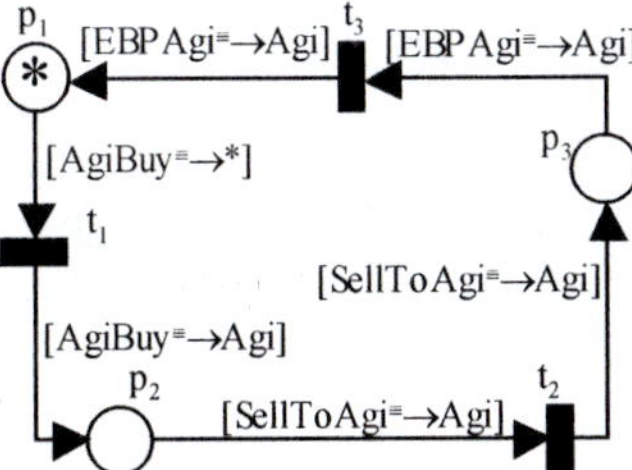

existence of an entity, called Blackboard, whose role is to allow a mobile agent to inform its buying intentions to the buyer agents within the market. A simple model for this function is shown in Figure 14; all its transitions are locally synchronized with mobile agent transitions.

Particular Strategies for Various Application Fields

We will overview the strategies proposed for obtaining nLNS models of systems from diverse nature that have in common the existence of mobile entities that require a detailed description of their behaviour. Such systems are batch processes, mobile robot systems, and urban traffic simulation.

Modeling Batch Processes

Batch Production Systems

Batch processes play an important role in the chemical and food process industries (oil refineries, pharmaceutical plants, petrochemical plants, gas plants, etc.). A batch process is defined as a discontinuous process that transform a finite amount of input substances or raw materials into finished products by means the execution of an ordered set of processing activities over a finite period of time, using one or more units of equipment.

Generally, large batch processes are multi-purpose chemical plants, where several products are manufactured concurrently within the same plant; the plant is divided into production units called process cells including equipment and transfer lines. The product obtained by a batch process is called a batch, which is defined as an entity that represents the processed material at any point into the process. Next, we overview several basic concepts used in batch manufacturing systems, namely recipes, resources, and process plan.

Recipes. A recipe or product specification is an entity that contains the minimum set of information that uniquely defines the manufacturing requirements for a specific product. There are four types of recipes:

- **General recipe.** This is an enterprise level recipe that serves as the basis for lower level recipes.
- **Site recipe.** This recipe is specific to a particular site.
- **Master recipe.** This recipe is targeted to a specific process cell. It assigns virtually the equipment and indicates the various ingredients, which have to be used to make the product.
- **Control recipe.** This recipe is a copy or instantiation of a master recipe.

The general and site recipes are equipment-independent, whereas the master and control recipes are equipment-dependent.

Resources. Two generic classes of resources are considered:

- **Processors.** These are devices that perform physical or logical changes in product properties (reactors, containers, etc.).
- **Transport devices.** Their main task is to open and close connections between processors to move material.

For a recipe to be able to use a resource, the resource must first be booked in order to prevent others recipes from using it, since most resources can only be used by one recipe at a time. During the execution of recipes (production of batches), recipes are responsible for the booking and unbooking of resources. Thus, recipes can be viewed as a control entity into a coordination system for batch processes.

Process plan. A process plan is defined as a partially ordered set of operations sequences (recipes) that specify a pre-established route into the plant; it allows transforming raw material into a final batch or product.

Modeling Strategy

A model specifying software for batch control mainly describes resource management and procedure sequencing. For simplicity, we consider a three-level model (Villanueva, 2003; López, 2005). Thus, of a natural way, the first level models the plant layout by describing the plant decompositions into process cells and the cell interconnection.

The second-level nets describe the behaviour of mobile agents that guide a batch thorough the plant and enable the execution of recipes within the pertinent cell.

The third-level nets represent the routes to follow within the plant (process plans) and detailed treatments to apply to the batch (recipes) within the process cells using specific equipment. This is sketched in Figure 15.

The agent net describes an entity that goes with the batch through plant into the cells; the agent uses the description of both the plan process and the recipes for routing the batch, booking resources, and unbooking these resources. Resources located into the cells are also

Figure 15. Batch production system decomposition and component hierarchy

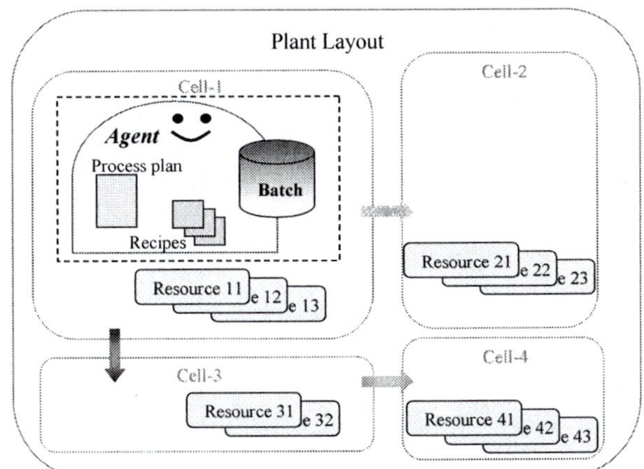

described by third-level nets. The agent coordinates the execution of the recipes according to the process plan. For more sophisticated control strategies dealing with large and complex production systems, the agent net may also handle roadmaps and interaction protocols for online decision-making.

Once this description of the modules is performed, the resulting models are related by the labelling of transitions and/or by the inclusion within other nets as tokens.

Mobile Robot Systems

The coordination of multiple mobile robots evolving into a structured environment is a challenging research topic involving a wide variety of techniques and approaches addressing problems related with the activities performed by robots, namely, sensing, task planning, decision-making, interaction, and mission execution control. In Almeyda (2002) and López-Mellado (2005), the use of nLNS is proposed for specifying the coordination of these tasks in order to facilitate the development of a distributed software coordination system.

Robot Mission Coordination

Consider a set of mobile robots (A_i) that evolve into a structured environment represented by a connected set of rooms (r_j) or stations of a floor building (Figure 16). The robots can navigate through the rooms and execute tasks (τ_k). The tasks are predefined sequences of operations (o_r) that may need resources located into the rooms, and/or may be performed in collaboration with other robots. For instance, $\mathcal{T}_2 = [o_1\ o_3\ (o_4 + o_5)\ o_7]$ means that Task 2 consists of the sequences $[o_1\ o_3\ o_4\ o_7]$ or $[o_1\ o_3\ o_5\ o_7]$.

Figure 16. A simple mobile robot system

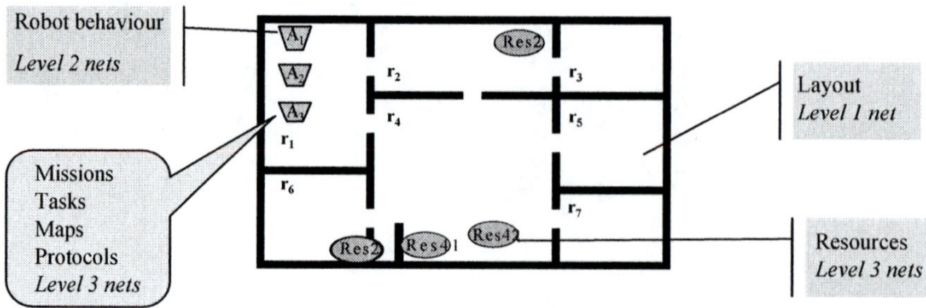

Every robot execute missions $\mathcal{M}_s$, which consists of a sequence of room sub-goals and tasks to be executed into the room; $\mathcal{M}_1 = r_3\ \mathcal{T}_4\ \mathcal{T}_5\ r_6\ \mathcal{T}_2\ r_1$ can express for instance a mission that consists in the displacement to the Room 3 where Tasks 4 and 5 must be executed, then the displacement to the Room 6 for executing Task 2, and finally, return to Room 1.

Robots may interact with resources or with other robots. Interactions among robots may be of diverse complexity going from simple synchronisation for carrying out an operation to complex negotiation protocols. The robots may need resources to execute some operations into the rooms; for this example, consider that there is one resource in Room 2 and two resources in Room 4.

Suppose that all the robots have the same basic capabilities, that is, they can perform the same operations, but the tasks are individually programmed in every robot; they eventually know to perform the same tasks. Every robot accepts one mission at a time in any room. The gates between the rooms are enough large for permitting the transit of more than one robot.

Modeling Strategy

A nLNS model may be defined at three levels. For the previously discussed system, the first-level net describes the environment where the robots evolve and the resources stay, the second-level nets model the agents that manage the general of the mobile robots, and the third-level nets represent specific features of a given robot, namely, missions, tasks, and roadmaps. Figure 16 describes the hierarchy of the nets of a three-level model of a multi-robot system. The models of robots handle nets describing missions, tasks, access roadmaps, and interaction protocols.

The first-level net is obtained from the system layout; the structure of this net associates each room with a place and each gate to two transitions for describing the access to the rooms; the places may contain agent nets representing the robots and object nets representing resources. The behaviour of a mobile robot is described by a level 2 net "moving" within the layout model; the model must represent the possible states that the robot controller follows to execute missions thorough the floor building; the marking is composed by level 3 nets representing the mission, the tasks the robot is able to perform, and the navigation roadmap.

Urban Traffic Simulation

Analysis and optimisation of urban traffic systems (UTS) have been often addressed via simulation. In order to analyse UTS in detail, the microscopic approach allows the simulation of the behaviour of vehicles, the performance of street and intersections, and the effectiveness of traffic lights control policies. Under this approach, UTS can be considered as discrete event systems, thus PN can be used for the specification of a software system for simulation.

A model for UTS micro-simulation must describe the traffic network including control signals and the users (vehicles) displacing within the network. If this model is expressed as nLNS, the software components for a micro-simulator may be conceived adopting an agent based approach; mobile agents will individually represent the vehicles by establishing diverse behaviour defined as travel plans, driving style (speed profile, changing lane procedures, etc.), and so forth (López-Neri, 2005).

A nLNS model specifies at level 1 the traffic network; the places represent the streets and the intersections; and the transitions and arcs describe the direction of the vehicles flow. At level 2, the nets describe the general behaviour of the agents representing the vehicles and other stationary software agents managing either the streets or the intersections. The agent nets representing users handle nets of level 3 which describe individual procedures that determine the behaviour of diverse kinds of vehicles within the traffic network; similarly, the street manager agents and intersection agents handle nets of level 3 used for the interaction with the vehicles agents and the traffic lights model. These notions are illustrated in Figure 17, which shows a level 1 net that models a fragment of UTS regarding a simple intersection of two one-way streets. Transitions t5 and t6 control the input of vehicles to the corresponding street segments.

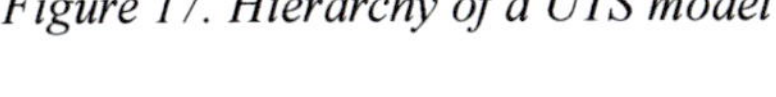

Figure 17. Hierarchy of a UTS model

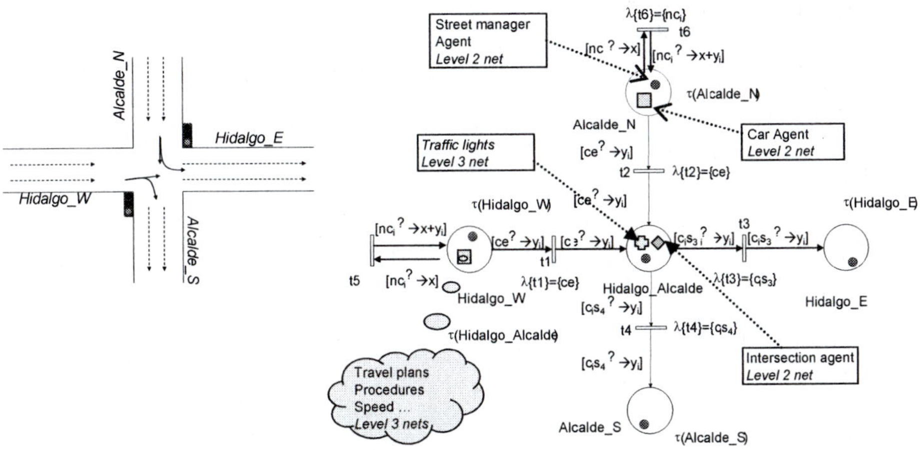

Implementation Issues

Multi-mobile agent-based software has been developed from models expressed in nLNS using JADE (Bellifemine, 1999), which is a middleware for the development of agent applications in compliance with the FIPA specifications for interoperable intelligent multi-agent systems. Its set of APIs and tools for debugging and deployment allows the development of distributed MAS.

A methodology was defined for mapping nLNS elements into classes and concepts provided by JADE. For the time being, it is considered three level models; an outline of this methodology is given (Sánchez, 2004):

- **Level 1 net:** Every place of the environment model, representing a host, corresponds to a container in JADE; the containers hold diverse kinds of agents. The set of all the containers composes an agent platform in which a container must be declared as main container.
- **Level 2 nets:** Every agent model is implemented as subclasses of the class Agent of JADE. The initial marking of every agent net corresponds to variable instances that represent plans, tasks, and protocols of the agents.
- **Level 3 nets:** The nets modeling plans, tasks, and protocols are implemented as *Behaviours*. The plans are implemented using some subclasses of *CompositeBehaviours*, in which the *ChildrenBehaviours* control the resuming of the agent tasks as well as the displacement of an agent net to another container. The tasks, according to their complexity, may be implemented as objects of the class *SimpleBehaviour* or the subclass *CompositeBehaviour* (when a task performs parallel operations or interacts with other agents through protocols). Protocols are directly implemented using the classes included in JADE; protocols that are not included may be implemented using the class *SimpleBehaviour.* The DF service included in JADE is able to perform the function of a blackboard where the agents offer theirs services to other agents.

The case study presented in this chapter was implemented following the described methodology; for every component of the model the corresponding classes were defined. The software was distributed into a set of PC interconnected through a LAN; several tests were performed using different number of agents.

Future Trends

The modeling formalism and methodologies presented in this chapter set up a first stage toward the automation of the development life cycle of multi-mobile agent systems. The specification of a system using nLNS and the remainder stages should be supported by a tool allowing the visual edition of a model, its simulation, and the generation of the specified software. Generated software could be built as a model interpreter scheme in which the model codification is handled by a generic distributed token player.

Regarding the implementation of nLNS models, several issues should be explored, namely, the handling of new agents identity when they are cloned, and the agents mobility within environments composed by heterogeneous platforms.

Another concern that has still not been addressed is the analysis of nLNS models' properties (liveness, boundedness, cyclicness, etc.); although determining such properties is a difficult issue due to the complexity of a nLNS model, it is possible to define a model construction method that guaranties the preservation of the properties of the model components (nets of different levels) when they are integrated into a complete model.

Conclusion

We presented a multi-level Petri net-based formalism called nLNS, and we proposed a methodology for modeling interactive mobile agent systems. The formalism induces a modular and hierarchical modeling strategy in which the modules are first conceived separately, then the labelling of transitions declare the relationships among modules, and the nesting of nets establishes their hierarchy. The obtained models are independent to programming languages.

The modeling approach is suitable for the development life cycle of large and complex agent-based software systems including mobile agents that perform collaboration or negotiation. It has been shown the application of nLNS to various systems of diverse nature which include mobile entities that exhibit complex behaviour and it is worthy to describe. Although the presented case study and the outlined examples deal with three level models, additional levels may be added when the size of the system and the complexity grows.

References

Almeyda, H. I. (2002, September). *A three-level net system for the modelling of mobile agents* (in Spanish). MSc. thesis. CINVESTAV-IPN, Guadalajara, México.

Bellifemine, F., Poggi, A., & Rimassa, G. (1999). JADE — A FIPA compliant agent framework. In *Proceedings of the 4th International Conference on the Practical Application of Intelligent Agent and Multi Agent Technology (PAAM99)*, London (pp. 97-108).

Chávez, A., & Maes, P. (1996). Kasbah: An agent marketplace for buying and selling goods. In *Proceedings of the First International Conference on the Practical Application of Intelligent Agents and Multi-Agent Technology (PAAM'96).*

Di Marzo, G., Muhugusa, M., & Tschudin, C. F. (1998). A survey of theories for mobile agents. *WWW Journal, Special Issue on Distributed WWW Processing: Applications and Techniques of Web Agents*, 139-153.

Ferber, J. (1999). *Multi-agent systems. An introduction to distributed artificial intelligence.* Addison-Wesley.

FIPA ORG. (2002a). *FIPA contract net interaction protocol specification* (Doc. No. SC00029H).

FIPA ORG. (2002b). *FIPA request interaction protocol specification* (Doc. No. SC00026H).

Hiraishi, K. (2000, October). A Petri-net-based model for the mathematical analysis of multi-agent systems. In *Proceedings of the IEEE International Conference on Systems, Man & Cybernetics,* Nashville, TN.

Kölher, M., Moldt, D., & Rölke, H. (2001, June). Modelling the structure and behavior of Petri net agents. In *Proceedings of 22nd ICATPN 2001,* Newcastle upon Tyne, UK (pp. 25-29).

Kummer, O. (2001). Introduction to Petri nets and reference nets. *Sozionikaktuell, 1,* 7-16.

Lomazova, I. (2000). Nested Petri nets — A formalism for specification and verification of multi-agent distributed systems. *Fundamenta informaticae, 43,*195-214.

López, E., Villanueva, N., Almeyda, H. (2005). Modelling of batch production systems using Petri nets with dynamic tokens. *Mathematics and Computers in Simulation. IMACS-Elsevier Science, 67*(6), 541-558.

López-Mellado, E., & Almeyda, H. (2005). A three-level net formalism for the modelling of multiple mobile robot systems. *International Journal of Computer Integrated Manufacturing, 18*(2),137-146.

López-Neri, E., López-Mellado, E., & Ramírez-Treviño, A. (2005, July). Hierarchical models of urban traffic systems for agent based simulation. In *Proceedings of the Workshop Optimization of Urban Traffic Systems,* Puerto Vallarta, Mexico (pp. 1-12).

Milojicic, D., Douglis, F., & Wheeler, R. (1999). *Mobility: Processes, computers, and agents.* Addison-Wesley.

Moldt, D., & Weinberg, F. (1997, June). Multi-agent-systems based on coloured Petri nets. In *Proceedings of the 18th ICATPN,* Toulouse, France (LNCS 1248, pp. 82-101).

Sánchez, R. (2004, August). *Multilevel specification of interaction protocols in mobile agent systems.* (in Spanish). MSc thesis, Cinvestav Unidad Guadalajara, México.

Sánchez, R., & López, E. (2004, October). Modular and hierarchical modeling of interactive mobile agents. In *Proceedings of the International Conference on Systems, Man, and Cybernetics,* The Hague, The Netherlands (pp. 1740-1745).

Valk, R. (1998). Petri nets as token objects: An introduction to elementary object nets. In *Proceedings of the International Conference on Application and Theory of Petri Nets* (pp. 1-25). Springer-Verlag.

Villanueva, N. I. (2003, December) *Multilevel modelling of batch processes* (in Spanish). MSc. thesis, Cinvestav Unidad Guadalajara, México.

Xu, D., & Yi, D. (2000, October 8-11) Modeling mobile agent systems with high level Petri nets. In *Proceedings of the IEEE International Conference on Systems, Man, and Cybernetics,* Nashville, TN (Vol. 4, pp. 3177-3182).

Chapter XIV

Development of an Intelligent Information System for Object-Oriented Software Design

Gary P. Moynihan, The University of Alabama, USA
Bin Qiao, The University of Alabama, USA
Matthew E. Elam, The University of Alabama, USA
Joel Jones, The University of Alabama, USA

Abstract

The purpose of this research was to apply an artificial intelligence approach to improve the efficiency of design pattern selection used in the development of object-oriented software. Design patterns provide a potential solution to the limitations occurring with traditional software design approaches. Current methods of design pattern selection tend to be intuitive and based on the experience of the individual software engineer. This expertise is very specialized and frequently unavailable to many software development organizations. A prototype expert system was developed in order to automate this process of selecting suitable patterns to be applied to the design problem under consideration. It guides the designer through the pattern selection process through inquiry regarding the nature of the design problem. The prototype system also provides the capabilities to browse patterns, view the relationship between patterns, and generate code based on the pattern selected. The routine application of such a system is viewed as a means to improve the productivity of software development by increasing the use of accepted design patterns.

Introduction

Software design is an iterative process, such that the requirements are transformed into a model for constructing the software. First, the design is represented at a very high level of abstraction. At this level, the design can be directly traced to specific data, functional, and behavioral requirements. Being an iterative process, the design undergoes changes over the duration of the design phase. Eventually, the design representations are expressed at a much lower level of abstraction. At this level, the connection between the requirements and the design is less obvious (Vliet, 2001).

Object-oriented design differs from traditional (i.e., procedural) software design methods, by achieving a number of different levels of modularity. This modularity can be defined as dividing software into separately named and addressable modules. These components then can be assembled to form the complete system. Although object-oriented software design is frequently viewed as easier than alternative approaches, designing any software is a difficult task, regardless of technique. For example, Jones, Hilton, and Lutz (1998) point out that "the promise of the object-oriented approach to the systems analysis hinges on correctly partitioning the problem domain into essential classes and objects. Most developers agree that this is no easy task." Despite these difficulties, experienced object-oriented designers produce good designs that are hard to achieve for a novice designer. Frequently, they will use recurring patterns of communicating objects and classes. Such patterns are applicable to specific design problems, and thus make the object-oriented designs more elegant, flexible, and ultimately reusable. These patterns allow experienced designers to reuse successful designs by basing new designs on their prior experience.

A software design pattern book by Gamma, Helm, Johnson, and Vlissides (1995) discusses 23 fundamental design patterns carefully selected from numerous object-oriented systems. It is regarded by many as the accepted baseline for this type of approach (e.g., Budinsky, Finnie, Vlissides, & Yu, 1996). Each of these fundamental patterns can be applied only under certain circumstances, so it has its own applicability criteria. Each pattern is also associated with its consequences. A subset of these patterns is related to each other, such that the application of one pattern makes the subsequent application of relevant patterns beneficial to the overall design. These patterns provide a valuable tool for the practicing software design professional. As the benefits of design patterns are becoming more and more apparent, the utilization of these patterns to develop components of reusable object-oriented software has become an emerging trend. Previous research done in this area is now being incorporated for commercial applications. Some of the associated advantages are discussed by Cline (1996). However, of these 23 fundamental design patterns that can be used to develop reusable object-oriented software, only a few of the patterns can be adopted while developing a specific application. A software designer should not have to become expert in all of the patterns in order to select the appropriate one for his or her specific application. A logical alternative is the automation of this knowledge and expertise.

Literature Search

An extensive literature review was carried out via both Internet and manual searches. The focus of this search was to identify and compare different levels of software reuse, as well as the different design pattern approaches that were applied. Three widely utilized software reuse techniques (i.e., component-based reuse, framework-based reuse, and pattern-based reuse) were identified. The review of these approaches indicated that an automated procedure, which can guide the selection of the appropriate design patterns, is highly desirable to the software industry. The literature search further confirmed that there had been limited work done on automating this area of design. Budinsky et al. (1996) developed an information system that automates the implementation of design patterns. For a specific pattern, the user inputs application-oriented information, from which the software tool generated all of the pattern-prescribed code automatically. The software utilized a hypertext rendition of the design patterns in order to give designers an integrated online reference and developmental tool. The automatic code generation improved the utility of the design patterns. Eden, Gil, and Yehundai (1997) presented a prototype tool that supported the specification of design patterns and their realization in a given program. The prototype automated the application of design patterns without obstructing the source code text from the programmer. They further described the identification and application of pattern specification language routines by the principles of the meta-programming approach (Eden et al., 1997). The automated tool maintained a library of routines and supported their modification, application, and debugging.

Design patterns are introduced frequently in reengineering legacy code. This improves the clarity of the design and helps in future developments. Cinneide and Nixon (1999) automated the transformations required to introduce design patterns in reengineered legacy code. The authors presented a procedure for this design pattern transformation, and have constructed a prototype system, referred to as design pattern tool (DPT). The DPT software applied design pattern transformations to Java programs. Their procedure has been applied successfully to structure-oriented patterns, such as Gamma et al.'s (1995) creational patterns (Cinneide & Nixon, 1999).

Work has also been conducted in developing software for the detection of design patterns in an existing code base. Brown (1996) constructed a Smalltalk-based system that detected several of the patterns identified by Gamma et al. (1995). Smith and Stotts (2003) applied the theorem prover OTTER to analyze C++ programs, based on their underlying design patterns. Similarly, a combination of static and dynamic analyses was used by Heuzeroth Lowe, and Mandel (2003) to detect design patterns.

These predecessor software tools are helpful in automating the application of design patterns. They enable the user to automatically generate code, to a certain degree, once a specific design pattern is selected, or to locate such patterns in previously generated code. However, these software tools are not applicable to the selection of design patterns. Since the number of patterns discovered is steadily increasing, it becomes progressively more difficult for a novice designer to continually master all of them. A software tool is required that can effectively reduce the number patterns to few appropriate ones.

Research Objective and Approach

An expert system is a computer-based system that can emulate a human problem-solver by applying knowledge and reasoning normally known and used by experts in that specific field. As these systems progressively penetrate the manufacturing environment, they represent an increasingly practical tool for a variety of functions, including design (Moynihan, 1993). The knowledge base, inference engine, interface, and support environment represent the components of a traditional expert system. The knowledge base is the repository for the problem-specific heuristics. These heuristics are normally obtained from a human domain expert, then structured and input by the knowledge engineer through the system's interface and support environment (Jackson, 1999). The inference engine provides the control mechanism for the expert system by identifying the heuristics to be activated, as well as the sequence of activation. The working memory contains the facts associated with the current problem under consideration (Moynihan, 1993).

There are relatively few applications of expert systems for the selection of design patterns. This is probably due to the recent nature of the design pattern concept. Kramer and Prechelt (1996) developed a prototype system to enhance the maintainability of existing software by incorporating the structural design patterns identified by Gamma et al. (1995). This system provides a heuristic approach for discovering design patterns in existing software. A similar procedure can be utilized in the selection of design patterns for their application during the design stage of new software. A few code generators are also available, which document a number of patterns and allow the generation of code from a specified pattern, for example, Budinsky et al.'s (1996). However, these applications are all based on the fact that users know which pattern to use and how to use it. In most cases, users may not have sufficient knowledge to make this determination. They need a software tool which can lead them to the proper selection of a pattern and tell them how to implement it. Thus, such code generators, as mentioned in the literature, are unable to provide sufficient support to users. A total solution for this problem area will require an implementation module as a supplement to the expert system core. A preliminary design for such an expert system for software architecture design was proposed by Bachmann, Bass, and Klein (2003).

The objective of this project was to investigate the application of expert system technology to the selection of design patterns. To support this objective, a prototype expert system was developed that can select suitable design patterns from a pool of candidate patterns, based upon inputs characterizing the problem at hand. This research was based on a proof-of-concept work (Suki, 2003) and targeted a more comprehensive expert system. More features were added to guide the implementation of design patterns.

Development Approach and System Architecture

Accepted practices in expert system development identify three major steps: knowledge engineering, system development, and system verification and validation. The key concepts, relationships and heuristics, are identified during the initial knowledge engineering phase. This phase was completed rapidly due to incorporation of the predecessor research by Suki (2003). The 23 design patterns, identified by Gamma et al. (1995), form the basis for this research. Eight patterns (i.e., abstract factory, adapter, composite, decorator, factory method, observer, strategy, and template method) within this group were selected because of their simplicity and frequent occurrence in many object-oriented designs. Gamma et al. (1995) note that for a novice designer, or a student of software design, these patterns provide a good beginning. The literature (e.g., Budinsky et al., 1996; Cinneide & Nixon, 1999) provided guidance on the selection of these patterns and the path followed by expert designers in their selection. This was the primary source of knowledge for forming the underlying heuristics. The resulting prototype expert system focuses on determining the knowledge associated within these eight design patterns and factors that drive the process of applying design patterns. When the reasoning reaches its result, the target pattern(s) are displayed to the users. A UML (unified modeling language) diagram (Rational Software Corporation, 1995), combined with other implementation instructions, is also provided to illustrate how the selected pattern(s) work. Finally, a code generator provides users sample programs for the selected pattern(s).

During the development phase, the acquired knowledge was organized. The selection process incorporates a rule-based scheme of knowledge representation. The selection of a rule-based system was felt appropriate after considering other schemas. The environment chosen for the actual development was object-oriented. Resident object-oriented capabilities (e.g., encapsulation, inheritance, and polymorphism) allow data hiding, sharing of attributes in a common class, and varying implementation of "functions" depending on the calling object (Jackson, 1999). Inference rules and objects were constructed and formalized. These rules were incorporated as attributes of the objects, thus combining the benefits of both approaches.

One major purpose of the general system design phase was to establish definitions and descriptions of the proposed system. A series of commercial off-the-shelf software products were reviewed and considered for purchase. Recommendation of specific software was based on an investigation of functionality, installation, and integration characteristics, as well as compatibility with existing hardware, software, and communications investments. The resulting functional system design (FSD) document was developed to further identify the overall system architecture, processing considerations, and definition of displays and reports. The functional system design carries the design to a sufficiently detailed level to support the actual programming of the system. The identified requirements and functionality were utilized for the subsequent programming phase.

The prototype system for the selection of design patterns is comprised of three primary components: the knowledge base, the inference engine, and the user interface. This is consistent with most expert system applications. In this application, the knowledge base is partitioned into three specific lobes. These lobes span the categories of domain-specific knowledge and execution-specific knowledge. Domain-specific knowledge refers to the knowledge about design patterns. It was obtained from the literature baseline, as well as domain expert interviews, during the knowledge acquisition phase.

The three lobes addressed reflect knowledge to differentiate patterns, knowledge of the characteristics of patterns, and knowledge of the relationship between patterns. The knowledge to differentiate patterns is used to select an appropriate pattern for the user's applications. It includes properties that classify patterns into different subgroups. It also has the capability to heuristically check each pattern's applicability and consequences. The system initially attempts to determine the approach of the user toward the selection of design patterns. The knowledge relevant to approaches allows the system to reduce the search of suitable patterns to a more limited subset. The applicability and consequences testing knowledge lobe contains the characteristics of the design patterns. It has the knowledge that is required to judge whether or not a design pattern is suitable to the problem at hand. It consists of eligibility criteria for all the design patterns that are in the scope of this study. This knowledge base also contains consequences associated with each design pattern such as the effects of using composite pattern.

The knowledge of characteristics of patterns consists of knowledge relating to each specific pattern, including a UML representation, the intent of the pattern, objects that participate in the pattern, collaboration of these objects, and C++ sample codes for the pattern. There are two types of relationships between patterns: alternative and supplement. An alternative relationship indicates that one pattern can be replaced by another with regard to the problem specifications. For example, there can be a choice between using the Iterator and Visitor that can only be made by knowing the complexity of the behavior to be performed on the elements of the structure being acted on. A supplement relationship represents the relation that one pattern can be used to support another, and that often these two patterns are used together. Thus, if Composite is the selected pattern, then Visitor would be indicated as a related one. Both of these relationships are contained in the third knowledge lobe.

The execution-specific knowledge base captures all the knowledge that is not domain-specific. This knowledge facilitates the processing of the system. Some examples of this type of knowledge can be the established goals, the relationship between the user interface and the knowledge elements, and the relationship between various screens. As the knowledge domain increases, the execution-specific knowledge overhead also increases.

These knowledge lobes are triggered in a sequential order during the execution of the system. The inference engine serves as the processing and control mechanism for this execution. There are primarily three types of inference engines that can be used to conduct the search: forward chaining, backward chaining, and hybrid chaining. In backward chaining, the knowledge base is examined to see if it can establish a value for the goal attribute by moving backwards toward the initial data state (Jackson, 1999). For this project, a backward-chaining search was used. As a first step, the goals and sub-goals are identified. Then, working backwards based on the evaluated numerical calculations, the conclusions and recommendations are drawn.

The inference engine interacts with the user via user interfaces. This interaction allows the inference engine to understand the problem that the user is trying to solve. The predefined goals drive the search process of the inference engine. In the case of the expert system for the selection of design patterns, the inference engine tries to achieve three goals by completion of the execution cycle. These goals are executed in a sequential order. These goals are interrelated, and the outcome of one can thus affect the execution of the other goals. This execution sequence guides the direction of the search for the inference engine. Depending on the goals, the chain is formed in the knowledge base.

The user interface facilitates the contact between the system and the user. Depending on the functionality, the user interfaces are categorized as input and output screens. The input screens are driven by goals that are being investigated. The expert system for the selection of design patterns uses dynamic input screens to display question prompts on a generalized screen. The dynamic nature of the input screen also provides real-time information on the status of the search.

During the programming phase, the formal knowledge representations were translated into computer code. Use of Visual Basic 6.0 facilitated system construction. It utilizes Microsoft Windows to provide a flexible, intuitive, and expandable environment for delivering knowledge-based systems. The system was developed and delivered on an IBM compatible microcomputer with a Pentium main processor. UML was utilized in this research to provide a graphical representation of the classes in the pattern. In addition, a code generator was also integrated with the expert system. Pieces of sample code provide a concrete example of the pattern. As noted by Gamma et al. (1995), "studying the code helps you learn how to implement the pattern," and depict example code fragments in C++. The code generator, developed in this research, adopts this same approach, since C++ is one of the most popular programming languages currently used (Ziring, 1998). Further, the C++ programming language offers a very broad range of object-oriented programming features, such as data abstraction, polymorphism, and inheritance, which make it suitable for implementing design patterns.

System Overview

System initiation activates the main module, from where the other three primary modules can be accessed (Figure 1). Once the user enters the system, the opening screen is displayed. Three screen options are available. Users can click on the Exit button to terminate the execution of the expert system. The About screen indicates the objectives and relevant background of the system. To initiate the expert system, users can click on the Start button. This leads the users to the Main Menu screen. An instruction box is located at the bottom of the Main Menu screen. This layout is consistent throughout the system. According to the instructions on this specific screen, users can click on the Back button to return to the Start screen, or they can click on any of other three buttons to invoke the functional modules: (1) the Select Pattern module, which guides users in selecting patterns and implementing selected patterns in their applications; (2) the Learn Single Pattern module, which teaches users the characteristic of each pattern; and (3) the Learn Relationships module, which shows the relationships between patterns.

The Select Pattern Module is designed to assist users in selecting an appropriate pattern for their applications. This expert system leads to the selection of design patterns by asking users a series of questions concerned with a specific problem to be solved (see Figure 2). The primary goal for the system is to determine which of the patterns is suitable to the

Figure 1. Main module

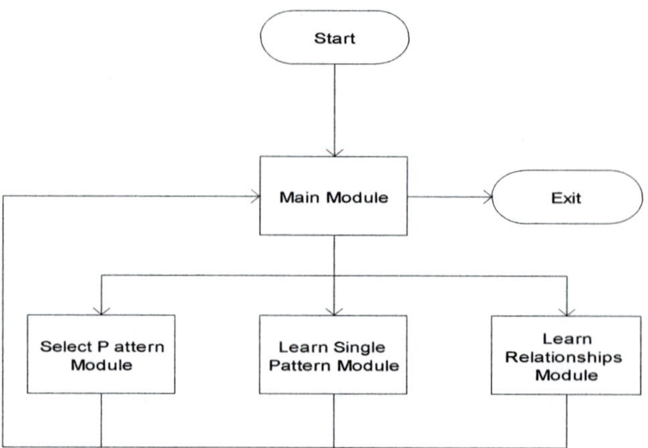

Figure 2. Sample query display

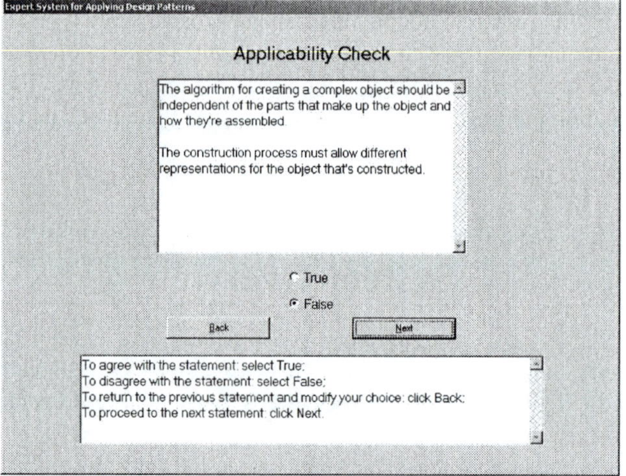

problem under consideration. Starting with multiple design patterns, the system tries to achieve a specific goal. This is consistent with the backward chaining approach frequently used by many diagnostic expert systems (Jackson, 1999). There are also additional goals to be achieved after completion of this primary goal. Since the search for these goals is similar to that of the primary goal, the solution direction for these goals similarly incorporates backward chaining. An option is also given to select a related pattern that can either replace or support the selected pattern.

Gamma et al. (1995) suggest that the patterns included in their book can be classified into three categories, depending on their purpose. These three categories are: (1) creational patterns, which concern the process of object creation; (2) structural patterns, which deal with the composition of classes or objects; and (3) behavioral patterns, used to characterize the

Figure 3. Pattern found display

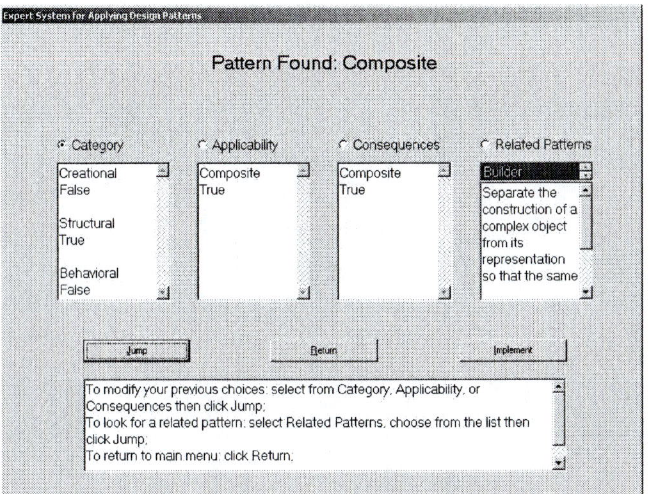

ways in which classes or objects interact and distribute responsibility. Thus, a Category Check screen is shown to differentiate patterns according to their purpose. Then, a series of statements are displayed. By agreeing or disagreeing with these statements, users are led to an intermediate result, that is, a particular pattern is identified in the knowledge base. In order to verify whether the pattern is appropriate for the users' applications, the applicability and consequences of the pattern still needs to be checked. A selected pattern may fail either of these two checks, indicating there is no proper pattern in the current knowledge base. A subsequent Pattern Not Found screen is invoked to inform users of the result.

Conversely, if the pattern passes both checks, a Pattern Found screen is invoked (Figure 3). In both screens, users can select the Category Check, Applicability Check, or Consequences Check option, then click on the Jump button to return to the previous decision and make modifications. However, in the Pattern Found screen, users have two more options. They can decide to implement current pattern by clicking on the Implement button. If they are interested in selecting a related pattern, all patterns that relate to the current pattern are listed in the list box below the Related Pattern option. Selecting a different item in the list box changes the content of the resulting edit box. By reviewing the related patterns shown in this edit box, users are able to determine whether or not they want to use this pattern in their applications. If they decide to do so, they will select the Related Pattern option, and then click on the Jump button. The system will proceed to checking the applicability and consequences of the pattern. When it passes both checks, a Pattern and Related Pattern Found screen will be invoked. In both the Pattern Found screen and the Pattern and Related Pattern Found screen, the explanation of reasoning is provided. Clicking on the Implement button invokes the "Implementation of Patterns" screen.

The Implementation of Patterns screen contains the instructions to implement a design pattern (Figure 4). As indicated at the bottom of the screen, selected patterns (include pattern and related pattern) are identified in the list box. The UML diagram is illustrated in the middle

Figure 4. Implementation of patterns display

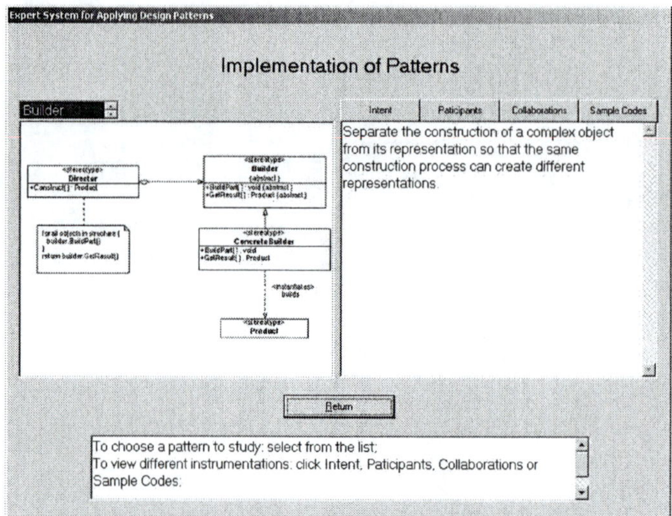

left of the screen. In the middle right of the screen, users can check the intent of the pattern, objects that participate in the pattern, collaboration of these objects, and C++ sample codes for the pattern by clicking on the respective buttons.

The Learn Single Pattern module shows users the implementation instructions of all patterns within the scope of this research. It reuses the Implementation of Patterns screen. The only difference is that all available patterns are identified in the list box. The Learn Relationships module is used to educate users regarding the relationships between patterns. Lines used to connect patterns indicate the relationship between each pair of patterns. By clicking on these lines, users can view a short description of the relationship in the edit box below the diagram.

Verification and Validation

Verification and validation are formal methods used to determine whether computer systems will satisfy user requirements. They provide a gating stage of the software development cycle. Verification confirms the correctness of the system according to the original design specifications. All components of an expert system are subject to verification: the knowledge base, the inference engine, and the user interface (Medsker & Liebowitz, 1994). The knowledge base is verified by examining the consistency, correctness, and completeness of the knowledge. It involves detecting errors such as redundancy, contradiction, and circular dependency. The inference engine is verified by examining the reasoning process of the system. It assesses not only if the expert system is producing correct intermediate and final results but also if the expert system is using the correct reasoning process. The user interface is verified by examining the functionality of every component in the appropriate screens and reports. Two approaches were utilized to accomplish verification of this prototype system: static and dynamic analysis (Smith & Kandel, 1993). Static analysis was utilized to verify the knowledge base. It does not involve the execution of the expert system, merely review of the code and associated documentation. Dynamic analysis involves the execution of the expert system. It is performed to determine if the expert system is producing the correct answers and using the correct reasoning process. All components of the prototype system were verified after the development was completed. Each module was tested using predesigned cases. Predesigned test cases were also utilized to verify the inference engine while conducting system testing. Upon indication of any errors, a structured problem resolution procedure was conducted.

The validation process establishes that the system's functionality will address the original engineering problem and the user's needs. According to the literature, there are two validation strategies available for consideration: validation against expert performance and validation by field testing (Prerau, 1990). They can be used alone or in combination, depending upon the application. Validation against expert performance can be achieved by comparing the expert system against operational expert judgments, comparing test case results, or comparing against project expert judgments. Validation by field testing involves running the program under actual or equivalent operational conditions. The field trial may be conducted either during initial production use or in parallel. A validation against expert performance was conducted to evaluate the prototype system developed during this research. This included utilization of predesigned test cases. These compared to the outcomes of the system with the expected results from the Gamma et al. (1995) design patterns book. A validation against expert performance was conducted by a variety of design pattern practitioners. The outcomes of the system were compared to their judgments. System validation indicated that a correct system was developed according to user's requirements.

The prototype system and associated documentation were reviewed by external evaluators. This validation against expert performance was conducted by 11 design pattern practitioners with a variety of levels of expertise, from students to professional software developers. These evaluators were self-selected by responding to a request on the pattern-discussion electronic mailing, hosted at the University of Illinois. Those who replied to the message, and expressed their interest in reviewing the system, were sent the program and relevant documentation. Feedback was collected and analyzed. The overall evaluation indicates that the system is generating the correct results and will provide a useful tool in assisting in the selection and implementation of design patterns. Several reviewers also provided suggestions for improving the system. These included screen design, displaying status of the search, and error messages. The suggestions resulting from the face validation were carefully considered, and the system was modified accordingly.

A predictive validation was conducted. This involved comparing the results from test cases in the literature, with the actual system output. These test cases resulted in execution and outcomes consistent with the proven results documented by Gamma et al. (1995) and Vlissides (1998), for example:

- **Test Case 1:** In this test case, the application was required to create different representations of a complex object using the same construction process. With this problem requirement in mind, the user confirmed the statement for category check of a creational pattern. The system investigated the Builder pattern's applicability as a suitable pattern, and then considered its consequences. When the user confirmed that the pattern was relevant to his application, and that the associated consequences were acceptable, the Builder became the selected pattern.

- **Test Case 2:** The problem under consideration required an application to compose objects into tree structures to represent part-whole hierarchies. An object that could access the elements of the tree structure was also required. This led to the display of the applicability and consequences check screens for the Composite pattern. Upon confirming that the pattern was applicable and that the consequences were acceptable, the Composite became the selected pattern. Since the Iterator pattern supports the implementation of the Composite pattern, the system tested the Iterator pattern for its application as a related pattern. When this supporting pattern also was found suitable, and its consequences acceptable, the system recommended a composite design pattern supported by an Iterator pattern as an appropriate solution for this problem.

Future Trends

The original set of software design patterns described by Gamma et al. (1995) tended to be general purpose in nature. The trend in current object-oriented design pattern research has transitioned to specialized applications. Martin, Riehle, and Buschmann (1997) introduce a series of such domain-specific patterns. For example, several design patterns for transportation systems and fire alarms are described. Rising (2000) continues this trend with specialized topics on patterns for finite state machines, parallel processing, and patterns about patterns.

These design patterns have normally been applied to the development of the underlying software for traditional types of information systems. Peters, Skowron, and Stepaniuk (2003) note that this approach "represents a well-understood paradigm useful in constructing components of a system." An emerging area of research involves the development of a whole new catalog of patterns for designing intelligent systems (IS). "Elaboration of IS patterns, augmentation of the IS pattern catalogue, refinement and extension of pattern maps, and consideration of properties of classification schemes are part of the future work in this research" (Peters, 2003). The level of complexity inherent in this research direction implies an even greater need for automated tools for its practical application. This may ultimately lead to the unique situation of intelligent information systems being used to design other intelligent information systems.

Conclusion

Catalogs containing new software design patterns continue to be published (e.g., Rising, 2000). Among various software reuse techniques, pattern-based reuse has the best flexibility and can be generally applied. It is less specific and is applicable in different languages and different domains. This work is an initial step at addressing the design pattern application problem, that is, leading a designer to the relevant pattern which is applicable to the problem at hand.

The prototype expert system, developed in this research, automates the design pattern selection and implementation process. Domain knowledge from human experts is incorporated into the system, and can be easily accessed via the user interface. It provides users with detailed guidance on which design pattern or which combination of patterns is appropriate to solve the problem under consideration. The implementation portion of the system also supports users in applying design pattern to real programs. It facilitates the application of design patterns and makes pattern-based software reuse more workable.

Considerable work remains in order to address a comprehensive catalog of patterns. The scope of this research was limited to a relatively small portion of design patterns that have been discovered. The expert system includes eight design patterns, which are regarded to be a frequently encountered subset of the patterns available for consideration (Gamma et al., 1995). A reasonable extension of this research is to enlarge the group of candidate design patterns. The increased number of design patterns will also raise the complexity of the knowledge base exponentially. Such techniques as partitioning of the knowledge base may need to be applied. A knowledge base maintenance facility, as suggested by some of the system validators, can also be incorporated. This facility would permit users to update the knowledge base, so as to correct existing rules or add new ones.

References

Bachmann, F., Bass, L., & Klein, M. (2003). *Preliminary design of ARCHE: A software architecture design assistant* (Tech. Rep. No. CUM/SEI-2003-TR-021). Pittsburgh, PA: Software Engineering Institute, Carnegie Mellon University.

Brown, K. (1996). *Reverse-engineering and automated design pattern detection in Smalltalk.* Master's thesis, Department of Computer Science, North Carolina State University, Raleigh.

Budinsky, F., Finnie, M., Vlissides, J., & Yu, P. (1996). Automatic code generation from design patterns. *IBM Systems Journal, 35*(2), 151-171.

Cinneide, M., & Nixon, P. (1999). A methodology for the automated introduction of design patterns. In *Proceedings of the IEEE International Conference on Software Maintenance.* Oxford, UK (pp. 463-472).

Cline, M. (1996). The pros and cons of adopting and applying design patterns in the real world. *Communications of ACM, 39*(10), 47-49.

Eden, A., Gil, J., & Yehundai, A. (1997). Automating the application of design patterns. *Journal of Object-Oriented Programming, 10*(2), 44-46.

Gamma, E., Helm, R., Johnson, R., & Vlissides, J. (1995). *Design patterns: Elements of reusable object-oriented software.* Reading, MA: Addison-Wesley.

Heuzeroth, D., Lowe, W., & Mandel, S. (2003). Generating design pattern detectors from pattern specifications. In *Proceedings of the 18th IEEE International Conference on Automated Software Engineering* (pp. 245-248).

Jackson, P. (1999). *Introduction to expert systems.* Reading, MA: Addison-Wesley.

Jones, T., Hilton, T., & Lutz, C. (1998). Discovering objects: Which identification and refinement strategies do analysts really use? *Journal of Database Management, 9*(3), 3-14.

Kramer, C., & Prechalt, L. (1996). Design recovery by automated search for structural design patterns in object-oriented software. In *Proceedings of the 3rd Working Conference on Reverse Engineering*, Monterey, CA (pp. 208-215).

Martin, R., Riehle, D., & Buschmann, F. (1997). *Pattern languages of program design 3.* Reading, MA: Addison-Wesley.

Medsker, L., & Liebowitz, J. (1994). *Design and development of experts systems and neural networks.* New York: Macmillan.

Moynihan, G. P. (1993). Application of expert systems to engineering design. In H. R. Parsaei & W. G. Sullivan (Eds.), *Concurrent engineering: Contemporary issues and modern design tools* (pp. 375-385). London: Chapman & Hall.

Peters, J. F. (2003). Design patterns in intelligent systems. In N. Zhong, Z. Ras, S. Tsumoto, & E. Suzuki (Eds.), *Foundations of intelligent systems* (pp. 262-269). Berlin: Springer.

Peters, J. F., Skowron, A. & Stepaniuk, J. (2003). Types, classification and information systems: A rough set approach. In *Proceedings of the Workshop on Rough Sets and Knowledge Discovery*, Warsaw, Poland (pp. 167-172).

Prerau, D. (1990). *Developing and managing expert systems.* Reading, MA: Addison-Wesley.

Rational Software Corporation (1995). *The unified method.* Lexington, MA: Rational Software Corporation.

Rising, L. (2000). *The pattern almanac 2000.* Reading, MA: Addison-Wesley.

Smith, J. M., & Stotts, D. (2003). SPQR: *Flexible automated design pattern extraction from source code.* Technical Report TR03-016. Department of Computer Science, University of North Carolina, Chapel Hill.

Smith, S., & Kandel, A. (1993). *Verification and validation of rule-based expert systems.* Boca Raton, FL: CRC Press.

Suki, A. (2003). *Expert system for the selection of design patterns.* Master's thesis, Department of Industrial Engineering, The University of Alabama, Tuscaloosa.

Vliet, H. (2001). *Software engineering principles and practice* (2nd ed.). Chichester, UK: John Wiley & Sons.

Vlissides, J. (1998). *Pattern matching: Design patterns applied.* Boston: Addison-Wesley.

Ziring, N. (1998). *Dictionary of programming languages.* Retrieved from http://cgibin.erols.com/ziring/cgi-bin/cep/cep.pl? _alpha=c

Chapter XV

An Agent Based Formal Approach for Modeling and Verifying Integrated Intelligent Information Systems

Leandro Dias da Silva, Federal University of Campina Grande, Brazil

Elthon Allex da Silva Oliveira, Federal University of Campina Grande, Brazil

Hyggo Almeida, Federal University of Campina Grande, Brazil

Angelo Perkusich, Federal University of Campina Grande, Brazil

Abstract

In this chapter, a formal agent-based approach for the modeling and verification of intelligent information systems using coloured Petri nets is presented. The use of a formal method allows analysis techniques such as automatic simulation and verification, increasing the confidence on the system behavior. The agent-based modeling allows separating distribution, integration, and intelligent features of the system, improving model reuse, flexibility, and maintenance. As a case study, an intelligent information control system for parking meters price is presented.

Introduction

Intelligent information systems (IIS) have been used in several different domains such as communication, sensor networks, decision-making processes, traffic control, business, and manufacturing systems, among others. Most IIS are distributed because the data is collected, processed, and used at different locations by different entities. These entities are autonomous and communicate among them to perform specific tasks. This scenario of an integrated IIS (IIIS) gives rise to several problems and difficulties to be addressed by the development team. Communication, scheduling, synchronization, databases, workflow, and real-time systems are some of the fields that usually have to be addressed in the development of an IIIS.

The agent-based development has been successfully applied to develop information systems with the characteristics mentioned (Jennings, 2001). Agents are intelligent entities, which are distributed and integrated to other agents. Therefore, developing information systems using the agent abstraction is quite convenient.

On the other hand, there are some features related to IIIS which are not explicitly addressed by the agent approach, such as dependability. Within this context, formal methods have been successfully used to promote confidence on the system behavior. More specifically, the coloured Petri nets (CPN) formal method (Jensen 1992, 1997) is pointed out as suitable for distributed and concurrent systems, which are inherent features of IIIS.

This chapter presents an agent-based approach for formal specification and verification of IIIS using coloured Petri nets. A generic agent-based skeleton CPN model comprising integration and distribution functionalities has been defined. Using this model, it is possible to model and verify agent-based IIIS by only modeling the intelligent functionalities. Distribution, integration and intelligent features are well encapsulated in CPN sub models. Thus, the proposed approach simplifies the IIIS modeling activity and improves its flexibility and maintenance. In order to illustrate the usage of the proposed approach, the modeling and verification of a control parking system is presented.

The remainder of the chapter is organized as follows. In the Background, some related works are discussed and background concepts are presented informally. After, the agent-based formal approach for modeling and verifying IIIS is presented. Next, the modeling and verification of a parking meter control system is presented and some verification results are discussed. In Future Trends, there are some insights and suggestions for future work. In the last section, the chapter is concluded and summarized.

Background

Coloured Petri Nets

Coloured Petri nets (CPN) (Jensen 1992, 1997) are a formal method with a mathematical base and a graphical notation for the specification and analysis of systems with characteristics such as concurrent, parallel, distributed, asynchronous, timed, among others. For the mathematical definition, the reader can refer to Jensen (1992, 1997). The graphical notation is a bipartite graph with places, represented as ellipses, and transitions, represented as rectangles. Transitions represent actions and the marking of the places represent the state of the model. A marking of a place at a given moment are the tokens present at that place. A token can be a complex data type in CPN/ML Language (Christensen & Haagh, 1996). Each place has an associated color set that represents the kind of tokens the place can have. The transitions can have guards and code associated to it. Guards are Boolean expression that must be true for the transition to fire. Code can be a function that is executed every time the transition fires. Arcs go from places to transitions and from transitions to places and never from transition to transition or place to place, and can have complicated expressions and function calls associated to it.

For a transition to fire, it is necessary that all input places, that is, places that have arcs that go from the place to the transition, have the number of tokens greater than or equal to the weight of the arc, $w(p,t)$, and the guard of the transition must be true. When these characteristics hold the transition is said to be enabled to fire. An enabled transition can fire at any time and not necessarily immediately. Once a transition fires, it removes $w(pi,t)$ from each input place pi, and the output places, that is, places that have arcs from the transition to the place, receive tokens according to the arc expression from the transition to the place: $w(t,p)$.

A CPN model can also have a hierarchy. Two mechanisms — substitution transitions and fusion places — can be used to structure the model in a more organized way. Substitution transitions are transitions that represent another CPN model, called a page. The page where the transition belongs to is called super-page and the page represented by the transition is called sub-page. In the sub-page there are places that can be input, output, or input/output places. These places are associated to input and output places of the transition in the super-page called sockets. Fusion places are places that are physically different but have always the same marking. A change in the marking of one place is reflected in all places that belong to that fusion set. These two mechanisms are just visual, and for simulation and model checking purpose the model is glued together and the hierarchy is considered a flat CPN model. This extension with hierarchy is called hierarchical coloured Petri nets (Jensen 1992, 1997), and there is a tool set to edit and analyze such models called Design/CPN (Jensen et al., 1999).

In Figure 1, a simple HCPN model is illustrated. In this figure, place *P3* is the input socket and place *P4* is the output socket of the substitution transition *T2* in the super-page. The place *P5* in the sub-page is the input place associated to *P3* in the super-page, and the place *P6* is the output place associated to place *P4,* respectively. The inscriptions *Int* closer to each place is the color set of the place and states that the places can have integer tokens. The expression *1`(2)* close to *P2* is the initial marking of this place. That means that in the initial state this place have a marking consisting of one token which value is *2*.

The expression [$i>0$] is the guard for transition *T1*. It is easy to see that at the initial marking *T1* is enabled to fire because there are tokens in the two input places that satisfy the input weight functions $w(P1,T1) = 1$ and $w(P2,T2) = 1$, and the guard [$i>0$] as $i=3$ in the initial marking. Once this transition fires one token is removed from *P1* and *P2* and one token is added to *P3* which value is the sum between the two input token $i+j$, where i and j are declared as integers in the declaration node. This node is where all the declarations of colors (the data types), variables, and functions are written.

Figure 1. HCPN model

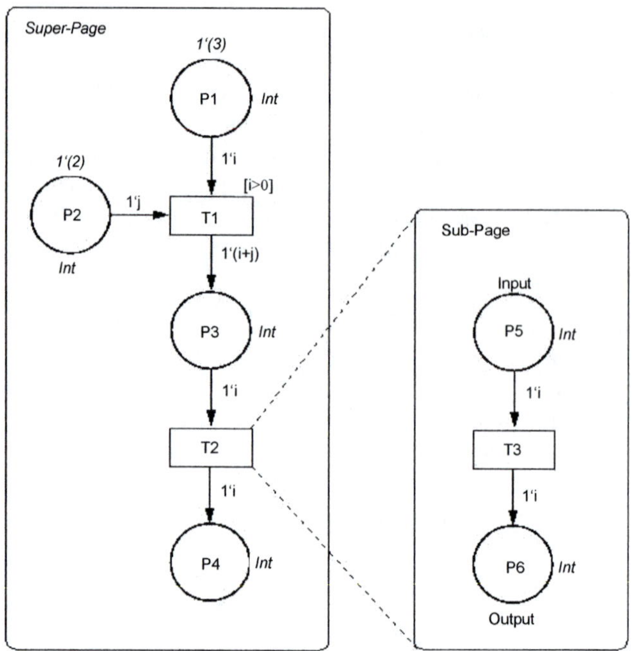

The sub-page can be an arbitrarily complicated CPN model with its own substitution transitions. Moreover the tokens can have complex data types such as tuples, records, lists, and user-defined types using primitive types.

Model Checking

With simulation, it is possible to investigate the behavior of the model. However, based on this analysis, it is not possible to guarantee that the properties are valid for all possible behavior of the model. Therefore, model checking (Clarke, Grumberg, & Peled, 1999) is used to prove that the desired properties of the model hold for every possible behavior.

The model checking activity consists of three steps. First, a model *M* must be developed. Second, the properties *S* to be verified must be specified in some logic. Third, model checking is performed. Therefore, model checking is used to verify if a given model models the specification: $M \models S$.

To verify the desired properties, through model checking, it is used the Design/CPN tool package is used to generate the state space and its temporal language library named ASK/CTL (Christensen & Mortensen, 1996) is used to perform model checking.

Based on the example shown in Figure 1 and a simplified ASK/CTL syntax, some examples of properties specifications are as follows:

$Pa = Marking.P1\ 1`()$

$Pb = Marking.P6\ 1`()$

$S = AND\ (Pa,\ EV(Pb))$

where *Pa* and *Pb* are atomic propositions and *S* is the property specification. *Pa* means that there is a token with any value in places *P1* and *P6*. *S* specifies that *Pa* is true and *Pb* is eventually true. This formula evaluated to true if *Pa* is true and at some point in the future *Pb* becomes true. Otherwise it is false. This example specifies that every token in the initial place always generate a token in the final place of the model. Moreover, it is important to note that this model can be a complicated model and to verify this kind of property can be useful.

Related Work

There are some works related to our approach. In Adam, Atluri, and Huang (1998), for example, it is presented a Petri net-based formal framework for modeling and analyzing workflows. The modeling and analysis activities are used to identify inconsistent dependency specifications among workflow tasks; to test if the workflow terminates in an acceptable state; and to test if it is feasible to execute a workflow with specified temporal constraints, for a given time.

In DEEN (2005), it is presented a multi-agent model of a distributed information system. The objective is to define the agent-based behavior of the distributed system, which must operate correctly and effectively in an error-prone industrial environment, based on a problem-solving model that is also proposed in DEEN (2005).

Another work, presented in Delena and Pratt (2005), focuses on to promote advanced model-based decision support systems by addressing problems such as lack of model reusability. The main motivation for such work is that the existing solutions for decision support systems are only suitable for specific domains and tools. Thus, the idea is to provide a general methodology for decision support, according to the real needs of the decision-makers, in a feasible manner.

Colored Petri nets have also been used to model some previous works such as Almeida, Silva, Perkusich, and Costa (2005) and Almeida, Silva, Silva Oliveira, and Perkusich (2005). In Almeida et al. (2005), a set of guidelines are presented for the modeling and verification of multi-agent systems, focusing on planning activities. In Almeida et al. (2005), a modeling and verification process for component-based systems is presented, with application to embedded control and automation systems.

In this chapter, a formal approach based on Petri nets and multi-agents systems is considered for the specification and analysis of IIIS. This approach is described in the next section.

Agent-Based Modeling and Verification Approach

The Agent Architecture

Many researchers have claimed that the agent-based approach is adequate for complex, distributed, and interaction-centric software development (Jennings, 2001). According to this approach, a system is composed of a society of distributed and autonomous agents that interact to reach their goals and provide the system functionalities. Also, agents are intelligent entities. Therefore, developing IIIS using the agent abstraction is quite convenient.

There are several architectures for agent-based systems. In the context of this work, we consider an adaptation of the MATHEMA architecture (Costa, Lopes, &Ferneda, 1995). It has been applied to various domains, such as algebra (Costa et al., 1995), musical harmony (Costa et al., 2002), and Petri nets (Costa, Perkusich, & Figueiredo, 1996), and promotes a clear encapsulation of the integration, distribution, and intelligent system functionalities.

Each agent in our architecture is composed of three systems: intelligent, social, and distribution. The intelligent system implements the functionalities of the system domain, according to the specific IIIS needs: decision support, business intelligence, problem solving, and so forth. The social system implements the functionalities for agent interaction and integration. The distribution system implements the functionalities to promote the communication among the agents.

Considering the integration and distribution features are inherent of all IIIS, the intelligent system can be seen as the *customizable part* of the agent architecture. Thus, a generic architecture must define customization points where domain-specific IIIS functionalities could

Figure 2. Agent architecture

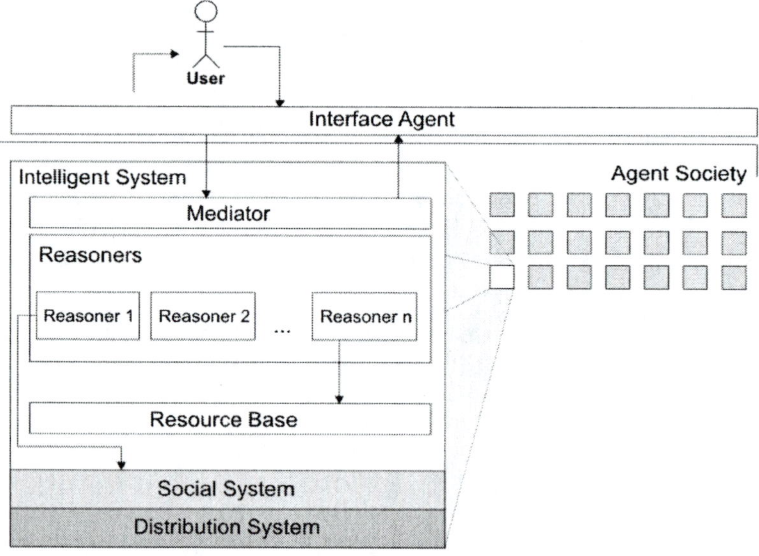

be placed to be integrated to the rest of the architecture. For that, the intelligent system is divided into the following entities, which are also illustrated in Figure 2.

- **Mediator:** It implements the interaction mechanisms with the interface agent and thus with the user. It also selects the suitable reasoner in order to respond to the user requests. The interface agent is just a simple agent responsible to interact with the user.
- **Reasoners:** They are the components that implement the domain-specific functionalities of the intelligent tutoring system. As the reasoners could be different for each application, these components are the customizable points of the architecture. For example, if an IIIS requires a decision-making support, a reasoner that implements such support must be integrated to the architecture.
- **Resource base:** It is responsible to store information.

Modeling and Verification Approach

Based on the agent-based generic architecture, we have modeled a generic CPN model for IIIS. The modeling activity has been performed using the design/CPN tool. The hierarchy page for the generic CPN model for IIIS is shown in Figure 3.

As mentioned before, the customizable entities are the reasoners. In Figure 3, the unique reasoner model is in the *decision-making* page. By changing and inserting new reasoners, it is possible to model the intelligent features of a specific IIIS. Since the distribution and integration features are common to all IIIS, we focus here in how to customize the model for the intelligent feature. The detailed models for all pages described in the hierarchy page can be found in Silva, Almeida, and Perkusich (2003).

The reasoners are modeled as CPN *substitution transitions*. In this way, according to the IIIS specific needs, new pages can be modeled and integrated to the model. Also, this makes possible to maintain the separation between intelligent, integration, and distribution features of the IIIS model.

In order to model and verify an IIIS using our approach, the following steps must be accomplished.

1. **Identify the agents:** The agents must be identified according to the IIIS requirements. It can be performed through defined roles involved with the IIIS specific domain and then define an agent or a set of agents to play each role. There are several methodologies for identifying agents based on system requirements, such as Tropos (Giunchiglia, Mylopoulos, & Perini, 2002).
2. **Identify agent reasoners:** When agents are identified, the reasoners can be defined by analyzing the intelligent requirements for each agent or agent role.
3. **Model agent reasoners:** Build a CPN model for each reasoner. Since the distribution and integration features are already modeled, this is the main activity of the IIIS modeling.

Figure 3. Hierarchy page for the generic CPN model

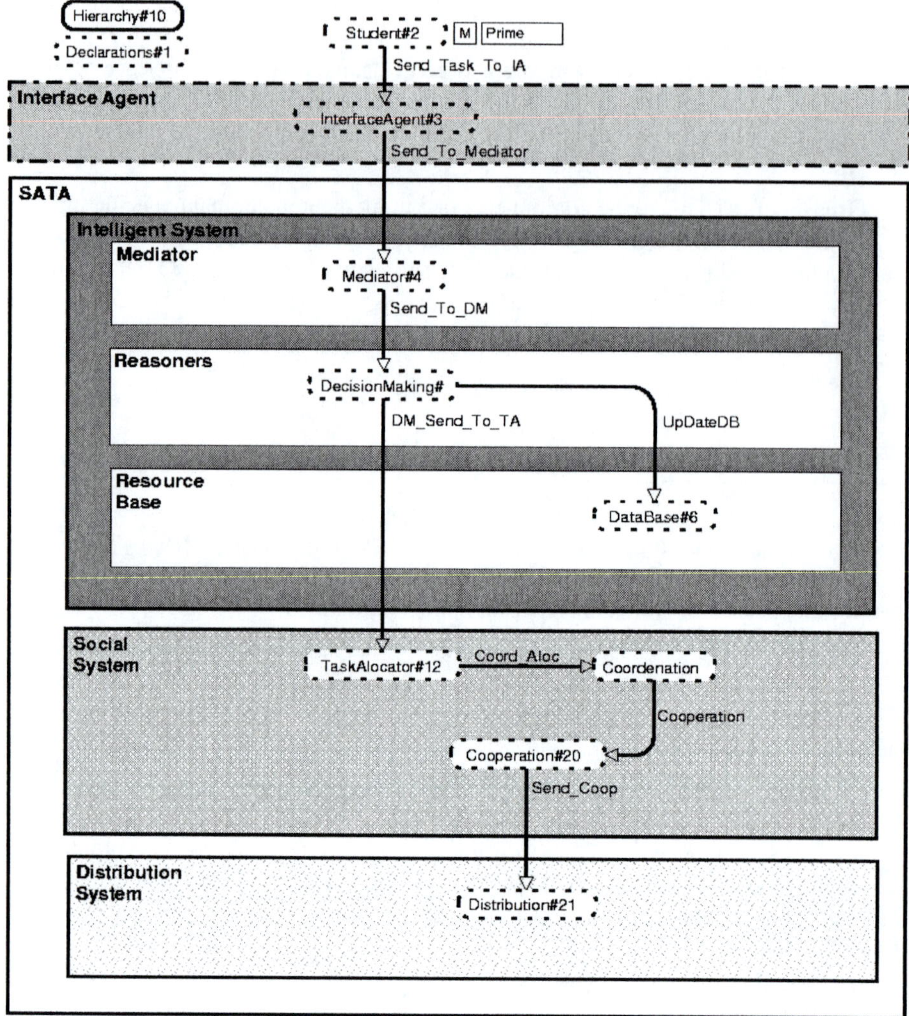

4. **Integrate the reasoners models to the generic CPN model:** Integrate the reasoners models to the CPN generic model by defining substitution transitions for each reasoner and linking the mediator, resource base, and social system according to the reasoners needs.

5. **Analyze the whole model:** Use the design/CPN tool to analyze the model and identify potential design errors.

Figure 4. Parking meters

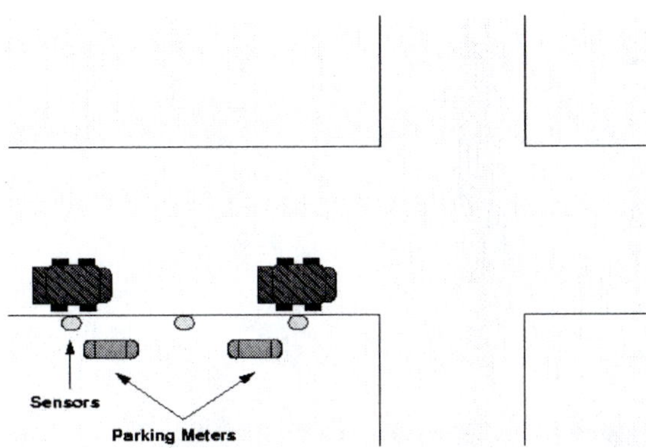

Case Study: Control Parking System

Parking has becoming a serious problem even for small cities. An initial solution is to charge for parking. When it is not a solution anymore, increasing the parking charges and constructing parking structures near busy places are possible solutions.

However, parking structures are sometimes not good because they are expensive and change the view and architecture of the city. Just keep increasing the price is also not a permanent solution because employees and other people cannot pay more money for parking.

An efficient solution is to change the price charged by the parking meters depending on the number of available spaces (Smith, 2005). In this case, 15% is considered the ideal number for specialists. Therefore, every time the number of spaces available goes above, the price can be decreased, and when it goes below 15%, the price can be increased.

The system for parking prices control is composed of sensors, parking meters, and a control system. In Figure 4, the parking scenario with sensors and meters is illustrated.

The sensors send the information regarding its space to the control system that keep track of all information sent by sensors and can decide which parking meter should increase or decrease the price shown.

Model

The problem with parking is that people have encountered difficulty in finding available spaces to park their vehicles. As a solution, all the places where people usually park are marked as a space and they are grouped in some parking zones.

A sensor is put in each one of these spaces with the purpose of monitoring its status. It monitors if the space is available or not. A parking meter is used to show the price to be paid. The idea of this solution is that for each parking zone, or group of parking spaces, the sensors send data to a central computer periodically informing if their respective space are available or not.

The central computer increases or decreases the price of parking according to the ratio of available spaces in each parking zone. In this example, if there are just 15% of available spaces to park in a specific parking zone, the price of vacancies is increased for that parking zone. Otherwise, if there are more than 15% of available spaces, the price is reduced. The act of increasing or reducing the price is done every time the central computer receives data from the sensors. So, the price will be constantly changed depending on the search for spaces to park.

Using the approach described, the steps to develop and analyze this application are:

1. **Identify the agents:** sensors, parking meters, and the decision agent
2. **Identify agent reasoners:** the decision agent
3. **Model agent reasoners:** This model can be seen in Figure 8.
4. **Integrate the reasoners models to the generic CPN model:** This integration is done by the main page as seen in Figure 5, using fusion places, and this whole model is integrated in the model shown in Figure 5 with substitution transitions at the reasoner part.
5. **Analyze the whole model:** This is discussed in the next section.

Figure 5. Main page

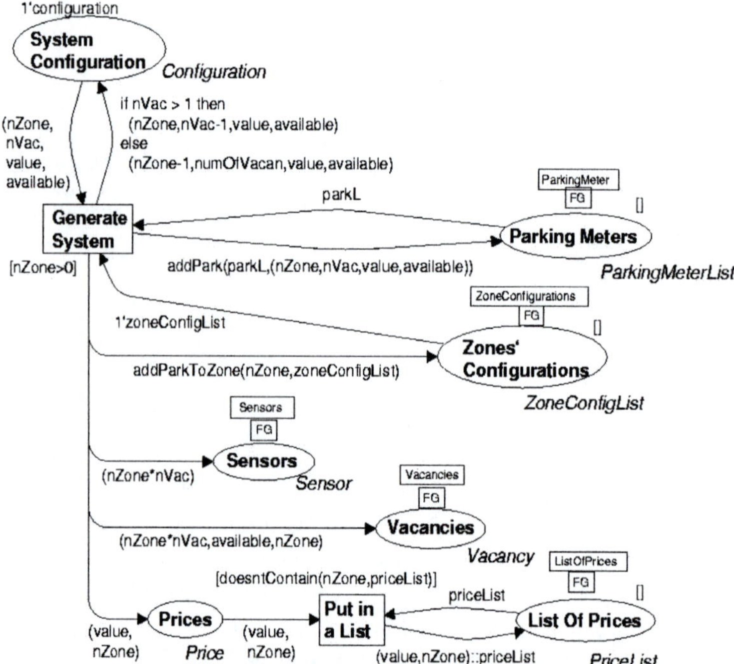

In Figure 5, the page where sensor agents, parking zones, and their vacancies and configurations, the parking meters agents and a list of prices for each parking zone are created is presented.

In the system configuration place, there is a token that has four fields: nZone, nVac, value, and available. The first field determines the number of parking zones to be created. The second means the number of vacancies for each parking zone. The third and fourth ones mean the initial price paid for using the vacancy and the status of the vacancy, respectively.

The *generate system* transition creates *nVac* vacancies for each one of the *nZone* parking zones. The guard *[nZone>0]* guarantees that the process of creation will stop for *nZone* less than or equal to zero.

In Figure 6, the page that describes the sensor behavior is presented. The part of the page surrounded by a dashed box generates a random value that models the status of the vacancy. The value *true* means it is available, *false* means it is not available. The *verify vacancy* transition verifies if the vacancy that corresponds to a sensor, by verifying their identifier values, is available or not. This verified status is sent to the *decision agent* page (central computer) that determines the new price according to the number of available vacancies.

In Figure 7, the page that describes the *decision agent* behavior is presented. It is this agent that controls when the price of a parking zone must be increased or reduced. On the *zones' configuration* place there is a token that has a list of the configuration of parking zones. This configuration has three fields: the parking zone identifier, the number of available vacancies, and the number of unavailable vacancies inside that parking zone. The unique transition of the page, named *update prices*, and the arc expression (*updatePrices(zoneConfigList,proceList)*) verify if the configuration of each parking zone is according to the specified threshold. As

Figure 6. Sensor agent page

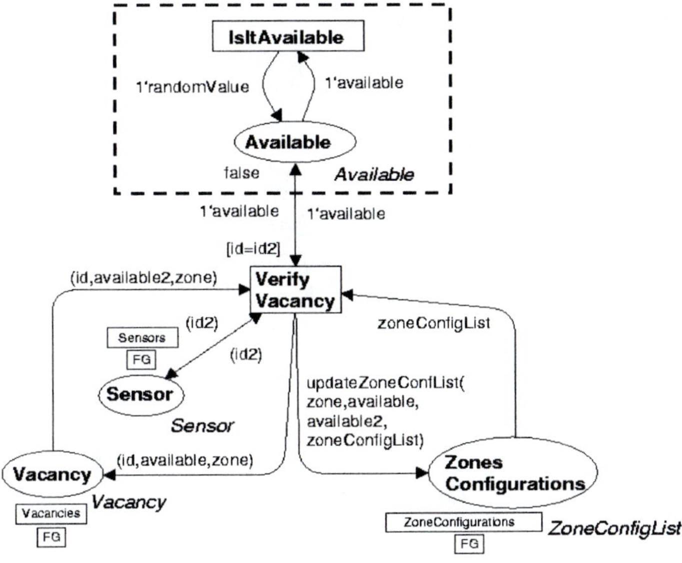

Figure 7. Decision agent page

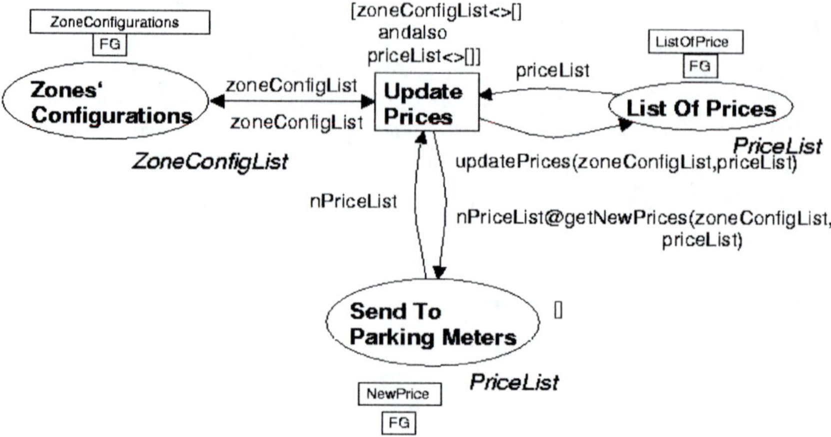

Figure 8. Parking meter agent page

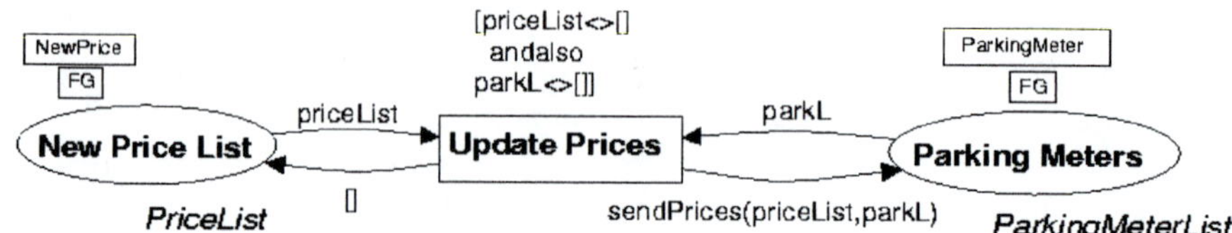

mentioned, if there are less than 15% of available vacancies in a parking zone, the price is increased, otherwise the price is decreased.

There is also a place named *list of prices*. The prices of all parking zones are on it in a list form. The transition updates this list and send a list with the newest prices, by the arc expression *nPriceList@getNewPrices(zoneConfigList,proceList)*, to all the parking meters of the parking zones that had their prices changed.

In the Figure 8, the *parking meter agent* page is presented. This agent receives a message from the *decision agent* with the new price list of the parking zones. If this list is not empty (see the *update prices* transition guard), the list that contains all the vacancies prices is updated with the new prices. So, it means that each one of the parking meters has changed its screen showing the new price. All this is done by the *update prices* transition.

It is important to note that any number of sensors and parking meters can be present in the system, and they can enter and leave the system without compromising the rest of the system. Also, the business strategy can change and the price can be controlled for a different number of available parking spaces instead of 15%. This change is also transparent for sensors and parking meters. Moreover, other agents can be considered such as a management agent for reporting and auditing purposes.

This model-based approach promotes a better organization and validation of the system as well as a good way to deal with changes in the system or requirements. Every time some change is incorporated to the requirement, the part of the model related to it can be changed and the analysis can be performed again to ensure that the changes respect the desired system behavior.

Analysis

Simulation

Many simulations were done and some things were observed: every time, for each zone it was created *numOfVac* vacancies; for each vacancy, it was created a parking meter and a sensor; and it was always created a list of prices, each one for each vacancy and a list of zone configurations, each one for each parking zone.

By simulating the model, it was detected that when a parking zone price changes, the price of the other parking zone vacancy does not change. And if a parking zone price is changed, maybe this new price does not appear in the parking meter visor because of a newer price. In other words, suppose the price is US$1. And it is changed to US$2. Before this new price is passed to the parking meter, it is changed back to $1, so the first change will not be passed to the users of the vacancies.

A weird feature was detected — the surrounded box of the sensor agent page that monitors if a vacancy is available or not looks preferring true values. Therefore, the model checking technique has to be applied in order to verify all possible behaviors.

Model Checking

Simulation cannot guarantee that all the possible execution traces of the model were explored. Therefore, it is necessary to generate a state space of the CPN model, also known as occurrence graph. In this kind of graph, each one of the nodes represents a possible state of the model.

With the state space in hands, it is used a temporal logic language to specify the desired properties, in this case it is used a library called ASK/CTL (Christensen & Mortensen, 1996). The specified properties were: (a) every time a sensor agent sends data with the vacancy status, the decision agent receives it; (b) every time the decision agent changes the price of a specific parking zone, all the parking meters of that parking zone receive a response message with the new price to be showed; the most important property is that (c) every time the available the number of vacancies reaches 15% or less of the total of vacancies in a certain parking zone, the price is increased, otherwise it is reduced; and (d) it is possible to have all the vacancies not available.

The logical propositions and formulas used to perform model checking for the CPN model are described in what follows. For the sake of convenience and simplicity a CTL-like notation is used.

a. This property is guaranteed because the place that represents the output of sensor agent and the place that represents the correspondent input of decision agent belong to the same set of fusion places. In other words, this property is satisfied due to the fusion place concept.

b. Property specification:

  - *Pa* = Decision agent changes the parking value
  - *Pb* = All parking meters of a parking zone receives the change
  - *S = AL(IMP(Pa,EV(Pb))*

  In other words, *Pa* is always true, consequently (*IMP* means implies) *Pb* will be true. This property is evaluated to false. The decision agent can change a parking zone price and before this price is sent to the parking meters, the decision agent can change the price again. So, the first change is not visible to the user of the vacancy.

c. Property specification:

  - *Pa1* = Number of vacancies equal to or less than 15 percent
  - *Pb1* = Price is increased
  - *Pa2* = Number of vacancies is greater than 15 percent
  - *Pb2* = Price is reduced
  - *S1 = AL(IMP(Pa1,EV(Pb1)))*
  - *S2 = AL(IMP(Pa2,EV(Pb2)))*
  - *S = AND(S1,S2);*

  This property is evaluated to be true.

d. The property is that there is just one parking zone and there are 10 vacancies in it.

  - *Pa* = The parking zone has no available vacancy.
  - *S = EV(Pa)*

  This property is evaluated to be true. Eventually, it can occur that none of the vacancies areavailable.

Future Trends

As a future trend, some other characteristics can be taken into account such as management information that can also be stored in a database for reporting and auditing purposes. Another agent can be inserted to do this task without changing the rest of the model. This flexibility promoted by the multi-agent framework together with the advantages of a formal method as Petri nets, make this approach a good way to deal with the challenges of the IIIS. Therefore, other classes of IIIS can be addressed using it.

There is an external communication library for the design/CPN tool called Comms/CPN (Gallasch & Kristensen, 2001). Using this library, it is possible to communicate the CPN model with an external application and, therefore, make the model control the system for parking prices itself. In this case, a mathematical correct proved model is the control system itself and there is no gap between design and implementation.

Conclusion

In this chapter, a formal multi-agent-based specification and validation approach is presented for the domain of intelligent information systems. An application of a control system for parking meters prices is used to illustrate the approach. A multi-agent development promotes a good way to deal with changes. In the case of this work, the model is formal, and it is possible to perform some analysis such as automatic simulation and model checking to ensure that desired properties of the system hold in the model.

The use of a formal model for specification and verification as presented in this chapter for the domain of intelligent information systems promotes trustworthiness in the system behavior. This is important for decision-making systems where a business strategy must be ensured. Moreover, with the multi-agent framework, changes can be applied to specific parts of the model while the rest of the model does not change. This local changes characteristic is important for complex distributed system to keep control on changes. Finally, when changes are done, the model can be used to analyze the behavior to ensure that the new changes respect the system properties.

An intelligent control system for parking prices control is presented to illustrate the advantages of using this approach to the IIIS domain. This system consists of autonomous sensor agents, parking meter agents, and a control agent. They interact with each other to ensure a minimum number of parking places to be available at busy shopping areas by increasing and decreasing the price. The formal model-based approach is used to specify and analyze this system and some analysis results are presented.

References

Adam, N. R., Atluri, V., & Huang, W.-K. (1998). Modeling and analysis of workflows using Petri nets. *Journal of Intelligent Information Systems: Special issue on workflow management systems, 10*(2), 131-158.

Almeida, H., Silva, L., Perkusich, A., & Costa, E. (2005). A formal approach for the modelling and verification of multiagent plans based on model checking and Petri nets. In R. Choren, A. Garcia, C. Lucena, & A. Romanovsky (Eds.), *Software engineering for multi-agent systems, III: Research issues and practical applications* (vol. 3390, pp. 162-179). Heidelberg, Germany: Springer GMBH.

Almeida, H. O. de, Silva, L. D. da, Silva Oliveira, E. A. da, & Perkusich, A. (2005). Formal approach for component based embedded software modelling and analysis. In *Proceedings of the IEEE International Symposium on Industrial Electronics* (*ISIE 2005*) (pp. 1337-1342). Dubrovinik, Croatia: IEEE Press.

Christensen, S., & Haagh, T. B. (1996). *Design/CPN overview of CPN ML syntax, version 3.0.* Aarhus, Denmark: University of Aarhus, Department of Computer Science.

Christensen, S., & Mortensen, K. H. (1996). *Design/CPN ASK-CTL manual*. Aarhus, Denmark: University of Aarhus, Department of Computer Science.

Clarke, E. M., Grumberg, O., & Peled, D. A. (1999). *Model checking*. Cambridge, MA: The MIT Press.

Costa, E. B., et al. (2002) A multi-agent cooperative intelligent tutoring system: The case of musical harmony domain. In *Proceedings of 2nd Mexican International Conference on Artificial Intelligence (MICAI'02)*, Merida (LNCS 2313, pp. 367-376). Heidelberg, Germany: Springer GMBH.

Costa, E. B., Lopes, M. A., Ferneda, E. (1995) Mathema: A learning environment base on a multi-agent architecture. In *Proceedings of the 12th Brazilian Symposium on Artificial Intelligence (SBIA '95)* (pp. 141-150). Campinas, Brazil: Springer GMBH.

Costa, E. B., Perkusich, A., Figueiredo, J. C. A (1996). A multi-agent based environment to aid in the design of Petri nets based software systems. In *Proceedings of the 8th International Conference on Software Engineering and Knowledge Engineering (SEKE'96)* (pp. 253-260). Buenos Aires, Argentina: IEEE Press.

Deen, S. (2005). An engineering approach to cooperating agents for distributed information systems. *Journal of Intelligent Information Systems*, *25*(1), 5-45.

Delena, D., & Pratt, D. B. (2006, February). An integrated and intelligent DSS for manufacturing systems. *Expert Systems with Applications, 30*(2), 325-336.

Gallasch, G., & Kristensen, L. M. (2001, August). Comms/CPN: A communication infrastructure for external communication with Design/CPN. In *Proceedings of the 3rd Workshop and Tutorial on Practical Use of Coloured Petri Nets and the CPN Tools* (pp. 75-90). Aarhus, Denmark: University of Aarhus, Department of Computer Science.

Giunchiglia, F., Mylopoulos, J., & Perini, A. (2002) The Tropos software development methodology: Processes, models and diagrams. In *Proceedings of the 1st International Joint Conference on Autonomous Agents and Multiagent Systems* (pp. 35-36). Bologna, Italy.

Jennings, N. R. (2001) An agent-based approach for building complex software systems. *Communications of the ACM*, *44*(4), 35-41.

Jensen, K. (1992). *Coloured Petri nets: Basic concepts, analysis, methods and practical use (vol. 1).* Heidelberg, Germany: Springer GMBH.

Jensen, K. (1997). *Coloured Petri nets: Basic concepts, analysis, methods and practical use (vol. 2).* Heidelberg, Germany: Springer GMBH.

Jensen, K., et al. (1999). *Design/CPN 4.0*. Retrieved December 17, 2005, from http://www.daimi.au.dk/designCPN/

Murata, T. (1989, April). Petri nets: Properties, analysis and applications. *Proceedings of the IEEE*, *77*(4), 541-580.

Smith, M. (2005, August). *Will a new generation of curbside sensors end our parking problems — or help the government monitor our every move?* Retrieved December, 17, 2005, from http://www.sfweekly.com/Issues/2005-08-17/news/smith.html

Chapter XVI

Intelligent Remote Monitoring and Maintenance Systems

Chengliang Liu, Shanghai JiaoTong University, China

Xuan F. Zha, National Institute of Standards and Technology, University of Maryland, USA & Shanghai JiaoTong University, China

Abstract

Internet-based intelligent fault diagnosis and maintenance technologies are keys for enterprises to achieve global leadership in market competition and manufacturing productivity for business in the 21st century. E-products, e-manufacturing, and e-service have been the goals of enterprises: (1) Next generation products must be network-based products — e-products. The vast developments of IT technology-based hardware and software make the controller of Internet-based products cheaper; (2) Common facilities such as Internet and World Wide Web, 3G (GPS, GPRS, and GIS) make e-maintenance or e-service cheaper and easier; (3) "Server-Web-user" methodology makes e-manufacturing possible, convenient, and efficient. To achieve these goals, smart software and NetWare are needed to provide proactive maintenance capabilities such as performance degradation measurement, fault recovery, self-maintenance, and remote diagnostics. This chapter presents methodologies and techniques for the development of an Internet server controller-based intelligent remote monitoring and maintenance system. Discussion involves how to make innovations and de-

velop products and manufacturing systems using Internet-based intelligent technologies and how to ensure product quality, coordinate activities, reduce costs, and change maintenance practice from the breakdown reaction to prevention. A hybrid intelligent approach using hardware and software agents (watchdog agent) is adopted. The server controller is Web-enabled, and its core is an embedded network model. The software agent is implemented through a package of Smart Prognostics Algorithms. The package consists of embedded computational prognostic algorithms developed using neural network based, time-series based, wavelet-based and hybrid joint time-frequency methods, and so forth, and a software toolbox for predicting degradation of devices and systems. The effectiveness of the proposed scheme is verified in a real testbed system.

Introduction

Globalization and fast growth of the Internet technologies and information technologies have added unprecedented challenges to industry. In the past decade, the impact of Web-based e-system technologies has accelerated the development process of products including product design, manufacturing, and business operations. Business automation is forcing companies to shift operations from the traditional "factory integration" philosophy to a "virtual factory" supply chain management philosophy (NRC, 1990). The technological advances to achieve this highly collaborative design and manufacturing environment are based on multimedia type information-based engineering tools and a highly reliable communication system to enable distributed procedures in concurrent engineering design, remote operation of manufacturing processes, and operation of distributed production systems. This transition is dependent upon the advancement of next-generation manufacturing practices on "e-factory and e-automation," which is focused on the use of information to collaboration on a global basis. Quality is no longer an objective; it is a prerequisite for competing in the global marketplace. In addition, the complexity of today's products has greatly attracted consumers' attention to the service cost of the product's life cycle. A new paradigm on robust engineering to focus on e-intelligence for integrated product design, manufacturing, and service is becoming a new benchmark strategy for manufacturing companies to compete in the 21st century (Lee, 1998, 1999, 2000).

Industry and government are constantly under economic pressures to reduce costs while increasing service and productivity. Because of the low labor cost, multinational companies establish many sub-factories in the developing countries and outsource some of their businesses. With the development of globally integrated activities manufacturing equipment becomes more complex and more costly to build and maintain. A leading manufacturing organization supported with global customer service should be flexible enough in management and labor practices, and possess the ability to develop and produce virtually defect-free products quickly in response to opportunities and needs of the changing world market. Because of the rapid growth of the global market, the fast responsive maintenance and service are becoming more and more important for companies to sustain their manufacturing productivity and customer satisfaction to compete globally (Lee, 2003). An intelligent e-maintenance system is a need for next-generation products and manufacturing systems. Future smart manufacturing companies necessitate a set of core intelligences to address the issues of smart business performance within the integrated design, manufacturing, and service business system. This set of core intelligences is called "5Ps," namely predictability, producibility, productivity, pollution prevention, and performance. With such a scientific understanding of the manufacturing business, it is vital to select the optimum strategies for innovations across product life cycle.

Innovations in product service systems must be provided for customers with better solutions. Smart product software can predict the failure of a system in advance. Such "prognostic" capability gives an ability to provide a new kind of aftermarket service to guarantee product and operations performance. A customer's need extends for the life of a product and requires a system design that takes into account the aftermarket support. Service and maintenance are important practices to maintain product and process quality and customers' satisfaction. In order to ensure the product quality, coordinate the activities, reduce costs, and change maintenance practice from breakdown reaction to breakdown prevention, there is currently a great need to remotely monitor, predict, detect, maintain, and diagnose faults of manufacturing equipment.

Machines degrade as a result of aging and wear, decrease of the performance reliability, and increase of the potentials for faults and failures. Economic effects, related to machine availability and reliability as well as corrective maintenance costs, have prompted facilities and factories to improve maintenance techniques and operations to monitor machine degradation and detect faults. The majority of unscheduled maintenance measures are very expensive and can cause a complete shutdown of the production line. By using the intelligent remote monitoring and maintenance system (IRMMS), maintenance can be scheduled in advance of sudden failure, and the necessity to replace parts at intervals based on the mean time between failures (MTBF) can be reduced. Instead, parts will need to be replaced only when necessary. Remote users and facilities can ensure the performance of consumer products, manufacturing equipment, quality of operations, and productivity of the plant by monitoring the degradation of manufacturing equipment. In addition to the current Internet-based interactive technology, IRMMS would enable service engineers to contact and/or monitor manufacturing equipment at a remote location, from virtually anywhere in the world. They do not need to visit the site, and the clients just need contact through telephone or network for simple diagnosis and maintenance advice. Therefore, with RMMS, the machinery and equipment characteristics could be well understood so that the operation of machinery could be optimized to reduce costs while improving product and service quality. The main merits of a reliable monitoring and maintenance system being incorporated within a machine or equipment are summarized as follows:

1. Prolonging equipment and machine life.
2. Increasing machine availability and enhance performance.
3. Reducing overall maintenance requirements and costs.
4. Extending the period between shutdowns.
5. Reducing emergency shutdowns and lost production.
6. Prolonging machine operation by corrective actions.
7. Early detection of problems can help to plan and effectively apply downtime, material, and labor.

8. Parts or components with long lead times can be ordered well in advance and help reduce inventory costs.
9. Significant cost savings, as highlighted by the mentioned benefits.
    a. Next generation products must be network products — e-products. The vast development of IT technology-based hardware and software makes the controller of Internet-based products cheaper.
    b. Common facilities such as Internet and World Wide Web, 3G (GPS, GPRS, and GIS) make e-service or e-maintenance cheaper and easier.
    c. "Server-Web-user" methodologies make the e-manufacturing possible, convenient, and efficient.

The main objective of this work is to develop methodologies and technologies to reduce the downtime of equipment near zero with the following procedures: (1) developing Internet-based server controller; (2) developing prognostics on-a-chip watchdog agent for product behavior assessment and performance degradation; (3) evaluating the analysis; (4) establishing a tele-service engineering system (TSES) testbed; (5) developing integrated intelligent maintenance software system. This chapter reports the development of an Internet server controller-based intelligent remote monitoring and maintenance system. A peer-to-peer multi-agent methodology using hardware and software agents (watchdog agent) is proposed, and some technologies are developed for implementing the proposed methodology.

The organization of the chapter is as follows. The next section reviews the related previous research and current research status. Then, we provide an overview and strategies for tele-service engineering system, and discuss the description and modeling of machine performance. We discuss machine performance description and modeling. Next, we describe the structure of remote monitoring fault diagnostics and maintenance system (RMFDMS). We present key technologies for developing the RMFDMS. A prognostics on-a-chip watchdog agent will be developed for assessing and evaluating product behavior and performance degradation. A testbed of the RMFDMS is also described. The last two sections provide future trends in the domain and give concluding remarks.

Brief Review

To date, many manufacturing companies are still performing service and maintenance activities based on a reactive approach. The fundamental issues to resolve these problems are inadequate information and understanding about the behaviors of products and manufacturing equipment on a daily basis. How to measure the performance degradation of components and machines is still an issue to be unsolved. Developers also lack the validated predictive models and tools that can tell what would happen when the process parameters take specified values. Research is required to understand the factors involved in product and machine breakdowns and to develop smart and reconfigurable monitoring tools that reduce or eliminate the production downtime, and thus reduce the dimensional variation due to the process degradation. To achieve these goals, smart software and NetWare are needed to provide proactive maintenance capabilities such as performance degradation measurement, fault recovery, self-maintenance, and remote diagnostics. These features would allow manufacturing and process industries to develop proactive maintenance strategies to guarantee the product and process performance and ultimately eliminate unnecessary system breakdowns. When aging occurs, the component and machine generally progress through a series of degradation states before failure occurs.

The performance of mechatronics products degrades as a result of aging, distortion, crack, impact, and wear, which decreases the reliability and increase the potential for faults and failures. Near-zero downtime and highest possible quality become a necessity for both service providers and manufacturers. Most mechatronics products today contain sophisticated sensors, high performance processors, and network interface capabilities. It is possible to perform remote monitoring and maintenance with less cost. Under these circumstances, condition-based maintenance (CBM), based on the sensing and assessing of the current state of the system, emerges an appropriate and efficient tool for achieving near-zero breakdown time through a significant reduction, and, when possible, elimination of downtime due to process or machine failure (Bengtsson, 2002). With a well-implemented CBM system, a company can save up to 20% in smaller production losses, improved quality, decreased stock of spare parts, and so forth (Bengtsson, 2002), but the CBM approach involves estimating a machine's current condition based upon the recognition of indications of failure (Engel, Gilmartin, Bongort, & Hess, 2000). To implement the predictive CBM techniques requires experts and a priori knowledge about the assessed machine or process because the corresponding failure modes must be known to assess the current machine or process's performance. For this reason, many CBM methods are application-specific and non-robust.

The traditional method was reactive maintenance, which performed only when equipment fails. This results in both high production costs and significant service downtime caused by equipment and process breakdowns. On the other hand, the preventative maintenance is intended to reduce or eliminate machine or process breakdowns and downtimes through maintenance operations scheduled regardless of the actual state of the machine or process. The preventative maintenance intervals are determined using the reliability theory and the information about the machine or process life cycle. This practice often results in an unnecessary loss of productivity either because the maintenance is performed when the process or machine is still functioning at an acceptable level or because unanticipated breakdowns occur before the scheduled maintenance operations are performed. For these reasons, Lee (1998) proposed a new methodology of detecting and quantifying failures toward an approach centered on the assessment and prediction of the performance degradation of a process, machine, or service. Lee and Ni also established a NSF I/UCRC Center for intelligent maintenance systems (IMS) (see www.imscenter.net). The IMS includes three areas: e-product, e-manufacturing, and e-maintenance. Fortune Magazine cited that IMS technology is one of the three key technologies of manufacturing. The e-maintenance or e-service must be based on e-product. Lee and Ni (2004) also give the Watchdog Agent™ structure for e-product and e-service. The Watchdog Agent™ has three tasks: multi-sensor assessment of performance degradation, forecasting of performance degradation, and diagnosis of the reasons of performance degradation. Multi-sensor assessment of performance degradation is accomplished through modules performing processing of multiple sensory inputs, extraction of features relevant to description of product's performance, and sensor fusion and performance assessment. Each of these modules is realized in several different ways to facilitate the use of watchdog agents in a wide variety of products and applications, with various requirements and limitations with respect to the character of signals, available processing power, memory and storage capabilities, limited space, power consumption, and so forth (Lee 1996, 1998, 1999; Lee & Ni, 2004). Sensory processing module transforms sensor signals into domains that are most informative of product's performance. Time-series analysis (Pandit & Wu, 1993) or frequency domain analysis (Casoetto, Djurdjanovic, Mayor, Lee, & Ni, 2003) could be used to process stationary signals (signals with time invariant frequency content) (Marple, 1987), while wavelet (Burrus, 1998) or joint time-frequency (Cohen, 1995) domains could be used to describe non-stationary signals (signals with time-varying frequency content) (Djurdjanovic & Lee 2002; Wang, Yu, Koc, & Lee, 2002; Lee, 1996). Radjou (2002) proposed a collaborative product life cycle model for equipment life modeling. There are some research works that have been done on forecasting of performance degradation (Charan & Tichy, 1998; Koc & Lee, 2000; Lee, 1998; NRC, 1990; Lee & Wang, 1999; Mobley, 1989: Lee & Kramer, 1992; Yan, Koç & Lee, 2002). Liu and Zha et al. (2004, 2005, 2006) established an IMS Web-station and developed several IMS platforms. Wang and Pham (1996, 1999) provided maintenance models for imperfect maintenance in production systems. Maillart and Pollock (2002) provided the cost-optimal condition monitoring method for predictive maintenance of two-phase systems. Badia and Berrade (2002) also offered an optimal method for revealed and unrevealed failures. Grall, Berenguer, and Dieulle (2002) made a case study for stochastically deteriorating systems. Chen and Trivedi (2002) and Monga and Zuo (1997) have given the reliability-based design of systems. Wildeman, Dekker, and Smith (1997) and Popova and Wilson (1999) provided the policies model for group replacement of parallel systems. The work by Wang and Pham et al. (2000, 2001) dealt with the optimal preparedness maintenance of multi-unit systems with imperfect maintenance and economic dependence. Kececioglu and Sun (1995) developed the opportunistic replacement model for the general discrete-time ball-bearing systems. Degbotse, Chen, and other experts have done some works on the dynamic preventive maintenance policy (Degbotse & Nachlas, 2003; Boland & El-Neweihi, 1998: Riane, Artiba, & Iassinovski, 2001; Chen, Chen, & Yuan, 2003). White and White (1989) did some work on decision processes. Research work was done for reliability assessments and maintenance strategy (Duffuaa, Ben-Daya, Al-Sultan, & Andijani, 2001; Charles, Floru, Azzaro-Pantel, Pibouleau, & Domenech, 2003; Li & Li, 2002; Bevilacqua & Chandrupatla, 1999; Bevilacqua & Braglia, 2000; Deshpande & Modak, 2002). As the maintenance concepts and contents are different in deferent areas, Waeyenbergh and Pintelon (2002, 2004) proposed some comprehensive maintenance concepts and framework. In recent years, the proportional hazards model was developed for measurement errors (Horowitz & Lee 2004; Tanaka & Rao, 2005; Dupuy, 2005). One of IMS' works is maintenance scheduling; Jayabalan and Chaudhuri (1992) set up a cost optimization model for maintenance scheduling.

The salient feature of the modern manufacturing technology is widely used in computer-integrated manufacturing systems (CIMS). A major requirement for the success of CIMS is the maintenance of high reliability in the highly sophisticated equipment in the system. Computerized numerical control (CNC) machine and robots are the main units of CIMS. The conventional methods of fault detection in manufacturing processes provide for relatively coarse fault diagnosis based on the monitoring of outputs from sensors. Currently, sufficient sensing (with sensors) and computational technologies exist to allow an individual to instrument full-scale structures and record numerous input channel records.

Significant efforts have been made in machine condition monitoring and fault diagnosis. Although the concepts of monitoring and fault diagnosis have been thoroughly explored and expanded, the more labor-intensive task of data reduction, analysis, and interpretation remains largely unchanged. In addition, although there are many commercially available maintenance management software tools, but they lack integratability and interoperability with production control systems and have limited usage in managing maintenance logistics and service business.

Overview and Strategies on Tele-Service Engineering System

Figure 1 shows an intelligent tele-service engineering system which integrates clients, service, and enterprise to provide the whole life cycle support for a product. Company members can share all intellectual activities performed in this system. The attributes of the tele-service engineering system (TSES) include:

1. remote monitoring, fault diagnosis, and maintenance
2. integrated maintenance and production, including customers and suppliers
3. responsive service distributed over networks of cooperating facilities
4. teamwork among geographically and organizationally distributed units/agents

Figure 1. Tele-service engineering system (TSES)

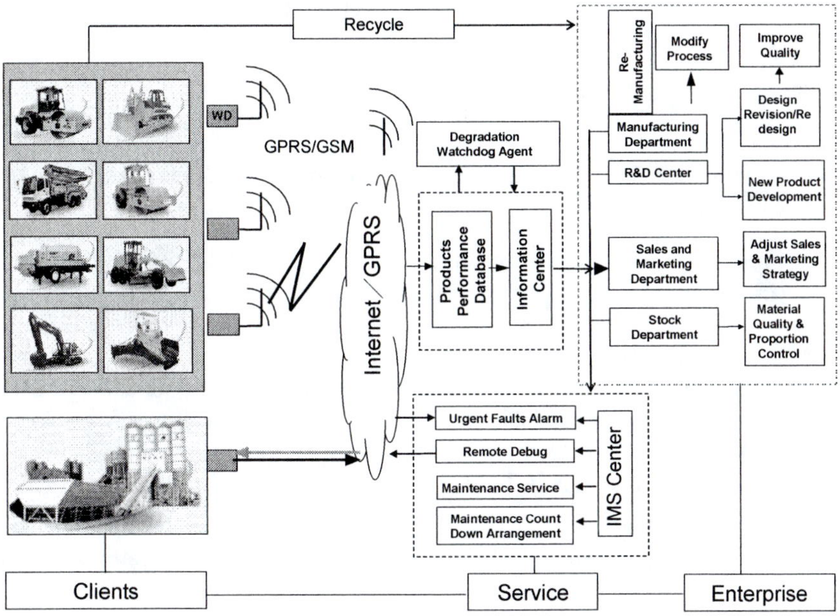

The core-enabling element of TSES is the smart computational agent that can predict the degradation or performance loss, not only the traditional diagnostics of failure or faults. A complete understanding and interpretation of states of degradation is necessary to accurately predict and prevent failure of a component or a machine once it has been identified as a critical element to the overall production system. The degradation is assessed through the performance assessment methods. A product's performance degradation behavior is often associated with a multi-symptom-domain information cluster, which consists of degradation behavior of functional components in a chain of actions. The acquisition of specific sensory information may contain multiple behavior information such as non-linear vibration, thermal or materials surface degradation, and misalignment. All information should be correlated for product behavior assessment and prognostics.

Today, the maintenance of products and machines is almost done locally for good reasons. Although one can imagine tele-operation, such as in unmanned space flights, it is probably unjustifiable for some time to come. The remote service is essential to TSES. When someone who is not at the site of the equipment wants to ensure that what is produced meets requirements (which may not be fully known to those at the site of the equipment), he or she must be able to evaluate operation parameters. However, there is an inevitable tension between over-specifying, which would not grant sufficient freedom to the local operators to optimize their process, and under-specifying, which could leave too much ambiguity. This problem exists today between suppliers and producers, with much consequence for conflict; it is becoming a central issue in TSES.

In practice, if a degradation condition is detected and measured, then proactive and corrective maintenance activities can be performed before a worse degradation condition or failures occur. To achieve a just-in-time lean maintenance and service operation, better decision-making tools in TSES are required to strategize resources through a supply-chain network system. Companies need to perform remote maintenance decision making to support technical and business personnel in managing maintenance and service logistics activities. In addition, a digital service modem can be used to integrate product's performance conditions with the customer support center via the Internet.

Machine Performance Description and Modeling

The fundamental research issue which hinders resolving monitoring and maintenance problems is an inadequate understanding of most maintenance activities. For example, it is not an easy job to identify which process parameters are most important and which are insensitive, and to obtain the validated predictive models that could report what will happen when the process parameters take on specified values. Hence the problem is not simply the one of designing a form that lists the available controls and requests values; it also involves creating sufficient understanding of each process to build an accurate performance predictive model. Once that is done, it will be relatively easy to standardize the communication interfaces.

The operational performance of components, machines, and processes can be divided into four states: normal operation state, degraded state, maintenance state, and failure state. Figure

Figure 2. Device time-performance curve

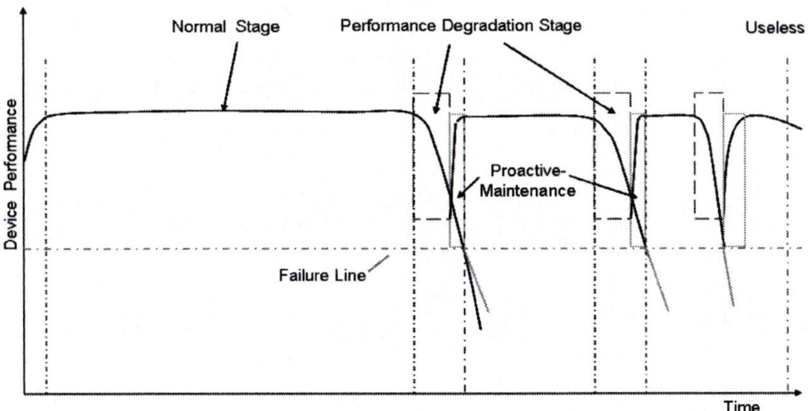

Figure 3. The performance of multi-equipment

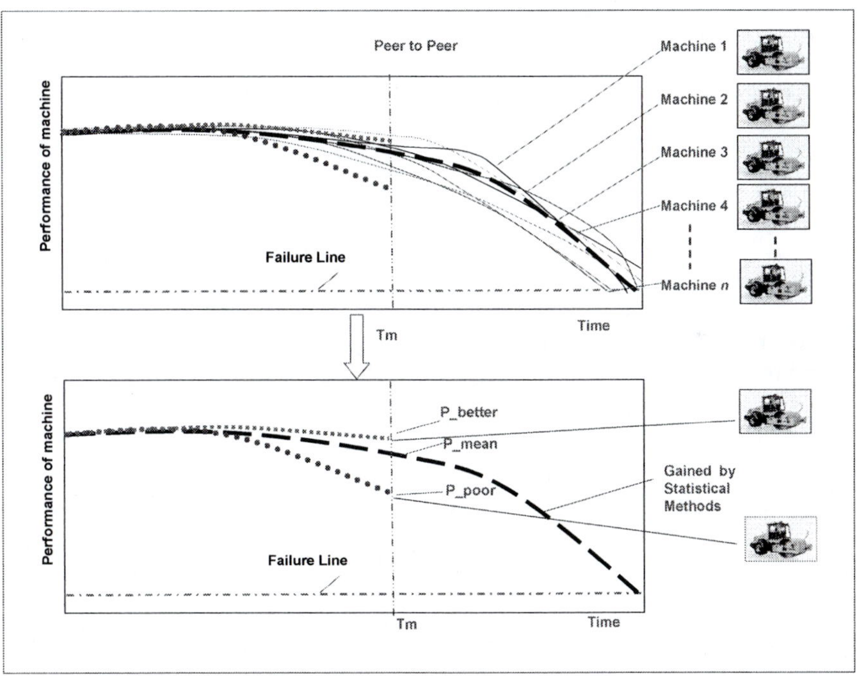

2 shows the time-performance curve, representing a degrading behavior of products. Figure 3 illustrates the performance of multiple equipments.

An equipment confidence value (CV) is defined as a function correlative with time (t) and feature parameters (M). Hence, we have,

Figure 4. Multi-sensor fusion for assessing the performance of single equipment

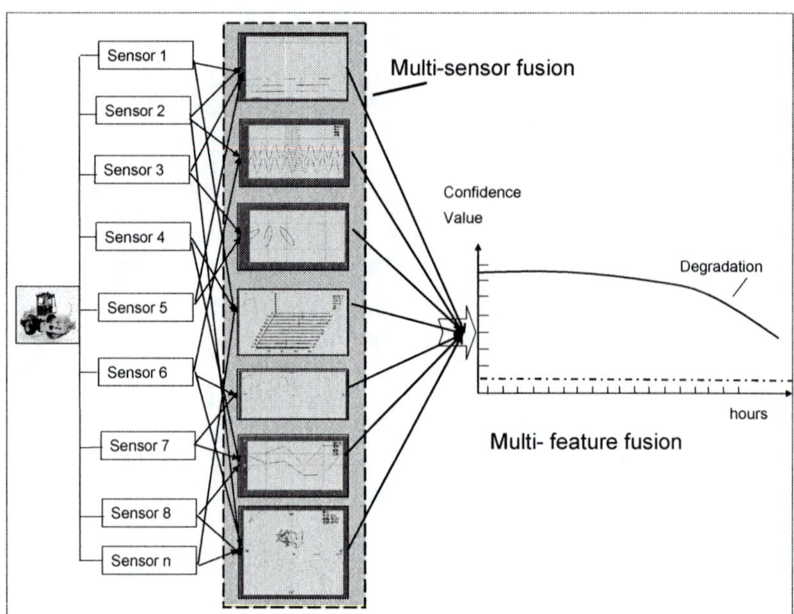

$$CV = P(t, M) = f(t, M_1, M_2, M_3, M_4, \ldots, M_n)$$

where M_i $(i=1,2,\ldots,n)$ is a feature parameter. The assessment of machine's performance information requires an integration of many different sensory devices and reasoning agents. Figure 4 shows a multi-sensor fusion approach for assessing the performance of equipment.

Remote Monitoring, Fault Diagnostics and Maintenance System (RMFDMS)

The system for remote monitoring, fault diagnostics, and maintenance (RMFDMS) can be divided into two parts according to its functionality. One is for remote monitoring and diagnosis, which includes signal collection, process, evaluation, and maintenance; the other is for remote control, which can control remote PC, PLC and video servers. This system can also be distributed into three parts according to its structure: remote monitoring center, transmission media, and operation site. Figure 5 shows a framework for the system.

Figure 5. Framework of the remote monitoring, fault diagnosis and maintenance system (RMFDMS)

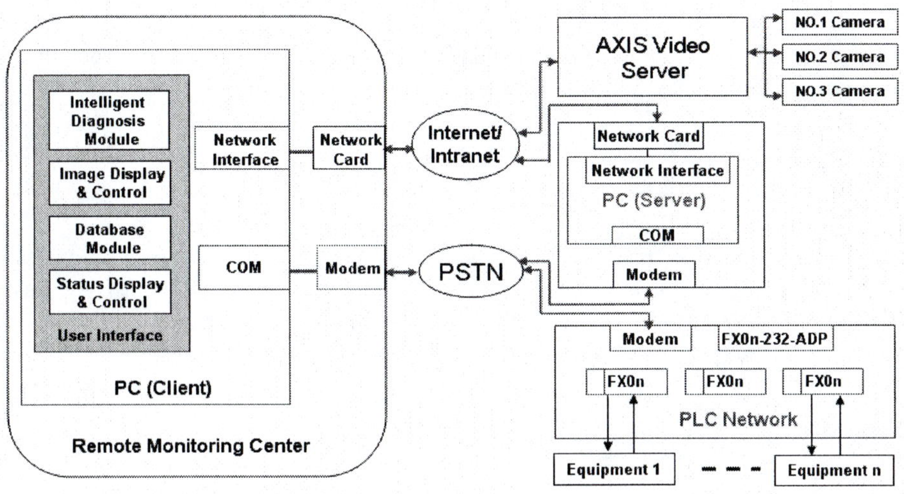

Remote Monitoring Center

This part serves as the cerebrum of the system which receives information from the operation site via Internet/Intranet or PSTN. It then processes that information according to specific arithmetic and sends out commands to the operation site in the light of processing results. It is made up of the following five modules:

1. **Image display & control module.** The function of this module is to timely display the image transmitted from the AXIS video server. In the meantime, it sends out control orders to the AXIS video server.
2. **Database module.** This module stores historic data in the database which can help the system make right decisions.
3. **Intelligent diagnosis module.** This is the core of the remote monitoring center, which can decide which part is wrong and provide reasoning advice for operators.
4. **Performance display & control module.** This module displays the real-time status of equipment and sends out orders to rectify it.
5. **User interface.** The user interface makes the operation become very convenient and useful.

Transmission Media

The main transmission media is the Internet in a long distance or the Intranet in a small range of area. PSTN is the secondary media that plays a role in an occasion when there is no Internet fetched or the Internet cannot be connected.

Operation Site

The operation site is the place where the actual operation is done. There are mainly three kinds of equipment in that place: AXIS video server, PC (server), and PLC. All devices can receive orders from the remote monitoring center and control the practical operation. They can be connected with Internet/Intranet or PSTN via network card or modem.

The System Structure for Mobile Equipment

The system architecture for mobile equipment consists of three layers (Figure 6):

1. **Equipment layer.** The main component in this layer is the Internet-based control module.
2. **Transport layer.** This layer includes the GSM/GPRS/CDMA module and the public network supporting the GSM/GPRS/CDMA services. It is a bridge layer between the field layer and the monitoring layer. Data can be transported bidirectionally via the transport layer.

Figure 6. The structure of the system for mobile equipment

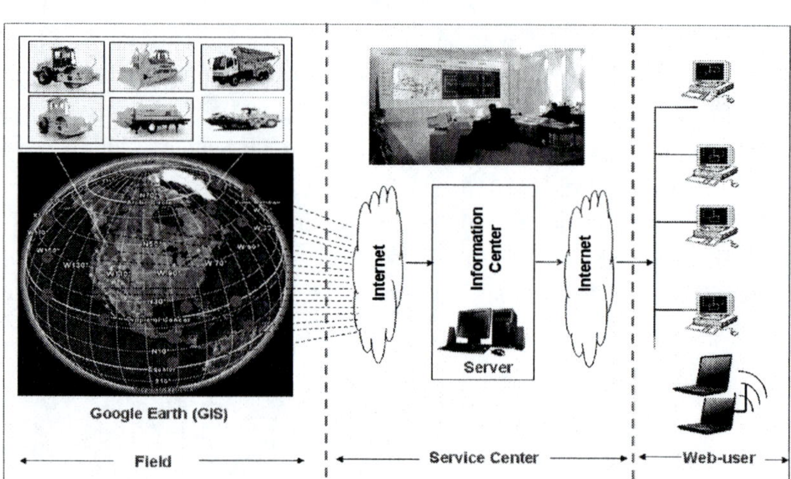

3. **Monitoring layer.** With the monitoring software and the server in this layer, the working condition can be displayed instantly and the parameters of the working system can be set remotely.

Key Technologies for Developing RMFDMS

Transmission and Control of Video Images and Voice

One of the important parts of remote monitoring is the transmission of video images and voice. The transmission of compressed format video images is realized through the re-development (or the secondary development) of video servers of AXIS communication. The transmission speed of video images is 15 frame/sec by Internet and 1 frame/2sec by PSTN. The voice data are also compressed and transmission is almost real-time on the Internet. With the PTZ device, the video camera, which has an adjustable focus and is linked to the video server, can be controlled thoroughly by the commands sent to the video server. Various commands are explained and executed by the video server and then result in corresponding camera motions, such as moving left/right or up/down or enlarging/shortening focus. Therefore, the omni-directional and nice status of the scene can be obtained.

Collection and Pre-Processing of Information

Though the information collected from different equipments is not the same, the problem of a large quantity of data is existent. Therefore, the corresponding data pre-processing modules of different equipment should be developed to meet the requirements of remote monitoring.

Data Transmission

The research need is therefore to construct models of remote performance assessment capability that can answer the questions posed remotely. In an actual use, these models will be employed iteratively to home in on the control parameter values that can produce the desired results. These models, like all of the others, must be interoperable and responsive to agents so that the remote user does not always have to communicate with them through a human intermediary.

Now, all of the controllers of important CNCs are PLC (e.g., SIEMENS, MITSUBISHI, etc.) and these newly produced equipments all have field bus interfaces (e.g., PROFIBUS) and supply remote communication modules. Users can make the secondary development based on this equipment. Data package can be sent by PLC to computer; in this case, the computer passively receives the data. Also, the computer can send data package actively to PLC for control, query, and so on. To transmit data correctly, two sides of the transmission have to obey the same communication protocol. Different PLCs commonly have different protocols, so that the computer should adjust itself according to different PLCs.

Construction of Field Bus for Product Line

The construction of field bus is the key part in the process of linking product line equipment into network. According to open and normative communication protocols, taking each equipment as its node and twisted-pair as its bus, the network realizes data transmission and information interchanging among local product line equipment and remote monitoring computers.

Settlement of the Real-Time Performance Problem

Real-time performance is the key to remote monitoring. To realize this performance, different networks should be constructed respectively according to different cases.

Internet-Based Server Controller

The Internet server controller is a Web-enabled embedded system. Its core is an embedded network model. As next-generation products are to be a B2D-based (business-to-device) global system, the server controller will be the base of next-generation products. Through the service controller, the service center can collect performance data and monitor all products/equipment dispersed all over the world at any time. This requires that the networked

Figure 7. Overall structure of the Internet-based server controller

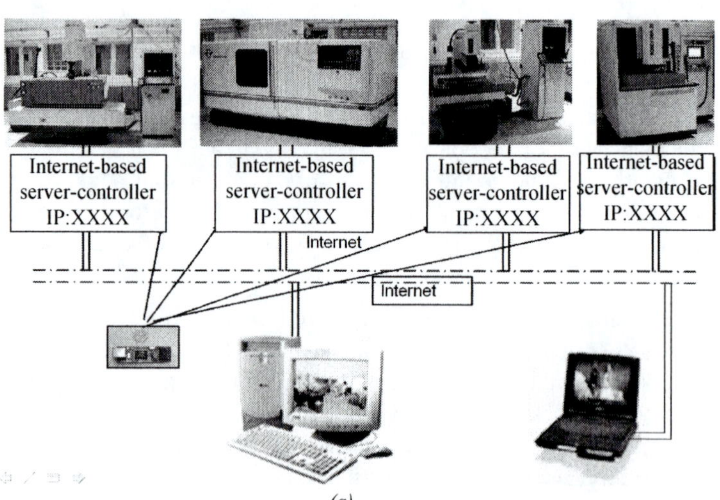

(a)

Figure 7. continued

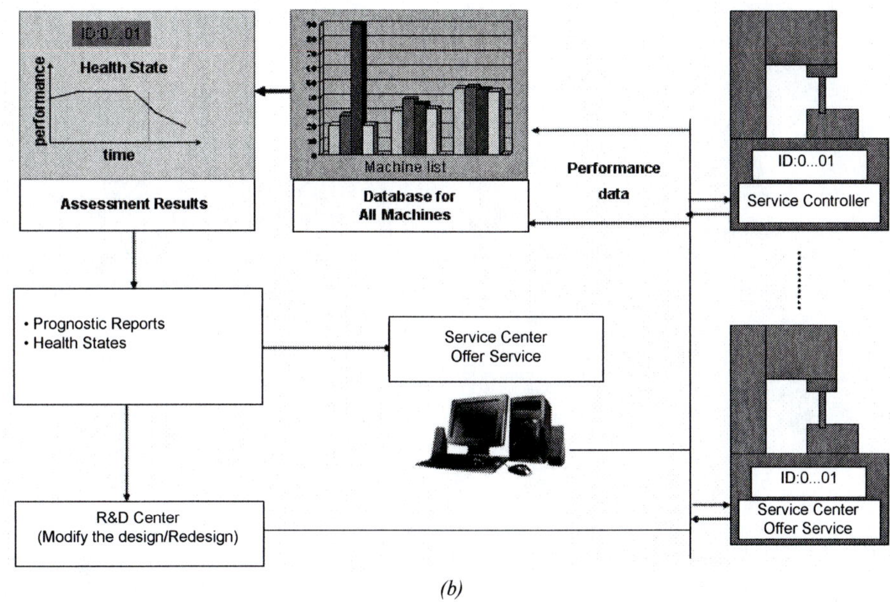

(b)

Figure 8. Hardware structure of the server controller

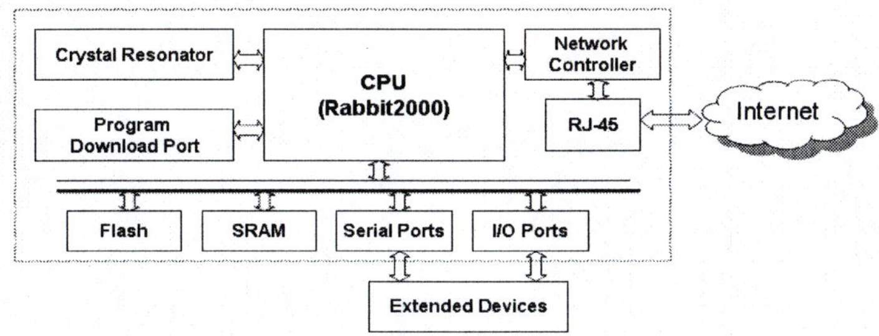

products have an IP when they are sold. The service center can also investigate the working states of any products and give the assessment results to the user.

Structure of the Embedded Network Model

The Internet-based server controller has the following functions: (1) It is a controller. (2) It is a Web-enabled server (i.e., it can be connected to Internet/Intranet). The product can be controlled in the remote site. (3) It can monitor the equipment by collecting and processing the performance data. Figure 8 shows the structure of the embedded network model. This

Figure 9. The flowchart of the agent program for the network device

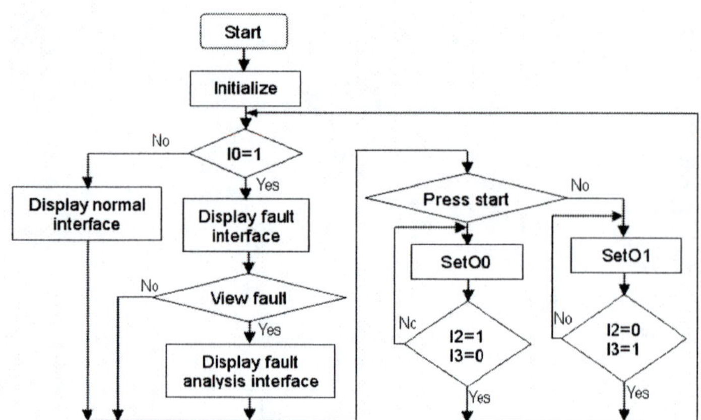

model is composed of nine parts, including CPU, flash, RAM, I/O, RJ-45, and so forth. In this model, RTL8019 is used as the network controller and RABBIT2000 is the CPU. Figure 9 gives a flowchart of the agent program for the network device.

Software System for Internet-Based Server Controller

The software of the Internet-based server controller is a multi-agent peer-to-peer system for coordinating and controlling the embedded network. Figure 10 illustrates the overall structure of the software system framework. The software agent is actually a package of *smart prognostics algorithms*, which consists of embedded computational prognostic algorithms and a software toolbox for predicting degradation of devices and systems. A toolbox that consists of different prognostics tools has been developed for predicting the degradation or performance loss on devices, process, and systems. These algorithms are developed using the *neural network* based, *time-series* based, *wavelet-based* and hybrid joint time-frequency methods. Figure 11 illustrates some prognostics algorithms of the software agent. The assessment of performance degradation is accomplished through several modules including processing of multiple sensory inputs, extraction of features relevant to description of product's performance, sensor fusion, and performance assessment. Each of these modules is realized in several different ways to facilitate the use of software agent in a wide variety of products and applications with various requirements and limitations with respect to the character of signals, available processing power, memory, and storage capabilities.

Recently, there have been many attempts to solve decision-making problems (assessment or evaluation and selection) by applying neural network and (fuzzy) rule-based expert systems techniques (Zha, 2003). The capabilities of rule-based (fuzzy) expert systems are inherently well-suited for decision-making problems. The major drawback, however, is that the programmer is required to define the functions underlying the multi-valued or ranked possibility optimization. Furthermore, expert-type rules use a comprehensive language system that may

Figure 10. The overall structure of the software system framework

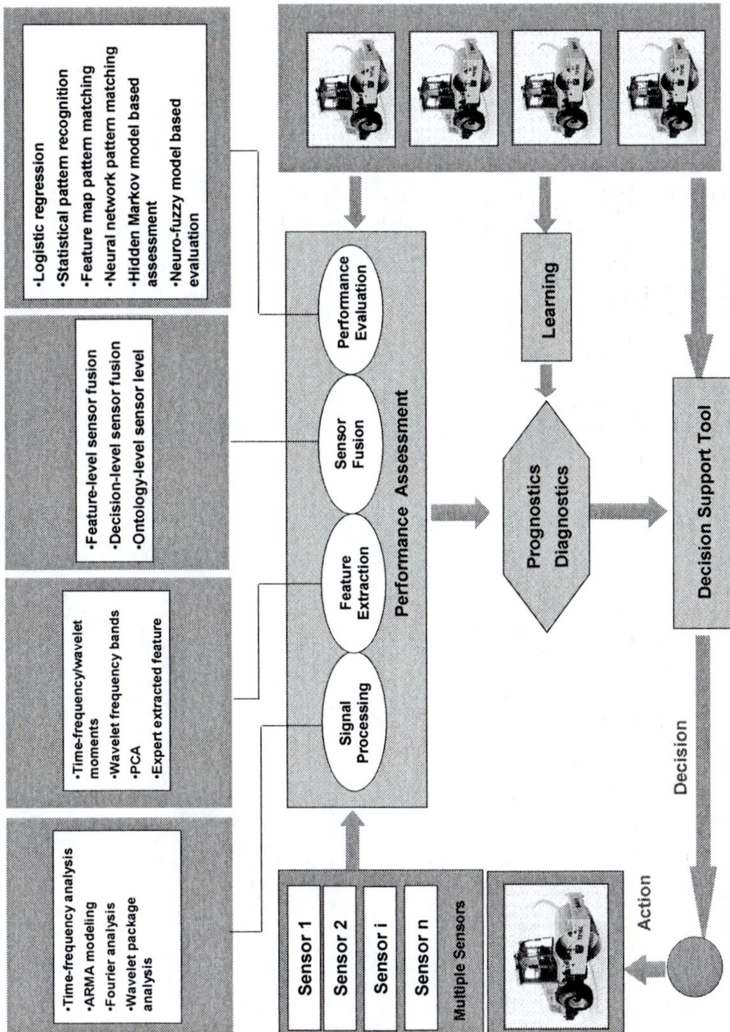

have built-in biases, embedded goals, and hidden information structures, which may result in errors (Zurada, 1992). Neural networks using mathematical relationships and mappings to design and optimize systems are capable of statistical decision-making given incomplete and uncertain information, and can be used to adapt to the user/designer's requirements. Unlike rule-based (fuzzy) expert systems, they evaluate all the conflict constraints or fusion information simultaneously, and model/learn the knowledge base using black-box techniques. They do not use rules in the formal sense so the evaluation or decision-making time can be greatly reduced from that of rule-based modeling. The strengths of neural networks accrue from the fact that they need not *priori* assumptions of models and from their capability to

Figure 11. Some prognostics algorithms of software agent

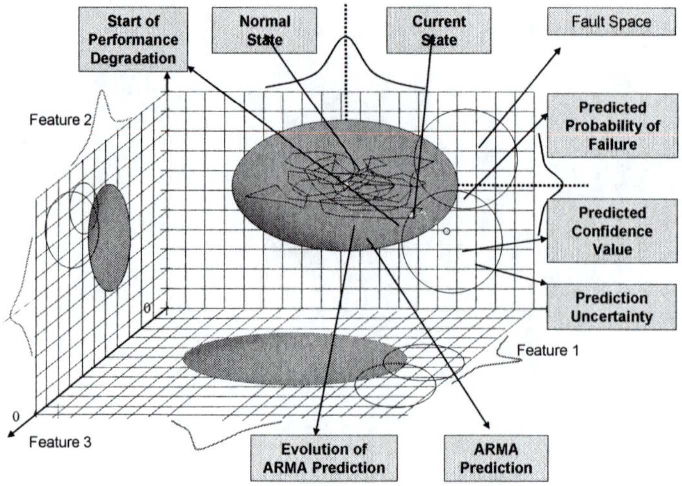

(a) Prognostics and forcasting methods

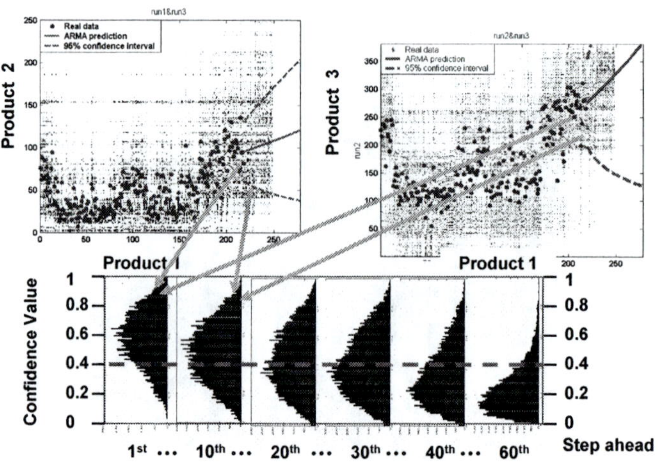

(b) Identify unacceptable behavior

infer complex, nonlinear underlying relationships. From the statisticians' point of view, neural networks are essentially statistical devices to perform inductive inference and are analogous to non-parametric, nonlinear regression models (Refenes, 1995; Zurada, 1992). However, existing neural schemes use two or more separate neural networks to accomplish some tasks respectively, and need to train them separately. This is tedious and costly, and sometimes very difficult. In order to overcome the suffered shortcomings or difficulties, more research endeavors are necessary to develop more general topologies of neural models,

Figure 11. Continued

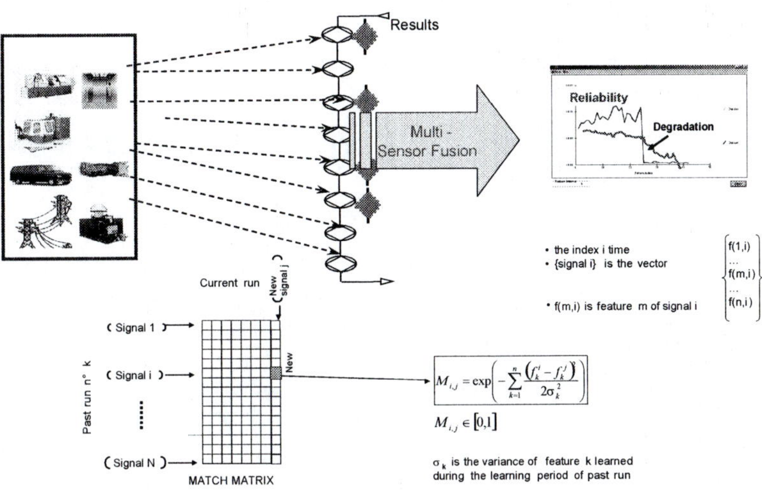

(c) Match matrix creation

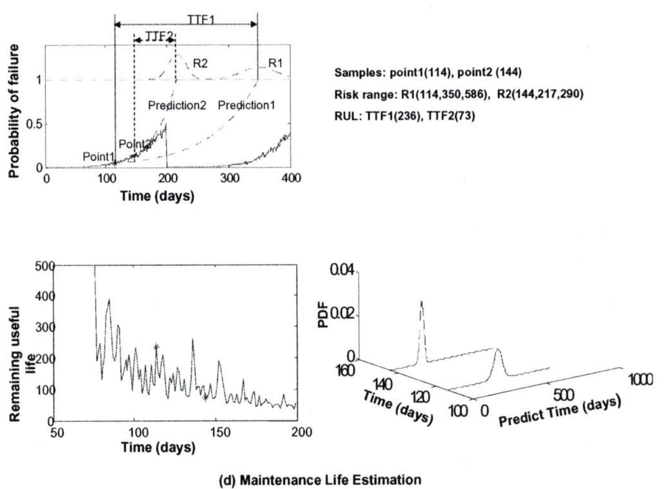

(d) Maintenance life estimation

learning algorithms, and approximation theories so that those models are applicable in the system modeling and control of complex systems. A new kind of hybrid neural networks is therefore required for decision support. It must also be conceded that rule-based (fuzzy) expert systems are much easier for humans to error-check than an ensemble of continuous equations in neural networks (Zarefar & Goulding, 1992). There is now a growing need in the intelligent community that complex decision-making problems require hybrid solutions (Zha, 2004). In view of these practical requirements and current research status and future trend of intelligent decision support, an evolutionary neuro-fuzzy network or fuzzy neural network (FNN) model has been developed for supporting computational intelligent decision-making and simulation. Details about the evolutionary neuro-fuzzy or fuzzy neural network model are discussed in Chapter XVII.

Remote Monitoring and Fault Prognostics: *Watchdog Agent*

To effectively measure the degradation of a machine, its behavior and associated information from operators and its working environment need to be assessed adaptively. The watchdog agent, a neural computing algorithm, has been developed to provide online composition and reasoning for product degradation assessment and prognostics, and enable manufacturers and customers to rapidly assess a product's performance and instantly figure out required maintenance activities. More specifically, this watchdog agent is a neural network-based "digital doctor" equipped with embedded computational prognostics algorithms and a toolbox for predicting the degradation or performance loss of devices and systems. The watchdog agent is integrated with wireless sensors to provide service sensor acquisition, processing, hashing, and health (good condition) reporting. The watchdog agent performs multi-input data generalization, hashing, and mapping, and represents the performance status information on a look-up table using a cerebellum computing approach. In addition, this agent could be connected with the Internet server so that the machine behavior and its performance information could be accessed and evaluated from a remote site.

Figure 12. The simplified hardware diagram of the watchdog agent

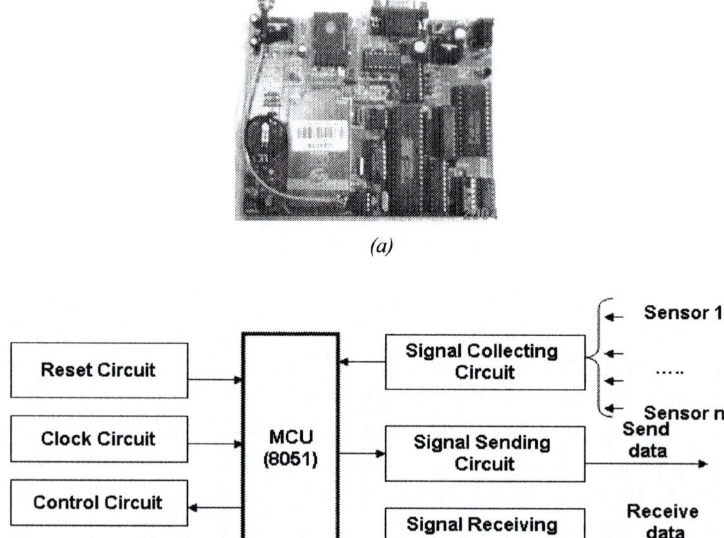

The controller is composed of seven parts: (1) MCU 8051: the CPU of the controller managing and controlling the actions of every part; (2) reset circuit: makes 8051 to restore the original state; (3) clock circuit: provides outside clock for 8051; (4) control circuit: sends control signal to start or stop the washing machine; (5) signal collecting circuit: collects the primal signals through sensors; (6) signal sending circuit: sends the result to the web chip then to the monitoring after signal is disposed in 8051; (7) signal receiving circuit: receives the control orders from the Web chip and then sends it to 8051. Figure 12 shows a simplified hardware diagram of the watchdog agent (assistant controller).

Testbed for Remote Monitoring and Maintenance System (RMMST)

The Overall Structure of RMMST

In this work, a testbed has been developed for the remote monitoring and maintenance system, in which many machines, instruments, or devices can be monitored. As shown in Figure 5, the system consists of two parts. The first part is an assistant controller mounted on the machine and connected with the controller of the machine. The assistant controller receives control signals from the network device and controls the operation mode of the machine. In the meantime, it receives sensory information from various sensors and sends it to the network device after processing. The second part is the network device developed on the base of a Web chip. This part acts as a tool that communicates with the monitoring PC through Internet. It realizes communication between the local PC and the remote PLC through the PSTN or Internet/Intranet. The local PC can query, control, and diagnose the remote PLC and equipment controller through two communication paths. Besides, RMMST supplies a new, convenient, and fast video transmission service based on the AXIS video server. The video images transferred are clear, steady, and fast, so the video transmission service deserves generalization. RMMST is developed in the environment of Visual C++ 6.0 and it is reliable, steady, and convenient to be embedded.

The Hardware of RMMST

Hardware Structure of RMMST

Figure 13 is the overall hardware structure of RMMST. It contains PC (client), Internet/Intranet, PSTN, Modem, Network card, AXIS Video Server, Camera, PC (server), and PLC.

Figure 13. The overall hardware structure of RMMST

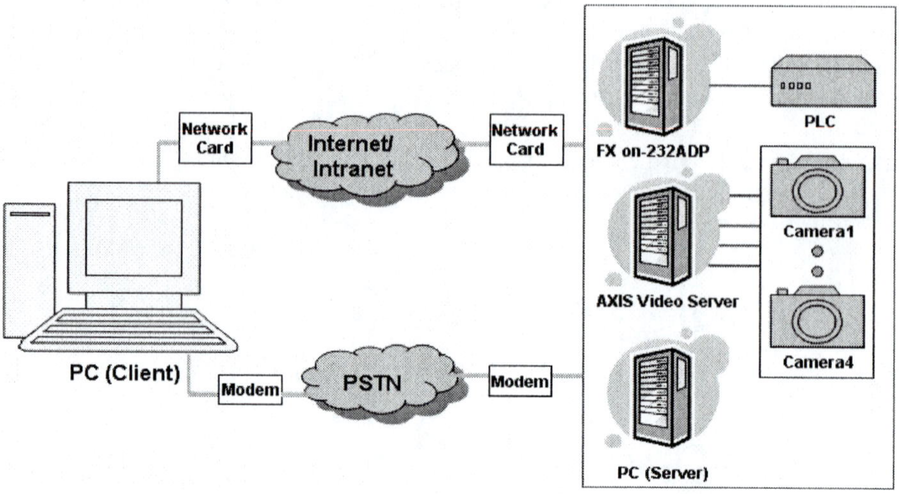

Communication from PC to PLC

To connect PC with PLC, the following work should be done at first:

1. Look and judge if the communication card configured in PC is matched with PLC, otherwise add a communication panel.
2. Write communication program for PC according to the communication protocol, while it is not necessary to write program for PLC because the communication mechanism is often set in it.
3. Select software platform provided by opened operation system and develop interface with the data exchanged with PLC.
4. To operate in remote site, we should connect PSTN through modem or via Internet/ Intranet.

In principle, there is no difficulty in connecting PC with PLC. It only needs to equip appropriative communication card and communication software to initialize and write program. However, configuring special communication card and communication software will cost too much. In fact, clients can do all the things by themselves; in the meantime, the following conditions must be met:

1. It is possible to interlink between PC-equipped VART and PLC with asynchronous communication fetch. The bus standard used by two sides is the same. It may be RS-232c, RS-422(RS-485), or 20mA ampere meter, otherwise exchange unit for bus standard should be used.

Figure 14. Structure of connection from PC to PLC

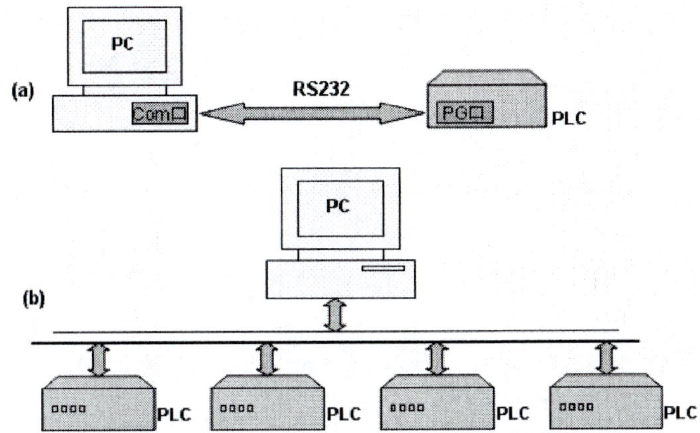

Figure 15. Connection from PC to PLC

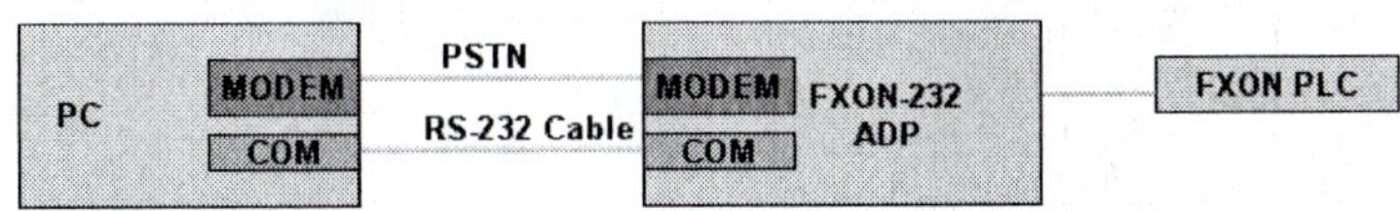

2. There should be the same baud rate, data file, number of data, stop number of data, and parity check. They should initialize their programs.

Clients often adopt two structures when they connect PC with PLC (see Figure 13). One is from point to point (one-to-one). In this kind of structure, com in PC is a joint with PG in PLC. Figure 14(a) shows this form. The other is from one point to multiple points (one-to-many). In this kind of structure, PC and several PLCs are connected into one serial bus. Figure 14(b) shows this form. It also is called principal and subordinate structure. FX series PLC produced by MITSUBISHI is selected. It can communicate only with the remote communication module Fxon-232ADP. Figure 15 shows the connection form from PC to PLC.

The communication cable should be produced according to the user's manual (see Table 1).

Communication from PC to PC

In RMMST, the client/server mode is adopted. The PC in the local monitoring center is the client, while the one in the remote site is the server. In this system, two PCs are connected through the Internet/Intranet or PSTN. Figure 16 is the connection form from PC to PC.

Table 1. (a) Cable connection form from PC to PLC; (b) cable connection form from modem to Fxon-232ADP

Programmable Controller Side			
Signal name	FX2N-232-BD	FX0N-232ADP	FX-232 ADP
FG	—		1
RXD	2	3	
TXD	3	2	
DTR	4	20	
GND	5	7	
DSR	6	6	

RS-232C Device Side					
Signal Name	Uses CS, RS		Signal Name	Uses DR, ER	
	9pin	25pin		9pin	25pin
FG	—	1	FG	—	1
RXD	2	3	RXD	2	3
TXD	3	2	TXD	3	2
RTS	7	4	DTR	4	20
GND	5	7	GND	5	7
CTS	8	5	DSR	6	6

(a)

Programmable Controller Side			
Signal Name	FX2N-232-BD	FX0N-232ADP	FX-232ADP
FG	—	1	
DCD	1	—	8
RXD	2	3	
TXD	3	2	
DTR	4	20	
GND	5	7	
DSR	6	6	

RS-232C Device Side					
Signal Name	Uses CS, RS		Signal Name	Uses DR, ER	
	9pin	25pin		9pin	25pin
FG	—	1	FG	—	1
DCD	1	8	DCD	1	8
RXD	2	3	RXD	2	3
TXD	3	2	TXD	3	2
RTS	7	4	DTR	4	20
GND	5	7	GND	5	7
CTS	8	5	DSR	6	6

(b)

Figure 16. Connection from PC to PC

PC (Client)
Network Card
Modem
Internet/Intranet
PSTN
Network Card
Modem
PC (Server)

Communication from PC to AXIS Video Server — AXIS 2401

In order to realize remote assistant diagnosis and provide operators a clear picture of the production site, the system of remote monitor should sustain multimedia which provides abundant information of Video and Audio. RMMST sustains Internet-based video transmission which can provide clear dynamic picture. AXIS 2401 produced by AXIS Communications in Sweden is adopted to provide a practical way to connect cameras with the Internet. On the basis of it, the secondary development can be carried out to produce many remote monitoring products. Now the virtues of AXIS 2401 are summarized as follows:

1. **Thin server.** AXIS 2401 is one variety of AXIS series. AXIS products provide a so-called "thin server" technology which permits all peripheral equipments to join into network, such as printer, memorizer, digital camera, CD-ROM driver, and scanner without PC or any servers.
2. **Plug and play.** AXIS 2401 video server can be fixed very easily. After it is connected with the video source and the 10/100mbps Ethernet network, and then allocated one IP address, we can enjoy clear dynamic pictures through the PC in the network. Its browser software may be Netscape Navigator or Microsoft Internet Explorer. It also provides a set of ActiveX controls to permit users to integrate picture into the user's program interface. If the camera is equipped with the cloud platform and its focus is adjusted automatically, we can control the scanning direction and focus through AXIS 2401.
3. **Open standards environment.** With support of the TCP/IP networking, SMTP e-mail, HTTP, and other Internet-related protocols, the AXIS2401 can be used in the mixed operation system environments, such as, Windows, UNIX, Macintosh, and OS/2.
4. **Wide range of applications.** AXIS2401 offers live video over the network to enhance and modernize traditional CCTV systems-and much more. AXIS2401 allows remote CCTV and video access directly from a standard Web browser. Users can access live images or remotely control CCTV at any time, anywhere. Accordingly, AXIS2401 can be used for: verifying intruder alarms, traffic surveillance, banking applications, parking lots, factory monitoring, industrial surveillance, visual security systems, image archiving, and so forth. SMTP e-mail is supported to allow images to be sent as e-mail attachments at predetermined times or events. The remote image monitoring module on the basis of AXIS2401 has two functions:
    1. **Assist fault diagnosis.** Operators can observe manufacturing equipment and key parts of the operation line by selecting suitable monitoring angle and position for cameras. Therefore, they may exactly judge the cause of equipments' faults in terms of the data collected by the special equipment.
    2. **Keep operational status.** Operators may get some valuable information by observing the running status in a small span of time before equipments are invalid. Figure 17 shows the connection form from PC to AXIS Video Server—AXIS2401. By the way, people can access AXIS2401 only through network.

Figure 17. Connection from PC to AXIS video server — AXIS2401

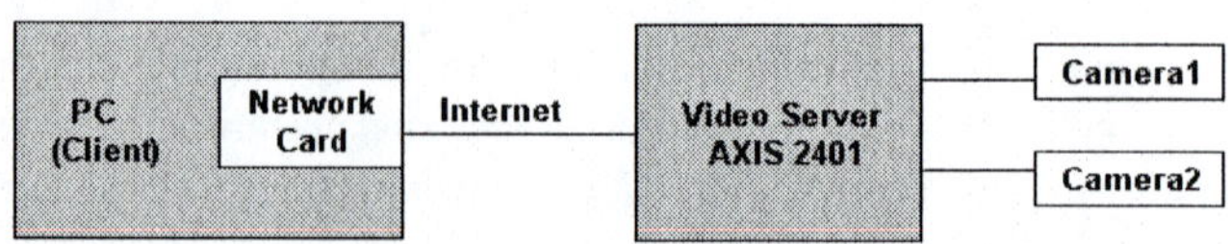

Figure 18. The main function flow chart of RMMST

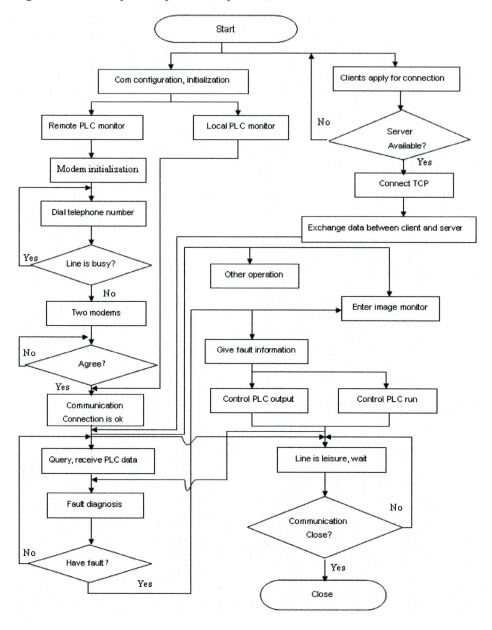

Start
Com configuration, initialization
Clients apply for connection
Remote PLC monitor
Local PLC monitor
No
Server
Available?
Yes
Modem initialization
Connect TCP
Dial telephone number
Exchange data between client and server
Yes
Line is busy?
Other operation
No
Enter image monitor
Two modems
Give fault information
No
Agree?
Yes
Control PLC output
Control PLC run
Communication
Connection is ok
Query, receive PLC data
Line is leisure, wait
Fault diagnosis
No
Communication
Close?
No
Have fault ?
Yes
Yes
Close

The Software of RMMST

The software of RMMST includes mainly three parts: serial communication module, network communication module, and image monitoring module. Figure 18 shows the main function flow chart of RMMST. These three parts will be introduced below respectively.

Serial Communication Module

This module realizes direct communication between local PC and local PLC or remote PLC. In local communication, the Com of PC is connected with FXon-232-ADP of PLC through RS-232C. In remote communication, the connection sequence is Com of PC, modem, PSTN, modem, and FXon-232-ADP (see Figure 13).

When the communication is successful, PC can query the data of all registers in PLC and control PLC for output, start, run and stop. Thereby PC can control the equipment with PLC as its controller indirectly and monitor its status. PLC can also send data to PC forwardly. When the equipment is out of order, PLC will do primary judgment and alarm PC, and then PC will read data for further judgment.

- **Implementation of RMMST communication thread.** A thread is created to monitor the communication event. Figure 19 is the framework of the communication thread. After the course starts, the main thread is created at first, and then the Com is initialized. The communication thread is created in a suitable place to monitor the communication event. When the communication thread receives new data, it sends WM_COMMRECVNOTIFY to the main thread. Similarly, it sends WM_COMMSENDNOTIFY to the main thread when the sending buffer is null. In the end, the main thread deletes the communication thread. In the following the creation, deletion and implementation of the communication thread will be introduced, including the communication thread variable, the communication event variable, and the user-defined communication message.

Figure 19. Framework of communication thread

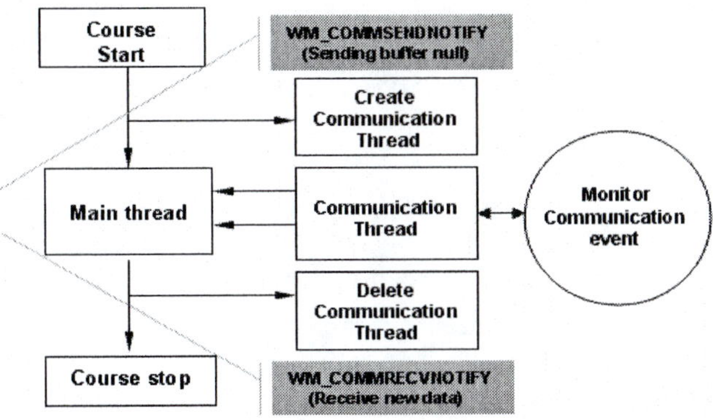

Figure 20. PC reads data from PLC

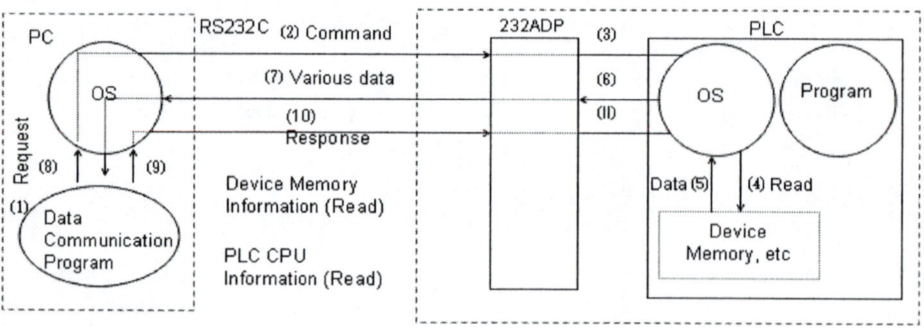

Figure 21. PC sends data to PLC

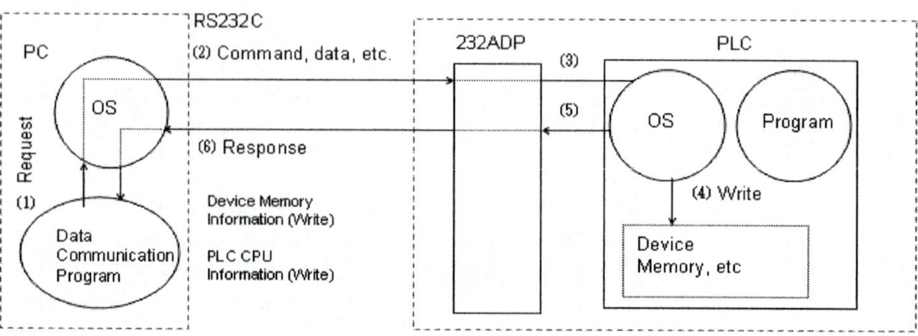

Figure 22. PLC sends data to PC

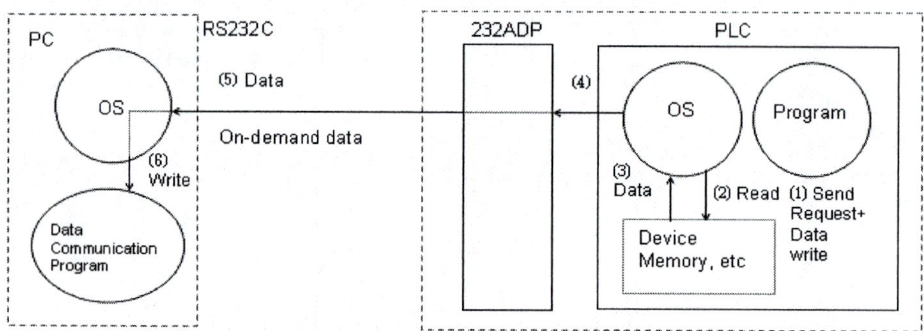

- **Data flow between PC to PLC.** Figures 20 through 22 show data flow between PC and the local PLC. The condition between PC and the remote PLC is the same.
- **Basic format of PLC communication protocol.** Figure 23 is the basic format of transmission data. Table 2 is the format of control protocol.

Figure 23. The basic format of transmission data

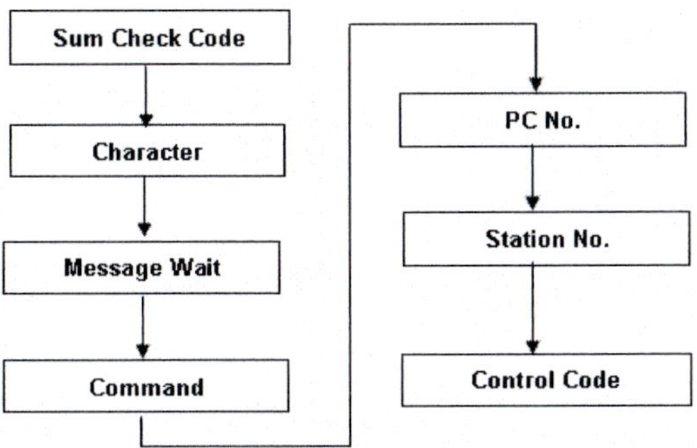

Table 2. The format of control protocol

Description	Control Protocol
To read data from PLC to PC	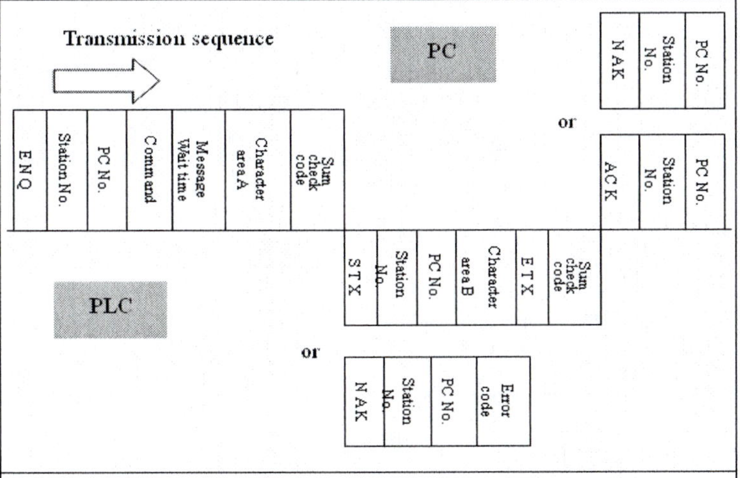 Transmission sequence PC: ENQ | Station No. | PC No. | Command | Message Wait time | Character area A | Sum check code PLC: STX | Station No. | PC No. | Character area B | ETX | Sum check code or NAK | Station No. | PC No. | Error code PC: ACK | Station No. | PC No. or NAK | Station No. | PC No.
To write data from PC to PLC	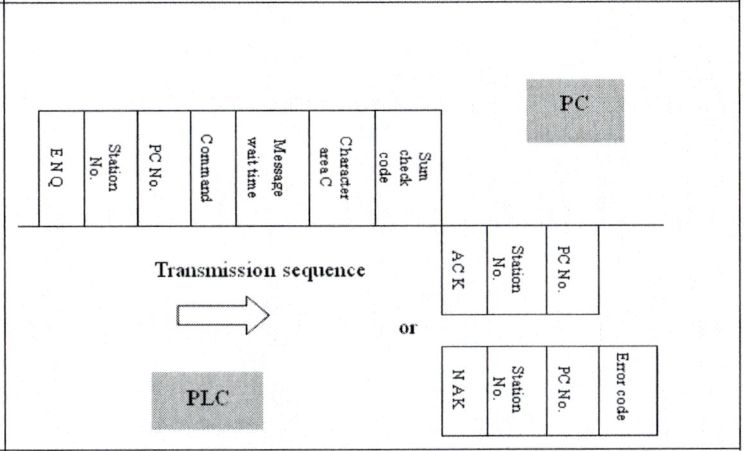 PC: ENQ | Station No. | PC No. | Command | Message wait time | Character area C | Sum check code Transmission sequence PLC: ACK | Station No. | PC No. or NAK | Station No. | PC No. | Error code

Figure 24. The framework of the link-oriented application call

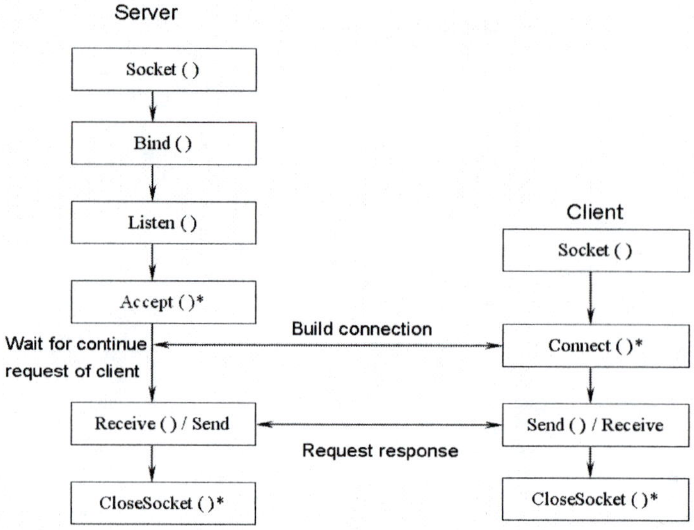

Table 3. Communication thread and its function

Function	Thread	Function of thread
Connect( )	ConnectThread( )	Connect server
Accept( )	WaitForConnectThread( )	Wait connection of client
Receive( )	ReadMessageThread( )	Receive information
Send( )	SendMessageThread( )	Send information

Network Communication Module

The network communication module of RMMST adopts the client/server mode and the TCP/IP protocol through Internet/Intranet. The module makes PC (client) connected with the remote PLC indirectly through PC (server). Figure 24 is a framework of the link-oriented application call.

Two sides can exchange data after call functions are connected according to the sequence. However, the operation is often blocked when the functions with "*"are called, especially socket works in synchronous block mode. RMMST uses the assistant thread to avoid this situation. RMMST also creates the corresponding thread for connect (), accept (), receive (), send (), and so on (see Table 3).

The communication between threads should be considered in multithread which may use global variable, pointer, and file map. RMMST uses pointer. When AfxBeginThread() is called, the communication can be run between the main thread and the assistant thread by transmitting the parameter of pointer.

Image Monitor Module

The AxisCamControl control provided by AXIS communications is developed to form the image monitoring module with the sustenance of AXIS video server. AxisCamControl control is one of the ActiveX controls. After registering and adding the AxisCamControl control to the communication application project, the program can be edited using the properties, methods, and events.

The Main Interfaces of RMMST

The Image Monitoring Interface

The role of the dialogue is to monitor the equipments in the remote production site. The cameras with cloud-platform are placed in the production site. The video image of equipments can be observed in the remote monitoring center by pressing the "Start" button after the IP address is configured in the "Server IP" frame on the interface. The series of buttons of direction control 1 can make the camera scan in four directions (up/down/left/right). Direction control 2 can make the camera to the furthest position. The "Reset" button can make the camera to the default position. The "Focus Control" buttons can push the focus far and drag it near. Figure 25 shows the image monitoring dialogue.

Figure 25. The image monitoring dialogue

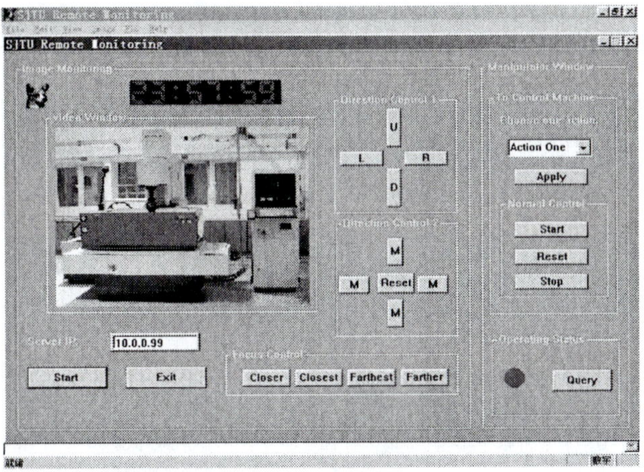

Figure 26. The PLC output control dialogue

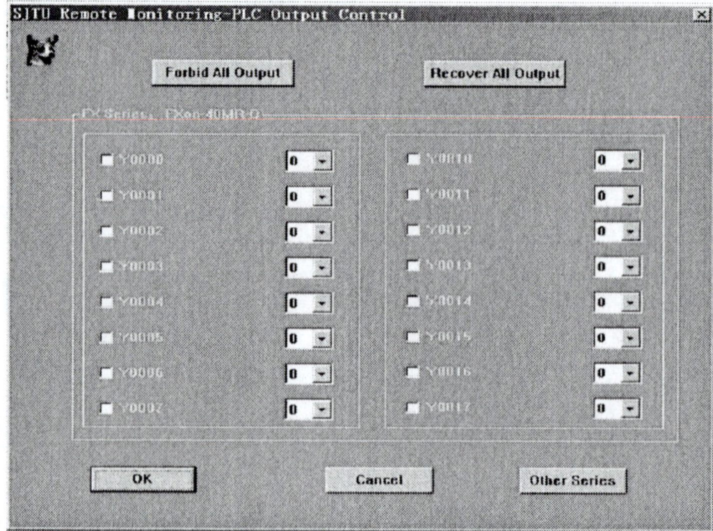

The PLC Output Control Interface

The PLC output can be controlled absolutely in RMMST. Selecting "0" means to forbid the output. On the contrast, selecting "1" is to permit the output. Moreover, there are two buttons "Forbid All Output" and "Recover All Output." Figure 26 shows the PLC output control dialogue.

The PLC Status Query Interface

The PLC status can be queried by selecting the register style and its beginning and ending numbers. The number of dots cannot go beyond 54 simultaneously. Otherwise, the system will alarm and you must reinstall. We can get much information about the equipments by analyzing the data. Figure 27 is the PLC status query dialogue.

Future Trends

In the future, the manufacturer must be responsible for the quality of products in the whole life cycle. All products can be traced. Therefore, e-products, e-manufacturing, and e-service will be the goals of the enterprises to achieve. To achieve these goals, smart hardware, software, and NetWare need to be developed. E-products require that all products' controllers

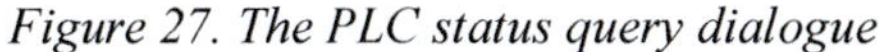

Figure 27. The PLC status query dialogue

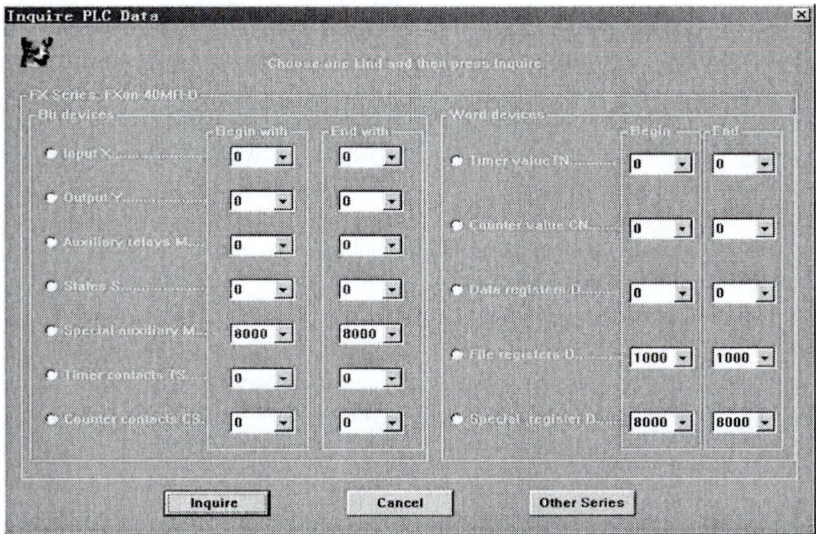

should be server controller; the server controller should have at least three functions: (1) It is a controller, which can make the machine run and archive all the actions. (2) It is a Web server, the host or client can land into the Web sever to set up or modify the Web page. (3) It is a monitor, which can monitor the performances of the product and send out all the information to server center. The server center expert system can make the decision and ensure the product quality, coordinate the activities, reduce costs, and change maintenance practice from breakdown reaction to breakdown prevention.

If all the machines are networked, then all the products can be traced. The e-service is necessary for future use. The Internet makes the distance between manufacture and client "zero." It saves the time and costs and also increases the reliability. The manufacturer should establish an e-service center. The e-service includes three parts: (1) Data base: All the data are obtained from client products over the Internet; all the products must have their unique ID numbers. (2) Expert system: It analyzes all information form client products and gives the decision. (3) Results usage: The analysis results are very useful for maintenance, design modification, or redesign, manufacturing, and supply chain. The future will be: "The manufacturing is e-work; the ERP makes the work easier."

Conclusion

This chapter presented the development of an Internet server controller-based intelligent monitoring and maintenance system for products. It also discussed how to develop products and manufacturing systems using Internet-based intelligent technologies and how to ensure product quality, coordinate activities, reduce costs,and change maintenance practice from the breakdown reaction to prevention. The intelligent monitoring and maintenance system was developed using the hybrid intelligent approach with integrating hardware and software agents (watchdog agent). The software agent is a package of smart prognostics algorithms, which consist of embedded computational prognostic algorithms and a software toolbox for predicting degradation of devices and systems. The algorithms are developed based on *neural network*, *time-series*, *wavelet,* and hybrid joint time-frequency methods. The intelligent maintenance system is an integrated intelligent environment. The effectiveness of the proposed approach is verified by developing an intelligent monitoring and maintenance system testbed for real machine and equipment.

Tomorrow's manufacturing industries must provide the life cycle support for the products they produced in a globalized enterprise. Information technology will play an indispensable role in supporting and enabling the complex practices of design and manufacturing by providing mechanisms to facilitate and manage the integrated system discipline. The need for improved understanding of a product's performance for after-market service will lead to digital service technology for reasons other than troubleshooting. Manufacturers and users will benefit from the increased equipment and process reliability that digital service technology offers. In addition, manufacturing suppliers will benefit from the opportunity to sell process solutions to their customers, not just equipment. The future work will be focused on the digital service technologies for the collaborative life cycle support of products and engineering systems (e.g., collaborative maintenance system in a global enterprise).

Acknowledgments

This work is supported by National Natural Science Foundation of China (Grant No. 50575145). Thanks also to all of my colleagues. We have a vigorous research team.

Note

Any opinions, findings, conclusions, or recommendations expressed in this material are those of the authors. No approval or endorsement by the National Institute of Standards and Technology is intended or implied.

References

Amari, S., & Fulton, W. (2003). Bounds on optimal replacement time of age replacement policy. In *Proceedings of The Annual Reliability and Maintainability Symposium on Product Quality and Integrity,* Tampa, FL (pp. 417-422).

Badia, F. G., & Berrade, M. D. (2002). Optimal inspection and preventive maintenance of units with revealed and unrevealed failures. *Reliability Engineering and System Safety, 78*(2), 157-163.

Belegundu, A. D., & Chandrupatla, T. R. (1999). *Optimization concepts and applications in engineering.* Upper Saddle River, NJ: Prentice Hall.

Bengtsson, M. (2002). Condition based maintenance on rail vehicles. In *IDPMTR 2002.*

Bevilacqua, M., & Braglia, M. (2000). The analytical hierarchy process applied to maintenance strategy selection. *Reliability Engineering and System Safety, 70*(1), 71-83.

Boland, P. J., & El-Neweihi, E. (1998). Statistical and information based (physical) minimal repair for k out of n systems. *Journal of Applied Probability, 35*(3), 731-740.

Burrus, C. S., Gopinath, R. A., & Haitao, G. (1998). *Introduction to wavelets and wavelet transforms — A Primer.* Upper Saddle River, NJ: Prentice Hall.

Casoetto, N., Djurdjanovic, D., Mayor, R., Lee, J., & Ni, J. (2003). *Multisensor process performance assessment through the use of autoregressive modeling and feature maps.* Paper presented at Transactions of SME/NAMRI (Paper No. 198).

Charan, R., & Tichy, N. (1998). Every business is a growth business. *Times Business.*

Charles, A. S., Floru, I. R., Azzaro-Pantel, C., Pibouleau, L., & Domenech, S. (2003). Optimization of preventive maintenance strategies in a multipurpose batch plant: Application to semiconductor manufacturing. *Computers and Chemical Engineering, 27*(4), 449-467.

Chen, D., & Trivedi, K. S. (2002). Closed-form analytical results for condition-based maintenance. *Reliability Engineering and System Safety, 76*(1), 43-51.

Chen, C. T., Chen, Y. W., & Yuan, J. (2003). On a dynamic preventive maintenance policy for a system under inspection. *Reliability Engineering and System Safety, 80*(2), 41-47.

Cohen, L. (1995). *Time-frequency analysis.* Englewood Cliffs, NJ: Prentice Hall.

Degbotse, A. T., & Nachlas, J. A. (2003). Use of nested renewals to model availability under opportunistic maintenance policies. In *Proceedings of The Annual Reliability and Maintenability Symposium on Product Quality and Integrity,* Tampa, FL (pp. 344-350).

Deshpande, V. S., & Modak, J. P. (2002). Application of RCM for safety consideration in a steel plant. *Reliability Engineering and System Safety, 78*(3), 325-334.

Djurdjanovic, D., Ni, J., & Lee, J. (2002). *Time-frequency based sensor fusion in the assessment and monitoring of machine performance degradation.* Paper presented at ASME Int. Mechanical Eng. Congress and Exposition (Paper No. IMECE2002-32032).

Duffuaa, S. O., Ben-Daya, M., Al-Sultan, K. S., & Andijani, A. (2001). A generic conceptual simulation model for maintenance systems. *Journal of Quality in Maintenance Engineering, 7*(3), 207-219.

Dupuy, J. F. (2005). The proportional hazards model with covariate measurement error. *Journal of Statistical Planning and Inference, 135*(2), 260-275.

Engel, S. J., Gilmartin, B. J., Bongort, K., & Hess, A. (2000). Prognostics, the real issues involved with predicting life remaining. In *Proceedings of the IEEE Aerospace Conference Proceedings* (Vol. 6, pp. 457-469).

Grall, A., Berenguer, C., & Dieulle, L. (2002). A condition-based maintenance policy for stochastically deteriorating systems. *Reliability Engineering and System Safety, 76*(1), 167-180.

Horowitz, J. L., & Lee, S. (2004). Semi-parametric estimation of a panel data proportional hazards model with fixed effects. *Journal of Econometrics, 119*(1), 155-198.

Jayabalan, V., & Chaudhuri, D. (1992). Cost optimization of maintenance scheduling for a system with assured reliability. *IEEE Transactions on Reliability, 41*(1), 21-25.

Kececioglu, D., & Sun, F. B. (1995). A general discrete-time dynamic programming model for the opportunistic replacement policy and its application to ball-bearing systems. *Reliability Engineering and System Safety, 47*(3), 175-185.

Koc, M., & Lee, J. (2000). *A system framework for next-generation e-maintenance systems.* Retrieved from http://www.uwm.edu/CEAS/ims/pdffiles/E-Maintenance.PDF

Lee, J. (1996). Measurement of machine performance degradation using a neural network model. *Journal of Computers in Industry, 30*(3), 193-209.

Lee, J. (1998). Teleservice engineering in manufacturing: Challenges and opportunities. *International Journal of Machine Tools & Manufacture, 38*(8), 901-910.

Lee, J. (2003, October 30). Advances and issues on remote monitoring and prognostics. In *Proceedings of 2003 International Conference on Intelligent Maintenance Systems.*

Lee, J., & Kramer, B. M. (1992). Analysis of machine degradation using a neural network based pattern discrimination model. *Journal of Manufacturing Systems, 12*(3), 379-387.

Lee, J., & Ni, J. (2002, March 25-27). Infotronics agent for tether-free prognostics. In *Proceeding of AAAI Spring Symposium on Information Refinement and Revision for Decision Making: Modeling for Diagnostics, Prognostics, and Prediction*, Stanford University, Palo Alto, CA.

Lee, J., & Ni, J. (2004, September 29-October 1). Infotronics-based intelligent maintenance system and its impacts to close-loop product life cycle system. In *Proceeding of Global Conference on Sustainable Product Development and Life Cycle Engineering,* Berlin, Germany.

Lee, J., & Wang, B. (1999). *Computer-aided maintenance: Methodologies and practices.* Kluwer Academic Publisher.

Liu, C. L., Zha, X. F., Miao, Y. B., & Lee, J. (2005). Internet server controller based intelligence maintenance system for information appliances products. *International Journal of Knowledge-Based and Intelligent Engineering Systems, 9*(2), 137-148.

Liu, C. L., Xie, K., Miao, Y. B., Zha, X. F., & Lee, J. (2006). Communication method for chaotic encryption in remote monitoring system for product e-manufacturing and e-maintenance. *Soft Computing, 10*(3), 224-229.

Liu, C. L., Xie, K., Zha, X. F., Feng, Z. J., & Lee, J. (2004, September 20-October 8). Study on Communication method for the chaotic encryption in remote monitoring systems. In *Proceedings of the 9th Online World Conference on Soft Computing in Industrial Applications.*

Liu, C. L., Zha, X. F., & Lee, J. (2004, September 20-October 8). Study on the Internet server controller based intelligent maintenance system for electrical appliances. In *Proceedings of the 9th Online World Conference on Soft Computing in Industrial Applications.*

Maillart, L. M., & Pollock, S. M. (2002). Cost-optimal condition-monitoring for predictive maintenance of 2-phase systems. *IEEE Transactions on Reliability, 51*(3), 322-330.

Marple, S. L. (1987). *Digital spectral analysis.* Englewood Cliffs, NJ: Prentice Hall.

Monga, A., & Zuo, M. J., (1997). Toogood R. Reliability based design of systems considering preventive maintenance and minimal repair. *International Journal of Reliability, Quality and Safety Engineering, 4*(1), 55-71.

NRC (1990). *The competitiveness edge: Research priorities for U.S. manufacturing.* National Academy Press.

NSF I/UCRC Center for Intelligent Maintenance Systems (2002). Available online at http://www.imscenter.net

Pandit, S. M., & Wu, S-M. (1993). *Time series and system analysis with application.* Malabar, FL: Krieger Publishing Co.

Pham, H., & Wang, H. (1996). Imperfect maintenance. *European Journal of Operational Research, 94*(3), 425-438.

Pham, H., & Wang, H.. (2000). Optimal (s; T) opportunistic maintenance of a k-out-of-n: G system with imperfect PM and partial failure. *Naval Research Logistics, 47*(3), 223-239.

Popova, E., & Wilson, J. G. (1999). Group replacement policies for parallel systems whose components have phase distributed failure times. *Annals of Operations Research, 91*, 163-190.

Radjou, N. (2002, May). The collaborative product life cycle. *Forrester Research.*

Refenes, A.-P. (1995). *Neural networks in the capital markets.* John Wiley & Sons.

Riane, F., Artiba, A., & Iassinovski, S. (2001). An integrated production planning and scheduling system for hybrid flowshop organizations. *International Journal of Production Economics, 74*(1-3), 33-48.

S K. (2002, June 24). Hot Technologies. *Fortune Magazine,* 162[F-H].

Tanaka, Y., & Rao, P. V. (2005). A proportional hazards model for informatively censored survival times. *Journal of Statistical Planning and Inference, 129*(1-2), 253-262.

Tsai, Y. T., Wang, K. S., & Tsai L. C. (2004). A study of availability-centered preventive maintenance for multi-component systems. *Reliability Engineering and System Safety, 84*(3), 261-270.

Waeyenbergh, G., & Pintelon, L. (2002). A framework for maintenance concept development. *International Journal of Production Economics, 77*(3), 299-313.

Waeyenbergh, G., & Pintelon, L. (2004). Maintenance concept development: A case study. *International Journal of Production Economics, 89*(3), 395-405.

Wang, H., & Pham, H. (1999). Some maintenance models and availability with imperfect maintenance in production systems. *Annals of Operations Research, 91*, 305-318.

Wang, X., Yu, G., Koc, M., & Lee, J. (2002). Wavelet neural network for machining performance assessment and its implication to machinery prognostic. In *Proceedings of the 5th International Conference on Managing Innovations in Manufacturing (MIM),* Milwaukee, Wisconsin (pp. 150-156).

Wang, H., Pham, H., & Izundu, A. E. (2001). Optimal preparedness maintenance of multi-unit systems with imperfect maintenance and economic dependence. In H. Pham (Ed.), *Recent advances in reliability and quality engineering* (pp. 75-92). NJ: World Scientific.

White, I. C., & White, D. J. (1989). Markov decision processes. *European Journal of Operational Research, 39*(1), 1-16.

Wildeman, R. E., Dekker, R., & Smith, A. C. J. M. (1997). A dynamic policy for grouping maintenance activities. *European Journal of Operational Research, 99*(3), 530-551.

Yan, J. H., Koç M., & Lee, J. (2002). Predictive algorithm for machine degradation detection using logistic regression. In *Proceedings of the 5th International Conference on Managing Innovations in Manufacturing (MIM),* Milwaukee, Wisconsin (pp. 172-178).

Zarefar, H., & Goulding, J. R. (1992). Neural networks in design of products: A case study. In A. Kusiak (Ed.), *Intelligent design and manufacturing* (pp. 179-201). John Wiley & Sons, Inc.

Zha, X. F. (2001). Neuro-fuzzy comprehensive assemblability and assembly sequence evaluation. *Artificial Intelligence in Engineering Design, Analysis, and Manufacturing (AIEDAM, An international Journal), 15*(5), 367-384.

Zha, X. F. (2002). Soft computing framework for intelligent human-machine system design: Simulation and optimization. *Soft Computing (A Fusion of Foundations, Methodologies and Applications: An International Journal, 7*(3), 187-198

Zha, X. F. (2004). A hybrid cross-mapping neural network model for computational intelligent design. *International Journal of Knowledge-Based and Intelligent Engineering Systems, 8*(1), 17-26.

Zha, X. F. (2004). Artificial intelligence and integrated intelligent systems in product design and development. In C. T. Leondes (Ed.), *Intelligent knowledge-based systems: Business and technology in new millennium, vol. IV: Intelligent Systems,* Chapter 1. USA: Kluwer Academic Publishers.

Zha, X. F. (2005) Manufacturing advisory service system for concurrent and collaborative design of MEMS services (vol. 1). In C. T. Leondes (Ed.), *MEMS/NEMS handbook: Techniques and applications.* USA: Springer/Kluwer Academic Publishers.

Zha, X. F. (2005). Soft computing in engineering design: A fuzzy neural network model for virtual product design and simulation. In A. Abraham & M. Koeppen (Eds.), *Soft computing in industrial application.* Springer Verlag.

Zha, X. F. (2005). Soft computing in engineering design: A hybrid dual cross-mapping neural network model. *Neural Computing and Applications, 14*(3), 176-188.

Zha, X. F., & Lim, S. Y. E. (2003). Intelligent design and planning of manual assembly systems: A neuro-fuzzy approach. *Computers & Industrial Engineering, 44*, 611-632.

Zha, X. F., Yang, Y. Q., & Choi, A. C. K. (1995). Intelligent quality control for robotized flexible assembly system. *Proceedings of 1st International Conference on Quality and Reliability* (Vol.1, pp. 324-332), Hong Kong.

Zhao, Y. X. (2003). On preventive maintenance policy of a critical reliability level for system subject to degradation. *Reliability Engineering and System Safety, 79*(3), 301-308.

Zuo, H. F., Zha, X. F., Shen, Q., & Li, B. C. (1991). An intelligent ferrography system for monitoring and diagnosing machinery wear with machine vision. In *Proceedings of 2nd International Conference on Technical Diagnosing (ICTD'91)*, Guilin, China (pp. 445-450).

Zurada, J. M. (1992). *Introduction to artificial neural system.* USA: West Publishing Company.

Section V:

Integrated Intelligent Product Design and Development

Chapter XVII

An Integrated Intelligent System Model and Its Applications in Virtual Product Design and Development

Xuan F. Zha, National Institute of Standards and Technology,
University of Maryland, USA & Shanghai JiaoTong University, China

Abstract

In this chapter, a novel integrated intelligent framework is first proposed for virtual engineering design and development based on the soft computing and hybrid intelligent techniques. Then, an evolutionary neuro-fuzzy (EFNN) model is developed and used for supporting modeling, analysis and evaluation, and optimization tasks in the design process, which combines fuzzy logic with neural networks and genetic algorithms. The developed system HIDS-EFNN provides a unified integrated intelligent environment for virtual engineering design and simulation. The focus of this chapter is to present a hybrid intelligent approach with evolutionary neuro-fuzzy modeling and its applications in virtual product design, customization, and simulation (product performance prediction). Case studies are provided to illustrate and verify the proposed model and approach.

Introduction

Design process is an iterative and highly interactive task. The designer has to consider countless constraints with usually opposing goals in the design process. Automatic design, analysis, evaluation, modification, and optimization of design parameters are important issues to be addressed during the design process. Thus, design is a process that includes not just the use of a quantitative technique but also the use of a qualitative technique. Over the past two decades, artificial intelligence (AI) techniques seem to have emerged as the main contender for conventional design techniques. Many efforts have been made to apply AI techniques such as expert system, fuzzy logic, neural network, and genetic algorithms to help accomplish some design tasks (Dagli, 1994; Wang & Takefuji, 1993; Zha, 2004b). While these techniques have produced encouraging results, the design problem is too complex to be solved by a single AI technique alone.

Each AI technique has particular strengths and weaknesses that make them suited for particular problems and not for others (Medesker, 1995). For instance, while neural networks are good at recognizing patterns, they are generally not good at explaining how they reach their decisions. On the other hand, fuzzy systems are good at explaining their decisions, but they cannot automatically acquire the rules they use to make those decisions. Thus, according to Goonatilake and Khebbal (1995), hybrid intelligent systems (HIS) may have to be used in which two or more AI techniques are integrated to overcome the limitations of each individual technique or in which different intelligent modules are used to collectively solve all the problems, with each solving the parts at which it is best. Here, the author prefers to use hybrid intelligent system (HIS) other than intelligent hybrid systems (IHS) as a hybrid system is in some cases referred to as a combination/integration of continuous and discrete systems. The high complexity and the inherent heterogeneity of many real world problems is one of the major challenges of current AI techniques. Due to the necessity of using different problem solving techniques, the interest in HIS is rapidly growing. HIS has been applied to many areas including process control, process fault diagnosis, prediction of economic data, and so forth. However, there is relatively little work on applying HIS to the design process.

This chapter aims to develop a hybrid intelligent model for supporting computational intelligent design and simulation. An evolutionary neuro-fuzzy or fuzzy neural network (EFNN) model is proposed with an integration of the neural networks, fuzzy logic, and genetic algorithms techniques for virtual product design, simulation, and customization.

The remaining parts of this chapter are organized as follows. The next section provides an overview of hybrid intelligent design systems. Then, a soft computing based integrated and hybrid intelligent framework for engineering design is proposed, followed by discussion of the evolutionary neuro-fuzzy (EFNN) model. After that, the implementation of the HIDS-EFNN design system is outlined and case studies for design and simulation using the developed model and system are provided. Finally the chapter is summarized and concluded.

Overview of Hybrid Intelligent Design Systems

This section provides an overview of hybrid intelligent design systems. The hybrid intelligent systems integrate knowledge-based systems, fuzzy logic, neural networks, genetic algorithms, and case-based among other techniques. Their effectiveness have been proven in a wide variety of real-world complex problems including planning and scheduling, representation and reasoning, intelligent interface, hybrid and integrated systems (CAD, database), and so forth. Hybrid intelligent systems are rapidly growing in importance and visibility in engineering design (Zha, 2004b). Akman, ten Hagen, and Veerkamp (1989) and Akman, ten Hagen, and Tomiyama, (1994) proposed the desirable functionalities of intelligent hybrid CAD systems and a unifying framework of intelligent, integrated, and interactive CAD (IIICAD) for describing and applying design knowledge. However, no details on the development and application of IIICAD systems are given. Zarefar and Goulding (1992) described the implementation of a neural network-based hybrid CAD design environment for mechanical power transmissions (gearbox design). The hybrid intelligent environment consisted of a fuzzy expert system and a back-propagation neural network. The research work provides a useful guide for applying hybrid intelligence to the design problem. Bahrami and Dagli (1993) reported on the application of fuzzy associative memory in conceptual design by mapping fuzzy functional requirements to crisp design solution. Their work established the basic foundation of intelligent CAD system, a tool that can assist designers in all phases of the design process. Relatively little work has been done in retrieving a crisp design solution based on the fuzzy input requirements and the simplicity of its practical implementation, making the system an attractive tool in the idea generation phase of the design process. Powell, Skolnick, and Tong (1995) proposed a unified approach for engineering design optimization based on their survey on the existing optimization techniques such as expert systems, numerical optimization, and genetic algorithms, which uses a combination of expert systems, numerical optimization, and genetic algorithms. This "unified" approach capitalizes on the individual advantages of each separate optimization technique but offset their disadvantages. It allows the user to concentrate on the design problem without having to worry about the selection and fine-tuning of optimization algorithms. Bahrami Lynch, and Dagli (1994) further examined the application of the hybrid neural networks in design and manufacturing. The system incorporates three neural network paradigms — fuzzy associative memory, back-propagation, and adaptive resonance theory (ART) — to achieve the integration of product-process design. The fuzzy associative memory approach is utilized for automation of mapping the marketing characteristics into predesigned structures. Adaptive resonance theory is utilized for object identification. A back-propagation neural network is used for camera calibration and another back-propagation network is used to control the speed of the robot arm based on the size of a work-piece. This unique application of neural networks in design and manufacturing can be extended for more sophisticated tools in concurrent engineering. The concepts introduced reinforce the need for the application of concurrent engineering methodologies and specific technologies based on artificial intelligence. Su and Wakelam (1999) applied integrated intelligent system approaches successfully for engineering design and manufacturing integration, which incorporate design and manufacture expertise and to integrate relevant CAD/CAE/CAM and AI techniques into the total design and manufacture process. The hybrid intelligent systems approach has been developed to integrate various activities involved in design and manufacture, including product design specification, conceptual design, detail design, process planning, costing, and CNC manufacture. It blends a rule-based system (RBS), artificial neural networks (ANNs), genetic algorithms (GAs), multimedia, and CAD/CAE/CAM packages into a single environment. The RBS and ANNs capture the design and manufacture expertise, while the other tasks are handled by relevant CAD/CAE/CAM software packages. The GA and Hypermedia are used for design optimization and to provide an effective means for user interfaces and data transfer. The RBS communicates with the others and works as a coordinator controlling the whole process. Chen and Occea (1999) proposed a soft computing framework for concurrent product design evolution and evaluation, and developed a concurrent design evaluation system (CONDENSE) that can help the designer in evaluating possible design solutions and design alternatives during the early stage of the design phase. A qualitative aspect evaluation is applied during the searching stage for solution principles and their combinations to help determine the design specifications, and a quantitative aspect evaluation is applied to provide information on performance, assemblability, manufacturability, and costs to facilitate design selection. The advantages of CONDENSE include speed-up of design and development, improvement of design quality, and facilitation of design selection. Based on the hybrid integration of neural networks and fuzzy expert system (i.e., neuro-fuzzy hybrid scheme) Zha and Lim (2002, 2003) developed a soft-computing framework for human machine system design and simulation. The complex human machine system is described by human and machine parameters within a comprehensive model, in which procedures and algorithms for human-machine system design, economical/ergonomic evaluation, and optimization are imposed in an integrated CAD and soft computing framework. With a combination of individual neural network and fuzzy logic techniques, the neuro-fuzzy hybrid soft-computing scheme implements a fuzzy if-then rules block for human-machine system design, evaluation, and optimization by trainable fuzzy neural network architecture. For training and test purposes, assembly tasks are simulated and carried out on a self-built multi-adjustable laboratory workstation with a flexible motion measurement and analysis system. The trained fuzzy neural network system is able to predict the operators' postures and joint angles of motion associated with a range of workstation configurations. The developed system provides a unified, intelligent computational framework for human machine system design and simulation.

In recent years, virtual product design is an emerging technology that allows engineers to visualize multi-dimensional properties of new products at its design stage without actually producing a prototype (Bateman, Bowden, Gogg, Harrell, & Mott, 1997; Law & Kelton, 1991; Li, Tay, & Ang, 2000). A recent report of US National Science Foundation (NSF) indicates that virtual intelligent design and cyber-infrastructure will play a pivotal role in supporting and shaping future predicative product realization systems and processes. In a virtual product design, a machine is virtually assembled; its performance is simulated using a simulation package and tested with new variable inputs. This allows manufacturers to reduce or bypass multiple physical prototype stages and achieve a significantly higher level of efficiency in product design by saving time and cost from the development cycle. A key issue of virtual product design and development is to accurately correlate the simulation output with the input conditions and after that to evaluate/predict the machine's behavior and performance under new conditions.

This research aims to develop a hybrid intelligent model for supporting computational intelligent design and simulation in a virtual environment.

Soft Computing Integrated and Hybrid Intelligent Framework for Engineering Design

In this section, based on the integrated and hybrid intelligent systems techniques, a novel soft-computing integrated intelligent scheme is proposed for engineering design process.

Soft Computing and Hybrid Intelligent Systems

There are many individual intelligent systems and approaches such as expert system, fuzzy logic, neural network, and genetic algorithms that can accomplish some design tasks (Dagli 1994; Wang & Takefuji, 1993; Zha, 2004b). However, due to particular computational properties of individual intelligent system techniques, hybrid intelligent solutions are required to solve complex design problems, which may integrate one or more of the above individual intelligent techniques.

The concept of soft computing introduced by Zadeh (1994) serves to highlight the emergence of computing methodologies in which the accent is on exploiting the tolerance for imprecision and uncertainty to achieve tractability, robustness, and low solution cost. At this juncture, the principal constituents of soft computing are fuzzy logic, neuro-computing, evolutionary computing, and probabilistic computing, with the latter subsuming belief networks, chaotic systems, and parts of learning theory. Soft computing techniques facilitate the use of fuzzy logic, neuro-computing, evolutionary computing, and probabilistic computing in combination, leading to the concept of hybrid intelligent systems. Such systems are rapidly growing in importance and visibility.

In this work, based on the hybrid integration of neural networks and knowledge-based expert system, a soft-computing framework is proposed for engineering design. The main objective of this work is to design and implement a hybrid intelligent system (HIS) for engineering design that is aimed at overcoming the limitations of the conventional design techniques. Its purpose is not to replace the conventional techniques but to supplement and complement them so that a much wider range of design situations can be adequately dealt with.

Integrated Intelligent Design Framework

A soft computing-based integrated intelligent framework, as shown in Figure 1, is proposed for engineering design with hybrid intelligent integration of neural networks and knowledge-based expert system as well as computer-aided design (CAD) techniques. Therefore, a systematic method for the design of product-process requires the concurrent integration of the following processes or procedures: product design, design for operation, process planning, task assignment and line balancing, equipment selection, production system design/layout, evaluation, and simulation.

Under this framework, the geometrical model from the CAD system constitutes the basis for product design. Considering this, the geometrical model has to be complemented to be as the product assembly model. This contains all the information necessary for designing

Figure 1. Soft computing-based integrated intelligent design framework

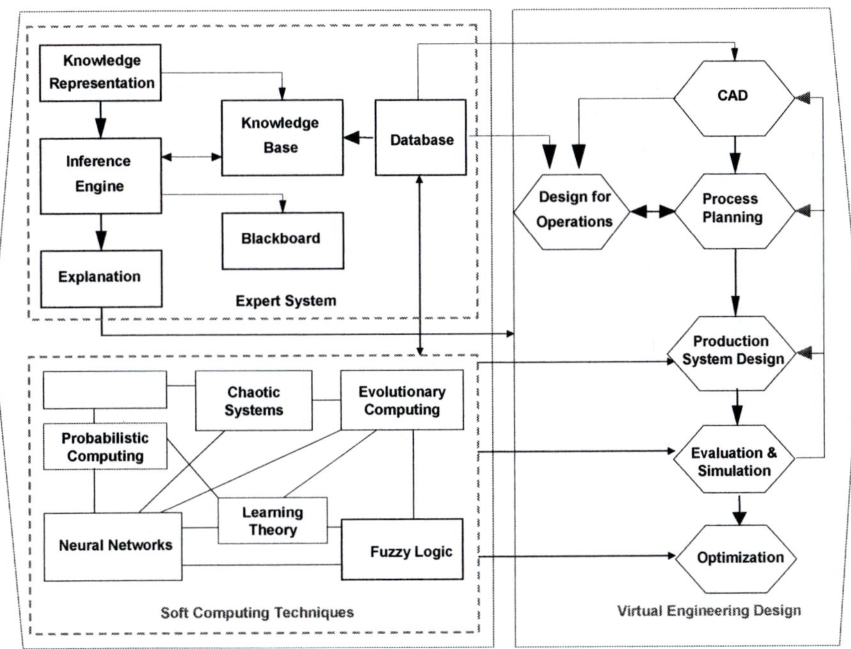

economic system. For example, the type of operation (e.g,. assembly), workstation, or the dimension of the equipment to provide parts depends on the dimension and the weight of the operating parts. Furthermore, information like the class of fit, the depth of insertion, and the positioning direction can be taken from the product model. To obtain all information and make them available for the design, it is possible to simulate the whole operation (e.g., assembly) process within an extended CAD system. The instrument used in this case is built up on the CAD system and offers all the functions needed to simulate and record the operation (e.g., assembly) process in addition to the CAD operations.

During this simulation, the operations and the relations between the operating parts can be specified or completed with further information (e.g., relations among operation tasks or the combinations of parts to subassemblies for assembly task). Based on this information, it is possible to derive the precedence diagram of the whole operation process. The precedence diagram is a directed graph that describes the logical and technological constraints among all tasks. This information and the additional description of the tasks are the basis for the computer-aided operation planning and simulation. The results have to be evaluated according to the multi-criterion's system goals. Some heuristic methods are required to find approximate solutions to these problems. For example, in manual workstation design and planning, the human workplace design and its optimization can then be carried out after obtaining the product and process information (e.g., geometric model and precedence constraints) (Zha, 2003).

An Evolutionary Neuro-Fuzzy Hybrid Intelligent Design Model

Overview

Recently, there have been many attempts to solve these problems by applying neural network and (fuzzy) rule-based expert systems techniques (Azoff, 1994; Kang, 1991; Refenes, 1995; Zha, 2003). The capabilities of rule-based (fuzzy) expert systems are inherently well suited to contribute to solutions to design problems. The major drawback, however, is that the programmer is required to define the functions underlying the multi-valued or ranked possibility optimization. Furthermore, expert-type rules use a comprehensive language system that may have built-in biases, embedded goals, and hidden information structures, which may result in errors (Zurada, 1992). Neural networks use mathematical relationships and mappings to design and optimize human-machine systems. They are capable of statistical decision-making given incomplete and uncertain design information, and can be designed to adapt to the user/designer's requirements. Unlike rule-based (fuzzy) expert systems, they evaluate all the design conflict constraints simultaneously, and model or learn the knowledge base using black-box techniques. They do not use rules in the formal sense, so the design time can be greatly reduced from that of rule-based modeling. The strengths of neural networks accrue from the fact that they need not *priori* assumptions of models and from their capability to infer complex, nonlinear underlying relationships. From the statisticians' point of view, neural networks are essentially statistical devices to perform inductive inference and are analogous to non-parametric, nonlinear regression models (Refenes, 1995; Zurada, 1992; Powell et al., 1995). However, existing neural schemes use two or more separate neural networks to accomplish some design tasks respectively, and need to train them separately. This is tedious and costly, and sometimes very difficult. In order to overcome the suffered shortcomings or difficulties, more research endeavors are necessary to develop more general topologies of neural models, learning algorithms, and approximation theories so that those models are applicable in the system modeling, design, and control of complex systems. A new kind of hybrid neural networks is therefore required for design support. It must also be conceded that rule-based (fuzzy) expert systems are much easier for humans to error-check than an ensemble of continuous equations in neural networks (Zarefar & Goulding, 1992). There is now a growing need in the intelligent design community that complex design problems require hybrid solutions (Zha, 2004b).

In view of these practical requirements and the current research status and future trend of intelligent design, this research aims to develop a hybrid intelligent model for supporting computational intelligent design and simulation in a virtual environment. In this work, an evolutionary neuro-fuzzy or fuzzy neural network model is developed and used for supporting modeling, analysis, and evaluation, and optimization tasks in the design process in the soft computing integrated intelligent design framework, which combines fuzzy logic with neural networks. Details about the evolutionary neuro-fuzzy or fuzzy neural network model are discussed in the next section.

The Neuro-Fuzzy Network Architecture

Figure 2 shows the architecture of the fuzzy neural network (FNN). It is basically a five-layer fuzzy rule-based neural network (Li, Ang, & Gay, 2005; Zha, 2003). In accordance with the common neural network notation in Zurada (1992), a node in layer *i* of the network has its input, $N^{(i)}$. The node performs a certain designated transformation/operation on its input (u_{ij}) weighted by their respective weight values (w_{ij}) and generates an output which is a function of its input, that is, output, $f(N^{(i)})$. Figure 3 shows the basic structure of a node in a conventional neural network. Generally, two steps are involved in neural computing. The first step is to transform the inputs into a function termed net-in or simply N:

$$N^k{}_j = f(u^k{}_{1j}.w^k{}_{1j},...,u^k{}_{ij}.w^k{}_{ij},...,u^k{}_{pj}.w^k{}_{pj}) \quad (1)$$

where superscript k indicates the layer number, and subscript i represents the node in the previous layer that sends input to node j in layer k; and p represents the number of inputs to the node. When the weight w_{ij} for all the u_{ij} is unit, we have:

$$N^k{}_j = f(u^k{}_{1j},...,u^k{}_{ij},...,u^k{}_{pj}) \quad (2)$$

Figure 2. The architecture of FNN

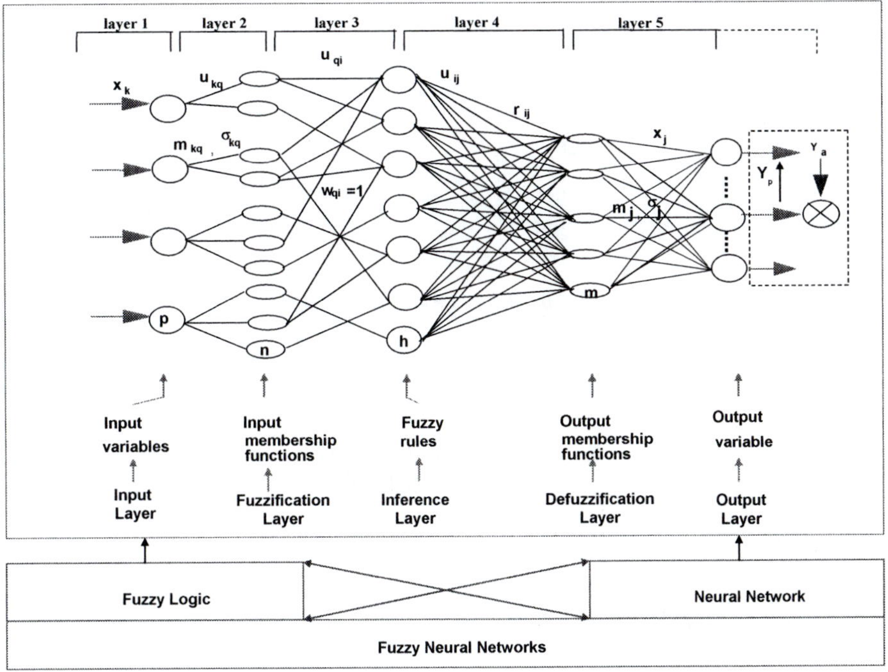

Figure 3. Basic structure of a neural node

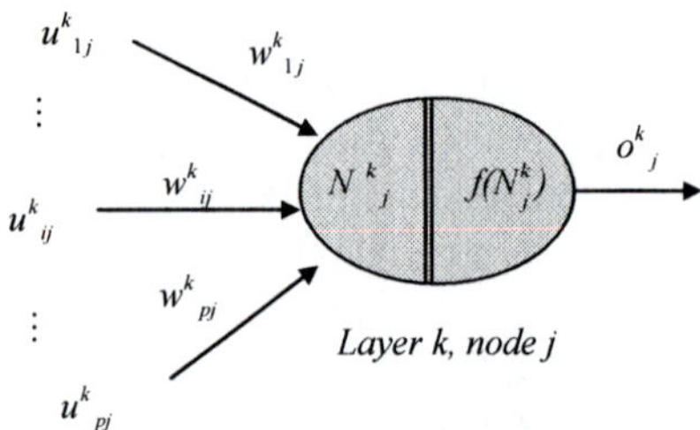

The second step is to generate the output o_j^k as a function of N:

$$o_j^k = f(N_j^k) \tag{3}$$

The output weighted by weight values will in turn become inputs to the relevant nodes in the immediate next layer according to the node connections in the network structure.

1. The nodes in Layer 1 transmit input values $\{x_k\}$ to next layer directly as $\{u_{kq}\}$, where $x_k = u_{kq}$. That is:

$$f(N_k^{(1)}) = N_k^{(1)} = x_k = u_{kq} \tag{4}$$

   where $k = 1, 2, \dots, p$; $q = 1, 2, \dots, n$

2. The nodes in Layer 2 are the input membership functions. They work as a fuzzifier to transform a numerical input into a fuzzy set. The membership functions are as follows:

   - Normal distributions with a range between 0 and 1.

$$N_q^{(2)} = -\frac{(u_{kq} - m_{kq})^2}{(\mathrm{d}_{kq})^2}, \; f(N_q^{(2)}) = e^{N_q^{(2)}} = u_{qi} \tag{5}$$

   Where $i = 1, 2, \dots, h$, $\{m_{kq}\}$ and $\{\sigma_{kq}\}$ are the means and variances of the input membership functions, respectively.

   - Sigmoid functions: $f(N_q^{(2)}) = 1/(1 + e^{-N_q^{(2)}}) = u_{qi}$
   - Trapezoidal or triangular functions (Zha & Lim, 2002, 2003).

3. The nodes in Layer 3 perform a fuzzy min-max operation on the node inputs, i.e. a fuzzy AND operation followed by a fuzzy OR operation:

$$N_i^{(3)} = min\{u_{qi} \cdot w_{qi}\} \tag{6}$$

$$f(N_i^{(3)}) = N_i^{(3)} = u_{ij} \tag{7}$$

$$u_{cj} = max(N_1^{(3)}, N_2^{(3)}, ..., N_h^{(3)}) \tag{8}$$

where $i = 1, 2, ..., h, j = 1, 2, ..., m$ and $c \in \{1, 2,...., h\}$. The link weight w_{qi} is unity. The node c is termed the winner node of the fuzzy min-max operation. It is noted that instead of min-max arbitrary triangular norm, co-norm could also be used here.

4. The nodes in Layer 4 represent the dampened outputs of the winner node.

$$N_j^{(4)} = u_{cj} \cdot r_{cj},\ f(N_j^{(4)}) = N_j^{(4)} = x_j \quad (i = c) \tag{9}$$

$j = 1, 2, ..., m$

The dampening coefficients are the rule values r_{ij}. The initial rule values are either random values or assigned directly by an expert. They can also be established outside the network from historical data and then incorporated into the network. The rule values are subsequently fine-tuned during learning.

5. The nodes in Layer 5 perform defuzzification of outputs. There are currently about 20 defuzzification methods (Leekwijck & Kerre, 1999, 2001). The defuzzification method used here is the centre of gravity method (Kosko, 1992), which uses the centroid of the membership function as the representative value. Thus if m_j and σ_j are the means and the variances of the output membership functions, respectively, then the defuzzified outputs are given by Equation 10 as follows:

$$\hat{y}(t) = f(N_{out}^{(5)}) = \frac{N_{out}^{(5)}}{\sum_{j=1}^{m} \sigma_j x_j} \tag{10}$$

where $N_{out}^{(5)} = \sum_{j=1}^{m} \sigma_j m_j x_j$ and $\{m_j \bullet \sigma_j\}$ are the link weights, $j = 1,2, ...,m$.

Training/Learning Algorithms

Fuzzy neural networks can be trained using various training/learning methods, such as the back propagation method (Horikawa, Furuhasshi, & Uchikawa, 1992), the Kohonen's feature maps method (Kohonen, 1988), and the conjugate gradient method (Leonard & Kramer, 1991). Standard back propagation remains the most widely used supervised learning method for neural networks (Refenes, 1995). In the following, based on the work in Li, Ang, and Gay (2005), we give the first two algorithms, that is, the back-propagation algorithm and the Kohonen's feature maps method (Horikawa et al., 1992; Kohonen, 1988).

The Supervised Learning

The objective of the supervised learning is to minimize the error function E as defined in Equation 11 by means of a learning algorithm.

$$E = \frac{1}{2}[y(t) - \hat{y}(t)\}^{2} \tag{11}$$

where $y(t)$ is the actual output, and $\hat{y}(t)$ is the predicted output. In FNN, the learning algorithm used is derived from the back-propagation algorithm (Refenes, 1995). Thus, if η is the assigned learning rate, the rule values r_{ij} are fine-tuned as follows:

$$r_{ij}(t+1) = r_{ij}(t) - \eta\frac{\partial E}{\partial r_{ij}} \tag{12}$$

$$\frac{\partial E}{\partial r_{ij}} = \frac{\partial E}{\partial f(N_j^{(4)})}\cdot\frac{\partial f(N_j^{(4)})}{\partial(N_j^{(4)})}\cdot\frac{\partial(N_j^{(4)})}{\partial r_{ij}} \tag{13}$$

From equations 12 and 13, we have:

$$r_{ij}(t+l) = r_{ij}(t) - \eta\frac{\partial E}{\partial r_{ij}} = r_{ij}(t) + \eta u_{ij}[Y_a(t) - Y_p(t)]\frac{(\sum_{j=1}^{m}\sigma_j x_j)\sigma_j m_j - (\sum_{j=l}^{m}\sigma_j m_j x_j)\ \sigma_j}{(\sum_{j=l}^{m}\sigma_j x_j)^2} \tag{14}$$

where:

- $u_{ij} = min[e^{-\frac{(x_k - m_{kq})^2}{(\sigma_{kq})^2}}]$, the net-input to the node of layer 4
- x_k = values of input in the 1st layer, $k = 1,2,\ldots,K$
- m_{kq} = mean of input membership function in the second layer
- δ_{kq} = Variance of input membership function in the second layer
- η = Learning rate
- r_{ij} = Rule value or damping coefficient
- $Y_a(t)$ = Actual output

- $Y_p(t)$ = Predicted output
- m_j = Mean of output membership function in the fifth layer
- σ_j = Variance of output membership function in the fifth layer
- x_j = Net-input to the layer-5 node

The learning process is iterated until an acceptable minimum error between the actual output Y_a and the predicted output Y_p is achieved.

Self-Organized Learning

The Kohonen's feature maps algorithm (Kohonen, 1988) is used here to find the number of membership functions and their respective means and variances. The algorithm is explained next.

For a given set of data $X = \{x_1, x_2, \ldots, x_n)$, initial mean values $m_1, m_2, \ldots, m_k$ are assigned arbitrarily, where $min\ \{x_1, x_2, \ldots, x_n) < m_i < max\ \{x_1, x_2, \ldots, x_n\}$.

The data are then grouped around the initial means according to:

$$|x_j - m_c| = \min_i \{\,|x_j - m_i|\,\} \quad 1 \le i \le k \text{ and } 1 \le j \le n \tag{15}$$

where m_c is the mean to which the datum x_j belongs. The following iterative process optimizes the data grouping and the mean values.

Let $x_j(t)$ be an input and $m_c(t)$ the value of m_c at iteration t (t = 0,1,2,…), then:

$$m_c(t+1) = m_c(t) + \alpha(t)[\,x_j(t) - m_c(t)] \tag{16}$$

if x_j belongs to the group of m_c, and:

$$m_c(t+1) = m_c(t) \tag{17}$$

if x_j does not belong to the group of m_c

$\alpha(t)[0<\alpha(t)<1]$ is a monotonically decreasing scalar learning rate. The iterations stop at either after a certain number of cycles decided by the user or when the condition $|m_c(t+1)-m_c(t)| \le \delta$ is satisfied, where δ is an error limit assigned by the user. The variances of membership functions can be determined by equation 18:

$$\sigma_i = \frac{1}{R}\sqrt{\frac{1}{p_i}\sum_{j=1}^{p_i}(x_j - m_i)^2} \quad 1 \le i \le k \tag{18}$$

where:

- σ_i = variance of membership function *i*
- m_I = mean of membership function *i*
- x_j = observed data sample
- k = total number of membership function nodes
- p_i = total number of data samples in *ith* membership function group
- R = overlap parameter

For a given input or output variable, the number of initial mean values (m_1, m_2, …, m_k) is assigned by trial-and-error. This involves striking a balance between learning time and accuracy. Too small a number results in an oversimplified structure and might therefore adversely affect accuracy. On the other hand, too large a number increases network complexity unnecessarily, resulting in a considerable increase in learning time with very little or no increase in accuracy.

Evolutionary Fuzzy Knowledge Base

Genetic algorithms (GAs) can be used to find or tune rules for an expert system, and expert systems can provide heuristics to improve the performance of a genetic system. For example, GAs can be applied for expert networks to find better membership values or certainty factors, and they can be used to optimize the (design) parameters in (design) problem-solving techniques. Here, we first discuss the former; the latter will be discussed in the next section.

Suppose that a rule is coded as a single chromosome. The rules are packed end-to-end to form the chromosome. Then, a simple GA can be used to evolve a population of chromosomes and yield a most-fit chromosome (a rule), which represents the relationship between the output and input fuzzy variables in rules. Fixed or static rules representing a priori knowledge are excluded from manipulation by the GA operators (crossover, mutation) but are included in the evaluation of a chromosome's fitness. In a simple GA, the length of the chromosome is fixed and thus the number of rules (R_1, R_2, …, R_n) packed in a chromosome is fixed. Therefore, the number of rules must be specified prior to training. A trail-and-error procedure can be used to estimate the number of rules required by running the GA several times with an arbitrarily large number of rules and examining the number of duplicated rules and cut connections. If the fuzzy knowledge based system is under saturated (i.e., contains disconnected or duplicated rules), then the number of rules will be decreased. Figure 4 illustrates a GA-based evolution for finding and tuning rules in the knowledge base.

$R_1, \ldots, R_i, \ldots, R_n$

|

110...,111,...010

|

if $X_1 = A_1$ and $X_2 = A_2$ and ... then $H_1 = C_1$

......

......

EFNN-Based Design Parameter Evolution and Optimization

According to Suh (1990), every design problem may be expressed through a set of design parameters. The design problem could be defined in terms of design parameters and their associative relationships of different formalisms. In every engineering design problem there is a space instantiated by the alternative solutions. It is quite common for these solution

Figure 4. GA-based evolution for rule-finding and tuning

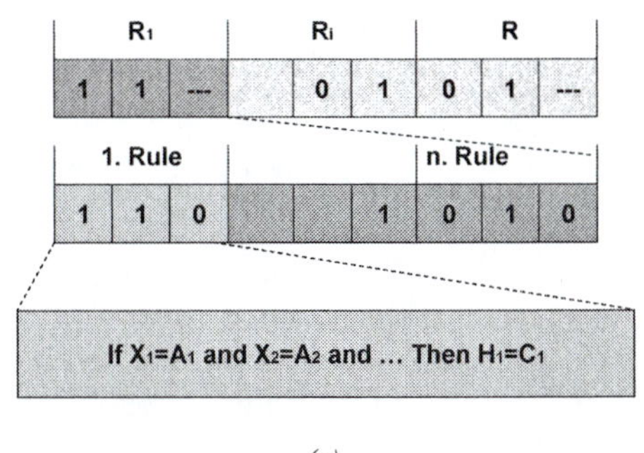

(a)

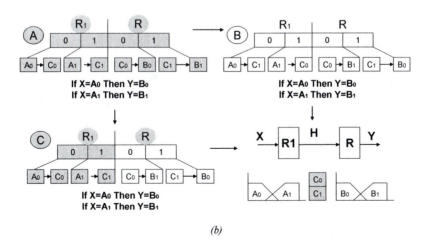

If X=A0 Then Y=B0
If X=A1 Then Y=B1

If X=A0 Then Y=B0
If X=A1 Then Y=B1

If X=A0 Then Y=B0
If X=A1 Then Y=B1

(b)

Figure 4. continued

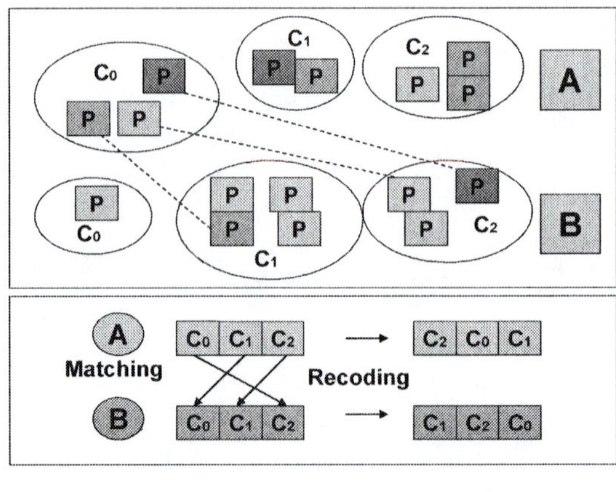

(c)

spaces to be highly non-linear, with discrete solution intervals, while the available design knowledge could be vague and expressed with formalisms other than analytical relations. As such, the optimal design solution must be searched by using a non-gradient-based heuristic algorithm that could avoid local extremes in the solution space, while having the possibility of balancing between speed and robustness.

In this work, based on the soft computing techniques, an EFNN-based design optimization and adaptation approach is used to confront several issues of parametric design, as shown in Figure 5. Genetic algorithms (GA) are deployed to find the optimum solution according to design objectives and custom optimization criteria. The best solutions obtained by the genetic optimization are recorded, and then the neuro-fuzzy or fuzzy neural network is employed to simplify and resolve the problem's complexity by substituting existing associative relations with a fuzzy rule system. Redesign may be performed by searching the optimum solution under the same criteria but using the simplified fuzzy structure.

The GA-based evolutionary neuro-fuzzy approach addresses design as a parametric optimization problem (Saridakis & Dentsoras, 2005). The optimal solution is extracted by varying a set of design parameters. Some of these design parameters are only used for defining other design parameters through associative relations and constraints that are critical for the design performance, noted as performance variables. Normally, the designers only have direct preferences on sets of values for the performance variables. This approach can facilitate: (a) the statement of the performance variables, (b) the solution search by applying preferences on target values for the stated performance variables, and (c) the recording of elite values of these performance variables during the genetic optimization process. The GA optimization results in an optimal solution and a set of "elite" values for variable primary and dependent design parameters (performance variables). This recorded set of values is used for training the fuzzy neural network that associates the primary performance variables with dependent performance variables without any intermediate design parameters or associations. The initial

Figure 5. GA-based optimization and neuro-fuzzy adaptation in design

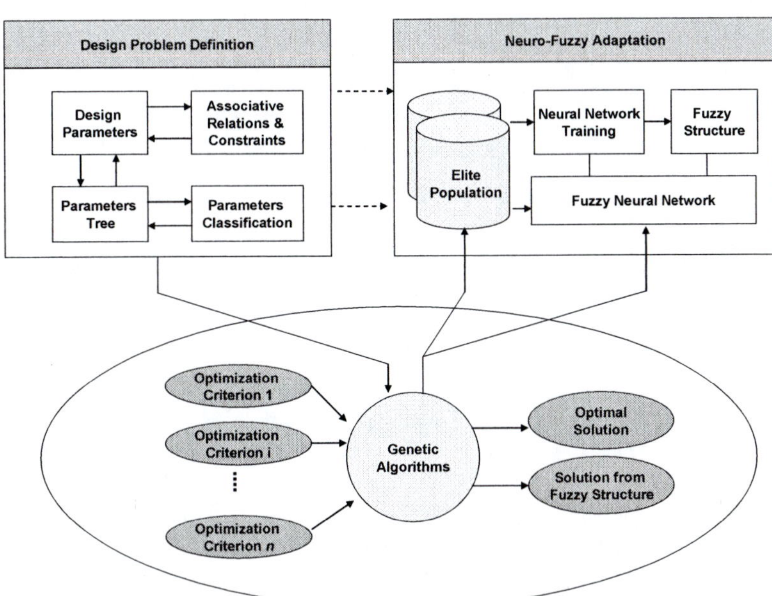

Figure 6. Design parameter hierarchical tree

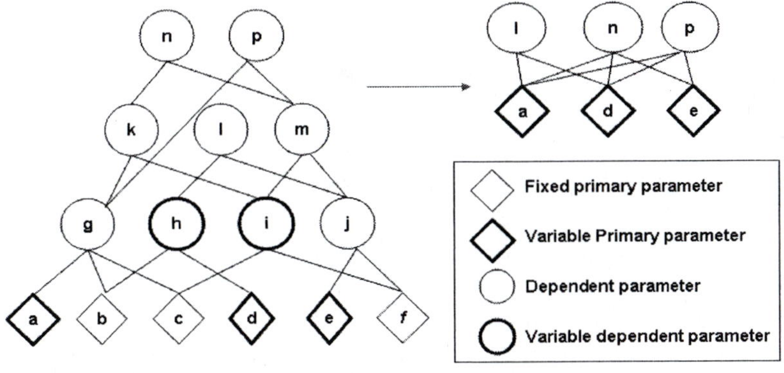

design problem is considered as evolved into a simplified fuzzy digraph with two-levels (Saridakis & Dentsoras, 2005) (see Figure 6).

To validate the algorithm and make a comparison, several techniques have been tested, such as ant colony, simulated annealing, tabu search, memetic algorithms, and pattern search. The results show that GAs were classified somewhere in the average. If used in combination with a traditional optimization technique, their adjustability in trading off speed with accuracy can be enhanced and their performance can be improved significantly. The GA is deployed only for optimization purposes, and they do not participate actively in the learning process. As far as the learning process is concerned, there are also many alternative approaches that can be deployed. It is true that inductive logic programming could deliver a design model suitable for redesign (despite the low learning rate). Other approaches based on hybrid neural networks could also be used. The neuro-fuzzy learning presented here dominated because of the following salient features (Saridakis & Dentsoras, 2005):

1. The fuzzy rules delivered by the trained ANN are extracted from elite solutions.
2. The fuzzy rules can be further calibrated rationally in redesign.
3. The fuzzy rules that model the simplified design model can also be used in a collaborative framework among designers with aggregation of the existing fuzzy sets under a specific aggregation strategy.

System Implementation

The hybrid intelligent design system (HIDS) is basically a combination of various independent and self-contained intelligent modules/subsystems coordinated by a control mechanism to perform all the sub-tasks in the design process. Each of the intelligent modules itself is

Figure 7. HIDS-EFNN design system implementation environment

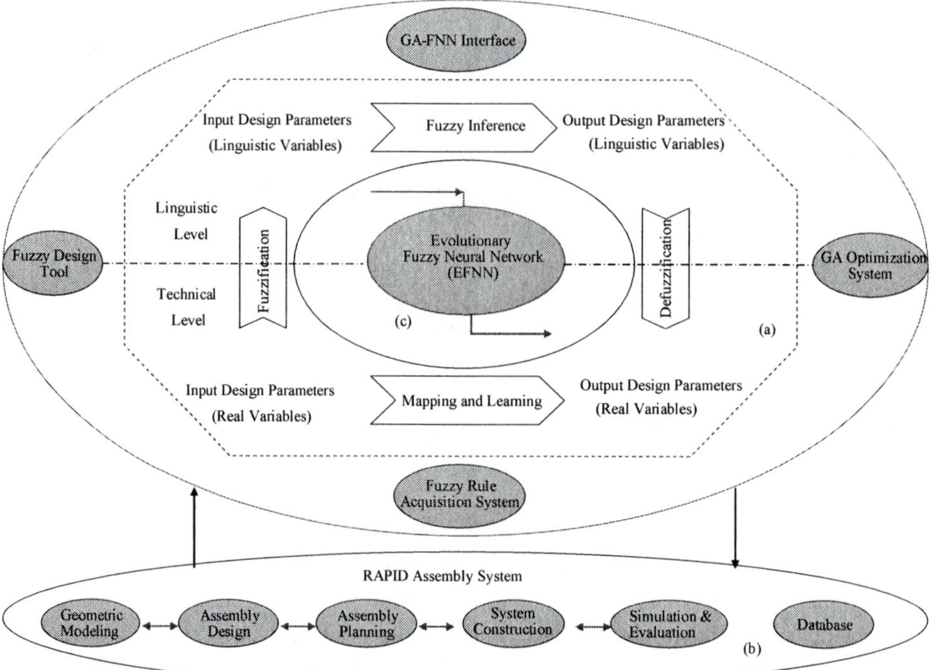

a HIS of AI techniques, working as a unified system to perform the sub-task for which it is designed. To facilitate the designer to solve the design problems, an evolutionary neuro-fuzzy (EFNN)-based HIDS, HIDS-EFNN, is developed, as shown in Figure 7. HIDS-EFNN is implemented through integrating modules or sub-systems such as: an FNN modeling and mapping system, a GA optimization system, a GA-FNN interface, a fuzzy design tool, a fuzzy rule acquisition system, and a CAD system. The fuzzy rule acquisition system is actually a knowledge learning system. Here, the self-developed RAPID assembly system (Zha, 1997, 1999, 2003, 2004d) is used as the CAD system for test purpose. It is noted that, with appropriate API, commercial CAD systems can also be supported. RAPID assembly system was originally developed for virtual assembly prototyping and planning with modules such as geometric modeling, assembly design, assembly sequence planning, assembly system construction, simulation and evaluation, ergonomic database (e.g., anthropometric data), and so forth. The application examples will be presented.

Applications and Case Studies

To verify the evolutionary neuro-fuzzy (FNN) model and the developed system, HIDS-EFNN, three case studies were carried out: (1) design of a four-linkage planar mechanism, (2) workstation table customization design, and (3) prediction of product performance.

Mechanism Design

The design of a four-linkage planar mechanism could be represented by four design parameters, that is, linkage lengths $a=a'$, $b=b'$ (unit), and angles c, $d=d' \in [0,180°]$. The design constraints require that linkage *b* does not intersect linkage *b*. Thus, the design has two patterns. If linkage *b* intersects *b*', the design is non-rational ("1" type), otherwise, it is rational ("0"). In fact, the design problem can be described as follows:

1. The rational design satisfies either: *b* and *b*' never intersect; or the intersecting point is not on the *b* or *b*' if intersects.
2. The non-rational design satisfies both: *b* and *b*' intersect; and the intersecting point is on the *b* or *b*' if intersects.
3. The distance $D_{bb'}$ between the intersecting point and the end point of b or b' can be used to describe the rationality degree of design (*r*), for example, very rational, more rational, less rational, and so forth, which corresponds to [0, 1].

Figure 8 shows the rational and non-rational designs, respectively. Some fuzzy rules (Figure 9) for the problem were derived as follows:

Figure 8. Four-linkage mechanism designs with the FNN model

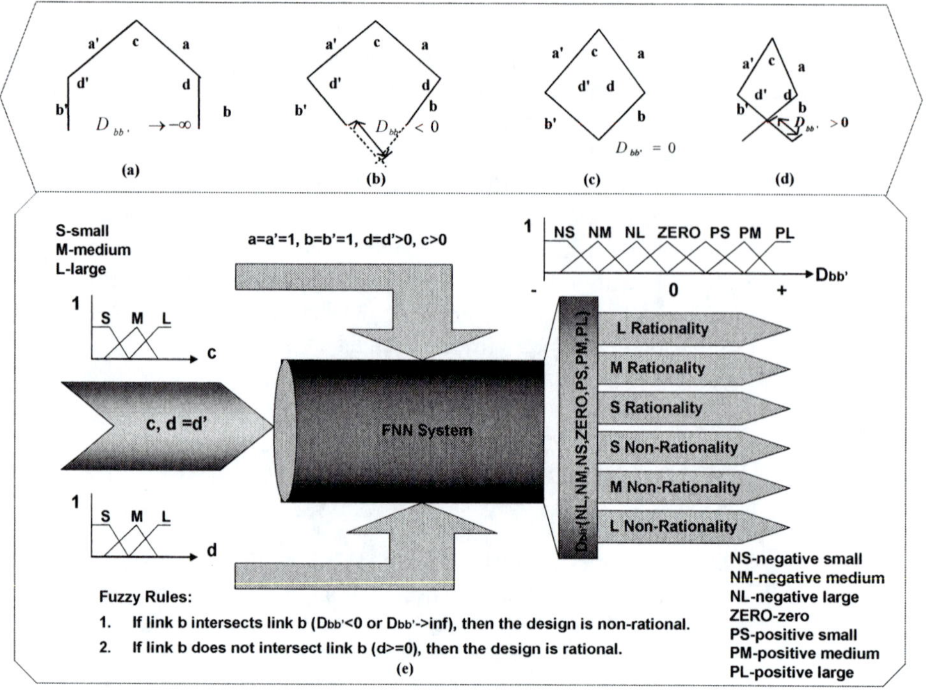

Fuzzy Rules:

R_1:

IF *a* is L (large) and *b* is L (large)
c is S (small) and *d* is L (large)
THEN $D_{bb'}$ is NL (negative large) and
r (the rationality degree) is PL (positive large).

R_2:

IF *c* is S (small) and *d* is M (medium)
THEN $D_{bb'}$ is PM(positive medium) and
r (the rationality degree) is NL (negative large).

……

A 5-input-1-ouput FNN can be constructed by using the proposed approach. The evolutionary neuro-fuzzy (EFNN) model is used to classify and evaluate the mechanism; the training patterns/samples are partially listed in Table 1. After training, the model can evaluate or

Figure 9. Design and control rules

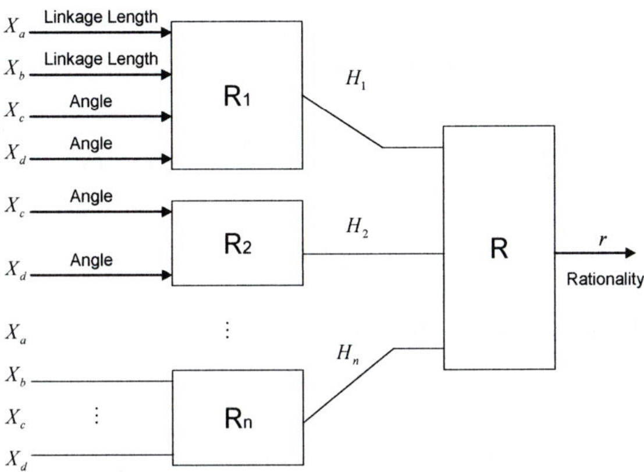

Figure 10. Redesign process using EFNN

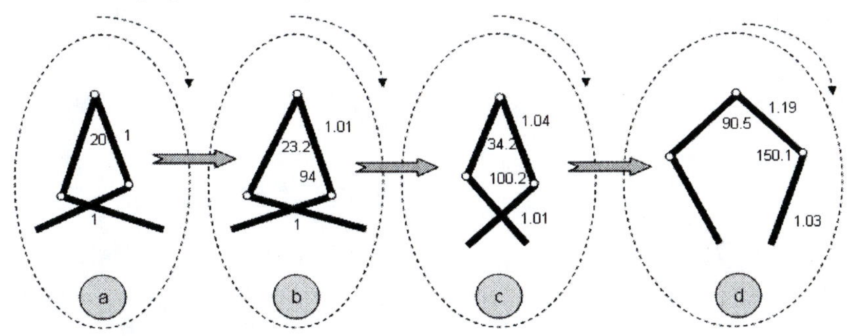

Table 1. Training patterns/samples

a	b	c	d	$D_{bb'}$	r
1	1	20	90	0.824	NL
1	1	20	170	$-\infty$	PL
1	1	100	90	-0.192	PS
1	1	100	170	-1.192	PL
1	1	20	91	0.823	NL
...	...	...	...		...

classify the non-rational and rational designs, and further rectify or modify or redesign the non-rational preliminary designs into the rational ones. Figure 10 shows a design process of using the EFNN model to modify/optimize the non-rational preliminary designs (e.g., a=1, b=1, c=20, d=90) into rational ones.

Workstation Table Customization Design

The essence of mass customization (MC) is to satisfy customers' requirements precisely without increasing costs, regardless of how unique these requirements may be. The design for the MC problem can be defined as: given a set of fuzzy functional requirements (FR) to generate and select the design solutions (DS) that can satisfy the input requirements. Figure

Figure 11. The HIDS-FNN design system used for conceptual workstation table customization design

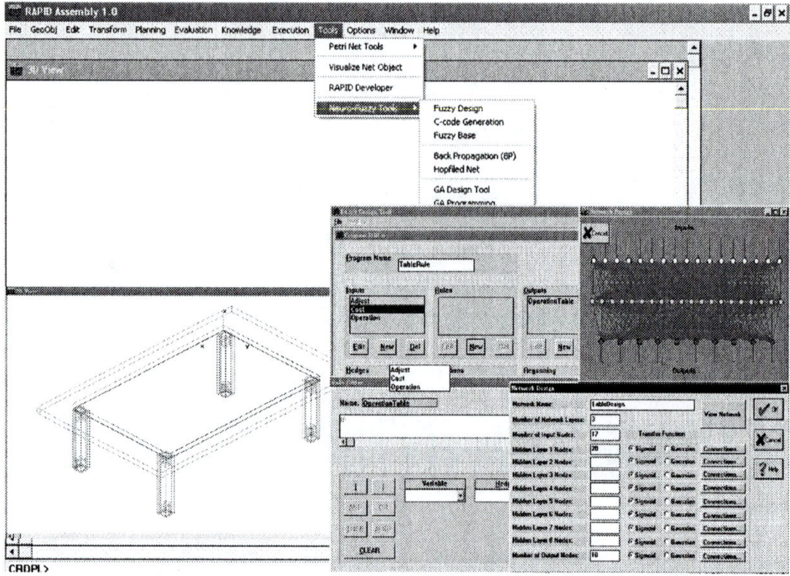

Table 2. Functional requirements, design constraints, and design solutions

Functional Requirements (FR)	FR={fr_i, i=1,2,...,6) ={adjustable, moveable, foldable, stability, stackable, comfortable}
Design Constraints (DC)	DC={dc_j, j=1,2, ...,11}={cost, size, weight, dining, office, workstation, home, classroom, public, typing, aesthetic}
Design Solutions (DS)	DS={ds_k, k=1,2,...,10}={operational table, executive table, contract table, simple office table, office table, stacking table, folding table, long table, classroom table, side table}

11 shows the HIDS-EFNN design system for conceptual workstation table customization design. To experiment with the concept for designing various classes of tables, we assume that the design has six generic functional requirements (FR), 11 design constraints (DC), and 10 design solutions (DS) generated (Table 2). Each design solution must satisfy a certain set of functional requirements and design constraints.

$$
\mathrm{M(FR\times DS)} = \begin{array}{r} \\ \mu_{fr_1}\text{(adjustable)} \\ \mu_{fr_2}\text{(moveable)} \\ \mu_{fr_3}\text{(foldable)} \\ \mu_{fr_4}\text{(stability)} \\ \mu_{fr_5}\text{(stackable)} \\ \mu_{fr_6}\text{(comfortable)} \end{array}
\begin{array}{c} \begin{array}{cccccccccc} ds_1 & ds_2 & ds_3 & ds_4 & ds_5 & ds_6 & ds_7 & ds_8 & ds_9 & ds_{10} \end{array} \\
\begin{pmatrix} 0 & 1.0 & 0 & 0.8 & 1.0 & 0 & 0 & 0 & 0 & 0 \\ 1.0 & 1.0 & 0 & 0 & 1.0 & 0 & 0 & 0 & 0 & 0 \\ 0 & 0 & 0 & 0 & 0 & 0 & 1.0 & 0 & 0 & 0 \\ 0 & 0 & 1.0 & 1.0 & 1.0 & 1.0 & 1.0 & 1.0 & 1.0 & 1.0 \\ 0 & 0 & 0 & 0 & 0 & 1.0 & 0 & 0 & 0 & 0 \\ 0 & 1.0 & 0 & 0 & 0 & 0 & 0 & 1.0 & 0 & 1.0 \end{pmatrix} \end{array}
$$

$$
\mathrm{M(DC\times DS)} = \begin{array}{r} \\ \mu_{dc_1}\text{(cost)} \\ \mu_{dc_1}\text{(size)} \\ \mu_{dc_1}\text{(weight)} \\ \mu_{dc_1}\text{(dining)} \\ \mu_{dc_1}\text{(office)} \\ \mu_{dc_1}\text{(relaxtion)} \\ \mu_{dc_1}\text{(home)} \\ \mu_{dc_1}\text{(classroom)} \\ \mu_{dc_1}\text{(public)} \\ \mu_{dc_1}\text{(typing)} \\ \mu_{dc_1}\text{(aesthetic)} \end{array}
\begin{array}{c} \begin{array}{cccccccccc} ds_1 & ds_2 & ds_3 & ds_4 & ds_5 & ds_6 & ds_7 & ds_8 & ds_9 & ds_{10} \end{array} \\
\begin{pmatrix} 0.9 & 0 & 0.8 & 1.0 & 0 & 1.0 & 1.0 & 0 & 1.0 & 0 \\ 0 & 0 & 0 & 0 & 0 & 1.0 & 1.0 & 0 & 1.0 & 0 \\ 0 & 0 & 1.0 & 1.0 & 0 & 1.0 & 1.0 & 0 & 0 & 0 \\ 0 & 0 & 0 & 0 & 0 & 0.8 & 0 & 0 & 0 & 0 \\ 1.0 & 1.0 & 1.0 & 1.0 & 1.0 & 0 & 0 & 0 & 0 & 0 \\ 0 & 0.7 & 0 & 0 & 0 & 0 & 0 & 1.0 & 0 & 0.5 \\ 0 & 0.3 & 0.5 & 0 & 0 & 0.5 & 1.0 & 1.0 & 0 & 1.0 \\ 0 & 0 & 0 & 0 & 0 & 0 & 0 & 1.0 & 0 & 0 \\ 0 & 0 & 0.5 & 1.0 & 0 & 0.5 & 0.8 & 1.0 & 0 & 0 \\ 1 & 0 & 0 & 0 & 0.8 & 0 & 0 & 0 & 0 & 0 \\ 0 & 1.0 & 0 & 0 & 0 & 0 & 0 & 0.8 & 0 & 1.0 \end{pmatrix} \end{array}
$$

$$
\mathrm{M(DS\times DS)} = \begin{array}{r} \\ ds_1 \\ ds_2 \\ ds_3 \\ ds_4 \\ ds_5 \\ ds_6 \\ ds_7 \\ ds_8 \\ ds_9 \\ ds_{10} \end{array}
\begin{array}{c} \begin{array}{cccccccccc} ds_1 & ds_2 & ds_3 & ds_4 & ds_5 & ds_6 & ds_7 & ds_8 & ds_9 & ds_{10} \end{array} \\
\begin{pmatrix} 1.0 & 0.3 & 0 & 0.7 & 0 & 0 & 0 & 0 & 0 & 0 \\ 0.3 & 1.0 & 0 & 0 & 0.6 & 0 & 0 & 0 & 0 & 0 \\ 0 & 0 & 1.0 & 0.7 & 0 & 0 & 0 & 0 & 0 & 0 \\ 0 & 0 & 0.7 & 1.0 & 0 & 0 & 0 & 0 & 0 & 0 \\ 0.7 & 0.5 & 0 & 0 & 1.0 & 0 & 0 & 0 & 0 & 0.8 \\ 0 & 0 & 0 & 0.6 & 0 & 1.0 & 0 & 0 & 0 & 0.6 \\ 0 & 0 & 0 & 0 & 0 & 0 & 1.0 & 0 & 0 & 0 \\ 0 & 0.5 & 0 & 0 & 0 & 0 & 0 & 1.0 & 0 & 0.6 \\ 0 & 0 & 0 & 0.6 & 0 & 0 & 0 & 0 & 1.0 & 0 \\ 0 & 0 & 0 & 0 & 0 & 0 & 0 & 0.6 & 0 & 1.0 \end{pmatrix} \end{array}
$$

Based on the fuzzy model, the fuzzy relationship matrix between requirements, constraints, and final solutions can be represented as matrices M(FR×DS), M(DC×DS), and M(DS×DS) in the fuzzy synthetic decision model. We further assume that the workstation table will be designed based on the crisp set of 10 pre-design tables above. For instance, the input requirement for designing a table may be stated as:

Design a very comfortable table that can be used more or less in operation and should cost $100 or so.

Thus, the functional requirements and constraints can be derived as: FR={fr_1}={table must be very comfortable}, DC={dc_1, dc_2}, dc_1=use more or less in operation; and dc_2=cost about $100. After requirements and design constraints are defined, the problem is to generate design solutions.

To solve the design problem formulated, the fuzzy synthetic model can be used to map a fuzzy set of requirements to a crisp set of table design alternatives. After analyzing various tables and discussing with marketing groups, fuzzy rules regarding the characteristics of tables can be identified. For instance, we have the following rule:

IF the desired table must be highly adjustable
& the cost is an important consideration
& it must be used mostly in a workstation
& it must be used for typing,
THEN the table is an office table.

From this rule, the membership function values can be derived: fr_1=highly adjustable, μ_{fr_1}=0.9; dc_1=the cost is an important consideration, μ_{dc_1}=0.8; dc_2=mostly to be used in workstation, μ_{dc_2}=1.0; dc_3=use for typing, μ_{dc_3}=0.5.

In the defined EFNN model, the input layer is designed to have 17 neurons, one neuron for every requirement. Each degree of membership is assigned to a separated neuron. The output layer is designed to have 11 neurons, one for every class of table. For example, the functional requirements and design constraints for an executive table are represented as:

Table 3. Experimental results

No	Functional Requirements	Design Solutions	Actual Designs	Remark
1	{0.7/fr_2, 0.5/fr_{16}}	ds_1, ds_5	ds_1	Operational table
2	{0.9/fr_1, 0.09/fr_{12}, 0.9/fr_{17}}	ds_2, ds_5	ds_2	Executive table
3	{0.85/fr_6, 0.9/fr_7}	ds_3, ds_{10}	ds_2	Error
4	{0.8/fr_4, 1.0/fr_7}	ds_3, ds_4, ds_6	ds_3	Contract table
5	{0.8/fr_1, 1.0/fr_2, 0.5/fr_{16}}	ds_1, ds_5	ds_5	Office table
6	{0.8/fr_1, 0.5/fr_2, 0.6/fr_7, 1.0/fr_{11}}	ds_4	ds_4	Simple office table
7	{0.9/fr_5, 0.8/fr_{10}}	ds_6	ds_6	Stacking table
8	{0.4/fr_5, 1.0/fr_{10}}	ds_{10}	ds_{10}	Side table
9	{0.4/fr_5, 0.5/fr_{10}}	ds_3, ds_6, ds_{10}	None	Error
10	{0.8/fr_4, 1.0/fr_{12}, 0.8/fr_{13}}	ds_3, ds_8, ds_{10}	ds_{10}	Classroom table
...	...	...	...	...

A_2= (1.0, 1.0, 0, 0, 0, 0, 1.0, 0, 0, 0, 1.0, 0.7, 0.3, 0, 0, 0, 1.0). The first value corresponds to f_{r_1} (ability to adjust the table), the second to f_{r_2} (ability to move the table), and so on. The design output for the executive table is represented as: B_2= (0.3, 1, 0, 0, 0.6, 0, 0, 0, 0, 0, 0). To experiment with the system, 10 fuzzy rules, one rule for each class of table, have been created. To test the system, 10 design scenarios with known solutions have been created, as described in Table 3. From the test results, the system was capable of successfully generating nine correct solutions. The overall system accuracy rate is better than 90%.

Performance Prediction/Evaluation for Hydraulic Products

Conventional evaluating/predicting methods suffer from several deficiencies and limitations, which make them inadequate for virtual product design in today's manufacturing requirements (Li et al., 2005). First, the design and manufacturing environment is so complex that an explicit model cannot always express the relationships between the outputs and the input factors. The conventional prediction methods like multiple regression models cannot be used. Second, design and manufacturing processes require a high accuracy to establish the relationship between machine inputs and outputs. Usually, conventional prediction methods cannot meet the accuracy requirements, especially when the data involved exhibit irregular pattern. It is, therefore, desirable to have a new evaluating/predicting method that can overcome these deficiencies and limitations.

The third example is to use the evolutionary neuro-fuzzy (EFNN) model to predict/evaluate product performance for virtual prototyping of the hydraulic system (Figure 12). The behavioral attributes of hydraulic components (pump, valve, cylinder, etc.) contribute most to the composable simulation for performance evaluation of the hydraulic systems (Xiang, Fok, & Yap, 2001; Xiang, Fok, & Thimmm, 2004). In this example, the EFNN

Figure 12. Virtual hydraulic components and systems (e-RAPID)

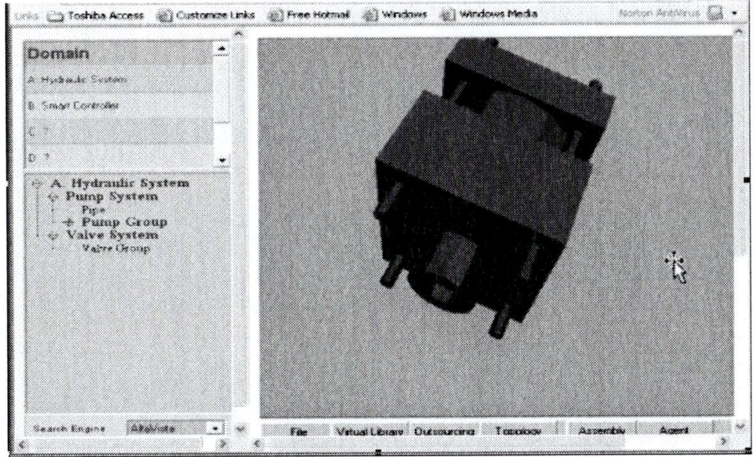

model is used to represent the behaviors of virtual components (pump and relief valve). For example, the pump experiences pressure variations during operation which affect the delivered flow-rate. Therefore, the virtual pump's behavior model should consider the dynamics relationship between the pressure and the flow-rate. The measured transient value of pressure (P) and flow-rate through pump (Q_p) are used to train the EFNN model for the virtual pump. Likewise the measured pressure (P) and flow-rate through relief valve (Q_r) are also used to train the EFNN model for the virtual relief valve. Hence, two final trained EFNN models can eventually be obtained for behavior representations of the virtual pump and virtual relief valve.

Specifically, in this application, we assume that five input variables such as media (fluid) material (x_1), size (x_2), running time (x_3), temperature (x_4) and flow-rate (x_5) have influence on the overall performance (pressure) index (y) of the hydraulic system in virtual prototyping. A total of 10,000 sample data sets are obtained through simulation using the simulation software package. The first 5,000 data samples obtained are used for training and the rest for testing. The data samples are first normalized to the range of [0, 1]. The number of membership function nodes is set as follows for each input variable after studying the distribution patterns of the data samples: 10 nodes for $\boldsymbol{x}_1$, 4 for $\boldsymbol{x}_2$, 10 for $\boldsymbol{x}_3$, 3 for $\boldsymbol{x}_4$, 4 for $\boldsymbol{x}_5$, and 3 for $\boldsymbol{y}$. Therefore, the maximum number of possible fuzzy rules was 4,800 which is 10×4×10×3×4. Membership functions are constructed for each variable. For example, two types of membership distribution functions: The triangular and the normal distribution functions are used for $\boldsymbol{x}_1$ before and after learning with an overlap parameter of 0.4. After the FNN model has been trained, test data are fed to the trained network to predict/evaluate the hydraulic system performance (pressure).

Figure 13 shows partial predicted results against the simulated results and the experimental results. R^2 is defined as a measure of the degree of fit between the estimated and actual values of the output target:

$$R^2 = \frac{[\sum (Y_i - \bar{Y})(\hat{Y}_i - \bar{Y})]^2}{\sum (Y_i - \bar{Y})^2 \sum (\hat{Y}_i - \bar{Y})^2} \qquad (0 \le R^2 \le 1) \tag{19}$$

Figure 13. Testing results of hydraulic system performance (pressure)

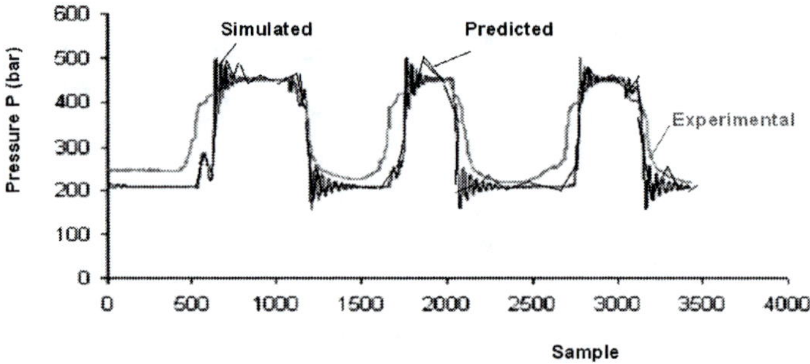

Table 4. Comparison the pressure between FNN and the regression model

Data Set	Y_A	Y_{EFNN}	Y_R
1	250.501	250.416	288.991
2	250.503	250.544	287.063
3	250.504	250.667	285.133
4	251.030	250.793	283.206
5	251.010	250.917	281.277
⋮	⋮	⋮	⋮
10000	472.000	472.125	459.099
Measures	**MSE**	**0.9471**	**83.5781**
	R^2	**0.9962**	**0.7640**

where Y is the hydraulic component or system performance (pressure), Y_i is the actual Y, $\hat{Y}_i$ is the estimated Y, and $\overline{Y}$ is the mean of Y. The error measures for the 5000 sets of test data are: MSE = 0.9468; R^2 = 0.9957.

Multiple regression models are traditional predicting models that are used to identify independent variables and their relationships with the dependent variable, and predict the independent variables for their future (Damodar, 1995). The multiple regression models used in this application were built using the commercial software package. The same data sets of the application were used. In multiple regression modeling, three evaluation measures are used: t-Test, F-Test and R^2. t-Test is used to test the significance of regression coefficients, F-Test the significance of the sum of the estimated coefficients, and $R^2 \in [0,1]$ is the degree of association between output variable Y and all the explanatory variables $\{X_i\}$. When $R^2 = 1$, the fitted regression line explains 100% of the variation in Y. On the other hand, when $R^2 = 0$, the model does not explain any of the variation in Y. The closer is R^2 to 1, the better the fit of the model.

We compared the performances of evolutionary neuro-fuzzy (EFNN) model and the multi-order regression model with the simulated pressure in Table 4. Y_A is the actual simulated hydraulic system performance; Y_{EFNN} is the predicted hydraulic system performance by the EFNN model; Y_R is the predicted performance by the regression model. The results show that the EFNN model performs much better than the multi-order regression model in terms of MSE and R^2 values. The superior performance of the EFNN may be attributed to the effectiveness of the EFNN architecture. The result of the application agrees with the general observation that multiple regression models are less accurate in cases where the predicting trend is irregular as is the case in this work.

Conclusion

In this chapter, a soft computing integrated and hybrid intelligent framework was first proposed for engineering design and simulation. Based on the hybrid intelligent system technique, an evolutionary neuro-fuzzy (evolutionary fuzzy neural network, EFNN) model which is basically an evolutionary five-layer fuzzy rule-based neural network has been developed and used for virtual product design for customization and product performance prediction in the virtual design environment. Thus, the EFNN model can be used as a toolkit for virtual product design and simulation. It brings trade-off analysis into the design process, allowing engineers to adopt a "predict and prevent" approach. Providing information about predicted physical effects, virtual development software facilitates design planning to optimize performance with fewer iterations and prototypes. By bringing multi-domain analysis to the engineer's desktop, the virtual prototyping system can optimize design performance, eliminate iterations, and shorten time to production. It can dramatically reduce the number and cost of physical prototypes, and accelerates verification of product design and development. The chapter also proposed a new neuro-fuzzy hybrid intelligent approach/system to the design for mass customization. The developed soft computing based design system, HIDS-EFNN, facilitates the application of the proposed EFNN model for design support. In summary, the proposed hybrid intelligent approach and the developed system in this work provides a better solution to the problems of virtual product design, simulation and mass customization.

Acknowledgment

Bulk of the work reported here was conducted at Nanyang Technological University and Singapore Institute of Manufacturing Technology, Singapore.

Note

No approval or endorsement by the National Institute of Standards and Technology is intended or implied.

References

Akman, V., ten Hagen, P. J. W., & Tomiyama, T. (1994). Desirable functionalties of intelligent CAD systems. In Dagli & Kusiak (Eds.), *Intelligent systems in design and manufacturing* (pp. 119-138).

Akman, V., ten Hagen, P. J. W., & Veerkamp, P. J. (Eds.). (1989). *Intelligent CAD systems II: Implementational issues.* Springer-Verlag.

Azoff, E. M. (1994). *Neural network time series forecasting of financial markets.* John Wiley & Sons.

Bahrami, A., & Dagli, C. H. (1993). From fuzzy input requirements to crisp design. *International Journal of Advanced Manufacturing Technology, 8*, 52-60.

Bahrami, A., Lynch, M., & Dagli, C. H. (1994). Integrating product and process design through intelligent systems. In C. H. Dagli & A. Kusiak (Eds.), *Intelligent systems in design and manufacturing* (pp. 237-260).

Bateman, R. E., Bowden, R. G., Gogg, T. J., Harrell, C. R., & Mott, J. R. A. (1997). *System improvement using simulation* (5th ed.). Promodel Corporation.

Chen, C., & Occea, L. G. (1999). *Soft computing for concurrent product design evaluation under a blackboard environment.* Paper presented at the 3rd International Conference on Engineering Design and Automation (EDA '99), Vancouver, Canada.

Dagli, C. H. (1994). *Artificial neural networks for intelligent manufacturing.* Chapman & Hall.

Damodar, N. G. (1995). *Basic econometrics* (3rd ed.). McGraw-Hill.

fuzzyTECH 4.22 (1996). *Reference manual.*

Goonatilake, S., & Khebbal, S. (1995). *Intelligent hybrid systems.* John-Wiley & Sons.

Horikawa, S., Furuhasshi, T., & Uchikawa, Y. (1992). On fuzzy modeling using fuzzy neural networks with the back-propagation algorithms. *IEEE Trans. on Neural Networks, 3*(5), 801-806.

Jang, J.-S. Roger. (1993). ANFIS: Adaptive-network-based fuzzy inference system. *IEEE Transactions on System Man Cybernetics, 23*, 665-685.

Kang, S. Y. (1991). *An investigation of the use of feedforward neural networks for forecasting.* PhD thesis, Kent State University.

Kohonen, T. (1988). *Self-organization and associative memory.* Berlin: Springer-Verlag.

Kosko, B. (1992). *Neural networks and fuzzy system.* Prentice-Hall International Editions.

Law, A. M., & Kelton, W. D. (1991). *Simulation modeling & analysis* (2nd ed.). McGraw-Hill International Editions.

Leekwijck, W. V., & Kerre, E. E. (1999). Defuzzification: Criteria and classification. *Fuzzy Sets and Systems, 108*, 159-178.

Leekwijck, W. V., & Kerre, E. E. (2001). Continuity focused choice of Maxima: Yet another defuzzification method. *Fuzzy Sets and Systems, 122*, 303-314.

Leonard, J. A., & Kramer, M. A. (1991). Improvement of the back-propagation algorithm for training neural networks. *Computer Chemical Engineering, 14*, 337-341.

Li, X., Ang, C. L., & Gay, R. (2005). An intelligent hybrid system for business forecasting. In C. T. Leondes (Ed.), *Intelligent knowledge-based systems: Business and technology in new millennium* (vol. IV). Kluwer Academic Publishers.

Li, X., Tay, A., & Ang, C. L. (2000). *A fuzzy neural network for virtual equipment design.* Research report. SIMTECH, Singapore.

Medesker, L. R. (1995). *Hybrid intelligent systems.* Kluwer Academic Publishers.

Powell, D. J., Skolnick, M. M., & Tong, S. S. (1995). A unified approach for engineering design. In Goonatillake & Khebbal (Eds.), *Intelligent hybrid systems* (pp. 107-120).

Refenes, A.-P. (1995). *Neural networks in the capital markets.* Chichester: John Wiley & Sons.

Rumelhart, D. E., Hinton, G. E., & Williams, R. J. (1986). Learning internal representations by error propagation. In *Parallel distributed processing* (vol. 1). Cambridge, MA: MIT Press.

Saridakis, K. M., & Dentsoras A. J. (2005, July 4-15). *Evolutionary neuro-fuzzy modeling in parametric design.* Presentation, 1st I*PROMS Virtual Int. Conf. on Intell. Production Machines & Systems, IPROMS.

Su, D. (1999). Design automation with the aids of multiple artificial intelligent techniques. *Concurrent Engineering: Research and Application, 7*(1), 23-30.

Su, D., & Wakelam, M. (1999). Evolutionary optimization within an intelligent hybrid system for design integration. *AIEDAM-Artificial Intelligence for Engineering Design, Analysis and Manufacturing, 13*(5), 351-363.

Suh, N. P. (1990). *The principle of design.* New York: Oxford University Press.

Wang, J., & Takefuji, Y. (1993). *Neural networks in design and manufacturing.* Singapore: World Scientific.

Xiang, W., Fok, S. C., & Yap, F. F. (2001). A fuzzy neural network approach to model hydraulic component from input-output data. *International Journal of Fluid Power, 2*(1), 37-47.

Xiang, W., Fok, S. C., & Thimmm, G. (2004). Agent-based composable simulation for virtual prototyping of fluid power system. *Computer in Industry, 54*(3), 237-251.

Yager, R. R., & Zadeh, L. A. (Eds.). (1991). *An introduction to fuzzy logic applications in intelligent systems.* Kluwer Academic Publishers.

Zadeh, L. A. (1965). Fuzzy sets. *Information and control, 8.*

Zadeh, L. A. (1994). Fuzzy logic, neural networks and soft computing. *Communication of ACM, 37*(3), 7784.

Zarefar, H., & Goulding, J. R. (1992). Neural networks in design of products: A case study. In A. Kusiak (Ed.), *Intelligent design and manufacturing* (pp. 179-201). John Wiley & Sons.

Zha, X. F. (1997). *Integrated intelligent design and assembly planning.* Research report. School of Mechanical and Production Engineering, Nanyang Technological University.

Zha, X. F. (2003). Soft computing framework for intelligent human-machine system design, simulation and optimization. *Soft Computing, 7*, 184-198

Zha, X. F. (2004a). A hybrid cross-mapping neural network model for computational intelligent design. *International Journal of Knowledge-based and Intelligent Engineering Systems, 8*(1), 17-26.

Zha, X. F. (2004b). Artificial intelligence and integrated intelligent systems in product design and development. In C. T. Leondes (Ed.), *Intelligent knowledge-based systems: Business and technology in new millennium* (vol. IV). Kluwer Academic Publishers.

Zha, X. F. (2004c, December 5-8). Hybrid intelligent systems in engineering design: A neuro-fuzzy model and its applications. The 4th International Conference on Hybrid Intelligent Systems (HIS'04), Kitakyushu, Japan.

Zha, X. F. (2004d). AI-supported Web-based virtual prototyping and planning for assembly. *The 14th International Conference on Flexible Automation and Intelligent Manufacturing,* Toronto.

Zha, X. F. (2005). Soft computing in engineering design: A fuzzy neural network model for virtual product design. In *Proceedings of Online World Conference on Soft Computing in Industrial Applications (WSC9), Advances in Soft Computing Series.* Germany: Springer Verlag.

Zha, X. F., & Lim, S. Y. E. (2002). Soft computing framework for intelligent human-machine system design and optimization (vol. 1). In C.T. Leondes (Ed.), *Intelligent systems: Technology and applications.* USA: CRC Press.

Zha, X. F., & Lim, S.Y. E. (2003). Intelligent design and planning of manual assembly workstation: A neuro-fuzzy approach. *Computers & Industrial Engineering, 44*, 611-632.

Zha, X. F., Li, L. L, & Lim, S. Y. E. (2004). A multi-agent intelligent environment for rapid assembly design, planning and simulation. In *Proceedings of 2004 ASME DETC/CIE* (Paper no. DETC-CIE57713).

Zurada, J. M. (1992). *Introduction to artificial neural system.* West Publishing Company.

Chapter XVIII

Document-Driven Design for Distributed CAD Services

Yan Wang, University of Central Florida, USA

Abstract

Current CAD systems only support interactive geometry generation, which is not ideal for distributed engineering services in enterprise-to-enterprise collaboration with a generic thin-client service-oriented architecture. This chapter presents a new feature-based modeling mechanism, document-driven design, to enable batch mode geometry construction for distributed CAD systems. A semantic feature model is developed to represent informative and communicative design intent. Feature semantics is explicitly captured as trinary relation, which provides good extensibility and prevents semantics loss. Data interoperability between domains is enhanced by schema mapping and multi-resolution semantics. This mechanism aims to enable asynchronous communication in distributed CAD environments with ease of design alternative evaluation and reuse, and improved system throughput and utilization.

Introduction

With the recent occurrence of outsourcing, collaborative product development among designers, manufacturers, suppliers, vendors, and other stakeholders is one of the keys for manufacturers to improve product quality, reduce cost, and shorten time-to-market in today's global competition. Collaborative design is the new design process where multidisciplinary stakeholders participate in design decision-making and share product information across enterprise boundaries in an Internet-enabled distributed environment.

Different from traditional standalone CAD systems, interaction between users and systems in collaborative design is a new challenge. Usually software systems may run in two modes: interactive mode, in which commands are entered and executed one at a time; and batch mode, in which commands are listed in a batch file sequentially and execution of the batch file finishes all commands automatically without user interaction. The issue of batch mode geometry generation for distributed CAD is discussed in this chapter. Current CAD systems only support interactive geometry generation. CAD users create geometric model by defining features step by step. These CAD systems can become fat clients in a distributed CAD environment in which clients perform the bulk of data processing operations locally. However, in a simple Web-based environment, thin-client CAD tools mainly with visualization functions cannot perform complex editing tasks locally. The majority of data processing requests are sent to the server. Synchronous communication will become the bottleneck of the overall system performance. Thus, synchronous and interactive model generation is not ideal for a distributed CAD system in which thin-client infrastructure is used in regular enterprise-to-enterprise collaboration.

Intense human involvement is a challenge to automate the geometry creation process. Usually as the first step of design implementation, geometry creation heavily depends on engineers' skills using CAD tools. In contrast, some other design processes, such as data translation, mesh model generation, finite element analysis and simulation, and process planning, can be done in batch mode with little human intervention. Batch mode processing can increase throughput of tools and reduce the cost of service providers. It also reduces human errors and enables better design data management and knowledge reuse.

Automation of the geometry creation process will enable the geometric modeling process to be easily incorporated in a distributed CAD environment such that the work load of the client and communication channel can be both reduced. It will enable an integrated automation loop of CAD, CAE, and optimization in the design alternative evaluation. In this chapter, we propose a new geometry generation mechanism, document-driven design, for batch mode feature-based geometric modeling considering ease of communication and reuse. Document-driven design (DDD) is the design process in which the model is high level and informational. Documents give specifications and instructions for model generation. In traditional model-driven design (MDD), the model is low level and normative. Model generation and evaluation are tightly coupled so that the modeling process has to be in an interactive mode. In the proposed DDD mechanism, the textual document is the only format of user input, and communication is based on the document. Document-driven process flow can simplify engineering design and analysis processes, thus accelerating design cycles. Furthermore, the semantics of features is not captured actively and maintained in existing modeling process. Interoperable feature model exchange and sharing still cannot be achieved with good scalability with existing one-to-one mapping methods. A semantic feature model is developed for the DDD mechanism in order to capture complete requirement information and geometry specification in the document with hierarchical native engineering semantics embedding.

The remainder of the chapter is organized as follows. First, we give an overview of related work on form feature representation and collaborative geometric modeling. Then, we present a semantic feature modeling scheme that allows batch mode geometry construction. Next, we demonstrate how to apply the document-driven design mechanism based on semantic feature model in collaborative design.

Background

Form Feature Representation

There are plenty of research efforts on form feature representation (Salomons, 1993; Shah & Mäntylä, 1995; Pratt & Anderson, 2001). In ASU Features Testbed Modeler (Shah & Rogers, 1988a, 1988b; Shah, 1990), features are defined in terms of parameters and rules about geometric shape. Interaction between features includes spatial relationship and volume-based CSG tree and Boolean operations. E-Rep (Hoffmann & Juan, 1993; Chen & Hoffmann, 1995; Hoffmann, 1997) distinguishes generated features, datum features, and modifying features and regards a CAD model as being built entirely by a sequence of feature insertion, modification, and deletion description. This system-independent feature description is then translated to explicit entity representation.

Several user-defined feature representation methods were proposed. Shah, Ali, and Rogers (1994) presented a declarative approach using geometric entities and algebraic constraints. Middleditch and Reade (1997) proposed a hierarchical structure for feature composition and emphasized the construct relationship of features. Hoffmann and Joan-Arinyo (1998a) define user-defined features by standard feature and constraints, and attributes procedurally. Bidarra, Idri, Noort, and Bronsvoort (1998) include validity constraints in user-defined features specification. Wang and Nnaji (2004) model intentional feature and geometric feature independently and embedded with parametric constraints.

Based on current framework of STEP standards, the ENGEN data model (EDM) (Shih & Anderson, 1997) extended STEP's current explicit entity representation by adding some predefined local features, such as round and chamfer in a bottom-up approach. PDES's form feature information model (FFIM) (NIST, 1988; Shah & Mathew, 1991) adopted a dual representation of explicit and implicit features. Explicit features are represented generally by face lists, while implicit features are categorized into depression, protrusion, passage, deformation, transition, and area features.

Some researchers used a hybrid CSG/B-Rep structure. Roy and Liu (1988) constructed CSG using form primitives and form features. A face-edge type data structure is used at the low-level B-Rep. These two data structures are linked by reference faces. Wang and Ozsoy (1991) used primitive features and form features to build the CSG structure. Dimension and orientation information are represented as constraint nodes in the CSG tree. A face-edge type data structure is used for lower level entities. The connection between two structures is built by pointers from set operator nodes in CSG to B-Rep data structure and from faces to feature faces. Gomes and Teixeira (1991) also developed a CSG/B-Rep scheme, in which CSG represents the high-level relationships between features, and the B-Rep model describes the details. An additional feature topological structure in parallel with the B-Rep model defines volume form features.

Feature Semantics

Feature-based modeling is able to associate functional and engineering information with parameters and features. However, the meaning of a feature cannot be consistently maintained in the modeling process. Feature semantics is domain dependent. Maintenance of semantics across domain boundaries is needed. Shah (1988) identified several transformation/mapping mechanisms between application-specific feature spaces. Bronsvoort and Jansen (1993), de Kraker, Dohmen, and Bronsvoort (1995), and Bronsvoort and Noort (2004) proposed a multiple-way feature conversion to support multiple feature views. Hoffmann and Joan-Arinyo (1998b, 2000) developed a product master model to associate different feature views. Within the domain of form feature, feature interaction during feature construction affects the interpretation of features. Bidarra and Bronsvoort (1999, 2000) embody richer semantics by creating feature models that are independent of geometric models. Feature validity is maintained by constraints. The history-independent feature evaluation is based on non-manifold geometry.

Collaborative Geometric Modeling

Initial research efforts on collaborative design were mainly done to support remote data access and visualization over the Internet. Reviews are available in references (Sriram, 2002; Yang & Xue, 2003; Fuh & Li, 2005). There has also been some work on geometric modeling for collaborative design. COCADCAM (Kao & Lin, 1998) allows distributed CAD/CAM users to work together on surface model co-editing through socket interface. CSM (Chan, Wong, & Ng, 1999) is an environment for multiple users to edit a shared solid object over the Web synchronously through CSG models. NetFEATURE (Lee, Han, Kim, & Park, 1999; Lee, Kim, & Han, 1999) includes Web-enabled feature modeling clients, neutral feature model servers, and database managers. Agents are defined on the server-side to serve clients for feature modeling by means of CORBA protocols. MUG (Anthony, Regli, John, & Lombeyda, 2001; Cera, Regli, Braude, Shapirstain, & Foster, 2002) is a multi-user environment for collaborative conceptual design and shape modeling. Users are able to exchange design semantics and modify the same geometric model synchronously. WebSpiff (Bidarra, van den Berg, & Bronsvoort, 2002, 2004) is a Web-based collaborative feature modeling system that supports interactive feature editing. Parametric representation of features is used for direct manipulation and communication. CADDAC (Agrawal, Ramani, & Hoffmann, 2002; Ramani, Agrawal, Babu, & Hoffmann, 2003) has a three-tier architecture and command objects are transmitted between the client and database to keep the consistency of local and master models. Li et al. (2004) developed a client/server modeling framework based on B-Rep representation. A face-based feature differentiation method is used to support interactive feature editing. CollFeature (Tang, Chou, & Dong, 2004) supports non-lock multi-user feature editing. Li, Gao, Li, & Yang (2004) developed a neutral feature operation mapping method for collaboration of heterogeneous systems.

This research only considers traditional interactive model construction. Batch-mode feature-based modeling offers several benefits including reduced human intervention, improved performance in distributed environments, ease of design alternative evaluation and reuse, and increased system throughput and utilization. As the distribution extensiveness of design activities increases, modeling mechanisms for complex models with ease of communication become important. The proposed DDD mechanism is to support lightweight CAD geometry construction in a service-oriented architecture with thin clients. A semantic feature model is developed to represent multi-level design intent, prevent semantics loss, and enhance data interoperability.

Semantic Feature Model

The semantic feature model intends to capture more design intent by providing an extensible modeling method to represent feature semantics. The fundamental difference between semantic modeling and traditional modeling methods is that traditional models represent relations between entities using binary relations while the semantic model uses trinary relations. The traditional binary relations of ER-alike data modeling simply model most relations as aggregation, which represents "is part of" relationships, and association, which represents "is related to" relationships. In contrast, the semantic model represents relations as subject-predicate-object triples which explicitly captures semantics in an extensible way. The difference is illustrated in Figure 1. In Figure 1a, feature relations are captured by binary aggregation and association in EXPRESS-G diagram. In Figure 1b, different types of arcs represent the predicates of semantic triples explicitly.

To be more precise, if E is a set of entities and $R = E \times E$ is a set of relations, the semantics of a semantic feature f can be defined as $m(f) = \{< s, p, o >\}$, where $s, o \in E, p \in R$. For each statement, s is subject, p is predicate, and o is object. The traditional feature models with binary relations only represent a subset of semantic feature models, in which $m(f) = \{< s, p', o >\}$ and $p' \in \{$ *aggregation*, *association*$\}$.

Semantic feature modeling needs to consider interoperability and extensibility. It needs to support dynamic schema evolution to capture new or evolving types of semantic information, be simple to use, and lightweight. The model should not make assumptions about the semantics of the metadata. It needs to be platform independent and provide interoperability between applications that manage and exchange metadata, and support well-formed relations for construction and query. Semantics are also local and context dependent. It should not be coded with special syntax in a tightly coupled way.

Static models cannot keep pace as new requirements arrive. The semantic feature model includes three aspects for interoperability and extensibility. Intent representation is the basic requirement of feature modeling. Semantic relation representation is the essence of extensibility to represent the open set of engineering semantics. And semantics interpretation derives new semantic relations from existing ones to ensure semantic completeness within one domain.

Figure 1. Comparison between binary relation in traditional model and trinary relation in semantic model

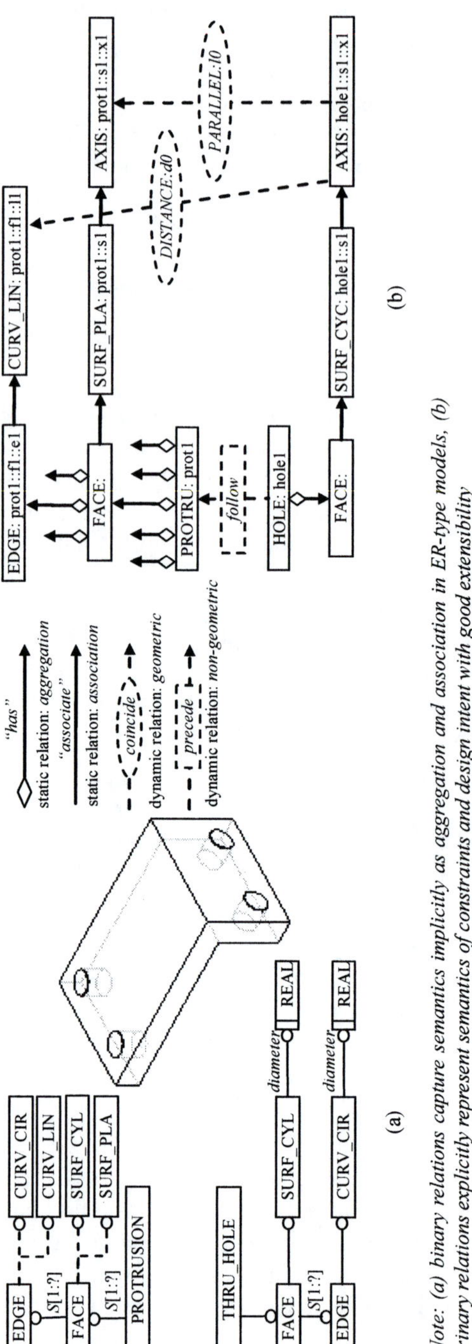

Note: (a) binary relations capture semantics implicitly as aggregation and association in ER-type models, (b) trinary relations explicitly represent semantics of constraints and design intent with good extensibility

Design Intent Representation

Semantic feature modeling is able to capture more semantics with extensible trinary relations so as to improve interoperability between different system domains. As illustrated in Figure 2, traditional CAD data interoperability problem is resolved based on the neutral geometry

Figure 2. Semantic richness is associated with information loss during data transformation.

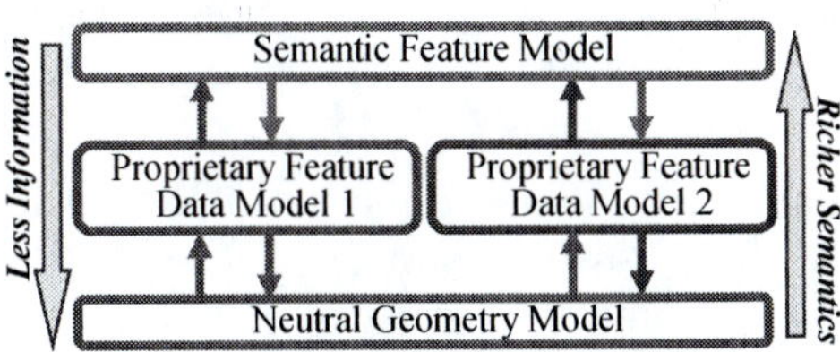

Figure 3. Two levels of design intent, informative and communicative, need to be captured in semantic model

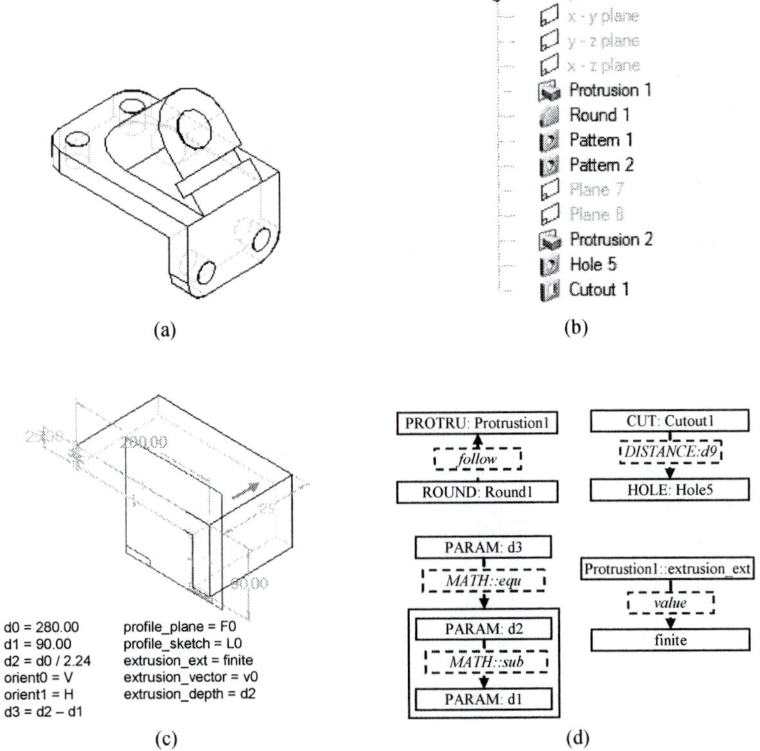

Note: (a) solid model of anchor; (b) informative design intent is the abstract intention in the plan; (c) communicative design intent is the intention manifested during the implementation; (d) semantic model represents design intent explicitly with subject-predicate-object triples

model (e.g., IGES and STEP). Information loss occurs when data is translated to languages or formats that have less expressible semantics. Semantic feature model intends to capture design semantics in an extensible way. Data interoperability is improved by modeling with richer semantics. The multi-level modeling structure also increases the transparency between feature definition and feature evaluation.

There are two levels of design intent: informative and communicative. Informative design intent is the abstract intention in the plan and contains the meaning of design. Communicative design intent is manifested during the implementation and includes the meaning of the designer. A semantic feature model can specify two levels of intent with properly defined feature schema. Capturing design intent requires extensible methods to represent semantics. As illustrated in Figure 3, two levels of design intent can be captured with extensible predicates.

The semantic feature model separates implicit/intentional features from explicit/geometric features. It is important to represent two categories of features independently so that feature specification can be both procedural and declarative. High-level informational intent is in the nature of specification, while low-level communicative intent is more related to operation. The semantic feature model for DDD intends to migrate the way of modeling features from traditional operation-oriented toward specification-oriented.

Semantic Relations

Semantic relation is the predicate in the semantic triple. The essence of flexibility and extensibility of the semantic feature model is the semantic relation between features, which in turn provides systematic approach for information retrieval. Basic semantic relations include static aggregation, generalization, association, and instantiation; hierarchical namespaces which delineate contexts of semantics; membership relations which express meta-level basic meanings of static associations; geometric relations that specify spatial association in Euclidean space; Boolean relations that specify the spatial occupation in Euclidean space; and temporal relations that capture the chronological dependency of feature evaluation.

Membership Schema

Membership schema is the semantic relation's vocabulary description language for feature classes. Membership schema defines properties that are used to specify classes. The associated class relations of inheritance and instantiation are also defined. The membership schema diagram in Figure 4 shows the scope of schema definition. In each knowledge domain, domain schema is a structured template defined by a collection of semantic categories. A semantic category is a grouping of vocabulary within a language, organizing words which are interrelated and defined by each other in various ways. A semantic class is words that share common semantic properties or attributes.

Membership relations are meta-level relations between features, which give rules for feature creation, categorization and division, and transformation between domains. Domain ontology of feature semantics thus can be defined based on membership relations. Examples are

Figure 4. Membership schema defines properties that are associated with semantic classes.

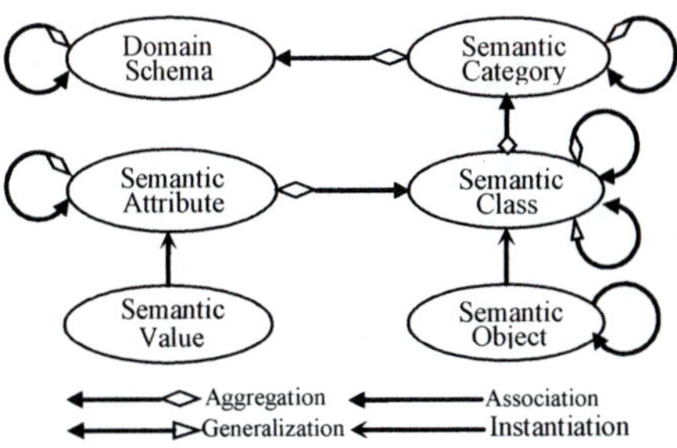

subcategory and identical. Feature f_1 is a subcategory of feature f_2 if and only if the semantics of f_1 infers the semantics of f_2, denoted as $m(f_1) \subseteq m(f_2)$. f_1 and f_2 are identical if $m(f_1) \subseteq m(f_2)$ and $m(f_1) \supseteq m(f_2)$. However, this universal requirement usually is too rigid for domain ontology mapping. If a semantic difference between $m(f_1)$ and $m(f_2)$ is defined as $m(f_1) \setminus m(f_2) := \{<s, p, o> \mid <s, p, o> \in m(f_1), <s, p, o> \notin m(f_2)\}$, and a domain-specific semantic zero ε in domain D is defined such that $\forall f \in D, \varepsilon \subseteq m(f)$, features f_1 and f_2 is identical if and only if $m(f_1) \setminus m(f_2) \subseteq \varepsilon$ and $m(f_2) \setminus m(f_1) \subseteq \varepsilon$. Extensibility is the prerequisite for membership schema since no standard cognitive notions for particular domains exist and conceptualization of terms varies in people's perception.

The membership schema can be used in feature mapping across domains. The definitions of features are different from CAD to CAD, from CAD to CAPP, and between other systems. The mapping process can be conducted based on membership schemata. For example, the definitions of form feature rib are different in two CAD systems, as shown in Figure 5. Establishing mapping between two features is necessary for interoperable data exchange. In schema models, semantic mapping can be based on graph topology, special relationships, and value types. Determining the identical relation between two rib features is the process of checking the similarity or isomorphism of two schema models. Relations between ontology domains thus can be established.

Geometric Relations

Geometric relations specify the various spatial associations in Euclidean space. These relations are constraints that dynamically change the connections between feature and entities. Geometric relations specify spatial relationships in intentional features as well as in evaluated features.

Boolean Relations

Union, intersect, and subtract are basic Boolean operations performed during feature evaluation. Boolean relation between features is one of the significant relations as well as one of

Figure 5. Membership schema can be used in feature mapping between different domains

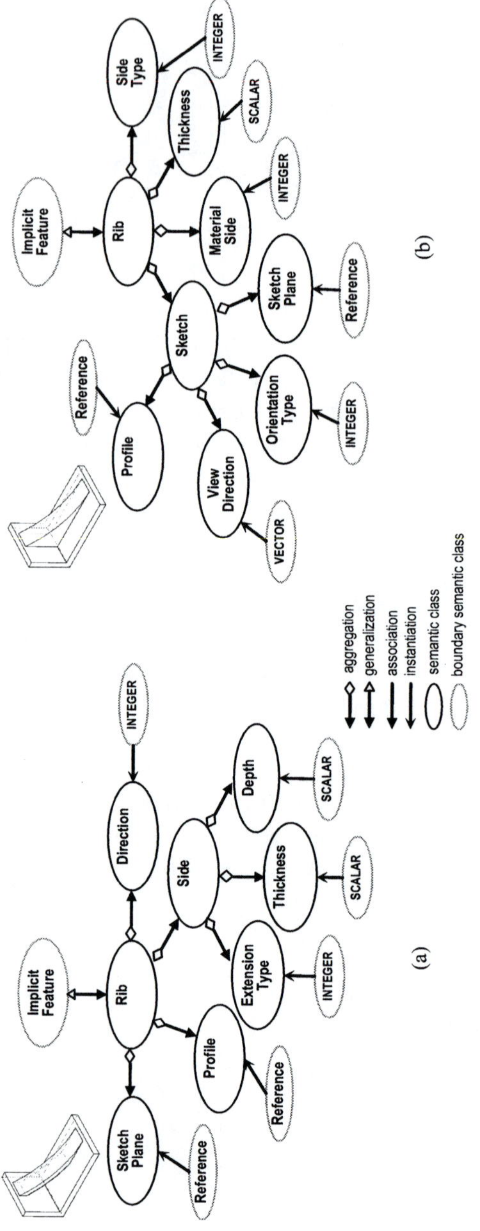

Note: (a) definition of feature rib in SolidEdge®, which supports finite thickness extension; (b) definition of feature rib in Pro/Engineer®, which does not support finite thickness extension. Extra feature cut may be needed to generate the geometry of (a).

the major problem sources in current feature-based modeling such as naming persistency. The non-commutative property of subtract makes feature evaluation sequence-dependent.

Temporal Relations

Temporal relations explicitly specify the chronological dependency between features as informative intent, which include precede, follow, co-occur, and independent. Temporal relations capture design history and ensure causal consistency of feature evaluation. Temporal relations are needed to complement the non-commutative property of the Boolean relation subtract.

Compound Relations

Compound relation allows complex features to be constructed based on basic feature definitions. Complex, but more precise, semantics are needed based on the fact that compound phrases are able to express delicate meanings that are not easy to infer from the meanings of its individual parts in natural languages. For example, semantics of "white-collar" are not just the intersection of semantics between "white" and "collar." New semantics, in addition to the semantics from the basic elements, are generated in a compound feature. Compound relations include adjective and substantive. An adjective compound is to qualify another feature and cannot exist independently, such as countersink, Philip head, and Trapezoidal runner. A substantive compound can exist independently as a complete part, such as button head rivet, Helical spring lock washer, and square neck bolt. Domain-specific features can be defined with compounds, and domain semantics structure can be built based on compound relations.

Semantics Interpretation and Data Exchange

Semantics interpretation is the process of transforming a general descriptive requirement from or to a more specific system-dependent formal semantic model. Interpretation needs to manage possible one-to-many mappings. Two examples of semantics ambiguity are shown in Figure 6. As illustrated in Figure 6a, one geometric model could be generated with different feature constructs (Type I ambiguity). The combination of low-level semantic features depends on user preference and construction sequence. In Figure 6b, one semantic feature can also create different geometric models with uncertain parameters caused by reference vagueness and numerical rounding errors in different systems (Type II ambiguity). Parameter modification of a feature could affect the features that have reference dependency on it. Different B-Rep models may be evaluated in different systems. While Type I ambiguity is a planning problem, Type II ambiguity is usually treated as naming persistency and model robustness problem.

Figure 6. Semantic interpretation helps to reduce ambiguity

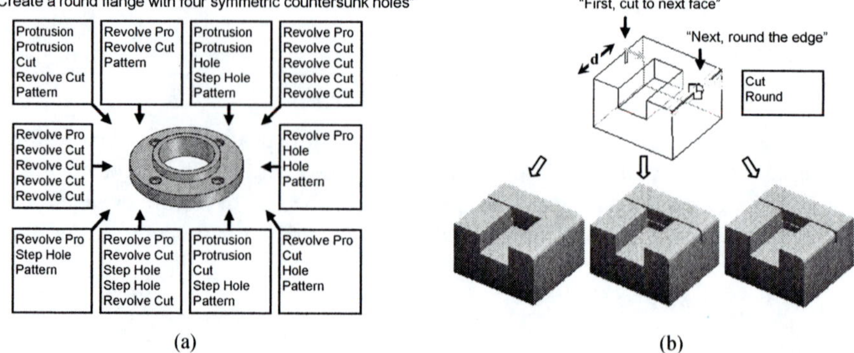

Note: (a) Type I ambiguity of semantic — different combinations of semantic features can generate the same geometry; (b) Type II ambiguity of semantics — different geometry is created from the same semantic feature, small variation of the parameter d *causes topological differences in systems such as SolidEdge® and Pro/Engineer®*

Semantics Composition and Decomposition

A hierarchical decomposition approach can be taken to accommodate Type I ambiguity. The purpose of systematic decomposition is to rationalize the design decision-making process such that arbitrary selection of semantics is avoided. Design intent needs to be captured with multiple resolutions. Based on compound relations, semantic features are constructed hierarchically. Thus, semantics can be referred to with different levels of details. Semantics inference derives new semantics from the existing one based on axioms and rules.

The feature composition process is described briefly as follows. For some adjective compound features $\{a, b, c,..., z\} \subset ACF$ and substantive compound features $\{A, B, C,..., Z\} \subset SCF$, if two non-communicative composition operators are defined as $\otimes : ACF \times ACF \rightarrow ACF$ and $\oplus : SCF \times ACF \rightarrow SCF$, the feature composition is the process in which new compound features are created with the two composition operators. Examples are $A \oplus a = B$ and $B \oplus\ = C$. A different way to create C is that $a \otimes b = c$ and $A \oplus c = C$. Note that only one substantive compound feature is created during the composition at any time. The associated planning problem to create A is to find an $X \in SCF$ and a $\{x, y, z,...\} \subset ACF$ such that $X \oplus x \oplus y \oplus z \oplus ... = A$. This includes the selection of both features and composition sequence.

Multi-resolution intent capturing can be achieved by feature representation with different levels of details. Establishing common semantic features between system domains is required to build the bridge. Figure 7 illustrates the algorithm of searching common compound features in order to exchange feature information between two CAD domains. Identical features are searched and generated from domain-specific features based on domain rules. A common substantive compound feature is found first with necessary composition operations (see Figure 7a). Once a common substantive compound feature is established, common adjective compound features can be searched further (see Figure 7b). As a result of the process, new compound features may be defined. These high-level and commonly agreed compound

Figure 7. Interoperable semantic feature model exchange based on common compound features

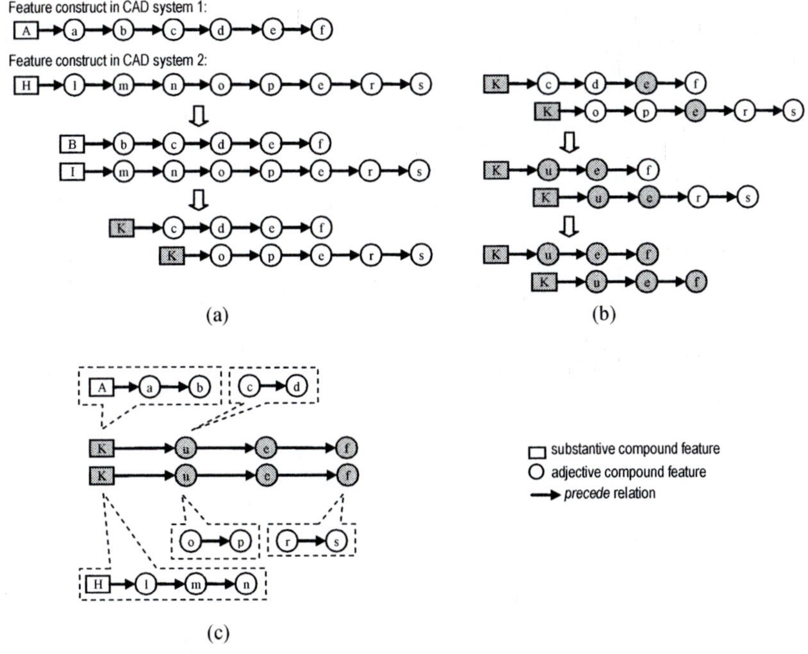

features then are used for information exchange between domains. Cross-domain semantics without domain-specific details is essential to data interoperability.

Semantics Simplification

Semantics simplification is the process of simplifying feature dependency, thus reducing Type II ambiguity. The depth of feature dependency trees should be minimized during the process. Based on the continuity of geometry and the principle of semantic ID (Wang & Nnaji, 2005), stable and persistent geometric entities need to be chosen as references whenever possible. As illustrated in Figure 8, the roots of the dependency tree usually are datum planes x, y, and z. By introducing datum features such as planes, curves, and points as references based on datum planes x, y, and z, the maximum depth of the tree can be reduced to two. Semantic equivalence relations allow for multiple ways of datum selection.

Simplified feature semantics enables history-independent modeling for global form features (e.g., extrusion, hole, cut, and loft) in which only global references are needed. In contrast, local form features (e.g., chamfer, fillet, rib, and pattern) require local references to other features. The depth of dependency trees can be reduced up to three if local features are involved.

Figure 8. Semantics simplification reduces the degrees of feature dependency.

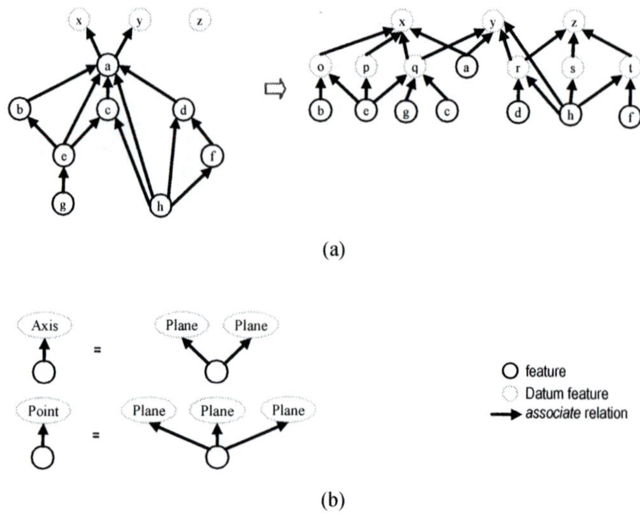

Note: (a) feature semantics can be simplified by introducing datum features; (b) examples of semantic equivalence

In summary, the interpretation process extracts and reorganizes feature semantics when semantics are transformed from or to system-dependent feature models, during which traditional feature models are derived based on semantic compound feature models. The geometry-oriented deduction inevitably loses some design intent. The main task here is not to prevent information loss. Instead, the major challenge is the accuracy of the derived data models. Derivation rules need to be designed to reduce ambiguity and uncertainty of interpretation and provide robust results. This is also related to semantic relation definition in specific domains.

With complete and multi-level feature construction information, the semantic feature model with intent and relation can be represented in single or multiple documents. Document-based design interaction between the client and server can be achieved simply through document processing in a distributed CAD environment.

Documentation of Semantic Model

The electronic document that records semantic model can be in any format. To facilitate interoperability, open standards, such as resource description framework (RDF)/eXtensible Markup Language (XML) (RDF) with commonly agreed schemata, are desirable, especially with the availability of low-cost parsing tools. While XML provides syntax markup, RDF enables semantics level markup. Based on the XML syntax, RDF is a general language for representing information on the Web. In a collaborative design environment, semantic entities and relations may be located in a distributed fashion. With the RDF/XML syntax,

Figure 9. Membership schema expressed in RDFS syntax

```
<?xml version="1.0"      encoding="ISO   - 8859 - 1" ?>
<!DOCTYPE rdf:RDF [
  <!ENTITY xsd "http://www.w3.org/2001/XMLSchema#">
  <!ENTITY rdf "http://www.w3.org/1999/02/22              - rdf  - syntax  - ns#">
 <!ENTITY rdfs "http://www.w3.org/2000/01/rdf              - schema#">
 <!ENTITY sf "http       ://www.e  - designcenter.info/schema/semantic          - feature  #">
]>
<rdf:RDF x   mlns:rdf="    &rdf;  " xmlns:rdfs="     &rdfs;   "  xml:base="   &sf;  ">
 < rdfs:Class rdf:ID="SFClass" rdfs:label="SFClass">
  <rdfs:subClassOf rdf:resource="&rdfs;Resource"/>
 </rdfs:Class>
 < rdfs  : Class rdf:ID="ImplicitFeature"          >
  <rdfs:subClassOf rdf:resource="            #SFClass"/>
 </rdfs:Class>
 < rdfs:Class rdf:ID="Reference"          >
  <rdfs:subClassOf rdf:resource="            #SFClass"/>
 </rdfs:Class>
 < rdfs:Class rdf:ID="Rib" rdfs:label="Rib">
  <rdfs:subClassOf rdf:re          source="  #ImplicitFeature"/>
 < /rdfs:Class>
 <rdfs:Class rdf:ID="Side" rdfs:label="Side">
  <rdfs:subClassOf rdf:resource="            #SFClass"/>
 </rdfs:Class>
<rdfs:Property rdf:ID="       pProfile" rdfs:label="       pProfile">
  <rdfs:domain rdf:resource="        #Rib"/>
  <rdfs:rang     e rdf:resource="    #Reference"/>
 </rdfs:Property>
 <rdf:Property rdf:ID="       pDirection" rdfs:label="        pDirection">
  <rdfs:domain rdf:resource="        #Rib"/>
  <rdfs:range rdf:resource="&xsd;int"/>
 </rdf:Property>
 < rdf:Property rdf:ID="       pThickness"   rdfs:label="pThic      kness" >
  <rdfs:domain rdf:resource="        #Side"/>
  <rdfs:range rdf:resource="&xsd;double"/>
 </rdf:Property>
 ...
 </rdf:RDF>
```

Document Type Definition (DTD) Entities
"SFClass" is a subclass of "Resource"
"ImplicitFeature" is a subclass of "SFClass"
"Reference" is a subclass of "SFClass"
"Rib" is a subclass of "ImplicitFeature"
"Side" is a subclass of "SFClass"
"Rib" has a "Reference" "pProfile"
"Rib" has an Integer value "pDirection"
"Side" has a Double value "pThickness"

entities and relations can be identified and linked over the Web. Feature-based geometric modeling can become a Web-based service.

RDFS for Membership Schema

RDF schema (RDFS) is RDF's vocabulary description language used to specify domain kinds and terms. It helps to construct the structure of the membership schema. The RDFS class and property system is similar to the type systems of object-oriented programming languages such as Java. RDF differs from many such systems in that instead of defining a class in terms of the properties its instances may have, the RDFS describes properties in terms of the classes of resource to which they apply using domain and range. For example, while a classical object-oriented system might typically define a feature class Sketch with an attribute called Direction of type Vector, a Direction property has a domain of Sketch and a range of Vector in RDFS definition. With this approach, it is easy to subsequently define additional properties with a domain of Sketch or a range of Vector without the need to redefine the original description of these classes. This property-centric approach enhances the extensibility of the RDF. Figure 9 shows an example of RDFS representation of the membership schema in Figure 5a.

RDF for Semantic Feature Model

RDF provides a generic data format that enables Web-based intelligent information modeling, which allows for interoperability of data, machine-understandable semantics for metadata, uniform query for resource discovery other than traditional text search, and integrated inference for decision-making. As a standard for serializing objects, RDF facilitates document-driven processes in a Web environment.

In general, as design migrates from abstract specification to concrete feature construction, the semantics of design is enriched gradually with reasoning. Being an important part of design knowledge representation, the semantics of features can be modeled in documents such that it is machine processible. Rule-based inference engines can be used to automate the evolvement of semantics. As illustrated in Figure 10, started from the fundamental requirement of a design or functional specification P^0, the compound feature is decomposed step-by-step toward system-specific feature construct. Based on rules, an inference engine can generate a new RDF document with richer semantics $m_{infer}^{\ i}$ from the ith level RDF document with semantics of $m(P^i)$. Then the $i+1^{th}$ level RDF document with semantics of $m(P^{i+1})$ is created with the semantic difference between $m_{infer}^{\ i}$ and $m(P^i)$. The original $m(P^i)$ is not necessary for the system to generate geometry. Nevertheless, to retain the original design intent, it is desirable to keep the associations among different RDF documents.

In practice, design reuse and data exchange are document archiving and sharing, and the compound feature decomposition is a process of document processing. As shown in the example of Figure 11, from abstract to concrete, high-level features of the flange in a RDF document are replaced by low-level features systematically based on inference rules in separate documents, which are specified with the generic premise-conclusion rule syntax used in some standard RDF tools such as Jena (HP Labs). Rules at different levels can also be combined and the reasoning process is shortened. While semantics are enriched as the feature model goes to detailed levels, informative intent is biased or lost as the semantics are gradually expressed by communicative intent.

Figure 10. The semantics are enriched gradually with multi-resolution RDF documents.

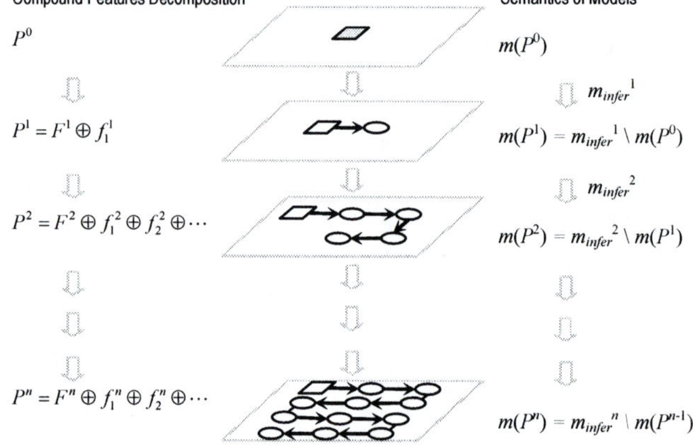

Figure 11. Feature representation and reasoning with RDF/XML documentation

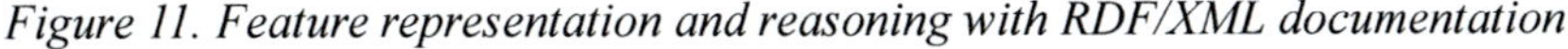

Level 0 features

```
<rdf:RDF
  xmlns:rdf="http://www.w3.org/1999/02/22-rdf-syntax-ns#"
  xmlns:sf="http://www.e-designcenter.info/schema/semantic-feature#"
  xml:base="http://www.e-designcenter.info/schema/semantic-feature#">
    <rdf:Description rdf:ID="Part">
      <sf:Has rdf:resource="#RoundFlange"/>
      <sf:Has rdf:resource="#SymCountersunkHole"/>
    </rdf:Description>
</rdf:RDF>
```

"Create a round flange with four symmetric countersunk holes"

Level 1 rules

```
[RoundFlange:
  (?a sf:Has sf:RoundFlange)  ->
    (?a sf:Has sf:RevolveProtrusion)]
[SymCountersunkHole:
  (?a sf:Has sf:SymCountersunkHole)  ->
    (?a sf:Has sf:CircularPattern)
    (?a sf:Has sf:DoubleStepHole)]
```

Level 1 features

```
<rdf:RDF
    xmlns:rdf="http://www.w3.org/1999/02/22-rdf-syntax-ns#"
    xmlns:sf="http://www.e-designcenter.info/schema/semantic-
feature#">
  <rdf:Description rdf:about="http://www.e-
designcenter.info/schema/semantic-feature#Part">
    <sf:Has rdf:resource="http://www.e-
designcenter.info/schema/semantic-feature#DoubleStepHole"/>
    <sf:Has rdf:resource="http://www.e-
designcenter.info/schema/semantic-feature#RevolveProtrusion"/>
    <sf:Has rdf:resource="http://www.e-
designcenter.info/schema/semantic-feature#CircularPattern"/>
  </rdf:Description>
</rdf:RDF>
```

Level 2 rules

```
[RevolveProtrusion:
  (?a sf:Has sf:RevolveProtrusion)  ->
    (sf:RevolveProtrusion sf:Has rpro:Profile)
    (sf:RevolveProtrusion sf:Has rpro:Axis)
    (sf:RevolveProtrusion sf:Has rpro:Angle)]
[CircularPattern:
  (?a sf:Has sf:CircularPattern)  ->
    (sf:CircularPattern sf:Has cptn:Plane)
    (sf:CircularPattern sf:Has cptn:Axis)
    (sf:CircularPattern sf:Has cptn:Count)]
[DoubleStepHole:
  (?a sf:Has sf:DoubleStepHole) ->
    (sf:DoubleStepHole sf:Associate dstp:Hole_1)
    (sf:DoubleStepHole sf:Associate dstp:Hole_2)
    (sf:DoubleStepHole sf:Associate dstp:Hole_3)]
```

Level 2 features

```
<rdf:RDF
    xmlns:rdf="http://www.w3.org/1999/02/22-rdf-syntax-ns#"
    xmlns:sf="http://www.e-designcenter.info/schema/semantic-
feature#" >
  <rdf:Description rdf:about="http://www.e-
designcenter.info/schema/semantic-feature#RevolveProtrusion">
    <sf:Has rdf:resource="http://www.e-
designcenter.info/schema/semantic-feature/RevolveProtrusion#Angle"/>
    <sf:Has rdf:resource="http://www.e-
designcenter.info/schema/semantic-
feature/RevolveProtrusion#Profile"/>
    <sf:Has rdf:resource="http://www.e-
designcenter.info/schema/semantic-feature/RevolveProtrusion#Axis"/>
  </rdf:Description>
  <rdf:Description rdf:about="http://www.e-
designcenter.info/schema/semantic-feature#DoubleStepHole">
    <sf:Associate rdf:resource="http://www.e-
designcenter.info/schema/semantic-feature/DoubleStepHole#Hole_2"/>
    <sf:Associate rdf:resource="http://www.e-
designcenter.info/schema/semantic-feature/DoubleStepHole#Hole_1"/>
    <sf:Associate rdf:resource="http://www.e-
designcenter.info/schema/semantic-feature/DoubleStepHole#Hole_3"/>
  </rdf:Description>
  <rdf:Description rdf:about="http://www.e-
designcenter.info/schema/semantic-feature#CircularPattern">
    <sf:Has rdf:resource="http://www.e-
designcenter.info/schema/semantic-feature/CircularPattern#Axis"/>
    <sf:Has rdf:resource="http://www.e-
designcenter.info/schema/semantic-feature/CircularPattern#Count"/>
    <sf:Has rdf:resource="http://www.e-
designcenter.info/schema/semantic-feature/CircularPattern#Plane"/>
  </rdf:Description>
</rdf:RDF>
```

Level 3 rules

```
[DoubleSteopHole_hole:
  (?a sf:Associate dstp:Hole_1)  ->
    (sf:Hole sf:HLE_TYPE_NEW xsd:string)
    (sf:Hole sf:HLE_STAN_TYPE xsd:string)
    (sf:Hole sf:HLE_THRDSERIS xsd:string)
    (sf:Hole sf:HLE_FITTYPE xsd:string)
    (sf:Hole sf:HLE_SCREWSIZE xsd:decimal)
    (sf:Hole sf:HLE_ADD_THREAD xsd:decimal)
    (sf:Hole sf:HLE_ADD_CBORE xsd:decimal)
    (sf:Hole sf:HLE_ADD_CSINK xsd:double)
    (sf:Hole sf:DIAMETER xsd:double)
    (sf:Hole sf:HLE_ADD_THREAD xsd:decimal)
    (sf:Hole sf:HLE_ADD_CBORE xsd:decimal)
    (sf:Hole sf:HLE_ADD_CSINK xsd:decimal)
    (sf:Hole sf:HLE_DRILLANGLE xsd:double)
    (sf:Hole sf:HLE_CSINKANGLE xsd:double)
    (sf:Hole sf:HLE_CSINKDIAM xsd:double)
    (sf:Hole sf:HLE_CBOREDEPTH xsd:double)
    (sf:Hole sf:HLE_CBOREDIAM xsd:double)
    (sf:Hole sf:HLE_DEPTH_FROM_TYPE xsd:string)
    (sf:Hole sf:HLE_DEPTH_FROM_VALUE xsd:double)
    (sf:Hole sf:HLE_DEPTH_FROM_REF sf:Reference)
    (sf:Hole sf:HLE_DEPTH_TO_TYPE xsd:string)
    (sf:Hole sf:HLE_DEPTH_TO_VALUE xsd:double)
    (sf:Hole sf:HLE_DEPTH_TO_REF sf:Reference)
    (sf:Hole sf:HLE_DEPTH xsd:double)
    (sf:Hole sf:HLE_DEPTH_REF sf:Reference)
    (sf:Hole sf:HLE_AXIS sf:Reference)
    (sf:Hole sf:HLE_REF_PLANE sf:Reference)
    (sf:Hole sf:HLE_DIM_REF1 sf:Reference)
    (sf:Hole sf:HLE_DIM_DIST1 xsd:double)
    (sf:Hole sf:HLE_DIM_REF1 sf:Reference)
    (sf:Hole sf:HLE_DIM_DIST1 xsd:double) ]
```

Level 3 features

```
<rdf:RDF
    xmlns:rdf="http://www.w3.org/1999/02/22-rdf-syntax-ns#"
    xmlns:sf="http://www.e-designcenter.info/schema/semantic-feature#" >
  <rdf:Description rdf:about="http://www.e-designcenter.info/schema/semantic-
feature#Hole">
    <sf:HLE_DEPTH_FROM_VALUE
rdf:resource="http://www.w3.org/2001/XMLSchema#double"/>
    <sf:DIAMETER rdf:resource="http://www.w3.org/2001/XMLSchema#double"/>
    <sf:HLE_AXIS rdf:resource="http://www.e-designcenter.info/schema/semantic-
feature#Reference"/>
    <sf:HLE_DRILLANGLE
rdf:resource="http://www.w3.org/2001/XMLSchema#double"/>
    <sf:HLE_CBOREDEPTH
rdf:resource="http://www.w3.org/2001/XMLSchema#double"/>
    <sf:HLE_DIM_REF1 rdf:resource="http://www.e-
designcenter.info/schema/semantic-feature#Reference"/>
    <sf:HLE_SCREWSIZE
rdf:resource="http://www.w3.org/2001/XMLSchema#decimal"/>
    <sf:HLE_CBOREDIAM rdf:resource="http://www.w3.org/2001/XMLSchema#double"/>
    <sf:HLE_DEPTH_FROM_REF rdf:resource="http://www.e-
designcenter.info/schema/semantic-feature#Reference"/>
    <sf:HLE_DIM_DIST1 rdf:resource="http://www.w3.org/2001/XMLSchema#double"/>
    <sf:HLE_DEPTH_TO_VALUE
rdf:resource="http://www.w3.org/2001/XMLSchema#double"/>
    <sf:HLE_ADD_CBORE
rdf:resource="http://www.w3.org/2001/XMLSchema#decimal"/>
    <sf:HLE_STAN_TYPE rdf:resource="http://www.w3.org/2001/XMLSchema#string"/>
    <sf:HLE_TYPE_NEW rdf:resource="http://www.w3.org/2001/XMLSchema#string"/>
    <sf:HLE_DEPTH rdf:resource="http://www.w3.org/2001/XMLSchema#double"/>
    <sf:HLE_DEPTH_REF rdf:resource="http://www.e-
designcenter.info/schema/semantic-feature#Reference"/>
    <sf:HLE_CSINKDIAM rdf:resource="http://www.w3.org/2001/XMLSchema#double"/>
    <sf:HLE_ADD_CSINK rdf:resource="http://www.w3.org/2001/XMLSchema#double"/>
    <sf:HLE_FITTYPE rdf:resource="http://www.w3.org/2001/XMLSchema#string"/>
    <sf:HLE_THRDSERIS rdf:resource="http://www.w3.org/2001/XMLSchema#string"/>
    <sf:HLE_DEPTH_TO_TYPE
rdf:resource="http://www.w3.org/2001/XMLSchema#string"/>
    <sf:HLE_DEPTH_TO_REF rdf:resource="http://www.e-
designcenter.info/schema/semantic-feature#Reference"/>
    <sf:HLE_REF_PLANE rdf:resource="http://www.e-
designcenter.info/schema/semantic-feature#Reference"/>
    <sf:HLE_ADD_CSINK
rdf:resource="http://www.w3.org/2001/XMLSchema#decimal"/>
    <sf:HLE_DEPTH_FROM_TYPE
rdf:resource="http://www.w3.org/2001/XMLSchema#string"/>
    <sf:HLE_ADD_THREAD
rdf:resource="http://www.w3.org/2001/XMLSchema#decimal"/>
    <sf:HLE_CSINKANGLE
rdf:resource="http://www.w3.org/2001/XMLSchema#double"/>
  </rdf:Description>
</rdf:RDF>
```

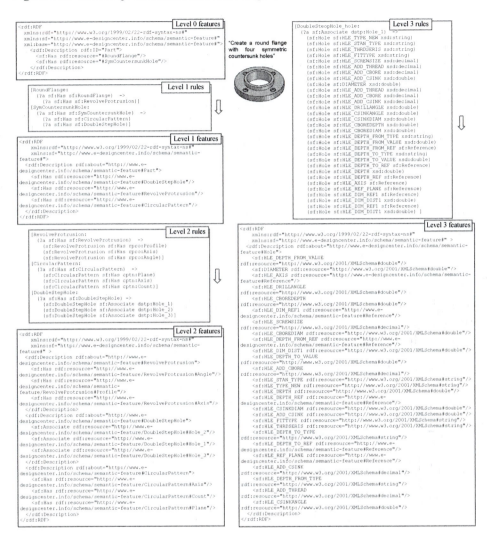

The top-down generic semantics decomposition needs to be supplemented with a bottom-up domain feature composition process in order to generate geometric model accurately. Documents that define system-specific features can be created and archived separately. They are linked to higher level RDF documents. During the document processing, if semantic features are detailed enough to refer to system-specific features, these system-specific documents are used to create geometry.

Figure 12. Document-centric interaction enables loosely-coupled asynchronous CAD services.

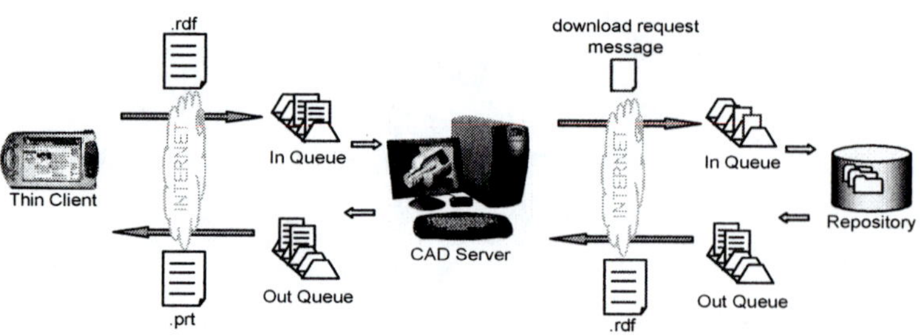

Document-Centric Interaction Model

In document-centric client-server interaction model, service consumers interact with service providers using documents that are meant to be processed as complete information. Documents could be design contents, operation request message, or both in common XML format. Simple object access protocol (SOAP) is such a communication protocol that is particularly suitable for XML-based messaging. As illustrated in Figure 12, the document-centric interaction model enables asynchronous CAD services in batch mode as well as other engineering services such as model translation, analysis, and simulation. Thin clients can send documents of semantic feature models in RDF format to a CAD server over networks. The CAD server will process the requests and generate CAD models in native or standard format. The CAD models can then be returned to clients. During the model generation, as the primary service, semantic features defined at remote repositories may be referred by the feature model from the client. Transparent to clients, new RDF resources may be allocated and used by the CAD server as secondary services.

Different from current Web document links, which only provide simple references for download at the syntax level, RDF provides semantic links such that meaningful information about resources can be obtained and intelligent Web services can be built.

Implementation

The document-driven geometric modeling mechanism based on the semantic feature model is tested within the research testbed called Pegasus at our research center. Pegasus is a service-oriented distributed e-design system, which is to test concepts, functions, and interoperability of research prototypes as well as commercial software for collaborative design (Nnaji, Wang, & Kim, 2004, 2005).

Figure 13. Service-oriented architecture for B2B engineering services

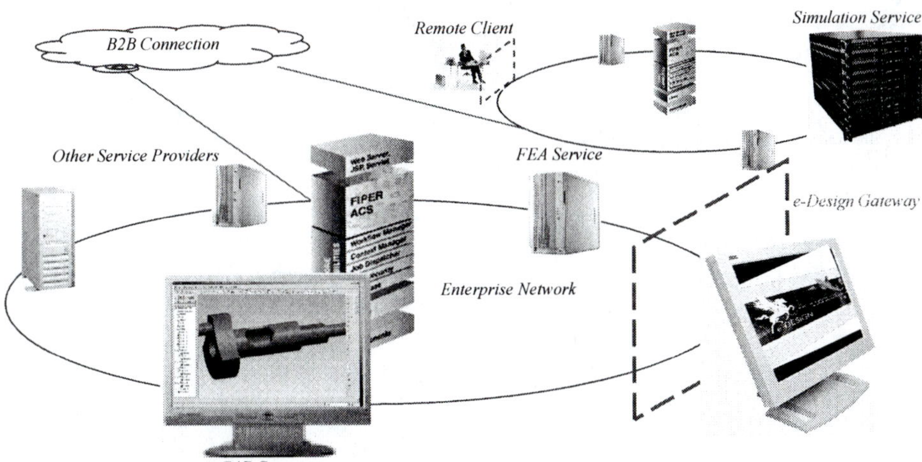

Service-Oriented Architecture

Service-oriented architecture (SOA) is an architectural style whose goal is to achieve loose coupling among interacting software agents. A service is a unit of work done by a service provider to achieve desired functions and end results for a service consumer. SOA is widely considered to be the best practice when solving integration problems of Web services. Similarly, transparent engineering services can be achieved with the same architecture. Data interoperability and process automation are the two most important principles to enable SOA. The semantic feature model for DDD intends to embrace these two principles.

We use FIPER® 1.6 (FIPER) as the backbone of the infrastructure for SOA. FIPER is a service-oriented distributed framework that supports federated engineering collaboration with design and analysis tools. Asynchronous communication is based on platform and language neutral message-oriented middleware (MOM) protocols. WebSphere Application Server® 5.1 and WebSphere MQ® are used. As shown in Figure 13, enterprise-to-enterprise collaboration is achieved with loosely coupled communication of SOA. Documents are used for the purposes of specification, request, storage, and presentation.

Document Processing

FIPER provides common and standard interfaces for interaction among tools as well as a process model to represent the design process in conjunction with product data. Existing tools can be easily integrated in the service supply chain. At the server side, a FIPER process model is defined, which include tasks of a document processor and a CAD service provider.

Figure 14. FIPER process model

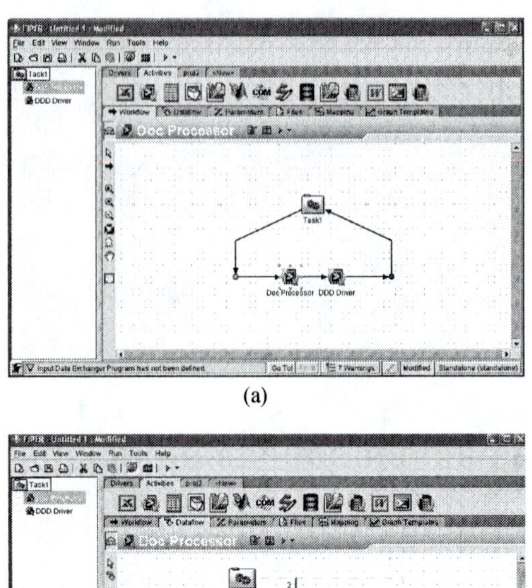

(a)

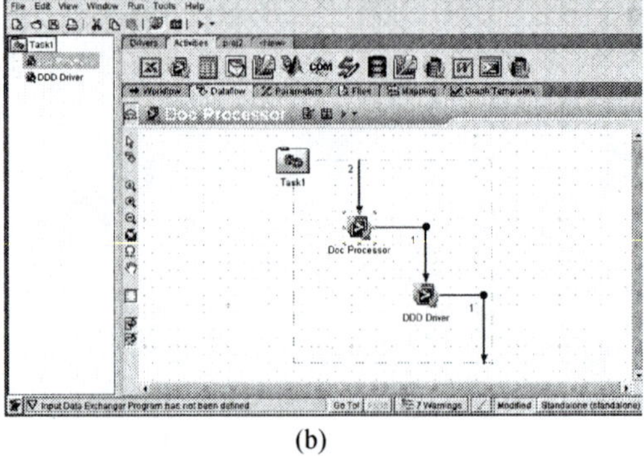

(b)

Note: (a) FIPER model defines components execution sequence; (b) definition of data flow between components as input and output

Figure 15. An overview of the DDD system

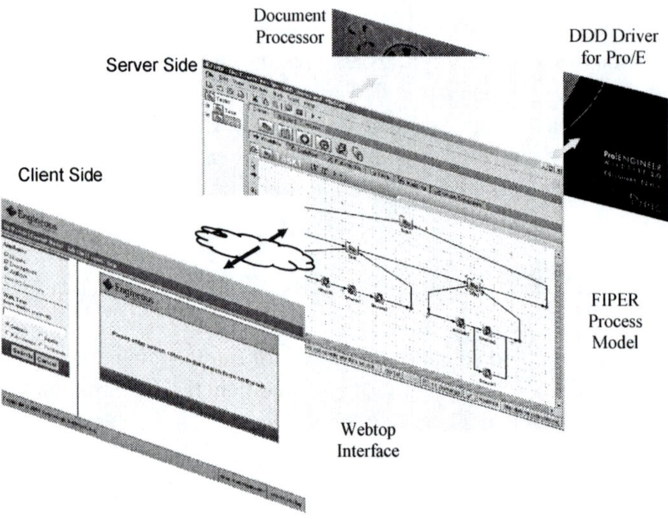

Figure 16. DDD mechanism enables lightweight model construction based on documents.

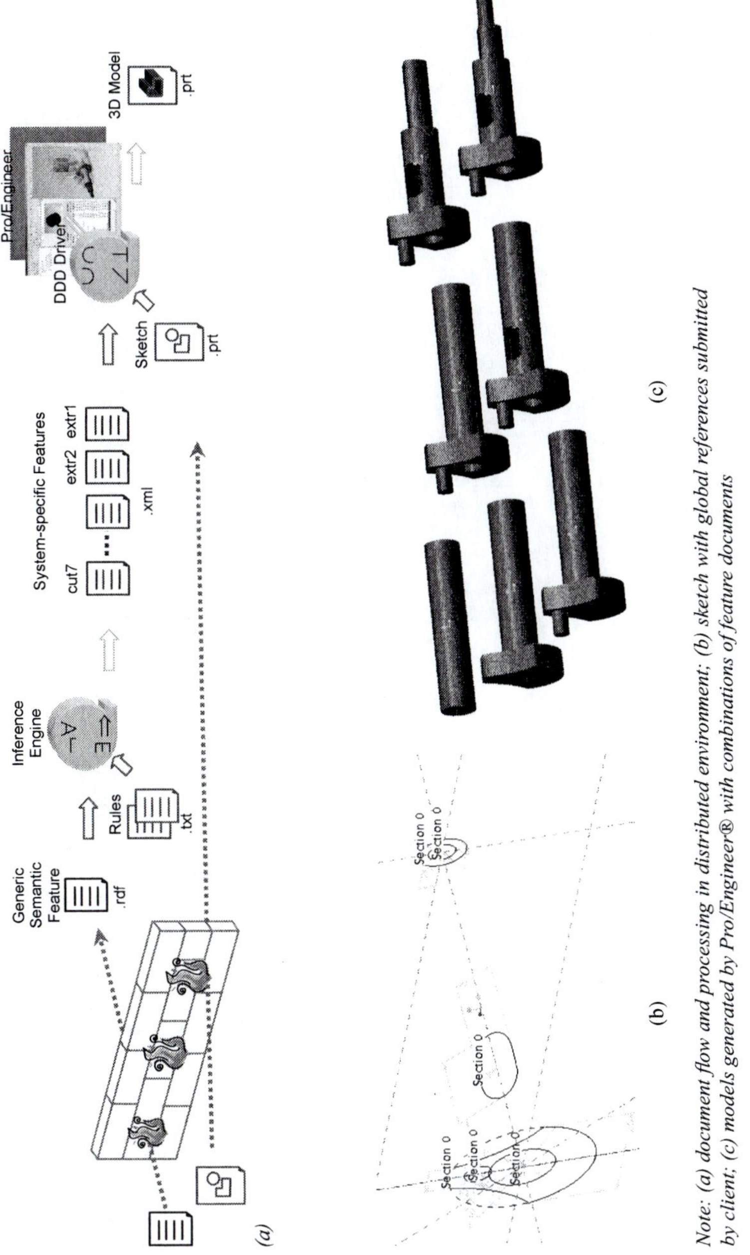

Note: (a) document flow and processing in distributed environment; (b) sketch with global references submitted by client; (c) models generated by Pro/Engineer® with combinations of feature documents

The FIPER process model defines functional components for a task and their execution sequence. It also defines data flow between components in the task, as shown in Figure 14.

An overview of the DDD system is shown in Figure 15. The document processor is developed based on Jena (HP Labs). Jena is an open source RDF Java toolkit for building semantic Web application. It provides programming APIs for processing RDF and RDFS, including a generic rule-based inference engine. Pro/Engineer® Wildfire 2.0 is integrated in the process model to provide CAD services as a Simcode component. Based on Pro/Toolkit® APIs, a DDD driver for pro/engineer is developed to process incoming feature documents and generate geometric models. At the client side, the process model is accessible to thin

Figure 17. A crankshaft model built with the DDD mechanism

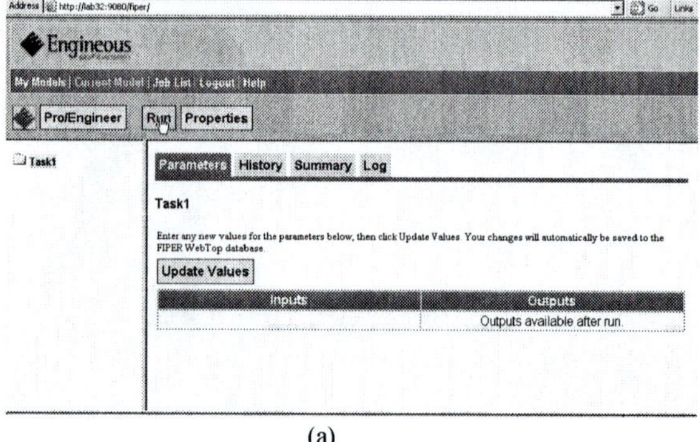

(a)

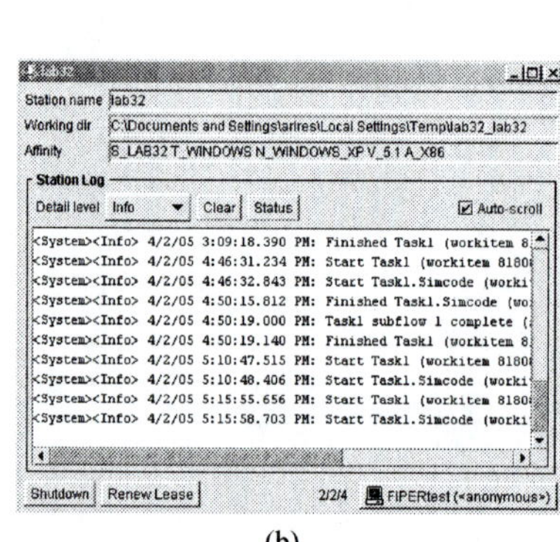

(b)

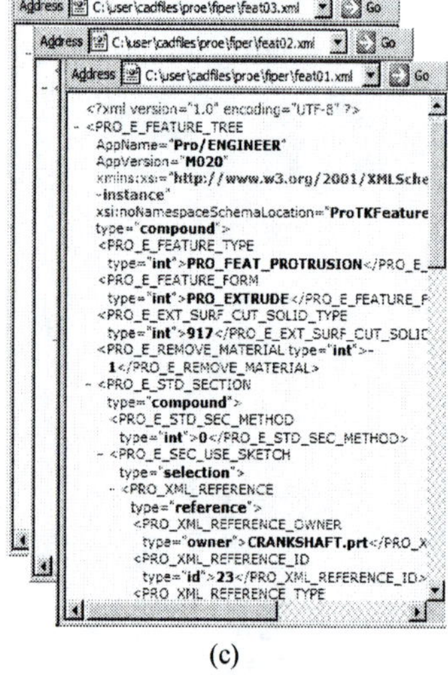

(c)

Note: (a) client requests DDD services from FIPER Webtop; (b) FIPER ACS and FIPER station direct DDD services to the service provider Pro/Engineer®; (c) system-specific individual features for Pro/Engineer® in XML documents; (d) Pro/Engineer® reads the 2D sketch file, and the DDD Driver processes feature documents in sequence automatically

Figure 17. continued

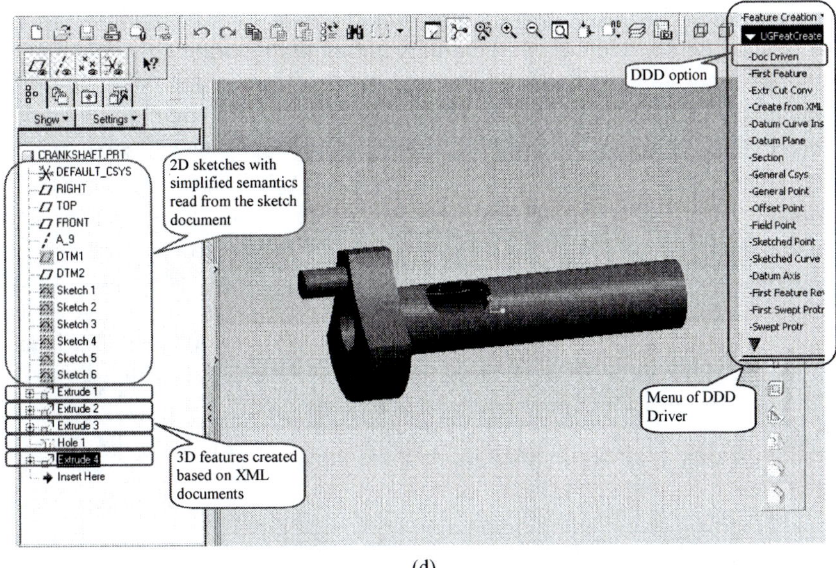

(d)

clients with FIPER WebTop Web service. Service transactions can be initiated simply through Web browsers.

The DDD mechanism enables batch-mode geometric model construction based on documents that contain specifications. As illustrated in Figure 16, a client submits documents of generic semantic features and 2D sketch as the input context alone with a FIPER process model to the server. During the FIPER model execution, the inference engine generates system-specific semantic features as one or more documents based on the inputs of features and rules. These feature documents then are fed into the DDD driver of pro/engineer along with the sketch. Different 3D models can be created with combinations of feature documents. Figure 17 shows how a crankshaft model is built with the DDD mechanism. After services are published at FIPER application control system (ACS), FIPER station can direct service requests from ACS to the service provider pro/engineer. The FIPER Simcode invokes pro/engineer and the sketch document is read into pro/engineer automatically. The selection of the document-driven option of DDD driver will allow it to create features one by one with each feature defined in one XML document. The client can request the DDD service with a simple Web browser. The DDD mechanism supports loosely coupled and asynchronous model generation as well as lightweight design data management and access, which enables thin-client-oriented distributed CAD services. Users can control the content of documents including the FIPER process model, 2D sketch specification, semantic feature model in RDF/XML, and inference rules.

Future Trends

In a grid computing environment — which is a new approach to provide virtualized infrastructure enabling people to utilize computing resources ubiquitously as utilities — CAD systems can become service providers and are available through networks in a pay-per-use fashion, in contrast to today's buy-and-own way. Thin client modeling environment can reduce the cost of using CAD services.

As computing and network resources become commodities, the use of engineering software tools in the future will be similar to today's utility consumption, which is based on service subscription. The advantage of this approach is that hardware and software maintenance tasks such as install, upgrade, and backup are all done by specialized service providers. Manufacturing enterprises do not have to have internal IT departments. Engineers use software services remotely based on their project needs. Specialized engineering service companies for design and analysis services will be formed.

Some new technical challenges are to be resolved for service-oriented engineering systems in the near future. First, current data models including STEP were designed for standalone CAD systems. Distributed databases need distributed data modeling schemes to optimize data access time and storage space. While the distributed database is totally different from centralized database, distributed geometric modeling (Wang & Nnaji, 2004) needs further exploration. Second, design data is modified by multiple designers. Most recent and correct versions should be maintained in either centralized or distributed repository. Consistency management and version control are important. Third, distributed design service requires design data to be shared by different parties. Intellectual property protection (Cera, Kim, Han, & Regli, 2004; Wang, Ajoku, Brustoloni, & Nnaji, 2006) is essential to build secure and trustworthy distributed engineering service systems.

Conclusion

This chapter presents a new feature-based modeling mechanism, document-driven design, to enable batch mode geometry construction for distributed CAD systems. This mechanism is to support loosely coupled lightweight CAD geometry generation in a service-oriented architecture with thin clients. A semantic feature model for document-driven design is developed to capture informative and communicative design intent. Feature semantics is explicitly represented as trinary relation, which provides good extensibility and prevents semantics loss. Data interoperability between domains is enhanced by schema mapping and multi-resolution semantics. Semantic feature models are represented in documents with standard RDF/XML syntax such that document processing and reasoning can be easily implemented. This mechanism aims to enable asynchronous communication in distributed CAD environments with ease of design alternative evaluation and reuse, reduced human errors, and improved system throughput and utilization.

References

Agrawal, A., Ramani, K., & Hoffmann, C. (2002). *CADDAC: Multi-client collaborative shape design system with server-based geometry kernel* (Paper No. DETC2002/CIE-34465). Paper presented at the ASME Design Engineering Technical Conferences & Computers and Information in Engineering Conference, Montreal, Canada.

Anthony, L., Regli, W. C., John, J. E., & Lombeyda, S. V. (2001). An approach to capturing structure, behavior, and function of artifacts in computer-aided design. *ASME Journal of Computers & Information Science in Engineering, 1*(2), 186-192.

Bidarra, R., & Bronsvoort, W. F. (1999). *History-independent boundary evaluation for feature modeling* (Paper No. DETC99/CIE-9122). Paper presented at the ASME Computers in Engineering Conference, Las Vegas, NV.

Bidarra, R., & Bronsvoort, W. F. (2000). Semantic feature modeling. *Computer.-Aided Design, 32*(3), 201-225.

Bidarra, R., Idri, A., Noort, A., & Bronsvoort, W. F. (1998). *Declarative user-defined feature classes* (Paper No. DETC98/CIE-5705). Paper presented at the ASME Computers in Engineering Conference, Atlanta, GA.

Bidarra, R., van den Berg, E., & Bronsvoort, W. F. (2002). A collaborative feature modeling system. *ASME Journal of Computers & Information Science in Engineering, 2*(3), 192-198.

Bidarra, R., van den Berg, E., & Bronsvoort, W. F. (2004). *Direct manipulation of feature models in Web-based collaborative design* (Paper No. DETC2004-57716). Paper presented at the ASME Design Engineering Technical Conferences & Computers and Information in Engineering Conference, Salt Lake City, UT.

Bronsvoort, W. F., & Jansen, F. W. (1993). Feature modelling and conversion — Key concepts to concurrent engineering. *Comp. in Ind., 21*(1), 61-86.

Bronsvoort, W. F., & Noort, A. (2004). Multiple-view feature modelling for integral product development. *Computer-Aided Design, 36*(10), 929-946.

Cera, C. D., Kim, T., Han, J. H., & Regli, W. C. (2004) Role-based viewing envelopes for information protection in collaborative modeling. *Computer-Aided Design, 36*(9), 873-886.

Cera, C. D., Regli, W. C., Braude, I., Shapirstain, Y., & Foster, C. V. (2002). A collaborative 3D environment for authoring design semantics. *IEEE Comp. Graphics & App., 22*(3), 42-55.

Chan, S., Wong, M., & Ng, V. (1999). Collaborative solid modeling on the WWW. In *Proceedings of the 14th ACM Symposium on Applied Computing*, San Antonio, TX (pp. 598-602).

Chen, X., & Hoffmann, C. M. (1995). Towards feature attachment. *Computer-Aided Design, 27*(9), 695-702.

de Kraker, K. J., Dohmen, M., & Bronsvoort, W. F. (1995). Multiple-way feature conversion to support concurrent engineering. In *Proceedings of the 3rd ACM Symposium on Solid Modeling & Applications*, Salt Lake City, UT (pp.105-114).

FIPER. Federated Intelligent Product Environment, Engineous Software. Retrieved from http://www.engineous.com/

Fuh, J. Y. H., & Li, W. D. (2005). Advances in collaborative CAD: The-state-of-the art. *Computer-Aided Design, 37*(5), 471-481.

Gomes, A. J. P., & Teixeira, J. C. G. (1991). Form feature modelling in a hybrid CSG/Brep Scheme. *Computers & Graphics, 15*(2), 217-229.

Hoffmann, C. M. (1997). EREP project overview. In D. Roller & P. Brunet (Eds.), *CAD systems development* (pp. 32-40). Berlin: Springer.

Hoffmann, C. M., & Joan-Arinyo, R. (1998a). On user-defined features. *Computer-Aided Design, 30*(5), 321-332.

Hoffman, C. M., & Joan-Arinyo, R. (1998b). CAD and the product master model. *Computer-Aided Design, 30*(11), 905-918.

Hoffmann, C. M., & Joan-Arinyo, R. (2000). Distributed maintenance of multiple product views. *Computer-Aided Design, 32*(7), 421-431.

Hoffmann, C. M., & Juan, R. (1993) EREP — An editable, high-level representation for geometric design and analysis. In P. Wilson, M. Wozny, & M. Pratt (Eds.), *Geometric modeling for product realization* (pp. 129-164). Rensselaerville, NY: North-Holland.

HP Labs. Jena-A Semantic Web Framework for Java. Retrieved from http://jena.sourceforge.net/

Kao, Y. C., & Lin, G. C. I. (1998). Development of a collaborative CAD/CAM system. *Robotics & Comp.-Int. Manuf., 14*(1), 55-68.

Lee, J. Y., Han, S. B., Kim, H., & Park, S. B. (1999) Network-centric feature-based modeling. In *Proceedings of the 7th IEEE Pacific Conference on Computer Graphics & Applications*, Seoul, Korea (pp. 280-289).

Lee, J. Y., Kim, H., & Han, S. B. (1999). *Web-enabled feature-based modeling in a distributed design environment* (Paper No. DETC99/DFM-8941). Paper presented at the ASME Design Engineering Technical Conferences, Las Vegas, NV.

Li, M., Gao, S., Li, J., & Yang, Y. (2004). *An approach to supporting synchronized collaborative design within heterogeneous CAD systems* (Paper No. DETC2004-57703). Paper presented at the ASME Design Engineering Technical Conferences & Computers and Information in Engineering Conference, Salt Lake City, UT.

Li, W. D., Ong, S. K., Fuh, J. Y. H., Wong, Y. S., Lu, Y. Q., & Nee, A. Y. C. (2004). Feature-based design in a distributed and collaborative environment. *Computer-Aided Design, 36*(9), 775-797.

Middleditch, A., & Reade, C. (1997). A kernel for geometric features. In *Proceedings of the 4th ACM Symposium on Solid Modeling & Applications*, Atlanta, GA (pp. 131-140).

NIST (1988). Product data exchange specification: The first working draft. National Institute of Standards and Technology Report, NISTIR88-4004.

Nnaji, B. O, Wang, Y., & Kim, K. Y. (2004). *Cost-effective product realization — Service-oriented architecture for integrated product life-cycle management.* Paper presented at the 7th IFAC Symposium on Cost Oriented Automation, Gatineau/Ottawa, Canada.

Nnaji, B. O, Wang, Y., & Kim, K. Y. (2005). E-design systems. In A. Badiru (Ed.), *The handbook of industrial and system engineering* (Chapter 28). Boca Raton, FL: Taylor & Francis.

Pratt, M. J., & Anderson, B. D. (2001). A shape modeling applications programming interface for the STEP standard. *Computer-Aided Design, 33*(7), 531-543.

Ramani, K., Agrawal, A., Babu, M., & Hoffmann, C. (2003). CADDAC: Multi-client collaborative shape design system with server-based geometry kernel. *ASME J. Comp. & Inf. Sci. in Eng., 3*(2), 170-173.

RDF. Resource description framework. World Wide Web Consortium (W3C). Retrieved from http://www.w3.org/RDF/

Roy, U., & Liu, C. R. (1988). Feature based representational scheme of a solid modeler for providing dimensioning and tolerancing information. *Robotics & Comp.-Integrated Manuf., 4*(3/4), 335-345.

Salomons, O. W., van Houten, F. J. A. M., & Kals, H. J. J. (1993). Review of research in feature based design. *J. Manuf. Sys., 12*(2), 113-132.

Shah, J. J. (1988). Feature transformations between application-specific feature spaces. *Computer-Aided Engineering Journal, 5*(6), 247-255.

Shah, J., Ali, A., & Rogers, M. (1994). Investigation of declarative feature modeling. In *Proceedings of the ASME Computers in Engineering Conference*, Minneapolis, MN (pp. 1-11).

Shah, J. J., & Mathew, A. (1991). Experimental investigation of the STEP form-feature information model. *Computer-Aided Design, 23*(4), 282-296.

Shah, J. J., & Mäntylä, M. (1995). *Parametric and feature-based CAD/CAM: Concepts, techniques, applications*. New York: John Wiley & Sons.

Shah, J. J., & Rogers, M. T. (1988a). Functional requirements and conceptual design of the feature-based modeling system. *Computer-Aided Engineering Journal, 5*(1), 9-15.

Shah, J. J., & Rogers, M. T. (1988b). Expert form feature modeling shell. *Computer-Aided Design, 20*(9), 515-524.

Shah, J., Rogers, M., Sreevalsan, P., Hsiao, D., Matthew, A., Bhatanagar, A., et al. (1990). An overview of the ASU features testbed. In P*roceedings of the ASME Computers in Engineering Conference*, Boston (pp. 233-242).

Shih, C. H., & Anderson, B. (1997). A design/constraint model to capture design intent. In *Proceedings of the 4th ACM Symposium on Solid Modeling & Applications*, Atlanta, GA (pp. 255-264).

Sriram, R. D. (2002). *Distributed and integrated collaborative engineering design*. Glenwood, MD: Sarven Publishers.

Tang, M., Chou, S.-C., & Dong, J.-X. (2004). Collaborative virtual environment for feature based modeling. In *Proceedings of the ACM SIGGRAPH*, Singapore (pp. 120-126).

Wang, Y., Ajoku, P. N., Brustoloni, J. C., & Nnaji, B. O. (2006, in press). Intellectual property protection in collaborative design through lean information modeling and sharing. *ASME J. Comp. & Inf. Sci. in Eng.*

Wang, N., & Ozsoy, M. (1991). A scheme to represent features, dimensions, and tolerances in geometric modeling. *J. Manuf. Sys., 10*(3), 233-240.

Wang, Y., & Nnaji, B. O. (2004). UL-PML: Constraint-enabled distributed design data model. *Int. J. Prod. Res., 42*(17), 3743-3763.

Wang, Y., & Nnaji, B. O. (2005). Geometry-based semantic ID for persistent and interoperable reference in feature-based parametric modeling. *Computer-Aided Design, 37*(10), 1081-1093.

Yang, H., & Xue, D. (2003). Recent research on developing Web-based manufacturing systems: A review. *Int. J. Prod. Res., 41*(15), 3601-3629.

Chapter XIX

Towards a Design Process for Integrating Product Recommendation Services in E-Markets

Nikos Manouselis, Informatics Laboratory,
Agricultural University of Athens, Greece

Constantina Costopoulou, Informatics Laboratory,
Agricultural University of Athens, Greece

Abstract

Online recommendation services (widely known as recommender systems) can support potential buyers by providing product recommendations that match their preferences. When integrated into e-markets, recommendation services may offer important added value. They can help online buyers to save time and make informed purchase decisions, as well as e-market operators to respond to buyer product queries in a more efficient manner, thus attracting more potential buyers. On the other hand, the variety of intelligent recommendation techniques that may be used to support such services can often prove complex and costly to implement. Toward this direction, this chapter proposes a design process for deploying intelligent recommendation services in existing e-markets, in order to reduce the complexity of such kinds of software development. To demonstrate the applicability of this approach, the proposed process is applied for the integration of a wine recommendation service in a Greek e-market with agricultural products.

Introduction

The rapid adoption of e-commerce practices and technologies has led to the development of numerous e-markets that offer a wide variety of products and services to the online buyers. From the buyers' perspective, this can lead to an often overwhelming amount of product information related to the purchase process. To facilitate searching, comparing, and selecting products in the context of e-markets, different types of integrated services or systems have been proposed. A particular class of such systems are the recommender systems, which facilitate the decision-making process of online buyers by providing recommendations about products matching their preferences (Schafer, Konstan, & Riedl, 2001). Recommender systems were originally defined as using the opinions of a community of users, to help individuals in that community to identify more effectively the content of interest from a potentially overwhelming set of choices (Resnick & Varian, 1997). Nowadays, the term has acquired a broader connotation, describing any system that produces individualized recommendations as output, or has the effect of guiding the user in a personalized way to interesting or useful items, in a large space of possible options (Burke, 2002).

Recommender systems use different types of techniques in order to provide personalised recommendations. According to Burke (2002), these techniques can be categorised as a content-based recommendation, collaborative recommendation, demographic recommendation, utility-based recommendation, as well as knowledge-based recommendation. Most of these techniques engage artificial intelligence (AI) methods in order to recommend products that best match each individual user's needs. For instance, recommender systems have previously engaged techniques, such as:

- decision tree induction and association rules mining, in order to identify users with similar interests and to extract rules that reflect their buying behavior (Changchien & Lu, 2001; Kim, Lee, Shaw, Chang, & Nelson, 2001; Cho, Kim, & Kim, 2002; Wang, Chuang, Hsu, & Keh, 2004);
- statistical methods, such as the calculation of user-to-user and item-to-item ratings' correlation, in order to create neighbourhoods of like-minded users (Herlocker, Konstan, & Riedl, 2002; Deshpande & Karypis, 2004; Miller, Konstan, & Riedl, 2004);
- classification methods, such as clustering algorithms and neural networks, to categorise users with similar preferences (Lee, Jun, Lee, & Kim, 2005; Martin-Guerrero et al., 2006; Lihua, Lu, Jing, & Zongyong, 2005); and
- taxonomy- and ontology-based approaches for representing user preferences and product spaces (Middleton, Shadbolt, & Roure, 2004; Hung, 2005).

This has led to a rich variety of AI-based approaches, which can be integrated in recommender systems.

On the other hand, surveys of online e-commerce systems (e.g., Holzmueller & Schluechter, 2002) reveal that most of the existing commercial e-market applications do not include a product recommendation service (i.e., a recommender system for products), or do not engage some intelligent technique to produce their product recommendations. This observation can be partially explained if we consider the inherent complexity of designing intelligent recommendation services, as well as the deployment and evaluation costs of such services. For instance, in the e-commerce domain there are several proposals of product recommendation algorithms (such as the ones proposed by Kim, Cho, Kim, Kim, & Suh, 2002; Cheung, Kwok, Law, & Tsui, 2003; Kim, Yum, Song, & Kim, 2005; Li, Lu, & Xuefeng, 2005) or stand-alone product recommendation systems (such as the approaches of Yen & Kong, 2002; Lee, 2004; Hung, 2005). Nevertheless, these are developed on a case-by-case basis, and include no guidelines related to how an intelligent product recommendation service can be designed, tested, and integrated into an existing e-market. Very few studies in the recommendation literature have addressed such issues (Stolze, 2002; Richard & Tchounikine, 2004). This can be an obstacle for e-market designers and developers, since the deployment of such services can often prove complex and confusing to them.

The aim of this chapter is to propose an efficient design process for deploying intelligent product recommendation services in existing e-markets. For this purpose, a set of design steps is suggested, based on a series of preliminary stages (Manouselis & Costopoulou, 2005) and an iterative software development approach, the rational unified process (RUP) (Boggs & Boggs, 2002). Then, these design steps are followed for integrating a wine recommendation service in an existing e-market. The remainder of this chapter is structured as follows. First, we give an overview of the preliminary stages and the process workflows of the RUP approach and identify a generic design process for integrating recommendation services in e-markets. Then, we demonstrate the application of the proposed design process in an already operating Greek e-market with agricultural products. Finally, we present the conclusions of this study and identify some future trends in this domain.

A Design Process for e-Market Recommendation Services

The Preliminary Stages

The value of product recommendation is mainly focused on saving time, responding to buyer product's queries quickly, making informed purchase decisions, and consequently attracting more potential buyers. As mentioned, although numerous product recommendation implementations have been proposed, they are mostly developed on a case-by-case basis. So far, there has been not any proposal for an overall process of integrating recommendation services in e-markets. An attempt has been made to address this issue by Manouselis and Costopoulou (2005), providing a preliminary set of design stages. These stages are briefly described as follows:

1. **Identification of actors and supported tasks.** This is responsible for the identification of the involved actors and the tasks to be supported in an existing e-market. The outcome of this stage is a formal specification of actors and their tasks, using the Unified Modeling Language (UML).

2. **Definition of recommendation items.** This is responsible for the identification of the product characteristics (attributes). The outcome is a formal specification of the recommended products' database, using entity-relationship (ER) diagrams.
3. **Development of recommendation algorithm.** This is responsible for the development of an algorithm that will be used to provide the recommendations. A number of candidate algorithm variations can also be developed, in accordance to related mathematical models (Herlocker et al., 2002). The outcomes of this stage are: (i) a flowchart of the recommendation algorithm, and (ii) the algorithm variations (optional).
4. **Rapid prototyping.** This is responsible for the implementation of the recommendation service components that take into account the architectural, functional, and technical requirements of the examined e-market. These components may refer to the recommended products' database, the recommendation algorithm or different algorithm variations, as well as the user interfaces. The outcome of this stage is a recommendation service prototype.
5. **Pilot evaluation.** This is responsible for performing an initial evaluation of the service prototype, either by using simulated or real data. As a result, design choices can be finalized. If any fine tuning is required, we can go back to the development of recommendation algorithm stage. The outcome of this stage is the final version of the recommendation service to be integrated in the e-market under study.

Although these stages can serve as a design approach for integrating product recommendation services in e-markets, they have not been supported with a set of systematic design and analysis tools (such as the UML ones), nor do they correspond to the stages of a systematic software development process. For this purpose, this chapter has further refined them.

The Rational Unified Process Approach

Software development involves a number of steps to be carried out, so that a software system is properly modeled, analysed, designed, specified, and implemented. UML is the de-facto software industry standard modeling language for visualizing, specifying, constructing, and documenting the elements of systems, in general, and software systems, in particular (Booch, Rumbaugh, & Jacobson, 1998). It provides a rich set of graphical artifacts to help in the elicitation and top-down refinement of software systems from requirements capture to the deployment of software components (Saleh, 2002). In UML, a system is described using different levels of abstraction and considering various views (i.e., business view, use case view, design and process view, implementation view). Each view is realized using different UML modeling tools (diagrams), such as use case diagrams, activity diagrams, sequence diagrams, collaboration diagrams, statechart diagrams, class diagrams, component diagrams, and deployment diagrams (Saleh, 2002).

UML is largely process-independent, meaning that it can be used with a number of software development processes. One of the most popular systematic approaches is the rational unified process (RUP) approach, a design and development process that is especially well suited to UML (Booch et al., 1998; Boggs & Boggs, 2002). The RUP development starts with six process workflows (i.e., business modeling, requirements or system use case modeling, analysis and design, implementation, test, and deployment) that adopt the various UML views, and continues with three more process workflows (i.e., configuration management, project management, and environment). The first six process workflows, which are directly related to the design and deployment of a system, are:

- **Business modeling** that describes the structure and dynamics of the business activities around the system. It results in business use case diagrams, activity diagrams, and analysis-level class diagrams with business entities.
- **Requirements or system use case modeling** that describes user requirements using use case diagrams. It results in identifying actors, use cases, and use case diagrams.
- **Analysis and design** that describes the structural and architectural aspects of the system. Analysis results in describing the flow of events in use cases by developing analysis-level sequence or collaboration diagrams. Design results in developing design-level sequence or collaboration diagrams, design-level class diagrams, statechart diagrams, component diagrams, and a deployment diagram.
- **Implementation** that takes into account the above UML diagrams in order to develop software components and integrate them in an initial version of the software system.
- **Test** that describes testing cases, procedures, and defect-tracking metrics.
- **Deployment** that covers the final system delivery and configuration.

The Proposed Design Process

The preliminary stages and the RUP process workflows have been studied in order to identify parts where the two approaches complement each other, as well as where they are overlapping. This led to the merging of the two approaches into a set of seven design steps aiming to facilitate the integration of a product recommendation service in an existing e-market. In Figure 1, the design process is presented following a waterfall model, where all design steps are also linked to the expected results of each step. These steps can be detailed as follows:

I. **Business modeling.** This step concentrates on the business activities that will be generally supported by the system (referred to here as the e-market business). It concerns the identification of business actors (anyone or anything that is external to the e-market business but interacts with it), business workers (roles within the e-market business), and business use cases (a group of related workflows within the e-market business that provide value to the business actors). The outcome of this step is a business use case diagram, which illustrates business use cases, business actors, and business workers for business activities, as well as the interactions between them. Activity diagrams can also be used to model the workflow through a particular business use case.

II. **System modeling.** This step specifies the scope of the system, using use cases and actors. Use cases include anything that is inside the system, whereas actors include

Figure 1. Design process of product recommendation service

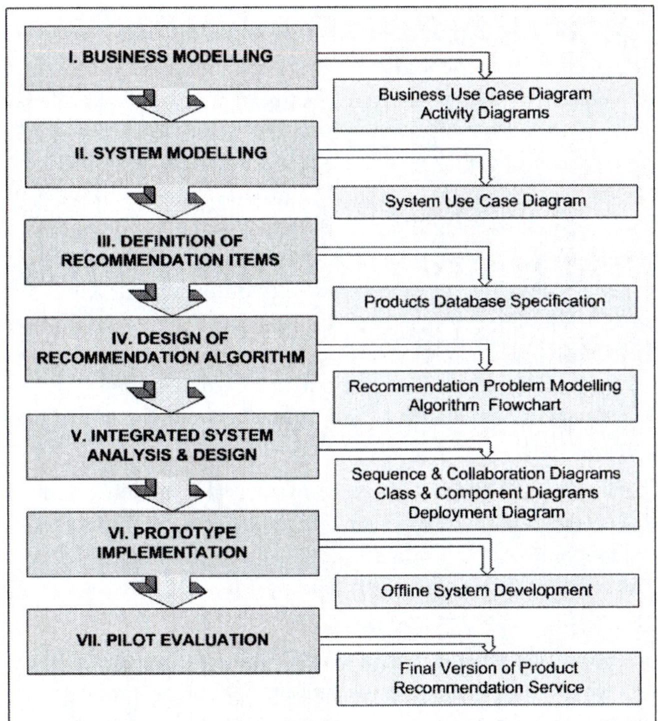

anything that is external, interacting with the system. The outcome of this step is a system use case diagram, which provides an overview of the identified actors and use cases, as well as the associations between them.

III. **Definition of recommendation items.** This step concerns the identification and modeling of the products to be recommended and their recommendation-relevant characteristics. Similarly (if required), the characteristics that will be stored to the buyers' profiles are also defined. This step is closely coupled with the enhancement of the databases of the e-market. Therefore, the outcome of this step is expected to be in the form of an ER diagram, which is generally used to describe the static aspects of databases.

IV. **Design of recommendation algorithm.** This step deals with the formulation of the recommendation problem, based on the supported use cases as defined in the business use case diagram, and the definition of the recommendation items during the previous step. Thus, we define the algorithm that will be used by the recommendation service in order to produce the recommendation. The outcome of this step is a model of the recommendation problem (e.g., in the form of a function synthesizing the various parameters) and a flowchart of the produced algorithm.

V. **Integrated system analysis and design.** This step involves the analysis and design of the e-market system, introducing new use cases, as well as sub-systems and software components required to implement them. At this point, each new use case of the e-market has to be supported by the appropriate (new or existing) sub-systems. During the e-market system analysis, the interactions between the involved actors and the e-market sub-systems are illustrated using sequence diagrams (for each new use case). Moreover, during the e-market design, a number of class diagrams have to be developed, representing the information that e-market sub-systems hold and exchange, by displaying the classes in a system. Additionally, there have to be developed one or more component diagrams, which will illustrate the components in the e-market system (the physical modules of software code) and the dependencies between them. Finally, another result of e-market design is a deployment diagram, which is concerned with the physical deployment of the system, the network layout, and the location of components in the network. This diagram illustrates all nodes of the e-market system network, the connections between them, and the processes that will run on each one.

VI. **Prototype implementation.** This step concerns the implementation of the recommendation service components, such as the recommended products' database, the recommendation algorithm or different algorithm variations, and the user interfaces. The outcome of this step is a service prototype, usually as a standalone off-line system module.

VII. **Pilot evaluation.** This step is related to performing an initial evaluation of the service prototype, using either simulated or real data. The appropriate variation of the recommendation algorithm is selected, and the user interface design and functionalities are finalized. If any fine tuning is required, we can go back to Step III. The outcome of this step is the final version of the product recommendation service, ready to be integrated into the e-market system.

A Case Study

In this section, the proposed design process is applied in a real case study. It refers to the integration of a wine recommendation service in a Greek e-market that offers agricultural products (*www.greekproducts.com*). This e-market provides access, among others, to a product catalog of Greek wines. The wines offered come from various producers and areas, and often have totally different characteristics. This e-market is an established one, which does not include a recommendation service so far. A potential buyer can browse categories of wines classified according to characteristics such as the variety name and price range. The results of browsing provide the user with a list of matching wines. In the following, the proposed design steps for integrating a wine recommendation service in this e-market are applied. All UML diagrams have been produced using the Rational Rose modeling tool.

Figure 2. Business use case diagram of the case study e-market

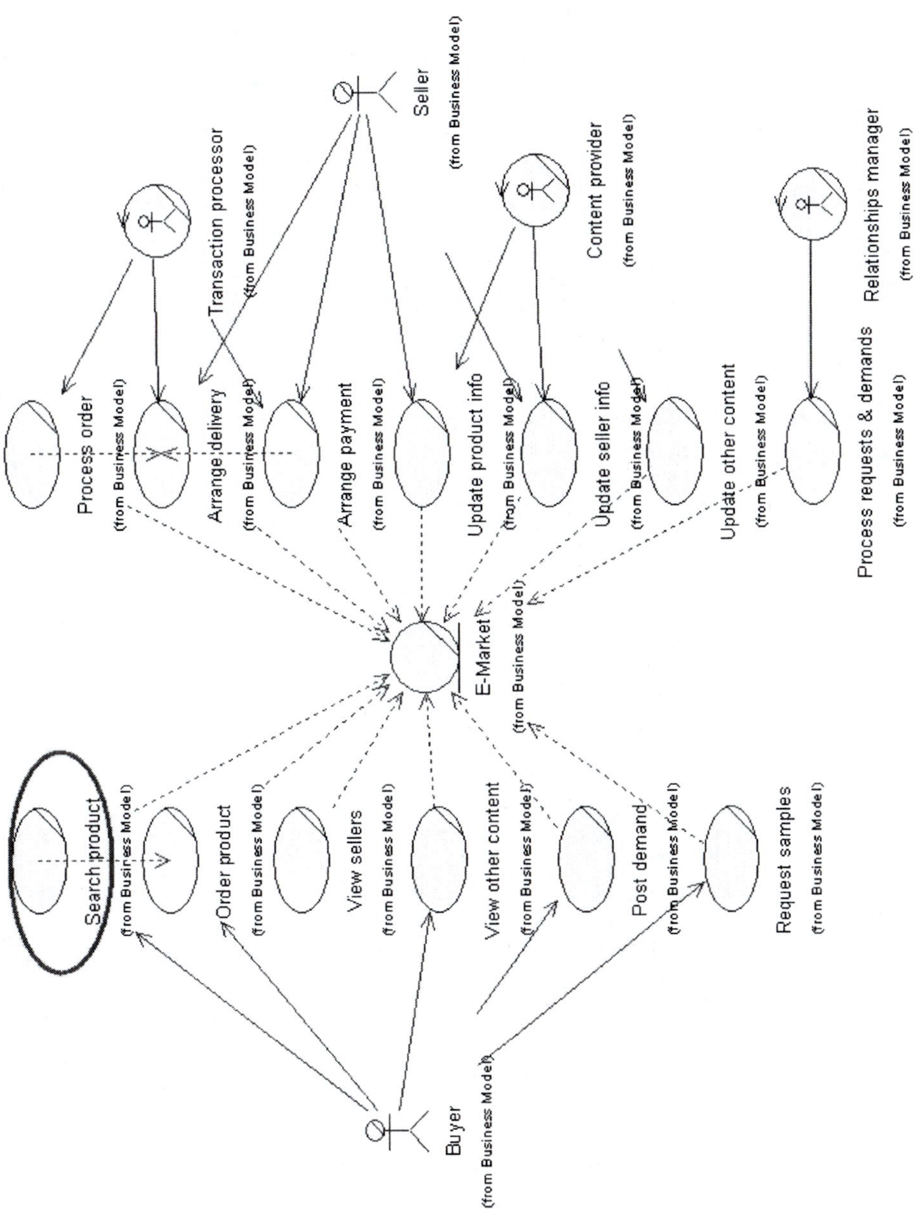

I. Business Modeling

From the buyer's perspective, the e-market business refers to an e-market that facilitates online users in finding appropriate products according to their needs. Thus, the business actors of the e-market under study that will take advantage of the e-market business are the following:

- **Buyer**, who is interested in finding Greek agricultural products in the e-market and is expected to be a consumer or a business entity (retailer, manufacturer, agent/broker, distributor, wholesaler etc.).
- **Seller**, who is offering Greek agricultural products to interested buyers through the e-market and is expected to be a producer, processor, or cooperative/association of producers.

Furthermore, the business workers of the e-market are the following:

- **Transaction processor**, who is responsible for receiving orders, processing them, and taking necessary actions for timely product delivery.
- **Relationships manager**, who is responsible for establishing contact with new business actors (either buyers or sellers).
- **Content provider**, who is responsible for the collection, authoring, and publication of the information in the e-market. This actor is responsible for collecting, publishing, and updating information about available products and about participating sellers. Moreover, he or she is responsible for all other kinds of content published in the e-market such as news, newsletter, sector studies, and health information.

The business use case diagram of the e-market under study provides an overview of the e-market business context and the way that the involved business actors are engaged (Figure 2). Marked in this diagram is the "Search product" business use case, which will be further analysed in this chapter, since it is the one mainly affected by the integration of the wine recommendation service. The workflow of each business use case can be further analysed in detail using activity diagrams.

II. System Modeling

Since our focus is on the integration of a wine recommendation service, use case modeling is engaged to demonstrate how new use cases can be introduced in the e-market system. For the "Search product" business use case, only the Buyer business actor, the Relationships manager business worker, and the Content provider business worker participate. All of them are involved in a number of system use cases related to the "Search product" business use case, which are:

- **Publish product** concerns the description of a product characteristics and the submission of this description to the e-market.
- **Update product** concerns the modification of some characteristics of a product.
- **Delete product** concerns the request for deletion of a product description from the e-market.
- **View product category** concerns viewing a category of a particular type of products in the e-market.
- **Browse** concerns browsing product categories and viewing lists of products in each category.
- **View product** concerns viewing the characteristics of a product, as stored in the e-market.

In order to integrate the wine recommendation service in the e-market, the following new use cases have to be added:

- **Make user profile** concerns submitting a registration request to the e-market so that a user profile is created.

Figure 3. Use case diagram related to "Search product" business use case

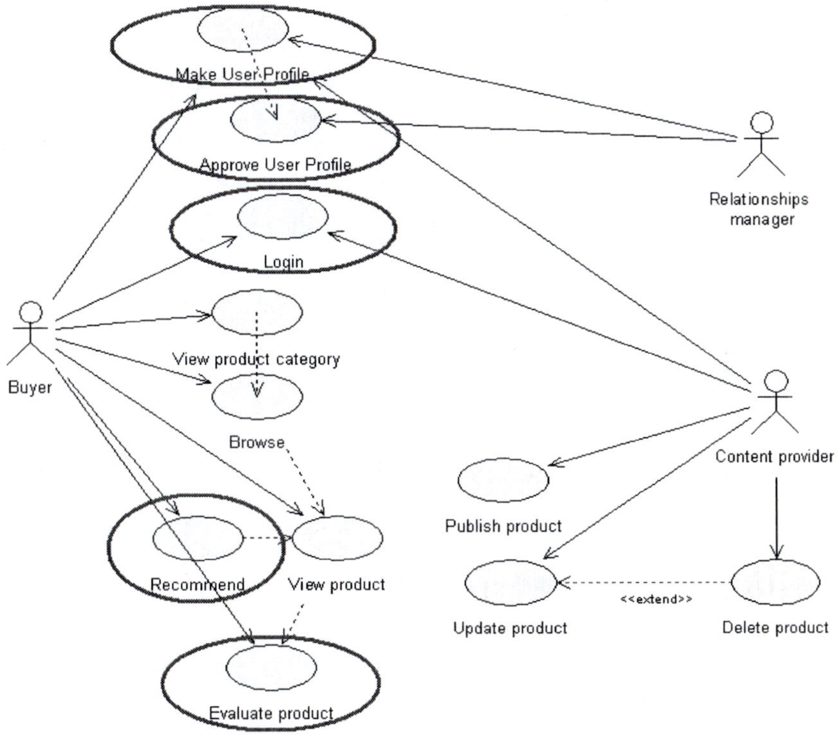

- **Approve user profile** concerns checking and approving (or not) a user registration request.
- **Login** concerns the logging in to the e-market process. It aims to allow only registered users to evaluate products and receive recommendations.
- **Evaluate product** concerns the submission of an evaluation (rating) of a product offered by the e-market.
- **Recommend** concerns the request for a recommendation of appropriate products, using already available product evaluations, so that a ranked list of recommended products is presented to the customer.

Figure 3 illustrates the use case diagram that is related to the "Search product" business use case. Marked in this diagram are the additional e-market system use cases required for the wine recommendation service.

III. Definition of Recommendation Items

The products candidate for recommendation in our case study are wines. In the e-market under study, wines are described using characteristics such as a unique ID, their name, their producer, a short description, and their price. The proposed wine recommendation service aims to follow the rationale of the Amazon recommendation service, which collects ratings of products from buyers who have tried them in order to help new buyers decide what to purchase.

In our case study, a more complex recommendation algorithm is engaged, based on multi-attribute utility theory (MAUT) (Keeney, 1992). It will produce wine recommendations based on multi-attribute subjective evaluations. This is the reason why a number of criteria that can affect buyers' choice have to be introduced. For the needs of this case study, eight criteria have been adopted from related literature (Baourakis, Matsatsinis, & Siskos, 1996), forming a set $\{g_1,..., g_8\}$ of criteria for wine evaluation (namely odor, quality, company image, packaging, authenticity, environmental influence, and price advertisement). According to Roy (1996), each criterion g_i $(i=1,...,8)$ is a non-decreasing real valued function, exhaustive, and non-redundant. We engage MAUT to represent the preference of the buyers upon the multiple criteria. Therefore, the total utility U of a wine a is defined as an additive value function of the following form:

$$U(a) = \sum_{i=1}^{8} w_i g_i(a) \qquad (1)$$

where $g_i(a)$ is the evaluation value of product a on criterion g_i, and w_i is a weight indicating the importance of criterion g_i for a particular buyer, with:

Figure 4. An ER diagram of the wine evaluations database

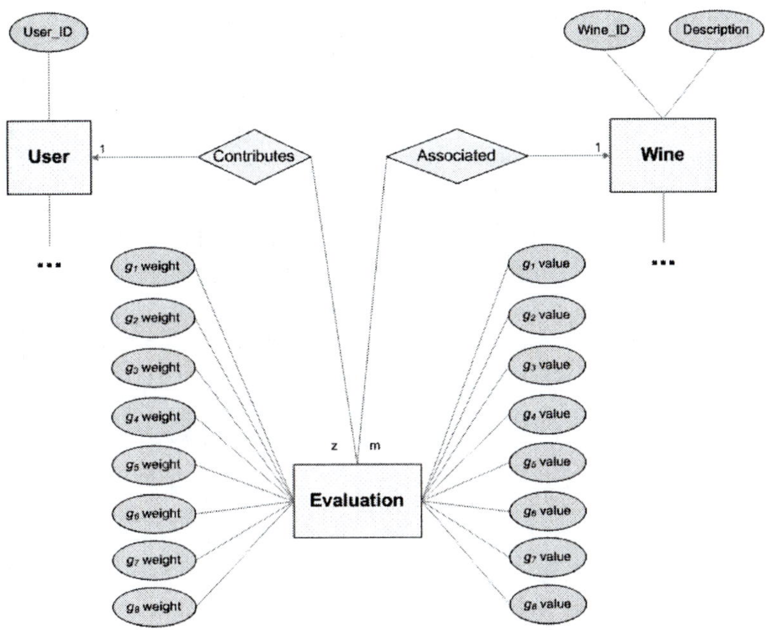

$$\sum_{i=1}^{8} w_i = 1 \tag{2}$$

The MAUT modeling affects the design of the recommendation service, since both the wine evaluations and the evaluator's importance weights have to be stored. This leads to the design of an appropriate database component to store wine evaluations. This component is specified using an ER diagram (Figure 4). A database component storing the buyer evaluations of wines upon these criteria is added to the system.

IV. Design of Recommendation Algorithm

In order to calculate the utility of a candidate product (wine) for a buyer who initiates the recommendation service, the following recommendation algorithm is considered: let m buyers to have provided evaluations for a particular product a. Now, the utility of the particular product a for each one of the buyers can be calculated. In the case where only one (m=1) evaluation exists, the utility for this buyer is given by formula 1. In the case where more than one (m>1) evaluations exist, the utilities U^k (k=1,…,m) for these buyers are calculated using formula 3:

Figure 5. The recommendation algorithm flow

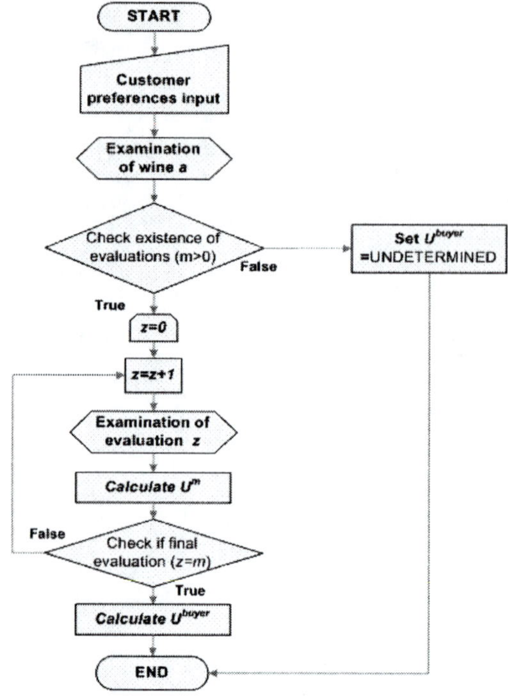

$$a \rightarrow \begin{cases} U^1 = \sum_{i=1}^{8} w_i^1 g_i^1(a) \\ \dots \\ U^m = \sum_{i=1}^{8} w_i^{z_j} g_i^{z_j}(a) \end{cases} \quad (3)$$

In order to predict the preferences of a new buyer in regards to the product *a*, the algorithm takes as input the utilities of the previous buyers, and produces as outcome the predicted utility U^{buyer}. A flowchart of this algorithm is depicted in Figure 5. Different formulas can be used for calculating U^{buyer}, leading to different variations of the algorithm that can be compared for performance.

V. Integrated System Analysis & Design

In the studied e-market system, use cases are supported by a set of sub-systems. The following e-market sub-systems are identified:

- **Interface sub-system**, responsible for the interaction with the users, passing information to and from the users to the e-market.

Figure 6. Sequence diagram for "Evaluate product" use case

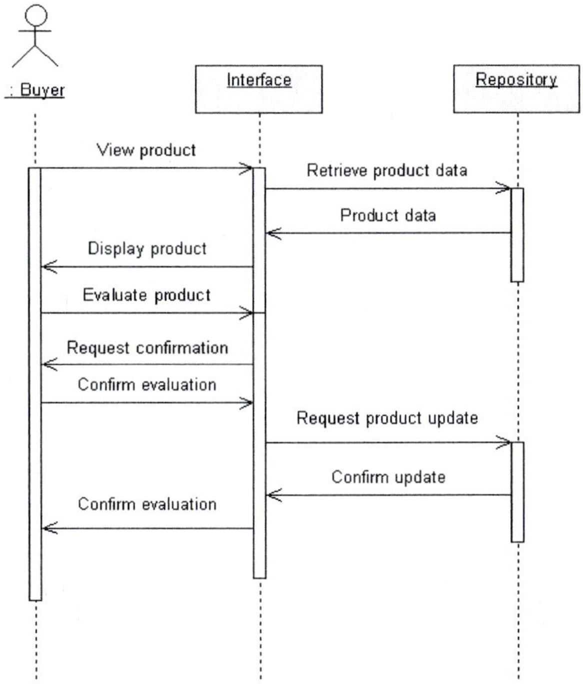

- **Search sub-system**, responsible for transforming user search interactions to queries that are understandable from e-market, as well as for returning the results to the interface sub-system.
- **Repository sub-system**, responsible for storing the descriptions and evaluations of products, providing data to the e-market interface according to the users' requests.

Sequence diagrams have been produced for each new use case. For brevity reasons, only the sequence diagram for the "Evaluate product" use case is presented (Figure 6). Moreover, for the e-market design, class diagrams have also been produced for the new use cases. Figure 8 presents the component diagram for the "Evaluate product" use case. More specifically, the user is authenticated and logs into the system, using the appropriate component user authentication (after the user information is checked in the users database). Then, the eight components that collect both the importance weight and the evaluation upon each criterion are appropriately storing them in the product evaluation database. Finally, Figure 9 presents the deployment diagram of the studied e-market system. At the server side, a MySQL server is the database server of the e-market that manages the e-market databases. At the same machine, an Apache Web server has been also installed, together with CGI scripting capabilities. On the client side, the user can view the e-market though a Web browser.

Figure 7. Class diagram for the "Evaluate product" use case (holds for all products, as well as for the wine case study)

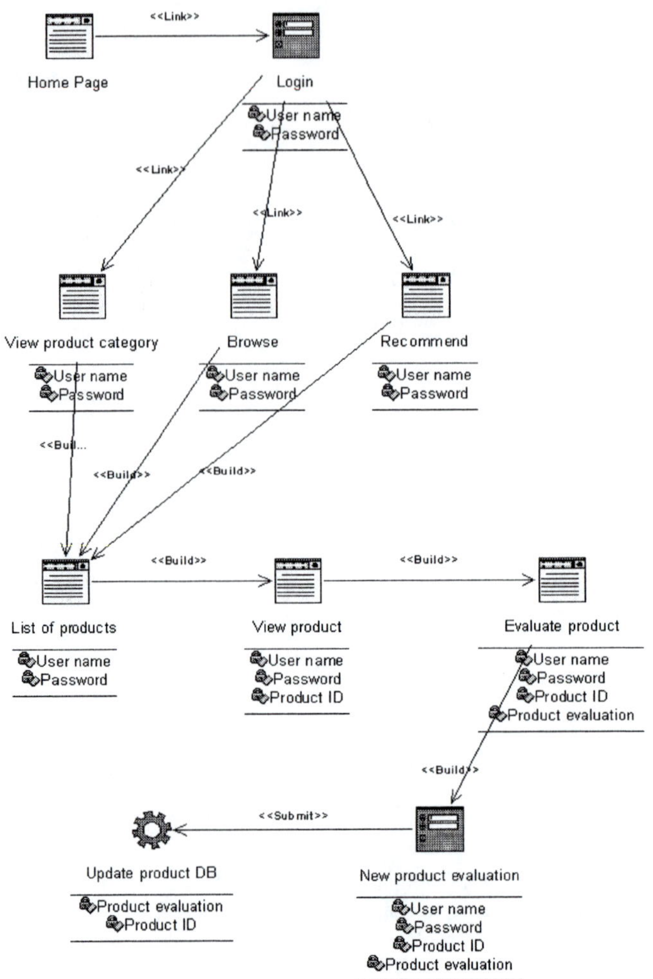

VI. Prototype Implementation

In this step, the prototype off-line version of the recommendation service has been implemented. Figure 10 provides an example of the wine recommendation user interface design. It demonstrates how on a regular screenshot of the e-market under study, a recommendation hint will appear next to a specific wine when the list of 'Search' results is presented to a buyer. The total suitability of a wine for the buyer is scaled to a value from *1* to *5* and represented as a number of stars (a visual cue often used in such systems).

Figure 8. Component diagram corresponding for "Evaluating product" use case (depicts only the components for only the wine case study, for other products additional ones will have to be included according to their evaluation criteria)

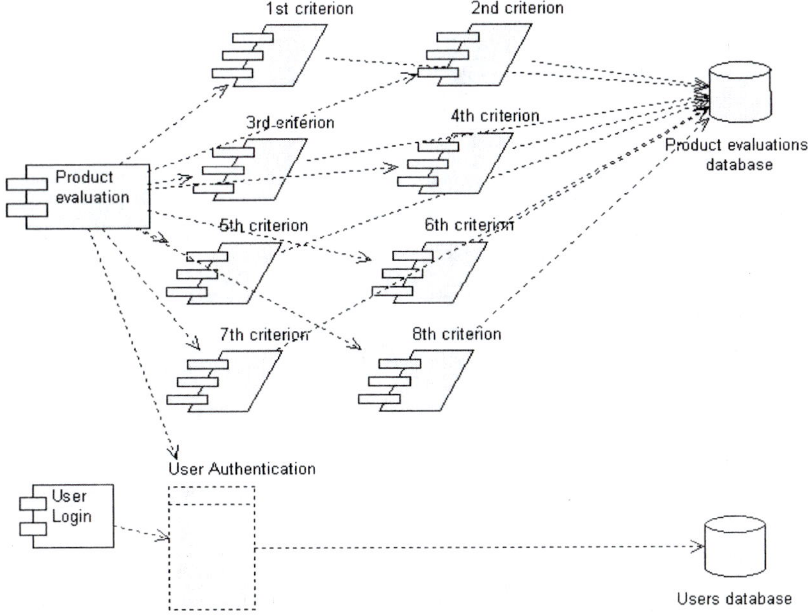

Figure 9. Deployment diagram of e-market

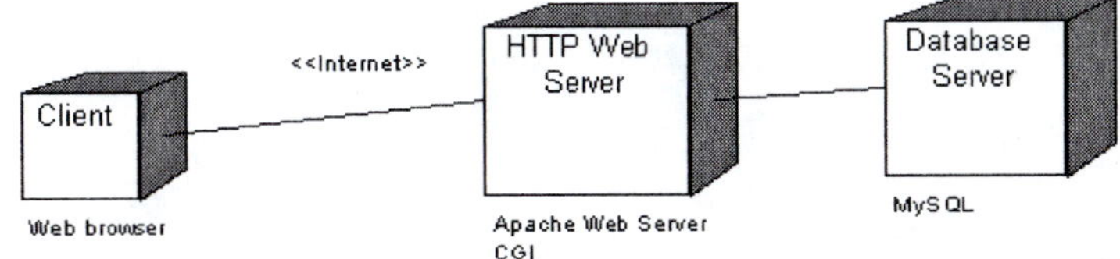

Figure 11 illustrates the way the wine recommendation service prototype can be integrated with the existing e-market architecture. In this figure, a layered view of the e-market with five levels of abstraction is presented: data storage, data management, supporting services, market services, and user interfaces. Each of these layers contains a number of e-market components, which have been enriched by the introduction of the additional system components (highlighted in Figure 11). For instance, the market services level included the "publish new wine," "browse wine list," and "view wine details" services. By integrating the recommendation service, an "evaluate wine" service has been added at this layer. Similarly, the "wine recommendation algorithm" has been added to the supporting services level, and the "wine

Figure 10. Interface design for wine recommendation results

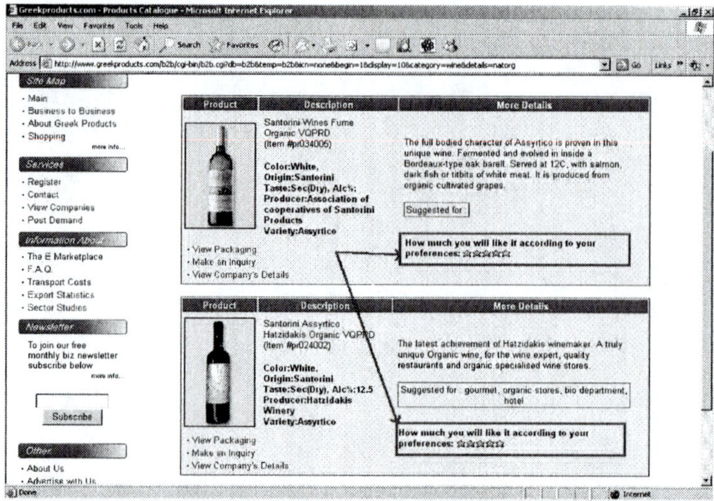

Figure 11. Wine recommendation integrated into layered e-market architecture

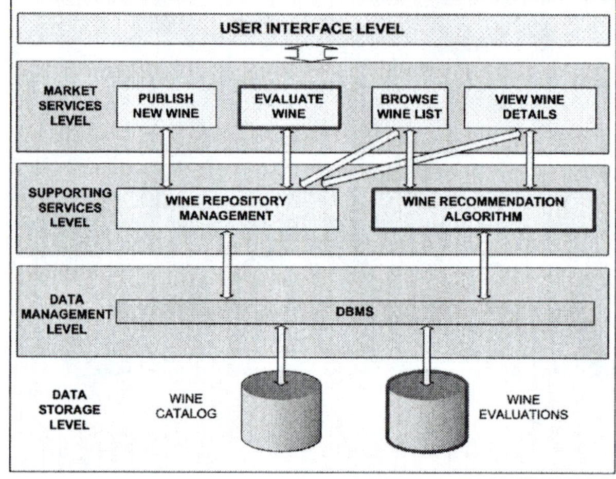

evaluations" to the data storage level. The new components of the studied e-market layered architecture have been implemented according to the results of the proposed design steps.

VII. Pilot Evaluation

This step deals with the selection of the appropriate variation of the wine recommendation algorithm. Simulated data about existing wines and their evaluations have been created and stored in the e-market system databases. More specifically, the wines' database has been populated with the descriptions of 10 wines $\{a_1, .., a_{10}\}$. It was assumed that a group of simulated buyers had previously provided evaluations for all 10 wines. Results comparing the recommendations of the algorithm variations to the actual preferences of buyers have been produced. The pilot evaluation results indicated which variation seems to be more suitable for the wine recommendation service of the examined e-market (Manouselis & Costopoulou, 2005). The integration of the proposed wine recommendation service in the e-market system has not yet taken place. The public deployment of this service in the e-market will be fully operative after the final decision of the e-market owners.

Conclusion

Recommender systems can offer important added value when integrated into e-markets. They can support potential buyers during the information gathering phase by providing product recommendations that match their preferences. However, the majority of the existing e-markets are not providing advanced recommendation services, although such services may offer a competitive advantage to an e-market. Some reasons might be the inherent complexity of intelligent recommendation services, as well as their deployment and evaluation costs. Currently, recommendation services are developed on a case-by-case basis, and to our knowledge there are no guidelines for integrating product recommendation services in e-markets.

To this direction, it is worth it to identify a framework for an efficient design process that will reduce the complexity of this kind of deployment. In particular, it is important to provide e-market designers with guidelines on how to efficiently design, develop, evaluate, and integrate recommendation services in existing e-markets. Thus, this chapter presented a design process for integrating intelligent product recommendation services in e-markets. This process is applied to a real e-market offering Greek agricultural products, for the deployment of a recommendation service of a particular type of products (i.e., wine). Similar services can be developed for other types of products. This work may be useful to two groups: academics/researchers studying product recommendation services for e-commerce applications; and e-market system designers and implementers considering the integration of product recommendation services in e-markets. Our next steps include the application of the proposed design process in other e-markets.

Future trends in the design and integration of intelligent recommendation services in e-markets include more focus on the aspects of evaluating different AI-based recommendation techniques, in order to choose the most appropriate one for deploying in a particular market context. This type of evaluation mainly includes two aspects:

- The evaluation of the different ways recommendations can be presented and explained to the buyers of the e-markets (small-scaled pilot experiments can help e-market designers to decide, for example, the appropriate interface design, as discussed by Herlocker, Konstan, & Riedl, 2000).

- The evaluation of various intelligent techniques for the recommendation algorithms so that the one providing higher accuracy and coverage results can be selected (simulation experiments can facilitate this design choice decisions, as discussed by Herlocker et al., 2002).

References

Baourakis, G., Matsatsinis, N. F., & Siskos, Y. (1996). Agricultural product development using multidimensional and multicriteria analyses: The case of wine. *European Journal of Operational Research, 94*(2), 321-334.

Boggs, W., & Boggs, M. (2002). *Mastering UML with Rational Rose*. Alameda, CA: SYBEX Inc.

Booch, G., Rumbaugh, J., & Jacobson, I. (1998). *The Unified Modelling Language user guide*. Boston: Addison Wesley.

Burke, R. (2002). Hybrid recommender systems: Survey and experiments. *User Modelling and User-Adapted Interaction, 12*, 331-370.

Changchien, S. W., & Lu, T.-C. (2001). Mining association rules procedure to support on-line recommendation by customers and products fragmentation. *Expert Systems with Applications, 20*, 325-335.

Cheung, K.-W., Kwok, J. T., Law, M. H., & Tsui, K.-C. (2003). Mining customer product ratings for personalized marketing. *Decision Support Systems, 35*, 231-243.

Cho, Y. H., Kim, J. K., & Kim, S. H. (2002). A personalised recommender system based on Web usage mining and decision tree induction. *Expert System with Applications, 23*, 329-342.

Deshpande, M., & Karypis, G. (2004). Item-based Top-N recommendation algorithms. *ACM Transactions on Information Systems, 22*(1), 143-177.

Herlocker, J., Konstan, J. A., & Riedl, J. (2000). *Explaining collaborative filtering recommendations*. Paper presented at the 2000 Conference on Computer Supported Cooperative Work.

Herlocker, J., Konstan, J. A., & Riedl, J. (2002). An empirical analysis of design choices in neighborhood-based collaborative filtering algorithms. *Information Retrieval, 5*, 287-310.

Herlocker, J. L., Konstan, J. A., Terveen, L. G., & Riedl, J. T. (2004). Evaluating collaborative filtering recommender systems. *ACM Transactions on Information Systems, 22*(1), 5-53.

Holzmueller, H. H., & Schluechter J. (2002). Delphi study about the future of B2B marketplaces in Germany. *Electronic Commerce Research & Applications, 1*, 2-19.

Hung, L. (2005). A personalized recommendation system based on product taxonomy for one-to-one marketing online. *Expert Systems with Applications, 29*(2), 383-392.

Keeney, R. L. (1992). *Value-focusedtThinking: A path to creative decision making*. Cambridge, MA: Harvard University Press.

Kim, J. K., Cho, Y. H., Kim, W. J., Kim, J. R., & Suh, J. H. (2002). A personalized recommendation procedure for Internet shopping support. *Electronic Commerce Research and Applications, 1*, 301-313.

Kim, J.W., Lee, B. H., Shaw, M. J., Chang, H.-L., & Nelson, M. (2001). Application of decision-tree induction techniques to personalized advertisements on Internet storefronts. *International Journal of Electronic Commerce, 5*(3), 45-62.

Kim, Y. S., Yum, B.-J., Song, J., & Kim, S. M. (2005). Development of a recommender system based on navigational and behavioral patterns of customers in e-commerce sites. *Expert Systems with Applications, 28*(2), 381-393.

Lee, J.-S., Jun, C.-H., Lee, J., & Kim, S. (2005). Classification-based collaborative filtering using market basket data. *Expert Systems with Applications, 29*, 700-704.

Lee, W.-P. (2004) Towards agent-based decision making in the electronic marketplace: Interactive recommendation and automated negotiation. *Expert Systems with Applications, 27*(4), 665-679.

Li, Y., Lu, L., & Xuefeng, L. (2005). A hybrid collaborative filtering method for multiple-interests and multiple-content recommendation in E-Commerce. *Expert Systems with Applications, 28*, 67-77.

Lihua, W., Lu, L., Jing, L., & Zongyong, L. (2005). Modeling multiple interests by an improved GCS approach. *Expert Systems with Applications, 29*, 757-767.

Manouselis, N., Costopoulou, C. (2005). *Designing Recommendation Services for e-Markets* (Tech. Rep.) Athens, Greece: Agricultural University of Athens, Informatics Laboratory.

Martin-Guerrero, J. D., Palomares, A., Balaguer-Ballester, E., Soria-Olivas, E., Gomez-Sanchis, J., & Soriano-Asensi, A. (in press). Studying the feasibility of a recommender in a citizen Web portal based on user modeling and clustering algorithms. *Expert Systems with Applications, 30*, 299-312.

Middleton, S. E., Shadbolt, N. R., & Roure, D. C. (2004). Ontological user profiling in recommender systems. *ACM Transactions on Information Systems, 22*(1), 54-88.

Miller, B. N., Konstan, J. A., & Riedl, J. (2004). PocketLens: Toward a personal recommender system. *ACM Transactions on Information Systems, 22*(3), 437-476.

Resnick, P., & Varian, H. R. (1997). Recommender systems. *Communications of the ACM, 40*(3), 56-58.

Richard, B., & Tchounikine, P. (2004). Enhancing the adaptivity of an existing Website with an epiphyte recommender system. *New Review of Hypermedia and Multimedia, 10*(1), 31-52.

Roy, B. (1996). *Multicriteria methodology for decision aiding*. Dordrecht, The Netherlands: Kluwer Academic Publishers.

Saleh, K. (2002). Documenting electronic commerce systems and software using the unified modelling language. *Information and Software Technology, 44*, 303-311.

Schafer, J. B., Konstan, J., & Riedl, J. (2001). E-commerce recommendation applications. *Data Mining and Knowledge Discovery, 5*, 115-153.

Stolze, M. (2002). Domain-oriented recommender applications: A framework for intimate recommending. In F. Ricci & B. Smith (Eds.), *Proceedings of the Adaptive Hypermedia Workshop on Recommendation and Personalization in eCommerce* (pp. 24-131). Computer Science Technical Report, Malaga: University of Malaga.

Wang, Y.-F., Chuang, Y.-L., Hsu, M.-H., & Keh, H.-C. (2004). A personalized recommender system for the cosmetic business. *Expert Systems with Applications, 26*, 427-434.

Yen, B. P.-C., & Kong, R. C. W. (2002). Personalization of information access for electronic catalogs on the Web. *Electronic Commerce Research and Applications, 1*, 20-40.

Chapter XX

A Stage Model for NPD Process Maturity and IKMS Implementation

Nassim Belbaly, UCLA Anderson Business School of Management, USA

Hind Benbya, UCLA Anderson Business School of Management, USA

Abstract

The objective of this chapter is to provide an analytical tool to assist organizations in their implementations of intelligent knowledge management systems (IKMS) along the new product development (NPD) process. Indeed, organizations rely on a variety of systems using artificial intelligence to support the NPD process that depends on the maturity stage of both the process and type of knowledge managed. Our framework outlines the technological and organizational path that organizations have to follow to integrate and manage knowledge effectively along their new product development process. In doing so, we also address the main limitations of the systems used to date and suggest the evolution toward a new category of KMS based on artificial intelligence that we refer to as intelligent knowledge management systems. We illustrate our framework with an analysis of several case studies.

Introduction

New product development (NPD) is seen among the essential processes for success, survival, and renewal of organizations, and firms have been constantly concerned with managing knowledge related to this process to drive performance and achieve time-to-market reduction. In this aim, organizations rely on a variety of information systems that range from simple knowledge repositories to more advanced knowledge management systems such as intelligent knowledge management systems.

While the importance of managing knowledge along the NPD process and using specific systems for this aim is widely acknowledged, few authors have so far attempted to characterize or relate the type of systems used with the characteristics of knowledge relying on the maturity of the NPD process. Such a framework will enable organizations not only to assess the maturity of their NPD process but also to support them in moving from one stage to the other and suggesting specific systems supporting each level of maturity. Today, these systems are called intelligent knowledge management systems (IKMS) because they rely more and more on artificial intelligence (AI) to overcome their limitations. In doing so, this chapter suggests an analytical framework for information systems implementation that depends on the maturity of the NPD process and the type of knowledge managed at each stage. Consequently, we examine some unexplored questions:

1. How can an organization move its NPD process from one stage to a more advanced stage?
2. Which systems should the organization adopt in each stage of its NPD life cycle?

The research on which this chapter is based relies on an in-depth analysis of the new product development process in five leading software and manufacturing companies. The remainder of this chapter proceeds as follows. First, we examine the literature related to the importance of managing knowledge during the new product development process, highlighting the tools and systems used and their main limitations. Next, we present our framework of analysis — the analytical framework for defining the maturity of the NPD process and the systems relying on artificial intelligence needed at each stage of the evolution process. We illustrate how this framework could be used through an analysis of five case studies. We finish with our discussion and conclusion summarizing our propositions, outlining the limitations of our study, and describing the implications for future research and for practice.

Knowledge Management and New Product Development

In many industries, the survival of firms is increasingly determined by their success in new product development (Cooper, 2001; Schilling & Hill, 1998). On average, more than one-third of a corporation's revenue comes from products that did not exist five years ago

Figure 1. A generic model of NPD process stage and gate

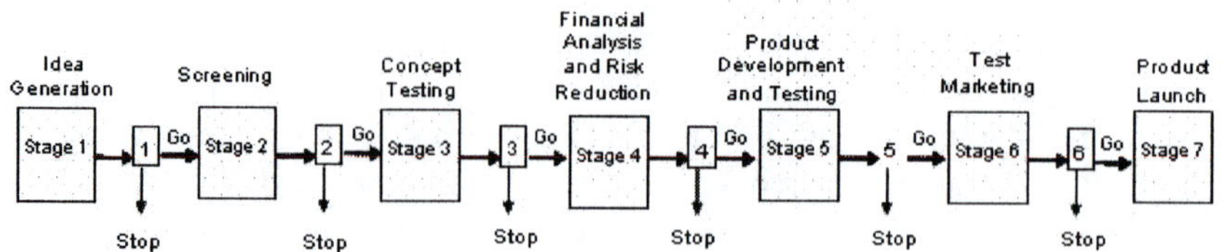

(Nambisan, 2003). This is particularly true for technology-driven firms, whose competition lies on the new product development (NPD) cycle time, and whose performance is a function of their ability to manage efficiently their NPD in getting to their markets faster as well as responding to their customer needs and expectations. NPD has also gained its importance by the fact that it covers a wide set of activities "beginning with the perception of a market opportunity and ending in the production, sales, and delivery of a product" (Ulrich & Eppinger, 2000). Due to competitive pressures, limited resources, and accelerating costs that characterize most NPD projects (Cooper & Kleinschmidt, 1986), firms increasingly use formalized and structured processes (Griffin, 1997). The NPD process corresponds to a conceptual and operational roadmap for moving a new product project from idea to launch (Cooper, 1994). This roadmap is scalable to suit the size and risk of the project (Cooper, 2001). This means that the number of stage gate processes depends on the critical decisions that have to be made. The outcome of each stage gate is a critical decision to either continue or abort the process, which in practice is reflected by major cost increase or decrease (Shake, 1999). Though they vary in their levels of complexity, virtually all NPD processes have two core features: activities and decisions — both of which are knowledge intensive. Figure 1 illustrates a generic NPD process.

Each stage of the NPD process requires the combination of knowledge and skills to perform useful actions to solve ill-structured problems. The solutions to these ill-structured problems are based on a combination of previous experience, formal knowledge, and specific and uncodified or tacit capabilities of the organization members (Marsh & Stock, 2000). These solutions are possible through an iteration of "doing, learning, and doing some more," with each iteration adding to the organization's capabilities (Wheelwright & Clark, 1992). In other words, NPD is a complex innovation process requiring the use of tacit and explicit knowledge in order to create and apply something that is new. This places a premium on the ability to effectively capture the knowledge created during the process so that it can be reused in the next generation of products to reduce development time.

Several studies put the emphasis on the criticality of managing knowledge developed during product design. Brockman and Morgan (2003) found a strong link between existing knowledge and NPD performance, while Marsh and Stock (2003) developed a model that outlines how organizations can integrate knowledge over time to ensure successful new product success and long-term competitive advantage. Nambisan (2003) argues that NPD is an emerging area where information systems (IS) could become a reference discipline and suggests four dimensions in which IS support NPD: process management, project management, information and knowledge management, and collaboration and communication. New evidence suggests that deploying information systems to support knowledge management in the context of NPD may actually represent enormous opportunities in terms of performance, generally, and time-to-market reduction, particularly. In what follows, we analyze the different categories of information systems used in the context of NPD and address their main limitations.

Information System and New Product Development

The information systems used to support NPD activities and processes, the NPD systems — referred to as product life cycle management (PLM) — have had a high adoption rate in different sectors and industries. These systems rely on several modules to support the NPD process that range from PLM planning, portfolio management, design, collaborative engineering, to manufacturing (PLM of Microsoft, Oracle, Matrixone, SAP, IBM, etc.). Despite their advantages, these systems remain focused on data and information processing and do not enable the management of strategic knowledge embedded within the NPD process. For this reason, organizations rely on a new category of information systems named knowledge management systems (KMS). KMS have the ability to foster the systematic identification of central knowledge and expertise, encourage the conversion of knowledge into manifest forms (e.g., explicit knowledge), and make information accessible to others in the firm in terms of knowledge reuse and as input for product knowledge development. Scott (1996) suggests that the ability to capture, reuse, maintain, and transfer knowledge is an essential element of the NPD process (Figure 2).

KMS Taxonomy and Main Limitations

In previous research, based on an analysis of several knowledge management systems, we classified KMS in three categories following the articulation of knowledge in tacit versus explicit dimensions. These are dynamic systems (e.g., yellow pages, communities of practice), process-oriented systems (e.g., lessons learned systems, processes description databases, and

Figure 2. Knowledge in new product development (adapted from Scott, 1996)

	Pre-product Design	Product Design	Post-Product Design
Knowledge	Lesson learned Project history Links to experts Customer needs Supplier competence Market intelligence	Product design rationale Process design rationale Causes for problems and failures in product testing	Manufacturability Product testing Root causes for engineering changes
IS	Groupware Intranet KMS	Simulations Prototypes Prod. Data Mgmt. Syst. Videoconferencing KMS	Prod. Data Mgmt. Syst. Videoconferencing KMS

Figure 3. Knowledge management systems classification and examples (Benbya et al., 2005)

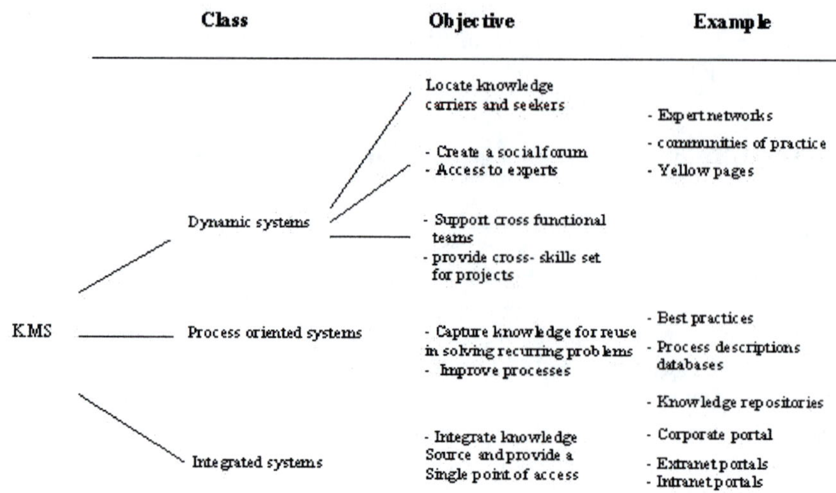

knowledge repositories), and integrative systems (corporate portal, Extranet, and Intranet portals) (Benbya, Passiante, & Belbaly, 2004; Benbya & Belbaly, 2005).

Dynamic Knowledge Management Systems

Dynamic knowledge management systems support mainly interactive communications between experts or team-based management and are consequently more concerned about the tacit dimension of knowledge. This category includes:

- Expertise location or what is called "yellow pages "or "people finder" that captures and inventories the knowledge, experience, and backgrounds of the firm's experts and acts as connectors between knowledge and expertise seekers and holders.
- Communities of practice that provide a social forum to a group of people who share a concern, a set of problems, and who deepen their knowledge and expertise in this area by interacting on an ongoing basis (Wenger, McDermott, & Snyder, 2002).

Process-Oriented Knowledge Management Systems

Organizations with significant intellectual capital require eliciting and capturing knowledge for reuse in new problems as well as recurring old problems. They are mainly codification-based systems focused on the technical side of knowledge and can be an important support for new product development. (e.g., a system to store marketing-oriented documents or more focused on research and development). These systems include: lessons learned systems, processes description databases, knowledge repositories, and best practices databases.

Integrative Knowledge Management Systems

The preceding KMS categories focused mainly on one dimension of knowledge over the other, either tacit knowledge in the case of expert networks and communities of practice or more explicit knowledge focused in the case of codification systems in databases. Today, most contemporary approaches to knowledge management system design rely on an integrative perspective on managing both explicit and tacit knowledge dimensions because it offers unrestricted possibilities for uniformly accessing knowledge across a variety of sources. This is the case of the corporate portal, which integrates different applications from collaboration tools to a database supporting knowledge embedded within business processes (Benbya et al., 2004).

While KMS have become an integral and recognized category of IS designed to manage knowledge in organizations, they still have some shortcomings that limit their functionality. Indeed, most of the traditional KMS are static and fall short in dealing with the exponential increase amount of information that come from distributed, heterogeneous, and voluminous information resources. This situation creates an information overload problem that the traditional KMS are not able to solve. The first generation of KMS is based on the existing data repositories and pre-assumed data needs. This means that if people require knowledge, they search for it through query sending and pull knowledge from the system, whereas the best response to a user's needs is quite often the synthesizing of data from a variety of distributed and heterogeneous sources. Conventional KMS are thus inflexible and stifle the efficient management of the knowledge management processes — creation, storage, transfer, and application (Alavi & Leidner, 2001) — that occur during the product development. To overcome these problems, organizations need to evolve toward the adoption of intelligent KMS based on artificial intelligence.

Toward Intelligent Knowledge Management Systems (IKMS)

From KMS to IKMS

The use of artificial intelligence in information systems gives the possibility to combine the implicit and explicit representations of knowledge. This combination is necessary to overcome the limits of traditional KMS that can store the information, rank it, display it, but cannot comprehend or process it. We refer to KMS that rely on AI as IKMS. By AI, we usually mean the three following dimensions: intelligent agents, logic, and reasoning.

These dimensions are found in Russel and Norvig (1995) who have classified the definitions of artificial intelligence in four categories from eight recent textbooks (Figure 4). These

Figure 4. Matrix of AI definitions

	Human performance	Rationality
Thought and reasoning	Systems that think like humans	Systems that think rationally
Behavior	Systems that act like humans	Systems that act rationally

definitions vary along two main dimensions that form the AI definition matrix. The left upside deal with thought processes and reasoning, and the left bottomside address behavior. Whereas the bottom left measure success in terms of human performance, the bottom left measure an ideal concept of intelligence called rationality. In this chapter, we focus on intelligent agents that can decide what to do and do it, adopting the view that intelligence is concerned mainly with rational action. Ideally, an intelligent agent takes the best possible action in a situation. This leads to the definition of an ideal rational agent (Russel & Norvig, 1995). For each possible percept sequence, an ideal rational agent should do whatever action is expected to maximize its performance measure on the basis of the evidence provided by the percept sequence and whatever built-in knowledge the agent has.

The representation of knowledge and the reasoning processes that bring knowledge to life are central to the entire field of artificial intelligence. Knowledge and reasoning are important for artificial agents because they enable successful behaviors that would be very hard to achieve otherwise. They deal with partially observable environments, and they combine general knowledge with current percepts to infer hidden aspects of the current state prior to selecting actions. They use knowledge-based agents that are able to accept new tasks in the form of explicitly described goals, achieve competence quickly by being told or learning new knowledge about the environment, and they can adapt to changes in the environment by updating their relevant knowledge. On another hand, the logic will be the primary vehicle for representing knowledge. A logical, knowledge-based agent begins with some knowledge of the world and of its own actions. It uses logical reasoning to maintain a description of the world as new percepts arrive, and to deduce a course of actions that will achieve its goals. The knowledge of logical agents is always definite — each proposition is either true or false in the world, although the agent may be agnostic about some propositions. Logic has the pedagogical advantage of being a simple example of a representation for knowledge-based agents, but logic has some severe limitations. Clearly, a large portion of the reasoning carried out by humans and other agents in partially observable environments depends on handling knowledge that is uncertain (Russel & Norvig, 2003).

We define an agent as anything that can be viewed as perceiving its environment through sensors and acting upon that environment through effectors (Russel & Norvig, 2003). Similarly, Franklin and Grasser (1997) defined an autonomous agent as a system situated within and a part of an environment that senses that environment and acts on it, over time, in pursuit of its own agenda and so as to affect what its senses in the future. Agents are already used to search for something in the Internet. Search engines themselves send their robots (or agents) to collect information and keep their databases up-to-date. Other kinds of agents are those in charge of representing a user in all his or her activities called user agents. They are created after a user logs in to a system and are responsible for interacting with him or her to receive any request and to act on behalf of the user they represent. They usually interface with another kind of agent that may be called profiling agents. These latter manage any information associated to the profile of a generic user, such as the credentials, address, preferences, and so on. User agents access the profile information in order to decide how to behave, with respect to the user they represent. Agents can also be helpful in the last phases of a knowledge management and information retrieval process, when data are returned to the requesting users. By cooperating with the user and profiling agents, a filtering agent can decide which data is relevant for the user and which is not, and make decisions about how to rank results according to the user profile-based policies. Additionally, ad hoc advertising agents could monitor an information source for updates to become available and notify a destination about it. They could either be reactive or proactive in this functionality. If reactive, they are more properly called notification agents, where the notifications come as a result of an explicit subscription by someone. If proactive, on the other hand, they assume an advertising role, since it is up to them to decide which users to contact and what content to transfer. All these agents contribute to the migration from static to dynamic KMS intelligence-based — referred to here as intelligent knowledge management systems (IKMS). In reality, IKMS rely on an integrated management that supports a diverse range of data and knowledge sources following a new information infrastructure based mainly on networked collaborative information models. These models rely on meeting various real-time delivery demands by using a team of multi-agents.

IKMS

The IKMS incorporate the view of multi-agent systems (MAS) that offer a highly flexible architecture for developing complex distributed applications. Thus, IKMS can deliver information just as it is required for tasks at hand. Agents can even move on the network carrying along the tasks they were assigned. They have proven that they can be quite helpful to perform routine tasks, which are normally carried out by human users.

This new generation of KMS relies on artificial intelligence in the form of intelligent agents as well as active knowledge resources represented with semantically rich meta-data to improve inaccuracies of information retrieval, and maximize the shareability of knowledge (Abar, Abe, & Kinoshita, 2004). These intelligent agents are also called software agents, and are able to increase the quality of services to help in the search and retrieval methods with KMS, as well as to assist in combining knowledge, leading consequently to the creation of new knowledge (Barthes & Tacla, 2002; Barbuceanu & Fox, 1994). They can also perform the processing of large quantities of information, searching over multiple sources spread all over the world, extracting selected portions of documents and so on.

Multi-agent systems (MAS) offer a highly flexible architecture for developing the complex distributed applications. At present, machines and software can store the information, rank it, display it, but cannot comprehend or process it. Therefore, IKMS will likely rely on conceptual models in the form of ontologies (Maedche, Motik, Stojanovic, Studer, & Volz, 2003). Ontologies[1] open the way to move from a document-oriented view of the KM to a content-oriented view, where knowledge items are structured, interlinked, combined, and used thereby facilitating agent interactions and communication with the sources, whereas semantic Web[2] technologies, especially ontologies and machine-processable relational

Figure 5. Functional architecture of IKMS (adapted form Abar et al., 2004)

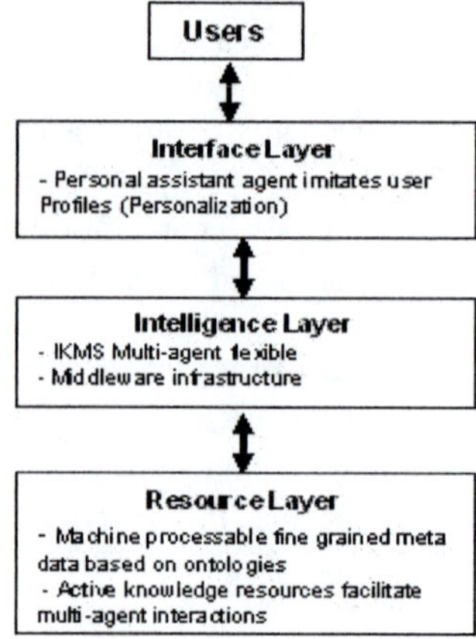

metadata[3], pave the way to enhanced KM solutions that are based on semantically related knowledge pieces of varying granularity (Davies, Fensel, & Harmelen, 2003). Hence, the impetus of next generation IKMS is the development of scalable, flexible, extensible, and interoperable distributed content management systems that know what to deliver to whom, using what mode, when, and how quickly. Figure 5 shows a three-layered functional architecture of the next generation knowledge management system (Abar et al., 2004). This architecture consists of the interface, intelligence, and resource layers. The interface layer stands for managing information in and out of the knowledge management system. When this information is relevant, timely, and actionable, it represents knowledge. At the interface layer, the KM system users interact with the system to create, explicate, use, retrieve, and share knowledge. The interface layer provides a universal mechanism for accessing all the layers and underlying processes for delivering the information. The personal assistant (PA) agent represents the interests of the user and provides the interface between the user and the system. It gradually learns how to better assist the user by observing and imitating the user, understanding user's interests and needs, and building up user's profiles. Through this layer, a virtual work environment is created which enables tacit knowledge sharing. Then, the intelligence layer which consists of multi-agent middleware infrastructure and that remains active all the time, behave concurrently in an autonomous manner to achieve a common goal regarding constantly changing user interests and heterogeneous knowledge resources. Agents can check the dynamic conditions of the knowledge management environment, reason to interpret those perceptions, solve problems, determine actions, and finally act accordingly. Some agents have an ability to learn from past mistakes at an explicit level, which is something very much in line with what a KM system is intended to help with. Finally, the structured resource layer contains organization's intellectual assets. The considerable size of the information space and the variety of resources residing in it, make network information access a daunting task. Therefore, knowledge should be organized by an appropriate taxonomy for the ease of its retrieval. By enhancing the existing information sources with meta-data, the agents are able to recognize and understand what information is and what is it about. This is because every agent understands and agrees on the meaning of a "term" the other agent is speaking because the term is officially described in a public ontology that can be referred to.

A Stage Model for NPD Process Maturity Model and IKMS Implementation

New Product Development (NPD) and Capability Maturity Model (CMM)

A number of studies have indicated the benefits of structured processes (Booz, Allen, & Hamilton, 1982). Griffin (1997) found that a structured, formal development process helps reduce development cycle time, and this effect is accentuated when the project involves the development of a relatively complex product. Eisenhardt and Tabrizi (1995) found in a study of the computer industry that firms using an "experiential strategy of multiple design iterations, extensive testing, frequent project milestones, a powerful project leader, and a multifunctional team" accelerated development. Finally, the Department of Defense guide for integrated product and process development (1996) specifically prescribes that continuous, measurable improvement should be an integral part of the NPD implementation. Defining and using process-focused metrics allows for early feedback and continuous monitoring and management of development activities and program maturation. Following this trend, various research studies and management writers have identified a large number of NPD best practices (e.g., Cooper, 1993; Dixon, 1990; Paulk, Curtis, Chrissis, & Weber, 1993). A special subcategory of NPD best practices has been normatively identified and categorized within the Software Engineering Institute (SEI) and is referred to as the capability maturity model (CMM) (Paulk et al., 1993). This model has its roots in Crosby's quality management maturity grid (Crosby, 1979). It assesses a software development organization to one of five levels of process maturity (initial, repeatable, defined, managed, and optimizing), and thus represents a way to gauge/predict performance on an ordinal scale. The CMM was designed to help organizations improve their products and service development, acquisition, and maintenance processes. Concepts covered by this model include systems engineering, software engineering, integrated product and process development, and supplier sourcing as well as traditional CMM concepts such as process management and project management (Figure 6). The capability maturity model is descriptive and normative, and defines the key practices that characterize and differentiate each successive level of process maturity. Thus, it provides a method for assessing firms' capabilities and the level of maturity of its NDP life cycle. The CMM defines maturity as "the extent to which a specific process is explicitly defined, managed, measured, controlled, and effective" (Paulk et al., 1993). At each level of maturity, both types of knowledge (tacit versus explicit; structured versus unstructured) are managed with a varied dominance at each stage and requiring different technologies.

Tacit knowledge consists of the hands-on skills, special know-how, heuristic, intuitions, and so on. It refers to personal knowledge that is hard to formalize or articulate (Polany, 1973). Tacit knowledge is transferred by shared experience, through, for example, apprenticeship or job training. Tacit knowledge in an organization ensures task effectiveness — that the right things are being done so that the work unit could attain its objectives — whereas explicit knowledge is used in the design of routines, standard operation procedures, and the structure of data records. Explicit knowledge enables the organization to enjoy a certain level of operational efficiency and control. It also promotes equable, consistent organizational responses. There are two types of explicit knowledge, one that is structured and an unstructured one.

Each level of the CMM is characterized by the dominance of a specific type of knowledge that the organization has to manage in order to move from one level to the other. In the following section, we relate the implementation of IKMS to the capability maturity model, developed by Carnegie Mellon University, and the type of knowledge (structured, unstructured, and tacit) that firms use during their life cycle (Figure 6). In doing so, we outline the technological and organizational path that an organization has to follow to integrate and manage knowledge effectively along its new product development maturity cycle (Figure 7).

Figure 6. The CMM maturity levels of NPD process

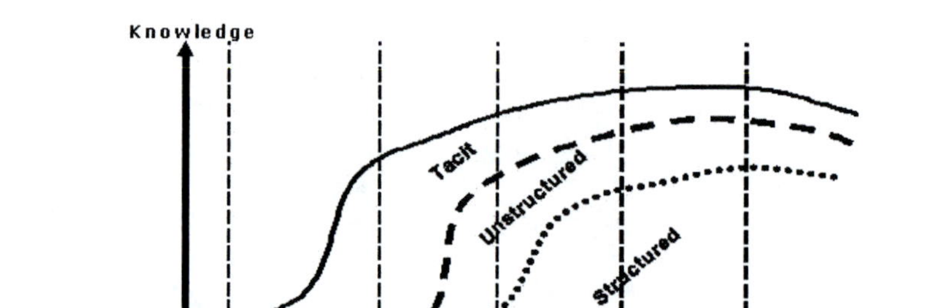

Figure 7. A stage model for implementing IKMS

		Initiation	Repeatable	Definition	Managed	Optimizing
Goals		Ad hoc management; production of products	Basic project management	Process standardization	Quantitative management	Continuous process improvement
Explicit	Structured	Data mining; electronic bulletin board	Expert systems; workflow systems; knowledge directories	Data warehouse; workflow	OLAP; personalization	Data integration; integrate structured and unstructured indexing
	Unstructured	Text mining	Document repositories	Taxonomies; quantitative mining	Portals personalization; content management; collaborative filtering	Discussion forums
Tacit		Collaboration; awareness; practice	Expert profile; story telling	Integrated expert and knowledge taxonomies	Expertise location	Combining new sources of knowledge

Level 1 — The Initial Level

At the initial level, the organization processes are usually ad hoc and chaotic and do not provide a stable environment for developing and maintaining the new product. Success in these organizations depends on the competence and heroics of the people in the organization and not on the use of proven processes. Such organizations frequently have difficulty making commitments that the staff can meet with an orderly engineering process, resulting in a series of crises. In spite of this ad hoc, chaotic environment, maturity level 1 organizations often produce products and services and are confronted with the management of their knowledge which is mostly tacit and unstructured explicit knowledge. The structured explicit knowledge is extracted through data mining and electronic bulletin board, whereas unstructured knowledge is managed through text mining inferential, using search engine. At this level, the tacit knowledge is exchanged through collaboration, awareness, and sharing of practices. Knowledge is extracted from the databases through data mining with agents based on algorithms, to discover numeric or propositional knowledge from non-distributed data and extract new knowledge.

Level 2 — The Repeatable Level

At maturity level 2, the repeatable level, policies for managing a new product development project and procedures to implement those policies are established. Planning and managing new projects is based on experience with similar projects. Process capability is enhanced by establishing basic process management techniques on a project-by-project basis. Thus, the organization may use some basic project management tools to track cost and schedule. An organization's new product projects in level 2 have already installed basic software management controls. Process discipline helps ensure that existing practices are retained during times of stress. When these practices are in place, projects are performed and managed according to their documented plans. The organizational requirements for achieving Level 2 are the establishment of policies that guide the projects in establishing the appropriate management processes. In terms of type of knowledge, the organizations at this level rely on expert systems, workflow systems, and knowledge repositories for managing the explicit structured knowledge. Concerning the unstructured knowledge, organizations rely on document repositories. The tacit level is based on the previous experience that concern the identification of the expertise needed to solve the problem, and the development of storytelling. Although expert systems can and have been applied to many areas within library and information science, the most popular areas have been online retrieval, reference, and referral services. Other areas which have received a relatively significant amount of attention are cataloging and classification, indexing and abstracting, collection development, acquisitions, and information management.

Level 3 — The Defined Level

At the defined level, the standard process for developing and maintaining new product development across the organization is understood and described in standards, procedures, tools, and methods. The organization's set of standard processes is established and improved over time to ensure its consistency across the organization. Projects establish their defined processes by tailoring the organization's set of standard processes according to tailoring guidelines. A defined new product process contains a coherent, integrated set of well-defined new product engineering and management processes. Within established product lines, cost, schedule, and functionality are under control, and new product quality is tracked. This process capability is based on a common, organization-wide understanding of the activities, roles, and responsibilities in a defined new product process. Also, an organization-wide training program is implemented to ensure that the staff and managers have the knowledge and skills required to fulfil their assigned roles. At this level, the organization is managing its structured knowledge by developing data warehouse workflows. For the unstructured knowledge, organizations are putting in place taxonomies and quantitative mining assessments. Concerning the tacit knowledge, they are integrating expert and knowledge taxonomies.

Level 4 — The Managed Level

At the managed level, the organization sets quantitative quality goals for both new products and processes. Productivity and quality are measured for important new product development process activities across all projects as part of an organizational measurement program. An organization-wide new product development process database is used to collect and analyze the data available from the projects' defined new product processes. These measurements establish the quantitative foundation for evaluating the projects' new product development processes. The use of precise measurements facilitate the effective management and control of the new product development effort. In particular, management can identify ways to adjust and adapt the process to particular projects without measurable losses of quality or deviations from specifications. This level of process capability allows an organization to predict trends in process and product quality within the quantitative bounds of these limits. It also needs to manage efficiently the knowledge that it has gathered and the one it needs. For this reason, organizations at this stage have to develop an efficient strategy to support their explicit structured knowledge by using OLAP[4] applications and personalization techniques. OLAP tools provide advanced functionality and multidimensional data analysis. They also offer the ability to page, rotate, and aggregate warehouse data to provide a "real life" view of the business situation for advanced analytical purposes. The agents used store knowledge for rational decision-making. At this stage, the organization relies also on integrated portals using content management, collaboration filtering, and personalization to manage its unstructured knowledge. For the tacit knowledge, the organization at this level relies on expertise location.

Level 5 — The Optimizing Level

At the optimizing level, the entire organization is focused on continuous process improvement. The organization has the means to identify weaknesses and strengthen the new product development processes proactively, with the goal of preventing the occurrence of defects. Data on the effectiveness of the new product development process is used to perform cost benefit analysis of new technologies and propose changes to the organization's new product development process. It also enables the elaboration of the qquantitative process improvement objectives. These objectives are continually revised to reflect changing business objectives and used as criteria in managing process improvement. The effects of deployed process improvements are measured and evaluated against the quantitative process-improvement objectives. Both the defined processes and the organization's set of standard processes are targets of measurable improvement activities. Process improvements to address common causes of process variation are identified, evaluated, and deployed. Concerning the management of structured knowledge, the organization has to focus on data integration and the indexing of structured and unstructured knowledge. The indexing agents provide an extra layer of abstraction on top of the services provided by search/indexing agents such as LYCOS and InfoSeek. The idea is to use the raw information provided by such engines, together with knowledge of the users' goals, preferences, and so forth to provide a personalized service. For the unstructured knowledge, the organization will be supporting discussion forum initiatives, whereas the tacit knowledge will concentrate on combining new sources of knowledge. We illustrate this framework through an analysis of several case studies.

Case Studies

As this study aims at suggesting a framework to support organizational knowledge management along their NPD life cycle and the technologies they require at each stage, five qualitative case studies have been conducted (Yin, 1994). These case studies are focused on a specific phase of the CMM because of the difficulty in finding one case covering all the stages and the time required for such analysis — longitudinal study. We have applied Eisenhardt's guidelines (1989) for theory-building case study research in conjunction with the guidelines by hypothesis-generation case study research offered by Yin (1994). This choice was motivated by the three criteria proposed by Yin (1994): "In general, case studies are the preferred strategy when 'how' or 'why' questions are being posed, when the investigator has little control over events, and when the focus is on a contemporary phenomenon within some real-life context." In gathering the data, standard techniques for conducting qualitative case study research were followed (Yin, 1994). In particular, data was collected via three of the six sources of evidence identified by Yin (1994): interviews, documents, and direct observation.

Hereafter, we illustrate with five case studies the CMM levels and associate each stage with the technologies used to support the management of knowledge through IKMS.

Level 1 — The Initial Level: NEC

NEC proactively carries out research and development working toward the creation of a ubiquitous society and the development of its IT and network integrated technology. NEC was confronted with a huge amount of information stored in large databases that should be analysed to become business knowledge at the early stage of its new product development. For this reason, NEC developed a strategy for data mining to support the organization of knowledge related to its new product development. The data mining research group of NEC has been developing fundamental data mining engines that focus on knowledge organization application domains. These engines rely on artificial technology to discover useful business knowledge mainly text data. For this purpose, NEC has developed an integrated set of tools that it has applied to its new product knowledge management. We have focused on three applications using agents to extract text data: survey analyzer (text mining engine), topic analyzer (topic trend analysis engine), and key semantics extraction engine, that have been applied by NEC as a support for knowledge management. Survey analyzer (association extraction) has been designed to conduct basic functions of text mining such as association rule discovery from static text database. The survey analyzer conducts three types of analysis: association rule induction, correspondence analysis, and co-occurrence analysis and typical sentence analysis, where keywords are extracted as the characteristics of given documents. However, a word is generally too small as a unit of extraction to catch semantic information about the target category, and a user might miss the point characteristics. The key semantics mining is supporting three tasks: key semantic extraction, redundancy reduction, and the phrase/sentence reconstruction. NEC has defined the key characteristics sub-structures of syntactic dependencies in the given documents, and has developed a key semantics mining system to supply more semantic information for users (Yamanishi & Morinaga, 2005). Both survey analyzer and key semantic mining systems analyze data given collectively. However, in a wide range of business areas including NPD, text data streams must be dealt with, and it is an important issue to discover topic trends and analyze their dynamics in real time. NEC has developed the topic analyzer which performs three tasks: topic structure identification, topic emergence detection, topic characterization; identifying the characteristics for each of the main topics.

Level 2 — The Repeatable Level: Xerox

Xerox has developed document management strategies to manage the document repositories. Xerox offers an array of innovative document solutions, services, and systems designed for offices and production-printing environments. Xerox is a printer company that knows everything about streaks and paper jams. All that knowledge has been codified and stored in very large databases that cover the "red streak problem." This knowledge is very well organized and codified in an application called DocuShare that deployed a world-class enterprise content management solution to help reduce costs, optimize information flows, and reduce risk. DocuShare is a Web-based document sharing tool that stores any document format and dynamically capture, manage, share, and deliver information, regardless of information source, corporate infrastructure, or user skill level or location. The DocuShare Archive Server allows to easily move content ready for archival onto a separate server, while actively preserving the context in which that information was initially stored in DocuShare (i.e., access control, location, metadata, and fully searchable indexing). The archive server maximizes project management and decision-making processes by letting users move outdated content visibly out of the way without permanently losing or destroying the information. Content can be manually archived as needed or flagged for automatic archival based on pre-set expiration dates.

Level 3 — The Defined Level: JPL NASA

The Jet Propulsion Laboratory of NASA has understood the need for developing strategies and practices for creating, collecting, and organizing information across NASA. The classification scheme of JPL taxonomy is meant to encompass all of NASA Web content (*NASA Web space*), including internal as well as external material. It is a means for tagging content so that it can be used and reused in different contexts. The overall objective was to develop a generic taxonomy from which specializations can be derived for specific purposes. Their taxonomy is open to extensibility and interoperability using standard facets (disciplines, functions, industries, locations, organizations, projects) and reusing existing standards and vocabulary sources (ACM[5] for computer science specializations, AFS[6] for functions, LOM[7] for educational roles, NAICS[8] for industries, SOC[9] for employee roles). It is also robust and in-depth by providing hierarchical granularity whenever possible, reusing the same concept multiple times in the scheme (so that the same concept has multiple parents), mapping abbreviations and other aliases as alternate terms or synonyms, using standard genre and document type categories in the information facet, and finally providing controlled vocabularies used to populate elements of more complex metadata schema such as the Dublin Core[10]. The benefits of this taxonomy development reside in meta data specifications for all NASA Web publishers, development of XML schema in accordance with DISA[11] registry (reuse where appropriate), enhancement of agency Web publishing processes, integration with NASA public portal content management system for reduced publishing cycles, coordinated message themes by the agency, better quality of Web materials, integration with the NASA search engine, Web site registration system. We can add that the JPL taxonomy is based on data dictionaries extended by ontologies that integrate engineering repositories, document repositories, e-mail archives, financial repositories and applications, multimedia assets, knowledge repositories and applications, searchable via Web services model and applications. This allows the creation of knowledge maps/ontologies for projects and disciplines that are interoperable with larger federal taxonomies commercial taxonomies.

Level 4 — The Managed Level: Nokia Research Center

Nokia Research Center was confronted by the issue of the use of efficient instrumentation for performance profiling. This means that Nokia had to deal with performance profiling which involves tracing software execution and the analysis of the obtained traces. The focus on the traces was due to the fact that traces affect system performance and distort software system execution. Nokia research team needed to minimize the effects of tracing on system's performance. To reach the minimization of the effect of tracing on the underlying system's performance, the team has added the agent software trace design and have implemented it to the overall software development process. First, the team has determined performance parameters of a running software system by gathering information on various types of events like component entry and exit function calls, execution states, message communication, resource usage, and so forth. This analysis has also taken in consideration that tracing reduces validity of performance profiling, but trace instrumentation comes at a cost (time changes behaviour of agent software, could violate real-time constraints and timing requirements in real-time systems). The Nokia team has also dealt with the complexity of software development that are affected by specific facts that make it more difficult because in the case of software development profiling is often performed by different individuals. Their task was to draw upon knowledge and skills that software developers and performance analysts bring with them and use this codified knowledge to create efficient trace instrumentation.

Level 5 — The Optimizing Level: Boeing

At this level of the CMM approach, Boeing has put in place a performance measurement system that drives measures at all levels of the organization and is part of the continuous process improvement. The organization has selected, analyzed, and aligned data and information to improve its performance using the five-step performance measurement system that uses intelligent agents able to gather, analyze, and facilitate decision-making. Their performance system begins with gathering requirements and expectations for stakeholders by facilitating the analysis of the data and information through the integration of the five-step performance. The first step is related to the leadership system and enterprise planning process that result in a set of action plans, performance goals, and metrics. The second step, named Goal Flow-down, communicates the goals and directions of their business, sites, and functions that are shared with their customers at each organizational level as appropriate. The third step, called Aerospace Support organization, measures goal and expectation at organizational, operational, and individual levels. Employee personal and professional development goals are also defined and documented through the performance development partnership process. The fourth step concerns measurement analysis and knowledge management systems, which provide performance status and other information needed for organizational decision-making and innovation. The fifth and final step is the performance review and communication, which is conducted at the Aerospace support, business, site, function, program, and organization / team levels and reported through the vision support plan system. The vision support plan is the Boeing system for collecting, monitoring, and reporting progress toward these goals that support the five-step performance with intelligent agents.

Conclusion

This chapter aims to provide an analytical framework corresponding to the maturity level of the new product development process (NPD), the type of knowledge dominant in each stage, and the information systems to be used to support the management of knowledge. While the importance of managing knowledge in the context of NPD is largely acknowledged and organizations rely on a variety of systems for this aim, few authors have so far attempted to characterize or relate the type of systems used with the characteristics of knowledge relying on the maturity of the NPD process. We rely in our analysis on the capability maturity model that assesses a software development organization to one of five levels of process maturity (i.e., initial, repeatable, defined, managed, and optimizing), and thus represents a way to gauge/predict performance on an ordinal scale and focuses on process management of the development process. We suggest the use of specific tools in each step for managing knowledge and the evolution toward intelligent knowledge management systems (IKMS).

IKMS overcome the limitations of most traditional KMS that are static and fall short in dealing with the exponential increase amount of information that come from distributed, heterogeneous, and voluminous information resources. They use artificial intelligence in the form of intelligent agents as well as active knowledge resources represented with semantically rich meta-data to improve inaccuracies of information retrieval and maximize the shareability of knowledge. We illustrate our analysis with several practical examples of leading companies in different stages of the maturity process. Our contribution is a first step toward developing an analytical framework for supporting the implementation of specific technologies supporting knowledge management along the NPD process and is mainly conceptual in nature. A further step and natural direction toward developing our analytical framework would be to apply it to a longitudinal case study analysis.

References

Abar, S., Abe, T., & Kinoshita, T. (2004). *A next generation knowledge management system architecture*. Paper presented at the 18th International Conference on Advanced Information Networking and Application (AINA'04).

Alavi, M., & Leidner D. E. (2001). Knowledge management and knowledge management systems: Conceptual foundations and research issues. *MIS Quarterly, 25*(1).

Barbuceanu, M., & Fox, M. S. (1994). *The information agent: An infrastructure for collaboration in the integrated enterprise*. Paper presented at the Cooperative Knowledge Based Systems, University of Keele, Staffordshire, UK, M. Deen (Ed.), DAKE Centre, Univ. of Keele.

Barthes, J-P., & Tacla, C. A. (2002). Agent-supported portals and knowledge management in complex R&D projects. *Computers in Industry, 48*(1), 3-16.

Benbya, H. (2005). *The dynamic interaction between institutional and cultural mechanisms in KMS effectiveness*. Academy of Management meeting, Honolulu, HI.

Benbya, H. (2005). Knowledge management support for new product development: Lessons from a case study in the aerospace industry. In *Proceedings of the San Diego International Systems Conference*.

Benbya, H., & Belbaly, N. (2005). Mechanisms for knowledge management systems effectiveness: An exploratory analysis. *Knowledge and Process Management Journal, 12*(3), 203-216.

Benbya, H., Passiante, G., & Belbaly, N. (2004). Corporate portal: A tool for knowledge management synchronization. *International Journal of Information Management, 24*, 201-220.

Brockman, B. K., & Morgan, R. M. (2003). The role off existing knowledge in new product innovativeness and performance. *Decision Sciences, 34*(2), 385-419.

Booz, A., & Hamilton, I. (1982). *New product development for the 1980s*. New York: Booz, Allen and Hamilton Inc.

Cooper, R. G. (1993). *Winning at new products: Accelerating the process idea from idea to launch*. Reading, MA: Addison-Wesley.

Cooper, R. G. (1994). New products: The factors that drive success. *International Marketing Review, 11*, 60-76.

Cooper, R. G. (2001). *Winning at new products* (3rd ed.). Reading, MA: Addison-Wesley Publishing Company.

Cooper, R. G., & Kleinschmidt, E. J. (1986). An investigation into the new product process: Steps, deficiencies, and impact. *Journal of Product and Innovation Management, 3*, 71-85.

Crosby, P. (1997). *Quality is free*. New York: McGraw-Hill.

Davies, J., Fensel, D., & Harmelen, F. V. (2003). *Towards the semantic Web: Ontology driven knowledge management*. John Wiley & Sons.

Department of Defense. (1996). *Integrated product and process development handbook.* DoD guide. Retrieved July 12, 2005, from http://www.arnet.gov/Library/OFPP/BestPractices/pbsc/library/dod-guide-to-integrated.pdf

Dixon, J. R., Nanni, A. J., & Vollman, T. E. (1990). *The new performance challenge measuring operations for world-class competition*. Homewood, IL: Dow Jones-Irwin.

Eisenhardt, K. M., & Tabrizi, B. (1995). Accelerating adaptive processes: Product innovation in the global computer industry. *Administrative Science Quarterly*.

Franklin, S., & Grasser, A. (1997). Is it an agent, or just a program: A taxonomy for autonomous agents. In J. Miller, M. Wooldridge, & N. Jennings (Eds.), *Intelligent agents III: Agent theories, architectures, and languages* (pp. 21-25). Berlin Heidelberg, Germany: SpringerVerlag.

Griffin, A. (1997). PDMA research on new product development practices: Updating trends and benchmarking best practices. *Journal of Product Innovation Management, 14*(4), 429-458.

Griffin, A., & Hauser, J. R. (1992). Patterns of communication among marketing engineering and manufacturing: A comparison between two new product teams. *Management Science, 38*(3), 360-373.

Maedche, A., Motik, B., Stojanovic, L., Studer, R., & Volz, R. (2003, March-April). Ontologies for enterprise knowledge management. *IEEE Intelligent Systems, 18*, 26-33.

Marsh, S. J., & Stock. G. (2003). Building dynamic capabilities in new product development through intertemporal integration. *Journal of Product Innovation Management, 20*(2), 136-148.

Nambisan, S. (2003). Information systems as a reference discipline for new product development. *MIS Quarterly, 27*(1), 1-18.

Paulk, M. C., Curtis, B., Chrissis, M. B., & Weber, C. V. (1993). *Capability maturity model for software. Version 1.1.* Software Engineering Institute Technical Report No. CMU/SEI-93-TR-24.

Schilling, M. A., & Hill, C. W. L. (1998). Managing the new product development process: Strategic imperatives. *Academy of Management Executive, 12*(3), 67-81.

Scott, J. E. (1996). *The role of information technology in organizational knowledge creation for new product development.* Paper presented at the 2nd Americas Conference on Information Systems.

Shake, S. (1999). *Articulating the new product development process.* Presentation.

Russel, S., & Norvig, P. (2003). *Artificial intelligence: A modern approach* (2nd ed.). Englewood Cliffs, NJ: Prentice Hall.

Ulrich, K. T., & Eppinger, S. D. (2000). *Product design and development*. New York: McGraw Hill.

Wenger, E., McDermott, R., & Snyder, W. (2002). *Cultivating communities of practice: A guide to managing knowledge*. Boston: Harvard Business School Press.

Wheelwright, S. C., & Clark, K. B. (1992). *Revolutionizing product development: Quantum leaps in speed, efficiency, and quality*. New York: The Free Press.

Yamanishi, K., & Morinaga, S. (2005). Data mining for knowledge organization. *NEC Journal of Advanced Technology, 2*(2), 129-136.

Endnotes

1 Ontology means a *specification of a conceptualization*. Thus, ontology is a description (like a formal specification of a program) of the concepts and relationships that can exist for an agent or a community of agents (Gruber, 1993).

2 Semantic Web provides a common framework that allows data to be shared and reused across application, enterprise, and community boundaries (W3C).

3 Metadata is machine understandable information for the Web that range from human-generated textual description of a resource to machine-generated data that may be useful only to software applications (W3C, Dublin Core Metadata).

4 OLAP stands for "On-Line Analytical Processing."

5 ACM (Association for Computing Machinery)

6 The AFS contains compliance data on air pollution point sources regulated by the United States state and local air regulatory agencies. AFS also includes data for management of operating permit applications and renewals.

7 LOM is the Lambert Operations Map produced in 1994 for the Glaciology traverse team shows topography and traverse routes.

8 North American Industry Classification System (NAICS)

9 Space Operations Contract (SOC)

10 The Dublin Core Metadata Initiative is an open forum engaged in the development of interoperable online metadata standards that support a broad range of purposes and business models.

11 DISA Registry Initiative is a program to deploy the technology outlined in the ebXML specifications for a standard online index of items needed by companies to do business in particular industries.

About the Authors

Xuan F. Zha is currently with the Manufacturing Engineering Laboratory at National Institute of Standards and Technology (NIST) and University of Maryland. He is also a guest professor of the Mechatronics Control Institute at Shanghai JiaoTong University, China. Prior to that, he was with Singapore Institute of Manufacturing Technology and Nanyang Technological University, Singapore. His current research interests are mainly in AI and intelligent systems applications, industrial informatics, micro/nano technology, and automation. He has authored or co-authored over 130 referred papers, including 25 book chapters and many reports in these areas. He serves regular reviewers for numerous international journals, conferences, book series, and research grants including IEEE and ASME transactions, journals, and conferences. He also served as many international conferences' program committee, session chairs, and guest editors of international journals. He is currently a senior member of IEEE and SME (Society of Manufacturing Engineers), a member of ASME (American Society of Mechanical Engineers), a member of Sigma Xi, a member of International Design Society, a member of World Federation on Soft Computing (WFSC), a member of Young Researchers Committee, among others.

* * * *

Alaa E. Abdel-Hakim received a bachelor's degree in 1996 from Assiut University in electrical engineering with honors. In 2000, he received a master's degree from the same university in electrical and computer engineering. Since the summer of 2002, he has been a research assistant and a PhD student at the CVIP Lab, University of Louisville. His current research includes feature extraction, object recognition, robotics, and computer vision. He is a member of the U.S. national engineering honor society, Tau Beta Pi.

Giovanni Acampora received a bachelor's degree in computer science in 2003 from the University of Salerno, Italy, where he is currently pursuing a PhD and working on the design of an ambient intelligence environment by using fuzzy control, evolutionary methodologies, and agent paradigm.

Ruth Aguilar-Ponce obtained a bachelor's degree in computer science from the Autonomous University of Puebla, Mexico in 1997. She obtained an MS in electronics from the National Institute for Research in Optics, Astrophysics and Electronics, Mexico, in 1999. She joined the Center for Advanced Computer Studies at the University of Louisiana - Lafayette, where she obtained a master's degree in computer engineering in 2004. Currently, she is a PhD candidate. Her research interests include sensor networks, communication protocols, system on a chip, signal, and image processing.

Norio Akamatsu received a BE in electrical engineering from the University of Tokushima, Japan (1966) and MS and PhD degrees in electrical engineering from Kyoto University, Japan (1968 and 1974, respectively). From 1968 to 1974, he was an associate lecturer at the Department of Electrical Engineering, University of Tokushima. Currently, he is professor at the Department of Information Science and Intelligent Systems, University of Tokushima. His research interests are neural networks and nonlinear circuits.

Hyggo Almeida received a master's degree in informatics from Federal University of Campina Grande, Brazil (2004), and received his bachelor's in computer science from Federal University of Alagoas, Maceió, Brazil (2002). Currently, he is a PhD student, since 2004, in electrical engineering in Federal University of Campina Grande, Brazil. His research is in the fields of component and multi-agent based dynamic software composition, software engineering for embedded systems, and pervasive computing.

John Atkinson is an associate professor in the Department of Computer Science at the Universidad de Concepción, Chile. His research topics focus on artificial intelligence, natural-language processing, text mining, and autonomous agents. Atkinson received a PhD in artificial intelligence from the University of Edinburgh, Scotland, UK. He is a member of the AAAI, ACM, and ACL.

Magdy Bayoumi is the director of the Center for Advanced Computer Studies (CACS) and Department Head of the Computer Science Department, University of Louisiana - Lafayette. He is also the Edmiston professor of computer engineering and Lamson professor. Dr. Bayoumi received bachelor's and master's degrees in electrical engineering from Cairo University, Egypt; an MSc in computer engineering from Washington University, St. Louis; and a PhD in electrical engineering from the University of Windsor, Canada. Dr. Bayoumi was the vice president for the technical activities of the IEEE Circuits and Systems Society. He is a fellow of the IEEE.

Nassim Belbaly is a visiting scholar at the Anderson Business School of Management at UCLA, where she is finalizing her PhD research on knowledge management systems effectiveness. She holds a master in electronic business from the e-Business Management School, Lecce, Italy, and a master in marketing from the IAE of Aix en Provence, France. His research activities are focused on knowledge management systems that supports new product development and improve their performance.

Hind Benbya is a visiting scholar at the Anderson Business School of Management at UCLA, where she is finalizing her PhD research on knowledge management systems effectiveness. She holds a master in electronic business from the e-Business Management School, Lecce, Italy, and a master in marketing from the IAE of Aix en Provence, France. Her research activities are focused on knowledge management systems implementation, information systems design and development and e-business management. Besides her research activities, she was involved in several applied and joint research projects with firms and academic institutions in Europe and the U.S. Her publications have appeared in the *International Journal of Information Management, Knowledge and Process Management Journal,* and *Information Technology and People,* among others.

Shu-Chuan Chu received a bachelor's degree in industrial management from the National Taiwan Institute of Technology, Taiwan, in 1988, and a PhD degree in informatics and engineering from the Flinders University of South Australia, Australia, in 2004. Currently, she is an assistant professor in the Department of Information Management, Cheng Shiu University, Taiwan. Her current research interests include data mining, swarm intelligence, soft computing, evolutionary computation, information hiding, and image processing.

André L. V. Coelho received a bachelor's degree in computer engineering in 1996, and earned master's and PhD degrees in electrical engineering (specialization in computer engineering) in 1998 and 2004, respectively, all from the State University of Campinas (Unicamp), Brazil. Currently, he is an invited research collaborator at the Master Program in Applied Informatics at the University of Fortaleza (Unifor), Brazil, conducting research in computational/swarm intelligence, metaheuristics, multiagent systems, machine learning, and data mining. He is a member of IEEE.

Constantina Costopoulou is an assistant professor at the Informatics Laboratory of the AUA. She holds a bachelor's degree in mathematics from the National and Kapodistrian University of Athens, Greece, a master's degree in software engineering from Cranfield Institute of Technology, UK, and a PhD from the National Technical University of Athens, Greece. Her research interests include rural area networks, Web services, intelligent agents, and e-services for the agricultural sector. She has published more than 60 papers in edited volumes, scientific journals, and refereed conferences. She has also served as the scientific responsible or member of the working group of several funded projects in the above research areas.

A. K. M. De Silva (BSc, Hons.; PhD; CEng; MIEE) gained her PhD in mechanical/manufacturing engineering from the University of Edinburgh, UK (1988), and her bachelor's degree (Hons.) in engineering science from Aberdeen University, UK (1982). She is currently a reader in engineering at the School of Engineering, Science and Design at Glasgow Caledonian University, UK. She is a member of the International Academy for Production Engineering (CIRP) and also a peer review college member of the UK Engineering and Physical Science Research Council (EPSRC). She has published widely and is a recognised authority in the area of unconventional machining processes.

Leandro Dias da Silva received his bachelor's degree in computer science from Federal University of Alagoas, Brazil, in 2000, and his master's in electrical engineering from Federal University of Campina Grande, in 2002. Currently, he is a PhD student, in electrical engineering at Federal University of Campina Grande, Campina Grande, Brazil. His research is in the fields of formal software verification, model checking, coloured petri nets, component-based software systems, and embedded systems. Leandro spent a year at University of California at Santa Cruz working as visiting researcher in the timed interfaces project with Professor Luca de Alfaro.

Matthew E. Elam is an assistant professor in the Department of Industrial Engineering at The University of Alabama. He has taught, performed research, and consulted with industry in several statistics related areas and in other subject areas. He is founder and co-director of the Industrial Engineering Quality Engineering Laboratory and is a member of the Maintenance and Reliability Center at Alabama. He has served as a reviewer for several journals and on the editorial board of one journal. He is a member of several professional organizations and honor societies and is an American Society for Quality Certified Quality engineer.

Aly A. Farag was educated at Cairo University (bachelor's degree, electrical engineering), Egypt, Ohio State University, USA (master's degree, biomedical engineering), University of Michigan, USA (master's degree, bioengineering), and Purdue University, Indiana (PhD, electrical engineering). Farag joined the University of Louisville, Kentucky, in August 1990, where he is currently a professor of electrical and computer engineering. His research interests are concentrated in the fields of computer vision and medical imaging. Farag is the founder and director of the Computer Vision and Image Processing Laboratory (CVIP Lab) at the University of Louisville, which supports a group of more 20 graduate students and postdocs. His contribution has been mainly in the areas of active vision system design, volume registration, segmentation, and visualization, where he has authored or coauthored more than 80 technical articles in leading journals and international meetings in the fields of computer vision and medical imaging. Farag is an associate editor of *IEEE Transactions on Image Processing.* He is a regular reviewer for a number of technical journals and to national agencies including the U.S. National Science Foundation and the National Institute of Health. He is a senior member of the IEEE and SME, and a member of Sigma Xi and Phi Kappa Phi.

Minoru Fukumi received BE and ME degrees from the University of Tokushima, Japan (1984 and 1987, respectively), and the doctor degree from Kyoto University, Japan (1996). Since 1987, he has been with the Department of Information Science and Intelligent Systems, University of Tokushima. In 1996, he became an associate professor in the same department. He became professor in the same department in 2005. His research interests include neural networks, evolutionary algorithms and image processing. He is a member of the IEEE, SICE, ISCIE, and IEICE.

D. K. Harrison (BSc, Hons.; MSc; PhD; CEng; FIEE; FIMechE; FIES; CITP; MBCS) is currently the acting dean of the School of Engineering, Science and Design within Glasgow Caledonian University. He has spent most of his working career in the manufacturing industry. A graduate of UMIST, he has also worked within the Department of Mechanical Engineering at UMIST, where he was a consultant to many blue chip manufacturing companies. He joined Glasgow Caledonian University in 1994 where he has had a variety of roles. He is currently involved with a number of research projects, principally with industrial organisations, all of which have the common theme of design and manufacturing optimisation. This activity has led to him having successfully supervised 21 PhD students through to graduation. He is the joint author of the widely used textbook *Systems for Planning & Control in Manufacturing*. He has also edited several other books and conference proceedings and has published his work widely.

Yoshiteru Ishida received a PhD in applied mathematics and physics from Kyoto University, Japan, in 1986. He served as an assistant professor at Department of Applied Mathematics and Physics, Kyoto University, from 1983 to 1986 and at Division of Applied Systems Science from 1987 to 1993. From 1994 to 1998, he had been an associate professor at Graduate School of Information Science, Nara Institute of Science and Technology. Since 1998, he has been a professor at Department of Knowledge-based Information Engineering at Toyohashi University of Technology. Some of his publications include *Immunity-Based Systems: A Design Perspective*, Springer; and *Immunity-Based Systems—Intelligent Systems by Artificial Immune Systems*, Corona Pub. Co. (in Japanese).

Kiyotaka Izumi received a BE in electronic engineering from The Nagasaki Institute of Applied Science in 1991, an ME in electrical engineering from the Saga University in 1993, and a DE in Faculty of Engineering Systems and Technology from the Saga University in 1996. He was a research associate in the Department of Mechanical Engineering, Saga University from April 1996 to March 2001 and in the Department of Advanced Systems Control Engineering, Saga University from April 2001 to 2004. Currently, he is an associate professor in the Department of Advanced Systems Control Engineering, Saga University, Japan. His research interests are in intelligent control, fuzzy control, evolutionary computation, and their applications to the robot control.

Chandimal Jayawardena received his bachelor's and master's degrees in electronics and telecommunication engineering from the University of Moratuwa, Sri Lanka (1999 and 2003, respectively). From 1999 to 2001, he was with SriLankan Airlines Ltd., and from 2001 to

2003 he was with Sri Lanka Telecom Ltd. as an engineer. Currently, he is perusing his PhD studies at the Department of Advanced Systems Control Engineering, Saga University, Japan. His research interests include intelligent robots, machine learning, and tele-robotics. He is a chartered engineer and a member of IEE, IEEE, and Institution of Engineers Sri Lanka.

Joel Jones received his PhD from the University of Illinois with a specialty in programming language implementation. He was formerly an assistant professor at The University of Alabama, working on design pattern need detection and the use of compiler technology for mobile computing. He is currently a member of the technical staff at Wind River Inc. in Alameda, California.

Stephen Karungaru received a bachelor's degree in electronics and communication from Moi University in 1992. He then joined the Department of Electrical and Electronics Engineering, Jomo Kenyatta University of Agriculture and Technology as a teaching assistant. He received a master's degree and a PhD in information system design from the Department of Information Science and Intelligent Systems, University of Tokushima in 2001 and 2004, respectively. He is currently an assistant professor in the same department. His research interests include pattern recognition, neural networks, evolutionally computation, image processing, and robotics. He is a member of IEEE and IEEJ.

Ashok Kumar obtained a BTech degree in computer science and engineering from the Institute of Technology, India in 1990. From 1990 to 1994, he worked with Uptron India Limited, Lucknow in the capacities of engineer and senior engineer. He joined the Center for Advanced Computer Studies in 1994, where he obtained MS and PhD degrees in 1997 and 1999, respectively. After getting his PhD, Kumar worked with Cadence Design Systems in the capacity of a senior member of technical staff for research and development operations. Currently, he is a research faculty at the Center for Advanced Computer Studies.

Clodoaldo A. M. Lima received a bachelor's degree in electrical engineering from Federal University of Juiz de Fora (UFJF), Brazil (1997), and master's and PhD degrees in computer engineering from State University of Campinas (Unicamp), Brazil (2000 and 2004, respectively). He is currently a research collaborator at the Department of Computer Engineering and Industrial Automation, Unicamp. His current research interests include multivariate analysis, machine learning, committee machines, financial engineering, and control and identification systems.

Chengliang Liu is professor of mechanical and mechatronic engineering and director of the Institute of Mechatronics, Shanghai JiaoTong University, Shanghai, China. His research interests include: automation, sensory systems for monitoring and diagnosis, intelligent maintenance systems, intelligent robotic systems, automated inspection, intelligent control of manufacturing processes, agriculture equipment, and so forth. He has published over 60 technical papers.

Vincenzo Loia received a bachelor's degree in computer science from the University of Salerno, Italy (1984), and a PhD in computer science from the University of Paris VI (1989). Since 1989, he has been a faculty member at the University of Salerno, where he teaches operating systems and adaptive hybrid agents and is currently a full professor of computer science in the Department of Mathematics and Computer Science. He is co-founder of the Soft Computing Laboratory and founder of the Multi Agent Systems Laboratory, both in the Department of Mathematics and Computer Science. He has been a principal investigator for several industrial R&D projects and in academic research projects. He is the author of more than 100 original research papers in international journals, book chapters, and international conference proceedings. He has edited three research books in the areas of agent technology, the Internet, and soft computing methodologies. His current research interests focus on merging soft computing and agent technology to design technologically complex environments. Loia is chair of the Task Force "Intelligent Agents" of Emergent Technologies Technical Committee (ETTC), IEEE Computational Intelligence Society.

Ernesto López-Mellado received a bachelor's degree in electrical engineering in 1977 from the Instituto Tecnológico de Cd. Madero, Mexico, a master's degree from the Cinvestav, Mexico City, Mexico, in 1979; and the Docteur Ingénieur degree in automation from the University Paul Sabatier, France, in 1986. Currently, he is professor of computer sciences in Cinvestav Unidad Guadalajara, Mexico. His research interests include petri nets and intelligent systems applied to the design and analysis of control software for discrete event systems.

Nikos Manouselis is a researcher at the Informatics Laboratory of the Agricultural University of Athens. He has a diploma in electronics & computer engineering, a master's in operational research, as well as, a master's in electronics & computer engineering, from the Technical University of Crete, Greece. Manouselis has been previously affiliated with the Informatics & Telematics Institute of the Centre for Research & Technology, Greece, as well as the Decision Support Systems Laboratory and the Multimedia Systems & Applications Laboratory of the Technical University of Crete, Greece. His research interests involve the design, development, and evaluation of electronic services, and their applications for the agricultural sector.

T. K. K. R. Mediliyegedara (BSc, Hons.; MBA; MIEE) graduated in 2001 and specialised in production engineering from the University of Peradeniya, Sri Lanka. Then, he worked for the same university as a research assistant and then as a lecturer. He followed with a master's in control systems engineering and a MBA in general management at the same university. He is currently working for the Glasgow Caledonian University in UK as a research assistant, while following a PhD in intelligent process monitoring and controls.

J. A. McGeough is Regius professor of engineering, Centre for Materials Science and Engineering and School of Mechanical Engineering, The University of Edinburgh, UK.

Masoud Mohammadian's research interests lie in adaptive self-learning systems, fuzzy logic, genetic algorithms, neural networks, and their application in industrial, financial, and business problems, which involve real-time data processing, planning, and decision-making. His current research concentrates on the application of computational intelligence techniques for learning and adaptation of intelligent agents and web-based information filtering and data mining. He has chaired more than seven international conferences on computational intelligence and intelligent agents and published over 90 research papers in conferences, journals, and books, as well as edited 12 books in the area of computational intelligence and intelligent agents. Masoud has more than 12 years of academic experience, and he has served as program committee member and/or co-chair of a large number of national and international conferences.

Gary P. Moynihan is a professor in the Department of Industrial Engineering, The University of Alabama. He received bachelor's and MBA degrees from Rensselaer Polytechnic Institute, and a PhD from the University of Central Florida. While at The University of Alabama, he has taught, developed, and expanded courses in information systems design, project management, and engineering economics. His primary area of research interest is information systems design and analysis. Prior to joining The University of Alabama, Dr. Moynihan held positions in the aerospace, computer, and chemical processing industries.

Michele Nappi received a bachelor's degree in computer science from the University of Salerno, Salerno, Italy (1991), a master's degree in information and communication technology from I.I.A.S.S., E.R. Caianiello, Vietri sul Mare, Salerno, and a PhD degree in applied mathematics and computer science from the University of Padova, Italy. He is currently an associate professor of computer science at the University of Salerno. His research interests include pattern recognition, image processing, compression and indexing, multimedia databases, and visual languages.

Elthon Allex da Silva Oliveira received his bachelor's in computer science from Federal University of Alagoas, Brazil, in 2004. Currently, he is a master's student in informatics with Federal University of Campina Grande, Campina Grande, Brazil. His research is in the fields of formal software verification, code annotation languages, model checking, and Petri nets.

Jeng-Shyang Pan received a bachelor's degree in electronic engineering from the National Taiwan Institute of Technology (1986), a master's degree in communication engineering from National Chiao Tung University, Taiwan, ROC (1988), and a PhD in electrical engineering from the University of Edinburgh, UK (1996). Pan has authored or co-authored 50 journal papers, 120 conference papers, and four textbooks. He joints the editorial board for *International Journal of Innovative Computing, Information and Control,* LNCS Transactions on Data Hiding and Multimedia Security, Springer, *International Journal of Knowledge-Based Intelligent Engineering Systems,* IOS Press, *International Journal of Hybrid Intelligent System,* Advanced Knowledge International, and *Journal of Information Assurance and Security,* Dynamic Publishers Inc. He has been the director of the International Office for two years, director of Computer and Communication Center Research for one year, and chairman of Alumni Association Center for one year at National Kaohsiung University of Applied Sciences. In 2001, he got the Award of Outstanding Electrical Engineer from the Electrical Engineers' Association of ROC. Currently, he is a professor in the Department of Electronic Engineering, National Kaohsiung University of Applied Sciences, Taiwan, ROC. He is also the president of Kaohsiung-Miami Sister Cities Association. His current research interests include information hiding, data mining, pattern recognition, and image processing.

Angelo Perkusich received a PhD and master's degree in electrical engineering from Federal University of Paraíba, Brazil (1994 and 1987, respectively), and received his bachelor's degree in electrical engineering from the Engineering Faculty of Barretos (1982). From 1988 to 1990, he was an assistant professor of the Electronic and Systems Department at the Federal University of Pernambuco. From 1992 to 1993, he was a visiting research at the University of Pittsburgh, USA. From 1991 to 1994, he was an assistant professor of the Electrical Engineering Department at the Federal University of Paraíba, Campina Grande, Brazil. Since 1994, he is an adjunct professor in that department. He is a project leader/consultant at the affiliated Nokia project for the development of embedded systems applications for mobile devices.

Bin Qiao received a bachelor's degree in computer engineering from Shanghai Jiao Tong University, China, and a master's degree in industrial engineering from The University of Alabama. He has recently returned to Shanghai to pursue his professional career.

Mark Radle is an assistant professor of computer science at the University of Louisiana - Lafayette. Radle earned his bachelor's degree in computer science from the University of New Orleans and his master's and PhD degrees in computer science at the University of Louisiana at Lafayette. His research interests include affective computing, AI, and computer science education.

Stefano Ricciardi received a bachelor's degree in computer science from the University of Salerno, Italy. He worked for five years in the videogame industry as modeling and animation supervisor. He was an assistant professor of computer science at the University of Basilicata, Italy, for two years. He is currently a computer science researcher at the University of Salerno. His current research interests include computer-generated imaging, virtual reality aimed to cultural heritage fruition, and biometry through 3D-based approach.

Russel Stonier is an associate professor in the Department of Computer Science at Central Queensland University, Australia. He is a member of IEEE and the Computational Intelligence Society. Research interests include: intelligent and evolutionary computation techniques, adaptive and sliding mode control, Liapunov techniques in control and dynamical systems, fuzzy control of mobile and articulated robot, fuzzy image enhancement, hierarchical fuzzy modelling, fuzzy controllers for optimal control with time-delay. Russel has authored over 90 journal, conference, and book papers in the fields of control, robotics, and evolutionary computation. He was recently the general chair of AI2004 and Complex2004. Russel Stonier holds a bachelor of science degree with honours and a PhD in mathematics from the University of Queensland, Australia.

Yu Tang received a master's degree in computer science from Georgia State University in 2001. She is currently working toward her PhD at Georgia State University. Her main research interests are artificial intelligent, data mining, soft computing, and Web applications. She is a software developer in Georgia Department of Transportation.

J. Luis Tecpanecatl-Xihuitl received a bachelor's degree in electrical engineering from the Autonomous University of Puebla, Mexico and a master's degree in electronics from National Institute for research on Astrophysics, Optic, and Electronics, Mexico. He is currently a PhD candidate in computer engineering at the Center for Advanced Computer Studies, University of Louisiana at Lafayette. His research interests focus on multi-standard digital receivers, VLSI digital processing systems, and image processing.

Yan Wang is an assistant professor at the Department of Industrial Engineering and Management Systems, University of Central Florida. Prior to joining UCF, he was on the engineering faculty at the University of Pittsburgh. His primary research interests are in the areas of engineering design, simulation, and visualization. At the National Science Foundation Industry/University Cooperative Research Center for e-Design, he is the thrust leader of enabling information infrastructure for collaborative design. Wang received his PhD in industrial engineering from University of Pittsburgh, a master's in electrical engineering from Chinese Academy of Sciences, and a bachelor's in electrical engineering from Tsinghua University in China.

Keigo Watanabe received BE and ME degrees in mechanical engineering from the University of Tokushima, Tokushima, Japan (1976 and 1978, respectively), and the DE degree in aeronautical engineering from Kyushu University, Fukuoka, Japan (1984). Currently, he is a professor in the Department of Advanced Systems Control Engineering, Saga University, Japan. He has published more than 480 technical papers in transactions, journals, and international conference proceedings, and is the author or editor of 22 books. Watanabe is a member of the Society of Instrument and Control Engineers, Japan Society of Mechanical Engineers, Japan Society for Precision Engineering, Institute of Systems, Control and Information Engineers, the Japan Society for Aeronautical and Space Science, Robotics Society of Japan, Japan Society for Fuzzy Theory and Intelligent Informatics, and IEEE.

Yan-Qing Zhang is currently an associated professor of the Computer Science Department at Georgia State University, Atlanta. He received bachelor's and master's degrees in computer science and engineering from Tianjin University, China, in 1983 and 1986, respectively, and the PhD degree in computer science and engineering at the University of South Florida, USA, in 1997. His research interests include hybrid intelligent systems, neural networks, fuzzy logic, evolutionary computation, granular computing, kernel machines, bioinformatics, medical informatics, computational Web intelligence, data mining, and knowledge discovery. He has published eight book chapters, over 40 journal papers, and over 90 conference papers. He is also the co-author of the book *Compensatory Genetic Fuzzy Neural Networks and Their Applications* published by World Scientific in 1998 and the book *Interval Neutrosophic Sets and Logic: Theory and Applications in Computing* published by HEXIS in 2005, and the co-editor of the book *Computational Web Intelligence: Intelligent Technology for Web Applications* published by World Scientific in 2004. He has served as a reviewer for 35 international journals. He has served as a committee member in over 60 international conferences. He is a program co-chair of 2006 IEEE International Conference on Granular Computing 2005 and IEEE-ICDM Workshop on MultiAgent Data Warehousing and MultiAgent Data Mining. He received 2005 IEEE-Granular Computing Outstanding Service Award. He is a member of Bioinformatics and Bioengineering Technical Committee of the Computational Intelligence Society of IEEE and the Technical Committee on Pattern Recognition for Bioinformatics of the International Association of Pattern Recognition. He is a member of IEEE and ACM.

Fernando J. Von Zuben received his PhD in electrical engineering (1996) from the School of Electrical and Computer Engineering, State University of Campinas (Unicamp), SP, Brazil. He is currently an associate professor at the Department of Computer Engineering and Industrial Automation, Unicamp. The main topics of his research are computational intelligence, autonomous navigation, multivariate analysis, and control and identification of dynamic systems. He coordinates open-ended research projects in these topics, tracking real-world problems through interdisciplinary cooperation.

Index

C

D

E

F

G

H

I

J

K

L

M

N

O

P

R

S

T

U

V

W

X

WITHDRAWN